The
SUNDAY R
LECTIONARY
For Lay Ministers

Contents

FEASTS OF THE LORD AND SOLEMNITIES

Preface

Dear Parish Leader and Sunday Reader,

There are many ways in which the *Sunday Reader's Lectionary* may assist you and your community.

The principal aim of this book is to make the liturgy more meaningful for the faithful by helping them to discover, in the Sunday readings, the power of God's Word for their daily lives. Therefore, whenever possible, a life-situation is mentioned in the general introduction to each Sunday service, as one context in which the readings can be listened to and understood.

We trust that priests and community leaders will find this lectionary useful in their preparation for Sunday liturgy: the introductions provide a deeper understanding of the readings, as well as many points which can be used for the homily.

There are some features of this lectionary which need special explanation.

No introduction is provided for the Second Reading or Gospel

At first sight, this may seem strange. There are, however, good reasons for it.

The introduction to the Gospel is to be found in the general introduction to the whole service. It is very important that the congregation should have some idea of the main theme of the Gospel *before* the First Reading is proclaimed. As the theme of the Gospel is usually reflected in the First Reading, the general introduction helps the faithful to listen to this reading in the light of the Gospel.

On those Sundays and Feastdays when all three readings have the same theme, no special introduction to the Second Reading is necessary. On those days when the Second Reading has no connection with the Gospel theme, an introduction to this reading would not help but would only confuse people – even though the themes might be important in themselves. It follows that if the theme of the celebration is taken from the Second Reading, our introduction, which is based on the Gospel, should be ignored or altered.

We have provided no separate introduction to the Gospel, so that the preacher may be free to choose whatever aspect of the Gospel reading he prefers.

7

Notes for Community Leaders
This book also contains various 'Notes for Community Leaders' which are to be found at intervals. They are placed so as to ensure that they will not easily be overlooked (as introductory material often is). These 'Notes' contain suggestions for making the liturgy ever more of a community celebration.

These special pages cover the following topics:
1 Sharing roles with others makes the liturgy beautiful (p.10)
2 About introductions to the readings (p.11)
3 A group writes the introduction to a reading (p.278)
4 What to avoid in introductions (p.279)
5 About the response after the reading (p.456)
6 The Alleluia or Gospel Acclamation (p.457)
7 How can people's daily experience flow into our Sunday worship? (p.532)
8 Lay ministry is not only a liturgical task (p.533)

We should like to encourage local readers to make up their own introduction to the Sunday readings. This book gives just one example of how this might be done. If local situations are reflected in the introduction, it will be so very much easier for the congregation to gain an insight into the meaning of the readings and to receive light for their lives.

Simplicity, scientific exegesis, and Sunday liturgy
The introductions in this lectionary avoid theological language. They attempt to express the fruits of exegesis in simple language, in order to meet people where they are. Our principle was that the introductions should help the faithful to 'open up' to the message, arousing interest so that they are able to listen more attentively to God's word.

In the drafting of texts, the simplicity of language, the choice of examples, and in the illustrations, Third World conditions have been preferred whenever a choice has had to be made. The book has grown out of the work of the Lumko Pastoral Institute in a Third World situation, and it is an attempt to meet real needs, particularly in situations where lay ministers may be conducting the Sunday service on their own. This simplicity and directness should commend the introductions also to those in more developed areas who are charged with preparing the readings for Sunday worship.

These introductions are not meant to take the place of deeper Bible study, which is to be heartily encouraged. A great variety of commentaries and scripture guides are available for group study and other purposes.

We hope and pray that this *Sunday Reader's Lectionary* will help congregations to gain true mental and spiritual 'access to sacred scripture' as called for by the Fathers of Vatican II (*Dei Verbum* 22).

O. Hirmer and F. Lobinger
Lumko Missiological Institute

Sharing Roles with Others Makes the Liturgy Beautiful and is a Sign of the Kingdom

Introduction to the service — Opening and greeting — Act of Reconciliation —

The Eucharist is the celebration of God's family. In this celebration there is a common faith, a common task, a common joy. There is a communal spirit of celebrating.

This communal spirit of celebrating should be extended so that tasks are decided on together and fulfilled together. In the same way, celebrations are conducted together, under the presiding role of the bishop or priest.

It is therefore important that the Christian community avoids assigning too many tasks to one person: tasks and roles should be shared out amongst the whole community.

This is also our message to the world at large: we are convinced that God wants us to create a spirit of equality and brotherhood at our places of work, in our villages and cities, in our political institutions and in our countries.

About Introductions to the Readings

Why we should have an introduction to the reading

- To show that the reading will be relevant to people's lives.
  We only listen to what is important for our own life.

- To make the congregation listen more carefully to the reading.
  The introduction does not give food, but it arouses hunger for food.

- To direct attention to the main idea of the reading.
  Often the main idea can only be discovered after the Gospel is read, but by then the first reading is forgotten.

Ways of giving an introduction to the readings

People must be able to distinguish the introduction from the reading. If there is only one reader, he or she should give the first words of the introduction from memory while looking at the audience.

The reader may even give the whole introduction in his or her own words, but should avoid extending it into a sermon, where the actual reading becomes a kind of appendix to his or her words.

The reader should make sure that there is a pause between the introduction and the reading.

To distinguish even more clearly between the introduction and the reading, two people may come forward — one reading the introduction, the other the reading. Both should remain at the lectern until the reading is finished.

THE SEASON OF ADVENT

First Sunday of Advent   A

Introduction to the Service

We cannot live without hope. We are always waiting and hoping for something beautiful and enjoyable. Without hope our lives become miserable and boring.

On this first Sunday of Advent we are invited to renew our hope in God and his promises.

The word *Advent* means 'coming'. We are waiting and hoping for the coming of the Lord in our midst, to lead us to a great and wonderful future.

This hope in God makes our lives meaningful and exciting.

Penitential Rite

Let us confess before God that our hope in him is not strong enough.

- Father in heaven, we trust more in our clever plans than in your Word.   (*Silence*)
  Lord, have mercy …

- Father of love, we trust more in our money and in our weapons of war than in your protection.   (*Silence*)
  Christ, have mercy …

- Father of joy, we trust more in our own paradise of luxury and impurity than in your promise.   (*Silence*)
  Lord, have mercy …

FIRST READING

We have good reason to be afraid of the future. Why, for instance, are we building weapons which can destroy the whole world and all its peoples? Why are millions of soldiers preparing and training for war?

The question we ask is: will there ever be a time when all peoples on earth will live together as brothers and sisters?

The prophet Isaiah asked the same question. God gave him a message which we shall now proclaim.

We read from the book of Isaiah, chapter two.
*
The vision of Isaiah son of Amoz, concerning Judah and Jerusalem.

In the days to come
the mountain of the Temple of the Lord
shall tower above the mountains
and be lifted higher than the hills.
All the nations will stream to it,
peoples without number will come to it; and they will say:

> 'Come, let us go up to the mountain of the Lord,
> to the Temple of the God of Jacob
> that he may teach us his ways
> so that we may walk in his paths;
> since the Law will go out from Zion,
> and the oracle of the Lord from Jerusalem.'

He will wield authority over the nations
and adjudicate between many peoples;
these will hammer their swords into ploughshares,
their spears into sickles.
Nation will not lift sword against nation,
there will be no more training for war.

O House of Jacob, come,
let us walk in the light of the Lord.

This is the word of the Lord. *Isaiah 2:1-5*

Responsorial Psalm

℟ **I rejoiced when I heard them say:**
'Let us go to God's house.'

1 I rejoiced when I heard them say:
'Let us go to God's house.'
And now our feet are standing
within your gates, O Jerusalem. ℟

2 It is there that the tribes go up,
the tribes of the Lord.
For Israel's law it is,
there to praise the Lord's name.
There were set the thrones of judgement
of the house of David. ℟

3 For the peace of Jerusalem pray:
'Peace be to your homes!
May peace reign in your walls,
in your palaces, peace!' ℟

4   For love of my brethren and friends
     I say: 'Peace upon you!'
     For love of the house of the Lord
     I will ask for your good.   ℞   *Ps 121:1-2. 4-5. 6-9. ℞ cf. v.1*

SECOND READING

We read from the letter of St Paul to the Romans, chapter thirteen.
*
You know 'the time' has come: you must wake up now: our
salvation is even nearer than it was when we were converted.
The night is almost over, it will be daylight soon – let us give up
all the things we prefer to do under cover of the dark; let us arm
ourselves and appear in the light. Let us live decently as people
do in the daytime: no drunken orgies, no promiscuity or licen-
tiousness, and no wrangling or jealousy. Let your armour be the
Lord Jesus Christ.

This is the word of the Lord.   *Romans 13:11-14*

Gospel Acclamation
    Alleluia, alleluia!
    Let us see, O Lord, your mercy
    and give us your saving help.
    Alleluia!   *Ps 84:8*

GOSPEL

We read from the holy Gospel according to Matthew, chapter twenty-
four.
*
Jesus said to his disciples: 'As it was in Noah's day, so will it be
when the Son of Man comes. For in those days before the Flood
people were eating, drinking, taking wives, taking husbands,
right up to the day Noah went into the ark, and they suspected
nothing till the Flood came and swept all away. It will be like this
when the Son of Man comes. Then of two men in the fields one is
taken, one left; of two women at the millstone grinding, one is
taken, one left.

'So stay awake, because you do not know the day when your
master is coming. You may be quite sure of this that if the
householder had known at what time of the night the burglar
would come, he would have stayed awake and would not have
allowed anyone to break through the wall of his house. Therefore, you too must stand ready because the Son of Man is
coming at an hour you do not expect.'

This is the Gospel of the Lord.   *Matthew 24:37-44*

Second Sunday of Advent   A

Introduction to the Service

In this time of Advent we are watching and waiting for the Saviour who can bring unity between the nations and among ourselves.

Such unity seems to be impossible.

And yet today we shall receive the message which proclaims to us: 'Peace is possible - it is close at hand'.

Penitential Rite

Let us examine our conscience:

Father, you are so close to us but our hearts are far from you. Help us to repent and to return to you and to your way of life.

- Did we find it hard to make peace and to forgive others? (*Silence*)

- Were we afraid to admit our mistakes?   (*Silence*)

- Did we create disunity by being jealous and touchy?   (*Silence*)

Let us acknowledge our failures.   **I confess**...

FIRST READING

'There is no justice in this world', many people complain. 'It does not pay to be good. Wickedness rules the world'.

However, in our First Reading the prophet Isaiah has a different message. There is somebody who will stand up for the poor of the land, who will judge the wicked. The new world of peace will undoubtedly come.

Isaiah also talks about animals which are by nature enemies and kill each other. They, too, will live together in peace. These animals, however, are symbols of the peoples and nations who will be able to live together in peace in God's new world.

We read from the book of Isaiah, chapter eleven.
*
A shoot springs from the stock of Jesse,
a scion thrusts from his roots:
on him the spirit of the Lord rests,
a spirit of wisdom and insight,
a spirit of counsel and power,
a spirit of knowledge and of the fear of the Lord.
(The fear of the Lord is his breath.)

He does not judge by appearances,
he gives no verdict on hearsay,
but judges the wretched with integrity,
and with equity gives a verdict for the poor of the land.
His word is a rod that strikes the ruthless;
his sentences bring death to the wicked.

Integrity is the loincloth round his waist,
faithfulness the belt about his hips.

The wolf lives with the lamb,
the panther lies down with the kid,
calf and lion cub feed together
with a little boy to lead them.
The cow and the bear make friends,
their young lie down together.
The lion eats straw like the ox.
The infant plays over the cobra's hole;
into the viper's lair
the young child puts his hand.
They do no hurt, no harm,
on all my holy mountain,
for the country is filled with the knowledge of the Lord
as the waters swell the sea.
That day, the root of Jesse
shall stand as a signal to the peoples.
It will be sought out by the nations
and its home will be glorious.

This is the word of the Lord. *Isaiah 11:1-10*

Responsorial Psalm
℟ **In his days justice shall flourish
and peace till the moon fails.**

1 O God, give your judgement to the king,
to a king's son your justice,
that he may judge your people in justice
and your poor in right judgement. ℟

2 In his days justice shall flourish
and peace till the moon fails.
He shall rule from sea to sea,
from the Great River to earth's bounds. ℟

3   For he shall save the poor when they cry
    and the needy who are helpless.
    He will have pity on the weak
    and save the lives of the poor.   ℟

4   May his name be blessed for ever
    and endure like the sun.
    Every tribe shall be blessed in him,
    all nations bless his name.   ℟

Ps 71:1-2. 7-8. 12-13. 17. ℟ cf. v.7

SECOND READING

We read from the letter of St Paul to the Romans, chapter fifteen.
*

Everything that was written long ago in the scriptures was meant
to teach us something about hope from the examples scripture
gives of how people who did not give up were helped by God.
And may he who helps us when we refuse to give up, help you
all to be tolerant with each other, following the example of Christ
Jesus, so that united in mind and voice you may give glory to the
God and Father of our Lord Jesus Christ.

It can only be to God's glory, then, for you to treat each other
in the same friendly way as Christ treated you. The reason Christ
became the servant of circumcised Jews was not only so that God
could faithfully carry out the promises made to the patriarchs, it
was also to get the pagans to give glory to God for his mercy, as
scripture says in one place: For this I shall praise you among the
pagans and sing your name.

This is the word of the Lord.   *Romans 15:4-9*

Gospel Acclamation
    Alleluia, alleluia!
    Prepare a way for the Lord,
    make his paths straight,
    and all mankind shall see the salvation of God.
    Alleluia!   *Lk 3:4. 6*

GOSPEL

We read from the holy Gospel according to Matthew, chapter three.
*

In due course John the Baptist appeared; he preached in the
wilderness of Judaea and this was his message: 'Repent, for the
kingdom of heaven is close at hand.' This was the man the

prophet Isaiah spoke of when he said:

> A voice cries in the wilderness:
> Prepare a way for the Lord,
> make his paths straight.

This man John wore a garment made of camel-hair with a leather belt round his waist, and his food was locusts and wild honey. Then Jerusalem and all Judaea and the whole Jordan district made their way to him, and as they were baptised by him in the river Jordan they confessed their sins. But when he saw a number of Pharisees and Sadducees coming for baptism he said to them, 'Brood of vipers, who warned you to fly from the retribution that is coming? But if you are repentant, produce the appropriate fruit, and do not presume to tell yourselves, "We have Abraham for our father," because, I tell you, God can raise children for Abraham from these stones. Even now the axe is laid to the roots of the trees, so that any tree which fails to produce good fruit will be cut down and thrown on the fire. I baptise you in water for repentance, but the one who follows me is more powerful than I am, and I am not fit to carry his sandals; he will baptise you with the Holy Spirit and fire. His winnowing-fan is in his hand; he will clear his threshing-floor and gather his wheat into the barn; but the chaff he will burn in a fire that will never go out.'

This is the Gospel of the Lord. *Matthew 3:1-12*

Third Sunday of Advent   A

Introduction to the Service
Today we celebrate the third Sunday of Advent. Christmas is near. We prepare ourselves to receive our Saviour with joy and happiness.

Misery, sickness and disappointments destroy our happiness. And yet, our hearts still long for everlasting joy.

We are hungry and thirsty for joy without end.

Penitential Rite
Let us ask ourselves:

● Where do we look for joy and satisfaction in our lives? (*Silence*)

● Do we abuse other people to make ourselves happy? (*Silence*)

● Do we run after the wrong kind of happiness, happiness which will eventually destroy us? *(Silence)*

Let us ask for forgiveness:

● Father in heaven, you are the fountain of all joy. We have forgotten you in our search for happiness.
    Lord, have mercy …

● Father, we push you aside and do not trust in your promises.
    Christ, have mercy …

● Father, we have looked for joy where we will never find it.
    Lord, have mercy …

FIRST READING

Sometimes we feel miserable, like people in the desert who have lost their way. For instance if we suddenly fall ill, and all our strength is turned to weakness. Disappointments turn our joy into tears. There are situations in life where we feel like the lame, the deaf and the blind.

In this situation, which the prophet compares to a 'wilderness', we hear a message of great joy.

We read from the book of Isaiah, chapter thirty-five.
★
Let the wilderness and the dry-lands exult,
let the wasteland rejoice and bloom,
let it bring forth flowers like the jonquil,
let it rejoice and sing for joy.

The glory of Lebanon is bestowed on it,
the splendour of Carmel and Sharon;
they shall see the glory of the Lord,
the splendour of our God.

Strengthen all weary hands,
steady all trembling knees
and say to all faint hearts,
'Courage! Do not be afraid.

'Look your God is coming,
vengeance is coming,
the retribution of God;
he is coming to save you.'

Then the eyes of the blind shall be opened,

the ears of the deaf unsealed,
then the lame shall leap like a deer
and the tongues of the dumb sing for joy,
for those the Lord has ransomed shall return.

They will come to Zion shouting for joy,
everlasting joy on their faces;
joy and gladness will go with them
and sorrow and lament be ended.

This is the word of the Lord. *Isaiah 35: 1-6. 10*

Responsorial Psalm
℟ **Come, Lord, and save us.**

or

℟ **Alleluia!**

1 It is the Lord who keeps faith for ever,
who is just to those who are oppressed.
It is he who gives bread to the hungry,
the Lord, who sets prisoners free. ℟

2 It is the Lord who gives sight to the blind,
who raises up those who are bowed down,
the Lord, who protects the stranger
and upholds the widow and orphan. ℟

3 It is the Lord who loves the just
but thwarts the path of the wicked.
The Lord will reign for ever,
Zion's God, from age to age. ℟ *Ps 145:6-10. ℟ cf. Is 35:4*

SECOND READING
We read from the letter of St James, chapter five.
*
Be patient, brothers, until the Lord's coming. Think of a farmer:
how patiently he waits for the precious fruit of the ground until it
has had the autumn rains and the spring rains! You too have to be
patient; do not lose heart, because the Lord's coming will be
soon. Do not make complaints against one another, brothers, so
as not to be brought to judgement yourselves; the Judge is
already to be seen waiting at the gates. For your example,
brothers, in submitting with patience, take the prophets who
spoke in the name of the Lord.

This is the word of the Lord. *James 5:7-10*

Gospel Acclamation
Alleluia, alleluia!
The spirit of the Lord has been given to me.
He has sent me to bring good news to the poor.
Alleluia! *Is 61:1 (Lk 4:18)*

GOSPEL

We read from the holy Gospel according to Matthew, chapter eleven.
*
John in his prison had heard what Christ was doing and he sent his disciples to ask him, 'Are you the one who is to come, or have we got to wait for someone else?' Jesus answered, 'Go back and tell John what you hear and see; the blind see again, and the lame walk, lepers are cleansed, and the deaf hear, and the dead are raised to life and the Good News is proclaimed to the poor; and happy is the man who does not lose faith in me.'

As the messengers were leaving, Jesus began to talk to the people about John: 'What did you go out into the wilderness to see? A reed swaying in the breeze? No? Then what did you go out to see? A man wearing fine clothes? Oh no, those who wear fine clothes are to be found in palaces. Then what did you go out for? To see a prophet? Yes, I tell you, and much more than a prophet: he is the one of whom scripture says: Look, I am going to send my messenger before you; he will prepare your way before you. I tell you solemnly, of all the children born of women, a greater than John the Baptist has never been seen; yet the least in the kingdom of heaven is greater than he is.'

This is the Gospel of the Lord. *Matthew 11:2-11*

Fourth Sunday of Advent A

Introduction to the Service
This time of Advent is a time of waiting and searching for God. Sometimes he seems to be very far away from us.

There are even people who complain: 'How can God allow all this misery on earth? If there is a God, let him come down. He should give us a sign that he is really with us. It would be easy for him to make all things right.'

Do we, at times, think in the same way?

In our celebration today the name of the Redeemer will be proclaimed to us. His name is not 'God-far-away' but Emmanuel: 'God is with us'.

Penitential Rite

Let us examine our conscience:

- God gives us many signs of his love, but we do not see them. (*Silence*)

- God gives us the powerful sign of his Word. But we do not see or listen. (*Silence*)

- God gives us Jesus, his Son, the greatest sign of his love. But we do not accept him fully. We ask for other signs. (*Silence*)

Let us confess that we have sinned. **I confess**...

FIRST READING

A child is the most beautiful sign of love. The love between a father and mother becomes visible in their baby. It is a wonderful and living sign of love.

God has given the whole of humankind this beautiful sign of his love.

We read from the book of Isaiah, chapter seven.
*
The Lord spoke to Ahaz and said, 'Ask the Lord your God for a sign for yourself coming either from the depths of Sheol or from the heights above.' 'No,' Ahaz answered 'I will not put the Lord to the test.'

Then Isaiah said:

'Listen now, House of David:
are you not satisfied with trying the patience of men
without trying the patience of my God, too?
The Lord himself, therefore,
will give you a sign.
It is this: the maiden is with child
and will soon give birth to a son
whom she will call Emmanuel,
a name which means "God-is-with-us".'

This is the word of the Lord. *Isaiah 7:10-14*

Responsorial Psalm
℟ **Let the Lord enter!**
He is the king of glory.

1 The Lord's is the earth and its fullness,
the world and all its peoples.
It is he who set it on the seas;
on the waters he made it firm. ℟

2 Who shall climb the mountain of the Lord?
Who shall stand in his holy place?
The man with clean hands and pure heart,
who desires not worthless things. ℟

3 He shall receive blessings from the Lord
and reward from the God who saves him.
Such are the men who seek him,
seek the face of the God of Jacob. ℟

Ps 23:1-6. ℟ cf. vv.7. 10

SECOND READING
We read from the letter of St Paul to the Romans, chapter one.
*
From Paul, a servant of Christ Jesus who has been called to be an
apostle, and specially chosen to preach the Good News that God
promised long ago through his prophets in the scriptures.

This news is about the Son of God, who, according to the
human nature he took, was a descendent of David: it is about
Jesus Christ our Lord who, in th order of the spirit, the spirit of
holiness that was in him, was proclaimed Son of God in all his
power through his resurrection from the dead. Through him we
received grace and our apostolic mission to preach the obedience
of faith to all pagan nations in honour of his name. You are one of
these nations, and by his call belong to Jesus Christ. To you all,
then, who are God's beloved in Rome, called to be saints, may
God our Father and the Lord Jesus Christ send grace and peace.

This is the word of the Lord. *Romans 1:1-7*

Gospel Acclamation
Alleluia, alleluia!
The virgin will conceive and give birth to a son
and they will call him Emmanuel,
a name which means 'God-is-with-us'.
Alleluia! *Mt 1:23*

GOSPEL

We read from the holy Gospel according to Matthew, chapter one.

*

This is how Jesus Christ came to be born. His mother Mary was betrothed to Joseph; but before they came to live together she was found to be with child through the Holy Spirit. Her husband Joseph, being a man of honour and wanting to spare her publicity, decided to divorce her informally. He had made up his mind to do this when the angel of the Lord appeared to him in a dream, and said 'Joseph son of David, do not be afraid to take Mary home as your wife, because she has conceived what is in her by the Holy Spirit. She will give birth to a son and you must name him Jesus, becaus he is the one who is to save his people from their sins.' Now all this took place to fulful the words spoken by the Lord through the prophet:

The virgin will conceive and give birth to a son
and they will call him Emmanuel,

a name which means 'God-is-with-us'. When Joseph woke up he did what the angel of the Lord had told him to do: he took his wife to his home.

This is the Gospel of the Lord. *Matthew 1:18-24*

THE SEASON OF CHRISTMAS
25 December *Solemnity*

Nativity of Our Lord   A, B, C

Mass at Midnight

Introduction to the Service

We have come together tonight to celebrate the birth of our Lord and Saviour. In a poor stable in Bethlehem Christ was born of the Virgin Mary.

We are here tonight to greet and welcome the new-born king. We are here to show him our love and our willingness to accept him into our community.

There was no room for the Holy Family at the inn. This is very sad. But it is also the source of great joy, for in the stable at Bethlehem, Christ joined all those who have no home, all those who have little money, all those who are pushed aside by others, all those who have no place in the city of the rich and powerful.

Penitential Rite

Before we enter the stable of Bethlehem, let us ask ourselves:

- Did we give shelter to people who had no home?   (*Silence*)

- Did we push aside people who were poor and powerless?   (*Silence*)

- Did we welcome little children as God's gift and as a blessing?   (*Silence*)

Let us ask for forgiveness from the Lord for all that we have done wrong and for all that we have failed to do: **I confess**...

FIRST READING

Our reading shows us the deep meaning of Christ's birth.

This reading was first addressed to people who had been taken into captivity, ill-treated, oppressed and even killed by their enemies.

We read from the book of the prophet Isaiah, chapter nine.
*
The people that walked in darkness
has seen a great light;

on those who live in a land of deep shadow
a light has shone.
You have made their gladness greater,
you have made their joy increase;
they rejoice in your presence
as men rejoice at harvest time,
as men are happy when they are dividing the spoils.
For the yoke that was weighing on him,
the bar across his shoulders,
the rod of his oppressor,
these you break as on the day of Midian.
For all the footgear of battle,
every cloak rolled in blood,
is burnt
and consumed by fire.
For there is a child born for us,
a son given to us
and dominion is laid on his shoulders;
and this is the name they give him:
Wonder-Counsellor, Mighty-God,
Eternal-Father, Prince-of-Peace.
Wide is his dominion
in a peace that has no end,
for the throne of David
and for his royal power,
which he establishes and makes secure
in justice and integrity.
From this time onwards and for ever,
the jealous love of the Lord of hosts will do this.

This is the word of the Lord.   *Isaiah 9:1-7*

Responsorial Psalm
℟   **Today a saviour has been born to us;**
he is Christ the Lord.

1   O sing a new song to the Lord,
sing to the Lord all the earth.
O sing to the Lord, bless his name.   ℟

2   Proclaim his help day by day,
tell among the nations his glory
and his wonders among all the peoples.   ℟

3 Let the heavens rejoice and earth be glad,
   let the sea and all within it thunder praise,
   let the land and all it bears rejoice,
   all the trees of the wood shout for joy
   at the presence of the Lord for he comes,
   he comes to rule the earth. ℟

4 With justice he will rule the world,
   he will judge the peoples with his truth. ℟

Ps 95:1-3. 11-13. ℟ Lk 2:11

SECOND READING

We read from the letter of St Paul to Titus, chapter two.
*

God's grace has been revealed, and it has made salvation possible
for the whole human race and taught us that what we have to do
is to give up everything that does not lead to God, and all our
worldly ambitions; we must be self-restrained and live good and
religious lives here in this present world, while we are waiting in
hope for the blessing which will come with the Appearing of the
glory of our great God and saviour Christ Jesus. He sacrificed
himself for us in order to set us free from all wickedness and to
purify a people so that it could be his very own and would have
no ambition except to do good.

   This is the word of the Lord.   *Titus 2:11-14*

Gospel Acclamation
   Alleluia, alleluia!
   I bring you news of great joy:
   today a saviour has been born to us, Christ the Lord.
   Alleluia!   *Lk 2:10-11*

GOSPEL

We read from the holy Gospel according to Luke, chapter two.
*

Caesar Augustus issued a decree for a census of the whole world
to be taken. This census – the first – took place while Quirinius
was governor of Syria, and everyone went to his own town to be
registered. So Joseph set out from the town of Nazareth in Galilee
and travelled up to Judaea, to the town of David called
Bethlehem, since he was of David's House and line, in order to be
registered together with Mary, his betrothed, who was with
child. While they were there the time came for her to have her

child, and she gave birth to a son, her first-born. She wrapped
him in swaddling clothes, and laid him in a manger because there
was no room for them at the inn. In the countryside close by there
were shepherds who lived in the fields and took it in turns to
watch their flocks during the night. The angel of the Lord
appeared to them and the glory of the Lord shone round them.
They were terrified, but the angel said, 'Do not be afraid. Listen, I
bring you news of great joy, a joy to be shared by the whole
people. Today in the town of David a saviour has been born to
you; he is Christ the Lord. And here is a sign for you: you will
find a baby wrapped in swaddling clothes and lying in a manger.'
And suddenly with the angel there was a great throng of the
heavenly host, praising God and singing:

'Glory to God in the highest heaven,
and peace to men who enjoy his favour'.

This is the Gospel of the Lord.   *Luke 2:1-4*

Mass at Dawn

Introduction to the Service

Today we come together, filled with great joy, to celebrate the
birth of our Lord Jesus Christ. This is the day which the Lord has
made! Let us rejoice and be glad!

In our celebration today we try to re-live what happened in
Bethlehem.

For instance, this morning when you said to each other: 'Come
on, let's go to church' you did the same as the shepherds of
Bethlehem. They said to one another: 'Let's go to Bethlehem and
see for ourselves'. With the shepherds we find Mary, Joseph and
the child in the manger. With them we kneel down in humble faith
and welcome Christ into our midst.

Penitential Rite

Before we enter the stable of Bethlehem, let us examine our
conscience:

● Are we ready to welcome Christ with a humble and pure
heart? (*Silence*)

● Are we concerned about people who are forced to live in
miserable houses, like Jesus in the stable at Bethlehem? (*Silence*)

Let us ask the Lord to cleanse our hearts and minds that we may welcome him with joy.   **I confess**…

FIRST READING

Our reading reminds us that Christ is the bridegroom who has come to visit his bride. Therefore, in this reading, the people of God are called the 'Daughter of Zion', the 'sought-after', and the 'City-not-forsaken'.

We read from the book of Isaiah, chapter sixty-two.
*

This the Lord proclaims
to the ends of the earth:

> Say to the daughter of Zion, 'Look,
> your saviour comes,
> the prize of his victory with him,
> his trophies before him'.
> They shall be called 'The Holy People',
> 'The Lord's Redeemed'.
> And you shall be called 'The-sought-after',
> 'City-not-forsaken'.

This is the word of the Lord.   *Isaiah 62:11-12*

Responsorial Psalm
   ℟   **This day new light will shine upon the earth:**
        the Lord is born for us.

1   The Lord is king, let earth rejoice,
     the many coastlands be glad.
     The skies proclaim his justice;
     all peoples see his glory.   ℟

2   Light shines forth for the just
     and joy for the upright of heart.
     Rejoice, you just, in the Lord;
     give glory to his holy name.   ℟   *Ps 96:1. 6. 11-12*

SECOND READING

We read from the letter of St Paul to Titus, chapter three.
*

When the kindness and love of God our saviour for mankind were revealed, it was not because he was concerned with any righteous actions we might have done ourselves; it was for no reason except his own compassion that he saved us, by means of the cleansing water of rebirth and by renewing us with the Holy Spirit which he has so generously poured over us through Jesus Christ our saviour. He did this so that we should be justified by his grace, to become heirs looking forward to inheriting eternal life.

This is the word of the Lord. *Titus 3:4-7*

Gospel Acclamation
Alleluia, alleluia!
Glory to God in the highest heaven,
and peace to men who enjoy his favour.
Alleluia! *Lk 2:14*

GOSPEL
We read from the holy Gospel according to Luke, chapter two.
*
Now when the angels had gone from them into heaven, the shepherds said to one another, 'Let us go to Bethlehem and see this thing that has happened which the Lord has made known to us.' So they hurried away and found Mary and Joseph, and the baby lying in the manger. When they saw the child they repeated what they had been told about him, and everyone who heard it was astonished at what the shepherds had to say. As for Mary, she treasured all these things and pondered them in her heart. And the shepherds went back glorifying and praising God for all they had heard and seen; it was exactly as they had been told.

This is the Gospel of the Lord. *Luke 2:15-20*

Mass During the Day

Introduction to the Service
Today we have come together to welcome Christ our Lord. We have hurried to the stable at Bethlehem and found Joseph, Mary and the baby lying in a manger.
Who is this child of Bethlehem?
In the Gospel today, the Apostle John reveals the deep and wondrous truth about the child. John tells us that this baby is the Word of God, made flesh. He is the same Word through whom everything was created, the same Word who gave life to every living creature, the same Word through whom we can all become children of God.
And so today we come together to accept Jesus as our Saviour and to welcome him into our midst.

Penitential Rite

Let us ask ourselves:

● How often did we reject Jesus and his word?   (*Silence*)

● Have we helped other people to find Christ?   (*Silence*)

Let us ask for forgiveness for rejecting Christ so often. **I confess**…

FIRST READING

Many fathers and mothers talk to their children and explain to them what happened at Christmas. In this way they share the good news with their children. In our community some teach the catechism, others preach, others share the Word of God in small communities. In this way, they all announce the good news of Christ's coming.

Our reading talks about these messengers of God and of the joy they bring.

We read from the book of Isaiah, chapter fifty-two.
*
How beautiful on the mountains,
are the feet of one who brings good news,
who heralds peace, brings happiness,
proclaims salvation,
and tells Zion,
'Your God is king!'
Listen! Your watchmen raise their voices,
they shout for joy together,
for they see the Lord face to face,
as he returns to Zion.
Break into shouts of joy together,
you ruins of Jerusalem;
for the Lord is consoling his people,
redeeming Jerusalem.
The Lord bares his holy arm
in the sight of all the nations,
and all the ends of the earth shall see
the salvation of our God.

This is the word of the Lord.   *Isaiah 52:7-10*

Responsorial Psalm
℟ **All the ends of the earth have seen
the salvation of our God.**

1 Sing a new song to the Lord
for he has worked wonders.
His right hand and his holy arm
have brought salvation. ℟

2 The Lord has made known his salvation;
has shown his justice to the nations.
He has remembered his truth and love
for the house of Israel. ℟

3 All the ends of the earth have seen
the salvation of our God.
Shout to the Lord all the earth,
ring out your joy. ℟

4 Sing psalms to the Lord with the harp,
with the sound of music.
With trumpets and the sound of the horn
acclaim the King, the Lord. ℟   *Ps 97:1-6. ℟ v.3*

SECOND READING

We read from the letter to the Hebrews, chapter one.
*
At various times in the past and in various different ways, God
spoke to our ancestors through the prophets; but in our own
time, the last days, he has spoken to us through his Son, the Son
that he has appointed to inherit everything and through whom
he made everything there is. He is the radiant light of God's glory
and the perfect copy of his nature, sustaining the universe by his
powerful command; and now that he has destroyed the defilement of sin, he has gone to take his place in heaven at the right
hand of divine Majesty. So he is now as far above the angels as
the title which he has inherited is higher than their own name.

God has never said to any angel: You are my Son, today I have
become your father, or: I will be a father to him and he a son to
me. Again, when he brings the First-born into the world, he says:
Let all the angels of God worship him.

This is the word of the Lord.   *Hebrews 1:1-6*

Gospel Acclamation

Alleluia, alleluia!
A hallowed day has dawned upon us.
Come, you nations, worship the Lord,
for today a great light has shone down upon the earth.
Alleluia!

GOSPEL

We read from the holy Gospel according to John, chapter one.

*
*In the beginning was the Word:
the Word was with God
and the Word was God.
He was with God in the beginning.
Through him all things came to be,
not one thing had its being but through him.
All that came to be had life in him
and that life was the light of men,
a light that shines in the dark,
a light that darkness could not overpower.*

A man came, sent by God.
His name was John.
He came as a witness,
as a witness to speak for the light,
so that everyone might believe through him.
He was not the light,
only a witness to speak for the light.

*The Word was the true light
that enlightens all men;
and he was coming into the world
He was in the world
that had its being through him,
and the world did not know him.
He came to his own domain
and his own people did not accept him.
But to all who did accept him
he gave power to become children of God,
to all who believe in the name of him
who was born not out of human stock
or urge of the flesh
or will of man
but of God himself.

The Word was made flesh,
he lived among us,
and we saw his glory,
the glory that is his as the only Son of the Father,
full of grace and truth.*

John appears as his witness. He proclaims:
'This is the one of whom I said:
He who comes after me
ranks before me
because he existed before me.'

Indeed, from his fullness we have, all of us, received–
yes, grace in return for grace,
since, though the Law was given through Moses,
grace and truth have come through Jesus Christ.
No one has ever seen God;
it is the only Son, who is nearest to the Father's heart,
who has made him known.

   This is the Gospel of the Lord.   John 1:1-18

*Shorter Form, verses 1-5. 9-14. Read between *.

Sunday in the Octave of Christmas   *Feast*

The Holy Family
of Jesus, Mary and Joseph   A

Where there is no Sunday occurring between 25 December and 1 January, this feast is celebrated on 30 December, with one reading only before the Gospel.

Introduction to the Service

We all belong to a family. We grew up in a family and know the people who are related to us. We also know the difficulties which families have to face. There are misunderstandings and troubles between parents and children, between father and mother, between one family and another.

Jesus also belonged to a family. Joseph, the carpenter, Mary and Jesus are called the Holy Family of Nazareth. Today we remember this Holy Family in our celebration.

We know that there were difficulties even in the Holy Family.

Jesus, for instance, remained behind in the Temple without the permission of his parents. But we can also be sure that Mary, Joseph and Jesus could sort out possible misunderstandings and difficulties. With Jesus in their midst, the family of Nazareth was able to do things well and to solve their problems in a spirit of love.

Penitential Rite

Let us examine our conscience:

- What are we doing at home in order to keep Jesus in our midst? Do we pray together at home? Do we read and share God's Word together?   (*Silence*)

- Do we appreciate the Sacrament of Marriage as a sign of Christ's presence in our families?   (*Silence*)

Let us ask for forgiveness for so often excluding Christ from our families.   **I confess**...

FIRST READING

We say: 'Children must obey their father and mother.'
    Our reading, however, does not talk about 'obeying' parents. Instead it talks about 'honouring' and 'respecting' our father and mother. This is much more than just obeying them.

We read from the book of Ecclesiasticus, chapter three.
*
The Lord honours the father in his children,
and upholds the rights of a mother over her sons.
Whoever respects his father is atoning for his sins,
he who honours his mother is like someone amassing a fortune.
Whoever respects his father will be happy with children of his
    own,
he shall be heard on the day when he prays.
Long life comes to him who honours his father,
he who sets his mother at ease is showing obedience to the
    Lord.
My son, support your father in his old age,
do not grieve him during his life.
Even if his mind should fail, show him sympathy,
do not despise him in your health and strength;
for kindness to a father shall not be forgotten
but will serve as reparation for your sins.

    This is the word of the Lord.   *Ecclesiasticus 3:2-6. 12-14*

Responsorial Psalm

℞   **O blessed are those who fear the Lord
and walk in his ways!**

1   O blessed are those who fear the Lord
and walk in his ways!
By the labour of your hands you shall eat.
You will be happy and prosper.   ℞

2   Your wife like a fruitful vine
in the heart of your house;
your children like shoots of the olive,
around your table.   ℞

3   Indeed thus shall be blessed
the man who fears the Lord.
May the Lord bless you from Zion
all the days of your life!   ℞   *Ps 127:1-5. ℞ cf. v.1*

SECOND READING

We read from the letter of St Paul to the Colossians, chapter three.
*
You are God's chosen race, his saints; he loves you and you
should be clothed in sincere compassion, in kindness and
humility, gentleness and patience. Bear with one another; forgive
each other as soon as a quarrel begins. The Lord has forgiven
you; now you must do the same. Over all these clothes, to keep
them together and complete them, put on love. And may the
peace of Christ reign in your hearts, because it is for this that you
were called together as parts of one body. Always be thankful.

Let the message of Christ, in all its richness, find a home with
you. Teach each other, and advise each other, in all wisdom.
With gratitude in your hearts sing psalms and hymns and
inspired songs to God; and never say or do anything except in the
name of the Lord Jesus, giving thanks to God the Father through
him.

Wives, give way to your husbands, as you should in the Lord.
Husbands, love your wives and treat them with gentleness.
Children, be obedient to your parents always, because that is
what will please the Lord. Parents, never drive your children to
resentment or you will make them feel frustrated.

This is the word of the Lord.   *Colossians 3:12-21*

Gospel Acclamation
Alleluia, alleluia!
May the peace of Christ reign in your hearts;
let the message of Christ find a home with you.
Alleluia!

Col. 3:15. 16

GOSPEL

We read from the holy Gospel according to Matthew, chapter two.
*
After the wise men had left, the angel of the Lord appeared to Joseph in a dream and said, 'Get up, take the child and his mother with you, and escape into Egypt, and stay there until I tell you, because Herod intends to search for the child and do away with him.' So Joseph got up and, taking the child and his mother with him, left that night for Egypt, where he stayed until Herod was dead. This was to fulfil what the Lord had spoken through the prophet:

I called my son out of Egypt.

After Herod's death, the angel of the Lord appeared in a dream to Joseph in Egypt and said, 'Get up, take the child and his mother with you and go back to the land of Israel, for those who wanted to kill the child are dead'. So Joseph got up and, taking the child and his mother with him, went back to the land of Israel. But when he learnt that Archelaus had succeeded his father Herod as ruler of Judaea he was afraid to go there, and being warned in a dream he left for the region of Galilee. There he settled in a town called Nazareth. In this way the words spoken through the prophets were to be fulfilled:

He will be called a Nazarene.

This is the Gospel of the Lord. *Matthew 2:13-15. 19-23*

1 January: Octave of Christmas

Solemnity of Mary, Mother of God   A, B, C

Introduction to the Service
Today we begin a new year. We begin it with a feast of 'Mary, Mother of God'.

A week ago we celebrated the birth of Jesus. Today we remember his mother and say 'thank you' to her. We praise her as the 'Mother of God'. We thank her for giving us Jesus.

Some people may wonder why we call Mary, 'Mother of God'. What is the reason for this? The reason is that the child of Bethlehem was both true man and true God at the same time.

Mary has borne us the Son of God. Therefore today we praise her and say: 'Mary, Mother of God, pray for us sinners. Pray for us now. Pray for us every single day of the coming year.'

Penitential Rite

Let us give ourselves to God with a humble and contrite heart:

Father in heaven. Look on us with mercy and love. Forgive us for what we have done wrong during the past year. Make good and supplement what we have failed to do.   (*Silence*)

I confess...

FIRST READING

Today we wish each other a happy New Year. This is good. Our reading is doing the same. It wishes us, however, much more than just a quick 'Happy New Year'.

We read from the book of Numbers, chapter six.
*
The Lord spoke to Moses and said, 'Say this to Aaron and his sons: "This is how you are to bless the sons of Israel. You shall say to them:

May the Lord bless you and keep you.
May the Lord let his face shine on you and be gracious to
    you.
May the Lord uncover his face to you and bring you peace."

This is how they are to call down my name on the sons of Israel, and I will bless them.'

This is the word of the Lord.   *Numbers 6:22-27*

Responsorial Psalm

℟   **O God, be gracious and bless us.**

1   God, be gracious and bless us
    and let your face shed its light upon us.
    So will your ways be known upon earth
    and all nations learn your saving help.   ℟

2 Let the nations be glad and exult
for you rule the world with justice.
With fairness you rule the peoples.
you guide the nations on earth.

3 Let the peoples praise you, O God;
let all the peoples praise you.
May God still give us his blessing
till the ends of the earth revere him. ℞

Ps 66:2-3. 5. 6. 8. ℞ v.2

SECOND READING

We read from the letter of St Paul to the Galatians, chapter four.
★
When the appointed time came, God sent his Son, born of a
woman, born a subject of the Law, to redeem the subjects of the
Law and to enable us to be adopted as sons. The proof that you
are sons is that God has sent the Spirit of his Son into our hearts:
the spirit that cries, 'Abba, Father', and it is this that makes you a
son, you are not a slave any more; and if God has made you son,
then he has made you heir.

This is the word of the Lord. *Galatians 4:4-7*

Gospel Acclamation
Alleluia, alleluia!
At various times in the past
and in various different ways,
God spoke to our ancestors through the prophets;
but in our own time, the last days,
he has spoken to us through his Son.
Alleluia! *Heb 1:1-2*

GOSPEL

We read from the holy Gospel according to Luke, chapter two.
★
The shepherds hurried away to Bethlehem and found Mary and
Joseph, and the baby lying in the manger. When they saw the
child they repeated what they had been told about him, and
everyone who heard it was astonished at what the shepherds had
to say. As for Mary, she treasured all these things and pondered
them in her heart. And the shepherds went back glorifying and
praising God for all they had heard and seen; it was exactly as
they had been told.

When the eighth day came and the child was to be circumcised, they gave him the name Jesus, the name the angel had given him before his conception.

This is the Gospel of the Lord. *Luke 2: 16-21*

Second Sunday after Christmas   *A, B, C*

Introduction to the Service

Today we celebrate the second Sunday after Christmas. We continue to rejoice in the birth of our Saviour.

For many people, this child of Bethlehem is just another child, one who became very famous in the course of his life. For Christians, however, this child is more than that. Who is he?

This is the message which we shall hear today: 'He ... was born not out of human stock or urge of the flesh ... The Word was made flesh and lived among us.'

Therefore we proclaim today: this child of Bethlehem is the Word of God made visible, God himself has come to us.

God spoke the Word: 'I want to be with my people.' And this Word became flesh in Jesus.

God spoke the Word: 'I want all people to see and hear how great is my love for you.' And this Word of God became flesh in Jesus.

Penitential Rite

Let us ask ourselves:

● Do we allow God to speak to us in our conscience?   (*Silence*)

● Do we search for God's Word in the scriptures?   (*Silence*)

● Do we allow God's Word to become flesh in our actions and our words?   (*Silence*)

Let us ask for forgiveness for closing ourselves to God's Word and ignoring his call.   **I confess**...

FIRST READING

Our reading talks about wisdom as if it were a person coming forth from the mouth of God, visiting people and settling down in the city. In this wisdom we can see Christ himself, coming forth from God; the Word of God made flesh among us.

We read from the book of Ecclesiasticus, chapter twenty-four.
*
Wisdom speaks her own praises,
in the midst of her people she glories in herself.
She opens her mouth in the assembly of the Most High,
she glories in herself in the presence of the Mighty One;

> 'Then the creator of all things instructed me,
> and he who created me fixed a place for my tent.
> He said, "Pitch your tent in Jacob,
> make Israel your inheritance.'
> From eternity, in the beginning, he created me,
> and for eternity I shall remain.
> I ministered before him in the holy tabernacle,
> and thus was I established on Zion.
> In the beloved city he has given me rest,
> and in Jerusalem I wield my authority.
> I have taken root in a privileged people
> in the Lord's property, in his inheritance.'

This is the word of the Lord.   *Ecclesiasticus 24:1-2 8-12*

Responsorial Psalm
℟ **The Word was made flesh,
and lived among us.**

or

℟ **Alleluia!**

1 O praise the Lord, Jerusalem!
   Zion, praise your God!
   He has strengthened the bars of your gates,
   he has blessed the children within you. ℟

2 He established peace on your borders,
   he feeds you with finest wheat.
   He sends out his word to the earth
   and swiftly runs his command. ℟

3 He makes his word known to Jacob,
   to Israel his laws and decrees.
   He has not dealt thus with other nations;
   he has not taught them his decrees. ℟

Ps 147:12-15. 19-20. ℟ Jn 1:14

SECOND READING

We read from the letter of St Paul to the Ephesians, chapter one.

*
Blessed be God the Father of our Lord Jesus Christ, who has blessed us with all the spiritual blessings of heaven in Christ. Before the world was made, he chose us, chose us in Christ, to be holy and spotless, and to live through love in his presence, determining that we should become his adopted sons, through Jesus Christ, for his own kind purposes, to make us praise the glory of his grace, his free gift to us in the Beloved.

That will explain why I, having once heard about your faith in the Lord Jesus, and the love that you show towards all the saints, have never failed to remember you in my prayers and to thank God for you. May the God of our Lord Jesus Christ, the Father of glory, give you a spirit of wisdom and perception of what is revealed, to bring you to full knowledge of him. May he enlighten the eyes of your mind so that you can see what hope his call holds for you, what rich glories he has promised the saints will inherit.

This is the word of the Lord.   *Ephesians 1:3-6.15-18*

Gospel Acclamation
Alleluia, alleluia!
Glory be to you, O Christ, proclaimed to the pagans;
Glory be to you, O Christ, believed in by the world.
Alleluia!   *cf. 1 Tim 3:16*

GOSPEL

We read from the holy Gospel according to John, chapter one.

*
*In the beginning was the Word:
the Word was with God
and the Word was God.
He was with God in the beginning.
Through him all things came to be,
not one thing had its being but through him.
All that came to be had life in him
and that life was the light of men,
a light that shines in the dark,
a light that darkness could not overpower.*

A man came, sent by God.
His name was John.

He came as a witness,
as a witness to speak for the light,
so that everyone might believe through him.
He was not the light,
only a witness to speak for the light.

*The Word was the true light
that enlightens all men;
and he was coming into the world.
He was in the world
that had its being through him,
and the world did not know him.
He came to his own domain
and his own people did not accept him.
But to all who did accept him
he gave power to become children of God,
to all who believe in the name of him
who was born not out of human stock
or urge of the flesh
or will of man
but of God himself.
The Word was made flesh,
he lived among us,
and we saw his glory,
the glory that is his as the only Son of the Father,
full of grace and truth.*

John appears as his witness. He proclaims:
'This is the one of whom I said:
He who comes after me
ranks before me
because he existed before me.'

Indeed, from his fullness we have, all of us, received –
yes, grace in return for grace,
since though the Law was given through Moses,
grace and truth have come through Jesus Christ.
No one has ever seen God;
it is the only Son, who is nearest to the Father's heart,
who has made him known.

   This is the Gospel of the Lord.   *John 1:1-18*

Shorter Form, verses 1-5. 9-14. Read between *.

6 January or the Sunday between 2 January and 8 January   *Solemnity*

The Epiphany of the Lord   *A, B, C*

Introduction to the Service

Today we celebrate the feast of the Epiphany. We will hear of a bright star which led wise men to Bethlehem where they found the infant Christ.

What is the meaning of this feast of the 'Epiphany'? Let me explain it to you.

Perhaps you have heard people talking about Christ in a very strange way. You may have heard them saying: 'Christ cannot be the Saviour of our nation. He is the God of the Jews. We need our own Christ, our own Saviour who can liberate our nation.'

Our feast today, the feast of the Epiphany, proclaims a different message: we see the star in the sky and this star helps people from different races and nations to find Christ. We see the chief priests and the scribes searching in the Bible which told them where to find their Saviour and king.

This, therefore, is the meaning of Epiphany: Christ appears as a great light. All nations and races come to him and accept him as their Saviour and king.

Penitential Rite

Let us ask ourselves:

● We have seen the light and have found Christ. What have we done to bring the good news to other nations and races? (*Silence*)

● Have I been a guiding star to others, showing them the right way? (*Silence*)

Let us ask for forgiveness for not showing others the way to Christ.   **I confess**…

FIRST READING

Our reading was first proclaimed amid the ruins of Jerusalem. The people of Israel were defeated and their city destroyed. In this troubled situation the prophet announced his message. He spoke of a great light which would appear in Jerusalem, beckoning to all nations and races.

We read from the book of Isaiah, chapter sixty.
*

Arise, shine out Jerusalem, for your light has come,
the glory of the Lord is rising on you,
though night still covers the earth
and darkness the peoples.

Above you the Lord now rises
and above you his glory appears.
The nations come to your light
and kings to your dawning brightness.

Lift up your eyes and look round:
all are assembling and coming towards you,
your sons from far away
and daughters being tenderly carried.

At this sight you will grow radiant,
your heart throbbing and full;
since the riches of the sea will flow to you;
the wealth of the nations come to you;

camels in throngs will cover you,
and dromedaries of Midian and Ephah;
everyone in Sheba will come,
bringing gold and incense
and singing the praise of the Lord.

This is the word of the Lord.   *Isaiah 60:1-6*

Responsorial Psalm
℟   **All nations shall fall prostrate before you, O Lord.**

1   O God, give your judgement to the king,
     to a king's son your justice,
     that he may judge your people in justice
     and your poor in right judgement.   ℟

2   In his days justice shall flourish
     and peace till the moon fails.
     He shall rule from sea to sea,
     from the Great River to earth's bounds.   ℟

3   The kings of Tarshish and the sea coasts
     shall pay him tribute.
     The kings of Sheba and Seba
     shall bring him gifts.

Before him all kings shall fall prostrate,
all nations shall serve him.   ℟

4   For he shall save the poor when they cry
and the needy who are helpless.
He will have pity on the weak
and save the lives of the poor.   ℟

Ps 71:1-2. 7-8. 10-13. ℟ cf. v.11

SECOND READING

We read from the letter of St Paul to the Ephesians, chapter three.
*
You have probably heard how I have been entrusted by God with
the grace he meant for you, and that it was by a revelation that I
was given the knowledge of the mystery. This mystery that has
now been revealed through the Spirit to his holy apostles and
prophets was unknown to any men in past generations; it means
that pagans now share the same inheritance, that they are parts
of the same body, and that the same promise has been made to
them, in Christ Jesus, through the gospel.

This is the word of the Lord.   *Ephesians 3:2-3. 5-6*

Gospel Acclamation
Alleluia, alleluia!
We saw his star as it rose
and have come to do the Lord homage.
Alleluia!   *Mt 2:2*

GOSPEL

We read from the holy Gospel according to Matthew, chapter two.
*
After Jesus had been born at Bethlehem in Judaea during the
reign of King Herod, some wise men came to Jerusalem from the
east. 'Where is the infant king of the Jews?' they asked. 'We saw
his star as it rose and have come to do him homage.' When King
Herod heard this he was perturbed, and so was the whole of
Jerusalem. He called together all the chief priests and the scribes
of the people, and enquired of them where the Christ was to be
born. 'At Bethlehem in Judaea,' they told him 'for this is what the
prophet wrote:

And you, Bethlehem, in the land of Judah
you are by no means least among the leaders of Judah,
for out of you will come a leader

who will shepherd my people Israel.'

Then Herod summoned the wise men to see him privately. He asked them the exact date on which the star had appeared, and sent them on to Bethlehem. 'Go and find out all about the child,' he said 'and when you have found him, let me know, so that I too may go and do him homage.' Having listened to what the king had to say, they set out. And there in front of them was the star they had seen rising; it went forward and halted over the place where the child was. The sight of the star filled them with delight, and going into the house they saw the child with his mother Mary, and falling to their knees they did him homage. Then, opening their treasures, they offered him gifts of gold and frankincense and myrrh. But they were warned in a dream not to go back to Herod, and returned to their own country by a different way.

This is the Gospel of the Lord. *Matthew 2:1-12*

Sunday after 6 January   First Sunday in Ordinary Time   *Feast*

The Baptism of the Lord   A

This feast is omitted when the Epiphany is celebrated on this Sunday.

Introduction to the Service

Today we celebrate the feast of our Lord's baptism in the river Jordan. We could also think of it as the feast of our Lord's baptism *and* confirmation.

Many of us remember the day when we were confirmed. Others in our community are preparing themselves for receiving this great sacrament of confirmation.

Baptism and confirmation belong together. This we can clearly see on the occasion when Jesus was baptised in the river Jordan. After John had baptised him, the Holy Spirit came down on Jesus and strengthened him.

Today, Jesus publicly began his mission. He was sent by the Father to overcome evil with good, to proclaim the will of God, to face jealousy, persecution and death. It was for this task that Jesus was strengthened at his baptism by the Holy Spirit.

This feast of our Lord's baptism, therefore, reminds us of our own baptism and confirmation.

Penitential Rite

Let us ask ourselves:

- In baptism God has accepted us as his beloved sons and daughters. Do we behave as God's children? (*Silence*)

- We are called to stand up against evil and hatred as Christ did. Do we accept this task for which we were strengthened in the sacrament of confirmation? (*Silence*)

We ask for forgiveness for forgetting the task which God gave us in the sacrament of baptism and confirmation. **I confess**...

FIRST READING

In our reading today the prophet Isaiah talks about the promised Messiah and his task in the world. This task is not limited to the healing of the sick but includes the healing of sick nations which long for justice.

We read from the book of Isaiah, chapter forty-two.

*
Thus says the Lord:

> Here is my servant whom I uphold,
> my chosen one in whom my soul delights.
> I have endowed him with my spirit
> that he may bring true justice to the nations.
>
> He does not cry out or shout aloud,
> or make his voice heard in the streets.
> He does not break the crushed reed,
> nor quench the wavering flame.
>
> Faithfully he brings true justice;
> he will neither waver, nor be crushed
> until true justice is established on earth,
> for the islands are awaiting his law.
>
> I, the Lord, have called you to serve the cause of right;
> I have taken you by the hand and formed you;
> I have appointed you as covenant of the people and light of
> the nations,
>
> to open the eyes of the blind,
> to free captives from prison,
> and those who live in darkness from the dungeon.

This is the word of the Lord.   *Isaiah 42:1-4. 6-7*

Responsorial Psalm
℟ **The Lord will bless his people with peace.**

1 O give the Lord you sons of God,
    give the Lord glory and power;
    give the Lord the glory of his name.
    Adore the Lord in his holy court. ℟

2 The Lord's voice resounding on the waters,
    the Lord on the immensity of waters;
    the voice of the Lord, full of power,
    the voice of the Lord, full of splendour. ℟

3 The God of glory thunders.
    In his temple they all cry: 'Glory!'
    The Lord sat enthroned over the flood;
    the Lord sits as king for ever. ℟   *Ps 28:1-4. 9-10. ℟ v.11*

SECOND READING

We read from the Acts of the Apostles, chapter ten.
*
Peter addressed Cornelius and his household: 'The truth I have
now come to realise' he said 'is that God does not have
favourites, but that anybody of any nationality who fears God
and does what is right is acceptable to him.

'It is true, God sent his word to the people of Israel, and it was
to them that the good news of peace was brought by Jesus Christ
– but Jesus Christ is Lord of all men. You must have heard about
the recent happenings in Judaea; about Jesus of Nazareth and
how he began in Galilee, after John had been preaching baptism.
God had anointed him with the Holy Spirit and with power, and
because God was with him, Jesus went about doing good and
curing all who had fallen into the power of the devil.'

This is the word of the Lord.   *Acts 10:34-38*

Gospel Acclamation
    Alleluia, alleluia!
    The heavens opened and the Father's voice resounded:
    'This is my Son, the Beloved. Listen to him.'
    Alleluia!
                                                 cf. Mk 9:8

GOSPEL

We read from the holy Gospel according to Matthew, chapter three.

*

Jesus came from Galilee to the Jordan to be baptised by John. John tried to dissuade him. 'It is I who need baptism from you,' he said 'and yet you come to me!' But Jesus replied, 'Leave it like this for the time being; it is fitting that we should, in this way, do all that righteousness demands.' At this, John gave in to him.

As soon as Jesus was baptised he came up from the water, and suddenly the heavens opened and he saw the Spirit of God descending like a dove and coming down on him. And a voice spoke from heaven, 'This is my Son, the Beloved; my favour rests on him.'

This is the Gospel of the Lord.   *Matthew 3:13-17*

THE SEASON OF LENT

Ash Wednesday   A, B, C

Introduction to the Service

Today is Ash Wednesday. We shall bless the ashes and place them on our heads.

With this ceremony we solemnly begin the time of Lent, the forty days of repentance for us as individuals and for the whole Christian community.

The ashes remind us of our own death. Without God we shall remain dust. The ashes also remind us of all the worthless things which we do or collect during our lives. This time of Lent is a chance to seek things which will last. It also encourages us to do things better.

For instance, it is not enough just to give to the poor. If we do that because we want to boast about it, our good works will burn to ashes before God. The same will happen to our prayers. Even the most beautiful and longest prayers offered up during our services will burn to ashes before God if we do not give him our heart and love.

This time of Lent is a time of repentance, a time for putting things right, a time for pulling out what is wrong and burning it to ashes.

Penitential Rite

Let us ask ourselves:

- What is wrong in my life? What should I pull out and burn to ashes? (*Silence*)

- Is there anything which I should rectify with my neighbours. Is there anything which disturbs the peace between them and me? (*Silence*)

Let us ask for forgiveness for all that is worthless like ashes in our lives.   **I confess**…

FIRST READING

When the people of Israel were oppressed by their enemies they cried out to God for help. They knew that God would come to their aid. However, they also knew that they themselves would have to

51

walk in God's way and do his will. It is for this reason, as our reading tells us, that the people of Israel proclaimed a time of fasting for the whole nation.

We read from the book of Joel, chapter two.
*
'Now, now – it is the Lord who speaks –
come back to me with all your heart,
fasting, weeping, mourning.'
Let your hearts be broken not your garments torn,
turn to the Lord your God again,
for he is all tenderness and compassion,
slow to anger, rich in graciousness,
and ready to relent.
Who knows if he will not turn again, will not relent,
will not leave a blessing as he passes,
oblation and libation
for the Lord your God?
Sound the trumpet in Zion!
Order a fast,
proclaim a solemn assembly,
call the people together,
summon the community,
assemble the elders,
gather the children,
even the infants at the breast.
Let the bridegroom leave his bedroom
and the bride her alcove.
Between vestibule and altar let the priests,
the ministers of the Lord, lament.
Let them say,
'Spare your people, Lord!
Do not make your heritage a thing of shame,
a byword for the nations.
Why should it be said among the nations,
"Where is their God?" '
Then the Lord, jealous on behalf of his land,
took pity on his people.

This is the word of the Lord.   *Joel 2:12-18*

Responsorial Psalm
    ℟   **Have mercy on us, O Lord, for we have sinned.**

1   Have mercy on me, God, in your kindness.
    In your compassion blot out my offence.
    O wash me more and more from my guilt
    and cleanse me from my sin.   ℟

2   My offences truly I know them;
    my sin is always before me.
    Against you, you alone, have I sinned:
    what is evil in your sight I have done.   ℟

3   A pure heart create for me, O God,
    put a steadfast spirit within me.
    Do not cast me away from your presence,
    nor deprive me of your holy spirit.   ℟

4   Give me again the joy of your help;
    with a spirit of fervour sustain me.
    O Lord, open my lips
    and my mouth shall declare your praise.   ℟

    Ps 50:3-6. 12-14. 17. ℟ v.3

SECOND READING

We read from the second letter of St Paul to the Corinthians, chapters five and six.
★
We are ambassadors for Christ; it is as though God were appealing through us, and the appeal that we make in Christ's name is: be reconciled to God. For our sake God made the sinless one into sin, so that in him we might become the goodness of God. As his fellow workers, we beg you once again not to neglect the grace of God that you have received. For he says: At the favourable time, I have listened to you; on the day of salvation I came to your help. Well, now is the favourable time; this is the day of salvation.

This is the word of the Lord.   *2 Corinthians 5:20–6:2*

Gospel Acclamation
    Praise to you, O Christ, king of eternal glory!
    A pure heart create for me, O God,
    and give me again the joy of your help.
    Praise to you, O Christ, king of eternal glory!   *Ps 50:12. 14*

or

    Praise to you, O Christ, king of eternal glory!

Harden not your hearts today,
but listen to the voice of the Lord.
Praise to you, O Christ, king of eternal glory!   *cf. Ps 94:8*

GOSPEL

We read from the holy Gospel according to Matthew, chapter six.
*
Jesus said to his disciples:

'Be careful not to parade your good deeds before men to attract their notice; by doing this you will lose all reward from your Father in heaven. So when you give alms, do not have it trumpeted before you; this is what the hypocrites do in the synagogues and in the streets to win men's admiration. I tell you solemnly, they have had their reward. But when you give alms, your left hand must not know what your right is doing; your almsgiving must be secret, and your Father who sees all that is done in secret will reward you.

'And when you pray, do not imitate the hypocrites: they love to say their prayers standing up in the synagogues and at the street corners for people to see them. I tell you solemnly, they have had their reward. But when you pray go to your private room and, when you have shut your door, pray to your Father who is in that secret place, and your Father who sees all that is done in secret will reward you.

'When you fast do not put on a gloomy look as the hypocrites do: they pull long faces to let men know they are fasting. I tell you solemnly, they have had their reward. But when you fast, put oil on your head and wash your face, so that no one will know you are fasting except your Father who sees all that is done in secret; and your Father who sees all that is done in secret will reward you.'

This is the Gospel of the Lord.   *Matthew 6:1-6. 16-18*

First Sunday of Lent   A

Introduction to the Service

Everyone has a family name. It comes from one person, who was the first to be called by this name. Today, the many members of our family are named after him. It is possible that the first ancestor not only gave us his name, but also imparted to us a part of his character. We notice, for example, that the members of one particular family are known to lack courage. It is possible that this common strength or weakness of a whole family has its roots in their ancestor.

Today, on this first Sunday of Lent, we look at our ancestors in the faith. We look at the first Adam, and realize that our present weakness stems from him.

Then we look at our second ancestor, the second Adam, who is Christ. From him we receive our hope.

Penitential Rite

At the beginning of our service we call on Christ's power and his mercy:

● Lord, we have stretched out our hand to the forbidden fruit of pride:
    Lord, have mercy ...

● Christ, we have turned to the forbidden tree of lust.
    Christ, have mercy ...

● Lord, we have listened to the lies of the evil one.
    Lord, have mercy ...

FIRST READING

In our homes, we listen eagerly to the stories told about our forefathers. We listen to these stories because they explain what we are today. These stories seem to speak about things long past, but in fact they say to us: what you do today has its roots in what was done long ago.

With this in mind let us listen to the ancient story of the book of Genesis, chapter two and three.

The Lord God fashioned man of dust from the soil. Then he breathed into his nostrils a breath of life, and thus man became a living being.

The Lord God planted a garden in Eden which is in the east, and there he put the man he had fashioned. The Lord God caused to spring up from the soil every kind of tree, enticing to look at and good to eat, with the tree of life and the tree of the knowledge of good and evil in the middle of the garden.

The serpent was the most subtle of all the wild beasts that the Lord God had made. It asked the woman, 'Did God really say you were not to eat from any of the trees in the garden?' The woman answered the serpent, 'We may eat the fruit of the trees in the garden. But of the fruit of the tree in the middle of the garden God said, "You must not eat it, nor touch it, under pain of death".' Then the serpent said to the woman, 'No! You will not die! God knows in fact that on the day you eat it your eyes will be opened and you will be like gods, knowing good and evil.' The woman saw that the tree was good to eat and pleasing to the eye, and that it was desirable for the knowledge that it could give. So she took some of its fruit and ate it. She gave some also to her husband who was with her, and he ate it. Then the eyes of both of them were opened and they realised that they were naked. So they sewed fig-leaves together to make themselves loin-cloths.

This is the word of the Lord.   *Genesis 2:7-9. 3:17*

Responsorial Psalm
℟ **Have mercy on us, O Lord, for we have sinned.**

1 Have mercy on me, God, in your kindness.
   In your compassion blot out my offence.
   O wash me more and more from my guilt
   and cleanse me from my sin.   ℟

2 My offences truly I know them;
   my sin is always before me.
   Against you, you alone, have I sinned;
   what is evil in your sight I have done.   ℟

3 A pure heart create for me, O God,
   put a steadfast spirit within me.
   Do not cast me away from your presence,
   nor deprive me of your holy spirit.   ℟

4 Give me again the joy of your help;
   with a spirit of fervour sustain me.
   O Lord, open my lips
   and my mouth shall declare your praise.   ℟

                        Ps 50:3-6. 12-14. 17. ℟ cf. v.3

SECOND READING

We read from the letter of St Paul to the Romans, chapter five.
*
Sin entered the world through one man, and through sin death, and thus death has spread through the whole human race because everyone has sinned. Sin existed in the world long before the Law was given. There was no law and so no one could

be accused of the sin of 'law-breaking', yet death reigned over all from Adam to Moses, even though their sin, unlike that of Adam, was not a matter of breaking a law.

Adam prefigured the One to come, but the gift itself considerably outweighed the fall. If it is certain that through one man's fall so many died, it is even more certain that divine grace, coming through the one man, Jesus Christ, came to so many as an abundant free gift. The results of the gift also outweigh the results of one man's sin: for after one single fall came judgement with a verdict of condemnation, now after many falls comes grace with its verdict of acquittal. *If it is certain that death reigned over everyone as the consequence of one man's fall, it is even more certain that one man, Jesus Christ, will cause everyone to reign in life who receives the free gift that he does not deserve, of being made righteous. Again, as one man's fall brought condemnation on everyone, so the good act of one man brings everyone life and makes them justified. As by one man's disobedience many were made sinners, so by one man's obedience many will be made righteous.

This is the word of the Lord.*   *Romans 5:12-19*

*Shorter Form, verses 12. 17-19. Read between *.*

Gospel Acclamation
Praise to you, O Christ, king of eternal glory!
Man does not live on bread alone
but on every word that comes from the mouth of God.
Praise to you, O Christ, king of eternal glory!   *Mt 4:4*

GOSPEL
We read from the holy Gospel according to Matthew, chapter four.
*
Jesus was led by the Spirit out into the wilderness to be tempted by the devil. He fasted for forty days and forty nights, after which he was very hungry, and the tempter came and said to him, 'If you are the Son of God, tell these stones to turn into loaves.' But he replied, 'Scripture says:

Man does not live on bread alone
but on every word that comes from the mouth of God.'

The devil then took him to the holy city and made him stand on the parapet of the Temple. 'If you are the Son of God' he said 'throw yourself down; for scripture says:

He will put you in his angels' charge,
and they will support you on their hands
in case you hurt your foot against a stone.'

Jesus said to him, 'Scripture also says:

You must not put the Lord your God to the test.'

Next, taking him to a very high mountain, the devil showed him
all the kingdoms of the world and their splendour. 'I will give you
all these' he said, 'if you fall at my feet and worship me.' Then
Jesus replied, 'Be off, Satan! For scripture says:

You must worship the Lord your God,
and serve him alone.'

Then the devil left him, and angels appeared and looked after
him.

This is the Gospel of the Lord. *Matthew 4:1-11*

Second Sunday of Lent   A

Introduction to the Service

When suffering is about to come upon us, we look for friends.
Who will be with us in the difficult times ahead?

It is the second Sunday of Lent; soon we will remember the time
when Jesus was rejected by the Jewish leaders, condemned and
crucified. Who will be with him in this time of suffering?

We find an answer to this question in today's Gospel reading,
when we hear about Jesus' transfiguration on the mountainside.
There, on the mountain, it became apparent who would be with
Christ in his suffering. Moses will be with him when the high
priests reject him. Elias will be with him when Pontius Pilate
condemns him. And above all, the Father will be with him at all
times.

Penitential Rite

Let us, at the beginning of this service, reflect on the way in
which we bear our own suffering:

● Lord, when we were sick or in difficulties, we sometimes forgot
  that you are always at our side.   (*Silence*)
  Lord, have mercy …

● We believe that our bodies, too, will be transfigured, because
  your glory already dwells in us. Yet, in times of suffering we

failed to think of this truth.   (*Silence*)
   Christ, have mercy ...

● We know that no suffering can separate us from your love. Yet
we sometimes doubted your loving providence.   (*Silence*)
   Lord, have mercy ...

FIRST READING

Abraham knew that he had to expect many hardships and much
suffering when he was told by God to leave his home for the sake
of his faith. God promised to be with him. But would Abraham
dare to trust in God and leave his home for the promised land?

We read from the twelfth chapter of the book of Genesis.
*

The Lord said to Abram, 'Leave your country, your family and
your father's house, for the land I will show you. I will make you
a great nation; I will bless you and make your name so famous
that it will be used as a blessing.

   'I will bless those who bless you:
   I will curse those who slight you.
   All the tribes of the earth
   shall bless themselves by you.'

So Abram went as the Lord told him.

This is the word of the Lord.   *Genesis 12:1-4*

Responsorial Psalm
   ℟   **May your love be upon us, O Lord,**
         as we place all our hope in you.

1   The word of the Lord is faithful
    and all his works to be trusted.
    The Lord loves justice and right
    and fills the earth with his love.   ℟

2   The Lord looks on those who revere him,
    on those who hope in his love,
    to rescue their souls from death,
    to keep them alive in famine.   ℟

3   Our soul is waiting for the Lord.
    The Lord is our help and our shield.
    May your love be upon us, O Lord,
    as we place all our hope in you.   ℟

                        Ps 32:4-5. 18-20. 22. ℟ v.22

SECOND READING

We read from the second letter of St Paul to Timothy, chapter one.
*
With me, bear the hardships for the sake of the Good News, relying on the power of God who has saved us and called us to be holy – not because of anything we ourselves have done but for his own purpose and by his own grace. This grace had already been granted to us, in Christ Jesus, before the beginning of time, but it has only been revealed by the Appearing of our saviour Christ Jesus. He abolished death, and he has proclaimed life and immortality through the Good News.

This is the word of the Lord.   *2 Timothy 1:8-10*

Gospel Acclamation

Glory and praise to you, O Christ!
From the bright cloud the Father's voice was heard:
'This is my Son, the Beloved. Listen to him.'
Glory and praise to you, O Christ!   *Mt 17:5*

GOSPEL

We read from the holy Gospel according to Matthew, chapter seventeen.
*
Jesus took with him Peter and James and his brother John and led them up a high mountain where they could be alone. There in their presence he was transfigured; his face shone like the sun and his clothes became as white as the light. Suddenly Moses and Elijah appeared to them; they were talking with him. Then Peter spoke to Jesus. 'Lord,' he said 'it is wonderful for us to be here; if you wish, I will make three tents here, one for you, one for Moses and one for Elijah.' He was still speaking when suddenly a bright cloud covered them with shadow, and from the cloud there came a voice which said, 'This is my Son, the Beloved; he enjoys my favour. Listen to him'. When they heard this, the disciples fell on their faces, overcome with fear. But Jesus came up and touched them. 'Stand up,' he said 'do not be afraid.' And when they raised their eyes they saw no one but only Jesus.

As they came down from the mountain Jesus gave them this order. 'Tell no one about the vision until the Son of Man has risen from the dead.'

This is the Gospel of the Lord.   *Matthew 17:1-9*

Third Sunday of Lent   A

Introduction to the Service

We cannot live without water.

In times of drought our cattle and our crops die, our gardens wilt. We need rain, we need wells and foundations.

We can think of God as a life-giving fountain. In our coming Easter celebrations we come to this fountain of life. Some of us will be baptised during this Easter Vigil. Those of us who are already baptised will renew our baptismal promises.

Penitential Rite

Today, as we begin this Lenten service, we examine our lives as Christians:

● Did we always turn to God as our fountain when we were sad? When we were in doubt? Did we turn to him when we were tempted, or when we were tired? Or did we turn to other sources?   (*Silence*)

● Did we allow the living Spirit of God to flow in us? Did we allow God's love to grow in us, in our relationship with others, and in our prayer life?   (*Silence*)

● Let us confess that we have sinned.   **I confess**...

FIRST READING

When you drill a bore-hole, you have reason to be proud of your achievement in getting water. But it will not be your own achievement if you get water in a lifeless desert by knocking at a hard and dry rock. It will be a miracle. The water you receive in this way is a wondrous gift. You did nothing at all to obtain it.

When we seek God's life in baptism, we stand before God in the same spirit of humility. Baptism is God's work, not ours.

Let us read about this event in the desert, from the book of Exodus, chapter seventeen.

*

Tormented by thirst, the people complained against Moses. 'Why did you bring us out of Egypt?' they said. 'Was it so that I should die of thirst, my children too, and my cattle?' Moses appealed to the Lord. 'How am I to deal with this people?' he said. 'A little more and they will stone me!' The Lord said to Moses, 'Take with you some of the elders of Israel and move on to the forefront of the people; take in your hand the staff with which you struck the river, and go. I shall be standing before you there on the rock, at Horeb. You must strike the rock, and water will flow from it for the people to drink.' This is what Moses did, in the sight of the elders of Israel. The place was named Massah and Meribah because of the grumbling of the sons of Israel and because they put the Lord to the test by saying, 'Is the Lord with us, or not?'

This is the word of the Lord.   *Exodus 17:3-7*

Responsorial Psalm
℟   **O that today you would listen to his voice:**
     'Harden not your hearts.'

1   Come, ring out our joy to the Lord;
    hail the rock who saves us.
    Let us come before him, giving thanks,
    with songs let us hail the Lord.   ℟

2   Come in; let us bow and bend low;
    let us kneel before the God who made us
    for he is our God and we
    the people who belong to his pasture,
    the flock that is led by his hand.   ℟

3   O that today you would listen to his voice!
    'Harden not your hearts as at Meribah,
    as on that day at Massah in the desert
    when your fathers put me to the test;
    when they tried me, though they saw my work.'   ℟
                          Ps 94:1-2. 6-9. ℟ v.8

SECOND READING
We read from the letter of St Paul to the Romans, chapter five.
*
Through our Lord Jesus Christ by faith we are judged righteous and at peace with God, since it is by faith and through Jesus that we have entered this state of grace in which we can boast about looking forward to God's glory. This hope is not deceptive, because the love of God has been poured into our hearts by the Holy Spirit which has been given us. We were still helpless when at his appointed moment Christ died for sinful men. It is not easy to die even for a good man – though of course for someone really

worthy, a man might be prepared to die – but what proves that
God loves us is that Christ died for us while we were still sinners.

This is the word of the Lord.   *Romans 5:1-2. 5-8*

Gospel Acclamation
Glory to you, O Christ, you are the Word of God!
Lord, you are really the saviour of the world;
give me the living water, so that I may never get thirsty.
Glory to you, O Christ, you are the Word of God!
cf. Jn 4:42. 15

GOSPEL
We read from the holy Gospel according to John, chapter four.
*
*Jesus came to the Samaritan town called Sychar, near the land
that Jacob gave to his son Joseph. Jacob's well is there and Jesus,
tired by the journey, sat straight down by the well. It was about
the sixth hour. When a Samaritan woman came to draw water,
Jesus said to her, 'Give me a drink.' His disciples had gone into
the town to buy food. The Samaritan woman said to him, 'What?
You are a Jew and you ask me, a Samaritan, for a drink?' – Jews,
in fact, do not associate with Samaritans. Jesus replied:

'If you only knew what God is offering
and who it is that is saying to you:
Give me a drink,
you would have been the one to ask,
and he would have given you living water.'

'You have no bucket, sir,' she answered 'and the well is deep:
how could you get this living water? Are you a greater man than
our father Jacob who gave us this well and drank from it himself
with his sons and his cattle?' Jesus replied:

'Whoever drinks this water
will get thirsty again;
but anyone who drinks the water that I shall give
will never be thirsty again:
the water that I shall give
will turn into a spring inside him, welling up to eternal life.'

'Sir,' said the woman 'give me some of that water, so that I may
never get thirsty and never have to come here again to draw
water.'* 'Go and call your husband' said Jesus to her 'and come

back here.' The woman answered, 'I have no husband.' He said to her, 'You are right to say, "I have no husband"; for although you have had five, the one you have now is not your husband. You spoke the truth there.' *'I see you are a prophet, sir' said the woman. 'Our fathers worshipped on this mountain, while you say that Jerusalem is the place where one ought to worship.' Jesus said:

> 'Believe me, woman, the hour is coming
> when you will worship the Father
> neither on this mountain nor in Jerusalem.

*Many Samaritans of that town had believed in him on the strength of the woman's testimony when she said, 'He told me all I have ever done,' so, when the Samaritans came up to him, they begged him to stay with them. He stayed for two days, and when he spoke to them many more came to believe; and they said to the woman, 'Now we no longer believe because of what you told us; we have heard him ourselves and we know that he really is the saviour of the world.'

This is the Gospel of the Lord.*   *John 4:5-42*

Shorter Form, verses 1.6-9. 13-17. 34-38. Read between.

Fourth Sunday of Lent A

Introduction to the Service

Today is already the fourth Sunday of Lent and there are only three weeks left before the great Easter Vigil. During that Vigil some of us will be baptised and we will all renew our baptismal promises.

In the baptismal ceremony we are anointed with Holy Oil, and our eyes are touched.

To be anointed means to be sent. This is why Jesus was called 'the Anointed One', anointed by the Father before all time. When Greek people want to say 'the Anointed One' they say *christos*.

We, too, were anointed and sent out when we were baptised. Our eyes were opened and we were sent out into the world to do God's will

Penitential Rite

Do we always live like people whose eyes were opened, and who were sent out by God?   Let us call on the Lord's mercy.

● Lord, you took away our blindness and opened our eyes to the truth. Yet we have often fallen back into blindness. (*Silence*)
Lord, have mercy …

● Christ, the Anointed One, you have anointed and sent forth each one of us. Yet we have often sinned by doing nothing, by not going to those we saw in need, by not preaching the good news to others. (*Silence*)
Christ, have mercy …

● Lord, by opening our eyes and anointing us you gave us a great gift. Yet we have sometimes brought shame on ourselves and on you. (*Silence*)
Lord, have mercy …

FIRST READING

When David was anointed King of Israel, he was still young. But he was anointed to be king for his whole life. It was a consecration which could never come to an end, just as we are anointed once and for all in baptism.

We read from the first book of Samuel, chapter sixteen.
*
The Lord said to Samuel, 'Fill your horn with oil and go. I am sending you to Jesse of Bethlehem, for I have chosen myself a king among his sons.' When Samuel arrived, he caught sight of Eliab and thought, 'Surely the Lord's anointed one stands there before him,' but the Lord said to Samuel, 'Take no notice of his appearance or his height for I have rejected him; God does not see as man sees; man looks at appearances but the Lord looks at the heart.' Jesse presented his seven sons to Samuel, but Samuel said to Jesse, 'The Lord has not chosen these.' He then asked Jesse, 'Are these all the sons you have?' He answered, 'There is still one left, the youngest; he is out looking after the sheep.' Then Samuel said to Jesse, 'Send for him; we will not sit down to eat until he comes.' Jesse had him sent for, a boy of fresh complexion, with fine eyes and pleasant bearing. The Lord said, 'Come, anoint him, for this is the one.' At this, Samuel took the horn of oil and anointed him where he stood with his brothers; and the spirit of the Lord seized on David and stayed with him from that day on.

This is the word of the Lord. *1 Samuel 16:1. 6-7. 10-13*

Responsorial Psalm
℟   **The Lord is my shepherd;
there is nothing I shall want.**

1 The Lord is my shepherd;
   there is nothing I shall want.
   Fresh and green are the pastures
   where he gives me repose.
   Near restful waters he leads me,
   to revive my drooping spirit.   ℟

2 He guides me along the right path;
   he is true to his name.
   If I should walk in the valley of darkness
   no evil would I fear.
   You are there with your crook and your staff;
   with these you give me comfort.   ℟

3 You have prepared a banquet for me
   in the sight of my foes.
   My head you have anointed with oil;
   my cup is overflowing.   ℟

4 Surely goodness and kindness shall follow me
   all the days of my life.
   In the Lord's own house shall I dwell
   for ever and ever.   ℟   *Ps 22. ℟ v.1*

SECOND READING

We read from the letter of St Paul to the Ephesians, chapter five.
*
You were darkness once, but now you are light in the Lord; be
like children of light, for the effects of the light are seen in
complete goodness and right living and truth. Try to discover
what the Lord wants of you, having nothing to do with the futile
works of darkness but exposing them by contrast. The things
which are done in secret are things that people are ashamed even
to speak of; but anything exposed by the light will be illuminated
and anything illuminated turns into light. That is why it is said:

   Wake up from your sleep,
   rise from the dead,
   and Christ will shine on you.

This is the word of the Lord.   *Ephesians 5:8-14*

Gospel Acclamation

Glory to you, O Christ, you are the Word of God!
I am the light of the world, says the Lord;
anyone who follows me will have the light of life.
Glory to you, O Christ, you are the Word of God!   *Jn 8:12*

GOSPEL

We read from the holy Gospel according to John, chapter nine.
*
| *As Jesus went along, he saw a man who had been blind from birth.* His disciples asked him, 'Rabbi, who sinned, this man or his parents, for him to have been born blind?' 'Neither he nor his parents sinned,' Jesus answered 'he was born blind so that the works of God might be displayed in him.

'As long as the day lasts
I must carry out the work of the one who sent me;
the night will soon be here when no one can work.
As long as I am in the world
I am the light of the world.'

Having said this, *he spat on the ground, made a paste with the spittle, put this over the eyes of the blind man and said to him, 'Go and wash in the Pool of Siloam' (a name that means 'sent'). So the blind man went off and washed himself, and came away with his sight restored.

His neighbours and people who earlier had seen him begging said, 'Isn't this the man who used to sit and beg?' Some said, 'Yes, it is the same one.' Others said, 'No, he only looks like him.' The man himself said, 'I am the man.'* So they said to him, 'Then how do your eyes come to be open?' 'The man called Jesus' he answered 'made a paste, daubed my eyes with it and said to me, "Go and wash at Siloam"; so I went, and when I washed I could see.' They asked, 'Where is he?' 'I don't know' he answered.

They brought the man who had been blind to the Pharisees. It had been a sabbath day when Jesus made the paste and opened the man's eyes, so when the Pharisees asked him how he had come to see, he said, 'He put a paste on my eyes, and I washed, and I can see.' Then some of the Pharisees said, 'This man cannot be from God: he does not keep the sabbath.' Others said, 'How could a sinner produce signs like this?' And there was disagreement among them, So they spoke to the blind man again, 'What have you to say about him yourself, now that he has opened your eyes?' 'He is a prophet' replied the man.

However, the Jews would not believe that the man had been blind and had gained his sight, without first sending for his parents and asking them, 'Is this man really your son who you say was born blind? If so how is it that he is now able to see?' His parents answered, 'We know he is our son and we know he was born blind, but we don't know how it is that he can see now, or who opened his eyes. He is old enough: let him speak for himself.' His parents spoke like this out of fear of the Jews, who had already agreed to expel from the synagogue anyone who should acknowledge Jesus as the Christ. This was why his parents said, 'He is old enough; ask him.'

So the Jews again sent for the man and said to him, 'Give glory to God! For our part, we know that this man is a sinner.' The man answered, 'I don't know if he is a sinner; I only know that I was blind and now I can see.' They said to him, 'What did he do to you? How did he open your eyes?' He replied, 'I have told you once and you wouldn't listen. Why do you want to hear it all again? Do you want to become his disciples too?' At this they hurled abuse at him: 'You can be his disciple,' they said 'we are disciples of Moses: we know that God spoke to Moses, but as for this man, we don't know where he comes from.' The man replied, 'Now here is an astonishing thing! He has opened my eyes and you don't know where he comes from! We know that God doesn't listen to sinners, but God does listen to men who are devout and do his will. Ever since the world began it is unheard of for anyone to open the eyes of a man who was born blind; if this man were not from God, he couldn't do a thing.' *'Are you trying to teach us,' they replied 'and you a sinner through and through, since you were born!' And they drove him away.

Jesus heard they had driven him away, and when he found him he said to him, 'Do you believe in the Son of Man?' 'Sir,' the man replied 'tell me who he is so that I may believe in him.' Jesus said, 'You are looking at him; he is speaking to you.' The man said, 'Lord, I believe', and worshipped him.*

Jesus said:

'It is for judgement
that I have come into this world,
so that those without sight may see
and those with sight turn blind.'

Hearing this, some Pharisees who were present said to him, 'We are not blind, surely?' Jesus replied:

> 'Blind? If you were,
> you would not be guilty,
> but since you say, "We see",
> your guilt remains.'

  This is the Gospel of the Lord.   *John 9:1-41*

*Shorter Form, verses 1. 6-9. 13-17. 34-38. Read between *.

Fifth Sunday of Lent   A

Introduction to the Service
Easter is the feast of the Resurrection. This time of Lent is the preparation time for the feast of the Resurrection.

In order to prepare ourselves, we fast, we change our ways, and we reflect: what does it mean to rise with Christ? What kind of life should someone lead if they say that they have died with Christ and have risen with him?

Penitential Rite
As we begin this service, we examine our lives:

● Do our lives reflect the joy which is expected of people who believe that they have risen with Christ?   (*Silence*)

● Do we remove from our lives those actions which can only be called 'dead works'?   (*Silence*)

● Do we extend to our neighbours the warm love, the friendliness, the active help, which is expected of those who live with the Risen Christ?   (*Silence*)

Let us confess that we have sinned.   **I confess**...

FIRST READING
The nation of Israel was dead. It was defeated and scattered. There seemed to be no hope that it would ever come to life again.

But God said: 'I am going to open your graves. I will raise you from your graves.'

God gives the same message of hope to each one of us who is ready to turn towards him.

We read from the book of the prophet Ezekiel, chapter thirty-seven.
*
The Lord says this: I am now going to open your graves; I mean to raise you from your graves, my people, and lead you back to the soil of Israel. And you will know that I am the Lord, when I open your graves and raise you from your graves, my people. And I shall put my spirit in you, and you will live, and I shall resettle you on your own soil; and you will know that I, the Lord, have said and done this – it is the Lord who speaks.

This is the word of the Lord.   *Ezekiel 37:12-14*

Responsorial Psalm
℞ **With the Lord there is mercy
and fullness of redemption.**

1 Out of the depths I cry to you, O Lord,
Lord, hear my voice!
O let your ears be attentive
to the voice of my pleading. ℞

2 If you, O Lord, should mark our guilt,
Lord, who would survive?
But with you is found forgiveness:
for this we revere you. ℞

3 My soul is waiting for the Lord,
I count on his word.
My soul is longing for the Lord
more than watchman for daybreak.
(Let the watchman count on daybreak
and Israel on the Lord.) ℞

4 Because with the Lord there is mercy
and fullness of redemption,
Israel indeed he will redeem
from all its iniquity. ℞   *Ps 129. ℞ v.7*

SECOND READING
We read from the letter of St Paul to the Romans, chapter eight.
*
People who are interested only in unspiritual things can never be pleasing to God. Your interests, however, are not in the unspiritual, but in the spiritual, since the Spirit of God has made his home in you. In fact, unless you possessed the Spirit of Christ

you would not belong to him. Though your body may be dead it is because of sin, but if Christ is in you then your spirit is life itself because you have been justified; and if the Spirit of him who raised Jesus from the dead is living in you, then he who raised Jesus from the dead will give life to your own mortal bodies through his Spirit living in you.

This is the word of the Lord.   *Romans 8:8-11*

Gospel Acclamation
Glory and praise to you, O Christ!
I am the resurrection and the life, says the Lord;
who ever believes in me will never die.
Glory and praise to you, O Christ!   *Jn 11:25. 26*

GOSPEL
We read from the holy Gospel according to John, chapter eleven.
*
There was a man named Lazarus who lived in the village of Bethany with the two sisters, Mary and Martha, and he was ill. – It was the same Mary, the sister of the sick man Lazarus, who anointed the Lord with ointment and wiped his feet with her hair. *The sisters sent this mesage to Jesus, 'Lord, the man you love is ill.' On receiving the message, Jesus said, 'This sickness will end not in death but in God's glory, and through it the Son of God will be glorified.'

Jesus loved Martha and her sister and Lazarus, yet when he heard that Lazarus was ill he stayed where he was for two more days before saying to the disciples, 'Let us go to Judaea.'* The disciples said, 'Rabbi, it is not long since the Jews wanted to stone you; are you going back again?' Jesus replied:

'Are there not twelve hours in the day?
A man can walk in the daytime without stumbling
because he has the light of this world to see by;
but if he walks at night he stumbles,
because there is no light to guide him'.

He said that and then added, 'Our friend Lazarus is resting, I am going to wake him.' The disciples said to him 'Lord, if he is able to rest he is sure to get better.' The phrase Jesus used referred to the death of Lazarus, but they thought that by 'rest' he meant 'sleep', so Jesus put it plainly, 'Lazarus is dead, and for your sake I am glad I was not there because now you will believe.

But let us go to him.' Then Thomas – known as the Twin – said to
the other disciples, 'Let us go too, and die with him.'

*On arriving, Jesus found that Lazarus had been in the tomb
for four days already.* Bethany is only about two miles from
Jerusalem, and many Jews had come to Martha and Mary to
sympathise with them over their brother. *When Martha heard
that Jesus had come she went to meet him. Mary remained sitting
in the house. Martha said to Jesus, 'If you had been here, my
brother would not have died, but I know that, even now,
whatever you ask of God, he will grant you.' 'Your brother' said
Jesus to her 'will rise again.' Martha said, 'I know he will rise
again at the resurrection on the last day.' Jesus said:

'I am the resurrection and the life.
If anyone believes in me, even though he dies he will live,
and whoever lives and believes in me
will never die.
Do you believe this?'

'Yes Lord,' she said 'I believe that you are the Christ, the Son of
God, the one who was to come into this world.'*

When she had said this, she went and called her sister Mary,
saying in a low voice, 'The Master is here and wants to see you.'
Hearing this, Mary got up quickly and went to him. Jesus had not
yet come into the village; he was still at the place where Martha
had met him. When the Jews who were in the house sympa-
thising with Mary saw her get up so quickly and go out, they
followed her, thinking that she was going to the tomb to weep
there.

Mary went to Jesus, and as soon as she saw him she threw
herself at his feet, saying, 'Lord if you had been here, my brother
would not have died.' At the sight of her tears, and those of the
Jews who followed her, *Jesus said in great distress, with a sigh
that came straight from the heart, 'Where have you put him?'
They said, 'Lord, come and see.' Jesus wept; and the Jews said,
'See how much he loved him!' But there were some who
remarked, 'He opened the eyes of the blind man, could he not
have prevented this man's death?' Still sighing, Jesus reached the
tomb: it was a cave with a stone to close the opening. Jesus said,
'Take the stone away.' Martha said to him 'Lord by now he will
smell; this is the fourth day.' Jesus replied 'Have I not told you
that if you believe you will see the glory of God?' So they took
away the stone. Then Jesus lifted up his eyes and said:

'Father, I thank you for hearing my prayer.
I knew indeed that you always hear me.
But I speak
for the sake of all these who stand round me,
so that they may believe it was you who sent me.'

When he had said this, he cried in a loud voice, 'Lazarus, here! Come out!' The dead man came out, his feet and hands bound with bands of stuff and a cloth round his face. Jesus said to them, 'Unbind him, let him go free.'

Many of the Jews who had come to visit Mary and had seen what he did believed in him.

This is the Gospel of the Lord.*   *John 11:1-45*

***Shorter Form, verses 3-7. 17. 20-7. 33-45. Read between ***

HOLY WEEK

Passion Sunday (Palm Sunday)   A, B, C

(The introduction to the Palm Procession can be found in the Sacramentary.)

FIRST READING

In our first reading we hear what the prophet Isaiah foretold about the suffering of Christ.

When we listen to this reading we can imagine Christ surrounded by his enemies, insulted and beaten up by them. We see Christ standing in their midst like a rock, strong and firm.

We read from the book of Isaiah, chapter fifty.

*

The Lord has given me
a disciple's tongue.
So that I may know how to reply to the wearied
he provides me with speech.
Each morning he wakes me to hear,
to listen like a disciple.
The Lord has opened my ear.
For my part, I made no resistance,
neither did I turn away.
I offered my back to those who struck me,
my cheeks to those who tore at my beard;
I did not cover my face
against insult and spittle.
The Lord comes to my help,
so that I am untouched by the insults.
So, too, I set my face like flint;
I know I shall not be shamed.

This is the word of the Lord.   *Isaiah 50:4-7*

Responsorial Psalm

℟   **My God, my God, why have you forsaken me?**

1   All who see me deride me.
    They curl their lips, they toss their heads.
    'He trusted in the Lord, let him save him;
    let him release him if this is his friend.'   ℟

2 Many dogs have surrounded me,
   a band of the wicked beset me.
   They tear holes in my hands and my feet.
   I can count every one of my bones. ℟

3 They divide my clothing among them.
   They cast lots for my robe.
   O Lord, do not leave me alone,
   my strength, make haste to help me! ℟

4 I will tell of your name to my brethren
   and praise you where they are assembled.
   'You who fear the Lord give him praise;
   all sons of Jacob, give him glory.
   Revere him, Israel's sons.' ℟   *Ps 21:8-9. 17-20. 23-24. ℟ v.2*

SECOND READING

Our second reading is a beautiful hymn which was sung by the
early Christians. They praised the Lord for making himself a slave
on the cross.
  But they could never think of the cross without also praising his
glorious resurrection.

We read from the letter of St Paul to the Philippians, chapter two.
*
His state was divine,
yet Christ Jesus did not cling
to his equality with God
but emptied himself
to assume the condition of a slave,
and became as men are,
and being as all men are,
he was humbler yet,
even to accepting death,
death on a cross.
But God raised him high
and gave him the name
which is above all other names
so that all beings
in the heavens, on earth and in the underworld,
should bend the knee at the name of Jesus
and that every tongue should acclaim
Jesus Christ as Lord,
to the glory of God the Father.

  This is the word of the Lord.   *Philippians 2:6-11*

Gospel Acclamation

Praise to you, O Christ, king of eternal glory:
Christ was humbler yet,
even to accepting death, death on a cross.
But God raised him high
and gave him the name which is above all names.
Praise to you, O Christ, king of eternal glory.   *Phil 2:8-9*

GOSPEL

Year A

The passion of our Lord Jesus Christ according to Matthew
*
N One of the Twelve, the man called Judas Iscariot, went to the chief priests and said:

O What are you prepared to give me if I hand him over to you?

N They paid him thirty silver pieces, and from that moment he looked for an opportunity to betray him.
    Now on the first day of Unleavened Bread the disciples came to Jesus to say,

C Where do you want us to make the preparations for you to eat the passover?

N He replied:

J Go to so-and-so in the city and say to him, 'The Master says: My time is near. It is at your house that I am keeping Passover with my disciples'.

N The disciples did what Jesus told them and prepared the Passover. When the evening came he was at table with the twelve disciples. And while they were eating he said:

J I tell you solemnly, one of you is about to betray me.

N They were greatly distressed and started asking him in turn,

C Not I, Lord, surely?

N He answered:

J Someone who has dipped his hand into the dish with me, will betray me. The Son of Man is going to his fate, as the scriptures say he will, but alas for that man by whom the Son of Man is betrayed! Better for that man if he had never been born!

N Judas, who was to betray him, asked in his turn,

O Not I, Rabbi, surely?

N Jesus answered:

N Narrator.   J Jesus.   O Other single speaker.
C Crowd, or more than one other speaker.

J   They are your own words.

N   Now as they were eating, Jesus took some bread, and when he had said the blessing he broke it and gave it to the disciples and said:

J   Take it and eat; this is my body.

N   Then he took a cup, and when he had returned thanks he gave it to them saying:

J   Drink all of you from this, for this is my blood, the blood of the covenant, which is to be poured out for many for the forgiveness of sins. From now on, I tell you, I shall not drink wine until the day I drink the new wine with you in the kingdom of my Father.

N   After psalms had been sung they left for the Mount of Olives. Then Jesus said to them,

J   You will all lose faith in me this night, for the scripture says: I shall strike the shepherd and the sheep of the flock will be scattered. But after my resurrection I shall go before you to Galilee.

N   At this, Peter said:

O   Though all lose faith in you, I will never lose faith.

N   Jesus answered him,

J   I tell you solemnly, this very night, before the cock crows, you will have disowned me three times.

N   Peter said to him,

O   Even if I have to die with you, I will never disown you.

N   And all the disciples said the same.

    Then Jesus came with them to a small estate called Gethsemane; and he said to his disciples,

J   Stay here while I go over there to pray.

N   He took Peter and the two sons of Zebedee with him. And sadness came over him, and great distress. Then he said to them:

J   My soul is sorrowful to the point of death. Wait here and keep awake with me.

N   And going on a little further he fell on his face and prayed:

J   My Father, if it is possible let this cup pass me by. Nevertheless, let it be as you, not I, would have it.

N   He came back to the disciples and found them sleeping, and he said to Peter:

J   So you had not the strength to keep awake with me one hour? You should be awake, and praying not to be put to the test. The spirit is willing, but the flesh is weak.

N   Again, a second time, he went away and prayed:

J   My father, if this cup cannot pass by without my drinking it, your will be done!

N   And he came again back and found them sleeping, their eyes were so heavy. Leaving them there, he went away again and prayed for the third time, repeating the same words. Then he came back to the disciples and said to them,

J   You can sleep on now and take your rest. Now the hour has come when the Son of Man is to be betrayed into the hands of sinners. Get up! Let us go! My betrayer is already close at hand.

N   He was still speaking when Judas, one of the Twelve, appeared, and with him a large number of men armed with swords and clubs, sent by the chief priests and elders of the people. Now the traitor had arranged a sign with them. He had said:

O   'The one I kiss, he is the man. Take him in charge.'

N   So he went straight up to Jesus and said:

O   Greetings, Rabbi,

N   and kissed him. Jesus said to him,

J   My friend, do what you are here for.

N   Then they came forward, seized Jesus and took him in charge. At that, one of the followers of Jesus grasped his sword and drew it; he struck out at the high priest's servant, and cut off his ear. Jesus then said:

J   Put your sword back, for all who draw the sword will die by the sword. Or do you think that I cannot appeal to my Father who would promptly send more than twelve legions of angels to my defence? But then, how would the scriptures be fulfilled that say this is the way it must be?

N   It was at this time that Jesus said to the crowds:

J   Am I a brigand, that you had to set out to capture me with swords and clubs? I sat teaching in the Temple day after day and you never laid hands on me.

N   Now all this happened to fulfil the prophecies in scripture. Then all the disciples deserted him and ran away.

    The men who had arrested Jesus led him off to Caiaphas the high priest, where the scribes and the elders were assembled. Peter followed him at a distance, and when he reached the high priest's palace, he went in and sat down with the attendants to see what the end would be.

The chief priests and the whole Sanhedrin were looking for evidence against Jesus, however false, on which they might pass the death-sentence. But they could not find any, though several lying witnesses came forward. Eventually two stepped forward and made a statement,

O This man said: 'I have power to destroy the Temple of God and in three days build it up'.

N The high priest then stood up and said to him:

O Have you no answer to that? What is this evidence these men are bringing against you?

N But Jesus was silent. And the high priest said to him:

O I put you on oath by the living God to tell us if you are the Christ, the Son of God.

N Jesus answered:

J The words are your own. Moreover, I tell you that from this time onward you will see the Son of Man seated at the right hand of the Power and coming on the clouds of heaven.

N At this, the high priest tore his clothes and said:

O He has blasphemed. What need of witnesses have we now? There! You have just heard the blasphemy. What is your opinion?

N They answered:

C He deserves to die.

N Then they spat in his face and hit him with their fists; others said as they struck him:

C Play the prophet, Christ! Who hit you then?

N Meanwhile Peter was sitting outside in the courtyard, and a servant-girl came up to him and said:

O You too were with Jesus the Galilean.

N But he denied it in front of them all, saying:

O I do not know what you are talking about.

N When he went out to the gateway another servant-girl saw him and said to the people there:

O This man was with Jesus the Nazarene.

N And again, with an oath, he denied it,

O I do not know the man.

N A little later the bystanders came up and said to Peter:

C You are one of them for sure! Why, your accent gives you away.

N Then he started calling down curses on himself and swearing:

O I do not know the man.

N At that moment the cock crew, and Peter remembered what Jesus had said, 'Before the cock crows you will have disowned me three times.' And he went outside and wept bitterly.

When morning came, all the chief priests and the elders of the people met in council to bring about the death of Jesus. They had him bound, and led him away to hand him over to Pilate, the governor. When he found that Jesus had been condemned, Judas his betrayer was filled with remorse and took the thirty pieces of silver back to the chief priests and elders, saying:

O I have sinned. I have betrayed innocent blood.

N They replied:

C What is that to us? That is your concern.

N And flinging down the silver pieces in the sanctuary he made off, and went and hanged himself. The chief priests picked up the silver pieces and said:

C It is against the Law to put this into the treasury; it is blood money.

N So they discussed the matter and bought the potter's field with it as a graveyard for foreigners, and this is why the field is called the Field of Blood today. The words of the prophet Jeremiah were then fulfilled: And they took the thirty silver pieces, the sum at which the precious One was priced by children of Israel, and they gave them for the potter's field, just as the Lord directed me.

Jesus, then, was brought before the governor, and the governor put to him this question:

O Are you the king of the Jews?

N Jesus replied:

J It is you who say it.

N But when he was accused by the chief priests and the elders he refused to answer at all. Pilate then said to him:

O Do you not hear how many charges they have brought against you?

N But to the governor's complete amazement, he offered no reply to any of the charges.

At festival time it was the governor's practice to release a prisoner for the people, anyone they chose. Now there was at that time a notorious prisoner whose name was Barabbas. So when the crowd gathered, Pilate said to them,

O Which do you want me to release for you: Barabbas or Jesus who is called Christ?

N For Pilate knew it was out of jealousy that they had handed him over. Now as he was seated in the chair of judgement, his wife sent him a message,

O Have nothing to do with that man; I have been upset all day by a dream I had about him.

N The chief priests and the elders, however, had persuaded the crowd to demand the release of Barabbas and the execution of Jesus. So when the governor spoke and asked them:

O Which of the two do you want me to release for you?

N They said:

C Barabbas.

N Pilate said to them:

O What am I to do with Jesus who is called Christ?

N They all said:

C Let him be crucified!

N Pilate asked:

O Why? What harm has he done?

N But they shouted all the louder,

C Let him be crucified!

N Then Pilate saw that he was making no impression, that in fact a riot was imminent. So he took some water, washed his hands in front of the crowd and said:

O I am innocent of this man's blood. It is your concern.

N And the people, to a man, shouted back:

C His blood be on us and on our children!

N Then he released Barabbas for them. He ordered Jesus to be first scourged and then handed over to be crucified.

The governor's soldiers took Jesus with them into the Praetorium and collected the whole cohort round him. Then they stripped him and made him wear a scarlet cloak, and having twisted some thorns into a crown they put this on his head and placed a reed in his right hand. To make fun of him they knelt to him saying:

C Hail, king of the Jews!

N And they spat on him and took the reed and struck him on the head with it. And when they had finished making fun of him, they took off the cloak and dressed him in his own clothes and led him away to crucify him.

On their way out, they came across a man from Cyrene, Simon by name, and enlisted him to carry his cross. When they had reached a place called Golgotha, that is, the place of the skull, they gave him wine to drink. When they had finished crucifying him they shared out his clothing by casting lots, and then sat down and stayed there keeping guard over him. Above his head was placed the charge against him; it read: 'This is Jesus, the King of the Jews'. At the same time two robbers were crucified with him, one on the right and one on the left.

The passers-by jeered at him; they shook their heads and said:

C   So you would destroy the Temple and rebuild it in three days! Then save yourself! If you are God's son, come down from the cross!

N   The chief priests with the scribes and elders mocked him in the same way, saying:

C   He saved others; he cannot save himself. He is the King of Israel; let him come down from the cross now, and we will believe in him. He put his trust in God; now let God rescue him if he wants him. For he did say, 'I am the son of God'.

N   Even the robbers who were crucified with him taunted him in the same way.

From the sixth hour there was darkness over all the land until the ninth hour. And about the ninth hour, Jesus cried out in a loud voice:

J   Eli, Eli, lama sabachthani?

N   That is: 'My God, my God, why have you deserted me?' When some of those who stood there heard this, they said:

C   The man is calling on Elijah,

N   and one of them quickly ran to get a sponge which he dipped in vinegar and, putting it on a reed, gave it him to drink. The rest of them said:

C   Wait! See if Elijah will come to save him.

N   But Jesus, again crying out in a loud voice, yielded up his spirit.

All kneel and pause a moment.

N   At that, the veil of the Temple was torn in two from top to bottom; the earth quaked; the rocks were split; the tombs opened and the bodies of many holy men rose from the dead, and these, after his resurrection, came out of the tombs, entered the Holy City and appeared to a number of people.

Meanwhile the centurion, together with the others guarding Jesus, had seen the earthquake and all that was taking place, and they were terrified and said:

C   In truth this was a son of God.

N And many women were there, watching from a distance, the same women who had followed Jesus from Galilee and looked after him. Among them were Mary of Magdala, Mary the mother of James and Joseph, and the mother of Zebedee's sons.

When it was evening, there came a rich man of Arimathaea called Joseph, who had himself become a disciple of Jesus. This man went to Pilate and asked for the body of Jesus. Pilate thereupon ordered it to be handed over. So Joseph took the body, wrapped it in a clean shroud and put it in his own new tomb which he had hewn out of the rock. He then rolled a large stone across the entrance of the tomb and went away. Now Mary of Magdala and the other Mary were there, sitting opposite the sepulchre.

Next day, that is, when Preparation Day was over, the chief priests and the Pharisees went in a body to Pilate and said to him,

C Your Excellency, we recall that this impostor said, while he was still alive, 'After three days I shall rise again'. Therefore give the order to have the sepulchre kept secure until the third day, for fear his disciples come and steal him away and tell the people, 'He has risen from the dead'. This last piece of fraud would be worse than what went before.

N Pilate said to them:

O You may have your guards. Go and make all as secure as you know how.

N So they went and made the sepulchre secure, putting seals on the stone and mounting a guard.

Matthew 26:14–27:66 ℞

Shorter form

The passion of our Lord Jesus Christ according to Matthew
*
Jesus was brought before Pontius Pilate, the governor, and the governor put to him this question, 'Are you the king of the Jews?' Jesus replied, 'It is you who say it.' But when he was accused by the chief priests and the elders he refused to answer at all. Pilate then said to him, 'Do you not hear how many charges they have brought against you?' But to the governor's complete amazement, he offered no reply to any of the charges.

At festival time it was the governor's practice to release a prisoner for the people, anyone they chose. Now there was at that a time notorious prisoner whose name was Barabbas. So when the crowd gathered, Pilate said to them, 'Which do you want me to release for you: Barabbas, or Jesus who is called Christ?' For Pilate knew it was out of jealousy that they had handed him over.

Now as he was seated in the chair of judgement, his wife sent him a message, 'Have nothing to do with that man; I have been upset all day by a dream I had about him.'

The chief priests and the elders, however, had persuaded the crowd to demand the release of Barabbas and the execution of Jesus. So when the governor spoke and asked them, 'Which of the two do you want me to release for you?' they said 'Barabbas'. 'But in that case,' Pilate said to them 'what am I to do with Jesus who is called Christ?' They all said, 'Let him be crucified!' 'Why?' he asked 'What harm has he done?' But they shouted all the louder, 'Let him be crucified!' Then Pilate saw that he was making no impression, that in fact a riot was imminent. So he took some water, washed his hands in front of the crowd and said, 'I am innocent of this man's blood. It is your concern.' And the people, to a man, shouted back, 'His blood be on us and on our children!' Then he released Barabbas for them. He ordered Jesus to be first scourged and then handed over to be crucified.

The governor's soldiers took Jesus with them into the Praetorium and collected the whole cohort round him. Then they stripped him and made him wear a scarlet cloak, and having twisted some thorns into a crown they put this on his head and placed a reed in his right hand. To make fun of him they knelt to him saying, 'Hail, king of the Jews!' And they spat on him and took the reed and struck him on the head with it. And when they had finished making fun of him, they took off the cloak and dressed him in his own clothes and led him away to crucify him.

On their way out, they came across a man from Cyrene, Simon by name, and enlisted him to carry his cross. When they had reached a place called Golgotha, that is, the place of the skull, they gave him wine to drink mixed with gall, which he tasted but refused to drink. When they had finished crucifying him they shared out his clothing by casting lots, and then sat down and stayed there keeping guard over him.

Above his head was placed the charge against him; it read: 'This is Jesus, the King of the Jews.' At the same time two robbers were crucified with him, one on the right and one on the left.

The passers-by jeered at him; they shook their heads and said 'So you would destroy the Temple and rebuild it in three days! Then save yourself! If you are God's son, come down from the cross!' The chief priests with the scribes and elders mocked him in the same way. 'He saved others,' they said 'he cannot save himself. He is the king of Israel; let him come down from the cross now, and we will believe in him. He put his trust in God; now let God rescue him if he wants him. For he did say, "I am the son of God." ' Even the robbers who were crucified with him taunted him in the same way.

From the sixth hour there was darkness over all the land until the ninth hour. And about the ninth hour, Jesus cried out in a loud voice, 'Eli, Eli, lama sabachthani?' that is, 'My God, my God, why have you deserted me?' When some of those who stood there heard this, they said, 'The man is calling on Elijah,' and one of them quickly ran to get a sponge which he dipped in vinegar and putting it on a reed, gave it him to drink. 'Wait!' said the rest of them 'and see if Elijah will come to save him.' But Jesus again crying out in a loud voice, yielded up his spirit.

All kneel and pause a moment.

At that, the veil of the Temple was torn in two from top to bottom; the earth quaked; the rocks were split; the tombs opened and the bodies of many holy men rose from the dead, and these, after his resurrection, came out of the tombs, entered the Holy City and appeared to a number of people. Meanwhile the centurion, together with the others guarding Jesus, had seen the earthquake and all that was taking place, and they were terrified and said, 'In truth this was a son of God.'

Matthew 27:11-54

Year B

The passion of our Lord Jesus Christ according to Mark
*

N It was two days before the Passover and the feast of Unleavened Bread, and the chief priests and scribes were looking for a way to arrest Jesus by some trick and have him put to death. For they said,

N Narrator. J Jesus. O Other single speaker.
C Crowd, or more than one speaker.

C It must not be during the festivities, or there will be a disturbance among the people.

N Jesus was at Bethany in the house of Simon the leper; he was at dinner when a woman came in with an alabaster jar of very costly ointment, pure nard. She broke the jar and poured the ointment on his head. Some who were there said to one another indignantly,

C Why this waste of ointment? Ointment like this could have been sold for over three hundred denarii and the money given to the poor;

N and they were angry with her. But Jesus said,

J Leave her alone. Why are you upsetting her? What she has done for me is one of the good works. You have the poor with you always and you can be kind to them whenever you wish, but you will not always have me. She has done what was in her power to do; she has anointed my body beforehand for its burial. I tell you solemnly, wherever throughout all the world the Good News is proclaimed, what she has done will be told also, in remembrance of her.

N Judas Iscariot, one of the Twelve, approached the chief priests with an offer to hand Jesus over to them. They were delighted to hear it, and promised to give him money; and he looked for a way of betraying him when the opportunity should occur.

On the first day of Unleavened Bread, when the Passover lamb was sacrificed, his disciples said to him,

C Where do you want us to go and make the preparations for you to eat the passover?

N So he sent two of his disciples, saying to them,

J Go into the city and you will meet a man carrying a pitcher of water. Follow him, and say to the owner of the house which he enters, 'The Master says: Where is my dining room in which I can eat the passover with my disciples?' He will show you a large upper room furnished with couches, all prepared. Make the preparations for us there.

N The disciples set out and went to the city and found everything as he had told them, and prepared the Passover.

When evening came he arrived with the Twelve. And while they were at table eating, Jesus said,

J I tell you solemnly, one of you is about to betray me, one of you eating with me.

N They were distressed and asked him, one after another,

O Not I, surely?

N He said to them,

J It is one of the Twelve, one who is dipping into the same dish with me. Yes, the Son of Man is going to his fate, as the scriptures say he will, but alas for that man by whom the Son of Man is betrayed! Better for that man if he had never been born!

N And as they were eating he took some bread, and when he had said the blessing he broke it and gave it to them, saying,

J Take it; this is my body.

N Then he took a cup, and when he had returned thanks he gave it to them, and all drank from it, and he said to them,

J This is my blood, the blood of the covenant, which is to be poured out for many. I tell you solemnly, I shall not drink any more wine until the day I drink the new wine in the kingdom of God.

N After psalms had been sung they left for the Mount of Olives. And Jesus said to them,

J You will all lose faith, for the scripture says, 'I shall strike the shepherd and the sheep will be scattered'. However after my resurrection I shall go before you to Galilee.

N Peter said,

O Even if all lose faith, I will not.

N And Jesus said to him,

J I tell you solemnly, this day, this very night, before the cock crows twice, you will have disowned me three times.

N But he repeated still more earnestly,

O If I have to die with you, I will never disown you.

N And they all said the same.
    They came to a small estate called Gethsemane, and Jesus said to his disciples,

J Stay here while I pray.

N Then he took Peter and James and John with him. And a sudden fear came over him, and great distress. And he said to them,

J My soul is sorrowful to the point of death. Wait here, and keep awake.

N And going on a little further he threw himself on the ground and prayed that, if it were possible, this hour might pass him by. He said,

J Abba (Father)! Everything is possible for you. Take this cup away from me. But let it be as you, not I, would have it.

N He came back and found them sleeping, and he said to Peter,

J   Simon, are you asleep? Had you not the strength to keep awake one hour? You should be awake, and praying not to be put to the test. The spirit is willing but the flesh is weak.

N   Again he went away and prayed, saying the same words. And once more he came back and found them sleeping, their eyes were so heavy; and they could find no answer for him. He came back a third time and said to them,

J   You can sleep on now and take your rest. It is all over . The hour has come. Now the Son of Man is to be betrayed into the hands of sinners. Get up! Let us go! My betrayer is close at hand already.

N   Even while he was still speaking, Judas, one of the Twelve, came up with a number of men armed with swords and clubs, sent by the chief priests and the scribes and the elders. Now the traitor had arranged a signal with them. He had said,

O   'The one I kiss, he is the man. Take him in charge, and see he is well guarded when you lead him away.'

N   So when the traitor came, he went straight up to Jesus and said,

O   Rabbi!

N   and kissed him. The others seized him and took him in charge. Then one of the bystanders drew his sword and struck out at the high priest's servant, and cut off his ear.
    Then Jesus spoke,

J   Am I a brigand that you had to set out to capture me with swords and clubs? I was among you teaching in the Temple day after day and you never laid hands on me. But this is to fulfil the scriptures.

N   And they all deserted him and ran away. A young man who followed him had nothing on but a linen cloth. They caught hold of him, but he left the cloth in their hands and ran away naked.
    They led Jesus off to the high priest; and all the chief priests and the elders and the scribes assembled there. Peter had followed him at a distance, right into the high priest's palace, and was sitting with the attendants warming himself at the fire.
    The chief priests and the whole Sanhedrin were looking for evidence against Jesus on which they might pass the death-sentence. But they could not find any. Several, indeed, brought false evidence against him, but their evidence was conflicting. Some stood up and submitted this false evidence against him,

C We heard him say, 'I am going to destroy this Temple made by human hands, and in three days build another, not made by human hands'.

N But even on this point their evidence was conflicting. The high priest then stood up before the whole assembly and put this question to Jesus,

O Have you no answer to that? What is this evidence these men are bringing against you?

N But he was silent and made no answer at all. The high priest put a second question to him,

O Are you the Christ the Son of the Blessed One?

N Jesus said,

J I am, and you will see the Son of Man seated at the right hand of the Power and coming with the clouds of heaven.

N The high priest tore his robes, and said,

O What need of witnesses have we now? You heard the blasphemy. What is your finding?

N And they all gave their verdict: he deserved to die.
Some of them started spitting at him and, blindfolding him, began hitting him with their fists and shouting,

C Play the prophet!

N And the attendants rained blows on him.
While Peter was down below in the courtyard, one of the high-priest's servant-girls came up. She saw Peter warming himself there, stared at him and said,

O You too were with Jesus, the man from Nazareth.

N But he denied it, saying

O I do not know, I do not understand what you are talking about.

N And he went out into the forecourt. The servant-girl saw him and again started telling the bystanders,

O This fellow is one of them.

N But he again denied it. A little later the bystanders themselves said to Peter,

C You are one of them for sure! Why, you are a Galilean.

N But he started calling curses on himself and swearing,

O I do not know the man you speak of.

N At that moment the cock crew for the second time, and Peter recalled how Jesus had said to him, 'Before the cock crows twice, you will have disowned me three times'. And he burst into tears.
First thing in the morning, the chief priest together with the elders and scribes, in short the whole Sanhedrin, had their

plan ready. They had Jesus bound and took him away and handed him over to Pilate.

Pilate questioned him,

O Are you the king of the Jews?

N He answered,

J It is you who say it.

N And the chief priests brought many accusations against him. Pilate questioned him again,

O Have you no reply at all? See how many accusations they are bringing against you!

N But to Pilate's amazement, Jesus made no further reply.

At festival time Pilate used to release a prisoner for them, anyone they asked for. Now a man called Barabbas was then in prison with the rioters who had committed murder during the uprising. When the crowd went up and began to ask Pilate the customary favour, Pilate answered them,

O Do you want me to release for you the king of the Jews?

N For he realised it was out of jealousy that the chief priests had handed Jesus over. The chief priests, however, had incited the crowd to demand that he should release Barabbas for them instead. Then Pilate spoke again.

O But in that case, what am I to do with the man you call king of the Jews?

N They shouted back.

C Crucify him!

N Pilate asked them,

O Why? What harm has he done?

N But they shouted all the louder,

C Crucify him!

N So Pilate, anxious to placate the crowd, released Barabbas for them and, having ordered Jesus to be scourged, handed him over to be crucified.

The soldiers led him away to the inner part of the palace, that is, the Praetorium, and called the whole cohort together. They dressed him up in purple, twisted some thorns into a crown and put it on him. And they began saluting him,

C Hail, king of the Jews!

N They struck his head with a reed and spat on him; and they went down on their knees to do him homage. And when they had finished making fun of him, they took off the purple and dressed him in his own clothes.

They led him out to crucify him. They enlisted a passer-by, Simon of Cyrene, father of Alexander and Rufus, who was coming in from the country, to carry his cross. They brought Jesus to the place called Golgotha, which means the place of the skull.

They offered him wine mixed with myrrh, but he refused it. Then they crucified him, and shared out his clothing, casting lots to decide what each should get. It was the third hour when they crucified him. The inscription giving the charge against him read: 'The King of the Jews.' And they crucified two robbers with him, one on his right and one on his left.

The passers-by jeered at him; they shook their heads and said,

C Aha! So you would destroy the Temple and rebuild it in three days! Then save yourself: come down from the cross!

N The chief priests and the scribes mocked him among themselves in the same way. They said,

C He saved others, he cannot save himself. Let the Christ, the king of Israel, come down from the cross now, for us to see it and believe.

N Even those who were crucified with him taunted him.

When the sixth hour came there was darkness over the whole land until the ninth hour. And at the ninth hour Jesus cried out in a loud voice,

J Eloi, Eloi, lama sabachthani?

N This means 'My God, my God, why have you deserted me?' When some of those who stood by heard this, they said,

C Listen, he is calling on Elijah.

N Someone ran and soaked a sponge in vinegar and, putting it on a reed, gave it him to drink, saying,

O Wait and see if Elijah will come to take him down.

N But Jesus gave a loud cry and breathed his last.

All kneel and pause a moment.

N And the veil of the Temple was torn in two from top to bottom. The centurion, who was standing in front of him, had seen how he had died, and he said,

O In truth this man was a son of God.

N There were some women watching from a distance. Among them were Mary of Magdala, Mary who was the mother of James the younger, and Joset, and Salome. These used to follow him and look after him when he was in Galilee. And there were many other women there who had come up to Jerusalem with him.

It was now evening, and since it was Preparation Day (that is the vigil of the sabbath), there came Joseph of Arimathaea, a prominent member of the Council, who himself lived in the hope of seeing the kingdom of God, and he boldly went to Pilate and asked for the body of Jesus. Pilate, astonished that he should have died so soon, summoned the centurion and enquired if he was already dead. Having been assured of this by the centurion, he granted the corpse to Joseph who brought a shroud, took Jesus down from the cross, wrapped him in the shroud and laid him in a tomb which had been hewn out of the rock. He then rolled a stone against the entrance to the tomb. Mary of Magdala and Mary the mother of Joset were watching and took note of where he was laid.

Mark 14:1–15:47

Shorter form

The passion of our Lord Jesus Christ according to Mark
*
First thing in the morning, the chief priests together with the elders and scribes, in short the whole Sanhedrin, had their plan ready. They had Jesus bound and took him away and handed him over to Pilate.

Pilate questioned him, 'Are you the king of the Jews?' 'It is you who say it' he answered. And the chief priests brought many accusations against him. Pilate questioned him again, 'Have you no reply at all? See how many accusations they are bringing against you!' But to Pilate's amazement, Jesus made no further reply.

At festival time Pilate used to release a prisoner for them, anyone they asked for. Now a man called Barabbas was then in prison with the rioters who had committed murder during the uprising. When the crowd went up and began to ask Pilate the customary favour, Pilate answered them, 'Do you want me to release for you the king of the Jews?' For he realised it was out of jealousy that the chief priests had handed Jesus over. The chief priests, however, had incited the crowd to demand that he should release Barabbas for them instead. Then Pilate spoke again. 'But in that case,' he said to them 'what am I to do with the man you call king of the Jews?' They shouted back, 'Crucify him!' 'Why?' Pilate asked them 'What harm has he done?' But they shouted all the louder, 'Crucify him!' So Pilate, anxious to placate the crowd, released Barabbas for them and, having ordered Jesus to be scourged, handed him over to be crucified.

The soldiers led him away to the inner part of the palace, that is, the Praetorium, and called the whole cohort together. They dressed him up in purple, twisted some thorns into a crown and put it on him. And they began saluting him, 'Hail, king of the Jews!' They struck his head with a reed and spat on him; and they went down on their knees to do him homage. And when they had finished making fun of him, they took off the purple and dressed him in his own clothes.

They led him out to crucify him. They enlisted a passer-by, Simon of Cyrene, father of Alexander and Rufus, who was coming in from the country, to carry his cross. They brought Jesus to the place called Golgotha, which means the place of the skull.

They offered him wine mixed with myrrh, but he refused it. Then they crucified him, and shared out his clothing, casting lots to decide what each should get. It was the third hour when they crucified him. The inscription giving the charge against him read: 'The King of the Jews'. And they crucified two robbers with him, one on his right and one on his left.

The passers-by jeered at him; they shook their heads and said, 'Aha! So you would destroy the Temple and rebuild it in three days! Then save yourself: come down from the cross!' The chief priests and the scribes mocked him among themselves in the same way. 'He saved others,' they said 'he cannot save himself. Let the Christ, the king of Israel, come down from the cross now, for us to see it and believe.' Even those who were crucified with him taunted him.

When the sixth hour came there was darkness over the whole land until the ninth hour. And at the ninth hour Jesus cried out in a loud voice, 'Eloi, Eloi, lama sabachthani?' which means, 'My God, my God, why have you deserted me?' When some of those who stood by heard this, they said, 'Listen he is calling on Elijah'. Someone ran and soaked a sponge in vinegar and, putting it on a reed, gave it him to drink saying, 'Wait and see if Elijah will come to take him down.' But Jesus gave a loud cry and breathed his last.

All kneel and pause a moment.

And the veil of the Temple was torn in two from top to bottom. The centurion, who was standing in front of him, had seen how he had died, and he said, 'In truth this man was a son of God.'

Mark 15:1-39

Year C

The passion of our Lord Jesus Christ according to Luke

*

N When the hour came Jesus took his place at table, and the apostles with him. And he said to them,

J I have longed to eat this passover with you before I suffer; because, I tell you, I shall not eat it again until it is fulfilled in the kingdom of God.

N Then, taking a cup, he gave thanks and said,

J Take this and share it among you, because from now on, I tell you, I shall not drink wine until the kingdom of God comes.

N Then he took some bread, and when he had given thanks, broke it and gave it to them, saying,

J This is my body which will be given for you; do this as a memorial of me.

N He did the same with the cup after supper, and said,

J This cup is the new covenant in my blood which will be poured out for you.

And yet, here with me on the table is the hand of the man who betrays me. The Son of Man does indeed go to his fate even as it has been decreed, but alas for that man by whom he is betrayed!

N And they began to ask one another which of them it could be who was to do this thing.

A dispute arose also between them about which should be reckoned the greatest, but he said to them,

J Among pagans it is the kings who lord it over them, and those who have authority over them are given the title Benefactor. This must not happen with you. No; the greatest among you must behave as if he were the youngest, the leader as if he were the one who serves. For who is the greater: the one at table or the one who serves? The one at table, surely? Yet here I am among you as one who serves!

You are the men who have stood by me faithfully in my trials; and now I confer a kingdom on you, just as my Father conferred one on me: you will eat and drink at my table in my kingdom, and you will sit on thrones to judge the twelve tribes of Israel.

N Narrator. **J** Jesus. **O** Other single speaker.
C Crowd, or more than one speaker.

Simon, Simon! Satan, you must know, has got his wish to sift you all like wheat; but I have prayed for you, Simon, that your faith may not fail, and once you have recovered, you in your turn must strengthen your brothers.

N He answered,

O Lord, I would be ready to go to prison with you, and to death.

N Jesus replied,

J I tell you, Peter, by the time the cock crows today you will have denied three times that you know me.

N He said to them,

J When I sent you out without purse or haversack or sandals, were you short of anything?

N They answered,

C No.

N He said to them,

J But now if you have a purse, take it: if you have a haversack, do the same; if you have no sword, sell your cloak and buy one, because I tell you these words of scripture have to be fulfilled in me: He let himself be taken for a criminal. Yes, what scripture says about me is even now reaching its fulfilment.

N They said,

C Lord, there are two swords here now.

N He said to them,

J That is enough!

N He then left the upper room to make his way as usual to the Mount of Olives, with the disciples following. When they reached the place he said to them,

J Pray not to be put to the test.

N Then he withdrew from them, about a stone's throw away, and knelt down and prayed, saying,

J Father, if you are willing, take this cup away from me. Nevertheless, let your will be done, not mine.

N Then an angel appeared to him coming from heaven to give him strength. In his anguish he prayed even more earnestly, and his sweat fell to the ground like great drops of blood.

When he rose from prayer he went to the disciples and found them sleeping for sheer grief. He said to them,

J Why are you asleep? Get up and pray not to be put to the test.

N He was still speaking when a number of men appeared, and at the head of them the man called Judas, one of the Twelve, who went up to Jesus to kiss him. Jesus said,

J Judas, are you betraying the Son of Man with a kiss?
N His followers, seeing what was happening, said,
C Lord, shall we use our swords?
N And one of them struck out at the high priest's servant, and cut off his right ear. But at this Jesus spoke,
J Leave off! That will do!
N And touching the man's ear he healed him.

  Then Jesus spoke to the chief priests and captains of the Temple guard and elders who had come for him. He said.
J Am I a brigand that you had to set out with swords and clubs? When I was among you in the Temple day after day you never moved to lay hands on me. But this is your hour; this is the reign of darkness.
N They seized him then and led him away, and they took him to the high priest's house. Peter followed at a distance. They had lit a fire in the middle of the courtyard and Peter sat down among them, and as he was sitting there by the blaze a servant-girl saw him, peered at him and said,
O This person was with him too.
N But he denied it, saying,
O Woman, I do not know him.
N Shortly afterwards, someone else saw him and said,
O You are another of them.
N But Peter replied,
O I am not, my friend.
N About an hour later, another man insisted, saying,
O This fellow was certainly with him. Why, he is a Galilean.
N Peter said,
O My friend, I do not know what you are talking about.
N At that instant, while he was still speaking, the cock crew, and the Lord turned and looked straight at Peter, and Peter remembered what the Lord had said to him, 'Before the cock crows today, you will have disowned me three times'. And he went outside and wept bitterly.

  Meanwhile the men who guarded Jesus were mocking and beating him. They blindfolded him and questioned him, saying,
C Play the prophet. Who hit you then?
N And they continued heaping insults on him.

  When day broke there was a meeting of the elders of the people, attended by the chief priests and scribes. He was brought before their council, and they said to him,
C If you are the Christ, tell us.

N He replied,

J If I tell you, you will not believe me, and if I question you, you will not answer. But from now on, the Son of Man will be seated at the right hand of the Power of God.

N Then they all said,

C So you are the Son of God then?

N He answered,

J It is you who say I am.

N They said,

C What need of witnesses have we now? We have heard it for ourselves from his own lips.

N The whole assembly then rose, and they brought him before Pilate.

They began their accusation by saying,

C We found this man inciting our people to revolt, opposing payment of tribute to Caesar, and claiming to be Christ, a king.

N Pilate put to him this question,

O Are you the king of the Jews?

N He replied,

J It is you who say it.

N Pilate then said to the chief priests and the crowd,

O I find no case against this man.

N But they persisted,

C He is inflaming the people with his teaching all over Judaea; it has come all the way from Galilee, where he started, down to here.

N When Pilate heard this, he asked if the man were a Galilean; and finding that he came under Herod's jurisdiction he passed him over to Herod who was also in Jerusalem at that time.

Herod was delighted to see Jesus; he had heard about him and had been wanting for a long time to set eyes on him; moreover, he was hoping to see some miracle worked by him. So he questioned him at some length; but without getting any reply. Meanwhile the chief priests and the scribes were there, violently pressing their accusations. Then Herod, together with his guards, treated him with contempt and made fun of him; he put a rich cloak on him and sent him back to Pilate. And though Herod and Pilate had been enemies before, they were reconciled that same day.

Pilate then summoned the chief priests and the leading men and the people. He said,

O You brought this man before me as a political agitator. Now I have gone into the matter myself in your presence and found no case against him. Nor has Herod either, since he has sent him back to us. As you can see, the man has done nothing that deserves death, so I shall have him flogged and then let him go.

N But as one man they howled,

C Away with him! Give us Barabbas!

N This man had been thrown into prison for causing a riot in the city and for murder.

Pilate was anxious to set Jesus free and addressed them again, but they shouted back.

C Crucify him! Crucify him!

N And for the third time he spoke to them,

O Why? What harm has this man done? I have found no case against him that deserves death, so I shall have him punished and let him go.

N But they kept on shouting at the top of their voices, demanding that he should be crucified, and their shouts were growing louder.

Pilate then gave his verdict: their demand was to be granted. He released the man they asked for, who had been imprisoned for rioting and murder, and handed Jesus over to them to deal with as they pleased.

As they were leading him away they seized on a man, Simon from Cyrene, who was coming in from the country, and made him shoulder the cross and carry it behind Jesus. Large numbers of people followed him, and of women too who mourned and lamented for him. But Jesus turned to them and said,

J Daughters of Jerusalem, do not weep for me; weep rather for yourselves and for your children. For the days will surely come when people will say, 'Happy are those who are barren, the wombs that have never borne, the breasts that have never suckled!' Then they will begin to say to the mountains, 'Fall on us!'; to the hills, 'Cover us!' For if men use the green wood like this, what will happen when it is dry?

N Now with him they were also leading out two other criminals to be executed.

When they reached the place called The Skull, they crucified him there and the criminals also, one on the right, the other on the left. Jesus said,

J Father, forgive them; they do not know what they are doing.

N Then they cast lots to share out his clothing. The people stayed there watching him. As for the leaders, they jeered at him, saying,

C He saved others; let him save himself if he is the Christ of God, the Chosen One.

N The soldiers mocked him too, and when they approached to offer him vinegar they said,

C If you are the king of the Jews, save yourself.

N Above him there was an inscription: 'This is the King of the Jews.'

One of the criminals hanging there abused him, saying,

O Are you not the Christ? Save yourself and us as well.

N But the other spoke up and rebuked him,

O Have you no fear of God at all? You got the same sentence as he did, but in our case we deserved it: we are paying for what we did. But this man has done nothing wrong. Jesus, remember me when you come into your kingdom.

N He replied

J Indeed, I promise you, today you will be with me in paradise.

N It was now about the sixth hour and, with the sun eclipsed, a darkness came over the whole land until the ninth hour. The veil of the Temple was torn right down the middle; and when Jesus had cried out in a loud voice, he said,

J Father, into your hands I commit my spirit.

N With these words he breathed his last.

All kneel and pause a moment.

When the centurion saw what had taken place, he gave praise to God and said,

O This was a great and good man.

N And when all the people who had gathered for the spectacle saw what had happened, they went home beating their breasts.

All his friends stood at a distance; so also did the women who had accompanied him from Galilee, and they saw all this happen.

Then a member of the council arrived, an upright and virtuous man named Joseph. He had not consented to what the others had planned and carried out. He came from Arimathaea, a Jewish town, and he lived in the hope of seeing the kingdom of God. This man went to Pilate and asked for the body of Jesus. He then took it down, wrapped it in a shroud and put him in a tomb which was hewn in stone in which no one had yet been laid. It was Preparation Day and the sabbath was imminent.

Meanwhile the women who had come from Galilee with Jesus were following behind. They took note of the tomb and of the position of the body.

Then they returned and prepared spices and ointments. And on the sabbath day they rested, as the law required.

Luke 22:14–23:56

Shorter form

The passion of our Lord Jesus Christ according to Luke
*
The elders of the people and the chief priests and scribes rose, and they brought Jesus before Pilate.

They began their accusation by saying, 'We found this man inciting our people to revolt, opposing payment of tribute to Caesar, and claiming to be Christ, a king.' Pilate put to him this question, 'Are you the king of the Jews?' 'It is you who say it' he replied. Pilate then said to the chief priests and the crowd, 'I find no case against this man.' But they persisted, 'He is inflaming the people with his teaching all over Judaea; it has come all the way from Galilee, where he started, down to here.' When Pilate heard this, he asked if the man were a Galilean; and finding that he came under Herod's jurisdiction he passed him over to Herod who was also in Jerusalem at that time.

Herod was delighted to see Jesus; he had heard about him and had been wanting for a long time to set eyes on him; moreover, he was hoping to see some miracle worked by him. So he questioned him at some length; but without getting any reply. Meanwhile the chief priests and the scribes were there, violently pressing their accusations. Then Herod, together with his guards, treated him with contempt and made fun of him; he put a rich cloak on him and sent him back to Pilate. And though Herod and Pilate had been enemies before, they were reconciled that same day.

Pilate then summoned the chief priests and the leading men and the people. 'You brought this man before me' he said 'as a political agitator. Now I have gone into the matter myself in your presence and found no case against the man in respect of all the charges you bring against him. Nor has Herod either, since he has sent him back to us. As you can see, the man has done nothing that deserves death, so I shall have him flogged and then let him go.' But as one man they howled, 'Away with him! Give us Barabbas!' (This man had been thrown into prison for causing a riot in the city and for murder.)

Pilate was anxious to set Jesus free and addressed them again, but they shouted back, 'Crucify him! Crucify him!' And for the third time he spoke to them, 'Why? What harm has this man done? I have found no case against him that deserves death, so I shall have him punished and then let him go.' But they kept on shouting at the top of their voices, demanding that he should be crucified. And their shouts were growing louder.

Pilate then gave his verdict: their demand was to be granted. He released the man they asked for, who had been imprisoned for rioting and murder, and handed Jesus over to them to deal with as they pleased.

As they were leading him away they seized on a man, Simon from Cyrene, who was coming in from the country, and made him shoulder the cross and carry it behind Jesus. Large numbers of people followed him, and of women too, who mourned and lamented for him. But Jesus turned to them and said, 'Daughters of Jerusalem, do not weep for me; weep rather for yourselves and for your children. For the days will surely come when people will say, "Happy are those who are barren, the wombs that have never borne, the breasts that have never suckled!" Then they will begin to say to the mountains, "Fall on us!"; to the hills, "Cover us!" For if men use the green wood like this, what will happen when it is dry?' Now with him they were also leading out two other criminals to be executed.

When they reached the place called The Skull, they crucified him there and the two criminals also, one on the right, the other on the left. Jesus said, 'Father forgive them; they do not know what they are doing.' Then they cast lots to share out his clothing.

The people stayed there watching him. As for the leaders, they jeered at him. 'He saved others,' they said 'let him save himself if he is the Christ of God, the Chosen One.' The soldiers mocked him too and when they approached to offer him vinegar they said, 'If you are the king of the Jews, save yourself.' Above him there was an inscription: 'This is the King of the Jews.'

One of the criminals hanging there abused him. 'Are you not the Christ?' he said. 'Save yourself and us as well.' But the other spoke up and rebuked him. 'Have you no fear of God at all?' he said. 'You got the same sentence as he did, but in our case we deserved it; we are paying for what we did. But this man has done nothing wrong. Jesus,' he said 'remember me when you come into your kingdom.' 'Indeed, I promise you,' he replied 'today you will be with me in paradise.'

It was now about the sixth hour and, with the sun eclipsed, a darkness came over the whole land until the ninth hour. The veil of the Temple was torn right down the middle; and when Jesus had cried out in a loud voice, he said, 'Father, into your hands I commit my spirit.' With these words he breathed his last.

All kneel and pause a moment.

When the centurion saw what had taken place, he gave praise to God and said, 'This was a great and good man.' And when all the people who had gathered for the spectacle saw what had happened, they went home beating their breasts.

All his friends stood at a distance; so also did the women who had accompanied him from Galilee, and they saw all this happen.

Luke 23:1-49

THE EASTER TRIDUUM

Holy Thursday   A, B, C

Evening Mass of the Lord's Supper

Introduction to the Service

Today we come together to celebrate the Last Supper which the Lord ate shortly before he suffered. It was on this occasion that Jesus washed the feet of his disciples.

At the end of the meal Jesus said: 'Do this as a memorial of me. I have given you an example so that you may copy what I have done for you.' This was the 'Last Will' of the Lord before he died for us.

A person's 'Last Will' is sacred. Sons and daughters remember the last words of their dying parents. They try and do everything that their parents told them to do before they died.

It is for this reason that we are here today around the table of the Lord. We wish to do what Jesus has done. He gave himself for us, sharing with us all he had, body and blood, his whole life and love.

Penitential Rite

Let us prepare ourselves to celebrate the Last Supper in the right way.

● Are we willing to share with others our daily bread?   (*Silence*)

● Are we willing to share with others positions of authority and power?   (*Silence*)

● Are we willing to serve others by helping them to live a successful life?   (*Silence*)

Let us ask the Lord to make us clean and to wash away our selfishness and greed.   **I confess**...

FIRST READING

In our first reading we hear about the 'Passover Meal' in which the Israelites celebrated their passover from slavery to freedom. This was the Passover Meal which Jesus ate with his disciples before he ate the Last Supper.

The Last Supper is the Passover Meal for Christians, for in it we celebrate our passover from death to life – together with the Lord.

We read from the book of Exodus, chapter twelve.

The Lord said to Moses and Aaron in the land of Egypt, 'This month is to be the first of all the others for you, the first month of your year. Speak to the whole community of Israel and say, "On the tenth day of this month each man must take an animal from the flock, one for each family: one animal for each household. If the household is too small to eat the animal, a man must join with his neighbour, the nearest to his house, as the number of persons requires. You must take into account what each can eat in deciding the number for the animal. It must be an animal without blemish, a male one year old; you may take it from either sheep or goats. You must keep it till the fourteenth day of the month when the whole assembly of the community of Israel shall slaughter it between the two evenings. Some of the blood must then be taken and put on the two doorposts and the lintel of the houses where it is eaten. That night, the flesh is to be eaten, roasted over the fire; it must be eaten with unleavened bread and bitter herbs. You shall eat it like this: with a girdle round your waist, sandals on your feet, a staff in your hand. You shall eat it hastily; it is a passover in honour of the Lord. That night, I will go through the land of Egypt and strike down all the first-born in the land of Egypt, man and beast alike, and I shall deal out punishment to all the gods of Egypt, I am the Lord. The blood shall serve to mark the houses that you live in. When I see the blood I will pass over you and you shall escape the destroying plague when I strike the land of Egypt. This day is to be a day of remembrance for you, and you must celebrate it as a feast in the Lord's honour. For all generations you are to declare it a day of festival, for ever."

This is the word of the Lord.   *Exodus 12:1-8. 11-14*

Responsorial Psalm
  ℟   **The blessing-cup that we bless**
      is a communion with the blood of Christ.

1 How can I repay the Lord
   for his goodness to me?
   The cup of salvation I will raise;
   I will call on the Lord's name.   ℟

2 O precious in the eyes of the Lord
   is the death of his faithful.

Your servant, Lord, your servant am I;
you have loosened my bonds.   ℟

3   A thanksgiving sacrifice I make:
I will call on the Lord's name.
My vows to the Lord I will fulfil
before all his people.   ℟

Ps 115:12-13. 15-18. ℟ cf. 1 Cor 10:16

SECOND READING

In our second reading we hear the words which Jesus spoke during the Last Supper. Every priest uses these words when he celebrates the Holy Eucharist. In the Holy Eucharist these words become real. Christ offers us his own body and blood.

We read from the first letter to the Corinthians, chapter eleven.
*
This is what I received from the Lord, and in turn passed on to you: that on the same night that he was betrayed, the Lord Jesus took some bread, and thanked God for it and broke it, and he said, 'This is my body, which is for you; do this as a memorial of me.' In the same way he took the cup after supper, and said, 'This cup is the new covenant in my blood. Whenever you drink it, do this as a memorial of me.' Until the Lord comes, therefore, every time you eat this bread and drink this cup, you are proclaiming his death.

This is the word of the Lord.   *1 Corinthians 11:23-26*

Gospel Acclamation
Praise and honour to you, Lord Jesus!
I give you a new commandment:
love one another just as I have loved you, says the Lord.
Praise and honour to you, Lord Jesus!   *Jn 13:34*

GOSPEL

We read from the holy Gospel according to John, chapter thirteen.
*
It was before the festival of the Passover, and Jesus knew that the hour had come for him to pass from this world to the Father. He had always loved those who were his in the world, but now he showed how perfect his love was.

They were at supper, and the devil had already put it into the mind of Judas Iscariot son of Simon, to betray him. Jesus knew that the Father had put everything into his hands, and that he had come from God and was returning to God, and he got up from table, removed his outer garment and, taking a towel, wrapped it round his waist; he then poured water into a basin and began to wash the disciples' feet and to wipe them with the towel he was wearing.

He came to Simon Peter, who said to him, 'Lord, are you going to wash my feet?' Jesus answered, 'At the moment you do not know what I am doing, but later you will understand.' 'Never!' said Peter 'You shall never wash my feet.' Jesus replied, 'If I do not wash you, you can have nothing in common with me.' 'Then, Lord,' said Simon Peter 'not only my feet, but my hands and my head as well!' Jesus said, 'No one who has taken a bath needs washing, he is clean all over. You too are clean, though not all of you are.' He knew who was going to betray him, that was why he said, 'though not all of you are.'

When he had washed their feet and put on his clothes again he went back to the table. 'Do you understand' he said 'what I have done to you? You call me Master and Lord, and rightly; so I am. If I, then, the Lord and Master, have washed your feet, you should wash each other's feet. I have given you an example so that you may copy what I have done to you.'

This is the Gospel of the Lord.   *John 13:1-15*

Good Friday   A, B, C

Celebration of the Lord's Passion

FIRST READING

We have come together today to celebrate the suffering and death of our Saviour.

Hundreds of years before Christ became man on earth, the prophet Isaiah foretold the sufferings of Jesus.

While listening to our first reading let us imagine how Jesus was tormented and crushed. But at the same time let us also remember, alongside Jesus, all those people who today are disfigured, despised, rejected, pierced with bullets and crushed by oppression.

We read from the book of Isaiah, chapters fifty-two and fifty-three.
*
See, my servant will prosper,
he shall be lifted up, exalted, rise to great heights.

As the crowds were appalled on seeing him
– so disfigured did he look
that he seemed no longer human –
so will the crowds be astonished at him,
and kings stand speechless before him;
for they shall see something never told
and witness something never heard before:
'Who could believe what we have heard,
and to whom has the power of the Lord been revealed?'

Like a sapling he grew up in front of us,
like a root in arid ground.
Without beauty, without majesty (we saw him),
no looks to attract our eyes;
a thing despised and rejected by men,
a man of sorrows and familiar with suffering,
a man to make people screen their faces;
he was despised and we took no account of him.

And yet ours were the sufferings he bore,
ours the sorrows he carried.
But we, we thought of him as someone punished,
struck by God, and brought low.
Yet he was pierced through for our faults,
crushed for our sins.

On him lies a punishment that brings us peace,
and through his wounds we are healed.
We had all gone astray like sheep,
each taking his own way,
and the Lord burdened him
with the sins of all of us.
Harshly dealt with, he bore it humbly,
he never opened his mouth,
like a lamb that is led to the slaughter-house,
like a sheep that is dumb before its shearers
never opening its mouth

By force and by law he was taken;
would anyone plead his cause?
Yes, he was torn away from the land of the living;
for our faults struck down in death.
They gave him a grave with the wicked,
a tomb with the rich,
though he had done no wrong
and there had been no perjury in his mouth.
The Lord has been pleased to crush him with suffering.
If he offers his life in atonement,
he shall see his heirs, he shall have a long life
and through him what the Lord wishes will be done.

His soul's anguish over
he shall see the light and be content.
By his sufferings shall my servant justify many,
taking their faults on himself.

Hence I will grant whole hordes for his tribute,
he shall divide the spoil with the mighty,
for surrendering himself to death
and letting himself be taken for a sinner,
while he was bearing the faults of many
and praying all the time for sinners.

    This is the word of the Lord.   *Isaiah 52:13-53:12*

Responsorial Psalm
   ℟ **Father, into your hands I commend my spirit.**

1   In you, O Lord, I take refuge.
    Let me never be put to shame.

In your justice, set me free.
Into your hands I commend my spirit.
It is you who will redeem me, Lord.   ℟

2   In the face of all my foes
    I am a reproach,
    an object of scorn to my neighbours
    and of fear to my friends.   ℟

3   Those who see me in the street
    run far away from me.
    I am like a dead man, forgotten in men's hearts,
    like a thing thrown away.   ℟

4   But as for me, I trust in you, Lord,
    I say: 'You are my God.'
    My life is in your hands, deliver me
    from the hands of those who hate me.   ℟

5   Let your face shine on your servant.
    Save me in your love.
    Be strong, let your heart take courage,
    all who hope in the Lord.   ℟

                    Ps 30:2. 6. 12-13. 15-17. 25. ℟ Lk 23:46

SECOND READING

There are many people who suffer in silence. Silent tears are shed
by widows, by people in hospitals and prisons and by people who
are forgotten by their friends and who feel lonely.

   In our second reading we hear that Christ is with all those
people who suffer silently. St Paul tells us: 'During his life on
earth, he offered up prayer and entreaty, aloud and in silent tears.'

We read from the letter to the Hebrews, chapters four and five.
*
Since in Jesus, the Son of God, we have the supreme high priest
who has gone through to the highest heaven, we must never let
go of the faith that we have professed. For it is not as if we had a
high priest who was incapable of feeling our weaknesses with us;
but we have one who has been tempted in every way that we are,
though he is without sin. Let us be confident, then, in approaching the throne of grace, that we shall have mercy from him and
find grace when we are in need of help.

   During his life on earth, he offered up prayer and entreaty,
aloud and in silent tears, to the one who had the power to save

him out of death, and he submitted so humbly that his prayer was heard. Although he was Son, he learnt to obey through suffering; but having been made perfect, he became for all who obey him the source of eternal salvation.

This is the word of the Lord.   *Hebrews 4:14-16; 5:7-9*

Gospel Acclamation
  Glory and praise to you, O Christ!
  Christ was humbler yet,
  even to accepting death, death on a cross.
  But God raised him high
  and gave him the name which is above all names.
  Glory and praise to you, O Christ!   *Phil 2:8-9*

GOSPEL

The passion of our Lord Jesus Christ according to John
*
N Jesus left with his disciples and crossed the Kedron valley. There was a garden there, and he went into it with his disciples. Judas the traitor knew the place well, since Jesus had often met his disciples there, and he brought the cohort to this place together with a detachment of guards sent by the chief priests and the Pharisees, all with lanterns and torches and weapons. Knowing everything that was going to happen to him, Jesus then came forward and said,
J Who are you looking for?
N They answered,
C Jesus the Nazarene.
N He said,
J I am he.
N Now Judas the traitor was standing among them. When Jesus said, 'I am he', they moved back and fell to the ground. He asked them a second time,
J Who are you looking for?
N They said,
C Jesus the Nazarene.
N Jesus replied,
J I have told you that I am he. If I am the one you are looking for, let these others go.

N Narrator.   J Jesus.   O Other single speaker.
C Crowd, or more than one speaker.

N This was to fulfil the words he had spoken: 'Not one of those you gave me have I lost'.

Simon Peter, who carried a sword, drew it and wounded the high priest's servant, cutting off his right ear. The servant's name was Malchus. Jesus said to Peter,

J Put your sword back in its scabbard; am I not to drink the cup that the Father has given me?

N The cohort and its captain and the Jewish guards seized Jesus and bound him. They took him first to Annas, because Annas was the father-in-law of Caiaphas, who was high priest that year. It was Caiaphas who had suggested to the Jews, 'It is better for one man to die for the people'.

Simon Peter, with another disciple, followed Jesus. This disciple, who was known to the high priest, went with Jesus into the high priest's palace, but Peter stayed outside the door. So the other disciple, the one known to the high priest, went out, spoke to the woman who was keeping the door and brought Peter in. The maid on duty at the door said to Peter,

O Aren't you another of that man's disciples?

N He answered,

O I am not.

N Now it was cold, and the servants and guards had lit a charcoal fire and were standing there warming themselves; so Peter stood there too, warming himself with the others.

The high priest questioned Jesus about his disciples and his teaching. Jesus answered,

J I have spoken openly for all the world to hear; I have always taught in the synagogue and in the Temple where all the Jews meet together: I have said nothing in secret. But why ask me? Ask my hearers what I taught: they know what I said.

N At these words, one of the guards standing by gave Jesus a slap in the face, saying,

O Is that the way to answer the high priest?

N Jesus replied,

J If there is something wrong in what I said, point it out; but if there is no offence in it, why do you strike me?

N Then Annas sent him, still bound, to Caiaphas, the high priest.

As Simon Peter stood there warming himself, someone said to him,

O Aren't you another of his disciples?

N He denied it saying,

O I am not.
N One of the high priest's servants, a relation of the man whose ear Peter had cut off, said,
O Didn't I see you in the garden with him?
N Again Peter denied it; and at once a cock crew.

They then led Jesus from the house of Caiaphas to the Praetorium. It was now morning. They did not go into the Praetorium themselves or they would be defiled and unable to eat the passover. So Pilate came outside to them and said,

O What charge do you bring against this man?
N They replied,
C If he were not a criminal, we should not be handing him over to you.
N Pilate said,
O Take him yourselves, and try him by your own Law.
N The Jews answered,
C We are not allowed to put a man to death.
N This was to fulfil the words Jesus had spoken indicating the way he was going to die.

So Pilate went back into the Praetorium and called Jesus to him, and asked,

O Are you the king of the Jews?
N Jesus replied,
J Do you ask this of your own accord, or have others spoken to you about me?
N Pilate answered,
O Am I a Jew? It is your own people and the chief priests who have handed you over to me: what have you done?
N Jesus replied,
J Mine is not a kingdom of this world; if my kingdom were of this world, my men would have fought to prevent me being surrendered to the Jews. But my kingdom is not of this kind.
N Pilate said,
O So you are a king then?
N Jesus answered,
J It is you who say it. Yes, I am a king. I was born for this, I came into the world for this; to bear witness to the truth, and all who are on the side of truth listen to my voice.
N Pilate said,
O Truth? What is that?
N And with that he went out again to the Jews and said,
O I find no case against him. But according to a custom of yours I

should release one prisoner at the Passover; would you like me, then, to release the king of the Jews?

N At this they shouted:

C Not this man, but Barabbas.

N Barabbas was a brigand.

Pilate then had Jesus taken away and scourged; and after this, the soldiers twisted some thorns into a crown and put it on his head, and dressed him in a purple robe. They kept coming up to him and saying,

C Hail, king of the Jews!

N and they slapped him in the face.

Pilate came outside again and said to them,

O Look, I am going to bring him out to you to let you see that I find no case.

N Jesus then came out wearing the crown of thorns and the purple robe. Pilate said,

O Here is the man.

N When they saw him the chief priests and the guards shouted,

C Crucify him! Crucify him!

N Pilate said,

O Take him yourselves and crucify him: I can find no case against him.

N The Jews replied,

C We have a Law, and according to the Law he ought to die, because he has claimed to be the son of God.

N When Pilate heard them say this his fears increased. Re-entering the Praetorium, he said to Jesus,

O Where do you come from?

N But Jesus made no answer. Pilate then said to him,

O Are you refusing to speak to me? Surely you know I have power to release you and I have power to crucify you?

N Jesus replied

J You would have no power over me if it had not been given you from above; that is why the one who handed me over to you has the greater guilt.

N From that moment Pilate was anxious to set him free, but the Jews shouted,

C If you set him free you are no friend of Caesar's; anyone who makes himself king is defying Caesar.

N Hearing these words, Pilate had Jesus brought out, and seated himself on the chair of judgement at a place called the Pavement, in Hebrew Gabbatha. It was Passover Preparation

Day, about the sixth hour. Pilate said to the Jews.

O Here is your king.

N They said,

C Take him away, take him away. Crucify him!

N Pilate said,

O Do you want me to crucify your king?

N The chief priests answered,

C We have no king except Caesar.

N So in the end Pilate handed him over to them to be crucified.

They then took charge of Jesus, and carrying his own cross he went out of the city to the place of the skull, or, as it was called in Hebrew, Golgotha, where they crucified him with two others, one on either side with Jesus in the middle. Pilate wrote out a notice and had it fixed to the cross; it ran: 'Jesus the Nazarene, King of the Jews.' This notice was read by many of the Jews, because the place where Jesus was crucified was not far from the city, and the writing was in Hebrew, Latin and Greek. So the Jewish chief priests said to Pilate,

C You should not write 'King of the Jews', but 'This man said: I am King of the Jews'.

N Pilate answered,

O What I have written, I have written.

N When the soldiers had finished crucifying Jesus they took his clothing and divided it into four shares, one for each soldier. His undergarment was seamless, woven in one piece from neck to hem; so they said to one another,

C Instead of tearing it, let's throw dice to decide who is to have it.

N In this way the words of scripture were fulfilled:

They shared out my clothing among them.
They cast lots for my clothes.

This is exactly what the soldiers did.

Near the cross of Jesus stood his mother and his mother's sister, Mary the wife of Clopas, and Mary of Magdala. Seeing his mother and the disciple he loved standing near her, Jesus said to his mother,

J Woman, this is your son.

N Then to the disciple he said,

J This is your mother.

N And from that moment the disciple made a place for her in his home.

After this, Jesus knew that everything had now been completed, and to fulfil the scripture perfectly he said:

J I am thirsty.

N A jar full of vinegar stood there, so putting a sponge soaked in vinegar on a hyssop stick they held it up to his mouth. After Jesus had taken the vinegar he said,

J It is accomplished;

N and bowing his head he gave up the spirit.

All kneel and pause a moment.

N It was Preparation Day, and to prevent the bodies remaining on the cross during the sabbath – since that sabbath was a day of special solemnity – the Jews asked Pilate to have the legs broken and the bodies taken away. Consequently the soldiers came and broke the legs of the first man who had been crucified with him and then of the other. When they came to Jesus, they found that he was already dead, and so instead of breaking his legs one of the soldiers pierced his side with a lance; and immediately there came out blood and water. This is the evidence of one who saw it – trustworthy evidence, and he knows he speaks the truth – and he gives it so that you may believe as well. Because all this happened to fulfil the words of scripture:

Not one bone of his will be broken,

and again, in another place scripture says:

They will look on the one whom they have pierced.

After this, Joseph of Arimathaea, who was a disciple of Jesus – though a secret one because he was afraid of the Jews – asked Pilate to let him remove the body of Jesus. Pilate gave permission, so they came and took it away. Nicodemus came as well – the same one who had first come to Jesus at night-time – and he brought a mixture of myrrh and aloes, weighing about a hundred pounds. They took the body of Jesus and wrapped it with the spices in linen cloths, following the Jewish burial custom. At the place where he had been crucified there was a garden, and in the garden a new tomb in which no one had yet been buried. Since it was the Jewish Day of Preparation and the tomb was near at hand, they laid Jesus there.

John 18:1-19:42

Easter Sunday   A, B, C

During the Night

The Easter Vigil

FIRST READING

In our first reading we praise God as the creator of heaven and earth. He made us in his own image and likeness.

What God started at the beginning of creation, he completed at Easter. Through the resurrection of Christ the whole of creation has become new. Easter is the second creation.

Through the resurrection of Christ, God's image and likeness has become perfect within us.

We read from the book of Genesis, chapters one and two.
*
| *In the beginning God created the heavens and the earth.* Now the earth was a formless void, there was darkness over the deep, and God's spirit hovered over the water.

God said, 'Let there be light', and there was light. God saw that light was good, and God divided light from darkness. God called light 'day', and darkness he called 'night'. Evening came and morning came: the first day.

God said, 'Let there be a vault in the waters to divide the waters in two.' And so it was. God made the vault, and it divided the waters above the vault from the waters under the vault. God called the vault 'heaven'. Evening came and morning came: the second day.

God said, 'Let the waters under heaven come together into a single mass, and let dry land appear.' And so it was. God called the dry land 'earth' and the mass of waters 'seas', and God saw that it was good.

God said, 'Let the earth produce vegetation: seed-bearing plants, and fruit trees bearing fruit with their seed inside, on the earth.' And so it was. The earth produced vegetation: plants bearing seed in their several kinds, and trees bearing fruit with their seed inside in their several kinds. God saw that it was good. Evening came and morning came: the third day.

God said, 'Let there be lights in the vault of heaven to divide day from night, and let them indicate festivals, days and years. Let them be lights in the vault of heaven to shine on the earth.' And so it was. God made the two great lights: the greater light to govern the day, the smaller light to govern the night, and the stars. God set them in the vault of heaven to shine on the earth, to govern the day and the night and to divide light from darkness. God saw that it was good. Evening came and morning came: the fourth day.

God said, 'Let the waters teem with living creatures, and let birds fly above the earth within the vault of heaven.' And so it was. God created great sea-serpents and every kind of living creature with which the waters teem, and every kind of winged creature. God saw that it was good. God blessed them, saying 'Be fruitful, multiply, and fill the waters of the seas; and let the birds multiply upon the earth.' Evening came and morning came: the fifth day.

God said, 'Let the earth produce every kind of living creature: cattle, reptiles, and every kind of wild beast.' And so it was. God made every kind of wild beast, every kind of cattle, and every kind of land reptile. God saw that it was good.

*God said, 'Let us make man in our own image, in the likeness of ourselves, and let them be masters of the fish of the sea, the birds of heaven, the cattle, all the wild beasts and all the reptiles that crawl upon the earth.'

God created man in the image of himself,
in the image of God he created him,
male and female he created them.

God blessed them, saying to them, 'Be fruitful, multiply, fill the earth and conquer it. Be masters of the fish of the sea, the birds of heaven and all living animals on the earth.' God said, 'See, I give you all the seed-bearing plants that are upon the whole earth, and all the trees with seed-bearing fruit; this shall be your food. To all wild beasts, all birds of heaven and all living reptiles on the earth I give all the foliage of plants for food.' And so it was. God saw all he had made, and indeed it was very good. Evening came and morning came: the sixth day.

Thus heaven and earth were completed with all their array. On the seventh day God completed the work he had been doing. He rested on the seventh day after all the work he had been doing.

This is the word of the Lord.*   *Genesis 1:1-2:2*

**Shorter Form, verses 1. 26-31. Read between *.*

Responsorial Psalm

℟ **Send forth your spirit, O Lord,**
and renew the face of the earth.

1 Bless the Lord, my soul!
Lord God, how great you are,
clothed in majesty and glory,
wrapped in light as in a robe! ℟

2 You founded the earth on its base,
to stand firm from age to age.
You wrapped it with the ocean like a cloak:
the waters stood higher than the mountains. ℟

3 You make springs gush forth in the valleys:
they flow in between the hills.
On their banks dwell the birds of heaven;
from the branches they sing their song. ℟

4 From your dwelling you water the hills;
earth drinks its fill of your gift.
You make the grass grow for the cattle
and the plants to serve man's needs. ℟

5 How many are your works, O Lord!
In wisdom you have made them all.
The earth is full of your riches.
Bless the Lord, my soul! ℟

Ps 103:1-2. 5-6. 10. 12-14. 24. 35. ℟ cf. v.30

Prayer

Let us pray.
Almighty and eternal God,
you created all things in wonderful beauty and order.
Help us now to perceive
how still more wonderful is the new creation
by which in the fullness of time
you redeemed your people
through the sacrifice of our passover, Jesus Christ,
who lives and reigns for ever and ever. ℟ **Amen.**

or

Let us pray.

Lord God,
the creation of man was a wonderful work,
his redemption still more wonderful.
May we persevere in right reason
against all that entices to sin
and so attain to everlasting joy.
We ask this through Christ our Lord. ℟ **Amen.**

SECOND READING

There is a long road leading to salvation. This road starts with Abraham and leads to Christ.

In our reading we shall hear how God tested the faith of Abraham by asking him to sacrifice his only son. When we listen to this story we think of Christ. God loved the world so much that he did not even spare his only beloved son.

We read from the book of Genesis, chapter twenty-two.
*
God put Abraham to the test. 'Abraham, Abraham,' he called. 'Here I am' he replied. 'Take your son,' God said 'your only child Isaac, whom you love, and go to the land of Moriah. There you shall offer him as a burnt offering, on a mountain I will point out to you.'

Rising early next morning Abraham saddled his ass and took with him two of his servants and his son Isaac. He chopped wood for the burnt offering and started on his journey to the place God had pointed out to him. On the third day Abraham looked up and saw the place in the distance. Then Abraham said to his servants, 'Stay here with the donkey. The boy and I will go over there; we will worship and come back to you.'

Abraham took the wood for the burnt offering, loaded it on Isaac, and carried in his own hands the fire and the knife. Then the two of them set out together. Isaac spoke to his father Abraham, 'Father' he said. 'Yes, my son' he replied. 'Look,' he said 'here are the fire and the wood, but where is the lamb for the burnt offering?' Abraham answered, 'My son, God himself will provide the lamb for the burnt offering.' Then the two of them went on together.

*When they arrived at the place God had pointed out to him, Abraham built an altar there, and arranged the wood. Then he bound his son Isaac and put him on the altar on top of the wood. Abraham stretched out his hand and seized the knife to kill his son.

But the angel of the Lord called to him from heaven, 'Abraham, Abraham' he said. 'I am here' he replied. 'Do not raise your hand against the boy' the angel said. 'Do not harm him, for now I know you fear God. You have not refused me your son, your only son.' Then looking up, Abraham saw a ram caught by its horns in a bush. Abraham took the ram and offered it as a burnt-offering in place of his son.*

Abraham called this place 'The Lord provides', and hence the saying today: On the mountain the Lord provides.

*The angel of the Lord called Abraham a second time from heaven. 'I swear by my own self – it is the Lord who speaks – because you have done this, because you have not refused me your son, your only son, I will shower blessings on you, I will make your descendants as many as the stars of heaven and the grains of sand on the seashore. Your descendants shall gain possession of the gates of their enemies. All the nations of the earth shall bless themselves by your descendants, as a reward for your obedience.'

This is the word of the Lord.*   *Genesis 22:1-18*

*Shorter Form, verses 1-2. 9-13. 15-18. Read between *.

Responsorial Psalm
℟ **Preserve me, God, I take refuge in you.**

1 O Lord, it is you who are my portion and cup;
   it is you yourself who are my prize.
   I keep the Lord ever in my sight:
   since he is at my right hand, I shall stand firm. ℟

2 And so my heart rejoices, my soul is glad;
   even my body shall rest in safety.
   For you will not leave my soul among the dead,
   nor let your beloved know decay. ℟

3 You will show me the path of life,
   the fullness of joy in your presence,
   at your right hand happiness for ever. ℟

                                    Ps 15:5. 8-11. ℟ v.1

Prayer
Let us pray.
God and Father of all who believe in you,

you promised Abraham that he would become the father of all
     nations,
and through the death and resurrection of Christ
you fulfil that promise:
everywhere throughout the world you increase your chosen
     people.
May we respond to your call
by joyfully accepting your invitation to the new life of grace.
We ask this through Christ our Lord.   ℟ **Amen.**

THIRD READING

The following reading is a dramatic story of how the people of
Israel were saved from their slavery in Egypt.
     In a hidden way, this story talks about baptism. In the water of
baptism we cross over to the land of God.

We read from the book of Exodus, chapters fourteen and fifteen.
*
The Lord said to Moses, 'Why do you cry to me so? Tell the sons
of Israel to march on. For yourself, raise your staff and stretch out
your hand over the sea and part it for the sons of Israel to walk
through the sea on dry ground. I for my part will make the heart
of the Egyptians so stubborn that they will follow them. So shall I
win myself glory at the expense of Pharaoh, of all his army, his
chariots, his horsemen. And when I have won glory for myself, at
the expense of Pharaoh and his chariots and his army, the
Egyptians will learn that I am the Lord.'
     Then the angel of the Lord, who marched at the front of the
army of Israel, changed station and moved to their rear. The pillar
of cloud changed station from the front to the rear of them, and
remained there. It came between the camp of the Egyptians and
the camp of Israel. The cloud was dark, and the night passed
without the armies drawing any closer the whole night long.
Moses stretched out his hand over the sea. The Lord drove back
the sea with a strong easterly wind all night, and he made dry
land of the sea. The waters parted and the sons of Israel went on
dry ground right into the sea, walls of water to right and to left of
them. The Egyptians gave chase: after them they went, right into
the sea, all Pharaoh's horses, his chariots, and his horsemen. In
the morning watch, the Lord looked down on the army of the
Egyptians from the pillar of fire and of cloud, and threw the army
into confusion. He so clogged their chariot wheels that they could
scarcely make headway. 'Let us flee from the Israelites,' the

Egyptians cried 'the Lord is fighting for them against the Egyptians!' 'Stretch out your hand over the sea,' the Lord said to Moses 'that the waters may flow back on the Egyptians and their chariots and their horsemen.' Moses stretched out his hand over the sea and, as day broke, the sea returned to its bed. The fleeing Egyptians marched right into it, and the Lord overthrew the Egyptians in the very middle of the sea. The returning waters overwhelmed the chariots and the horsemen of Pharaoh's whole army, which had followed the Israelites into the sea; not a single one of them was left. But the sons of Israel had marched through the sea on dry ground, walls of water to right and to left of them. That day, the Lord rescued Israel from the Egyptians, and Israel saw the Egyptians lying dead on the shore. Israel witnessed the great act that the Lord had performed against the Egyptians, and the people venerated the Lord; they put their faith in the Lord and in Moses, his servant.

It was then that Moses and the sons of Israel sang this song in honour of the Lord: *Exodus 14:15–15:1*

The choir takes up the Responsorial Psalm immediately.

Responsorial Psalm
℟   **I will sing to the Lord, glorious his triumph!**

1   I will sing to the Lord, glorious his triumph!
     Horse and rider he has thrown into the sea!
     The Lord is my strength, my song, my salvation.
     This is my God and I extol him,
     my father's God and I give him praise.   ℟

2   The Lord is a warrior! The Lord is his name.
     The chariots of Pharaoh he hurled into the sea,
     the flower of his army is drowned in the sea.
     The deeps hide them; they sank like a stone.   ℟

3   Your right hand, Lord, glorious in its power,
     your right hand, Lord, has shattered the enemy.
     In the greatness of your glory you crushed the foe.   ℟

4   You will lead your people and plant them on your mountain,
     the place, O Lord, where you have made your home,
     the sanctuary, Lord, which your hands have made.
     The Lord will reign for ever and ever.   ℟
                                        Ex 15:1-6. 17-18. ℟ v.1

Prayer

Let us pray.

Father,
even today we see the wonders
of the miracles you worked long ago.
You once saved a single nation from slavery,
and now you offer that salvation to all through baptism.
May the peoples of the world become true sons of Abraham
and prove worthy of the heritage of Israel.
We ask this through Christ our Lord.   ℟   **Amen.**

or

Let us pray.

Lord God,
in the new covenant
you shed light on the miracles you worked in ancient times:
the Red Sea is a symbol of our baptism,
and the nation you freed from slavery
is a sign of your Christian people.
May every nation
share the faith and privilege of Israel
and come to new birth in the Holy Spirit.
We ask this through Christ our Lord.   ℟   **Amen.**

FOURTH READING

Easter is like a wedding feast. Through the death and resurrection of Christ we have become God's beloved people. We are now loved and adorned like a bride. The reading tells us of God's message of forgiveness.

'Now your creator will be your husband ... With great love I will take you back.

We read from the book of Isaiah, chapter fifty-four.
*
Thus says the Lord:

Now your creator will be your husband,
his name, the Lord of hosts;
your redeemer will be the Holy One of Israel,
he is called the God of the whole earth.
Yes, like a forsaken wife, distressed in spirit,
the Lord calls you back.
Does a man cast off the wife of his youth?
says your God.

I did forsake you for a brief moment,
but with great love will I take you back.
In excess of anger, for a moment
I hid my face from you.
But with everlasting love I have taken pity on you,
says the Lord, your redeemer.

I am now as I was in the days of Noah
when I swore that Noah's waters
should never flood the world again.
So now I swear concerning my anger with you
and the threats I made against you;

for the mountains may depart,
the hills be shaken,
but my love for you will never leave you
and my covenant of peace with you will never be shaken,
says the Lord who takes pity on you.

Unhappy creature, storm-tossed, disconsolate,
see, I will set your stones on carbuncles
and your foundations on sapphires.
I will make rubies your battlements,
your gates crystal,
and your entire wall precious stones.
Your sons will all be taught by the Lord.
The prosperity of your sons will be great.
You will be founded on integrity;
remote from oppression, you will have nothing to fear;
remote from terror, it will not approach you.

This is the word of the Lord.   *Isaiah 54:5-14*

Responsorial Psalm

℟   **I will praise you, Lord, you have rescued me.**

1   I will praise you, Lord, you have rescued me
     and have not let my enemies rejoice over me.
     O Lord, you have raised my soul from the dead,
     restored me to life from those who sink into the grave.   ℟

2   Sing psalms to the Lord, you who love him,
     give thanks to his holy name.
     His anger lasts but a moment; his favour through life.
     At night there are tears, but joy comes with dawn.   ℟

3   The Lord listened and had pity.
    The Lord came to my help.
    For me you have changed my mourning into dancing,
    O Lord my God, I will thank you for ever.   ℟
                              Ps 29:2. 4-6. 11-13. ℟ v.2

Prayer
Let us pray.
Almighty and eternal God,
glorify your name by increasing your chosen people
as you promised long ago.
In reward for their trust,
may we see in the Church the fulfilment of your promise.
We ask this through Christ our Lord.   ℟   **Amen.**

*Prayers may also be chosen from those given after the following
readings, if the readings are omitted.*

FIFTH READING

Our next reading records a vision of the prophet Isaiah. What
Isaiah saw in this vision has been fulfilled in Christ. It is Christ who
can satisfy the longing of our hearts, Christ whom we can find
among us if we search for him. It is Christ who implements the
plan God has for the world and for us all.

We read from the book of Isaiah, chapter fifty-five.
*
Thus says the Lord:

Oh, come to the water all you who are thirsty;
though you have no money, come!
Buy corn without money, and eat,
and, at no cost, wine and milk.
Why spend money on what is not bread,
your wages on what fails to satisfy?
Listen, listen to me, and you will have good things to eat
and rich food to enjoy.
Pay attention, come to me;
listen, and your soul will live.

With you I will make an everlasting covenant
out of the favours promised to David.
See, I have made of you a witness to the peoples,
a leader and a master of the nations.
See, you will summon a nation you never knew,

those unknown will come hurrying to you,
for the sake of the Lord your God,
of the Holy One of Israel who will glorify you.

Seek the Lord while he is still to be found,
call to him while he is still near.
Let the wicked man abandon his way,
the evil man his thoughts.
Let him turn back to the Lord who will take pity on him,
to our God who is rich in forgiving;
for my thoughts are not your thoughts,
my ways not your ways – it is the Lord who speaks.
Yes, the heavens are as high above earth
as my ways are above your ways,
my thoughts above your thoughts.

Yes, as the rain and the snow come down from the heavens and
do not return without watering the earth, making it yield and
giving growth to provide seed for the sower and bread for the
eating, so the word that goes from my mouth does not return to
me empty, without carrying out my will and succeeding in what
it was sent to do.

This is the word of the Lord.   *Isaiah 55:1-11*

Responsorial Psalm
℞   **With joy you will draw water from the wells of salvation.**

1   Truly God is my salvation,
    I trust, I shall not fear.
    For the Lord is my strength, my song,
    he became my saviour.
    With joy you will draw water
    from the wells of salvation.   ℞

2   Give thanks to the Lord, give praise to his name!
    Make his mighty deeds known to the peoples,
    declare the greatness of his name.   ℞

3   Sing a psalm to the Lord
    for he has done glorious deeds,
    make them known to all the earth!
    People of Zion, sing and shout for joy
    for great in your midst is the Holy One of Israel.   ℞

                              Is 12:2-6. ℞ v.3

Prayer
Let us pray.
Almighty, ever-living God,
only hope of the world,
by the preaching of the prophets
you proclaimed the mysteries we are celebrating tonight.
Help us to be your faithful people,
for it is by your inspiration alone
that we can grow in goodness.
We ask this through Christ our Lord.   ℟ **Amen.**

SIXTH READING

The prophet Baruch asked the people of Israel why they were
defeated by their enemies and why they had to live as captives in a
strange country.

He then gives them the answer, saying: 'You have forsaken the
fountain of wisdom!'

For us Christians, the fountain of wisdom is the risen Lord. If we
hold on to his commands and follow his advice, we shall find life
and will enjoy peace in the nation.

We read from the book of the prophet Baruch, chapters three and four.
*
Listen, Israel, to commands that bring life;
hear, and learn what knowledge means.
Why, Israel, why are you in the country of your enemies,
growing older and older in an alien land,
sharing defilement with the dead,
reckoned with those who go to Sheol?
Because you have forsaken the fountain of wisdom.
Had you walked in the way of God,
you would have lived in peace for ever.
Learn where knowledge is, where strength,
where understanding, and so learn
where length of days is, where life,
where the light of the eyes and where peace.
But who has found out where she lives,
who has entered her treasure house?

But the One who knows all knows her,
he has grasped her with his own intellect,
he has set the earth firm for ever
and filled it with four-footed beasts,
he sends the light – and it goes,
he recalls it – and trembling it obeys;

the stars shine joyfully at their set times:
when he calls them, they answer, 'Here we are';
they gladly shine for their creator.
It is he who is our God,
no other can compare with him.
He has grasped the whole way of knowledge,
and confided it to his servant Jacob,
to Israel his well-beloved;
so causing her to appear on earth
and move among men.

This is the book of the commandments of God,
the Law that stands for ever;
those who keep her live,
those who desert her die.
Turn back, Jacob, seize her,
in her radiance make your way to light:
do not yield your glory to another,
your privilege to a people not your own.
Israel, blessed are we:
what pleases God has been revealed to us.

This is the word of the Lord.   *Baruch 3:9-15. 32–4:4*

Responsorial Psalm
℟ **You have the message of eternal life, O Lord.**

1 The law of the Lord is perfect,
   it revives the soul.
   The rule of the Lord is to be trusted,
   it gives wisdom to the simple. ℟

2 The precepts of the Lord are right,
   they gladden the heart.
   The command of the Lord is clear,
   it gives light to the eyes. ℟

3 The fear of the Lord is holy,
   abiding for ever.
   The decrees of the Lord are truth
   and all of them just. ℟

4 They are more to be desired than gold,
   than the purest of gold
   and sweeter are they than honey,
   than honey from the comb. ℟   *Ps 18:8-11. ℟ Jn 6:69*

Prayer

Let us pray.

Father,
you increase your Church
by continuing to call all people to salvation.
Listen to our prayers
and always watch over those you cleanse in baptism.
We ask this through Christ our Lord. ℞ **Amen.**

SEVENTH READING

It is the risen Lord who has called us together tonight. He is ready to remove from our bodies our hearts of stone and to give us hearts of flesh instead. It is he who calls us together from all nations and makes us God's people.

We read from the book of the prophet Ezekiel, chapter thirty-six.
*

The word of the Lord was addressed to me as follows: 'Son of man, the members of the House of Israel used to live in their own land, but they defiled it by their conduct and actions. I then discharged my fury at them because of the blood they shed in their land and the idols with which they defiled it. I scattered them among the nations and dispersed them in foreign countries. I sentenced them as their conduct and actions deserved. And now they have profaned my holy name among the nations where they have gone, so that people say of them, "These are the people of the Lord; they have been exiled from his land." But I have been concerned about my holy name, which the House of Israel has profaned among the nations where they have gone. And so, say to the House of Israel, "The Lord says this: I am not doing this for your sake, House of Israel, but for the sake of my holy name, which you have profaned among the nations where you have gone. I mean to display the holiness of my great name, which has been profaned among the nations, which you have profaned among them. And the nations will learn that I am the Lord – it is the Lord who speaks – when I display my holiness for your sake before their eyes. Then I am going to take you from among the nations and gather you together from all the foreign countries, and bring you home to your own land. I shall pour clean water over you and you will be cleansed; I shall cleanse you of all your defilement and all your idols. I shall give you a new heart, and put a new spirit in you; I shall remove the heart of stone from your bodies and give you a heart of flesh instead. I shall put my spirit in you, and make you keep my laws and sincerely respect my observances. You will live in the land which I gave your ancestors. You shall be my people and I will be your God.'''

This is the word of the Lord. *Ezekiel 36:16-28*

Responsorial Psalm

℞ **Like the deer that yearns for running streams, so my soul is yearning for you, my God.**

1 My soul is thirsting for God.
the God of my life;
when can I enter and see
the face of God? ℞

2 These things will I remember
as I pour out my soul:
how I would lead the rejoicing crowd
into the house of God,
amid cries of gladness and thanksgiving,
the throng wild with joy. ℞

3 O send forth your light and your truth;
let these be my guide.
Let them bring me to your holy mountain
to the place where you dwell. ℞

4 And I will come to the altar of God,
the God of my joy.
My redeemer, I will thank you on the harp,
O God, my God. ℞ *Pss 41:3. 5; 42:3. 4.* ℞ *41:2*

If a Baptism takes place, the Responsorial Psalm which follows the Fifth Reading above, or Ps 50 as follows, is used.

Responsorial Psalm

℞ **A pure heart create for me, O God.**

1 A pure heart create for me, O God,
put a steadfast spirit within me.
Do not cast me away from your presence,
nor deprive me of your holy spirit. ℞

2 Give me again the joy of your help.
with a spirit of fervour sustain me,

that I may teach transgressors your ways
and sinners may return to you.   ℟

3 For in sacrifice you take no delight,
   burnt offering from me you would refuse,
   my sacrifice, a contrite spirit.
   A humbled, contrite heart you will not spurn.   ℟

Ps 50:12-15. 18. 19. ℟ *v.12*

Prayer
Let us pray.
God of unchanging power and light,
look with mercy and favour on your entire Church.
Bring lasting salvation to mankind,
so that the world may see
the fallen lifted up,
the old made new,
and all things brought to perfection,
through him who is their origin,
our Lord Jesus Christ,
who lives and reigns for ever and ever.   ℟ **Amen.**

or

Let us pray.
Father,
you teach us in both the Old and the New Testament
to celebrate this passover mystery.
Help us to understand your great love for us.
May the goodness you now show us
confirm our hope in your future mercy.
We ask this through Christ our Lord.   ℟ **Amen.**

or

Let us pray.
Almighty and eternal God,
be present in this sacrament of your love.
Send your Spirit of adoption
on those to be born again in baptism.
And may the work of our humble ministry
be brought to perfection by your mighty power.
We ask this through Christ our Lord.   ℟ **Amen.**

NEW TESTAMENT READING

It is a very old custom in our Church that the catechumens are baptised during this Easter Vigil.

St Paul gives us the reason for it in his letter to the Romans, chapter six.

*
When we were baptised in Christ Jesus we were baptised in his death; in other words, when we were baptised we went into the tomb with him and joined him in death, so that as Christ was raised from the dead by the Father's glory, we too might live a new life.

If in union with Christ we have imitated his death, we shall also imitate him in his resurrection. We must realise that our former selves have been crucified with him to destroy this sinful body and to free us from the slavery of sin. When a man dies, of course, he has finished with sin.

But we believe that having died with Christ we shall return to life with him: Christ, as we know, having been raised from the dead will never die again. Death has no power over him any more. When he died, he died, once for all, to sin, so his life now is life with God; and in that way, you too must consider yourselves to be dead to sin but alive for God in Christ Jesus.

This is the word of the Lord. *Romans 6:3-11*

After the epistle all rise, and the priest solemnly intones the Alleluia which is repeated by all present.

Responsorial Psalm
℟   **Alleluia, alleluia, alleluia!**

1   Give thanks to the Lord for he is good,
    for his love has no end.
    Let the sons of Israel say:
    'His love has no end.'   ℟

2   The Lord's right hand has triumphed;
    his right hand raised me up.
    I shall not die, I shall live
    and recount his deeds.   ℟

3   The stone which the builders rejected
    has become the corner stone.
    This is the work of the Lord,
    a marvel in our eyes.   ℟   *Ps 117:1-2. 16-17. 22-23*

GOSPEL

Year A

We read from the holy Gospel according to Matthew, chapter twenty-eight.
★

After the sabbath, and towards dawn on the first day of the week, Mary of Magdala and the other Mary went to visit the sepulchre. And all at once there was a violent earthquake, for the angel of the Lord, descending from heaven, came and rolled away the stone and sat on it. His face was like lightning, his robe white as snow. The guards were so shaken, so frightened of him, that they were like dead men. But the angel spoke; and he said to the women, 'There is no need for you to be afraid. I know you are looking for Jesus, who was crucified. He is not here, for he has risen, as he said he would. Come and see the place where he lay, then go quickly and tell his disciples, "He has risen from the dead and now he is going before you to Galilee; it is there you will see him." Now I have told you.' Filled with awe and great joy the women came quickly away from the tomb and ran to tell the disciples.

And there, coming to meet them, was Jesus. 'Greetings' he said. And the women came up to him and, falling down before him, clasped his feet. Then Jesus said to them, 'Do not be afraid; go and tell my brothers that they must leave for Galilee; they will see me there.'

This is the Gospel of the Lord.   *Matthew 28:1-10*

Year B

We read from the holy Gospel according to Mark, chapter sixteen.
★

When the sabbath was over, Mary of Magdala, Mary the mother of James, and Salome, bought spices with which to go and anoint him. And very early in the morning on the first day of the week they went to the tomb, just as the sun was rising.

They had been saying to one another, 'Who will roll away the stone for us from the entrance to the tomb?' But when they looked they could see that the stone – which was very big – had already been rolled back. On entering the tomb they saw a young man in a white robe seated on the right-hand side, and they were struck with amazement. But he said to them, 'There is no need for alarm. You are looking for Jesus of Nazareth, who was crucified: he has risen, he is not here. See, here is the place where they laid him. But you must go and tell his disciples and Peter, "He is going before you to Galilee; it is there you will see him, just as he told you." '

This is the Gospel of the Lord. *Mark 16:1-7*

Year C

We read from the holy Gospel according to Luke, chapter twenty-four.
*

On the first day of the week, at the first sign of dawn, the women went to the tomb with the spices they had prepared. They found that the stone had been rolled away from the tomb, but on entering discovered that the body of the Lord Jesus was not there. As they stood there not knowing what to think, two men in brilliant clothes suddenly appeared at their side. Terrified, the women lowered their eyes. But the two men said to them, 'Why look among the dead for someone who is alive? He is not here; he has risen. Remember what he told you when he was still in Galilee: that the Son of Man had to be handed over into the power of sinful men and be crucified, and rise again on the third day?' And they remembered his words.

When the women returned from the tomb they told all this to the Eleven and to all the others. The women were Mary of Magdala, Joanna, and Mary the mother of James. The other women with them also told the apostles, but this story of theirs seemed pure nonsense, and they did not believe them.

Peter, however, went running to the tomb. He bent down and saw the binding cloths, but nothing else; he then went back home, amazed at what had happened.

This is the Gospel of the Lord. *Mark 24:1-12*

Homily
A homily should follow the readings.

Easter Sunday   A, B, C

Mass of the Day

Introduction to the Service

With great joy we have come together today to celebrate the resurrection of our Lord. The Lord is risen indeed, Alleluia!

Today we proclaim to the world a message of hope: Christ is risen, do not despair!

Today we proclaim eternal life to all who have died in faith.

Today we proclaim joy to all who think their life is a failure or a disaster.

Christ is alive in our midst. He has risen from the dead to be with us in body and soul, as man and as God. This is our faith, which we proclaim today.

Penitential Rite

Let us ask ourselves:

● Are we aware of Christ's presence whenever we come together in his name?   (*Silence*)

● Do we allow the risen Lord to inspire us in times of loneliness and difficulty?   (*Silence*)

● Do we see the risen Lord at work in all people who are doing good?   (*Silence*)

Let us ask for forgiveness for not rejoicing in the presence of the risen Lord and for not trusting in him.   **I confess**...

FIRST READING

We are keen to experience the presence of the risen Lord.

In our reading today we hear of the Apostles and how they experienced Christ's presence before and after his resurrection.

We read from the Acts of the Apostles, chapter ten.

*
Peter addressed Cornelius and his household: 'You must have heard about the recent happenings in Judaea; about Jesus of Nazareth and how he began in Galilee, after John had been preaching baptism. God had anointed him with the Holy Spirit and with power, and because God was with him, Jesus went

about doing good and curing all who had fallen into the power of the devil. Now I, and those with me, can witness to everything he did throughout the countryside of Judaea and in Jerusalem itself: and also to the fact that they killed him by hanging him on a tree, yet three days afterwards God raised him to life and allowed him to be seen, not by the whole people but only by certain witnesses God had chosen beforehand. Now we are those witnesses – we have eaten and drunk with him after his resurecction from the dead – and he has ordered us to proclaim this to his people and to tell them that God has appointed him to judge everyone, alive or dead. It is to him that all the prophets bear this witness: that all who believe in Jesus will have their sins forgiven through his name.'

This is the word of the Lord.   *Acts 10:34. 37-43*

Responsorial Psalm
   ℟   **This day was made by the Lord;**
         we rejoice and are glad.

or

   ℟   **Alleluia, alleluia, alleluia!**

1   Give thanks to the Lord for he is good,
      for his love has no end.
      Let the sons of Israel say:
      'His love has no end.'   ℟

2   The Lord's right hand has triumphed;
      his right hand raised me up.
      I shall not die, I shall live
      and recount his deeds.   ℟

3   The stone which the builders rejected
      has become the corner stone.
      This is the work of the Lord,
      a marvel in our eyes.   ℟   *Ps 117:1-2. 16-17. 22-23. ℟ v.24*

SECOND READING
We read from the letter of St Paul to the Colossians, chapter three.
*
Since you have been brought back to true life with Christ, you must look for the things that are in heaven, where Christ is, sitting at God's right hand. Let your thoughts be on heavenly

things, not on the things that are on the earth, because you have died, and now the life you have is hidden with Christ in God. But when Christ is revealed – and he is your life – you too will be revealed in all your glory with him.

This is the word of the Lord. *Colossians 3:1-4*

Alternative Reading

We read from the first letter of St Paul to the Corinthians, chapter five.
∗
You must know how even a small amount of yeast is enough to leaven all the dough, so get rid of all the old yeast, and make yourselves into a completely new batch of bread, unleavened as you are meant to be. Christ, our passover, has been sacrificed; let us celebrate the feast, by getting rid of all the old yeast of evil and wickedness, having only the unleavened bread of sincerity and truth.

This is the word of the Lord. *1 Corinthians 5:6-8*

The sequence is said or sung on this day. On the weekdays of the Octave of Easter, its use is optional.

SEQUENCE

Christians, to the Paschal Victim offer sacrifice and praise.
The sheep are ransomed by the Lamb;
and Christ, the undefiled,
hath sinners to his Father reconciled.
Death with life contended: combat strangely ended!
Life's own Champion, slain, yet lives to reign.
Tell us, Mary: say what thou didst see upon the way.
The tomb the Living did enclose;
I saw Christ's glory as he rose!
The angels there attesting;
shroud with grave-clothes resting.
Christ, my hope, has risen: he goes before you into Galilee.
That Christ is truly risen from the dead we know.
Victorious king, thy mercy show!
Amen.

Gospel Acclamation
Alleluia, alleluia!
Christ, our passover, has been sacrificed;
let us celebrate the feast then, in the Lord.
Alleluia!   *1 Cor 5:7-8*

GOSPEL

We read from the holy Gospel according to John, chapter twenty.
*
It was very early on the first day of the week and still dark, when
Mary of Magdala came to the tomb. She saw that the stone had
been moved away from the tomb and came running to Simon
Peter and the other disciple, the one Jesus loved. 'They have
taken the Lord out of the tomb' she said 'and we don't know
where they have put him.'

So Peter set out with the other disciple to go to the tomb. They
ran together, but the other disciple, running faster than Peter,
reached the tomb first; he bent down and saw the linen cloths
lying on the ground, but did not go in. Simon Peter who was
following now came up, went right into the tomb, saw the linen
cloths on the ground, and also the cloth that had been over his
head; this was not with the linen cloths but rolled up in a place by
itself. Then the other disciple who had reached the tomb first also
went in; he saw and he believed. Till this moment they had failed
to understand the teaching of scripture, that he must rise from
the dead.

This is the Gospel of the Lord.   *John 20:1-9*

THE SEASON OF EASTER

Second Sunday of Easter   A

Introduction to the Service

Today we celebrate the second Sunday of Easter. All the Sundays between Easter and Pentecost are called 'Sundays of Easter'.

It was during these fifty days between Easter and Pentecost that the newly baptised Christians in the early Church traditionally received special instructions. They were baptised at Easter and could now take part in the Holy Eucharist. Therefore, during this time between Easter and Pentecost special readings were chosen to initiate the newly baptised into the deeper meaning of our life with the risen Lord.

On these Sundays of Easter we are invited to join with those who are newly baptised and search with them for the deeper meaning of our faith.

Today, for instance, Jesus encourages us saying: 'Doubt no longer but believe ... Happy are those who have not seen and yet believe.'

Penitential Rite

Let us ask ourselves:

● Are we interested in deepening our faith in Christ and knowing more about him?   (*Silence*)

● Do we believe that Jesus is present among us now and whenever we come together in his name?   (*Silence*)

Let us ask the Lord to forgive us and to strengthen our faith.
I confess...

FIRST READING

Our reading shows us how faith in Christ can change our lives. Our faith helps us to live together in a new and wonderful way.

We read from the Acts of the Apostles, chapter two.
*
The whole community remained faithful to the teaching of the apostles, to the brotherhood, to the breaking of bread and to the prayers.

The many miracles and signs worked through the apostles made a deep impression on everyone.

The faithful all lived together and owned everything in common; they sold their goods and possessions and shared out the proceeds among themselves according to what each one needed.

They went as a body to the Temple every day but met in their houses for the breaking of bread; they shared their food gladly and generously; they praised God and were looked up to by everyone. Day by day the Lord added to their community those destined to be saved.

This is the word of the Lord.   *Acts 2:42-47*

Responsorial Psalm
℟   **Give thanks to the Lord for he is good,
for his love has no end.**

or

℟   **Alleluia, alleluia, alleluia!**

1   Let the sons of Israel say:
'His love has no end.'
Let the sons of Aaron say:
'His love has no end,'
Let those who fear the Lord say:
'His love has no end.'   ℟

2   I was thrust, thrust down and falling
but the Lord was my helper.
The Lord is my strength and my song;
he was my saviour.
There are shouts of joy and victory
in the tents of the just.   ℟

3   The stone which the builders rejected
has become the corner stone.
This is the work of the Lord,
a marvel in our eyes.
This day was made by the Lord;
we rejoice and are glad.   ℟   *Ps 117:2-4. 13-15. 22-24. ℟v.1*

SECOND READING
We read from the first letter of St Peter, chapter one.
*
Blessed be God the Father of our Lord Jesus Christ, who in his great mercy has given us a new birth as his sons, by raising Jesus

Christ from the dead, so that we have a sure hope and the promise of an inheritance that can never be spoilt or soiled and never fade away, because it is being kept for you in the heavens. Through your faith, God's power will guard you until the salvation which had been prepared is revealed at the end of time. This is a cause of great joy for you, even though you may for a short time have to bear being plagued by all sorts of trials; so that, when Jesus Christ is revealed, your faith will have been tested and proved like gold – only it is more precious than gold, which is corruptible even though it bears testing by fire – and then you will have praise and glory and honour. You did not see him, yet you love him; and still without seeing him, you are already filled with a joy so glorious that it cannot be described, because you believe; and you are sure of the end to which your faith looks forward, that is, the salvation of your souls.

This is the word of the Lord.   *1 Peter 1:3-9*

Gospel Acclamation
Alleluia, alleluia!
Jesus said: 'You believe because you can see me.
Happy are those who have not seen and yet believe.'
Alleluia!   *Jn 20:29*

GOSPEL
We read from the holy Gospel according to John, chapter twenty.
*
In the evening of that same day, the first day of the week, the doors were closed in the room where the disciples were, for fear of the Jews. Jesus came and stood among them. He said to them, 'Peace be with you,' and showed them his hands and his side. The disciples were filled with joy when they saw the Lord, and he said to them again, 'Peace be with you.

'As the Father sent me,
so am I sending you.'

After saying this he breathed on them and said:

'Receive the Holy Spirit.
For those whose sins you forgive,
they are forgiven;
for those whose sins you retain,
they are retained.'

Thomas, called the Twin, who was one of the Twelve, was not with them when Jesus came. When the disciples said, 'We have seen the Lord,' he answered, 'Unless I see the holes that the nails made in his hands and can put my finger into the holes they made, and unless I can put my hand into his side, I refuse to believe.' Eight days later the disciples were in the house again and Thomas was with them. The doors were closed, but Jesus came in and stood among them. 'Peace be with you,' he said. Then he spoke to Thomas, 'Put your finger here; look, here are my hands. Give me your hand; put it into my side. Doubt no longer but believe.' Thomas replied, 'My Lord and my God!'

Jesus said to him:

'You believe because you can see me.
Happy are those who have not seen and yet believe.'

There were many other signs that Jesus worked and the disciples saw, but they are not recorded in this book. These are recorded so that you may believe that Jesus is the Christ, the Son of God, and that believing this you may have life through his name.

This is the Gospel of the Lord.   *John 20:19-31*

Third Sunday of Easter A

Introduction to the Service

Today we celebrate the third Sunday of Easter.

Together with those who are newly baptised, we listen carefully to the message which we will receive in our celebration today. We will hear of the two disciples who went to the village of Emmaus.

We know what happened on the way. Jesus joined them. He accepted their invitation and had a meal with them. They recognised him at the breaking of bread.

This story of the two disciples on their way to Emmaus helped the newly baptised Christians to appreciate more fully the celebration of the Eucharist. It encouraged them to come together in their homes for the 'Breaking of Bread' on Sundays.

What we now call Holy Eucharist or Holy Mass, the early Christians called 'Breaking of Bread.'

Penitential Rite
Let us ask ourselves:

- Do we recognise the risen Lord in our midst when we celebrate the 'Breaking of Bread'? (*Silence*)

- Do we break our bread and share it with others who need our help? (*Silence*)

Let us ask for forgiveness for not sharing with others.
I confess...

FIRST READING

On the road to Emmaus Jesus told the two disciples: 'You foolish men. So slow to believe the full message of the prophets! They have already told you that the Christ has to suffer.'

In our reading today, Peter uses the same argument. He tells the people of Israel that King David foretold that Christ would rise from the dead.

We read from the Acts of the Apostles, chapter two.
*

On the day of Pentecost Peter stood up with the Eleven and addressed the crowd in a loud voice: 'Men of Israel, listen to what I am going to say: Jesus the Nazarene was a man commended to you by God by the miracles and portents and signs that God worked through him when he was among you, as you all know. This man, who was put into your power by the deliberate intention and foreknowledge of God, you took and had crucified by men outside the Law. You killed him, but God raised him to life, freeing him from the pangs of Hades; for it was impossible for him to be held in its power since, as David says of him:

I saw the Lord before me always,
for with him at my right hand nothing can shake me.
So my heart was glad
and my tongue cried out with joy:
my body, too, will rest in the hope
that you will not abandon my soul to Hades
nor allow your holy one to experience corruption.
You have made known the way of life to me,
you will fill me with gladness through your presence.'

'Brothers, no one can deny that the patriarch David himself is dead and buried: his tomb is still with us. But since he was a prophet, and knew that God had sworn him an oath to make one of his descendants succeed him on the throne, what he foresaw and spoke about was the resurrection of the Christ: he is the one who was not abandoned to Hades, and whose body did not experience corruption. God raised this man Jesus to life, and all of us are witnesses to that. Now raised to the heights by God's right hand, he has received from the Father the Holy Spirit, who was promised, and what you see and hear is the outpouring of that Spirit.'

This is the word of the Lord. *Acts 2:14.22-33*

Responsorial Psalm

℞ **Show us, Lord, the path of life.**

or

℞ **Alleluia!**

1 Preserve me, God, I take refuge in you.
I say to the Lord: 'You are my God.
O Lord, it is you who are my portion and cup;
it is you yourself who are my prize.' ℞

2 I will bless the Lord who gives me counsel,
who even at night directs my heart.
I keep the Lord ever in my sight:
since he is at my right hand, I shall stand firm. ℞

3 And so my heart rejoices, my soul is glad;
even my body shall rest in safety.
For you will not leave my soul among the dead,
nor let your beloved know decay. ℞

4 You will show me the path of life,
the fullness of joy in your presence,
at your right hand happiness for ever. ℞

Ps 15:1-2. 5. 7-11. ℞ v.11

SECOND READING

We read from the first letter of St Peter, chapter one.
*
If you are acknowledging as your Father one who has no favourites and judges everyone according to what he has done, you must be scrupulously careful as long as you are living away

from your home. Remember, the ransom that was paid to free you from the useless way of life your ancestors handed down was not paid in anything corruptible, neither in silver nor gold, but in the precious blood of a lamb without spot or stain, namely Christ; who, though known since before the world was made, has been revealed only in our time, the end of the ages, for your sake. Through him you now have faith in God, who raised him from the dead and gave him glory for that very reason – so that you would have faith and hope in God.

This is the word of the Lord.   *1 Peter 1:17-21*

Gospel Acclamation
Alleluia, alleluia!
Lord Jesus, explain the scriptures to us.
Make our hearts burn within us as you talk to us.
Alleluia!   *cf. Lk 24:32*

GOSPEL
We read from the holy Gospel according to Luke, chapter twenty-four.
*
Two of the disciples of Jesus were on their way to a village called Emmaus, seven miles from Jerusalem, and they were talking together about all that had happened. Now as they talked this over, Jesus himself came up and walked by their side; but something prevented them from recognising him. He said to them, 'What matters are you discussing as you walk along?' They stopped short, their faces downcast.

Then one of them, called Cleopas answered him, 'You must be the only person staying in Jerusalem who does not know the things that have been happening there these last few days.' 'What things?' he asked. 'All about Jesus of Nazareth' they answered 'who proved he was a great prophet by the things he said and did in the sight of God and of the whole people; and how our chief priests and our leaders handed him over to be sentenced to death, and had him crucified. Our own hope had been that he would be the one to set Israel free. And this is not all: two whole days have gone by since it all happened; and some women from our group have astounded us: they went to the tomb in the early morning, and when they did not find the body, they came back to tell us they had seen a vision of angels who declared he was alive. Some of our friends went to the tomb and found everything exactly as the women had reported, but of him they saw nothing.'

Then he said to them, 'You foolish men! So slow to believe the full message of the prophets! Was it not ordained that the Christ should suffer and so enter into his glory?' Then, starting with Moses and going through all the prophets, he explained to them the passages throughout the scriptures that were about himself.

When they drew near to the village to which they were going, he made as if to go on; but they pressed him to stay with them. 'It is nearly evening' they said 'and the day is almost over.' So he went in to stay with them. Now while he was with them at the table, he took the bread and said the blessing; then he broke it and handed it to them. And their eyes were opened and they recognised him; but he had vanished from their sight. Then they said to each other, 'Did not our hearts burn within us as he talked to us on the road and explained the scriptures to us?'

They set out that instant and returned to Jerusalem. There they found the Eleven assembled together with their companions, who said to them, 'Yes, it is true. The Lord has risen and has appeared to Simon.' Then they told their story of what had happened on the road and how they had recognised him at the breaking of bread.

This is the Gospel of the Lord. Luke 24:13-35

Fourth Sunday of Easter   A

Introduction to the Service

Today we celebrate the fourth Sunday of Easter.

Again, we join with those who are newly baptised to learn more about the faith during this time after Easter.

With them we ask the following questions:

'What happened when we were baptised? Why do we believe in Jesus? Is he the only one who can save us?'

In our celebration we shall hear the Lord's answer. He calls himself the Good Shepherd. All others are like thieves and brigands. He also calls himself the gate; the only gate leading to life.

It was in baptism that we entered through this gate and became members of Christ's flock.

Penitential Rite

Let us ask ourselves:

- Do we listen to the voice of the Good Shepherd who wants to guide us and show us the way? (*Silence*)

- Do we trust in Jesus as our only Saviour or do we follow people whom Christ would call 'thieves and brigands'? (*Silence*)

Let us ask for forgiveness for not listening to the voice of Christ. **I confess**...

FIRST READING

Our reading is the first missionary sermon to be recorded in the New Testament. Peter speaks to the crowd which had asked the question: 'What shall we do to be saved?

We read from the Acts of the Apostles, chapter two.
*

On the day of Pentecost Peter stood up with the Eleven and addressed the crowd with a loud voice: 'The whole House of Israel can be certain that God has made this Jesus whom you crucified both Lord and Christ.'

Hearing this, they were cut to the heart and said to Peter and the apostles, 'What must we do, brothers?' 'You must repent,' Peter answered 'and every one of you must be baptised in the name of Jesus Christ for the forgiveness of your sins, and you will receive the gift of the Holy Spirit. The promise that was made is for you and your children, and for all those who are far away, for all those whom the Lord our God will call to himself.' He spoke to them for a long time using many arguments, and he urged them, 'Save yourselves from this perverse generation.' They were convinced by his arguments, and they accepted what he said and were baptised. That very day about three thousand were added to their number.

This is the word of the Lord. *Acts 2:14.36-41*

Responsorial Psalm

℞   **The Lord is my shepherd;**
    there is nothing I shall want.

or

℞   **Alleluia!**

1   The Lord is my shepherd;
    there is nothing I shall want.
    Fresh and green are the pastures
    where he gives me repose.
    Near restful waters he leads me,
    to revive my drooping spirit.   ℞

2   He guides me along the right path;
    he is true to his name.
    If I should walk in the valley of darkness
    no evil would I fear.
    You are there with your crook and your staff;
    with these you give me comfort.   ℞

3   You have prepared a banquet for me
    in the sight of my foes.
    My head you have anointed with oil;
    my cup is overflowing.   ℞

4   Surely goodness and kindness shall follow me
    all the days of my life.
    In the Lord's own house shall I dwell
    for ever and ever.   ℞   *Ps 22:1-6. ℞ v.1*

SECOND READING

We read from the first letter of St Peter, chapter two.
*
The merit, in the sight of God, is in bearing punishment patiently
when you are punished after doing your duty.

This, in fact, is what you were called to do, because Christ
suffered for you and left an example for you to follow the way he
took. He had not done anything wrong, and there had been no
perjury in his mouth. He was insulted and did not retaliate with
insults; when he was tortured he made no threats but he put his
trust in the righteous judge. He was bearing our faults in his own
body on the cross, so that we might die to our faults and live for
holiness; through his wounds you have been healed. You had

gone astray like sheep but now you have come back to the shepherd and guardian of your souls.

This is the word of the Lord. *1 Peter 2:20-25*

Gospel Acclamation
Alleluia, alleluia!
I am the good shepherd, says the Lord;
I know my own sheep and my own know me.
Alleluia! *Jn 10:14*

GOSPEL
We read from the holy Gospel according to John, chapter ten.
*
Jesus said: 'I tell you most solemnly, anyone who does not enter the sheepfold through the gate, but gets in some other way is a thief and a brigand. The one who enters through the gate is the shepherd of the flock; the gatekeeper lets him in, the sheep hear his voice, one by one he calls his own sheep and leads them out. When he has brought out his flock, he goes ahead of them, and the sheep follow because they know his voice. They never follow a stranger but run away from him: they do not recognise the voice of strangers.'

Jesus told them this parable but they failed to understand what he meant by telling it to them.

So Jesus spoke to them again:

'I tell you most solemnly,
I am the gate of the sheepfold.
All others who have come
are thieves and brigands;
but the sheep took no notice of them.
I am the gate.
Anyone who enters through me will be safe:
he will go freely in and out
and be sure of finding pasture.
The thief comes
only to steal and kill and destroy.
I have come
so that they may have life
and have it to the full.'

This is the Gospel of the Lord. *John 10:1-10*

Fifth Sunday of Easter   A

Introduction to the Service

When we prepare for a long and difficult journey we may be worried and ask ourselves: 'Shall I arrive safely? Accidents can happen on the road. Will there be somewhere at the other end where I can stay?'

When we were baptised, we too began a long and difficult trip. It is good to ask ourselves: 'Do we have the strength to persevere to the end? Will we get tired on the road of God and give up?'

We have all experienced difficulties in living our faith. Doubts arose in our hearts. God seemed to be so far away. Nothing made sense any more. Our heart was troubled.

In this situation of doubts and distress we hear the Lord's message today: 'Do not let your heart be troubled. Trust in me. I am the Way.'

Penitential Rite

Let us examine ourselves:

● Is our heart troubled because we were insisting on going alone, without God?   (*Silence*)

● Do we have sleepless nights because we worry too much without trusting in the Lord?   (*Silence*)

Let us surrender ourselves into the hands of God by asking for forgiveness.   **I confess**…

FIRST READING

When many people joined the early Church, trouble started. Jealousy arose between people of different races. There were complaints and dissatisfaction.

Our reading tells us how the early Christians solved their problems.

We read from the Acts of the Apostles, chapter six.

*
About this time, when the number of disciples was increasing, the Hellenists made a complaint against the Hebrews: in the daily distribution their own widows were being overlooked. So the Twelve called a full meeting of the disciples and addressed them, 'It would not be right for us to neglect the word of God so as to give out food; you, brothers, must select from among yourselves

seven men of good reputation, filled with the Spirit and with wisdom; we will hand over this duty to them, and continue to devote ourselves to prayer and to the service of the word.' The whole assembly approved of this proposal and elected Stephen, a man full of faith and of the Holy Spirit, together with Philip, Prochorus, Nicanor, Timon, Parmenas, and Nicolaus of Antioch, a convert to Judaism. They presented these to the apostles, who prayed and laid their hands on them.

The word of the Lord continued to spread: the number of disciples in Jerusalem was greatly increased, and a large group of priests made their submission to the faith.

This is the word of the Lord. *Acts 6:1-7*

Responsorial Psalm

℟ **May your love be upon us, O Lord, as we place all our hope in you.**

or

℟ **Alleluia!**

1 Ring out your joy to the Lord, O you just;
for praise is fitting for loyal hearts.
Give thanks to the Lord upon the harp,
with a ten-stringed lute sing him songs. ℟

2 For the word of the Lord is faithful
and all his works to be trusted.
The Lord loves justice and right
and fills the earth with his love. ℟

3 The Lord looks on those who revere him,
on those who hope in his love,
to rescue their souls from death,
to keep them alive in famine. ℟

Ps 32:1-2. 4-5. 18-19. ℟ v.22

SECOND READING

We read from the first letter of St Peter, chapter two.
*
The Lord is the living stone, rejected by men but chosen by God and precious to him; set yourselves close to him so that you too, the holy priesthood that offers the spiritual sacrifices which Jesus Christ has made acceptable to God, may be living stones making a spiritual house. As scripture says: See how I lay in Zion a

precious cornerstone that I have chosen and the man who rests his trust on it will not be disappointed. That means that for you who are believers, it is precious; but for unbelievers, the stone rejected by the builders has proved to be the keystone, a stone to stumble over, a rock to bring men down. They stumble over it because they do not believe in the word; it was the fate in store for them.

But you are a chosen race, a royal priesthood, a consecrated nation, a people set apart to sing the praises of God who called you out of the darkness into his wonderful light.

This is the word of the Lord.   *1 Peter 2:4-9*

Gospel Acclamation
Alleluia, alleluia!
Jesus said: 'I am the Way, the Truth and the Life.
No one can come to the Father except through me.'
Alleluia!   *Jn 14:6*

GOSPEL
We read from the holy Gospel according to John, chapter fourteen.
*
Jesus said to his disciples:

'Do not let your hearts be troubled.
Trust in God still, and trust in me.
There are many rooms in my Father's house;
if there were not, I should have told you.
I am now going to prepare a place for you,
and after I have gone and prepared you a place,
I shall return to take you with me;
so that where I am
you may be too.
You know the way to the place where I am going.'

Thomas said, 'Lord, we do not know where you are going, so how can we know the way?' Jesus said:

'I am the Way, the Truth and the Life.
No one can come to the Father except through me.
If you know me, you know my Father too.
From this moment you know him and have seen him.'

Philip said, 'Lord, let us see the Father and then we shall be satisfied.' 'Have I been with you all this time, Philip,' said Jesus to him 'and you still do not know me?

'To have seen me is to have seen the Father,
so how can you say, "Let us see the Father"?
Do you not believe
that I am in the Father and the Father is in me?
The words I say to you I do not speak as from myself:
it is the Father, living in me, who is doing this work.
You must believe me when I say
that I am in the Father and the Father is in me;
believe it on the evidence of this work, if for no other reason.

'I tell you most solemnly,
whoever believes in me
will perform the same works as I do myself,
he will perform even greater works,
because I am going to the Father.'

This is the Gospel of the Lord.   *John 14:1-2*

Sixth Sunday of Easter   A

Introduction to the Service

In the early Church the Sacraments of Baptism and Confirmation were given together during the Easter Vigil. Why?

Baptism and confirmation belong together as Easter and Pentecost belong together. Therefore it became customary in the early Church to lay hands on the newly baptised and to ask the power of the Holy Spirit to come down on them.

It is through the Holy Spirit that Jesus lives in us and we in him. In today's Gospel reading Jesus tells us: 'On that day you will understand that I am in my Father and you in me and I in you.'

Penitential Rite

Let us ask ourselves

● Have I ever experienced deep joy in my heart because God lives in me?   (*Silence*)

● Do I accept my fellow Christians as my brothers and sisters because the same Spirit of God lives in them?   (*Silence*)

Let us ask for forgiveness for ignoring God's Spirit within us.
I confess…

FIRST READING

In our reading we shall hear how the Apostles administered the Sacrament of Confirmation.

We read from the Acts of the Apostles, chapter eight.

*

Philip went to a Samaritan town and proclaimed the Christ to them. The people united in welcoming the message Philip preached, either because they had heard of the miracles he worked or because they saw them for themselves. There were, for example, unclean spirits that came shrieking out of many who were possessed, and several paralytics and cripples were cured. As a result there was great rejoicing in that town.

When the apostles in Jerusalem heard that Samaria had accepted the word of God, they sent Peter and John to them, and they went down there, and prayed for the Samaritans to receive the Holy Spirit, for as yet he had not come down on any of them: they had only been baptised in the name of the Lord Jesus. Then they laid hands on them, and they received the Holy Spirit.

This is the word of the Lord.   *Acts 8:5-8.14-17*

Responsorial Psalm
℟   **Cry out with joy to God all the earth.**

or

℟   **Alleluia!**

1   Cry out with joy to God all the earth,
    O sing to the glory of his name.
    O render him glorious praise.
    Say to God: 'How tremendous your deeds!   ℟

2   'Before you all the earth shall bow;
    shall sing to you, sing to your name!'
    Come and see the works of God,
    tremendous his deeds among men.   ℟

3   He turned the sea into dry land,
    they passed through the river dry-shod.
    Let our joy then be in him;
    he rules for ever by his might.   ℟

4   Come and hear, all who fear God.
    I will tell what he did for my soul:
    Blessed be God who did not reject my prayer
    nor withhold his love from me.   ℟   *Ps 65:1-7. 16. 20. ℟ v.1*

SECOND READING

We read from the first letter of St Peter, chapter three.

*

Reverence the Lord Christ in your hearts, and always have your answer ready for people who ask you the reason for the hope that you all have. But give it with courtesy and respect and with a clear conscience, so that those who slander you when you are living a good life in Christ may be proved wrong in the accusations that they bring. And if it is the will of God that you should suffer, it is better to suffer for doing right than for doing wrong.

Why, Christ himself, innocent though he was, had died once for sins, died for the guilty, to lead us to God. In the body he was put to death, in the spirit he was raised to life.

This is the word of the Lord. *1 Peter 3:15-18*

Gospel Acclamation
Alleluia, alleluia!
Jesus said: 'If anyone loves me he will keep my word,
and my Father will love him, and we shall come to him.'
Alleluia! *Jn 14:23*

GOSPEL

We read from the holy Gospel according to John, chapter fourteen.

*

Jesus said to his disciples:

'If you love me you will keep my commandments.
I shall ask the Father,
and he will give you another Advocate
to be with you for ever,
that Spirit of truth
whom the world can never receive
since it neither sees nor knows him;
but you know him,
because he is with you, he is in you.
I will not leave you orphans;
I will come back to you.
In a short time the world will no longer see me;
but you will see me,
because I live and you will live.
On that day
you will understand that I am in my Father
and you in me and I in you.

Anybody who receives my commandments and keeps them
will be one who loves me;
and anybody who loves me will be loved by my Father,
and I shall love him and show myself to him.'

This is the Gospel of the Lord.   *John 14:15-21*

*When the Ascension of the Lord is celebrated on the Seventh
Sunday of Easter, the Second Reading and Gospel assigned to the
Seventh Sunday may be read on the Sixth Sunday.*

The Ascension of the Lord   A

Introduction to the Service

There are great celebrations when the leader of a nation is
installed. A king is led to his throne, a President has to swear an
oath and other leaders are solemnly led into their new office.
Sometimes the whole nation takes part by listening to the radio or
watching the celebration on TV.

Today we celebrate the installation of Christ as the great Lord of
all nations; Christ has ascended into heaven and takes his seat at
the right hand of God. All honour and power are given to him.

On this day of Ascension we rejoice with all people in heaven
and all nations on earth. We acclaim Jesus as our Lord.

Penetential Rite

We ask ourselves:

● Do we accept Jesus as our Lord by allowing him to rule our
lives?   (*Silence*)

● Do we trust in him in time of trouble?   (*Silence*)

● Do we expect Christ to judge all our words and actions when he
comes back in glory?   (*Silence*)

Let us ask for mercy.   **I confess**…

FIRST READING

When we say good-bye to a friend we remain standing until they
have gone out of sight.

We should NOT do the same when we celebrate the ascension
of Jesus in heaven today. He is with us in a new way until he
comes back in glory.

We read from the Acts of the Apostles, chapter one.
★
In my earlier work, Theophilus, I dealt with everything Jesus had done and taught from the beginning until the day he gave his instructions to the apostles he had chosen through the Holy Spirit, and was taken up to heaven. He had shown himself alive to them after his Passion by many demonstrations: for forty days he had continued to appear to them and tell them about the kingdom of God. When he had been at table with them, he had told them not to leave Jerusalem, but to wait there for what the Father had promised. 'It is' he had said 'what you have heard me speak about: John baptised with water but you, not many days from now, will be baptised with the Holy Spirit.'

Now having met together, they asked him, 'Lord, has the time come? Are you going to restore the kingdom to Israel?' He replied, 'It is not for you to know times or dates that the Father has decided by his own authority, but you will receive power when the Holy Spirit comes on you, and then you will be my witnesses not only in Jerusalem but throughout Judaea and Samaria, and indeed to the ends of the earth.'

As he said this he was lifted up while they looked on, and a cloud took him from their sight. They were still staring into the sky when suddenly two men in white were standing near them and they said, 'Why are you men from Galilee standing here looking into the sky? Jesus who has been taken up from you into heaven, this same Jesus will come back in the same way as you have seen him go there.'

This is the word of the Lord.   *Acts 1:1-11*

Responsorial Psalm
  ℟ **God goes up with shouts of joy;**
     the Lord goes up with trumpet blast.

or

  ℟ **Alleluia!**

1 All peoples, clap your hands,
   cry to God with shouts of joy!
   For the Lord, the Most High, we must fear,
   great king over all the earth. ℟

2 God goes up with shouts of joy;
   the Lord goes up with trumpet blast.

Sing praise for God, sing praise,
sing praise to our king, sing praise.   ℟

3   God is king of all the earth.
Sing praise with all your skill.
God is king over the nations;
God reigns on his holy throne.   ℟   *Ps 46:2-3. 6-9. ℟v. 6*

SECOND READING
We read from the letter of St Paul to the Ephesians, chapter one.
*
May the God of our Lord Jesus Christ, the Father of glory, give
you a spirit of wisdom and perception of what is revealed, to
bring you to full knowledge of him. May he enlighten the eyes of
your mind so that you can see what hope his call holds for you,
what rich glories he has promised the saints will inherit and how
infinitely great is the power that he has exercised for us believers.
This you can tell from the strength of his power at work in Christ,
when he used it to raise him from the dead and to make him sit at
his right hand, in heaven, far above every Sovereignty, Authority, Power, or Domination, or any other name that can be
named, not only in this age, but also in the age to come. He has
put all things under his feet, and made him as the ruler of
everything, the head of the Church; which is his body, the
fullness of him who fills the whole creation.

This is the word of the Lord.   *Ephesians 1:17-23*

Gospel Acclamation
Alleluia, alleluia!
Go, make disciples of all the nations;
I am with you always; yes, to the end of time.
Alleluia!   *Mt 28:19-20*

GOSPEL
We read from the holy Gospel according to Matthew, chapter twenty-
eight.
*
The eleven disciples set out for Galilee, to the mountain where
Jesus had arranged to meet them. When they saw him they fell
down before him, though some hesitated. Jesus came up and
spoke to them. He said, 'All authority in heaven and on earth has
been given to me. Go, therefore, make disciples of all the nations;
baptise them in the name of the Father and of the Son and of the

Holy Spirit, and teach them to observe all the commands I gave you. And know that I am with you always; yes, to the end of time.'

This is the Gospel of the Lord.   *Matthew 28:16-20*

Seventh Sunday of Easter   A

Introduction to the Service

Last Thursday we celebrated the Ascension of our Lord. Next Sunday will be Pentecost, the feast of the Holy Spirit. These ten days between Ascension and Pentecost are a time of waiting.

Think of a time when you were anxiously waiting for a dear friend. Your whole heart was waiting for him or her. You looked out through the window, opened the door in the hope you might see your friend coming or even went out to meet him or her.

It must have been with such a spirit of expectation and longing that the disciples of the Lord waited in the Upper Room, united in continuous prayer, waiting for the Spirit.

Penitential Rite

Let us examine our conscience:

- Are we one heart and soul when we pray together in our celebration?   (*Silence*)

- Do we unite ourselves in love with those people who voice a petition during our celebration?   (*Silence*)

- How do we prepare ourselves for the coming feast of Pentecost?   (*Silence*)

Let us make ourselves one and pray for one another.
I confess…

FIRST READING

We cannot pour wine into a cup which is still full of water. God cannot pour out his Spirit into people who are still full of themselves. Therefore the disciples of Jesus prayed in the Upper Room, emptying themselves by opening up to God with a longing heart.

We read from the Acts of the Apostles, chapter one.
*

After Jesus was taken up into heaven, the apostles went back from the Mount of Olives, as it is called, to Jerusalem, a short distance away, no more than a sabbath walk; and when they reached the city they went to the upper room where they were staying; there were Peter and John, James and Andrew, Philip and Thomas, Bartholomew and Matthew, James son of Alphaeus and Simon the Zealot, and Jude son of James. All these joined in continuous prayer, together with several women, including Mary the mother of Jesus, and with his brothers.

This is the word of the Lord.   *Acts 1:12-14*

Responsorial Psalm
  ℟   **I am sure I shall see the Lord's goodness**
       in the land of the living.

or

  ℟   **Alleluia!**

1   The Lord is my light and my help;
     whom shall I fear?
     The Lord is the stronghold of my life;
     before whom shall I shrink?   ℟

2   There is one thing I ask of the Lord,
     for this I long,
     to live in the house of the Lord,
     all the days of my life,
     to savour the sweetness of the Lord,
     to behold his temple.   ℟

3   O Lord, hear my voice when I call;
     have mercy and answer.
     Of you my heart has spoken;
     'Seek his face.'   ℟   *Ps 26:1. 4. 7-8. ℟ v.13*

SECOND READING

We read from the first letter of St Peter, chapter four.
*

If you can have some share in the sufferings of Christ, be glad, because you will enjoy a much greater gladness when his glory is revealed. It is a blessing for you when they insult you for bearing the name of Christ, because it means that you have the Spirit of glory, the Spirit of God resting on you. None of you should ever deserve to suffer for being a murderer, a thief, a criminal or an informer; but if anyone of you should suffer for being a Christian, then he is not to be ashamed of it; he should thank God that he has been called one.

This is the word of the Lord.   *1 Peter 4:13-16*

Gospel Acclamation
Alleluia, alleluia!
I will not leave you orphans, says the Lord;
I will come back to you, and your hearts will be full of joy.
Alleluia!   *cf. Jn 14:18*

GOSPEL

We read from the holy Gospel according to John, chapter seventeen.
*
Jesus raised his eyes to heaven and said:

'Father, the hour has come:
glorify your Son
so that your Son may glorify you;
and, through the power over all mankind that you have
    given him,
let him give eternal life to all those you have entrusted to
    him.
And eternal life is this:
to know you,
the only true God,
and Jesus Christ whom you have sent.
I have glorified you on earth
and finished the work
that you gave me to do.
Now, Father, it is time for you to glorify me
with that glory I had with you
before ever the world was.
I have made your name known
to the men you took from the world to give me.
They were yours and you gave them to me,
and they have kept your word.
Now at last they know
that all you have given me comes indeed from you;
for I have given them
the teaching you gave to me,

and they have truly accepted this, that I came from you,
and have believed that it was you who sent me.
I pray for them;
I am not praying for the world
but for those you have given me,
because they belong to you:
all I have is yours
and all you have is mine,
and in them I am glorified.
I am not in the world any longer,
but they are in the world,
and I am coming to you.'

This is the Gospel of the Lord.   *John 17:1-11*

Pentecost Sunday   A

Mass during the Day

Introduction to the Service

Today we celebrate the great feast of Pentecost. It is the feast of
God's Spirit. The power of evil spirits has come to an end.

We know how the evil spirit of envy can poison our heart. We
know the evil spirits of anger and greed. The spirit of hatred
destroys happiness and peace. We are afraid of these spirits of evil
and death.

Today, however, we praise the great deeds of God. He breathes
over us with the spirit of power. His breath is like storm and fire.
Today, the evil spirits become afraid, their power is broken.

We have come together to open ourselves to God. We allow him
to breathe on us as he breathed upon the first Christians in
Jerusalem.

Penetential Rite

Let us prepare ourselves for the coming of the Spirit.

- Is there within us a spirit of joy and gratitude?   (*Silence*)

- Is there within us a spirit of love and unity?   (*Silence*)

- Is there within us a spirit of going out to other people, joyfully
  telling them about Christ?   (*Silence*)

Let us open ourselves to God by asking his forgiveness.
I confess...

FIRST READING

Our reading is challenging us.

Do we as Christians just come to church and sing and pray together? Or do we open the door and go out to other people who do not yet follow the way of Christ? When did we last talk about Christ to our children or our neighbours?

We read from the Acts of the Apostles, chapter two.
*
When Pentecost day came round, the apostles had all met in one room, when suddenly they heard what sounded like a powerful wind from heaven, the noise of which filled the entire house in which they were sitting; and something appeared to them that seemed like tongues of fire; these separated and came to rest on the head of each of them. They were all filled with the Holy Spirit, and began to speak foreign languages as the Spirit gave them the gift of speech.

Now there were devout men living in Jerusalem from every nation under heaven, and at this sound they all assembled, each one bewildered to hear these men speaking his own language. They were amazed and astonished. 'Surely' they said 'all these men speaking are Galileans? How does it happen that each of us hears them in his own native language? Parthians, Medes and Elamites; people from Mesopotamia, Judaea and Cappadocia, Pontus and Asia, Phrygia and Pamphylia, Egypt and the parts of Libya round Cyrene; as well as visitors from Rome – Jews and proselytes alike – Cretans and Arabs; we hear them preaching in our own language about the marvels of God.'

This is the word of the Lord.   *Acts 2:1-11*

Responsorial Psalm
   ℟ **Send forth your Spirit, O Lord,**
      and renew the face of the earth.

or

   ℟ **Alleluia.**

1 Bless the Lord, my soul!
    Lord God, how great you are,
    How many are your works, O Lord!
    The earth is full of your riches. ℟

2 You take back your spirit, they die,
    returning to the dust from which they came.
    You send forth your spirit, they are created;
    and you renew the face of the earth. ℟

3 May the glory of the Lord last for ever!
   May the Lord rejoice in his works!
   May my thoughts be pleasing to him.
   I find my joy in the Lord. ℟

Ps 103:1. 24. 29-31. 34. ℟ cf v.30

SECOND READING

We read from the first letter of St Paul to the Corinthians, chapter
twelve.
*
No one can say, 'Jesus is Lord' unless he is under the influence of
the Holy Spirit.

There is a variety of gifts but always the same Spirit; there are
all sorts of service to be done, but always to the same Lord;
working in all sorts of different ways in different people, it is the
same God who is working in all of them. The particular way in
which the Spirit is given to each person is for a good purpose.

Just as a human body, though it is made up of many parts, is a
single unit because all these parts, though many, make one body,
so it is with Christ. In the one Spirit we were all baptised, Jews as
well as Greeks, slaves as well as citizens, and one Spirit was given
to us all to drink.

This is the word of the Lord.   *1 Corinthians 12:3-7. 12-13*

SEQUENCE

The sequence may be said or sung.

Holy Spirit, Lord of light,
    From the clear celestial height
Thy pure beaming radiance give.

Come, thou Father of the poor,
    Come with treasures which endure;
Come, thou light of all that live!

Thou, of all consolers best,
    Thou, the soul's delightful guest,
Dost refreshing peace bestow;

Thou in toil art comfort sweet;
    Pleasant coolness in the heat;
Solace in the midst of woe.

Light immortal, light divine,
    Visit thou these hearts of thine,
And our inmost being fill:

If thou take thy grace away,
    Nothing pure in man will stay;
All his good is turned to ill.

Heal our wounds, our strength renew;
    On our dryness pour thy dew;
Wash the stains of guilt away:

Bend the stubborn heart and will;
    Melt the frozen, warm the chill;
Guide the steps that go astray.

Thou, on us who evermore
    Thee confess and thee adore,
With thy sevenfold gifts descend:

Give us comfort when we die;
    Give us life with thee on high;
Give us joys that never end.

Gospel Acclamation
Alleluia, alleluia!
Come, Holy Spirit, fill the hearts of your faithful
and kindle in them the fire of your love.
Alleluia!

GOSPEL
We read from the holy Gospel according to John, chapter twenty.
*
In the evening of the first day of the week, the doors were closed
in the room where the disciples were, for fear of the Jews. Jesus
came and stood among them. He said to them, 'Peace be with
you,' and showed them his hands and his side. The disciples
were filled with joy when they saw the Lord, and he said to them
again, 'Peace be with you.

'As the Father sent me,
so am I sending you.'

After saying this he breathed on them and said:

'Receive the Holy Spirit.
For those whose sins you forgive,
they are forgiven;
for those whose sins you retain,
they are retained.'

This is the Gospel of the Lord.   *John 20:19-23*

SOLEMNITIES OF THE LORD IN ORDINARY TIME

Sunday after Pentecost   *Solemnity*

The Most Holy Trinity   A

Introduction to the Service

Today we celebrate the feast of the Blessed Trinity. We proclaim our faith: there is only one God, but in God there is God the Father, God the Son and God the Holy Spirit.

This feast of the Blessed Trinity helps us to think of God in the right way: God is not an old man with a long beard, sitting on a throne and feeling lonely.

Rather, this feast of the Blessed Trinity tells us the opposite: God is a community. Life, joy and mutual love are vibrating in God. Within God there is an everlasting feast to which we are all invited.

This is our salvation: God the Father, Son and Holy Spirit wants to share his life with us. The Lord has revealed this wonderful message when he tells us in the gospel: 'God loved the world so much, that he gave his only Son, so that everyone who believes in him may not be lost but may have eternal life.'

God, Son and Love. That is the Blessed Trinity.

Penitential Rite

Let us ask ourselves:

● Do we ever thank God that we were baptised in the name of the Father, the Son and the Holy Spirit?   (*Silence*)

● Do we ever allow God to love us, exposing ourselves to him in silent prayer?   (*Silence*)

● Is our faith in Christ strong enough so that we do not get lost?   (*Silence*)

Let us ask God to forgive us for the sake of Jesus.   **I confess**...

FIRST READING

In the Old Testament God had not revealed himself as the Blessed Trinity. However, in our reading we hear of God's tenderness and compassion for his people, whom he wanted to adopt. It was through this tender love that God the Father, Son and Spirit was already present among the people of Israel.

We read from the book of Exodus, chapter thirty-four.
*
With the two tablets of stone in his hands, Moses went up the mountain of Sinai in the early morning as the Lord had commanded him. And the Lord descended in the form of a cloud, and Moses stood with him there.

He called on the name of the Lord. The Lord passed before him and proclaimed, 'Lord, Lord, a God of tenderness and compassion, slow to anger, rich in kindness and faithfulness.' And Moses bowed down to the ground at once and worshipped. 'If I have indeed won your favour, Lord,' he said 'let my Lord come with us, I beg. True, they are a headstrong people, but forgive us our faults and our sins, and adopt us as your heritage.'

This is the word of the Lord.   *Exodus 34:4-6.8-9*

Responsial Psalm
1   You are blest, Lord God of our fathers.
    ℟   **To you glory and praise for evermore.**
    Blest your glorious holy name.
    ℟   **To you glory and praise for evermore.**

2   You are blest in the temple of your glory.
    ℟   **To you glory and praise for evermore.**
    You are blest on the throne of your kingdom.
    ℟   **To you glory and praise for evermore.**

3   You are blest who gaze into the depths.
    ℟   **To you glory and praise for evermore.**
    You are blest in the firmament of heaven.
    ℟   **To you glory and praise for evermore.**

                                    Dan 3:52-56. ℟ v.52

SECOND READING
We read from the second letter of St Paul to the Corinthians, chapter thirteen.
*
Brothers, we wish you happiness; try to grow perfect; help one another. Be united; live in peace, and the God of love and peace will be with you.

Greet one another with the holy kiss. All the saints send you greetings.

The grace of the Lord Jesus Christ, the love of God and the fellowship of the Holy Spirit be with you all.

This is the word of the Lord. *2 Corinthians 13:11-13*

Gospel Acclamation
Alleluia, alleluia!
Glory be to the Father, and to the Son, and to the Holy Spirit,
the God who is, who was, and who is to come.
Alleluia! *cf. Apoc 1:8*

GOSPEL

We read from the holy Gospel according to John, chapter three.
*
Jesus said to Nicodemus,

'God loved the world so much
that he gave his only Son,
so that everyone who believes in him may not be lost
but may have eternal life.
For God sent his Son into the world
not to condemn the world,
but so that through him the world might be saved.
No one who believes in him will be condemned;
but whoever refuses to believe is condemned already,
because he has refused to believe
in the name of God's only Son.'

This is the Gospel of the Lord. *John 3:16-18*

Thursday after Trinity Sunday *Solemnity*

The Body and Blood of Christ   A

Introduction to the Service
There are things which we do every day again and again without much thought. For instance, greeting our neighbours. We wish them a good morning or a good afternoon but our thoughts may be far away from them. We are in danger of acting very superficially.
   The same thing can happen with our celebration of the Eucharist and with receiving Holy Communion. It can become for us merely an outward tradition which we no longer think deeply about.

It is for this reason that we celebrate today the feast of *Corpus Christi*. This is a Latin word, meaning 'Body of Christ'. We celebrate this feast in order to appreciate again more deeply the body and blood of Christ whom we receive at holy Mass.

In our celebration today, the Lord reminds us that we cannot live without the Eucharist: without eating his body and drinking his blood.

Penitential Rite

Let us ask ourselves:

- How do we appreciate our Sunday Mass? Do we miss the Sunday Eucharist for any minor reason or inconvenience? (*Silence*)

- Do we help each other to make our Sunday Eucharist a joyful celebration in our community? (*Silence*)

- Do we allow Holy Communion to bring us closer together as brothers and sisters? (*Silence*)

Let us ask for forgiveness for not appreciating the Eucharist as we should. **I confess**...

FIRST READING

During the forty years in the desert, the people of Israel learnt how to trust and how to rely completely on God. They realised that they needed more than bread alone.

What do we think? What more do we need?

We read from the book of Deuteronomy, chapter eight.
*
Moses said to the people: 'Remember how the Lord your God led you for forty years in the wilderness, to humble you, to test you and know your inmost heart – whether you would keep his commandments or not. He humbled you, he made you feel hunger, he fed you with manna which neither you nor your fathers had known, to make you understand that man does not live on bread alone but that man lives on everything that comes from the mouth of the Lord.

'Do not then forget the Lord your God who brought you out of the land of Egypt, out of the house of slavery: who guided you through this vast and dreadful wilderness, a land of fiery serpents, scorpions, thirst; who in this waterless place brought you water from the hardest rock; who in this wilderness fed you with manna that your fathers had not known.'

This the word of the Lord.   *Deuteronomy 8:2-3.14-16*

Responsorial Psalm
℟   **O praise the Lord, Jerusalem!**

or

℟   **Alleluia!**

1   O praise the Lord, Jerusalem!
     Zion, praise your God!
     He has strengthened the bars of your gates,
     he has blessed the children within you.   ℟

2   He established peace on your borders,
     he feeds you with finest wheat.
     He sends out his word to the earth
     and swiftly runs his command.   ℟

3   He makes his word known to Jacob,
     to Israel his laws and decrees.
     He has not dealt thus with other nations;
     he has not taught them his decrees.   ℟
                                   Ps 147:12-15. 19-20. ℟ v.12

SECOND READING

We read from the first letter of St Paul to the Corinthians, chapter ten.
*
The blessing-cup that we bless is a communion with the blood of
Christ, and the bread that we break is a communion with the
body of Christ. The fact that there is only one loaf means that,
though there are many of us, we form a single body because we
all have a share in this one loaf.

This is the word of the Lord.   *1 Corinthians 10:16-17*

SEQUENCE

*The sequence may be said or sung in full, or using the shorter
form indicated by the asterisked verses.*

     Sing forth, O Zion, sweetly sing
     The praises of thy Shepherd-King,
          In hymns and canticles divine;
     Dare all thou canst, thou hast no song

Worthy his praises to prolong,
    So far surpassing powers like thine.

Today no theme of common praise
Forms the sweet burden of thy lays –
    The living, life-dispensing food –
That food which at the sacred board
Unto the brethren twelve our Lord
    His parting legacy bestowed.

Then be the anthem clear and strong,
Thy fullest note, thy sweetest song,
    The very music of the breast:
For now shines forth the day sublime
That brings remembrance of the time
    When Jesus first his table blessed.

Within our new King's banquet-hall
They meet to keep the festival
    That closed the ancient paschal rite:
The old is by the new replaced;
The substance hath the shadow chased;
    And rising day dispels the night.

Christ willed what he himself had done
Should be renewed while time should run,
    In memory of his parting hour:
Thus, tutored in his school divine,
We consecrate the bread and wine;
    And lo – a Host of saving power.

This faith to Christian men is given –
Bread is made flesh by words from heaven:
    Into his blood the wine is turned:
What though it baffles nature's powers
Of sense and sight? This faith of ours
    Proves more than nature e'er discerned.

Concealed beneath the two-fold sign,
Meet symbols of the gifts divine,
    There lie the mysteries adored:
The living body is our food;
Our drink the ever-precious blood;
    In each, one undivided Lord.

Not he that eateth it divides
The sacred food, which whole abides
    Unbroken still, nor knows decay;
Be one, or be a thousand fed,
They eat alike that living bread
    Which, still received, ne'er wastes away.

The good, the guilty share therein,
With sure increase of grace or sin,
    The ghostly life, or ghostly death:
Death to the guilty; to the good
Immortal life. See how one food
    Man's joy or woe accomplisheth.

We break the Sacrament; but bold
And firm thy faith shall keep its hold;
Deem not the whole doth more enfold
    Than in the fractured part resides:
Deem not that Christ doth broken lie;
'Tis but the sign that meets the eye;
The hidden deep reality
    In all its fullness still abides.

*Behold the bread of angels, sent
For pilgrims in their banishment,
The bread for God's true children meant,
    That may not unto dogs be given:
Oft in the olden types foreshowed;
In Isaac on the altar bowed,
And in the ancient paschal food,
    And in the manna sent from heaven.

*   Come then, good shepherd, bread divine,
Still show to us thy mercy sign;
Oh, feed us still, still keep us thine;
So may we see thy glories shine
    In fields of immortality;

*   O thou, the wisest, mightiest, best,
Our present food, our future rest,
Come, make us each thy chosen guest,
Co-heirs of thine, and comrades blest
    With saints whose dwelling is with thee.

Gospel Acclamation
Alleluia, alleluia!
I am the living bread which has come down from heaven,
says the Lord.
Anyone who eats this bread will live for ever.
Alleluia!   *Jn 6:51-52*

GOSPEL

We read from the holy Gospel according to John, chapter six.
★
Jesus said to the Jews:
'I am the living bread which has come down from heaven.
Anyone who eats this bread will live for ever;
and the bread that I shall give
is my flesh, for the life of the world.'

Then the Jews started arguing with one another: 'How can
this man give us his flesh to eat?' they said. Jesus replied:

'I tell you most solemnly,
if you do not eat the flesh of the Son of Man
and drink his blood,
you will not have life in you.
Anyone who does eat my flesh and drink my blood
has eternal life,
and I shall raise him up on the last day.
For my flesh is real food
and my blood is real drink.
He who eats my flesh and drinks my blood
lives in me
and I live in him.
As I, who am sent by the living Father,
myself draw life from the Father,
so whoever eats me will draw life from me.
This is the bread come down from heaven;
not like the bread our ancestors ate:
they are dead,
but anyone who eats this bread will live for ever.'

This is the Gospel of the Lord.   *John 6:51-58*

Friday after the Second Sunday after Pentecost　　　　　*Solemnity*

The Sacred Heart of Jesus　A

Introduction to the Service

Different people have different ideas of God. Some imagine God as the powerful creator who lives far beyond the stars. For others God is a great judge who will reward all our good deeds and punish what we have done wrong.

Today, however, we receive a different message. On this feast of the Sacred Heart of Jesus, the Lord shows us God as he really is. 'Come to me', he says, 'for I am gentle and humble of heart'.

This feast of the Sacred Heart reveals to us a God of gentle and tender love; a message which is perhaps harder for those who are learned and clever to understand.

Penitential Rite

Let us ask ourselves:

● Are we willing to accept God's love as children accept the love of their parents? (*Silence*)

● Do we talk a lot about God, while our hearts are far from him? (*Silence*)

By asking for God's forgiveness we give ourselves completely into his loving hands. **I confess**...

FIRST READING

It is difficult for a young man to give reasons why he fell in love with a certain young lady. There are no real reasons for falling in love.

In our reading Moses tells the people of Israel that God has fallen in love with them. And what was the reason? Not because the Israelites were such great and good people. There was no other reason but the boundless generosity of God's heart. 'God set his heart on you and chose you', said Moses.

We read from the book of Deuteronomy, chapter seven.

*

Moses said to the people: 'You are a people consecrated to the Lord your God; it is you that the Lord our God has chosen to be his very own people out of all the peoples on the earth.

'If the Lord set his heart on you and chose you, it was not

because you outnumbered other peoples: you were the least of all peoples. It was for love of you and to keep the oath he swore to your fathers that the Lord brought you out with his mighty hand and redeemed you from the house of slavery, from the power of Pharaoh king of Egypt. Know then that the Lord your God is God indeed, the faithful God who is true to his covenant and his graciousness for a thousand generations towards those who love him and keep his commandments, but who punishes in their own persons those that hate him; he makes him work out his punishment in person. You are therefore to keep and observe the commandments and statutes and ordinances that I lay down for you today.'

This is the word of the Lord.   *Deuteronomy 7:6-11*

Responsorial Psalm
℟ **The love of the Lord is everlasting
     upon those who hold him in fear.**

1 My soul, give thanks to the Lord,
   all my being, bless his holy name.
   My soul, give thanks to the Lord
   and never forget all his blessings. ℟

2 It is he who forgives all your guilt,
   who heals every one of your ills,
   who redeems your life from the grave,
   who crowns you with love and compassion. ℟

3 The Lord does deeds of justice,
   gives judgement for all who are oppressed.
   He made known his ways to Moses
   and his deeds to Israel's sons. ℟

4 The Lord is compassion and love,
   slow to anger and rich in mercy.
   He does not treat us according to our sins
   nor repay us according to our faults. ℟

                    Ps 102:1-4. 6-8. 10. ℟ v.17

SECOND READING
We read from the first letter of St John, chapter four.
*
My dear people,
let us love one another
since love comes from God

and everyone who loves is begotten by God and knows God.
Anyone who fails to love can never have known God,
because God is love.
God's love for us was revealed
when God sent into the world his only Son
so that we could have life through him;
this is the love I mean:
not our love for God,
but God's love for us when he sent his Son
to be the sacrifice that takes our sins away.
My dear people,
since God has loved us so much,
we too should love one another.
No one has ever seen God;
but as long as we love one another
God will live in us
and his love will be complete in us.
We can know that we are living in him
and he is living in us
because he lets us share his Spirit.
We ourselves saw and we testify
that the Father sent his Son
as saviour of the world.
If anyone acknowledges that Jesus is the Son of God,
God lives in him, and he in God.
We ourselves have known and put our faith in
God's love towards ourselves.
God is love
and anyone who lives in love lives in God,
and God lives in him.

This is the word of the Lord.   *1 John 4:7-16*

Gospel Acclamation
Alleluia, alleluia!
Shoulder my yoke and learn from me,
for I am gentle and humble in heart.
Alleluia!   *Mt 11:29*

GOSPEL

We read from the holy Gospel according to Matthew, chapter eleven.

*

Jesus exclaimed, 'I bless you, Father, Lord of heaven and of earth, for hiding these things from the learned and the clever and revealing them to mere children. Yes, Father, for that is what it pleased you to do. Everything has been entrusted to me by my Father; and no one knows the Son except the Father, just as no one knows the Father except the Son and those to whom the Son chooses to reveal him.

'Come to me, all you who labour and are overburdened, and I will give you rest. Shoulder my yoke and learn from me, for I am gentle and humble in heart, and you will find rest for your souls. Yes, my yoke is easy and my burden light.'

This is the Gospel of the Lord.   *Matthew 11:25-30*

SUNDAYS IN ORDINARY TIME

First Sunday in Ordinary Time

The Baptism of the Lord   A

See above, pp. 47.

Second Sunday in Ordinary Time   A

Introduction to the Service

Last Sunday we remembered the Baptism of the Lord in the river Jordan. Today we hear about the task which he was sent to fulfil. Jesus was sent to become the light of all nations and to gather them to God. He was sent to take away the sin of the world.

We, too, have a task to fulfil in life. It is a task which is given to us by God. Whether we plough the fields, repair a motorcar, work in an office or teach in school, it is a task given to us by God, and not just by the people who have employed us.

In any task which we fulfil, God wants us to serve others and make them happy.

Penitential Rite

Let us ask ourselves:

- How do we fulfil our task in life, whether that task is as a father or mother, as a teacher or student or where we work?   (*Silence*)

- Do we make people happy or unhappy?   (*Silence*)

- Are we a light to other people or do we lead them astray?   (*Silence*)

Let us ask for forgiveness for carrying out our task in life so poorly.   **I confess**…

FIRST READING

Isaiah speaks in our first reading about the task of the Messiah. He calls him a 'servant' of the people. His task will bring light and salvation not only to the tribes of Israel, but to the ends of the earth.

We read from the book of Isaiah, chapter forty-nine.
*

The Lord said to me, 'You are my servant, Israel,
in whom I shall be glorified';
I was honoured in the eyes of the Lord,
my God was my strength.
And now the Lord has spoken,
he who formed me in the womb to be his servant,
to bring Jacob back to him,
to gather Israel to him:

> 'It is not enough for you to be my servant,
> to restore the tribes of Jacob and bring back the survivors of
>   Israel;
> I will make you the light of the nations
> so that my salvation may reach to the ends of the earth.'

This is the word of the Lord. *Isaiah 49:3.5-6*

Responsorial Psalm

℟ **Here I am, Lord!
I come to do your will.**

1 I waited, I waited for the Lord
  and he stooped down to me;
  he heard my cry.
  He put a new song into my mouth,
  praise of our God. ℟

2 You do not ask for sacrifice and offerings,
  but an open ear.
  You do not ask for holocaust and victim.
  Instead, here am I. ℟

3 In the scroll of the book it stands written
  that I should do your will.
  My God, I delight in your law
  in the depth of my heart. ℟

4 Your justice I have proclaimed
  in the great assembly.
  My lips I have not sealed;
  you know it, O Lord. ℟ *Ps 39:2. 4. 7-10. ℟ vv.8. 9*

SECOND READING

We read from the first letter of St Paul to the Corinthians, chapter one.

*

I, Paul, appointed by God to be an apostle, together with brother Sosthenes, send greetings to the church of God in Corinth, to the holy people of Jesus Christ, who are called to take their place among all the saints everywhere who pray to our Lord Jesus Christ; for he is their Lord no less than ours. May God our Father and the Lord Jesus Christ send you grace and peace.

This is the word of the Lord.   *1 Corinthians 1:13*

Gospel Acclamation
Alleluia, alleluia!
Blessings on the King who comes,
in the name of the Lord!
Peace in heaven
and glory in the highest heavens!
Alleluia!

or

Alleluia, alleluia!
The Word was made flesh and lived among us;
to all who did accept him
he gave power to become children of God.
Alleluia!   *Jn 1:14. 12*

GOSPEL

We read from the holy Gospel according to John, chapter one.

*

Seeing Jesus coming towards him, John said, 'Look, there is the lamb of God that takes away the sin of the world. This is the one I spoke of when I said: A man is coming after me who ranks before me because he existed before me. I did not know him myself, and yet it was to reveal him to Israel that I came baptising with water.' John also declared, 'I saw the Spirit coming down on him from heaven like a dove and resting on him. I did not know him myself, but he who sent me to baptise with water had said to me, "The man on whom you see the Spirit come down and rest is the one who is going to baptise with the Holy Spirit." Yes, I have seen and I am the witness that he is the Chosen One of God.'

This is the Gospel of the Lord.   *John 1:29-34*

Third Sunday in Ordinary Time   A

Introduction to the Service

We have accepted the Word of Christ as Good News. This, however, does not mean that we experience only joy and happiness. The Good News is given to us as light and joy to strengthen us in our times of darkness and suffering.

Sometimes it becomes really dark within us. All light and joy disappear. We may be rejected by others, we may fail in our work, or sickness may strike us. There are times when we are swallowed up by darkness and fear.

In this situation we hear the message today: 'The people that walked in darkness has seen a great light'. 'Repent, the kingdom of heaven is close at hand.'

Penitential Rite

Let us ask ourselves:

● Where do we look for consolation in times of trouble?   (*Silence*)

● Do we accept Christ's Word as Good News which can bring us light and joy?   (*Silence*)

Let us ask for forgiveness for remaining in the darkness of sin. **I confess**…

FIRST READING

In our first reading today and in the Gospel we hear of the land of 'Zebulun and Naphtali'. These lands are the districts next to the Sea of Galilee; an area which Jesus liked very much and where he lived and worked for a long time.

Listening to our first reading we should remember the time when the prophet Isaiah wrote these words. It was a time of blood and misery. Zebulun and Naphthali were destroyed by their enemies and the people were killed or led away into a foreign country to be slaves.

Can there be any good news for such people?

We read from the book of Isaiah, chapter eight.
*
In days past the Lord humbled the land of Zebulun and the land of Naphtali, but in days to come he will confer glory on the Way of the Sea on the far side of Jordan, province of the nations.

The people that walked in darkness
has seen a great light;
on those who live in a land of deep shadow
a light has shone.
You have made their gladness greater,
you have made their joy increase;
they rejoice in your presence
as men rejoice at harvest time,
as men are happy when they are dividing the spoils.

For the yoke that was weighing on him,
the bar across his shoulders,
the rod of his oppressor,
these you break as on the day of Midian.

This is the word of the Lord.   *Isaiah 8:23-9:3*

Responsial Psalm
℞   **The Lord is my light and my help.**

1   The Lord is my light and my help;
whom shall I fear?
The Lord is the stronghold of my life;
before whom shall I shrink?   ℞

2   There is one thing I ask of the Lord,
for this I long,
to live in the house of the Lord,
all the days of my life,
to savour the sweetness of the Lord,
to behold his temple.   ℞

3   I am sure I shall see the Lord's goodness
in the land of the living.
Hope in him, hold firm and take heart.
Hope in the Lord!   ℞   *Ps 26:1. 4. 13-14. ℞ v.1*

SECOND READING

We read from the first letter of St Paul to the Corinthians, chapter one.
*
I appeal to you, brothers, for the sake of our Lord Jesus Christ, to
make up the differences between you, and instead of disagreeing
among yourselves, to be united again in your belief and practice.
From what Chloe's people have been telling me, my dear
brothers, it is clear that there are serious differences among you.

What I mean are all these slogans that you have, like: 'I am for Paul,' 'I am for Apollos,' 'I am for Cephas,' 'I am for Christ.' Has Christ been parcelled out? Was it Paul that was crucified for you? Were you baptised in the name of Paul?

For Christ did not send me to baptise, but to preach the Good News, and not to preach that in the terms of philosophy in which the crucifixion of Christ cannot be expressed.

This is the word of the Lord.   *1 Corinthians 1:10-13.17*

Gospel Acclamation
   Alleluia, alleluia!
   Jesus proclaimed the Good News of the kingdom,
   and cured all kinds of sickness among the people.
   Alleluia!   *Mt 4:23*

GOSPEL
We read from the holy Gospel according to Matthew, chapter four.
*
*Hearing that John had been arrested Jesus went back to Galilee, and leaving Nazareth he went and settled in Capernaum, a lakeside town on the borders of Zebulun and Naphtali. In this way the prophecy of Isaiah was to be fulfilled:

   Land of Zebulun! Land of Naphtali!
   Way of the sea on the far side of Jordan,
   Galilee of the nations!
   The people that lived in darkness
   has seen a great light;
   on those who dwell in the land and shadow of death
   a light has dawned.

From that moment Jesus began his preaching with the message, 'Repent, for the kingdom of heaven is close at hand.'*

As he was walking by the Sea of Galilee he saw two brothers, Simon, who was called Peter, and his brother Andrew; they were making a cast in the lake with their net, for they were fishermen. And he said to them, 'Follow me and I will make you fishers of men.' And they left their nets at once and followed him.

Going on from there he saw another pair of brothers, James son of Zebedee and his brother John; they were in their boat with their father Zebedee, mending their nets, and he called them. At once, leaving the boat and their father, they followed him.

He went round the whole of Galilee teaching in their synagogues, proclaiming the Good News of the kingdom and curing all kinds of diseases and sickness among the people.

This is the Gospel of the Lord.   *Matthew 4:12-33*

*Shorter Form, verses 12-17. Read between *

Fourth Sunday in Ordinary Time   A

Introduction to the Service

We like people who are humble. They are pleasant and kind. We feel at home with them. Humble people do not pretend to know everything. They listen to our opinion and appreciate what we do or say. Humble people can take correction and are not afraid to admit a mistake.

Today's Gospel praises those who are humble and gentle. 'Happy are the poor in spirit', says Jesus, 'happy the gentle, happy the peacemakers ... theirs is the kingdom of heaven.'

Penitential Rite

Let us ask ourselves:

● Are we humble and gentle in dealing with others?   (*Silence*)

● Are we too proud to accept correction or to admit a mistake?   (*Silence*)

● Are we too proud to bow before God and confess our sins in the Sacrament of Reconciliation?   (*Silence*)

Let us humble ourselves and admit our sins.   **I confess**...

FIRST READING

Sometimes we have the impression that humble people cannot get on in life. They will be trampled upon and pushed aside. How can they find shelter and defend themselves?
What is God's opinion about humility?

We read from the book of the prophet Zephaniah, chapters two and three.
*
Seek the Lord
all you, the humble of the earth,
who obey his commands.
Seek integrity,

seek humility:
you may perhaps find shelter
on the day of the anger of the Lord.
In your midst I will leave
a humble and lowly people,
and those who are left in Israel will seek refuge in the name of
    the Lord.
They will do no wrong,
will tell no lies;
and the perjured tongue will no longer
be found in their mouths.
But they will be able to graze and rest
with no one to disturb them.

    This is the word of the Lord.   *Zephaniah 2:3;3:12-13*

Responsorial Psalm
  ℟ **How happy are the poor in spirit;**
     theirs is the kingdom of heaven.

or

    ℟ **Alleluia!**

1 It is the Lord who keeps faith for ever,
    who is just to those who are oppressed.
    It is he who gives bread to the hungry,
    the Lord, who sets prisoners free.   ℟

2 It is the Lord who gives sight to the blind,
    who raises up those who are bowed down,
    the Lord, who protects the stranger
    and upholds the widow and orphan.   ℟

3 It is the Lord who loves the just
    but thwarts the path of the wicked.
    The Lord will reign for ever,
    Zion's God, from age to age.   ℟   *Ps 145:7-10. ℟ Mt 5:3*

SECOND READING

We read from the first letter of St Paul to the Corinthians, chapter one.
*
Take yourselves, brothers, at the time when you were called: how
many of you were wise in the ordinary sense of the word, how
many were influential people, or came from noble families? No, it
was to shame the wise that God chose what is foolish by human

reckoning, and to shame what is strong that he chose what is weak by human reckoning; those whom the world thinks common and contemptible are the ones that God has chosen – those who are nothing at all to show up those who are everything. The human race has nothing to boast about to God, but you, God has made members of Christ Jesus and by God's doing he has become our wisdom, and our virtue, and our holiness, and our freedom. As scripture says: if anyone wants to boast, let him boast about the Lord.

This is the word of the Lord.   *1 Corinthians 1:26-31*

Gospel Acclamation
Alleluia, alleluia!
Blessed are you, Father,
Lord of heaven and earth,
for revealing the mysteries of the kingdom
to mere children.
Alleluia!   *Mt 11:25*

or

Alleluia, alleluia!
Rejoice and be glad:
your reward will be great in heaven.
Alleluia!   *Mt 5:12*

GOSPEL
We read from the holy Gospel according to Matthew, chapter five.
*
Seeing the crowds, Jesus went up the hill. There he sat down and was joined by his disciples. Then he began to speak. This is what he taught them:

'How happy are the poor in spirit;
theirs is the kingdom of heaven.
Happy the gentle:
they shall have the earth for their heritage.
Happy those who mourn:
they shall be comforted.
Happy those who hunger and thirst for what is right:
they shall be satisfied.
Happy the merciful:
they shall have mercy shown them.
Happy the pure in heart:

they shall see God.
Happy the peacemakers:
they shall be called sons of God.
Happy those who are persecuted in the cause of right:
theirs is the kingdom of heaven.

'Happy are you when people abuse you and persecute you and speak all kinds of calumny against you on my account. Rejoice and be glad, for your reward will be great in heaven.'

This is the Gospel of the Lord.   *Matthew 5:1-12*

Fifth Sunday in Ordinary Time   A

Introduction to the Service

What happens to salt when we put it into food? It dissolves and makes the food more tasty. Another question: What happens to a candle when we light it? It eats itself up in order to give light to the people in the room.

The Lord tells us today: 'You are the salt of the earth'. He expects us to love others in an unselfish way, like salt which dissolves unselfishly in the food.

Penitential Rite

Let us examine our conscience:

● Last week, how often did we forget our own comfort in order to serve our neighbours or our community?   (*Silence*)

● Do we share our bread with the hungry?   (*Silence*)

● Do our words and actions cause people to praise God or do they cause them to curse?   (*Silence*)

Let us ask God's forgiveness for often not being light and salt.   **I confess**...

FIRST READING

In our reading the prophet Isaiah gives us many examples of how we can become light. He speaks about things which we should do at home and in public life.

We read from the book of Isaiah, chapter fifty-eight.

*
Thus says the Lord:

> Share your bread with the hungry,
> and shelter the homeless poor,
> clothe the man you see to be naked
> and turn not from your own kin.
> Then will your light shine like the dawn
> and your wound be quickly healed over.
>
> Your integrity will go before you
> and the glory of the Lord behind you.
> Cry, and the Lord will answer;
> call, and he will say, 'I am here.'
>
> If you do away with the yoke,
> the clenched fist, the wicked word,
> if you give your bread to the hungry,
> and relief to the oppressed,
> your light will rise in the darkness,
> and your shadows become like noon.

This is the word of the Lord.   *Isaiah 58:7-10*

Responsorial Psalm
    ℟   **The good man is a light in the darkness for the upright.**

or

    ℟   **Alleluia!**

1   He is a light in the darkness for the upright:
    he is generous, merciful and just.
    The good man takes pity and lends,
    he conducts his affairs with honour.   ℟

2   The just man will never waver:
    he will be remembered for ever.
    He has no fear of evil news;
    with a firm heart he trusts in the Lord.   ℟

3 With a steadfast heart he will not fear;
   open-handed, he gives to the poor;
   his justice stands firm for ever.
   His head will be raised in glory. ℟   *Ps 111:4-9. ℟ v.4*

SECOND READING

We read from the first letter of St Paul to the Corinthians, chapter two.
*

When I came to you, brothers, it was not with any show of
oratory or philosophy, but simply to tell you what God had
guaranteed. During my stay with you, the only knowledge I
claimed to have was about Jesus, and only about him as the
crucified Christ. Far from relying on any power of my own, I
came among you in great 'fear and trembling' and in my speeches
and the sermons that I gave, there were none of the arguments
that belong to philosophy; only a demonstration of the power of
the Spirit. And I did this so that your faith should not depend on
human philosophy but on the power of God.

This is the word of the Lord.   *1 Corinthians 2:1-5*

Gospel Acclamation
   Alleluia, alleluia!
   I am the light of the world, says the Lord,
   anyone who follows me
   will have the light of life.
   Alleluia!   *Jn 8:12*

GOSPEL

We read from the holy Gospel according to Matthew, chapter five.
*

Jesus said to his disciples: 'You are the salt of the earth. But if salt
becomes tasteless, what can make it salty again? It is good for
nothing, and can only be thrown out to be trampled underfoot by
men.

'You are the light of the world. A city built on a hill-top cannot
be hidden. No one lights a lamp to put it under a tub; they put it
on the lamp-stand where it shines for everyone in the house. In
the same way your light must shine in the sight of men, so that,
seeing your good works, they may give the praise to your Father
in heaven.'

This is the Gospel of the Lord.   *Matthew 5:13-16*

Sixth Sunday in Ordinary Time A

Introduction to the Service

How do we imagine God in our mind? Is he like a slave-driver who orders us around at random? No. God loves us and wants us to be happy. It is for this reason that he has given us his commandments. They are words of love.

If we keep these commandments we develop in ourselves all that is good and beautiful. By doing God's will we behave as God himself behaves.

Penitential Rite

We ask ourselves:

- Do we accept God's commandments as a burden or as a blessing? (*Silence*)

- Which commandments did we reject last week? (*Silence*)

- Do we appear outwardly as good and holy people while within us there is anger, envy and lust? (*Silence*)

Let us ask for forgiveness for rejecting God's will and love. **I confess**...

FIRST READING

Is it possible for us to keep God's commandments and to remain faithful? It often seems to be impossible when we are over-powered by anger and human weakness.

Our first reading speaks about this problem. God is challenging us. He has given us the freedom to choose between good and evil.

We read from the book of Ecclesiasticus, chapter fifteen.
*
If you wish, you can keep the commandments,
to behave faithfully is within your power.
He has set fire and water before you;
put out your hand to whichever you prefer.
Man has life and death before him;
whichever a man likes better will be given him.
For vast is the wisdom of the Lord;
he is almighty and all-seeing.
His eyes are on those who fear him,
he notes every action of man.
He never commanded anyone to be godless,

he has given no one permission to sin.

This is the word of the Lord.   *Ecclesiasticus 15:15-20*

Responsorial Psalm
℟   **They are happy who follow God's law!**

1   They are happy whose life is blameless,
     who follow God's law!
     They are happy those who do his will,
     seeking him with all their hearts.   ℟

2   You have laid down your precepts
     to be obeyed with care.
     May my footsteps be firm
     to obey your statutes.   ℟

3   Bless your servant and I shall live
     and obey your word.
     Open my eyes that I may consider
     the wonders of your law.   ℟

4   Teach me the demands of your statutes
     and I will keep them to the end.
     Train me to observe your law,
     to keep it with my heart.   ℟

Ps 118:1-2. 4-5. 17-18. 33-34. ℟ v.1

SECOND READING
We read from the first letter of St Paul to the Corinthians, chapter two.
*
We have a wisdom to offer those who have reached maturity: not
a philosophy of our age, it is true, still less of the masters of our
age, which are coming to their end. The hidden wisdom of God
which we teach in our mysteries is the wisdom that God
predestined to be for our glory before the ages began. It is a
wisdom that none of the masters of this age have ever known, or
they would not have crucified the Lord of Glory; we teach what
scripture calls: the things that no eye has seen and no ear has
heard, things beyond the mind of man, all that God has prepared
for those who love him.

These are the very things that God has revealed to us through
the Spirit, for the Spirit reaches the depths of everything, even
the depths of God.

This is the word of the Lord.   *1 Corinthians 2:6-10*

Gospel Acclamation

Alleluia, alleluia!
Speak, Lord, your servant is listening:
you have the message of eternal life.
Alleluia!   *1 Sam 3:9; Jn 6:68*

or

Alleluia, alleluia!
Blessed are you, Father,
Lord of heaven and earth,
for revealing the mysteries of the kingdom
to mere children.
Alleluia!   *cf. Mt 11:25*

GOSPEL

We read from the holy Gospel according to Matthew, chapter five.
*
Jesus said to his disciples: 'Do not imagine that I have come to abolish the Law or the Prophets. I have come not to abolish them but to complete them. I tell you solemnly, till heaven and earth disappear, not one dot, one little stroke, shall disappear from the Law until its purpose is achieved. Therefore, the man who infringes even one of the least of these commandments and teaches others to do the same will be considered the least in the kingdom of heaven; but the man who keeps them and teaches them will be considered great in the kingdom of heaven.

*'For I tell you, if your virtue goes no deeper than that of the scribes and Pharisees, you will never get into the kingdom of heaven.

'You have learnt how it was said to our ancestors: You must not kill; and if anyone does kill he must answer for it before the court. But I say this to you: anyone who is angry with his brother will answer for it before the court;* if a man calls his brother "Fool" he will answer for it before the Sanhedrin; and if a man calls him "Renegade" he will answer for it in hell fire. So then, if you are bringing your offering to the altar and there remember that your brother has something against you, leave your offering there before the altar, go and be reconciled with your brother first, and then come back and present your offering. Come to terms with your opponent in good time while you are still on the way to the court with him, or he may hand you over to the judge and the judge to the officer, and you will be thrown into prison. I tell you solemnly, you will not get out till you have paid the last penny.

'You have learnt how it was said: You must not commit adultery. But I say this to you: if a man looks at a woman lustfully, he has already committed adultery with her in his heart. If your right eye should cause you to sin, tear it out and throw it away; for it will do you less harm to lose one part of you than to have your whole body thrown into hell. And if your right hand should cause you to sin, cut it off and throw it away; for it will do you less harm to lose one part of you than to have your whole body go to hell.

'It has also been said: Anyone who divorces his wife must give her a writ of dismissal. But I say this to you: everyone who divorces his wife, except for the case of fornication, makes her an adulteress; and anyone who marries a divorced woman commits adultery.

'Again, you have learnt how it was said to our ancestors: You must not break your oath, but must fulfil your oaths to the Lord. But I say this to you: do not swear at all, either by heaven, since that is God's throne; or by the earth, since that is his footstool; or by Jerusalem, since that is the city of the great king. Do not swear by your own head either, since you cannot turn a single hair white or black. *All you need say is "Yes" if you mean yes, "No" if you mean no; anything more than this comes from the evil one.'

This is the Gospel of the Lord.*   *Matthew 5:17-37*

Shorter Form, verses 20-22. 27-28. 33-34. 37. Read between *.

Seventh Sunday in Ordinary Time   A

Introduction to the Service

God has a wonderful plan for us all. He wants us to develop fully as human beings and to become like him. However, our real sin is that we want to remain as we are and so we reject God's invitation to grow and develop in love.

But it is God's plan that we become holy and perfect as he is himself.

Penitential Rite

Let us ask ourselves:

● What did we do last week in order to grow spiritually?   (*Silence*)

● Did we pray from deep down in our hearts? (*Silence*)

● Did we take Christ as our example when we wanted to retaliate or take revenge? (*Silence*)

Let us ask God to heal us and to make us perfect as he is. **I confess**...

FIRST READING

We all have our heroes in life to whom we look up. For example, a young boy makes a professional soccer player his hero. He wants to play soccer as his hero does. A girl may take a beautiful film-star as her heroine. She wants to be as beautiful as her film-star.

In our first reading today we are invited to take God as our hero and star. He invites us to become good and beautiful, as he is.

We read from the book of Leviticus, chapter nineteen.

*

The Lord spoke to Moses; he said: 'Speak to the whole community of the sons of Israel and say to them: "Be holy, for I, the Lord your God, am holy.

"You must not bear hatred for your brother in your heart. You must openly tell him, your neighbour, of his offence; this way you will not take a sin upon yourself. You must not exact vengeance, nor must you bear a grudge against the children of your people. You must love your neighbour as yourself. I am the Lord." '

This is the word of the Lord.   *Leviticus 19:1-2.17-18*

Responsorial Psalm
    ℟   **The Lord is compassion and love.**

1   My soul, give thanks to the Lord,
    all my being, bless his holy name.
    My soul, give thanks to the Lord
    and never forget all his blessings.   ℟

2   It is he who forgives all your guilt,
    who heals every one of your ills,
    who redeems your life from the grave,
    who crowns you with love and compassion.   ℟

3   The Lord is compassion and love,
    slow to anger and rich in mercy.

He does not treat us according to our sins
nor repay us according to our faults. ℞

4   As far as the east is from the west
     so far does he remove our sins.
     As a father has compassion on his sons,
     the Lord has pity on those who fear him. ℞

Ps 102:1-4. 8. 10. 12-13. ℞ v.8

SECOND READING

We read from the first letter of St Paul to the Corinthians, chapter
three.
*
Didn't you realise that you were God's temple and that the Spirit
of God was living among you? If anybody should destroy the
temple of God, God will destroy him, because the temple of God
is sacred; and you are that temple.

Make no mistake about it: if any one of you thinks of himself
as wise, in the ordinary sense of the word, then he must learn to
be a fool before he really can be wise. Why? Because the wisdom
of this world is foolishness to God. As scripture says: The Lord
knows wise men's thoughts: he knows how useless they are, or
again: God is not convinced by the arguments of the wise. So
there is nothing to boast about in anything human: Paul, Apollos,
Cephas, the world, life and death, the present and the future, are
all your servants; but you belong to Christ and Christ belongs to
God.

This is the word of the Lord.   *1 Corinthians 3:16-23*

Gospel Acclamation
     Alleluia, alleluia!
     If anyone loves me he will keep my word,
     and my Father will love him,
     and we shall come to him.
     Alleluia!   *Jn 14:23*

or

     Alleluia, alleluia!
     When anyone obeys what Christ has said,
     God's love comes to perfection in him.
     Alleluia!   *1 Jn 2:5*

GOSPEL

We read from the holy Gospel according to Matthew, chapter five.

*
Jesus said to his disciples: 'You have learnt how it was said: Eye for eye and tooth for tooth. But I say this to you: offer the wicked man no resistance. On the contrary, if anyone hits you on the right cheek, offer him the other as well; if a man takes you to law and would have your tunic, let him have your cloak as well. And if anyone orders you to go one mile, go two miles with him. Give to anyone who asks, and if anyone wants to borrow, do not turn away.

'You have learnt how it was said: You must love your neighbour and hate your enemy. But I say this to you: love your enemies and pray for those who persecute you; in this way you will be sons of your Father in heaven, for he causes his sun to rise on bad men as well as good, and his rain to fall on honest and dishonest men alike. For if you love those who love you, what right have you to claim any credit? Even the tax collectors do as much, do they not? And if you save your greetings for your brothers, are you doing anything exceptional? Even the pagans do as much, do they not? You must therefore be perfect just as your heavenly Father is perfect.'

This is the Gospel of the Lord.   *Matthew 5:38-48*

Eighth Sunday in Ordinary Time   *A*

Introduction to the Service

Each one of us has come to church with our own difficulties. We need help and encouragement. We need guidance and strength.

In our celebration today we are invited to renew our trust in God. We are called on to hand ourselves over to God, completely, as children do when they are in trouble.

Penitential Rite

Let us examine our conscience:

● What are the difficulties which worry us most?   (*Silence*)

● Do we try to solve them without God's help and advice?   (*Silence*)

• Do we worry too much because we do not yet fully trust in God? (*Silence*)

Let us ask for forgiveness for not trusting in God's protection. **I confess**…

FIRST READING

It is easy to trust in God when things go well. It becomes difficult, however, when everything goes wrong.

For example, there was a time when everything went wrong for the people of Jerusalem. Their beloved city was destroyed and they were led away into captivity like animals.

In this hopeless situation Isaiah had a short but powerful message for them. This message is so beautiful that we should learn it by heart and remember it in times of trouble.

We read from the book of Isaiah, chapter forty-nine.
*
Zion was saying, 'The Lord has abandoned me,
the Lord has forgotten me.'
Does a woman forget her baby at the breast,
or fail to cherish the son of her womb?
Yet even if these forget,
I will never forget you.

This is the word of the Lord.   *Isaiah 49:14-15*

Responsorial Psalm
    ℟ **In God alone is my soul at rest.**

1 In God alone is my soul at rest;
    my help comes from him.
    He alone is my rock, my stronghold,
    my fortress: I stand firm. ℟

2 In God alone be at rest, my soul;
    for my hope comes from him.
    He alone is my rock, my stronghold,
    my fortress: I stand firm. ℟

3 In God is my safety and glory,
    the rock of my strength.
    Take refuge in God all you people.
    Trust him at all times.
    Pour out your hearts before him. ℟   *Ps 61:2-3. 6-9. ℟ v.6*

SECOND READING

We read from the first letter of St Paul to the Corinthians, chapter four.

★
People must think of us as Christ's servants, stewards entrusted with the mysteries of God. What is expected of stewards is that each one should be found worthy of his trust. Not that it makes the slightest difference to me whether you, or indeed any human tribunal, find me worthy or not. I will not even pass judgement on myself. True, my conscience does not reproach me at all, but that does not prove that I am acquitted; the Lord alone is my judge. There must be no passing of premature judgement. Leave that until the Lord comes: he will light up all that is hidden in the dark and reveal the secret intentions of men's hearts. Then will be the time for each one to have whatever praise he deserves, from God.

This is the word of the Lord.   *1 Corinthians 4:1-5*

Gospel Acclamation
Alleluia, alleluia!
Your word is truth, O Lord,
consecrate us in the truth.
Alleluia!
                                                        Jn 17:17

or

Alleluia, alleluia!
The word of God is something alive and active;
it can judge secret emotions and thoughts.
Alleluia!
                                                        Heb 4:12

GOSPEL

We read from the holy Gospel according to Matthew, chapter six.

★
Jesus said to his disciples: 'No one can be the slave of two masters: he will either hate the first and love the second, or treat the first with respect and the second with scorn. You cannot be the slave both of God and of money.

'That is why I am telling you not to worry about your life and what you are to eat, nor about your body and how you are to clothe it. Surely life means more than food, and the body more than clothing! Look at the birds in the sky. They do not sow or reap or gather into barns; yet your heavenly Father feeds them. Are you not worth much more than they are? Can any of you, for all his worrying, add one single cubit to his span of life? And why worry about clothing? Think of the flowers growing in the fields; they never have to work or spin; yet I assure you that not even Solomon in all his regalia was robed like one of these. Now if that is how God clothes the grass in the field which is there today and thrown into the furnace tomorrow, will he not much more look after you, you men of little faith? So do not worry; do not say, "What are we to eat? What are we to drink? How are we to be clothed?" It is the pagans who set their hearts on all these things. Your heavenly Father knows you need them all. Set your hearts on his kingdom first, and on his righteousness, and all these other things will be given you as well. So do not worry about tomorrow; tomorrow will take care of itself. Each day has enough trouble of its own.'

This is the Gospel of the Lord.   *Matthew 6:24-34*

Ninth Sunday in Ordinary Time   A

Introduction to the Service

We left our homes this morning to come to Church. We gave of our time this Sunday morning, in order to serve God. We know that it is not enough to have a baptismal certificate somewhere in our cupboard. We know that only the doing of God's will will count, not a piece of paper.

Now, as we are about to begin singing and praying, we remember these words of Christ: 'It is not those who say to me 'Lord, Lord' who will enter the kingdom of heaven, but the person who does the will of my Father in heaven.'

We begin our service by making up our mind that what we are about to say, we will also do.

Penitential Rite

Let us look back on the past week and ask ourselves:

- During this week were there occasions when we, although we are called by Christ's name, did not do his will?   (*Silence*)

- Were there occasions when we just said 'Lord, Lord', but no action followed?   (*Silence*)

Let us confess that we have sinned.   **I confess**...

FIRST READING

Have you ever experienced the blessing and joy that follows a decision to keep God's commandments? For instance, have you felt this after making peace with your neighbour?

You may also have experienced the curse and the misery which Moses talks of, at times when you decided not to keep God's commandments.

In our first reading we are invited to choose between blessing and curse, between joy and misery.

We read from the book of Deuteronomy, chapter eleven.

*

Moses said to the people: 'Let these words of mine remain in your heart and in your soul; fasten them on your hand as a sign and on your forehead as a circlet.

'See, I set before you today a blessing and a curse: a blessing, if you obey the commandments of the Lord our God that I enjoin on you today; a curse, if you disobey the commandments of the Lord your God and leave the way I have marked out for you today, by going after other gods you have not known. You must keep and observe all the laws and customs that I set before you today.'

This is the word of the Lord.   *Deuteronomy 11:18.26-28.32*

Responsorial Psalm
℞   **Be a rock of refuge for me, O Lord.**

1   In you, O Lord, I take refuge.
      Let me never be put to shame.
      In your justice, set me free,
      hear me and speedily rescue me.   ℞

2   Be a rock of refuge to me,
      a mighty stronghold to save me,
      for you are my rock, my stronghold.
      For your name's sake, lead me and guide me.   ℞

3   Let your face shine on your servant.
      Save me in your love.
      Be strong, let your heart take courage,
      all who hope in the Lord.   ℞   *Ps 30:2-4. 17. 25. ℞ v.3*

SECOND READING

We read from the letter of St Paul to the Romans, chapter three.
*
God's justice that was made known through the Law and the Prophets has now been revealed outside the Law, since it is the same justice of God that comes through faith to everyone, Jew and pagan alike, who believes in Jesus Christ. Both Jew and pagan sinned and forfeited God's glory, and both are justified through the free gift of his grace by being redeemed in Christ Jesus who was appointed by God to sacrifice his life so as to win reconciliation through faith since, as we see it, a man is justified by faith and not by doing something the Law tells him to do.

This is the word of the Lord.   *Romans 3:21-25.28*

Gospel Acclamation
    Alleluia, alleluia!
    If anyone loves me he will keep my word,
    and my Father will love him,
    and we shall come to him.
    Alleluia!
                                      Jn 14:23

or

    Alleluia, alleluia!
    I am the vine, you are the branches,
    says the Lord.
    Whoever remains in me, with me in him,
    bears fruit in plenty.
    Alleluia!
                                        Jn 15:5

GOSPEL

We read from the holy Gospel according to Matthew, chapter seven.
*
Jesus said to his disciples: 'It is not those who say to me, "Lord, Lord", who will enter the kingdom of heaven, but the person who does the will of my Father in heaven. When the day comes many will say to me, "Lord, Lord, did we not prophesy in your name, cast out demons in your name, work many miracles in your name?" Then I shall tell them to their faces: I have never known you; away from me, you evil men!

'Therefore, everyone who listens to these words of mine and acts on them will be like a sensible man who built his house on rock. Rain came down, floods rose, gales blew and hurled themselves against that house, and it did not fall: it was founded on rock. But everyone who listens to these words of mine and does not act on them will be like a stupid man who built his house on sand. Rain came down, floods rose, gales blew and struck that house, and it fell; and what a fall it had!'

This is the Gospel of the Lord.   *Matthew 7:21-27*

Tenth Sunday in Ordinary Time   A

Introduction to the Service

Every Sunday celebration begins with a pentitential service. We ask for God's forgiveness and cry for mercy.

However, the Lord tells us today that he will not forgive us just because we say long prayers. What he wants from us is that we show mercy towards our neighbours. He is not pleased if we only offer him nice ceremonies and songs; he wants love, not sacrifice.

Penitential Rite

Let us ask ourselves:

● Did we show mercy to somebody last week?   (*Silence*)

● Did we help people even when they were ungrateful?   (*Silence*)

● Did we despise others because they were from a different family or nation?   (*Silence*)

Let us ask for forgiveness for rejecting the Lord's advice: 'What I want is mercy, not sacrifice'.   **I confess**...

FIRST READING

In our first reading the prophet Hosea describes a penitential service conducted by the people of Ephraim and Judah. During such a service, cattle were slaughtered and burnt on the altar as a 'sacrifice'. By offering these sacrifices, people thought that God should forgive them.

The prophet Hosea, however, did not agree with them.

We read from the book of Hosea, chapter six.
*
Let us set ourselves to know the Lord;
that he will come is as certain as the dawn
his judgement will rise like the light,
he will come to us as showers come,
like spring rains watering the earth.

What am I to do with you, Ephraim?
What am I to do with you, Judah?
This love of yours is like a morning cloud,
like the dew that quickly disappears.
This is why I have torn them to pieces by the prophets,
why I slaughtered them with the words from my mouth,
since what I want is love, not sacrifice;
knowledge of God, not holocausts.

This is the word of the Lord. *Hosea 6:3-6*

Responsorial Psalm
℟ **I will show God's salvation to the upright.**

1 The God of gods, the Lord,
   has spoken and summoned the earth,
   from the rising of the sun to its setting.
   'I find no fault with your sacrifices,
   your offerings are always before me. ℟

2 'Were I hungry, I would not tell you,
   for I own the world and all it holds.
   Do you think I eat the flesh of bulls,
   or drink the blood of goats? ℟

3 'Pay your sacrifice of thanksgiving to God
   and render him your votive offerings.
   Call on me in the day of distress.
   I will free you and you shall honour me.' ℟
   Ps 49:1. 8. 12-15. ℟ v.23

SECOND READING
We read from the letter of St Paul to the Romans, chapter four.
*
Though it seemed Abraham's hope could not be fulfilled, he
hoped and he believed, and through doing so he did become the
father of many nations exactly as he had been promised: Your
descendants will be as many as the stars. Even the thought that
his body was past fatherhood – he was about a hundred years old
– and Sarah too old to become a mother, did not shake his belief.
Since God had promised it, Abraham refused either to deny it or
even to doubt it, but drew strength from faith and gave glory to
God, convinced that God had power to do what he had
promised. This is the faith that was 'considered as justifying

him'. Scripture however does not refer only to him but to us as well when it says that his faith was thus 'considered'; our faith too will be 'considered' if we believe in him who raised Jesus our Lord from the dead, Jesus who was put to death for our sins and raised to life to justify us.

This is the word of the Lord. *Romans 4:18-25*

Gospel Acclamation
Alleluia, alleluia!
Open our heart, O Lord,
to accept the words of your Son.
Alleluia! *cf. Acts 16:14*

or

Alleluia, alleluia!
The Lord has sent me to bring the good news to the poor,
to proclaim liberty to captives.
Alleluia! *Lk 4:18*

GOSPEL

We read from the holy Gospel according to Matthew, chapter nine.
*
As Jesus was walking on he saw a man named Matthew sitting by the customs house, and he said to him, 'Follow me.' And he got up and followed him.

While he was at dinner in the house it happened that a number of tax collectors and sinners came to sit at the table with Jesus and his disciples. When the Pharisees saw this, they said to his disciples, 'Why does your master eat with tax collectors and sinners?' When he heard this he replied, 'It is not the healthy who need the doctor, but the sick. Go and learn the meaning of the words: What I want is mercy, not sacrifice. And indeed I did not come to call the virtuous, but sinners.'

This is the Gospel of the Lord. *Matthew 9:9-13*

Eleventh Sunday in Ordinary Time   A

Introduction to the Service

It is good to ask ourselves the following questions: 'Why did we come to church? Why are we Christians?'

There may be many reasons. Perhaps our parents brought us to church, we feel happy coming to church or we want help from God.

However, what is the fundamental reason why we are here today? The main reason is that God has chosen us. He has called us to come round this altar.

Jesus called his twelve Apostles in a special way. But he has chosen and called each one of us as well. He has chosen us to be his beloved people; a 'kingdom of priests'.

We have the right to approach the altar and to offer ourselves to God. We are called to pray and offer our gifts in the name of *all* people on earth. Together with the priest we are a chosen people and a kingdom of priests.

Penitential Rite

Let us ask ourselves:

● Did I ever thank God that I know him and love him?   (*Silence*)

● Did I ever praise God for choosing me to be his own, his friend, his beloved son or daughter?   (*Silence*)

● During the Holy Eucharist, do I think only of myself or do I also think of others, praying for them and giving them to God?   (*Silence*)

Let us ask God's forgiveness for being so ungrateful to him. **I confess**…

FIRST READING

When a young man asks a young woman to marry him, he takes her aside and proposes marriage.

In the same way, it was as if God wanted to take the whole people of Israel aside, leading them into the wilderness where he proposed his covenant to them.

In the wilderness, God chose his people and made them his own. He called them to be his people and a 'kingdom of priests'.

We read from the book of Exodus, chapter nineteen.

*

From Rephidim the Israelites set out again; and when they reached the wilderness of Sinai, there in the wilderness they pitched their camp; there facing the mountain Israel pitched camp.

Moses then went up to God, and the Lord called to him from the mountain, saying, 'Say this to the House of Jacob, declare this to the sons of Israel, "You yourselves have seen what I did with the Egyptians, how I carried you on eagle's wings and brought you to myself. From this you know that now, if you obey my voice and hold fast to my covenant, you of all the nations shall be my very own, for all the earth is mine. I will count you a kingdom of priests, a consecrated nation."'

This is the word of the Lord. *Exodus 19:2-6*

Responsorial Psalm
℟ **We are his people:**
the sheep of his flock.

1 Cry out with joy to the Lord, all the earth.
Serve the Lord with gladness.
Come before him, singing for joy. ℟

2 Know that he, the Lord, is God.
He made us, we belong to him,
we are his people, the sheep of his flock. ℟

3 Indeed, how good is the Lord,
eternal his merciful love.
He is faithful from age to age. ℟ *Ps 99:2-3. 5. ℟ v.3*

SECOND READING

We read from the letter of St Paul to the Romans, chapter five.

*

We were still helpless when at his appointed moment Christ died for sinful men. It is not easy to die even for a good man – though of course for someone really worthy, a man might be prepared to die – but what proves that God loves us is that Christ died for us while we were still sinners. Having died to make us righteous, is it likely that he would now fail to save us from God's anger? When we were reconciled to God by the death of his Son, we were still enemies; now that we have been reconciled surely we may count on being saved by the life of his Son? Not merely because we have been reconciled but because we are filled with joyful trust in God through our Lord Jesus Christ, through whom we have already gained our reconciliation.

This is the word of the Lord. *Romans 5:6-11*

Gospel Acclamation
Alleluia, alleluia!
The sheep that belong to me listen to my voice,
says the Lord,
I know them and they follow me.
Alleluia! *Jn 10:27*

or

Alleluia, alleluia!
The kingdom of God is close at hand.
Repent, and believe the Good News.
Alleluia! *Mk 1:15*

GOSPEL

We read from the holy Gospel according to Matthew, chapters nine and ten.
*
When Jesus saw the crowds he felt sorry for them because they were harassed and dejected, like sheep without a shepherd. Then he said to his disciples, 'The harvest is rich but the labourers are few, so ask the Lord of the harvest to send labourers to his harvest.'

He summoned his twelve disciples, and gave them authority over unclean spirits with power to cast them out and to cure all kinds of diseases and sickness.

These are the names of the twelve apostles: first, Simon who is called Peter, and his brother Andrew; James the son of Zebedee, and his brother John; Philip and Bartholomew; Thomas, and Matthew the tax collector; James the son of Alphaeus, and Thaddaeus; Simon the Zealot and Judas Iscariot, the one who was to betray him. These twelve Jesus sent out, instructing them as follows:

'Do not turn your steps to pagan territory, and do not enter any Samaritan town; go rather to the lost sheep of the House of Israel. And as you go, proclaim that the kingdom of heaven is close at hand. Cure the sick, raise the dead, cleanse the lepers, cast out devils. You received without charge, give without charge.'

This is the Gospel of the Lord. *Matthew 9:36-10:8*

Twelfth Sunday in Ordinary Time   A

Introduction to the Service

Nine times we read in the Gospels that Jesus said to his disciples 'Do not be afraid'. Why did he have to repeat this so often? Is it still important for us today, to be strengthened against fear?

I think we will freely admit that we, too, need to be told: do not be afraid!

Penitential Rite

Let us think about our fears and ask for forgiveness:

● Have we failed God by having too little confidence in him? (*Silence*)

● Did we perhaps fear that evil spirits would harm us although we are in God's hands?   (*Silence*)

● Did we lack trust that God knows our difficulties?   (*Silence*)

● Did we fail to believe that he will never forsake us?   (*Silence*)

Let us confess that we have sinned: **I confess**...

FIRST READING

The prophet Jeremiah was beaten and put into prison for no other reason than for saying the hard truth to those in authority. What was his reaction when he was persecuted again and again?

We read from the book of Jeremiah, chapter twenty.
*
Jeremiah said:

I hear so many disparaging me,
' "Terror from every side!"
Denounce him! Let us denounce him!'
All those who used to be my friends
watched for my downfall,
'Perhaps he will be seduced into error.
Then we will master him
and take our revenge!'
But the Lord is at my side, a mighty hero;
my opponents will stumble, mastered,
confounded by their failure;

everlasting, unforgettable disgrace will be theirs.
But you, Lord of Hosts, you who probe with justice,
who scrutinise the loins and heart,
let me see the vengeance you will take on them,
for I have committed my cause to you.
Sing to the Lord,
praise the Lord,
for he has delivered the soul of the needy
from the hands of evil men.

This is the word of the Lord.   *Jeremiah 20:10-13*

Responsorial Psalm

℟   **In your great love, answer me, O God.**

1   It is for you that I suffer taunts,
    that shame covers my face,
    that I have become a stranger to my brothers,
    an alien to my own mother's sons.
    I burn with zeal for your house
    and taunts against you fall on me.   ℟

2   This is my prayer to you,
    my prayer for your favour.
    In your great love, answer me, O God,
    with your help that never fails:
    Lord, answer, for your love is kind;
    in your compassion, turn towards me.   ℟

3   The poor when they see it will be glad
    and God-seeking hearts will revive;
    for the Lord listens to the needy
    and does not spurn his servants in their chains.
    Let the heavens and the earth give him praise,
    the sea and all its living creatures.   ℟

                    Ps 68:8-10. 14. 17. 33-35. ℟ v.14

SECOND READING

We read from the letter of St Paul to the Romans, chapter five.
*
Sin entered the world through one man, and through sin death,
and thus death has spread through the whole human race
because everyone has sinned. Sin existed in the world long before
the Law was given. There was no law and so no one could be

accused of the sin of 'law-breaking', yet death reigned over all from Adam to Moses, even though their sin, unlike that of Adam, was not a matter of breaking a law.

Adam prefigured the One to come, but the gift itself considerably outweighed the fall. If it is certain that through one man's fall so many died, it is even more certain that divine grace, coming through the one man, Jesus Christ, came to so many as an abundant free gift.

This is the word of the Lord. *Romans 5:12-15*

Gospel Acclamation
Alleluia, alleluia!
The Word was made flesh and lived among us;
to all who did accept him
he gave power to become children of God.
Alleluia! *Jn 1:14.12*

or

Alleluia, alleluia!
The Spirit of truth will be my witness;
and you too will be my witnesses.
Alleluia! *Jn 15:26.27*

GOSPEL
We read from the holy Gospel according to Matthew, chapter ten.
*
Jesus instructed the Twelve as follows: 'Do not be afraid. For everything that is now covered will be uncovered, and everything now hidden will be made clear. What I say to you in the dark, tell in the daylight; what you hear in whispers, proclaim from the house-tops.

'Do not be afraid of those who kill the body but cannot kill the soul; fear him rather who can destroy both body and soul in hell. Can you not buy two sparrows for a penny? And yet not one falls to the ground without your Father knowing. Why, every hair on your head has been counted. So there is no need to be afraid; you are worth more than hundreds of sparrows.

'So if anyone declares himself for me in the presence of men, I will declare myself for him in the presence of my Father in heaven. But the one who disowns me in the presence of men, I will disown in the presence of my Father in heaven.'

This is the Gospel of the Lord. *Matthew 10:26-33*

Thirteenth Sunday in Ordinary Time A

Introduction to the Service

Who are we, now assembled in this holy place? We are the disciples of Christ. To be a disciple of Christ means to be with him, to learn from him, to be sent out by him.

All this we have tried to do during the past week. Now we have assembled to show our unity with Jesus and with each other. Christ says: 'who welcomes you, welcomes me.' He is one with us. Have we always been aware that Jesus is with us?

Penitential Rite

● Lord, you have said: 'Who welcomes you, welcomes me'. We sometimes forgot that you were with us, and we felt alone. (*Silence*)

Lord, have mercy...

● We are sent by you. But sometimes we forgot this truth and thought that others should be sent to us, not we to them. (*Silence*)

Christ, have mercy...

● Lord, you said: 'Whoever does not take his cross and follow me is not worthy of me.' Sometimes we were afraid of the cross of working with you. (*Silence*)

Lord, have mercy...

FIRST READING

The prophet Elisha had to undertake many journeys in his work for God. But it was difficult for a poor man to make these journeys in a country where wars raged, where people distrusted strangers, and where people were themselves poor.

How was the prophet received in those difficult times?

We read from the second book of Kings, chapter four.

*
One day as Elisha was on his way to Shunem, a woman of rank who lived there pressed him to stay and eat there. After this he always broke his journey for a meal when he passed that way. She said to her husband, 'Look, I am sure the man who is constantly passing our way must be a holy man of God. Let us build him a small room on the roof, and put him a bed in it, and a table and chair and lamp; whenever he comes to us he can rest there.'

One day when he came, he retired to the upper room and lay down. 'What can be done for her?' he asked. Gehazi, his servant, answered, 'Well, she has no son and her husband is old.' Elisha said, 'Call her.' The servant called her and she stood at the door. 'This time next year,' Elisha said 'you will hold a son in your arms.'

This is the word of the Lord.   *2 Kings 4:8-11.14-16*

Responsorial Psalm
℟   **I will sing for ever of your love, O Lord.**

1   I will sing for ever of your love, O Lord;
      through all ages my mouth will proclaim your truth.
      Of this I am sure, that your love lasts for ever,
      that your truth is firmly established as the heavens.   ℟

2   Happy the people who acclaim such a king,
      who walk, O Lord, in the light of your face,
      who find their joy every day in your name,
      who make your justice the source of their bliss.   ℟

3   For it is you, O Lord, who are the glory of their strength;
      it is by your favour that our might is exalted:
      for our ruler is in the keeping of the Lord;
      our king in the keeping of the Holy One of Israel.   ℟
                                          Ps 88:2-3. 16-19. ℟ v.2

SECOND READING
We read from the letter of St Paul to the Romans, chapter six.
*
When we were baptised in Christ Jesus we were baptised in his death; in other words, when we were baptised we went into the tomb with him and joined him in death, so that as Christ was raised from the dead by the Father's glory, we too might live a new life.

But we believe that having died with Christ we shall return to life with him: Christ, as we know, having been raised from the dead will never die again. Death has no power over him any more. When he died, he died, once for all, to sin, so his life now is life with God; and in that way, you too must consider yourselves to be dead to sin but alive for God in Christ Jesus.

This is the word of the Lord.   *Romans 6:3-4.8-11*

Gospel Acclamation
Alleluia, alleluia!
Open our heart, O Lord,
to accept the words of your Son.
Alleluia!   *cf. Acts 16:14*

or

Alleluia, alleluia!
You are a chosen race, a royal priesthood, a people set apart
to sing the praises of God
who called you out of darkness into his wonderful light.
Alleluia!   *1 Peter 2:9*

GOSPEL

We read from the holy Gospel according to Matthew, chapter ten.
*
Jesus instructed the Twelve as follows: 'Anyone who prefers
father or mother to me is not worthy of me. Anyone who prefers
son or daughter to me is not worthy of me. Anyone who does not
take his cross and follow in my footsteps is not worthy of me.
Anyone who finds his life will lose it; anyone who loses his life
for my sake will find it.

'Anyone who welcomes you welcomes me; and those who
welcome me welcome the one who sent me.

'Anyone who welcomes a prophet because he is a prophet will
have a prophet's reward; and anyone who welcomes a holy man
because he is a holy man will have a holy man's reward.

'If anyone gives so much as a cup of cold water to one of these
little ones because he is a disciple, then I tell you solemnly, he
will most certainly not lose his reward.'

This is the Gospel of the Lord.   *Matthew 10:37-42*

Fourteenth Sunday in Ordinary Time A

Introduction to the Service
'If you want to achieve something in life, you need to be a hard
and powerful person.' This is what many people say. But it is not
what Christ says. He praised the humble. And he was a humble,
gentle person himself.

We are his disciples. We have promised that we will follow his
way. But we have not always done so and therefore we now ask
for God's pardon and forgiveness.

Penitential Rite

- Lord, we ask for forgiveness for our pride. (*Silence*)

- We remember how often we wanted to achieve our aims by pushing others aside. (*Silence*)

- Gentleness was often missing in our lives and we ask for forgiveness. (*Silence*)

Let us confess that we have sinned. **I confess...**

FIRST READING

Should we love splendour or humility? We read now what some of the Israelites felt about this question.

They said that not even their king should love splendour, but should live in humility. They pointed to the example of their former king, David, who did not even want to ride a horse, but chose rather to ride a donkey.

Some Israelites disagreed and objected to the idea of a humble king.

We read from the prophet Zechariah, chapter nine.

*
The Lord says this:
'Rejoice heart and soul, daughter of Zion!
Shout with gladness, daughter of Jerusalem!
See now, your king comes to you;
he is victorious, he is triumphant,
humble and riding on a donkey,
on a colt, the foal of a donkey.
He will banish chariots from Ephraim
and horses from Jerusalem;
the bow of war will be banished.
He will proclaim peace for the nations.
His empire shall stretch from sea to sea,
from the River to the ends of the earth.'

This is the word of the Lord. *Zechariah 9:9-10*

Responsorial Psalm
℟ **I will bless your name for ever,
O God my King.**

or

℟ **Alleluia!**

1   I will give you glory, O God my King,
    I will bless your name for ever.
    I will bless you day after day
    and praise your name for ever.   ℟

2   The Lord is kind and full of compassion,
    slow to anger, abounding in love.
    How good is the Lord to all,
    compassionate to all his creatures.   ℟

3   All your creatures shall thank you, O Lord,
    and your friends shall repeat their blessing.
    They shall speak of the glory of your reign
    and declare your might, O God.   ℟

4   The Lord is faithful in all his words
    and loving in all his deeds.
    The Lord supports all who fall
    and raises all who are bowed down.   ℟

Ps 144:1-2. 8-11. 13-14. ℟ v.1

SECOND READING

We read from the letter of St Paul to the Romans, chapter eight.

Your interests are not in the unspiritual, but in the spiritual, since
the Spirit of God has made his home in you. In fact, unless you
possessed the Spirit of Christ you would not belong to him, and if
the Spirit of him who raised Jesus from the dead is living in you,
then he who raised Jesus from the dead will give life to your own
mortal bodies through his Spirit living in you.

So then, my brothers, there is no necessity for us to obey our
unspiritual selves or to live unspiritual lives. If you do live in that
way, you are doomed to die; but if by the Spirit you put an end to
the misdeeds of the body you will live.

This is the word of the Lord.   *Romans 8:9.11-13*

Gospel Acclamation
    Alleluia, alleluia!
    Blessed are you, Father, Lord of heaven and earth,
    for revealing the mysteries of the kingdom to mere children.
    Alleluia!   *cf. Mt 11:25*

GOSPEL

We read from the holy Gospel according to Matthew, chapter eleven.

＊

Jesus exclaimed, 'I bless you, Father, Lord of heaven and of earth, for hiding these things from the learned and the clever and revealing them to mere children. Yes, Father, for that is what it pleased you to do. Everything has been entrusted to me by my Father; and no one knows the Son except the Father, just as no one knows the Father except the Son and those to whom the Son chooses to reveal him.

'Come to me, all you who labour and are overburdened, and I will give you rest. Shoulder my yoke and learn from me, for I am gentle and humble in heart, and you will find rest for your souls. Yes, my yoke is easy and my burden light.'

This is the Gospel of the Lord.   *Matthew 11:25.30*

Fifteenth Sunday in Ordinary Time   A

Introduction to the Service

Nobody forced us to come to church today. We freely accepted the invitation of God. The inviting Word of God was sown in us like a small, seemingly powerless seed. The germination of the seed within us depends on our acceptance of the Word.

The fact that we are here is some sign that we are willing to let God's seed grow in us. At other times, however, we know that we were not good soil for God's Word, and so we have to ask for forgiveness.

Penitential Rite

● At times we were like stone before God's Word and were not open for it.   (*Silence*)

Lord, have mercy...

● At times we were like shallow ground and made little effort to allow God's Word to develop deep roots in us.   (*Silence*)

Christ, have mercy...

● At times we allowed thistles to get the upper hand and they choked your Word in us.   (*Silence*)

Lord, have mercy...

FIRST READING

A word has no power in itself. It can therefore be ignored. Even a word of God can at first be ignored by people. But God has ways of making sure that his Word will finally come true, even if it is at first rejected by people.

We read from the prophet Isaiah, chapter fifty-five.
*
Thus says the Lord: 'As the rain and the snow come down from the heavens and do not return without watering the earth, making it yield and giving growth to provide seed for the sower and bread for the eating, so the word that goes from my mouth does not return to me empty, without carrying out my will and succeeding in what it was sent to do.'

This is the word of the Lord. *Isaiah 55:10-11*

Responsorial Psalm
℟ **Some seed fell into rich soil
and produced its crop.**

1 You care for the earth, give it water,
you fill it with riches.
Your river in heaven brims over
to provide its grain. ℟

2 And thus you provide for the earth;
you drench its furrows,
you level it, soften it with showers,
you bless its growth. ℟

3 You crown the year with your goodness.
Abundance flows in your steps,
in the pastures of the wilderness it flows. ℟

4 The hills are girded with joy,
the meadows covered with flocks,
the valleys are decked with wheat.
They shout for joy, yes, they sing. ℟ *Ps 64:10-14. ℟ Lk 8:8*

SECOND READING

We read from the letter of St Paul to the Romans, chapter eight.
*
I think that what we suffer in this life can never be compared to the glory, as yet unrevealed, which is waiting for us. The whole creation is eagerly waiting for God to reveal his sons. It was not

for any fault on the part of creation that it was made unable to attain its purpose, it was made so by God; but creation still retains the hope of being freed, like us, from its slavery to decadence, to enjoy the same freedom and glory as the children of God. From the beginning till now the entire creation, as we know, has been groaning in one great act of giving birth; and not only creation, but all of us who possess the first-fruits of the Spirit, we too groan inwardly as we wait for our bodies to be set free.

This is the word of the Lord.   *Romans 8:18-23*

Gospel Acclamation
Alleluia, alleluia!
Speak, Lord, your servant is listening;
you have the message of eternal life.
Alleluia!   *1 Sam 3:9; Jn 6:68*

or

Alleluia, alleluia!
The seed is the word of God, Christ the sower;
whoever finds this seed will remain for ever.
Alleluia!

GOSPEL
We read from the holy Gospel according to Matthew, chapter thirteen.
*
*Jesus left the house and sat by the lakeside, but such crowds gathered round him that he got into a boat and sat there. The people all stood on the beach, and he told them many things in parables.

He said, 'Imagine a sower going out to sow. As he sowed, some seeds fell on the edge of the path, and the birds came and ate them up. Others fell on patches of rock where they found little soil and sprang up straight away, because there was no depth of earth; but as soon as the sun came up they were scorched and, not having any roots, they withered away. Others fell among thorns, and the thorns grew up and choked them. Others fell on rich soil and produced their crop, some a hundredfold, some sixty, some thirty. Listen, anyone who has ears!'*

Then the disciples went up to him and asked, 'Why do you talk to them in parables?' 'Because' he replied 'the mysteries of the kingdom of heaven are revealed to you, but they are not revealed to them. For anyone who has will be given more, and he will have more than enough; but from anyone who has not, even what he has will be taken away. The reason I talk to them in parables is that they look without seeing and listen without hearing or understanding. So in their case this prophecy of Isaiah is being fulfilled:

You will listen and listen again, but not understand,
see and see again, but not perceive.
For the heart of this nation has grown coarse,
their ears are dull of hearing, and they have shut their eyes,
for fear they should see with their eyes,
hear with their ears,
understand with their heart,
and be converted
and be healed by me.

'But happy are your eyes because they see, your ears because they hear! I tell you solemnly, many prophets and holy men longed to see what you see, and never saw it; to hear what you hear, and never heard it.

'You, therefore, are to hear the parable of the sower. When anyone hears the word of the kingdom without understanding, the evil one comes and carries off what was sown in his heart: this is the man who received the seed on the edge of the path. The one who received it on patches of rock is the man who hears the word and welcomes it at once with joy. But he has no root in him, he does not last; let some trial come, or some persecution on account of the word, and he falls away at once. The one who received the seed in thorns is the man who hears the word but the worries of this world and the lure of riches choke the word and so he produces nothing. And the one who received the seed in rich soil is the man who hears the word and understands it; he is the one who yields a harvest and produces now a hundredfold, now sixty, now thirty.'

This is the Gospel of the Lord.   *Matthew 13:1-23*

Shorter Form, verses 1-9. Read between *.

Sixteenth Sunday in Ordinary Time   A

Introduction to the Service

God is holy. He hates evil. Why then does he not remove by force evil things from this world? When we hear about murders, wars, or grave injustices, we want God to come with power and to exterminate those who do evil.

But would not God then have to annihilate us as well? Did not we, too, cause evil to others at one time or another? We begin to see the wisdom of God's patience with us.

In this Sunday service we stand in deep admiration before God who is infinitely holy and infinitely patient with those who fail to be holy.

Penitential Rite

● We bow before God as we remember the evil we have done.   (*Silence*)

● We bow before God as we remember how impatient we ourselves were with those who repeatedly harmed us.   (*Silence*)

● We bow low before God as we see the contrast between his way of dealing with evil, and our own ways.   (*Silence*)

Let us confess that we have sinned: **I confess**...

FIRST READING

Some rulers are very strict with those under them. They think this is the only way to conquer evil in a country. But we have seen that strictness alone cannot lead a country to happiness. The problem is how strictness can be combined with leniency and love.

In our reading from the book of Wisdom we hear somebody rejoicing in the way God is able to be both strict and lenient with us.

We read from the book of Wisdom, chapter twelve.
*
There is no god, other than you, who cares for everything,
to whom you might have to prove that you never judged
   unjustly.
Your justice has its source in strength,
your sovereignty over all makes you lenient to all.
You show your strength when your sovereign power is
   questioned

and you expose the insolence of those who know it;
but, disposing of such strength, you are mild in judgement,
you govern us with great lenience,
for you have only to will, and your power is there.
By acting thus you have taught a lesson to your people
how the virtuous man must be kindly to his fellow men,
and you have given your sons the good hope
that after sin you will grant repentance.

This is the word of the Lord.   *Wisdom 12:13.16-19*

Responsorial Psalm
℟ **O Lord, you are good and forgiving.**

1 O Lord, you are good and forgiving,
    full of love to all who call.
    Give heed, O Lord, to my prayer
    and attend to the sound of my voice. ℟

2 All the nations shall come to adore you
    and glorify your name, O Lord:
    for you are great and do marvellous deeds,
    you who alone are God. ℟

3 But you, God of mercy and compassion,
    slow to anger, O Lord,
    abounding in love and truth,
    turn and take pity on me. ℟   *Ps 85:5-6. 9-10. 15-16. ℟ v.5*

SECOND READING
We read from the letter of St Paul to the Romans, chapter eight.
*
The Spirit comes to help us in our weakness. For when we cannot
choose words in order to pray properly, the Spirit himself
expresses our plea in a way that could never be put into words,
and God who knows everything in our hearts knows perfectly
well what he means, and that the pleas of the saints expressed by
the Spirit are according to the mind of God.

This is the word of the Lord.   *Romans 8:26-27*

Gospel Acclamation
Alleluia, alleluia!
May the Father of our Lord Jesus Christ
enlighten the eyes of our mind,

so that we can see what hope his call holds for us.
Alleluia!   cf. Eph 1:17. 18

or

Alleluia, alleluia!
Blessed are you, Father,
Lord of heaven and earth,
for revealing the mysteries of the kingdom
to mere children.
Alleluia!   cf. Mt 11:25

GOSPEL

We read from the holy Gospel according to Matthew, chapter thirteen.
*
Jesus put a parable before the crowds, 'The kingdom of heaven may be compared to a man who sowed good seed in his field. While everybody was asleep his enemy came, sowed darnel all among the wheat, and made off. When the new wheat sprouted and ripened, the darnel appeared as well. The owner's servants went to him and said, "Sir, was it not good seed that you sowed in your field? If so, where does the darnel come from?" "Some enemy has done this" he answered. And the servants said, "Do you want us to go and weed it out?" But he said, "No, because when you weed out the darnel you might pull up the wheat with it. Let them both grow till the harvest; and at harvest time I shall say to the reapers: First collect the darnel and tie it in bundles to be burnt, then gather the wheat into my barn." '

He put another parable before them, 'The kingdom of heaven is like a mustard seed which a man took and sowed in his field. It is the smallest of all the seeds, but when it has grown it is the biggest shrub of all and becomes a tree so that the birds of the air come and shelter in its branches.'

He told them another parable, 'The kingdom of heaven is like the yeast a woman took and mixed in with three measures of flour till it was leavened all through.'

In all this Jesus spoke to the crowds in parables; indeed, he would never speak to them except in parables. This was to fulfill the prophecy:

I will speak to you in parables
and expound things hidden since the foundation of the world.

Then, leaving the crowds, he went to the house; and his disciples came to him and said, 'Explain the parable about the darnel in the field to us.' He said in reply, 'The sower of the good seed is the Son of Man. The field is the world; the good seed is the subjects of the kingdom; the darnel, the subjects of the evil one; the enemy who sowed them, the devil; the harvest is the end of the world; the reapers are the angels. Well then, just as the darnel is gathered up and burnt in the fire, so it will be at the end of time. The Son of Man will send his angels and they will gather out of his kingdom all things that provoke offences and all who do evil, and throw them into the blazing furnace, where there will be weeping and grinding of teeth. Then the virtuous will shine like the sun in the kingdom of their Father. Listen, anyone who has ears!'

This is the Gospel of the Lord.   *Matthew 13:24-43*

*Shorter Form, verses 24-30. Read between *.*

Seventeenth Sunday in Ordinary Time   A

Introduction to the Service

When you decided to come to church this morning, some of you may have had to make the difficult decision to leave other important matters behind. For some it may have meant deciding not to have a long sleep, or not to go out with a group of friends.

When you chose instead to come to this service, you were like the person who knew about a treasure hidden in a field, and who sold everything he had to buy that field.

However, at other times during this past week, you may not have made the right decision. You may have chosen the wrong path and therefore you now come before God to ask his forgiveness:

Penitential Rite

● Lord, you know that we sometimes made the wrong choice. We chose our selfish pleasure rather than the path of helping others.   (*Silence*)

    Lord, have mercy…

● Christ, in some of our decisions we lacked wisdom. We ignored the real treasures and chose what was of less value.   (*Silence*)

    Christ, have mercy…

● Lord, you offer us the treasure of living with you. Forgive us for not even recognising how much you offer us.   (*Silence*)
　　Lord, have mercy...

FIRST READING

When the young King Solomon was asked to choose between receiving riches and receiving wisdom, it was not an easy choice for him to make. Riches are something visible, which appeal immediately to all of us. Would he not be carried away by this desire which we all share?

We read in the first book of Kings, chapter three.
*
The Lord appeared to Solomon in a dream and said, 'Ask what you would like me to give you.' Solomon replied, 'Lord, my God, you have made your servant king in succession to David my father. But I am a very young man, unskilled in leadership. Your servant finds himself in the midst of this people of yours that you have chosen, a people so many its numbers cannot be counted or reckoned. Give your servant a heart to understand how to discern between good and evil, for who could govern this people of yours that is so great?' It pleased the Lord that Solomon should have asked for this. 'Since you have asked for this' the Lord said 'and not asked for long life for yourself or riches or the lives of your enemies, but have asked for a discerning judgement for yourself, here and now I do what you ask. I give you a heart wise and shrewd as none before you has had and none will have after you.'

This is the word of the Lord.　　　　　　　　　　*1 Kings 3:5.7-12*

Responsorial Psalm
　　℟　**Lord how I love your law!**

1　My part, I have resolved, O Lord,
　　is to obey your word.
　　The law from your mouth means more to me
　　than silver and gold.　℟

2　Let your love be ready to console me
　　by your promise to your servant.
　　Let your love come to me and I shall live
　　for your law is my delight.　℟

3 That is why I love your commands
more than finest gold.
That is why I rule my life by your precepts:
I hate false ways. ℟

4 Your will is wonderful indeed;
therefore I obey it.
The unfolding of your word gives light
and teaches the simple. ℟

Ps 118:57. 72. 76-77. 127-130. ℟ v.97

SECOND READING

We read from the letter of St Paul to the Romans, chapter eight.
*

We know that by turning everything to their good God co-operates with all those who love him, with all those that he has called according to his purpose. They are the ones he chose specially long ago and intended to become true images of his Son, so that his Son might be the eldest of many brothers. He called those he intended for this; those he called he justified, and with those he justified he shared his glory.

This is the word of the Lord. *Romans 8:28-30*

Gospel Acclamation
Alleluia, alleluia!
I call you friends, says the Lord,
because I have made known to you
everything I have learnt from my Father.
Alleluia! *Jn 15:15*

or

Alleluia, alleluia!
Blessed are you, Father,
Lord of heaven and earth,
for revealing the mysteries of the kingdom
to mere children.
Alleluia! *cf. Mt 11:25*

GOSPEL

We read from the holy Gospel according to Matthew, chapter thirteen.
*

*Jesus said to the crowds, 'The kingdom of heaven is like treasure hidden in a field which someone has found; he hides it again, goes off happy, sells everything he owns and buys the field.

'Again, the kingdom of heaven is like a merchant looking for fine pearls; when he finds one of great value he goes and sells everything he owns and buys it.*

'Again, the kingdom of heaven is like a dragnet cast into the sea that brings in a haul of all kinds. When it is full, the fishermen haul it ashore; then, sitting down, they collect the good ones in a basket and throw away those that are no use. This is how it will be at the end of time: the angels will appear and separate the wicked from the just to throw them into the blazing furnace where there will be weeping and grinding of teeth.

'Have you understood all this?' They said 'Yes.' And he said to them, 'Well then, every scribe who becomes a disciple of the kingdom of heaven is like a householder who brings out from his storeroom things both new and old.'

This is the Gospel of the Lord.   Matthew 13:44-52

*Shorter Form, verses 44-46. Read between *.

Eighteenth Sunday in Ordinary Time   A

Introduction to the Service

In many countries there is a shortage of food. Every day hundreds of children all over the world die of hunger. For many families the struggle for daily bread is the only thing they can think of. They cannot enjoy life.

In such times what does it mean for us, Christians, to gather round this table for the sacred meal of Holy Communion? What does it mean for us to open the Bible and to read about the miracle Christ performed when he fed thousands of hungry people in the desert?

In one sentence we can answer: our gathering here on this Sunday is a sign of hope, and a reminder of our task.

Penitential Rite

Before we take part in this meal, we prepare ourselves by reflecting:

● Do we open our eyes to see people in need, or do we try to ignore them?   (Silence)

● When we see people in need, are we prepared to do something about it?   (Silence)

● When our efforts to help are failing, do we easily abandon our sense of hope.   (*Silence*)

Let us confess that we have sinned.   **I confess**...

FIRST READING

This earth will definitely become a place where everybody has sufficient food. This is the powerful message of our first reading.
We read it in order to retain our sense of hope; God will succeed in his plans. We also read it in order to remember that it is our task to work against hunger and need.

We read from the book of the prophet Isaiah, chapter fifty-five.
*
Thus says the Lord:

Oh, come to the water all you who are thirsty;
though you have no money, come!
Buy corn without money, and eat,
and, at no cost, wine and milk.
Why spend money on what is not bread,
your wages on what fails to satisfy?
Listen, listen to me and you will have good things to eat
and rich food to enjoy.
Pay attention, come to me;
listen, and your soul will live.
With you I will make an everlasting covenant
out of the favours promised to David.

This is the word of the Lord.   *Isaiah 55:1-3*

Responsorial Psalm
℟   **You open wide your hand, O Lord,
     you grant our desires.**

1   The Lord is kind and full of compassion,
     slow to anger, abounding in love.
     How good is the Lord to all,
     compassionate to all his creatures.   ℟

2   The eyes of all creatures look to you
     and you give them their food in due time.
     You open wide your hand,
     grant the desires of all who live.   ℟

3   The Lord is just in all his ways
    and loving in all his deeds.
    He is close to all who call him,
    call on him from their hearts.   ℞   *Ps 144:8-9. 15-18. ℞ v.16*

SECOND READING

We read from the letter of St Paul to the Romans, chapter eight.
*
Nothing can come between us and the love of Christ, even if we
are troubled or worried, or being persecuted, or lacking food or
clothes, or being threatened or even attacked. These are the trials
through which we triumph, by the power of him who loved us.

For I am certain of this: neither death nor life, no angel, no
prince, nothing that exists, nothing still to come, not any power,
or height or depth, nor any created thing, can ever come between
us and the love of God made visible in Christ Jesus our Lord.

This is the word of the Lord.   *Romans 8:35.37-39*

Gospel Acclamation
    Alleluia, alleluia!
    Blessings on the King who comes,
    in the name of the Lord!
    Peace in heaven
    and glory in the highest heavens!
    Alleluia!   *Lk 19:38; 2:14*

or

    Alleluia, alleluia!
    Man does not live on bread alone,
    but on every word that comes from the mouth of God.
    Alleluia!   *Mt 4:4*

GOSPEL

We read from the holy Gospel according to Matthew, chapter fourteen.
*
When Jesus received the news of John the Baptist's death he
withdrew by boat to a lonely place where they could be by
themselves. But the people heard of this and, leaving the towns,
went after him on foot. So as he stepped ashore he saw a large
crowd; and he took pity on them and healed their sick.

When evening came, the disciples went to him and said, 'This
is a lonely place, and the time has slipped by; so send the people
away, and they can go to the villages to buy themselves some

food.' Jesus replied, 'There is no need for them to go: give them something to eat yourselves.' 'But they answered, 'All we have with us is five loaves and two fish.' 'Bring them here to me,' he said. He gave orders that the people were to sit down on the grass; then he took the five loaves and the two fish, raised his eyes to heaven and said the blessing. And breaking the loaves he handed them to his disciples who gave them to the crowds. They all ate as much as they wanted, and they collected the scraps remaining, twelve baskets full. Those who ate numbered about five thousand men, to say nothing of women and children.

This is the Gospel of the Lord.   *Matthew 14:13-21*

Nineteenth Sunday in Ordinary Time   A

Introduction to the Service

There are many different ways of encountering God. Each one of us has met God in one way or another. Some of us may have felt the presence of God at a time of great joy, others may have felt his presence through the goodness of other people, and again others may have encountered God in times of sickness and need. Even now we have gathered here to meet our Lord in Word and Sacrament.

Are we ready to meet him?

Penitential Rite

● Lord, we are sometimes so occupied with things that we do not even notice your presence.   (*Silence*)

Lord, have mercy...

● We feel ashamed to admit that there were even times when we rather wished not to feel your presence.   (*Silence*)

Christ, have mercy...

● At other times we knew that we could meet you in prayer, but we failed to do so.   (*Silence*)

Lord, have mercy...

FIRST READING

Prophets are people who are close to God. Yet they, too, were sometimes not sure in what way they could meet God. In our reading we hear how the prophet Elijah encountered God in a way which surprised him.

We read from the first book of the Kings, chapter nineteen.
*
When Elijah reached Horeb, the mountain of God, he went into
the cave and spent the night in it. Then he was told, 'Go out and
stand on the mountain before the Lord.' Then the Lord himself
went by. There came a mighty wind, so strong it tore the
mountains and shattered the rocks before the Lord. But the Lord
was not in the wind. After the wind came an earthquake. But the
Lord was not in the earthquake. After the earthquake came a fire.
But the Lord was not in the fire. And after the fire there came the
sound of a gentle breeze. And when Elijah heard this, he covered
his face with his cloak and went out and stood at the entrance of
the cave.

This is the word of the Lord. *1 Kings 19:9.11-13*

Responsorial Psalm
℟ **Let us see, O Lord, your mercy
and give us your saving help.**

1 I will hear what the Lord God has to say,
a voice that speaks of peace.
His help is near for those who fear him
and his glory will dwell in our land. ℟

2 Mercy and faithfulness have met;
justice and peace have embraced.
Faithfulness shall spring from the earth
and justice look down from heaven. ℟

3 The Lord will make us prosper
and our earth shall yield its fruit.
Justice shall march before him
and peace shall follow his steps. ℟ *Ps 84:9-14. ℟ v. 8*

SECOND READING
We read from the letter of St Paul to the Romans, chapter nine.
*
What I want to say is no pretence; I say it in union with Christ – it
is the truth – my conscience in union with the Holy Spirit assures
me of it too. What I want to say is this: my sorrow is so great, my
mental anguish so endless, I would willingly be condemned and
be cut off from Christ if it could help my brothers of Israel, my
own flesh and blood. They were adopted as sons, they were
given the glory and the covenants; the Law and the ritual were

drawn up for them, and the promises were made to them. They are descended from the patriarchs and from their flesh and blood came Christ who is above all, God for ever blessed! Amen.

This is the word of the Lord. *Romans 9:1-5*

Gospel Acclamation

Alleluia, alleluia!
Blessings on the King who comes, in the name of the Lord!
Peace in heaven and glory in the highest heavens!
Alleluia!

Lk 19:38

or

Alleluia, alleluia!
My soul is waiting for the Lord,
I count on his word.
Alleluia!

Ps 129:5

GOSPEL

We read from the holy Gospel according to Matthew, chapter fourteen.
*

Jesus made the disciples get into the boat and go on ahead to the other side while he would send the crowds away. After sending the crowds away he went up into the hills by himself to pray. When evening came, he was there alone, while the boat, by now far out on the lake, was battling with a heavy sea, for there was a headwind. In the fourth watch of the night he went towards them, walking on the lake, and when the disciples saw him walking on the lake they were terrified. 'It is a ghost' they said, and cried out in fear. But at once Jesus called out to them, saying, 'Courage! It is I! Do not be afraid.' It was Peter who answered. 'Lord ', he said 'if it is you, tell me to come to you across the water.' 'Come' said Jesus. Then Peter got out of the boat and started walking towards Jesus across the water, but as soon as he felt the force of the wind, he took fright and began to sink. 'Lord! Save me!' he cried. Jesus put out his hand at once and held him. 'Man of little faith,' he said 'why did you doubt?' And as they got into the boat the wind dropped. The men in the boat bowed down before him and said, 'Truly, you are the Son of God.'

This is the Gospel of the Lord. *Matthew 14:22-33*

Twentieth Sunday in Ordinary Time   A

Introduction to the Service

When we were on our way here this morning, we probably passed people who were not going to church. Some do not belong to any Church, others belong to other denominations. Can you still remember with what feelings you looked at them? Did you feel sorry for them? Or did you think you were better than them? Or did you think that they, too, may in some way be near God?

It is quite important how we look at those who do not worship together with us. We have to try to understand how God himself looks at this difference between us, his Church, and those who do not belong to it.

Penitential Rite

At the beginning of this service we prepare ourselves by asking God for his forgiveness.

● Were there instances when we failed to show understanding to those who are separated from us and therefore do not worship together with us? *(Silence)*

● Were there times when we were very proud of having the true faith and consequently despised others? *(Silence)*

● Were there times when we failed to love those who worshipped in a different way? *(Silence)*

Let us confess that we have sinned: **I confess**...

FIRST READING

In the Old Testament the people of God often thought that God would only accept *their* sacrifices, not those of foreign nations. They thought God would not allow foreigners to come to his holy mountain. The prophet tells us how God corrected their views.

We read from the prophet Isaiah, chapter fifty-six.
*
Thus says the Lord: Have a care for justice, act with integrity, for soon my salvation will come and my integrity be manifest.

Foreigners who have attached themselves to the Lord to serve him and to love his name and be his servants – all who observe the sabbath, not profaning it, and cling to my covenant – these I will bring to my holy mountain. I will make them joyful in my house of prayer. Their holocausts and their sacrifices will be accepted on my altar, for my house will be called a house of prayer for all the peoples.

This is the word of the Lord.   *Isaiah 56:1.6-7*

Responsorial Psalm
℟   **Let the peoples praise you, O God;
let all the peoples praise you.**

1   O God, be gracious and bless us
and let your face shed its light upon us.
So will your ways be known upon earth
and all nations learn your saving help.   ℟

2   Let the nations be glad and exult
for you rule the world with justice.
With fairness you rule the peoples,
you guide the nations on earth.   ℟

3   Let the peoples praise you, O God;
let all the peoples praise you.
May God still give us his blessing
till the ends of the earth revere him.   ℟

Ps 66:2-3. 5-6. 8. ℟ v.4

SECOND READING

We read from the letter of St Paul to the Romans, chapter eleven.
*
Let me tell you pagans this: I have been sent to the pagans as their apostle, and I am proud of being sent, but the purpose of it is to make my own people envious of you, and in this way save some of them. Since their rejection meant the reconciliation of the world, do you know what their admission will mean? Nothing less than a resurrection from the dead! God never takes back his gifts or revokes his choice.

Just as you changed from being disobedient to God, and now enjoy mercy because of their disobedience, so those who are disobedient now – and only because of the mercy shown to you – will also enjoy mercy eventually. God has imprisoned all men in their own disobedience only to show mercy to all mankind.

This is the word of the Lord.   *Romans 11:13-15.29-32*

Gospel Acclamation

Alleluia, alleluia!
The sheep that belong to me listen to my voice,
says the Lord,
I know them and they follow me.
Alleluia!

Jn 10:27

or

Alleluia, alleluia!
Jesus proclaimed the Good News of the kingdom,
and cured all kinds of sickness among the people.
Alleluia!

cf. Mt 4:23

GOSPEL

We read from the holy Gospel according to Matthew, chapter fifteen.
*
Jesus left Gennesaret and withdrew to the region of Tyre and Sidon. Then out came a Canaanite woman from that district and started shouting, 'Sir, Son of David, take pity on me. My daughter is tormented by a devil.' But he answered her not a word. And his disciples went and pleaded with him. 'Give her what she wants,' they said 'because she is shouting after us.' He said in reply, 'I was sent only to the lost sheep of the House of Israel.' But the woman had come up and was kneeling at his feet. 'Lord,' she said 'help me.' He replied, 'It is not fair to take the children's food and throw it to the house-dogs.' She retorted, 'Ah yes, sir; but even house-dogs can eat the scraps that fall from their master's table.' Then Jesus answered her, 'Woman, you have great faith. Let your wish be granted.' And from that moment her daughter was well again.

This is the Gospel of the Lord.   *Matthew 15:21-28*

Twenty-First Sunday in Ordinary Time   A

Introduction to the Service

Nobody likes to live in a house which is built on a shaky foundation, so that they constantly fear that the house may collapse on top of them at any time. Nobody likes to belong to a family which may dissolve at any moment. And nobody likes to belong to a Church community which may disintegrate at any time.

Our assembly around this altar is built on a firm foundation. It is built on Peter and the Apostles. Christ said: 'You are Peter and on this rock I will build my Church.'

Penitential Rite

As we are about to give thanks for our faith, we also humbly admit the defects in our own faith:

- Lord, our faith is not as firm as the faith of Peter. It is often timid and shaky. (*Silence*)
  Lord, have mercy...

- Christ, we do not confess our faith in you as clearly as Peter confessed it. At times we hid our faith, and at times we even denied it. (*Silence*)
  Christ, have mercy...

- Lord, when difficulties crop up, we do not always remain convinced that you are the Christ, the Son of the Living God. (*Silence*)
  Lord, have mercy...

FIRST READING

Each nation has its own ways of installing a new leader. The Israelites also had symbols which showed that a person was now entrusted with an office of leadership. God made use of the Israelites' symbols when he wanted to show that he was giving his authority to a person.

We read of such an instance in the book of the prophet Isaiah, chapter twenty-two.

Thus says the Lord of hosts to Shebna, the master of the palace:

I dismiss you from your office,
I remove you from your post,
and the same day I call on my servant
Eliakim son of Hilkiah.
I invest him with your robe,
gird him with your sash,
entrust him with your authority;
and he shall be a father
to the inhabitants of Jerusalem
and to the House of Judah.
I place the key of the House of David
on his shoulder;

should he open, no one shall close,
should he close, no one shall open.
I drive him like a peg
into a firm place;
he will become a throne of glory
for his father's house.

This is the word of the Lord.   *Isaiah 22:19-23*

Responsorial Psalm
℟   **Your love, O Lord, is eternal,**
     discard not the work of your hands.

1   I thank you, Lord, with all my heart,
     you have heard the words of my mouth.
     Before the angels I will bless you.
     I will adore before your holy temple.   ℟

2   I thank you for your faithfulness and love
     which excel all we ever knew of you.
     On the day I called, you answered;
     you increased the strength of my soul.   ℟

3   The Lord is high yet he looks on the lowly
     and the haughty he knows from afar.
     Your love, O Lord, is eternal,
     discard not the work of your hands.   ℟
                              Ps 137:1-3. 6. 8. ℟ v. 8

SECOND READING

We read from the letter of St Paul to the Romans, chapter eleven.
*
How rich are the depths of God – how deep his wisdom and
knowledge – and how impossible to penetrate his motives or
understand his methods! Who could ever know the mind of the
Lord? Who could ever be his counsellor? Who could ever give
him anything or lend him anything? All that exists comes from
him; all is by him and for him. To him be glory for ever! Amen.

This is the word of the Lord.   *Romans 11:33-36*

Gospel Acclamation
     Alleluia, alleluia!
     God in Christ was reconciling the world to himself,
     and he has entrusted to us the news that they are reconciled.
     Alleluia!   *2 Cor 5:19*

or

> Alleluia, alleluia!
> You are Peter
> and on this rock I will build my Church.
> And the gates of the underworld can never hold out against
>   it.
> Alleluia!
>
> Mt 16:18

GOSPEL

We read from the holy Gospel according to Matthew, chapter sixteen.
*

When Jesus came to the region of Caesarea Philippi he put this question to his disciples, 'Who do people say the Son of Man is?' And they said, 'Some say he is John the Baptist, some Elijah, and others Jeremiah or one of the prophets.' 'But you,' he said, 'who do you say I am?' Then Simon Peter spoke up, 'You are the Christ,' he said, 'the Son of the living God.' Jesus replied, 'Simon son of Jonah, you are a happy man! Because it was not flesh and blood that revealed this to you but my Father in heaven. So I now say to you: You are Peter and on this rock I will build my Church. And the gates of the underworld can never hold out against it. I will give you the keys of the kingdom of heaven; whatever you bind on earth shall be considered bound in heaven; whatever you loose on earth shall be considered loosed in heaven.' Then he gave the disciples strict orders not to tell anyone that he was the Christ.

This is the Gospel of the Lord.   *Matthew 16:13-20*

Twenty-Second Sunday in Ordinary Time   A

Introduction to the Service

We have gathered for worship on this Sunday, in order to give thanks to God for inviting us to the faith. But here is a question which we should ask ourselves: would we have joined the Church had we known that our membership would not only bring us joy but also suffering? We can also ask this in another way: if we were to be told today that we would have to suffer for the sake of our faith, what would we do?

During this service we will look at Christ's readiness to accept even suffering if necessary. We also look at our own readiness to suffer for our faith.

Penitential Rite

- Let us now remember a recent incident in our lives, when we wanted to avoid suffering for our faith. Perhaps we did not want to miss something enjoyable. (*Silence*)

- Or let us remember an incident when we refused to help others. We did not want to suffer any inconvenience in order to help others. We refused even the smallest kind of suffering. (*Silence*)

Let us confess that we have sinned. **I confess**...

FIRST READING

The task of the prophets often involved suffering. They were sent not only to announce joyful events, but also to remind people of their sins and injustices. They were often threatened with death because of this; their task brought them suffering.

We read from the book of the prophet Jeremiah, chapter twenty.
*
You have seduced me, Lord, and I have let myself be seduced;
you have overpowered me: you were the stronger.
I am a daily laughing-stock,
everybody's butt.
Each time I speak the word, I have to howl
and proclaim: 'Violence and ruin!'
The word of the Lord has meant for me
insult, derision, all day long.
I used to say, 'I will not think about him,
I will not speak in his name any more.'
Then there seemed to be a fire burning in my heart,
imprisoned in my bones.
The effort to restrain it wearied me,
I could not bear it.

    This is the word of the Lord   *Jeremiah 20:7-9*

Responsorial Psalm
℞ **For you my soul is thirsting, O Lord my God.**

1   O God, you are my God, for you I long;
      for you my soul is thirsting.
      My body pines for you
      like a dry, weary land without water. ℞

2 So I gaze on you in the sanctuary
   to see your strength and your glory.
   For your love is better than life,
   my lips will speak your praise. ℟

3 So I will bless you all my life,
   in your name I will lift up my hands.
   My soul shall be filled as with a banquet,
   my mouth shall praise you with joy. ℟

4 For you have been my help;
   in the shadow of your wings I rejoice.
   My soul clings to you;
   your right hand holds me fast. ℟   *Ps 62:2-6. 8-9. ℟ v.2*

SECOND READING

We read from the letter of St Paul to the Romans, chapter twelve.
*

Think of God's mercy, my brothers, and worship him, I beg you,
in a way that is worthy of thinking beings, by offering your living
bodies as a holy sacrifice, truly pleasing to God. Do not model
yourselves on the behaviour of the world around you, but let
your behaviour change, modelled by your new mind. This is the
only way to discover the will of God and know what is good,
what it is that God wants, what is the perfect thing to do.

   This is the word of the Lord.   *Romans 12:1-2*

Gospel Acclamation
   Alleluia, alleluia!
   May the Father of our Lord Jesus Christ
   enlighten the eyes of our mind,
   so that we can see
   what hope his call holds for us.
   Alleluia!   *cf. Eph 1:17.18*

GOSPEL

We read from the holy Gospel according to Matthew, chapter sixteen.
*
Jesus began to make it clear to his disciples that he was destined
to go to Jerusalem and suffer grievously at the hands of the elders
and chief priests and scribes, to be put to death and to be raised
up on the third day. Then, taking him aside, Peter started to
remonstrate with him. 'Heaven preserve you, Lord,' he said.
'This must not happen to you.' But he turned and said to Peter,

'Get behind me, Satan! You are an obstacle in my path, because the way you think is not God's way but man's.'

Then Jesus said to his disciples, 'If anyone wants to be a follower of mine, let him renounce himself and take up his cross and follow me. For anyone who wants to save his life will lose it; but anyone who loses his life for my sake will find it. What, then, will a man gain if he wins the whole world and ruins his life? Or what has a man to offer in exchange for his life?

'For the Son of Man is going to come in the glory of his Father with his angels, and, when he does, he will reward each one according to his behaviour.'

This is the Gospel of the Lord.   *Matthew 16:21-27*

Twenty-Third Sunday in Ordinary Time   A

Introduction to the Service
Where people live together we find trouble and misunderstanding. This can happen even between good friends.

We Christians are not better than other people. We have the same problems. However, as Christians we should be a sign to the world. We should show the world how we can solve our difficulties in a new way.

This is the message of our celebration today: as Christians we are called to solve our problems in the spirit of Christ and in loving fellowship. People should point to us and say: 'Look how these people help each other to overcome their difficulties.'

Penitential Rite
Let us examine our conscience:

● Do we try to bridge the gaps and heal the tensions which arise in our Christian community?   (*Silence*)

● Are we an example to other people by showing them how we, Christians, solve our problems in a new way?   (*Silence*)

Let us ask for forgiveness for trying to solve our problems in our own way, without following the way of Christ.   **I confess**...

FIRST READING
When our fellow Christians behave badly we are slow to help them. We find it hard to talk openly with them and help them to

return to the right path.

We find it easier to talk about them behind their back. Perhaps, we even say: 'That is not my business, am I my brother's watchman and bodyguard?'

What has our reading to say about this question?

We read from the book of Ezekiel, chapter thirty-three.
*
The word of the Lord was addressed to me as follows, 'Son of man, I have appointed you as sentry to the House of Israel. When you hear a word from my mouth, warn them in my name. If I say to a wicked man: Wicked wretch, you are to die, and you do not speak to warn the wicked man to renounce his ways, then he shall die for his sin, but I will hold you responsible for his death. If, however, you do warn a wicked man to renounce his ways and repent, and he does not repent, then he shall die for his sin, but you yourself will have saved your life.'

This is the word of the Lord. *Ezekiel 33:7-9*

Responsorial Psalm
℟ **O that today you would listen to his voice!**
Harden not your hearts.

1   Come, ring out our joy to the Lord;
    hail the rock who saves us.
    Let us come before him, giving thanks,
    with songs let us hail the Lord.   ℟

2   Come in; let us bow and bend low;
    let us kneel before the God who made us
    for he is our God and we
    the people who belong to his pasture,
    the flock that is led by his hand.   ℟

3   O that today you would listen to his voice!
    'Harden not your hearts as at Meribah,
    as on that day at Massah in the desert
    when your fathers put me to the test;
    when they tried me, though they saw my work.'   ℟

Ps 94:1-2. 6-9. ℟ *v.8*

SECOND READING

We read from the letter of St Paul to the Romans, chapter thirteen.
*
Avoid getting into debt, except the debt of mutual love. If you

love your fellow men you have carried out your obligations. All the commandments: You shall not commit adultery, you shall not kill, you shall not steal, you shall not covet, and so on, are summed up in this single command: You must love your neighbour as yourself. Love is the one thing that cannot hurt your neighbour; that is why it is the answer to every one of the commandments.

This is the word of the Lord. *Romans 13:8-10*

Gospel Acclamation
Alleluia, alleluia!
Your word is truth, O Lord,
consecrate us in the truth.
Alleluia! *Jn 17:17*

or

Alleluia, alleluia!
God in Christ was reconciling the world to himself,
and he has entrusted to us the news that they are reconciled.
Alleluia! *2 Cor 5:19*

GOSPEL

We read from the holy Gospel according to Matthew, chapter eighteen.
*
Jesus said to his disciples: 'If your brother does something wrong, go and have it out with him alone, between your two selves. If he listens to you, you have won back your brother. If he does not listen, take one or two others along with you: the evidence of two or three witnesses is required to sustain any charge. But if he refuses to listen to these, report it to the community; and if he refuses to listen to the community, treat him like a pagan or a tax collector.

'I tell you solemnly, whatever you bind on earth shall be considered bound in heaven; whatever you loose on earth shall be considered loosed in heaven.

'I tell you solemnly once again, if two of you on earth agree to ask anything at all, it will be granted to you by my Father in heaven. For where two or three meet in my name, I shall be there with them.'

This is the Gospel of the Lord. *Matthew 18:15-20*

Twenty-Fourth Sunday in Ordinary Time   A

Introduction to the Service

In our Sunday Celebration we offer each other the sign of peace. This sign can become very meaningful if we really want to make peace with all our brothers and sisters.

However, we sometimes get tired of making peace with others time after time. So we ask ourselves: how often should we forgive each other? It is a question which worries us.

In our celebration today the Lord will encourage us not to give up. He tells us not to get tired of making peace with others.

He does not get tired of forgiving us time and again.

He is the one who will forgive us seventy-seven times if we return to him with love.

Penitential Rite

Let us ask ourselves:

● Am I tired of making peace again and again with people at home and at work?   (*Silence*)

● Is there still anger and resentment in my heart towards my neighbour?   (*Silence*)

Let us ask for God's forgiveness. May he forgive us our trespasses as we forgive those who trespass against us. **I confess**...

FIRST READING

Our reading is taken from the book of Ecclesiasticus. Another name for this book is 'Wisdom of Sirach'.

The early Christians loved this book very much. They called it 'Ecclesiasticus' which means 'book for the Church community'. It gave them practical advice on how to live as Christians and how to solve their problems in the community.

We read from the book of Ecclesiasticus, chapters twenty-seven and twenty-eight.
*
Resentment and anger, these are foul things,
and both are found with the sinner.
He who exacts vengeance will experience the vengeance of the
  Lord,

who keeps strict account of sin.
Forgive your neighbour the hurt he does you,
and when you pray, your sins will be forgiven.
If a man nurses anger against another,
can he then demand compassion from the Lord?
Showing no pity for a man like himself,
can he then plead for his own sins?
Mere creature of flesh, he cherishes resentment;
who will forgive him his sins?
Remember the last things, and stop hating,
remember dissolution and death, and live by the
    commandments.
Remember the commandments, and do not bear your neighbour
    ill-will;
remember the covenant of the Most High, and overlook the
    offence.

This is the word of the Lord.   *Ecclesiasticus 27:30-28:7*

Responsorial Psalm
    ℟   **The Lord is compassion and love,
        slow to anger and rich in mercy.**

1   My soul, give thanks to the Lord,
    all my being, bless his holy name.
    My soul, give thanks to the Lord
    and never forget all his blessings.   ℟

2   It is he who forgives all your guilt,
    who heals every one of your ills,
    who redeems your life from the grave,
    who crowns you with love and compassion.   ℟

3   His wrath will come to an end;
    he will not be angry for ever.
    He does not treat us according to our sins
    nor repay us according to our faults.   ℟

4   For as the heavens are high above the earth
    so strong is his love for those who fear him.
    As far as the east is from the west
    so far does he remove our sins.   ℟   *Ps 102:1-4. 9-12. ℟ v.8*

SECOND READING

We read from the letter of St Paul to the Romans, chapter fourteen.
*
The life and death of each of us has its influence on others; if we live, we live for the Lord; and if we die, we die for the Lord, so that alive or dead we belong to the Lord. This explains why Christ both died and came to life, it was so that he might be Lord both of the dead and of the living.

This is the word of the Lord.   *Romans 14:7-9*

Gospel Acclamation
Alleluia, alleluia!
Speak, Lord, your servant is listening:
you have the message of eternal life.
Alleluia!   *1 Sam 3:9; Jn 6:68*

or

Alleluia, alleluia!
I give you a new commandment:
love one another, just as I have loved you,
says the Lord.
Alleluia!   *Jn 13:34*

GOSPEL

We read from the holy Gospel according to Matthew, chapter eighteen.
*
Peter went up to Jesus and said, 'Lord, how often must I forgive my brother if he wrongs me? As often as seven times?' Jesus answered, 'Not seven, I tell you, but seventy-seven times.

'And so the kingdom of heaven may be compared to a king who decided to settle his accounts with his servants. When the reckoning began, they brought him a man who owed ten thousand talents; but he had no means of paying, so his master gave orders that he should be sold, together with his wife and children and all his possessions, to meet the debt. At this, the servant threw himself down at his master's feet. "Give me time," he said, "and I will pay the whole sum." And the servant's master felt so sorry for him that he let him go and cancelled the debt. Now as this servant went out, he happened to meet a fellow servant who owed him one hundred denarii; and he seized him by the throat and began to throttle him. "Pay what you owe me," he said. His fellow servant fell at his feet and implored him, saying, "Give me time and I will pay you." But the other would not agree; on the contrary, he had him thrown into prison till he should pay the debt. His fellow servants were deeply distressed when they saw what had happened, and they went to their master and reported the whole affair to him. Then the master sent for him. "You wicked servant," he said, "I cancelled all that debt of yours when you appealed to me. Were you not bound, then, to have pity on your fellow servant just as I had pity on you?" And in his anger the master handed him over to the torturers till he should pay all his debt. And that is how my heavenly Father will deal with you unless you each forgive your brother from your heart.'

This is the Gospel of the Lord.   *Matthew 18:21-35*

Twenty-Fifth Sunday in Ordinary Time   A

Introduction to the Service
God's ways are high above our ways. God's thoughts are high above our thoughts.

We, for example, tend to be small-minded and stingy. We want to regulate everything with laws and regulations. But God's way is different. God is generous and broad-minded; God's generosity has no limits.

This is the message which the Lord gives us today: be generous, broad-minded and good. Therefore today, we ask the Lord to inspire us with his spirit of generosity.

Penitential Rite
Let us ask ourselves:

● Was I generous towards other people last week?   (*Silence*)

● Did I help others generously? Did I forgive generously? (*Silence*)

● Was I stingy last week, jealous and small-minded?   (*Silence*)

Let us present ourselves to God and ask forgiveness for our lack of generosity.   **I confess**...

FIRST READING
Often we have our own ways of dealing with people; our own

ideas of what we call justice, our own ideas of what we call generosity. We may even think that these, our ways and ideas, are the only right ones to create justice and happiness. But are they God's way as well?

We read from the book of Isaiah, chapter fifty-five.
*
Seek the Lord while he is still to be found,
call to him while he is still near.
Let the wicked man abandon his way,
the evil man his thoughts.
Let him turn back to the Lord who will take pity on him,
to our God who is rich in forgiving;
for my thoughts are not your thoughts,
my ways not your ways – it is the Lord who speaks.
Yes, the heavens are as high above earth
as my ways are above your ways,
my thoughts above your thoughts.

This is the word of the Lord.   *Isaiah 55:6-9*

Responsorial Psalm
℟   **The Lord is close to all who call him.**

1   I will bless you day after day
and praise your name for ever.
The Lord is great, highly to be praised,
his greatness cannot be measured.   ℟

2   The Lord is kind and full of compassion,
slow to anger, abounding in love.
How good is the Lord to all,
compassionate to all his creatures.   ℟

3   The Lord is just in all his ways
and loving in all his deeds.
He is close to all who call him,
who call on him from their hearts.   ℟

Ps 144:2-3. 8-9. 17-18. ℟ v.18

SECOND READING

We read from the letter of St Paul to the Philippians, chapter one.
*
Christ will be glorified in my body, whether by my life or by my death. Life to me, of course, is Christ, but then death would bring me something more; but then again, if living in this body means

doing work which is having good results – I do not know what I should choose. I am caught in this dilemma: I want to be gone and be with Christ, which would be very much the better, but for me to stay alive in this body is a more urgent need for your sake.

Avoid anything in your everyday lives that would be unworthy of the gospel of Christ.

This is the word of the Lord.   *Philippians 1:20-24.27*

Gospel Acclamation
Alleluia, alleluia!
Blessings on the King who comes,
in the name of the Lord!
Peace in heaven
and glory in the highest heavens!
Alleluia!
                                                                              Lk 19:38

or

Alleluia, alleluia!
Open our heart, O Lord,
to accept the words of your Son.
Alleluia!
                                                                        cf. Acts 16:14

GOSPEL
We read from the holy Gospel according to Matthew, chapter twenty.
*
Jesus said to his disciples: 'The kingdom of heaven is like a landowner going out at daybreak to hire workers for his vineyard. He made an agreement with the workers for one denarius a day, and sent them to his vineyard. Going out at about the third hour he saw others standing idle in the market place and said to them, "You go to my vineyard too and I will give you a fair wage." So they went. At about the sixth hour and again at about the ninth hour, he went out and did the same. Then at about the eleventh hour he went out and found more men standing round, and he said to them, "Why have you been standing here idle all day?" "Because no one has hired us" they answered. He said to them, "You go into my vineyard too". In the evening, the owner of the vineyard said to his bailiff, "Call the workers and pay them their wages, starting with the last arrivals and ending with the first." So those who were hired at about the eleventh hour came forward and received one denarius each. When the first came, they expected to get more, but they too received one denarius

each. They took it, but grumbled at the landowner. "The men who came last" they said "have done only one hour, and you have treated them the same as us, though we have done a heavy day's work in all the heat." He answered one of them and said, "My friend, I am not being unjust to you; did we not agree on one denarius? Take your earnings and go. I choose to pay the last-comer as much as I pay you. Have I no right to do what I like with my own? Why be envious because I am generous?" Thus the last will be first, and the first, last.'

This is the Gospel of the Lord.   *Matthew 20:1-16*

Twenty-Sixth Sunday in Ordinary Time   A

Introduction to the Service

We expect God to console and strengthen us. We do not like it very much if we are challenged and told that something is wrong with us. However, we know that in whatever God says or does God wants only what is best for us.

For instance today, Jesus asks us the question: 'Do you belong to those people who say loudly: "Yes Father, your will be done" but then you do what you like and say "NO" to me?'

This will always be our struggle as Christians. We talk a lot about God but find it hard to do his will. Others may not talk so much about God, they may not even belong to our Church, and yet they may do God's will better than we do.

For instance, the priests and elders were furious when Jesus told them that the tax-collectors and prostitutes had a better chance of being accepted by God than they had, even though they were pious people who spent their lives in the Temple.

Penitential Rite

Let us ask ourselves:

● Did we talk of God's will for us but then do the opposite of what we said? (*Silence*)

● When last did we come back to God in the Sacrament of Reconciliation, so as to make a new start to do God's will? (*Silence*)

Let us ask for forgiveness for all our failings.   **I confess**…

FIRST READING

The people of Israel sometimes imagined God to be like a book-keeper. They expected God to write down all their good deeds and good words and add them up. They trusted in the credit-balance which they thought they had with God.

It is for this reason that they complained bitterly when things went wrong in their lives. They accused God of being unjust. How could he possibly deal with them in such a way? What did God reply?

We read from the book of Ezekiel, chapter eighteen.

*

The word of the Lord was addressed to me as follows: 'You object, "What the Lord does is unjust." Listen, you House of Israel: is what I do unjust? Is it not what you do that is unjust? When the upright man renounces his integrity to commit sin and dies because of this, he dies because of the evil that he himself has committed. When the sinner renounces sin to become law-abiding and honest, he deserves to live. He has chosen to renounce all his previous sins; he shall certainly live; he shall not die.'

This is the word of the Lord.   *Ezekiel 18:25-28*

Responsorial Psalm
℞ **Remember your mercy, Lord.**

1 Lord, make me know your ways.
   Lord, teach me your paths.
   Make me walk in your truth, and teach me:
   for you are God my saviour. ℞

2 Remember your mercy, Lord,
   and the love you have shown from of old.
   Do not remember the sins of my youth.
   In your love remember me,
   because of your goodness, O Lord. ℞

3 The Lord is good and upright.
   He shows the path to those who stray,
   he guides the humble in the right path;
   he teaches his way to the poor. ℞   *Ps 24:4-9. ℞ v.6*

SECOND READING

We read from the letter of St Paul to the Philippians, chapter two.

*

If our life in Christ means anything to you, if love can persuade at all, or the Spirit that we have in common, or any tenderness and sympathy, then be united in your convictions and united in your love, with a common purpose and a common mind. That is the one thing which would make me completely happy. There must be no competition among you, no conceit; but everybody is to be self-effacing. Always consider the other person to be better than your self, so that nobody thinks of his own interests first but everybody thinks of other people's interests instead. In your minds you must be the same as Christ Jesus:

> His state was divine,
> yet he did not cling
> to his equality with God
> but emptied himself
> to assume the condition of a slave,
> and became as men are;
> and being as all men are,
> he was humbler yet,
> even to accepting death,
> death on a cross.
> But God raised him high
> and gave him the name
> which is above all other names
> so that all beings
> in the heavens, on earth and in the underworld,
> should bend the knee at the name of Jesus
> and that every tongue should acclaim
> Jesus Christ as Lord,
> to the glory of God the Father.

This is the word of the Lord.   *Philippians 2:1-11*

Shorter Form, verses 1-5. Read between *.

Gospel Acclamation
Alleluia, alleluia!
If anyone loves me he will keep my word.
and my Father will love him,
and we shall come to him.
Alleluia!

Jn 14:23

or

Alleluia, alleluia!
The sheep that belong to me listen to my voice,
says the Lord,
I know them and they follow me.
Alleluia!   *Jn 10:27*

GOSPEL

We read from the holy Gospel according to Matthew, chapter twenty-
one.
*
Jesus said to the chief priests and the elders of the people, 'What
is your opinion? A man had two sons. He went and said to the
first, "My boy, you go and work in the vineyard today." He
answered, "I will not go", but afterwards thought better of it and
went. The man then went and said the same thing to the second
who answered, "Certainly, sir", but did not go. Which of the two
did the father's will?' 'The first' they said. Jesus said to them, 'I
tell you solemnly, tax collectors and prostitutes are making their
way into the kingdom of God before you. For John came to you, a
pattern of true righteousness, but you did not believe him, and
yet the tax collectors and prostitutes did. Even after seeing that,
you refused to think better of it and believe in him.'

This is the Gospel of the Lord.   *Matthew 21:28-32*

Twenty-Seventh Sunday in Ordinary Time   A

Introduction to the Service

The Lord calls us today by a beautiful name. He calls us 'my
vineyard', meaning that we are his fields, his orchards, his
plantations. God has planted us in his kingdom; God has called us
together; God makes us grow and he expects good fruit.

Let us ask the question: is it at all possible that God's vineyard in
our country could disappear completely, that it could be uprooted
and destroyed? Is it possible that the Church in our nation could
die out?

Jesus answer is: 'Yes, it is possible. You may lose the chance
which I have given you. Other people, other nations may get this
chance instead.'

Penitential Rite
Let us ask ourselves:

● What good fruit have we brought forth for God during the past
 week? (*Silence*)

● Did we allow God's word to guide us last week? (*Silence*)

● Do we as a church community fulfil our task in this country of
 ours? Are we God's sign in this country, as we stand up for
 God's values and ideals? (*Silence*)

Let us ask for forgiveness for all the bad fruit which we brought
forth during the past week. **I confess**...

FIRST READING

Our reading is like the letter of a disappointed lover. God asks us:
'Where are the signs of your love? I expected justice and integrity
but found bloodshed and cries of distress instead'.

We read from the book of Isaiah, chapter five.
*
Let me sing to my friend
the song of his love for his vineyard.
My friend had a vineyard
on a fertile hillside.
He dug the soil, cleared it of stones,
and planted choice vines in it.
In the middle he built a tower,
he dug a press there too.
He expected it to yield grapes,
but sour grapes were all that it gave.

And now, inhabitants of Jerusalem
and men of Judah,
I ask you to judge
between my vineyard and me.
What could I have done for my vineyard
that I have not done?
I expected it to yield grapes.
Why did it yield sour grapes instead?

Very well, I will tell you
what I am going to do to my vineyard:
I will take away its hedge for it to be grazed on,
and knock down its wall for it to be trampled on.

I will lay it waste, unpruned, undug;
overgrown by the briar and the thorn.
I will command the clouds
to rain no rain on it.
Yes, the vineyard of the Lord of hosts
is the House of Israel,
and the men of Judah
that chosen plant.
He expected justice, but found bloodshed,
integrity, but only a cry of distress.

This is the word of the Lord.   *Isaiah 5:1-7*

Responsorial Psalm
℟   **The vineyard of the Lord is the House of Israel.**

1   You brought a vine out of Egypt;
     to plant it you drove out the nations.
     It stretched out its branches to the sea,
     to the Great River it stretched out its shoots.   ℟

2   Then why have you broken down its walls?
     It is plucked by all who pass by.
     It is ravaged by the boar of the forest,
     devoured by the beasts of the field.   ℟

3   God of hosts, turn again, we implore,
     look down from heaven and see.
     Visit this vine and protect it,
     the vine your right hand has planted.   ℟

4   And we shall never forsake you again:
     give us life that we may call upon your name.
     God of hosts, bring us back;
     let your face shine on us and we shall be saved.   ℟
                      Ps 79:9. 12-16. 19-20. ℟ Is 5:7

SECOND READING

We read from the letter of St Paul to the Philippians, chapter four.
*
There is no need to worry; but if there is anything you need, pray
for it, asking God for it with prayer and thanksgiving, and that
peace of God, which is so much greater than we can understand,
will guard your hearts and your thoughts, in Christ Jesus.
Finally, brothers, fill your minds with everything that is true,

everything that is noble, everything that is good and pure, everything that we love and honour, and everything that can be thought virtuous or worthy of praise. Keep doing all the things that you learnt from me and have been taught by me and have heard or seen that I do. Then the God of peace will be with you.

This is the word of the Lord.   *Philippians 4:6-9*

Gospel Acclamation

Alleluia, alleluia!
I call you friends, says the Lord,
because I have made known to you
everything I have learnt from my Father.
Alleluia!   *Jn 15:15*

or

Alleluia, alleluia!
I chose you from the world
to go out and bear fruit,
fruit that will last,
says the Lord.
Alleluia!   *cf. Jn 15:16*

GOSPEL

We read from the holy Gospel according to Matthew, chapter twenty-one.

Jesus said to the chief priests and the elders of the people, 'Listen to another parable. There was a man, a landowner, who planted a vineyard; he fenced it round, dug a winepress in it and built a tower; then he leased it to tenants and went abroad. When vintage time drew near he sent his servants to the tenants to collect his produce. But the tenants seized his servants, thrashed one, killed another and stoned a third. Next he sent some more servants, this time a larger number, and they dealt with them in the same way. Finally he sent his son to them. "They will respect my son" he said. But when the tenants saw the son, they said to each other, "This is the heir. Come on, let us kill him and take over his inheritance." So they seized him and threw him out of the vineyard and killed him. Now when the owner of the vineyard comes, what will he do to those tenants?' They answered, 'He will bring those wretches to a wretched end and lease the vineyard to other tenants who will deliver the produce to him when the season arrives.' Jesus said to them, 'Have you never read in the scriptures:

It was the stone rejected by the builders
that became the keystone.
This was the Lord's doing
and it is wonderful to see?

'I tell you, then, that the kingdom of God will be taken from you and given to a people who will produce its fruit.'

This is the Gospel of the Lord.   *Matthew 21:33-43*

Twenty-Eighth Sunday in Ordinary Time   A

Introduction to the Service

Life without feasts and celebrations is dull and boring. Feasts are joyful occasions. Friends who have not seen each other for a long time meet again. Food and drink are in good supply; there is singing and dancing. Feasts are like green mountains rising above dry and barren valleys.

We also know that food and drink are not enough for a feast. Unity, peace and love make a feast a real feast. Disunity, quarrels and tears spoil and destroy a feast.

This is the message of our celebration today: God has prepared a feast for us. He himself is an eternal feast. Our celebration together is a foretaste of this feast, where all tears will be wiped away and where death will be no more.

Penitential Rite

Let us ask ourselves:

- God invites us to his everlasting feast. Do we accept his invitation? *(Silence)*

- God invites us to find all joy and life in him. Do we accept his invitation? *(Silence)*

- Do we take part in this Holy Eucharist in such a way that it becomes a joyful feast for God's people? *(Silence)*

Let us ask for forgiveness for having refused God's invitation on many occasions. **I confess...**

FIRST READING

Our reading is about a vision of the prophet Isaiah. It describes the perfect feast which God has prepared for his people. We note in this vision that more is offered than just food and drink.

We read from the book of Isaiah, chapter twenty-five.
*
On this mountain,
the Lord of hosts will prepare for all people
a banquet of rich food, a banquet of fine wines,
of food rich and juicy, of fine strained wines.
On this mountain he will remove
the mourning veil covering all peoples,
and the shroud enwrapping all nations,
he will destroy Death for ever.
The Lord will wipe away
the tears from every cheek;
he will take away his people's shame
everywhere on earth,
for the Lord has said so.
That day, it will be said: See, this is our God
in whom we hoped for salvation;
the Lord is the one in whom we hoped.
We exult and we rejoice
that he has saved us;
for the hand of the Lord
rests on this mountain.

This is the word of the Lord.   *Isaiah 25:6-10*

Responsorial Psalm
  ℟ **In the Lord's own house shall I dwell
     for ever and ever.**

1 The Lord is my shepherd;
   there is nothing I shall want.
   Fresh and green are the pastures
   where he gives me repose.
   Near restful waters he leads me,
   to revive my drooping spirit.   ℟

2 He guides me along the right path;
   he is true to his name.
   If I should walk in the valley of darkness

no evil would I fear.
You are there with your crook and your staff;
with these you give me comfort. ℟

3 You have prepared a banquet for me
in the sight of my foes.
My head you have anointed with oil;
my cup is overflowing. ℟

4 Surely goodness and kindness shall follow me
all the days of my life
In the Lord's own house shall I dwell
for ever and ever. ℟   *Ps 22. ℟ v. 6*

SECOND READING

We read from the letter of St Paul to the Philippians, chapter four.
*
I know how to be poor and I know how to be rich too. I have been
through my initiation and now I am ready for anything anywhere: full stomach or empty stomach, poverty or plenty. There is
nothing I cannot master with the help of the One who gives me
strength. All the same, it was good of you to share with me in my
hardships. In return my God will fulfil all your needs, in Christ
Jesus, as lavishly as only God can. Glory to God, our Father, for
ever and ever. Amen.

This is the word of the Lord.   *Philippians 4:12-14. 19-20*

Gospel Acclamation

Alleluia, alleluia!
The Word was made flesh and lived among us;
to all who did accept him
he gave power to become children of God.
Alleluia!

Jn 1:12. 14

or

Alleluia, alleluia!
May the Father of our Lord Jesus Christ
enlighten the eyes of our mind,
so that we can see what hope his call holds for us.
Alleluia!   *cf. Eph 1:17.18*

GOSPEL

We read from the holy Gospel according to Matthew, chapter twenty-two.

*
Jesus said to the chief priests and elders of the people: 'The kingdom of heaven may be compared to a king who gave a feast for his son's wedding. He sent his servants to call those who had been invited, but they would not come. Next he sent some more servants. "Tell those who have been invited" he said "that I have my banquet all prepared, my oxen and fattened cattle have been slaughtered, everything is ready. Come to the wedding." But they were not interested: one went off to his farm, another to his business, and the rest seized his servants, maltreated them and killed them. The king was furious. He despatched his troops, destroyed those murderers and burnt their town. Then he said to his servants, "The wedding is ready; but as those who were invited proved to be unworthy, go to the crossroads in the town and invite everyone you can find to the wedding." So these servants went out on to the roads and collected together everyone they could find, bad and good alike; and the wedding hall was filled with guests. When the king came in to look at the guests he noticed one man who was not wearing a wedding garment, and said to him, "How did you get in here, my friend, without a wedding garment?" And the man was silent. Then the king said to the attendants, "Bind him hand and foot and throw him out into the dark, where there will be weeping and grinding of teeth." For many are called, but few are chosen.'

This is the Gospel of the Lord.   *Matthew 22:1-4*

*Shorter Form, verses 1-10. Read between *.

Twenty-Ninth Sunday in Ordinary Time   A

Introduction to the Service

In our celebration today we shall hear of two great political leaders, Cyrus, the king of Babylon and Caesar the Emperor of Rome.

We consider the question: what have political leaders to do with God? Don't political leaders and God fall into completely different categories?

God's Word today will throw light on this question. The Lord shows his respect for political leaders. On the other hand, however, we are told that all political leaders should regard themselves as tools in God's hand. He is the Lord; there is no other God besides him.

Penitential Rite
Let us ask ourselves:

● Some of you may be political leaders or may hold a government office. Do you accept your task as a call from God, who wants you to serve his people?   (*Silence*)

● Do we respect our leaders?   (*Silence*)

Let us ask for forgiveness for pushing God aside in public life.   **I confess**...

FIRST READING

In our reading we hear of Cyrus, the powerful king of Babylon. The amazing thing is that Cyrus was not a believer in the God of Israel. And yet, the prophet Isaiah calls him 'the anointed one ... whom the Lord has taken by his right hand' and to whom he has given a 'great title'.

We read from the book of Isaiah, chapter forty-five.
*
Thus says the Lord to his anointed, to Cyrus,
whom he has taken by his right hand
to subdue nations before him
and strip the loins of kings,
to force gateways before him
that their gates be closed no more:

It is for the sake of my servant Jacob,
of Israel my chosen one,
that I have called you by your name,
conferring a title though you do not know me.
I am the Lord, unrivalled;
there is no other God besides me.
Though you do not know me, I arm you
that men may know from the rising to the setting of the sun
that, apart from me, all is nothing.

This is the word of the Lord.   *Isaiah 45:1.4-6*

Responsorial Psalm
℟   **Give the Lord glory and power.**

1   O sing a new song to the Lord,
    sing to the Lord all the earth.
    Tell among the nations his glory
    and his wonders among all the peoples.   ℟

2   The Lord is great and worthy of praise,
    to be feared above all gods;
    the gods of the heathens are naught.
    It was the Lord who made the heavens.   ℟

3   Give the Lord, you families of peoples,
    give the Lord glory and power,
    give the Lord the glory of his name.
    Bring an offering and enter his courts.   ℟

4   Worship the Lord in his temple.
    O earth, tremble before him.
    Proclaim to the nations: 'God is king.'
    He will judge the peoples in fairness.   ℟
    Ps 95:1. 3-5. 7-10. ℟ v.7

SECOND READING

We read from the first letter of St Paul to the Thessalonians, chapter one.
*

From Paul, Silvanus and Timothy, to the Church in Thessalonika which is in God the Father and the Lord Jesus Christ; wishing you grace and peace from God the Father and the Lord Jesus Christ.

We always mention you in our prayers and thank God for you all, and constantly remember before God our Father how you have shown your faith in action, worked for love and persevered through hope, in our Lord Jesus Christ.

We know, brothers, that God loves you and that you have been chosen, because when we brought the Good News to you, it came to you not only as words, but as power and as the Holy Spirit and as utter conviction.

This is the word of the Lord.   *1 Thessalonians 1:1-5*

Gospel Acclamation
> Alleluia, alleluia!
> Your word is truth, O Lord,
> consecrate us in the truth.
> Alleluia!

Jn 17:17

or

> Alleluia, alleluia!
> You will shine in the world like bright stars
> because you are offering it the word of life.
> Alleluia!

Phil 2:15-16

GOSPEL

We read from the holy Gospel according to Matthew, chapter twenty-two.
*
The Pharisees went away to work out between them how to trap Jesus in what he said. And they sent their disciples to him, together with the Herodians, to say, 'Master, we know that you are an honest man and teach the way of God in an honest way, and that you are not afraid of anyone, because a man's rank means nothing to you. Tell us your opinion, then. Is it permissible to pay taxes to Caesar or not?' But Jesus was aware of their malice and replied, 'You hypocrites! Why do you set this trap for me? Let me see the money you pay the tax with.' They handed him a denarius and he said, 'Whose head is this? Whose name?' 'Caesar's' they replied. He then said to them, 'Very well, give back to Caesar what belongs to Caesar – and to God what belongs to God.'

> This is the Gospel of the Lord.

Matthew 22:15-21

Thirtieth Sunday in Ordinary Time   A

Introduction to the Service
There is a proverb which says: 'These people have done nothing in life. They have not even planted a tree!'

When people plant a tree they generally do so for others. Trees grow slowly. Those who plant trees often do not live to enjoy their fruit: others will reap the harvest. In this way, planting a tree is a sign of unselfish love.

It would be the greatest praise if people could say of us one day:

'This man has done great things in life. He lived for others.' Or 'This woman has done great things in life. She was always there for others.' Love makes the lives of such people meaningful and worth living.

I ask you to see today's message in the same light: 'Love God with all your heart ... and your neighbour as yourself.' This commandment is not a chain around our neck but a way of making our lives meaningful and precious.

Penitential Rite

Let us ask ourselves:

● Did we act out of love in a way which made our lives really meaningful last week?   (*Silence*)

● Is there anything which hinders us from loving God with our whole heart and with all our strength?   (*Silence*)

Let us ask forgiveness if we did not do something for others with real unselfish love.   **I confess**...

FIRST READING

Our reading gives us a powerful example of how we can love our neighbours. It speaks about strangers among us, and about people who are powerless in society. It also speaks about people who have to borrow money from those who are better off.

We read from the book of Exodus, chapter twenty-two.
★
The Lord said to Moses, 'Tell the sons of Israel this, "You must not molest the stranger or oppress him, for you lived as strangers in the land of Egypt. You must not be harsh with the widow, or with the orphan; if you are harsh with them, they will surely cry out to me, and be sure I shall hear their cry; my anger will flare and I shall kill you with the sword, your own wives will be widows, your own children orphans.

"If you lend money to any of my people, to any poor man among you, you must not play the usurer with him: you must not demand interest from him.

"If you take another's cloak as a pledge, you must give it back to him before sunset. It is all the covering he has; it is the cloak he wraps his body in; what else would he sleep in? If he cries to me, I will listen, for I am full of pity."'

This is the word of the Lord.   *Exodus 22:20-26*

Responsorial Psalm
℞ **I love you, Lord, my strength.**

1 I love you, Lord, my strength,
my rock, my fortress, my saviour.
My God is the rock where I take refuge;
my shield, my mighty help, my stronghold.
The Lord is worthy of all praise:
when I call I am saved from my foes. ℞

2 Long life to the Lord, my rock!
Praised be the God who saves me.
He has given great victories to his king
and shown his love for his anointed. ℞

Ps 17:2-4. 47. 51. ℞ v.2

SECOND READING

We read from the first letter of St Paul to the Thessalonians, chapter one.
*
You observed the sort of life we lived when we were with you, which was for your instruction, and you were led to become imitators of us, and of the Lord; and it was with the joy of the Holy Spirit that you took to the gospel, in spite of the great opposition all round you. This has made you the great example to all believers in Macedonia and Achaia since it was from you that the word of the Lord started to spread – and not only throughout Macedonia and Achaia, for the news of your faith in God has spread everywhere. We do not need to tell other people about it: other people tell us how we started the work among you, how you broke with idolatry when you were converted to God and became servants of the real, living God; and how you are now waiting for Jesus, his Son, whom he raised from the dead, to come from heaven to save us from the retribution which is coming.

This is the word of the Lord.   *1 Thessalonians 1:5-10*

Gospel Acclamation
Alleluia, alleluia!
Open our heart, O Lord,
to accept the words of your Son.
Alleluia!

cf. Acts 16:14

or

> Alleluia, alleluia!
> If anyone loves me he will keep my word,
> and my Father will love him,
> and we shall come to him.
> Alleluia!

Jn 14:23

GOSPEL

We read from the holy Gospel according to Matthew, chapter twenty-two.

*

When the Pharisees heard that Jesus had silenced the Sadducees they got together and, to disconcert him, one of them put a question, 'Master, which is the greatest commandment of the Law?' Jesus said, 'You must love the Lord your God with all your heart, with all your soul, and with all your mind. This is the greatest and the first commandment. The second resembles it: you must love your neighbour as yourself. On these two commandments hang the whole Law, and the Prophets also.'

This is the Gospel of the Lord. *Matthew 22:34-40*

Thirty-First Sunday in Ordinary Time   A

Introduction to the Service

People in authority have a great responsibility. Leaders in the Church and leaders in the Government are called to do God's work, each in their own particular way.

In our celebration today, the Lord gives these leaders guidance but also a solemn warning. They should not overstress their official dress or status. They themselves should do what they preach to others.

This is often our greatest fault. We show others the right way but we do the opposite ourselves. We criticise the faults of others but we commit the same faults ourselves.

Penitential Rite

Let us examine our conscience:

- Do we ourselves practise what we preach, and do what we teach others to do? *(Silence)*

- Are we more concerned about our status than we are about serving others and helping them to grow? *(Silence)*

Let us ask God's forgiveness for advising others but doing the opposite ourselves.   **I confess**…

FIRST READING

Among the twelve tribes of Israel was the tribe of the priests, the Levites. Members of this tribe had to serve in the Temple, read the word of God and offer sacrifices and incense. They also had political leadership.

Our reading today is a shocking warning for these priests and leaders.

We read from the book of the prophet Malachi, chapters one and two.
*
I am a great king, says the Lord of hosts, and my name is feared throughout the nations. And now, priests, this warning is for you. If you do not listen, if you do not find it in your heart to glorify my name, says the Lord of hosts, I will send the curse on you and curse your very blessing. You have strayed from the way; you have caused many to stumble by your teaching. You have destroyed the covenant of Levi, says the Lord of hosts. And so I in my turn have made you contemptible and vile in the eyes of the whole people in repayment for the way you have not kept to my paths but have shown partiality in your administration.

Have we not all one Father? Did not one God create us? Why, then, do we break faith with one another, profaning the covenant of our ancestors?

This is the word of the Lord.   *Malachi 1:14-2:2. 8-10*

Responsorial Psalm
℟   **Keep my soul in peace before you, O Lord.**

1   O Lord, my heart is not proud
    nor haughty my eyes.
    I have not gone after things too great
    nor marvels beyond me.   ℟

2   Truly I have set my soul
    in silence and peace.
    A weaned child on its mother's breast,
    even so is my soul.   ℟

3   O Israel, hope in the Lord
    both now and for ever.   ℟   *Ps 130*

SECOND READING

We read from the first letter of St Paul to the Thessalonians, chapter two.
*

Like a mother feeding and looking after her own children, we felt so devoted and protective towards you, and had come to love you so much, that we were eager to hand over to you not only the Good News but our whole lives as well. Let me remind you, brothers, how hard we used to work, slaving night and day so as not to be a burden on any one of you while we were proclaiming God's Good News to you.

Another reason why we constantly thank God for you is that as soon as you heard the message that we brought you as God's message, you accepted it for what it really is, God's message and not some human thinking; and it is still a living power among you who believe it.

This is the word of the Lord.   *1 Thessalonians 2:7-9. 13*

Gospel Acclamation
  Alleluia, alleluia!
  Speak, Lord, your servant is listening:
  you have the message of eternal life.
  Alleluia!   *1 Sam 3:9; Jn 6:68*

or

  Alleluia, alleluia!
  You have only one Father, and he is in heaven;
  you have only one Teacher, the Christ!
  Alleluia!   *Mt 23:9. 10*

GOSPEL

We read from the holy Gospel according to Matthew, chapter twenty-three.
*

Addressing the people and his disciples Jesus said, 'The scribes and the Pharisees occupy the chair of Moses. You must therefore do what they tell you and listen to what they say; but do not be guided by what they do: since they do not practise what they preach. They tie up heavy burdens and lay them on men's shoulders, but will they lift a finger to move them? Not they! Everything they do is done to attract attention, like wearing broader phylacteries and longer tassels, like wanting to take the place of honour at banquets and the front seats in the synagogues, being greeted obsequiously in the market squares and having people call them Rabbi.

'You, however, must not allow yourselves to be called Rabbi, since you have only one Master, and you are all brothers. You must call no one on earth your father, since you have only one Father, and he is in heaven. Nor must you allow yourselves to be called teachers, for you have only one Teacher, the Christ. The greatest among you must be your servant. Anyone who exalts himself will be humbled, and anyone who humbles himself will be exalted.'

This is the Gospel of the Lord.   *Matthew 23:1-12*

Thirty-Second Sunday in Ordinary Time   A

Introduction to the Service
There are many clever people in the world. Clever people pass their exams, they know how to make money, they can build houses and mend cars. Thank God that he has given us brains to do all these things.

We need to have brains. But we need more than that. We also need wisdom. Wise people know what is important in life. They will find those things which we cannot buy with money or borrow from our friends.

This is the message of our celebration today: be wise people and not fools. There are things which you cannot buy or borrow. Look for them!

Penitential Rite
Let us ask ourselves:

● Did we despise God's wisdom and chase after useless things?   (*Silence*)

● Did we keep the light of faith burning in us through prayer and worship?   (*Silence*)

Let us ask God to forgive our foolishness.   **I confess**…

FIRST READING
In our reading we hear of wisdom which goes around the city like a gentle woman. We are told to look out for her. Those who love her will find her.

We read from the book of Wisdom, chapter six.
*
Wisdom is bright, and does not grow dim.
By those who love her she is readily seen,
and found by those who look for her.
Quick to anticipate those who desire her, she makes herself
    known to them.
Watch for her early and you will have no trouble;
you will find her sitting at your gates.
Even to think about her is understanding fully grown;
be on the alert for her and anxiety will quickly leave you.
She herself walks about looking for those who are worthy of her
and graciously shows herself to them as they go,
in every thought of theirs coming to meet them.

This is the word of the Lord.   *Wisdom 6:12-16*

Responsorial Psalm
℞   **For you my soul is thirsting, O God, my God.**

1   O God, you are my God, for you I long;
    for you my soul is thirsting.
    My body pines for you
    like a dry, weary land without water.   ℞

2   So I gaze on you in the sanctuary
    to see your strength and your glory.
    For your love is better than life,
    my lips will speak your praise.   ℞

3   So I will bless you all my life,
    in your name I will lift up my hands.
    My soul shall be filled as with a banquet,
    my mouth shall praise you with joy.   ℞

4   On my bed I remember you.
    On you I muse through the night
    for you have been my help;
    in the shadow of your wings I rejoice.   ℞   *Ps 62:2-8. ℞ v.2*

SECOND READING

We read from the first letter of St Paul to the Thessalonians, chapter
four.
*
*We want you to be quite certain, brothers, about those who have

died, to make sure that you do not grieve about them, like the other people who have no hope. We believe that Jesus died and rose again, and that it will be the same for those who have died in Jesus: God will bring them with him.* We can tell you this from the Lord's own teaching, that any of us who are left alive until the Lord's coming will not have any advantage over those who have died. At the trumpet of God, the voice of the archangel will call out the command and the Lord himself will come down from heaven; those who have died in Christ will be the first to rise, and then those of us who are still alive will be taken up in the clouds, together with them, to meet the Lord in the air. So we shall stay with the Lord for ever. With such thoughts as these you should comfort one another.

This is the word of the Lord.   *1 Thessalonians 4:13-18*

*Shorter Form, verses 13-14. Read between *.

Gospel Acclamation

Alleluia, alleluia!
Stay awake and stand ready,
because you do not know the hour
when the Son of Man is coming.
Alleluia!   *Mt 24:42. 44*

GOSPEL

We read from the holy Gospel according to Matthew, chapter twenty-five.
*
Jesus told this parable to his disciples: 'The kingdom of heaven will be like this: Ten bridesmaids took their lamps and went to meet the bridegroom. Five of them were foolish and five were sensible: the foolish ones did take their lamps, but they brought no oil, whereas the sensible ones took flasks of oil as well as their lamps. The bridegroom was late, and they all grew drowsy and fell asleep. But at midnight there was a cry, "The bridegroom is here! Go out and meet him." At this, all those bridesmaids woke up and trimmed their lamps, and the foolish ones said to the sensible ones, "Give us some of your oil: our lamps are going out." But they replied, "There may not be enough for us and for you; you had better go to those who sell it and buy some for yourselves." They had gone off to buy it when the bridegroom arrived. Those who were ready went in with him to the wedding

hall and the door was closed. The other bridesmaids arrived later. "Lord, Lord," they said "open the door for us." But he replied, "I tell you solemnly, I do not know you." So stay awake, because you do not know either the day or the hour.'

This is the Gospel of the Lord.   *Matthew 25:1-13*

Thirty-Third Sunday in Ordinary Time   *A*

Introduction to the Service

At every Holy Mass we bring bread and wine to the altar and say 'We bring you these gifts, fruit of the earth and work of human hands.'

But we bring to the altar not only bread and wine, but all the work of our hands and minds as well. All the gifts and powers which we have received from God, we offer again in thanksgiving; all the abilities we have been given; everything which we call 'talents' in us. We are invited today to bring all these gifts and talents to God in praise and thanksgiving.

Some of us have the gift of being either a good mother or a good father. Others have the talent to sing, to pray aloud, to read the lessons. Others again have the talent to teach the faith in catechism classes, to visit the sick or to bury the dead.

All these talents of our community we present today to God and say: 'Thank you Father for all these gifts'.

Penitential Rite

Let us ask ourselves:

- How did we use our talents and gifts?   (*Silence*)

- Did we allow others in our community to develop their gifts as well?   (*Silence*)

Let us ask for God's forgiveness if we have buried our talents and not used them for the community.   **I confess**...

FIRST READING

In our reading we proclaim the praise of a woman who is a loving mother and a perfect wife. She is the perfect example of somebody who has made full use of the talents given by God.

We read from the book of Proverbs, chapter thirty-one.
*
A perfect wife – who can find her?
She is far beyond the price of pearls.
Her husband's heart has confidence in her,
from her he will derive no little profit.
Advantage and not hurt she brings him
all the days of her life.
She is always busy with wool and with flax,
she does her work with eager hands.
She sets her hands to the distaff,
her fingers grasp the spindle.
She holds out her hand to the poor,
she opens her arms to the needy.
Charm is deceitful, and beauty empty;
the woman who is wise is the one to praise.
Give her a share in what her hands have worked for,
and let her works tell her praises at the city gates.

This is the word of the Lord.   *Proverbs 31:10-13. 19-20. 30-31*

Responsorial Psalm
℟   **O blessed are those who fear the Lord.**

1   O blessed are those who fear the Lord
    and walk in his ways!
    By the labour of your hands you shall eat.
    You will be happy and prosper.   ℟

2   Your wife like a fruitful vine
    in the heart of your house;
    your children like shoots of the olive,
    around your table.   ℟

3   Indeed thus shall be blessed
    the man who fears the Lord.
    May the Lord bless you from Zion
    in a happy Jerusalem
    all the days of your life.   ℟   *Ps 127:1-5. ℟ v.1*

SECOND READING

We read from the first letter of St Paul to the Thessalonians, chapter
five.
*
You will not be expecting us to write anything to you, brothers,

about 'times and seasons', since you know very well that the Day of the Lord is going to come like a thief in the night. It is when people are saying, 'How quiet and peaceful it is' that the worst suddenly happens, as suddenly as labour pains come on a pregnant woman; and there will be no way for anybody to evade it.

But it is not as if you live in the dark, my brothers, for that Day to overtake you like a thief. No, you are all sons of light and sons of the day: we do not belong to the night or to darkness, so we should not go on sleeping, as everyone else does, but stay wide awake and sober.

This the word of the Lord. *1 Thessalonians 5:1-6*

Gospel Acclamation
Alleluia, alleluia!
Even if you have to die, says the Lord,
keep faithful, and I will give you
the crown of life.
Alleluia! *Apoc 2:10*

or

Alleluia, alleluia!
Make your home in me, as I make mine in you,
says the Lord.
Whoever remains in me bears fruit in plenty.
Alleluia! *Jn 15:4.5*

GOSPEL

We read from the holy Gospel according to Matthew, chapter twenty-five.
*
Jesus spoke this parable to his disciples: 'The kingdom of heaven is like a man on his way abroad who summoned his servants and entrusted his property to them. To one he gave five talents, to another two, to a third one; each in proportion to his ability. Then he set out.

The man who had received the five talents promptly went and traded with them and made five more. The man who had received two made two more in the same way. But the man who had received one went off and dug a hole in the ground and hid his master's money.

*Now a long time after, the master of those servants came

back and went through his accounts with them. The man who had received the five talents came forward bringing five more. "Sir," he said " you entrusted me with five talents; here are five more than I have made."*

His master said to him, "Well done, good and faithful servant; you have shown you can be faithful in small things, I will trust you with greater; come and join in your master's happiness." Next the man with the two talents came forward. "Sir," he said "you entrusted me with two talents; here are two more that I have made." His master said to him, "Well done, good and faithful servant; you have shown you can be faithful in small things, I will trust you with greater; come and join in your master's happiness." Last came forward the man who had the one talent. "Sir," said he "I had heard you were a hard man, reaping where you have not sown and gathering where you have not scattered; so I was afraid, and I went off and hid your talent in the ground. Here it is; it was yours, you have it back." But his master answered him, "You wicked and lazy servant! So you knew that I reap where I have not sown and gather where I have not scattered? Well then, you should have deposited my money with the bankers, and on my return I would have recovered my capital with interest. So now, take the talent from him and give it to the man who has the five talents. For to everyone who has will be given more, and he will have more than enough; but from the man who has not, even what he has will be taken away. As for this good-for-nothing servant, throw him out into the dark, where there will be weeping and grinding of teeth." '

| *This is the Gospel of the Lord.*   *Matthew 25:14-30*

*Shorter Form, verses 14-15, 19-20. Read between *.

Thirty-Fourth Sunday in Ordinary Time   Solemnity

Our Lord Jesus Christ, Universal King   A

Introduction to the Service
Today we have reached the end of the Church year. Next Sunday we shall begin the season of Advent.

On this last Sunday of the Church year we proclaim Christ as our king. In our celebration we shall see him coming in glory: judging and saving people.

How will he judge? How will he separate the good from the bad?

Will he put the Christians on one side and the non-Christians on the other side?

No. There will be a different separation. He will only ask one question: 'What did you do for others? Were you concerned about those who had no food, no clothes; those who were sick and miserable?'

Penitential Rite

Let us ask ourselves:

- Did I help only those who belong to my family or my race? (*Silence*)

- Did I recognize the face of Christ in all those people who suffer? (*Silence*)

Let us ask the Lord to make up for all we have not done. **I confess**…

FIRST READING

Some people complain that the Church today is only concerned about the poor, and forgets about the wealthy who also need guidance. In our reading we hear the Good Shepherd saying: 'I shall bandage the wounded and make the weak strong. I shall watch over the fat and healthy. I shall be a true shepherd.'

We read from the book of Ezekiel, chapter thirty-four.
*
The Lord says this: I am going to look after my flock myself and keep all of it in view. As a shepherd keeps all his flock in view when he stands up in the middle of his scattered sheep, so shall I keep my sheep in view. I shall rescue them from wherever they have been scattered during the mist and darkness. I myself will pasture my sheep, I myself will show them where to rest – it is the Lord who speaks. I shall look for the lost one, bring back the stray, bandage the wounded and make the weak strong. I shall watch over the fat and healthy. I shall be a true shepherd to them.

As for you, my sheep, the Lord says this: I will judge between sheep and sheep, between rams and he-goats.

This is the word of the Lord. *Ezekiel 34:11-12. 15-17*

Responsorial Psalm
    ℟   **The Lord is my shepherd;**
        there is nothing I shall want.

1   The Lord is my shepherd;
     there is nothing I shall want.
     Fresh and green are the pastures
     where he gives me repose.   ℟

2   Near restful waters he leads me,
     to revive my drooping spirit.
     He guides me along the right path;
     he is true to his name.   ℟

3   You have prepared a banquet for me
     in the sight of my foes.
     My head you have anointed with oil;
     my cup is overflowing.   ℟

4   Surely goodness and kindness shall follow me
     all the days of my life.
     In the Lord's own house shall I dwell
     for ever and ever.   ℟   *Ps 22:1-3. 5-6. ℟ v.1*

SECOND READING

We read from the first letter of St Paul to the Corinthians, chapter fifteen.
*
Christ has been raised from the dead, the first-fruits of all who have fallen asleep. Death came through one man and in the same way the resurrection of the dead has come through one man. Just as all men die in Adam, so all men will be brought to life in Christ; but all of them in their proper order: Christ as the first-fruits and then, after the coming of Christ, those who belong to him. After that will come the end, when he hands over the kingdom to God the Father, having done away with every sovereignty, authority and power. For he must be king until he has put all his enemies under his feet and the last of the enemies to be destroyed is death. And when everything is subjected to him, then the Son himself will be subject in his turn to the One who subjected all things to him, so that God may be all in all.

This is the word of the Lord.   *1 Corinthians 15:20-26. 28*

Gospel Acclamation

Alleluia, alleluia!
Blessings on him who comes in the name of the Lord!
Blessings on the coming kingdom of our father David!
Alleluia!

Mk 11:10

GOSPEL

We read from the holy Gospel according to Matthew, chapter twenty-five.

*

Jesus said to his disciples: 'When the Son of Man comes in his glory, escorted by all the angels, then he will take his seat on his throne of glory. All the nations will be assembled before him and he will separate men one from another as the shepherd separates sheep from goats. He will place the sheep on his right hand and the goats on his left. Then the King will say to those on his right hand, "Come, you whom my Father has blessed, take for your heritage the kingdom prepared for you since the foundation of the world. For I was hungry and you gave me food; I was thirsty and you gave me drink; I was a stranger and you made me welcome; naked and you clothed me, sick and you visited me, in prison and you came to see me." Then the virtuous will say to him in reply, "Lord, when did we see you hungry and feed you; or thirsty and give you drink? When did we see you a stranger and make you welcome; naked and clothe you; sick or in prison and go to see you?" And the King will answer, "I tell you solemnly, in so far as you did this to one of the least of these brothers of mine, you did it to me." Next he will say to those on his left hand, "Go away from me, with your curse upon you, to the eternal fire prepared for the devil and his angels. For I was hungry and you never gave me food; I was thirsty and you never gave me anything to drink; I was a stranger and you never made me welcome, naked and you never clothed me, sick and in prison and you never visited me." Then it will be their turn to ask, "Lord, when did we see you hungry or thirsty, a stranger or naked, sick or in prison, and did not come to your help?" Then he will answer, "I tell you solemnly, in so far as you neglected to do this to one of the least of these, you neglected to do it to me." And they will go away to eternal punishment, and the virtuous to eternal life.'

This is the Gospel of the Lord.

Matthew 25:31-46

A Group Writes the Introduction to a Reading

Instead of using the introduction given in the book, the group drafts a new one, which is related to the local situation.

Steps in drafting an introduction

1 The group first reads the text of the *Gospel*.

2 The group reads the text of the First Reading.

3 The group discusses: what is the main idea the congregation should discover when it hears the first reading, even though it has not yet heard the Gospel?

4 Individual work by each member of the group:
   a) Each person reflects silently:
   What kind of introduction does the congregation need in order to help them listen eagerly to the reading and to discover the reading's main theme?
   Does the congregation need a life-related question?
   Does the congregation need a question which raises an expectation?
   Should the congregation be told the main theme of the reading, or should they be left to discover this for themselves?
   Do any difficult words need to be explained?
   Does the reading's background need explanation?
   b) Each member of the group writes an introduction.

5 All the introductions are read aloud. The others listen as if they were members of the congregation.

6 The best introduction is chosen, according to the criteria listed on the opposite page.
   The group listens again to the introduction and makes improvements.
   The reading of the introduction and the First Reading is practised.

What to Avoid in an Introduction

- **Avoid making it too long.**
  You distract people from the Word of God!

- **Avoid giving a sermon.**
  God's Word first, then our own words!

- **Avoid saying what the reading will say.**
  Repetition is boring.
  Your task is only to arouse the hunger.
  God's Word is the food!

- **Avoid pious talk and generalities.**
  Pious talk in your introduction will put people to sleep! Adopt a style of language which people speak at home: respectful but down to earth.

- **Avoid too many ideas.**
  Use only one idea. Other good ideas can be used another time. People can only remember easily one idea at a time.

- **Avoid distractions.**
  No verse numbers: Book and chapter are sufficient: No second introduction: In the Sundays in Ordinary Time, the Second Reading is not connected with the First Reading or the Gospel. Hence, an introduction to the Second Reading will introduce new ideas and this will confuse people.

- **Connect your introduction with people's lives.**
  You will arouse greater interest if you can show people, through your introduction, that the reading will give an answer to their daily problems. Never give such an answer in the introduction itself. Just mention the problem and say that the reading has something to say about it.

THE SEASON OF ADVENT

First Sunday of Advent   B

Introduction to the Service

Today we begin the time of Advent. It is a time of waiting as we prepare ourselves for the coming of the Lord.

We know there will be four Sundays of Advent. We know that in four weeks time we will be celebrating the birth of Jesus in Bethlehem.

We do *not* know, however, when the Lord will come to each one of us asking: 'What did you do with your life? Your time is up. I have given you hands to work – what did you do with them? I have given you a family, friends and neighbours. How did you live with them? I have given you a task in life, how did you fulfil this task?'

Penitential Rite

Therefore, let us examine our conscience:

- Which talents has God given you in life?
  How have you used them?   (*Silence*)

- What people does God allow you to meet at home and at work?
  How have you treated these people?   (*Silence*)

- What task has God given you in life, what is your work?
  How have you fulfilled this task?   (*Silence*)

Let us ask for forgiveness for wasting the time and talents which God has given us.   **I confess**...

FIRST READING

Our reading is a powerful prayer for Advent. The people of Israel realised that they had abandoned God and strayed from his way.

In this reading we hear the people of Israel crying out for God, that he may come down to them and guide them again.

We read from the book of Isaiah, chapters sixty-three and sixty-four.
*
You, Lord, yourself are our Father,
Our Redeemer is your ancient name.
Why, Lord, leave us to stray from your ways
and harden our hearts against fearing you?
Return, for the sake of your servants,

the tribes of your inheritance.
Oh, that you would tear the heavens open and come down
– at your Presence the mountains would melt.
No ear has heard,
no eye has seen
any god but you act like this
for those who trust him.
You guide those who act with integrity
and keep your ways in mind.
You were angry when we were sinners;
we had long been rebels against you.
We were all like men unclean,
all that integrity of ours like filthy clothing.
We have all withered like leaves
and our sins blew us away like the wind.
No one invoked your name
or roused himself to catch hold of you.
For you hid your face from us
and gave us up to the power of our sins.
And yet, Lord, you are our Father;
we the clay, you the potter,
we are all the work of your hand.

This is the word of the Lord.   *Isaiah 63:16-17;64:1. 3-8*

Responsorial Psalm
℟   **God of hosts, bring us back;**
   let your face shine on us and we shall be saved.

1   O shepherd of Israel, hear us,
   shine forth from your cherubim throne.
   O Lord, rouse up your might,
   O Lord, come to our help.   ℟

2   God of hosts, turn again, we implore,
   look down from heaven and see.
   Visit this vine and protect it,
   the vine your right hand has planted.   ℟

3   May your hand be on the man you have chosen,
   the man you have given your strength.
   And we shall never forsake you again:
   give us life that we may call upon your name.   ℟
                           Ps 79:2-3. 15-16. 18-19. ℟ v. 4

SECOND READING

We read from the first letter of St Paul to the Corinthians, chapter one.
*
May God our Father and the Lord Jesus Christ send you grace and peace.

I never stop thanking God for all the graces you have received through Jesus Christ. I thank him that you have been enriched in so many ways, especially in your teachers and preachers; the witness to Christ has indeed been strong among you so that you will not be without any of the gifts of the Spirit while you are waiting for our Lord Jesus Christ to be revealed; and he will keep you steady and without blame until the last day, the day of our Lord Jesus Christ, because God by calling you has joined you to his Son, Jesus Christ; and God is faithful.

This is the word of the Lord.   *1 Corinthians 1:3-9*

Gospel Acclamation
Alleluia, alleluia!
Let us see, O Lord, your mercy
and give us your saving help.
Alleluia!   *Ps 84:8*

GOSPEL

We read from the holy Gospel according to Mark, chapter thirteen.
*
Jesus said to his disciples: 'Be on your guard, stay awake, because you never know when the time will come. It is like a man travelling abroad: he has gone from home, and left his servants in charge, each with his own task; and he has told the doorkeeper to stay awake. So stay awake, because you do not know when the master of the house is coming, evening, midnight, cockcrow, dawn; if he comes unexpectedly, he must not find you asleep. And what I say to you I say to all: Stay awake!'

This is the Gospel of the Lord.   *Mark 13:33-37*

Second Sunday of Advent   B

Introduction to the Service

Today is the second Sunday of Advent. We are invited to prepare a way for the Lord and make his path straight.

We have a definite choice: we have the freedom to accept God or to reject him. We have the freedom either to allow God to enter our lives or to reject him.

Penitential Rite

We ask ourselves:

- Is there anything in my life which is dishonest and wrong? (*Silence*)

- Is there anything in my life which I have to make good again? Is there anything which I have to return to somebody because it does not belong to me? (*Silence*)

- What am I going to do to restore the good name of my neighbour because I have destroyed his or her good name? (*Silence*)

Let us ask God's forgiveness for all our dishonest ways. **I confess**...

FIRST READING

Our reading is a real message for Advent. It is a message of hope and joy: God has seen our troubles and comes to help us.

This reading was first addressed to the people of Israel who were in great difficulties. They were defeated by their enemies, many of them had been cruelly killed, others had been led away in chains into life-long captivity. In this situation of national disaster, the prophet proclaims the message which we are going to hear now.

We read from the book of Isaiah, chapter forty.
*
'Console my people, console them'
says your God.
'Speak to the heart of Jerusalem
and call to her
that her time of service is ended,
that her sin is atoned for,
that she has received from the hand of the Lord
double punishment for all her crimes.'

A voice cries, 'Prepare in the wilderness
a way for the Lord.
Make a straight highway for our God
across the desert.
Let every valley be filled in,
every mountain and hill be laid low,
let every cliff become a plain,

and the ridges a valley;
then the glory of the Lord shall be revealed
and all mankind shall see it;
for the mouth of the Lord has spoken.'

Go up on a high mountain,
joyful messenger to Zion.
Shout with a loud voice,
joyful messenger to Jerusalem.
Shout without fear,
say to the towns of Judah,
'Here is your God.'

Here is the Lord coming with power,
his arm subduing all things to him.
The prize of his victory is with him,
his trophies all go before him.
He is like a shepherd feeding his flock,
gathering lambs in his arms,
holding them against his breast
and leading to their rest the mother ewes.

This is the word of the Lord. *Isaiah 40:1-5. 9-11*

Responsorial Psalm

℟   **Let us see, O Lord, your mercy
and give us your saving help.**

1   I will hear what the Lord God has to say,
a voice that speaks of peace,
peace for his people.
His help is near for those who fear him
and his glory will dwell in our land.   ℟

2   Mercy and faithfulness have met;
justice and peace have embraced.
Faithfulness shall spring from the earth
and justice look down from heaven.   ℟

3   The Lord will make us prosper
and our earth shall yield its fruit.
Justice shall march before him
and peace shall follow his steps.   ℟   *Ps 84:9-14. ℟ v.8*

SECOND READING

We read from the second letter of St Peter, chapter three.
*

There is one thing, my friends, that you must never forget: that with the Lord, 'a day' can mean a thousand years, and a thousand years is like a day. The Lord is not being slow to carry out his promises, as anybody else might be called slow; but he is being patient with you all, wanting nobody to be lost and everybody to be brought to change his ways. The Day of the Lord will come like a thief, and then with a roar the sky will vanish, the elements will catch fire and fall apart, the earth and all that it contains will be burnt up.

Since everything is coming to an end like this, you should be living holy and saintly lives while you wait and long for the Day of God to come, when the sky will dissolve in flames and the elements melt in the heat. What we are waiting for is what he promised; the new heavens and new earth, the place where righteousness will be at home. So then, my friends, while you are waiting, do your best to live lives without spot or stain so that he will find you at peace.

This is the word of the Lord.   *2 Peter 3:8-14*

Gospel Acclamation
Alleluia, alleluia!
Prepare a way for the Lord.
make his paths straight,
and all mankind shall see the salvation of God.
Alleluia!
                                                 Lk 3:4.6

GOSPEL

We read from the holy Gospel according to Mark, chapter one.
*

The beginning of the Good News about Jesus Christ, the Son of God. It is written in the book of the prophet Isaiah:

Look, I am going to send my messenger before you;
he will prepare your way.
A voice cries in the wilderness:
Prepare a way for the Lord,
make his paths straight,

and so it was that John the Baptist appeared in the wilderness, proclaiming a baptism of repentance for the forgiveness of sins. All Judaea and all the people of Jerusalem made their way to him, and as they were baptised by him in the river Jordan they confessed their sins. John wore a garment of camel-skin, and he lived on locusts and wild honey. In the course of his preaching he said, 'Someone is following me, someone who is more powerful than I am, and I am not fit to kneel down and undo the strap of his sandals. I have baptised you with water, but he will baptise you with the Holy Spirit.'

This is the Gospel of the Lord. *Mark 1:1-8*

Third Sunday of Advent   B

Introduction to the Service

Today is already the third Sunday of Advent. In our celebration we are invited to rejoice and to be happy at all times because the Lord is near.

Often, however, we do not feel like rejoicing. Our hearts are sad. The Lord seems to be very far away from us. We feel miserable and bad. We go and look for consolation and joy. Often we cannot find it. Even God seems to be absent.

Probably in Jesus' time people felt the same way. They were looking for the Redeemer and could not find him. But John the Baptist tells us, as he told them: Rejoice, your saviour is among you though you do not recognise him. But look, he is very close to you!

Penitential Rite

We ask ourselves:

● Did we invite Christ to stay within our homes?   (*Silence*)

● Did we allow Christ to take part in our meetings?   (*Silence*)

● Do we try to solve our problems in the spirit of Christ?   (*Silence*)

Let us ask for forgiveness for expelling Christ from our midst. **I confess**...

FIRST READING

Our reading proclaims a message truly fitting for Advent: God is sending the Redeemer to all who are sad, to all whose hearts are broken, to all who feel enslaved as if in prison.

We read from the book of Isaiah, chapter sixty-one.
*
The spirit of the Lord has been given to me,
for the Lord has anointed me.
He has sent me to bring good news to the poor,
to bind up hearts that are broken;

to proclaim liberty to captives,
freedom to those in prison;
to proclaim a year of favour from the Lord.

'I exult for joy in the Lord,
my soul rejoices in my God,
for he has clothed me in the garments of salvation,
he has wrapped me in the cloak of integrity,
like a bridegroom wearing his wreath,
like a bride adorned in her jewels.

'For as the earth makes fresh things grow,
as a garden makes seeds spring up,
so will the Lord make both integrity and praise
spring up in the sight of the nations.'

This is the word of the Lord. *Isaiah 61:1-2. 10-11*

Responsorial Psalm
℟   **My soul rejoices in my God.**

1   My soul glorifies the Lord,
    my spirit rejoices in God, my Saviour.
    He looks on his servant in her nothingness;
    henceforth all ages will call me blessed.   ℟

2   The Almighty works marvels for me.
    Holy his name!
    His mercy is from age to age,
    on those who fear him.   ℟

3   He fills the starving with good things,
    sends the rich away empty.
    He protects Israel, his servant,
    remembering his mercy.   ℟   *Lk 1:46-50. 53-54. ℟ Is 61:10*

SECOND READING

We read from the first letter of St Paul to the Thessalonians, chapter five.

*

Be happy at all times; pray constantly; and for all things give thanks to God, because this is what God expects you to do in Christ Jesus.

Never try to suppress the Spirit or treat the gift of prophecy with contempt; think before you do anything – hold on to what is good and avoid every form of evil.

May the God of peace make you perfect and holy; and may you all be kept safe and blameless, spirit, soul and body, for the coming of our Lord Jesus Christ. God has called you and he will not fail you.

This is the word of the Lord.   *1 Thessalonians 5:16-24*

Gospel Acclamation

Alleluia, alleluia!
The spirit of the Lord has been given to me.
He has sent me to bring good news to the poor.
Alleluia!   *Is 61:1 (Lk 4:18)*

GOSPEL

We read from the holy Gospel according to John, chapter one.

A man came, sent by God.
His name was John.
He came as a witness,
as a witness to speak for the light,
so that everyone might believe through him.
He was not the light,
only a witness to speak for the light.
This is how John appeared as a witness. When the Jews sent priests and Levites from Jerusalem to ask him, 'Who are you?' he not only declared, but he declared quite openly, 'I am not the Christ.' 'Well then,' they asked 'are you Elijah?' 'I am not' he said. 'Are you the Prophet?' He answered, 'No.' So they said to him, 'Who are you? We must take back an answer to those who sent us. What have you to say about yourself ?' So John said, 'I am, as Isaiah prophesied:

a voice that cries in the wilderness:
Make a straight way for the Lord.'

Now these men had been sent by the Pharisees, and they put this further question to him, 'Why are you baptising if you are not the Christ, and not Elijah, and not the prophet?' John replied, 'I baptise with water; but there stands among you – unknown to you – the one who is coming after me; and I am not fit to undo his sandal-strap.' This happened at Bethany, on the far side of the Jordan, where John was baptising.

This is the Gospel of the Lord.   *John 1:6-8. 19-28*

Fourth Sunday of Advent   B

Introduction to the Service

During this time of Advent we look forward to the birth of Christ. We do the same as Mary did when she was expecting her child. Together with Mary we are waiting for Christmas.

In our celebration we shall hear of the mystery of how Jesus began to grow in Mary's womb. The Holy Spirit overshadowed her. For nine months Mary carried Jesus under her heart, intimately united with him, protecting him, loving him and waiting for him.

The womb of the Virgin Mary was like a living temple in which God became flesh. It was not a temple made by people, it was a temple created by God.

In a similar way God wants to dwell among us today – if we accept him as Mary did. God wants to live right within us and among us.

Penitential Rite

Let us ask ourselves:

- How do we accept Christ when we receive Holy Communion?   (*Silence*)

- Do we accept Christ in our parish communities by coming together in his name, by praying together and sharing the Gospel together?   (*Silence*)

- Do we protect the life of unborn children?   (*Silence*)

Let us ask for forgiveness for giving Christ such a poor welcome.   **I confess**...

FIRST READING

King David wanted to build a house for God where the ark of the covenant could be kept. At first, the prophet Nathan agreed to this plan. Then, however, he disagreed.

He told David that God prefers to stay among the people, walking with them and living with them as he had done in the past.

God wanted to stay in the House of David – that is, to stay among the people.

We read from the second book of Samuel, chapter seven.

*

Once David had settled into his house and the Lord had given him rest from all the enemies surrounding him, the king said to the prophet Nathan, 'Look, I am living in a house of cedar while the ark of God dwells in a tent.' Nathan said to the king, 'Go and do all that is in your mind, for the Lord is with you.'

But that very night the word of the Lord came to Nathan:

'Go and tell my servant David, "Thus the Lord speaks: Are you the man to build me a house to dwell in? I took you from the pasture, from following the sheep, to be leader of my people Israel; I have been with you on all your expeditions; I have cut off all your enemies before you. I will give you fame as great as the fame of the greatest on earth. I will provide a place for my people Israel; I will plant them there and they shall dwell in that place and never be disturbed again; nor shall the wicked continue to oppress them as they did, in the days when I appointed judges over my people Israel; I will give them rest from all their enemies. The Lord will make you great; the Lord will make you a House. And when your days are ended and you are laid to rest with your ancestors, I will preserve the offspring of your body after you and make his sovereignty secure. I will be a father to him and he a son to me. Your House and your sovereignty will always stand secure before me and your throne be established for ever." '

This is the word of the Lord.   *2 Samuel 7:1-5. 8-12. 14. 16*

Responsorial Psalm

℟   **I will sing for ever of your love, O Lord.**

1   I will sing for ever of your love, O Lord;
     through all ages my mouth will proclaim your truth.
     Of this I am sure, that your love lasts for ever,
     that your truth is firmly established as the heavens.   ℟

2   'I have made a covenant with my chosen one;
    I have sworn to David my servant:
    I will establish your dynasty for ever
    and set up your throne through all ages.'   ℟

3   He will say to me: 'You are my father,
    my God, the rock who saves me.'
    I will keep my love for him always;
    for him my covenant shall endure.   ℟

Ps 88:2-5. 27. 29. ℟ cf. v.2

SECOND READING

We read from the letter of St Paul to the Romans, chapter sixteen.
*
Glory to him who is able to give you the strength to live according
to the Good News I preach, and in which I proclaim Jesus Christ,
the revelation of a mystery kept secret for endless ages, but now
so clear that it must be broadcast to pagans everywhere to bring
them to the obedience of faith. This is only what scripture has
predicted, and it is all part of the way the eternal God wants
things to be. He alone is wisdom; give glory therefore to him
through Jesus Christ for ever and ever. Amen.

This is the word of the Lord.   *Romans 16:25-27*

Gospel Acclamation
   Alleluia, alleluia!
   I am the handmaid of the Lord:
   let what you have said be done to me.
   Alleluia!   *Lk. 1:38*

GOSPEL

We read from the holy Gospel according to Luke, chapter one.
*
The angel Gabriel was sent by God to a town in Galilee called
Nazareth, to a virgin betrothed to a man named Joseph, of the
House of David; and the virgin's name was Mary. He went in and
said to her, 'Rejoice, so highly favoured! The Lord is with you.'
She was deeply disturbed by these words and asked herself what
this greeting could mean, but the angel said to her, 'Mary, do not
be afraid; you have won God's favour. Listen! You are to conceive
and bear a son, and you must name him Jesus. He will be great
and will be called Son of the Most High. The Lord God will give
him the throne of his ancestor David; he will rule over

the House of Jacob for ever and his reign will have no end.' Mary said to the angel, 'But how can this come about, since I am a virgin?' 'The Holy Spirit will come upon you' the angel answered 'and the power of the Most High will cover you with its shadow. And so the child will be holy and will be called Son of God. Know this too: your kinswoman Elizabeth has, in her old age, herself conceived a son, and she whom people called barren is now in her sixth month, for nothing is impossible to God.' 'I am the handmaid of the Lord,' said Mary 'let what you have said be done to me.' And the angel left her.

This is the Gospel of the Lord.   *Luke 1:26-38*

THE SEASON OF CHRISTMAS

Christmas Day

See above, pp. 25.

Sunday in the Octave of Christmas

The Holy Family
of Jesus, Mary and Joseph   B

Where there is no Sunday occurring between 25 December and 1 January, this feast is celebrated on 30 December, with one reading only before the Gospel.

Introduction to the Service

We all belong to a family. We grew up in a family and know the people who are related to us. We also know the difficulties which families have to face. There are misunderstandings and troubles between parents and children, between father and mother, between one family and another.

Jesus also belonged to a family. Joseph, the carpenter, Mary and Jesus are called the Holy Family of Nazareth. Today we remember this Holy Family in our celebration.

We know that there were difficulties even in the Holy Family. Jesus, for instance, remained behind in the Temple without the permission of his parents. But we can also be sure that Mary, Joseph and Jesus could sort out possible misunderstandings and difficulties. With Jesus in their midst, the family of Nazareth was able to do things well and to solve their problems in a spirit of love.

Penitential Rite

Let us examine our conscience:

● What are we doing at home in order to keep Jesus in our midst? Do we pray together at home? Do we read and share God's Word together?   (*Silence*)

● Do we appreciate the Sacrament of Marriage as a sign of Christ's presence in our families.   (*Silence*)

Let us ask for forgiveness for so often excluding Christ from our families.   **I confess**…

The First Reading, Psalm, Second Reading and Gospel Acclamation given for Year A, pp.34ff., may be used, with the Gospel below. Or the alternative readings given below may be used.

FIRST READING

Some married couples long for years to have their first child. When their wish is eventually granted they rejoice with a grateful heart. They realise that a child is a precious gift from God. In our reading we shall bear of such a couple.

We read from the book of Genesis, chapters fifteen and twenty-one.

★
The word of the Lord was spoken to Abram in a vision, 'Have no fear, Abram, I am your shield; your reward will be very great'.

'My Lord,' Abram replied 'what do you intend to give me? I go childless...' Then Abram said, 'See, you have given me no descendants; some man of my household will be my heir'. And then this word of the Lord was spoken to him, 'He shall not be your heir; your heir shall be of your own flesh and blood'. Then taking him outside he said, 'Look up to heaven and count the stars if you can. Such will be your descendants' he told him. Abram put his faith in the Lord, who counted this as making him justified.

The Lord dealt kindly with Sarah as he had said, and did what he had promised her. So Sarah conceived and bore a son to Abraham in his old age, at the time God had promised. Abraham named the son born to him Isaac, the son to whom Sarah had given birth.

This is the word of the Lord.   *Genesis 15:1-6. 21:1-3*

Responsorial Psalm
    ℟   **He, the Lord, is our God.**
         He remembers his covenant for ever.

1   Give thanks to the Lord, tell his name,
     make known his deeds among the peoples.
     O sing to him, sing his praise;
     tell all his wonderful works!   ℟

2   Be proud of his holy name,
     let the hearts that seek the Lord rejoice.
     Consider the Lord and his strength;
     constantly seek his face.   ℟

3   Remember the wonders he has done,
     his miracles, the judgements he spoke.
     O children of Abraham, his servant,
     O sons of the Jacob he chose.   ℟

4   He remembers his covenant for ever,
     his promise for a thousand generations,
     the covenant he made with Abraham,
     the oath he swore to Isaac.   ℟   *Ps 104:1-6. 8-9. ℟ vv.7.8*

SECOND READING

We read from the letter to the Hebrews, chapter eleven.
*
It was by faith that Abraham obeyed the call to set out for a
country that was the inheritance given to him and his
descendants, and that he set out without knowing where he was
going.

It was equally by faith that Sarah, in spite of being past the
age, was made able to conceive, because she believed that he who
had made the promise would be faithful to it. Because of this,
there came from one man, and one who was already as good as
dead himself, more descendants than could be counted, as many
as the stars of heaven or the grains of sand on the seashore.

It was by faith that Abraham, when put to the test, offered up
Isaac. He offered to sacrifice his only son even though the
promises had been made to him and he had been told: It is
through Isaac that your name will be carried on. He was
confident that God had the power even to raise the dead; and so,
figuratively speaking, he was given back Isaac from the dead.

This is the word of the Lord.   *Hebrews 11:8. 11-12. 17-19*

Gospel Acclamation
     Alleluia, alleluia!
     At various times in the past
     and in various different ways,
     God spoke to our ancestors through the prophets;
     but in our own time, the last days,
     he has spoken to us through his Son.
     Alleluia!
                                       Heb 1:1-2

GOSPEL

We read from the holy Gospel according to Luke, chapter two.
*
| *When the day came for them to be purified as laid down by the

Law of Moses, the parents of Jesus took him up to Jerusalem to present him to the Lord* – observing what stands written in the law of the Lord: Every first-born male must be consecrated to the Lord – and also to offer in sacrifice, in accordance with what is said in the Law of the Lord, a pair of turtledoves or two young pigeons. Now in Jerusalem there was a man named Simeon. He was an upright and devout man; he looked forward to Israel's comforting and the Holy Spirit rested on him. It had been revealed to him by the Holy Spirit that he would not see death until he had set eyes on the Christ of the Lord. Prompted by the Spirit he came to the Temple; and when the parents brought in the child Jesus to do for him what the Law required, he took him into his arms and blessed God; and he said:

'Now, Master, you can let your servant go in peace,
just as you promised;
because my eyes have seen the salvation
which you have prepared for all the nations to see,
a light to enlighten the pagans
and the glory of your people Israel.'

As the child's father and mother stood there wondering at the things that were being said about him, Simeon blessed them and said to Mary his mother, 'You see this child: he is destined for the fall and for the rising of many in Israel, destined to be a sign that is rejected – and a sword will pierce your own soul too – so that the secret thoughts of many may be laid bare.'

There was a prophetess also, Anna, the daughter of Phanuel, of the tribe of Asher. She was well on in years. Her days of girlhood over, she had been married for seven years before becoming a widow. She was now eighty-four years old and never left the Temple, serving God night and day with fasting and prayer. She came by just at that moment and began to praise God; and she spoke of the child to all who looked forward to the deliverance of Jerusalem.

*When they had done everything the Law of the Lord required, they went back to Galilee, to their own town of Nazareth. Meanwhile the child grew to maturity, and he was filled with wisdom; and God's favour was with him

This is the Gospel of the Lord.*   *Luke 2:22-40*

*Shorter Form, verses 22. 39-40. Read between *.*

1 January: Octave of Christmas

Solemnity of Mary, Mother of God

See above, pp. 37.

Second Sunday after Christmas

See above, pp.40.

6 January (or Sunday between 2 January and 8 January)

The Epiphany of the Lord

See above, pp. 44.

Sunday after 6 January   First Sunday in Ordinary Time   Feast

The Baptism of the Lord   B

This feast is omitted when the Epiphany is celebrated on this Sunday.

Introduction to the Service

Today we celebrate the feast of our Lord's baptism in the river Jordan. We could also think of it as the feast of our Lord's baptism *and* confirmation.

Many of us remember the day when we were confirmed. Others in our community are preparing themselves for receiving this great sacrament of confirmation.

Baptism and confirmation belong together. This we can clearly see on the occasion when Jesus was baptised in the river Jordan. After John had baptised him, the Holy Spirit came down on Jesus and strengthened him.

Today, Jesus publicly began his mission. He was sent by the Father to overcome evil with good, to proclaim the will of God, to face jealousy, persecution and death. It was for this task that Jesus was strengthened at his baptism by the Holy Spirit.

This feast of our Lord's baptism, therefore, reminds us of our own baptism and confirmation.

Penitential Rite

Let us ask ourselves:

● In baptism God has accepted us as his beloved sons and daughters. Do we behave as God's children?   (*Silence*)

● We are called to stand up against evil and hatred as Christ did. Do we accept this task for which we were strengthened in the sacrament of confirmation?   (*Silence*)

We ask for forgiveness for forgetting the task which God gave us in the sacrament of baptism and confirmation.   **I confess**...

The First Reading, Psalm, Second Reading and Gospel Acclamation given for Year A, pp.47ff., may be used, with the Gospel given below. Or the alternative readings given below may be used.

FIRST READING

Today, Christ begins his work in public. Will he succeed or will he fail in his mission? Will he satisfy the deepest desires of our hearts?

We read from the prophet Isaiah, chapter fifty-five.
★
Oh, come to the water all you who are thirsty;
though you have no money, come!
Buy corn without money, and eat,
and, at no cost, wine and milk.
Why spend money on what is not bread,
your wages on what fails to satisfy?
Listen, listen to me, and you will have good things to eat
and rich food to enjoy.
Pay attention, come to me;
listen, and your soul will live.

With you I will make an everlasting covenant
out of the favours promised to David.
See, I have made of you a witness to the peoples,
a leader and a master of the nations.
See, you will summon a nation you never knew,
those unknown will come hurrying to you,
for the sake of the Lord your God,
of the Holy One of Israel who will glorify you.

Seek the Lord while he is still to be found,
call to him while he is still near.
Let the wicked man abandon his way,
the evil man his thoughts.
Let him turn back to the Lord who will take pity on him,
to our God who is rich in forgiving;
for my thoughts are not your thoughts,
my ways not your ways – it is the Lord who speaks.
Yes, the heavens are as high above earth
as my ways are above your ways,
my thoughts above your thoughts.

Yes, as the rain and the snow come down from the heavens and do not return without watering the earth, making it yield and giving growth to provide seed for the sower and bread for the eating, so the word that goes from my mouth does not return to me empty, without carrying out my will and succeeding in what it was sent to do.

This is the word of the Lord.   *Isaiah 55:1-11*

Responsorial Psalm
℟ **With joy you will draw water**
    from the wells of salvation.

1 Truly, God is my salvation,
   I trust, I shall not fear.
   For the Lord is my strength, my song,
   he became my saviour.
   With joy you will draw water
   from the wells of salvation. ℟

2 Give thanks to the Lord, give praise to his name!
   Make his mighty deeds known to the peoples!
   Declare the greatness of his name. ℟

3 Sing a psalm to the Lord
   for he has done glorious deeds,
   make them known to all the earth!
   People of Zion, sing and shout for joy
   for great in your midst is the Holy One of Israel. ℟

Is 12:2-6, ℟ v.3

SECOND READING

We read from the first letter of St John, chapter five.
*
Whoever believes that Jesus is the Christ
has been begotten by God;
and whoever loves the Father that begot him
loves the child whom he begets.
We can be sure that we love God's children
if we love God himself and do what he has commanded us;
this is what loving God is –
keeping his commandments;
and his commandments are not difficult,
because anyone who has been begotten by God
has already overcome the world;
this is the victory over the world –
our faith.
Who can overcome the world?
Only the man who believes that Jesus is the Son of God:
Jesus Christ who came by water and blood,
not with water only,
but with water and blood;
with the Spirit as another witness –

since the Spirit is the truth –
so that there are three witnesses,
the Spirit, the water and the blood,
and all three of them agree.
We accept the testimony of human witnesses,
but God's testimony is much greater,
and this is God's testimony,
given as evidence for his Son.

This is the word of the Lord   *1 John 5:1-9*

Gospel Acclamation
   Alleluia, alleluia!
   John saw Jesus coming towards him, and said:
   This is the Lamb of God who takes away the sin of the
      world.
   Alleluia!
                                                cf. Jn 1:29

GOSPEL
We read from the holy Gospel according to Mark, chapter one.
*
In the course of his preaching John the Baptist said, 'Someone is
following me, someone who is more powerful than I am, and I
am not fit to kneel down and undo the strap of his sandals. I have
baptised you with water, but he will baptise you with the Holy
Spirit.'

   It was at this time that Jesus came from Nazareth in Galilee
and was baptised in the Jordan by John. No sooner had he come
up out of the water than he saw the heavens torn apart and the
Spirit, like a dove, descending on him. And a voice came from
heaven, 'You are my Son, the Beloved; my favour rests on you.'

This is the Gospel of the Lord.   *Mark 1:7-11*

THE SEASON OF LENT

Ash Wednesday

See above, pp. 51.

First Sunday of Lent   B

Introduction to the Service

Last Wednesday, Ash Wednesday, we solemnly began the period of Lent. We blessed the ashes and placed them on our heads. (*For those who could not attend on Wednesday, this can also be done today, the first Sunday of Lent.*)

The forty days of Lent are a time of self-control and training. With Christ, we want to train ourselves in our battle against evil.

Every sportsman who wants to win a prize must train and exercise self-control. He must not eat and drink too much, he must avoid alcohol and smoking and take exercise every day. Training and self-control give us a chance to win the prize.

Christ did the same. For forty days he remained in the wilderness, doing without those things which make life comfortable. In the desert he prepared himself for the great task which lay ahead of him.

Penitential Rite

Let us ask ourselves:

● Am I willing to make this time of Lent a time of self-control and self-discipline?   (*Silence*)

● Is there anything wrong in my life which I need to change?   (*Silence*)

● Can I save money for the poor by denying myself some comfort or luxury?   (*Silence*)

   I confess...

FIRST READING

During Lent we want to renew the commitment we made in baptism. Our reading today reminds us very closely of what happened to us in baptism.

In baptism we are saved through water, like Noah in the ark, and we begin a new life after being saved. In baptism God makes a covenant or love-pact with us as he did with Noah after the great flood. Lent is the time to renew this covenant we made with God.

We read from the book of Genesis, chapter nine.

God spoke to Noah and his sons, 'See, I establish my Covenant with you, and with your descendants after you; also with every living creature to be found with you, birds, cattle and every wild beast with you: everything that came out of the ark, everything that lives on the earth. I establish my Covenant with you: no thing of flesh shall be swept away again by the waters of the flood. There shall be no flood to destroy the earth again.'

God said, 'Here is the sign of the Covenant I make between myself and you and every living creature with you for all generations: I set my bow in the clouds and it shall be a sign of the Covenant between me and the earth. When I gather the clouds over the earth and the bow appears in the clouds, I will recall the Covenant between myself and you and every living creature of every kind. And so the waters shall never again become a flood to destroy all things of flesh.'

This is the word of the Lord.   *Genesis 9:8-15*

Responsorial Psalm
℟ **Your ways, Lord, are faithfulness and love**
   for those who keep your covenant.

1 Lord, make me know your ways.
   Lord, teach me your paths.
   Make me walk in your truth, and teach me:
   for you are God my saviour. ℟

2 Remember your mercy, Lord,
   and the love you have shown from of old.
   In your love remember me,
   because of your goodness, O Lord. ℟

3 The Lord is good and upright.
   He shows the path to those who stray,
   he guides the humble in the right path;
   he teaches his way to the poor. ℟   *Ps 24:4-9. ℟ cf. v.10*

SECOND READING

We read from the first letter of St Peter, chapter three.

Christ himself, innocent though he was, died once for sins, died for the guilty, to lead us to God. In the body he was put to death, in the spirit he was raised to life, and, in the spirit, he went to preach to the spirits in prison. Now it was long ago, when Noah was still building that ark which saved only a small group of eight people 'by water', and when God was still waiting patiently, that these spirits refused to believe. That water is a type of the baptism which saves you now, and which is not the washing off of physical dirt but a pledge made to God from a good conscience, through the resurrection of Jesus Christ, who has entered heaven and is at God's right hand, now that he has made the angels of the Dominations and Powers his subjects.

This is the word of the Lord.   *1 Peter 3:18-22*

Gospel Acclamation
Praise to you, O Christ, king of eternal glory!
Man does not live on bread alone,
but on every word that comes from the mouth of God.
Praise to you, O Christ, king of eternal glory!   *Mt 4:4*

GOSPEL
We read from the holy Gospel according to Mark, chapter one.
*
The Spirit drove Jesus out into the wilderness and he remained there for forty days, and was tempted by Satan. He was with the wild beasts, and the angels looked after him.

After John had been arrested, Jesus went into Galilee. There he proclaimed the Good News from God. 'The time has come' he said 'and the kingdom of God is close at hand. Repent, and believe the Good News.'

This is the Gospel of the Lord.   *Mark 1:12-15*

Second Sunday of Lent   B

Introduction to the Service
Today, on the second Sunday of Lent, we are invited by the Lord to climb the mountain of God with him. On this mountain, Jesus' disciples saw him transfigured. They had never seen Jesus like that before.

All of us have experienced God in one form or another. But did we ever come very close to him? Did we ever experience the power and joy of his presence? Did we ever want to stay with God, as did the three disciples on the mountain?

Perhaps, many of us have not yet experienced God in such a manner. We all, however, have the chance to experience God in a new and deeper way.

This is exactly what we want to do during this time of Lent. We are invited by the Lord to make a special effort to find God. We are invited to climb the mountain of God, together with Christ, making a special effort to come closer to God and to experience him in a new and deeper way.

Penitential Rite
Let us examine our conscience:

● Do I accept the invitation to make a special effort to find God during this time of Lent? (*Silence*)

● Is there anything in my life which hinders me in my effort to come closer to God? (*Silence*)

Let us ask for forgiveness, for finding it so hard to make a special effort to find God during this time of Lent. **I confess**...

FIRST READING
In our reading we meet a man who made an extraordinary effort to do God's will. He was prepared to give away the greatest treasure he had.

What are we prepared to give away in the name of God?

We read from the book of Genesis, chapter twenty-two.
*
God put Abraham to the test. 'Abraham, Abraham' he called. 'Here I am' he replied. 'Take your son,' God said 'your only child Isaac, whom you love, and go to the land of Moriah. There you shall offer him as a burnt offering, on a mountain I will point out to you.'

When they arrived at the place God had pointed out to him, Abraham built an altar there and arranged the wood. Then he stretched out his hand and seized the knife to kill his son.

But the angel of the Lord called to him from heaven. 'Abraham, Abraham' he said. 'I am here' he replied. 'Do not raise your hand against the boy' the angel said. 'Do not harm him, for now I know you fear God. You have not refused me your son, your only son.' Then looking up, Abraham saw a ram caught by its horns in a bush. Abraham took the ram and offered it as a burnt-offering in place of his son.

The angel of the Lord called Abraham a second time from heaven. 'I swear by my own self – it is the Lord who speaks – because you have done this, because you have not refused me your son, your only son, I will shower blessings on you, I will make your descendants as many as the stars of heaven and the grains of sand on the seashore. Your descendants shall gain possession of the gates of their enemies. All the nations of the earth shall bless themselves by your descendants, as a reward for your obedience.'

This is the word of the Lord.   *Genesis 22:1-2. 9-13. 15-18*

Responsorial Psalm
R̸   **I will walk in the presence of the Lord**
     in the land of the living.

1   I trusted, even when I said:
    'I am sorely afflicted.'
    O precious in the eyes of the Lord
    is the death of his faithful.   R̸

2   Your servant, Lord, your servant am I;
    you have loosened my bonds.
    A thanksgiving sacrifice I make:
    I will call on the Lord's name.   R̸

3   My vows to the Lord I will fulfil
    before all his people,
    in the courts of the house of the Lord,
    in your midst, O Jerusalem.   R̸   *Ps 115:10. 15-19. R̸ Ps 114:9*

SECOND READING
We read from the letter of St Paul to the Romans, chapter eight.
*
With God on our side who can be against us? Since God did not spare his own Son, but gave him up to benefit us all, we may be certain, after such a gift, that he will not refuse anything he can give. Could anyone accuse those that God has chosen? When God acquits, could anyone condemn? Could Christ Jesus? No! He not only died for us – he rose from the dead, and there at God's right hand he stands and pleads for us.

This is the word of the Lord.   *Romans 8:31-34*

Gospel Acclamation
    Glory and praise to you, O Christ!
    From the bright cloud the Father's voice was heard:
    'This is my Son, the Beloved. Listen to him!'
    Glory and praise to you, O Christ!   *Mt 17:5*

GOSPEL
We read from the holy Gospel according to Mark, chapter nine.
*
Jesus took with him Peter and James and John and led them up a high mountain where they could be alone by themselves. There in their presence he was transfigured: his clothes became dazz-

lingly white, whiter than any earthly bleacher could make them. Elijah appeared to them with Moses; and they were talking with Jesus. Then Peter spoke to Jesus. 'Rabbi', he said 'it is wonderful for us to be here; so let us make three tents, one for you, one for Moses and one for Elijah.' He did not know what to say; they were so frightened. And a cloud came, covering them in shadow; and there came a voice from the cloud, 'This is my Son, the Beloved. Listen to him.' Then suddenly, when they looked round, they saw no one with them any more but only Jesus.

As they came down the mountain he warned them to tell no one what they had seen, until after the Son of Man had risen from the dead. They observed the warning faithfully, though among themselves they discussed what 'rising from the dead' could mean.

This is the Gospel of the Lord.   *Mark 9:2-10*

Third Sunday of Lent   B

Introduction to the Service

Today, on the third Sunday of Lent, we meet Christ in the Temple. He is doing strange things there and the Jews are scandalised. Perhaps, we too, would have been scandalised.

How would we react if Christ were to come to our church services, social occasions or committee meetings saying, in quite a loud voice: 'Why do you turn my father's house into a market place?'

Penitential Rite

We ask ourselves:

● How much time do we spend in our meetings talking only about money and 'business'?   (*Silence*)

● How much time do we spend in our meetings praying and sharing the Gospel?   (*Silence*)

● Is our heart like a market place, full of worries and anxieties? Is there any place left for God?   (*Silence*)

Let us ask God's forgiveness for what we have done wrong. **I confess**...

FIRST READING

During this time of Lent the catechumens – people in the early

Church preparing for Baptism — were taught about the way in which Christians live.

Therefore, on this Sunday, the Ten Commandments were proclaimed. Our reading presents them like a freedom charter. God reminds his people: 'I have freed you from the slavery of Egypt. Continue on this way of freedom and keep my commandments'.

We read from the book of Exodus, chapter twenty.

*God spoke all these words. He said, 'I am the Lord your God who brought you out of the land of Egypt, out of the house of slavery.

'You shall have no gods except me.*

'You shall not make yourself a carved image or any likeness of anything in heaven or on earth beneath or in the waters under the earth; you shall not bow down to them or serve them. For I, the Lord your God, am a jealous God and I punish the father's fault in the sons, the grandsons, and the great-grandsons of those who hate me; but I show kindness to thousands of those who love me and keep my commandments.

'You shall not utter the name of the Lord your God to misuse it, for the Lord will not leave unpunished the man who utters his name to misuse it.

'Remember the sabbath day and keep it holy. For six days you shall labour and do all your work, but the seventh day is a sabbath for the Lord your God. You shall do no work that day, neither you nor your son nor your daughter nor your servants, men or women, nor your animals nor the stranger who lives with you. For in six days the Lord made the heavens and the earth and the sea and all that these hold, but on the seventh day he rested; that is why the Lord has blessed the sabbath day and made it sacred.

*'Honour your father and your mother so that you may have a long life in the land that the Lord your God has given to you.

'You shall not kill.

'You shall not commit adultery.

'You shall not steal.

'You shall not bear false witness against your neighbour.

'You shall not covet your neighbour's house. You shall not covet your neighbour's wife, or his servant, man or woman, or his ox, or his donkey, or anything that is his.'

This is the word of the Lord.*   *Exodus 20:1-17*

*Shorter Form, verses 1-3. 7-8. 12-17. Read between *.*

Responsorial Psalm
℞   **You, Lord, have the message of eternal life.**

1   The law of the Lord is perfect,
     it revives the soul.
     The rule of the Lord is to be trusted,
     it gives wisdom to the simple.   ℞

2   The precepts of the Lord are right,
     they gladden the heart.
     The command of the Lord is clear,
     it gives light to the eyes.   ℞

3   The fear of the Lord is holy,
     abiding for ever.
     The decrees of the Lord are truth
     and all of them just.   ℞

4   They are more to be desired than gold,
     than the purest of gold
     and sweeter are they than honey,
     than honey from the comb.   ℞   *Ps 18:8-11.* ℞ *Jn 6:68*

SECOND READING

We read from the first letter of St Paul to the Corinthians, chapter one.
*
While the Jews demand miracles and the Greeks look for wisdom, here are we preaching a crucified Christ; to the Jews an obstacle that they cannot get over, to the pagans madness, but to those who have been called, whether they are Jews or Greeks, a Christ who is the power and the wisdom of God. For God's foolishness is wiser than human wisdom, and God's weakness is stronger than human strength.

   This is the word of the Lord.   *1 Corinthians 1:22-25*

Gospel Acclamation
     Praise to you, O Christ, king of eternal glory!
     I am the resurrection and the life, says the Lord,
     whoever believes in me will never die.
     Praise to you, O Christ, king of eternal glory!   *Jn 11:25. 26*

or

     Praise to you, O Christ, king of eternal glory!
     God loved the world so much that he gave his only Son;
     everyone who believes in him has eternal life.
     Praise to you, O Christ, king of eternal glory!   *Jn 3:16*

GOSPEL

We read from the holy Gospel according to John, chapter two.

*

Just before the Jewish Passover Jesus went up to Jerusalem, and in the Temple he found people selling cattle and sheep and pigeons, and the money changers sitting at their counters there. Making a whip out of some cord, he drove them all out of the Temple, cattle and sheep as well, scattered the money changers' coins, knocked their tables over and said to the pigeon-sellers, 'Take all this out of here and stop turning my Father's house into a market.' Then his disciples remembered the words of scripture: Zeal for your house will devour me. The Jews intervened and said, 'What sign can you show us to justify what you have done?' Jesus answered, 'Destroy this sanctuary, and in three days I will raise it up.' The Jews replied, 'It has taken forty-six years to build this sanctuary: are you going to raise it up in three days?' But he was speaking of the sanctuary that was his body, and when Jesus rose from the dead, his disciples remembered that he had said this, and they believed the scripture and the words he had said.

During his stay in Jerusalem for the Passover many believed in his name when they saw the signs that he gave, but Jesus knew them all and did not trust himself to them; he never needed evidence about any man; he could tell what a man had in him.

This is the Gospel of the Lord.   *John 2:13-25*

Fourth Sunday of Lent   B

Introduction to the Service

The Sundays of Lent help us to prepare ourselves for celebrating Easter with deeper understanding.

Today, for instance, we hear the message of God's boundless generosity. We listen to the conversation between Jesus and Nicodemus. There we hear the words: 'God loved the world so much that he gave his only Son.'

This message of boundless generosity should not be taken for granted. For example, we know that we cannot take it for granted that all parents love their children. Many do not! Similarly we just cannot assume that our best friends would die for us if need should arise. And yet! God does.

What we shall experience at Easter is exactly that: God loves the world so much that he gave his only Son. Even if we crucify him, Christ will keep on loving us and inviting us to believe in him.

Penitential Rite

Let us examine our conscience:

● Do we appreciate the many good things people do for us at home, in shops and offices? (*Silence*)

● Do we appreciate that we are loved by God even though we do not deserve it? (*Silence*)

Let us ask for forgiveness for our thoughtlessness and ingratitude. **I confess**...

FIRST READING

Our reading is an example of God's boundless generosity.

The people of God, even their priests, had become unfaithful to the God of Israel. They ignored all God's warnings and so, to make them listen, God destroyed their Temple and they were led away, as slaves, into captivity.

Will God abandon his people for ever? In the reading we hear of the political leaders whom God uses to show his generosity.

We read from the second book of Chronicles, chapter thirty-six.
*

All the heads of the priesthood, and the people too, added infidelity to infidelity, copying all the shameful practices of the nations and defiling the Temple that the Lord had consecrated for himself in Jerusalem. The Lord, the God of their ancestors, tirelessly sent them messenger after messenger, since he wished to spare his people and his house. But they ridiculed the messengers of God, they despised his words, they laughed at his prophets, until at last the wrath of the Lord rose so high against his people that there was no further remedy.

Their enemies burned down the Temple of God, demolished the walls of Jerusalem, set fire to all its palaces, and destroyed everything of value in it. The survivors were deported by Nebuchadnezzar to Babylon; they were to serve him and his sons until the kingdom of Persia came to power. This is how the word of the Lord was fulfilled that he spoke through Jeremiah, 'Until this land has enjoyed its sabbath rest, until seventy years have gone by, it will keep sabbath throughout the days of its desolation.'

And in the first year of Cyrus king of Persia, to fulfil the word of the Lord that was spoken through Jeremiah, the Lord roused the spirit of Cyrus king of Persia to issue a proclamation and to have it publicly displayed throughout his kingdom: 'Thus speaks Cyrus king of Persia, "The Lord, the God of heaven, has given me all the kingdoms of the earth; he has ordered me to build him a Temple in Jerusalem, in Judah. Whoever there is among you of all his people, may his God be with him! Let him go up." '

This is the word of the Lord.   *2 Chronicles 36:14-16. 19-23*

Responsorial Psalm

℟   **O let my tongue
       cleave to my mouth
       if I remember you not!**

1   By the rivers of Babylon
     there we sat and wept,
     remembering Zion;
     on the poplars that grew there
     we hung up our harps.   ℟

2   For it was there that they asked us,
     our captors, for songs,
     our oppressors, for joy.
     'Sing to us,' they said,
     'one of Zion's songs.'   ℟

3   O how could we sing
     the song of the Lord
     on alien soil?
     If I forget you, Jerusalem,
     let my right hand wither!   ℟

4   O let my tongue
     cleave to my mouth
     if I remember you not,
     if I prize not Jerusalem
     above all my joys!   ℟   *Ps 136:1-6. ℟ v.6*

SECOND READING

We read from the letter of St Paul to the Ephesians, chapter two.
*
God loved us with so much love that he was generous with his mercy: when we were dead through our sins, he brought us to life with Christ – it is through grace that you have been saved – and raised us up with him and gave us a place with him in heaven, in Christ Jesus.

This was to show for all ages to come, through his goodness towards us in Christ Jesus, how infinitely rich he is in grace. Because it is by grace that you have been saved, through faith; not by anything of your own, but by a gift from God; not by

anything that you have done, so that nobody can claim the credit.
We are God's work of art, created in Christ Jesus to live the good
life as from the beginning he had meant us to live it.

This is the word of the Lord. *Ephesians 2:4-10*

Gospel Acclamation
Glory and praise to you, O Christ!
God loved the world so much that he gave his only Son;
everyone who believes in him has eternal life.
Glory and praise to you, O Christ! *Jn 3:16*

GOSPEL

We read from the holy Gospel according to John, chapter three.
*
Jesus said to Nicodemus:

'The Son of Man must be lifted up
as Moses lifted up the serpent in the desert,
so that everyone who believes may have eternal life in him.
Yes, God loved the world so much
that he gave his only Son,
so that everyone who believes in him may not be lost
but may have eternal life.
For God sent his Son into the world
not to condemn the world,
but so that through him the world might be saved.
No one who believes in him will be condemned;
but whoever refuses to believe is condemned already,
because he has refused to believe
in the name of God's only Son.
On these grounds is sentence pronounced:
that though the light has come into the world
men have shown they prefer
darkness to the light
because their deeds were evil.
And indeed, everybody who does wrong
hates the light and avoids it,
for fear his actions should be exposed;
but the man who lives by the truth
comes out into the light,
so that it may be plainly seen that what he does is done in
    God.'

This is the Gospel of the Lord. *John 3:14-21*

Fifth Sunday of Lent   B

Introduction to the Service

Today is already the fifth Sunday of Lent. The message we hear this Sunday will again help us to prepare ourselves for Easter. It will help us to understand more clearly what Christ did for us at Easter.

In the Gospel reading we will hear of some Greeks who wanted to see Jesus. This was extraordinary. Greeks were not of the same race as the Jews; they were regarded as strangers and heathens. But Jesus rejoiced.

In his spirit he saw himself dying on the cross, all races and nations assembled around the cross. Therefore he said: 'When I am lifted up from the earth – I shall draw all people to myself.' Jesus wanted to die for all races and nations and to bind them to himself with bonds of love.

Penitential Rite

Let us come to the cross of Jesus and ask for forgiveness:

● Lord Jesus, here we are. We are your people. We have different names and come from different families. Draw us to yourself.   (*Silence*)
    Lord, have mercy...

● Lord Jesus, how often you have wanted to draw us to yourself. We, however, refused.   (*Silence*)
    Christ, have mercy...

● Lord Jesus, we easily reject people of other races and nations. Forgive us and draw all of us to yourself.   (*Silence*)
    Lord, have mercy...

FIRST READING

In our reading we hear of a new covenant, and new 'love-pact' which God is going to make between himself and his people. While we listen to this reading we can imagine Christ on the cross, drawing all people to himself, making this 'love-pact' between himself and all nations and races.

We read from the book of Jeremiah, chapter thirty-one.
*
See, the days are coming – it is the Lord who speaks – when I will make a new covenant with the House of Israel and the House of Judah, but not a covenant like the one I made with their ancestors on the day I took them by the hand to bring them out of the land

of Egypt. They broke that covenant of mine, so I had to show them who was master. It is the Lord who speaks. No, this is the covenant I will make with the House of Israel when those days arrive – it is the Lord who speaks. Deep within them I will plant my Law, writing it on their hearts. Then I will be their God and they shall be my people. There will be no further need for neighbour to try to teach neighbour, or brother to say to brother, 'Learn to know the Lord!' No, they will all know me, the least no less than the greatest – it is the Lord who speaks – since I will forgive their iniquity and never call their sin to mind.

This is the word of the Lord. *Jeremiah 31:31-34*

Responsorial Psalm
℟ **A pure heart create for me, O God.**

1 Have mercy on me, God, in your kindness.
   In your compassion blot out my offence.
   O wash me more and more from my guilt
   and cleanse me from my sin. ℟

2 A pure heart create for me, O God,
   put a steadfast spirit within me.
   Do not cast me away from your presence,
   nor deprive me of your holy spirit. ℟

3 Give me again the joy of your help;
   with a spirit of fervour sustain me,
   that I may teach transgressors your ways
   and sinners may return to you. ℟ *Ps 50:3-4. 12-15. ℟ v.12*

SECOND READING
We read from the letter to the Hebrews, chapter five.
*
During his life on earth, Christ offered up prayer and entreaty, aloud and in silent tears, to the one who had the power to save him out of death, and he submitted so humbly that his prayer was heard. Although he was Son, he learnt to obey through suffering; but having been made perfect, he became for all who obey him the source of eternal salvation.

This is the word of the Lord. *Hebrews 5:7-9*

Gospel Acclamation
Glory to you, O Christ, you are the Word of God!
If a man serves me, says the Lord, he must follow me;

wherever I am, my servant will be there too.
Glory to you, O Christ, you are the Word of God!   *Jn 12:26*

GOSPEL

We read from the holy Gospel according to John, chapter twelve.

Among those who went up to worship at the festival were some
Greeks. These approached Philip, who came from Bethsaida in
Galilee, and put this request to him, 'Sir, we should like to see
Jesus.' Philip went to tell Andrew, and Andrew and Philip
together went to tell Jesus. Jesus replied to them:

'Now the hour has come
for the Son of Man to be glorified.
I tell you, most solemnly,
unless a wheat grain falls on the ground and dies,
it remains only a single grain;
but if it dies,
it yields a rich harvest.
Anyone who loves his life loses it;
anyone who hates his life in this world
will keep it for the eternal life.
If a man serves me, he must follow me,
wherever I am, my servant will be there too.
If anyone serves me, my Father will honour him.
Now my soul is troubled.
What shall I say:
Father, save me from this hour?
But it was for this very reason that I have come to this hour.
Father, glorify your name!'

A voice came from heaven, 'I have glorified it, and I will
glorify it again.'
People standing by, who heard this, said it was a clap of
thunder; others said, 'It was an angel speaking to him.' Jesus
answered, 'It was not for my sake that this voice came, but for
yours.

'Now sentence is being passed on this world;
now the prince of this world is to be overthrown.
And when I am lifted up from the earth,
I shall draw all men to myself.'

By these words he indicated the kind of death he would die.

This is the Gospel of the Lord.   *John 12:20-30*

HOLY WEEK

Passion Sunday (Palm Sunday)
See above, pp. 74.

THE EASTER TRIDUUM

Holy Thursday
(*Mass of the Lord's Supper*)

See above, pp. 103.

Good Friday
(*Celebration of the Lord's Passion*)

See above, pp. 107.

The Easter Vigil
See above, pp. 116.

Easter Day
See above, pp. 135.

THE SEASON OF EASTER

Second Sunday of Easter B

Introduction to the Service

Today is the second Sunday of Easter. We are assembled together in the same way as the Apostles were assembled, eight days after the resurrection of the Lord.

The Apostles closed the doors for fear of the Jews. Do we close our hearts because we have little faith? Even if we have doubts like Thomas, let us invite the Lord in with an open heart. We invite him to come into our midst, we ask him to breathe over us and to bring us his peace.

In our celebration today we shall hear the message: 'Happy are those who have not seen and yet believe'.

Penitential Rite

Let us ask ourselves:

- Do I believe the message that Christ is risen?   (*Silence*)

- Do I allow the risen Lord to breathe over me and inspire me with his word and spirit?   (*Silence*)

Let us ask God's forgiveness for our unbelief.   **I confess**...

FIRST READING

In our reading we hear of the early Church community and how they lived together after the resurrection of Christ. It is in such communities that people today still experience the presence of the risen Lord.

We read from the Acts of the Apostles, chapter four.
*
The whole group of believers was united, heart and soul; no one claimed for his own use anything that he had, as everything they owned was held in common.

The apostles continued to testify to the resurrection of the Lord Jesus with great power, and they were all given great respect.

None of their members was ever in want, as all those who owned land or houses would sell them, and bring the money from them, to present it to the apostles; it was then distributed to any members who might be in need.

This is the word of the Lord.   *Acts 4:32-35*

Responsorial Psalm

℟ **Give thanks to the Lord for he is good,
    for his love has no end.**

or

℟ **Alleluia, alleluia, alleluia!**

1 Let the sons of Israel say:
   'His love has no end.'
   Let the sons of Aaron say:
   'His love has no end.'
   Let those who fear the Lord say:
   'His love has no end.'   ℟

2 The Lord's right hand has triumphed;
   his right hand raised me up.
   I shall not die, I shall live
   and recount his deeds.
   I was punished, I was punished by the Lord,
   but not doomed to die.   ℟

3 The stone which the builders rejected
   has become the corner stone.
   This is the work of the Lord,
   a marvel in our eyes.
   This day was made by the Lord;
   we rejoice and are glad.   ℟   *Ps 117:2-4. 15-18. 22-24. ℟ v.1*

SECOND READING

We read from the first letter of St John, chapter five.
*
Whoever believes that Jesus is the Christ
has been begotten by God;
and whoever loves the Father that begot him
loves the child whom he begets.
We can be sure that we love God's children
if we love God himself and do what he has commanded us;
this is what loving God is –
keeping his commandments;
and his commandments are not difficult,
because anyone who has been begotten by God
has already overcome the world;
this is the victory over the world –
our faith.
Who can overcome the world?

only the man who believes that Jesus is the Son of God;
Jesus Christ who came by water and blood,
not with water only,
but with water and blood;
with the Spirit as another witness –
since the Spirit is the truth.

This is the word of the Lord.   *1 John 5:1-6*

Gospel Acclamation
Alleluia, alleluia!
Jesus said: 'You believe because you can see me.
Happy are those who have not seen and yet believe.'
Alleluia!   *Jn 20:29*

GOSPEL
We read from the holy Gospel according to John, chapter twenty.
*
In the evening of that same day, the first day of the week, the
doors were closed in the room where the disciples were, for fear
of the Jews. Jesus came and stood among them. He said to them,
'Peace be with you,' and showed them his hands and his side.
The disciples were filled with joy when they saw the Lord, and he
said to them again, 'Peace be with you.

'As the Father sent me,
so am I sending you,'

After saying this he breathed on them and said:

'Receive the Holy Spirit.
For those whose sins you forgive,
they are forgiven;
for those whose sins you retain,
they are retained.'

Thomas, called the Twin, who was one of the Twelve, was not
with them when Jesus came. When the disciples said, 'We have
seen the Lord,' he answered, 'Unless I see the holes that the nails
made in his hands and can put my finger into the holes they
made, and unless I can put my hand into his side, I refuse to
believe.' Eight days later the disciples were in the house again
and Thomas was with them. The doors were closed, but Jesus
came in and stood among them. 'Peace be with you,' he said.
Then he spoke to Thomas, 'Put your finger here; look, here are

my hands. Give me your hand; put it into my side. Doubt no longer but believe.' Thomas replied, 'My Lord and my God!' Jesus said to him:

'You believe because you can see me.
Happy are those who have not seen and yet believe.'

There were many other signs that Jesus worked and the disciples saw, but they are not recorded in this book. These are recorded so that you may believe that Jesus is the Christ, the Son of God, and that believing this you may have life through his name.

This is the Gospel of the Lord. *John 20:19-31*

Third Sunday of Easter B

Introduction to the Service

During the last week we have talked to many people at home, on the road, in shops etc. Some of these people listened carefully to us and understood us. Others, however, closed up. They did not understand us. Perhaps they did not want to understand us: they closed their hearts and minds and refused to listen to us.

What about ourselves as we stand here before God. Perhaps our eyes are closed so that we cannot recognise the risen Lord among us. Perhaps our ears are closed, so that we cannot listen to God's Word.

Penitential Rite

Let us ask God in this celebration to open our hearts and minds that we may recognise Jesus in our midst: (*Silence*)

● For closing our eyes and not seeing the great deeds which God has done for us.
   Lord, have mercy...

● For closing our ears and not listening to God's message of joy.
   Christ, have mercy...

● For closing our hearts when Jesus wanted to reveal himself to us.
   Lord, have mercy...

FIRST READING

When somebody dies, we see what is happening, and yet we do not really understand what death means. But we are totally lost when we hear about resurrection. What does it mean?

The Apostles, too, were asked this question. Today we hear Peter giving an unusual explanation when he says that in the resurrection of Jesus, the Father 'glorified' Jesus.

We read from the Acts of the Apostles, chapter three.

*
Peter said to the people: 'You are Israelites, and it is the God of Abraham, Isaac and Jacob, the God of our ancestors, who has glorified his servant Jesus, the same Jesus you handed over and then disowned in the presence of Pilate, after Pilate had decided to release him. It was you who accused the Holy One, the Just One, you who demanded the reprieve of a murderer while you killed the prince of life. God, however, raised him from the dead, and to that fact we are the witnesses.

'Now I know, brothers, that neither you nor your leaders had any idea what you were really doing; this was the way God carried out what he had foretold, when he said through all his prophets that his Christ would suffer. Now you must repent and turn to God, so that your sins may be wiped out.'

This is the word of the Lord.   *Acts 3:13-15. 17-19*

Responsorial Psalm
   ℟   **Lift up the light of your face on us, O Lord.**

or

   ℟   **Alleluia!**

1   When I call, answer me, O God of justice;
     from anguish you released me, have mercy and hear me!   ℟

2   It is the Lord who grants favours to those whom he loves;
     the Lord hears me whenever I call him.   ℟

3   'What can bring us happiness?' many say.
     Lift up the light of your face on us, O Lord.   ℟

4   I will lie down in peace and sleep comes at once,
     for you alone, Lord, make me dwell in safety.   ℟
                                        Ps 4:2. 4. 7. 9. ℟ v.7

SECOND READING
We read from the first letter of St John, chapter two.
*

I am writing this, my children,
to stop you sinning;
but if anyone should sin,
we have our advocate with the Father,
Jesus Christ, who is just;
he is the sacrifice that takes our sins away,
and not only ours,
but the whole world's.
We can be sure that we know God
only by keeping his commandments.
Anyone who says, 'I know him',
and does not keep his commandments,
is a liar,
refusing to admit the truth.
But when anyone does obey what he has said,
God's love comes to perfection in him.

  This is the word of the Lord.   *1 John 2:1-5*

Gospel Acclamation
 Alleluia, alleluia!
 Lord Jesus, explain the scriptures to us.
 Make our hearts burn within us as you talk to us.
 Alleluia!
               cf. Lk 24:32

GOSPEL
We read from the holy Gospel according to Luke, chapter twenty-four.
*

The disciples told their story of what had happened on the road and how they had recognised Jesus at the breaking of bread.

 They were still talking about this when Jesus himself stood among them and said to them, 'Peace be with you!' In a state of alarm and fright, they thought they were seeing a ghost. But he said, 'Why are you so agitated, and why are these doubts rising in your hearts? Look at my hands and feet; yes, it is I indeed. Touch me and see for yourselves; a ghost has no flesh and bones as you can see I have.' And as he said this he showed them his hands and feet. Their joy was so great that they could not believe it, and they stood dumbfounded; so he said to them, 'Have you anything here to eat?' And they offered him a piece of grilled fish, which he took and ate before their eyes.

Then he told them, 'This is what I meant when I said, while I was still with you, that everything written about me in the Law of Moses, in the Prophets and in the Psalms, has to be fulfilled.' He then opened their minds to understand the scriptures, and he said to them, 'So you see how it is written that the Christ would suffer and on the third day rise from the dead, and that, in his name, repentance for the forgiveness of sins would be preached to all the nations, beginning from Jerusalem. You are witnesses to this.'

This is the Gospel of the Lord.   *Luke 24:35-48*

Fourth Sunday of Easter   B

Introduction to the Service
In the past chiefs and kings were called 'shepherds' of their people. They were expected to keep their people together and even to die for them in battle.

Today, Jesus calls himself the 'Good Shepherd'. We have come here to church because we have heard his call. He wants to gather us around him and keep us together.

Penitential Rite
Let us ask ourselves:

- Did we come to church to 'attend a service' or to meet the living Christ among us?   (*Silence*)

- Last week, did we do things in our own name or did we allow the power of Jesus to work in us?   (*Silence*)

- If we have authority over people – whether in an office or a factory or a school – did we behave like big bosses or did we treat people the way the Good Shepherd has shown us?   (*Silence*)

We present ourselves into the merciful hands of God.
I confess...

FIRST READING
When a shepherd dies, his work among the flock is ended. Not so with Christ.

Peter explains to the Jews and to us how the risen Christ continues his work of healing among us.

We read from the Acts of the Apostles, chapter four.

*

Filled with the Holy Spirit, Peter said: 'Rulers of the people, and elders! If you are questioning us today about an act of kindness to a cripple, and asking us how he was healed, then I am glad to tell you all, and would indeed be glad to tell the whole people of Israel, that it was by the name of Jesus Christ the Nazarene, the one you crucified, whom God raised from the dead, by this name and by no other that this man is able to stand up perfectly healthy, here in your presence today. This is the stone rejected by you the builders, but which has proved to be the keystone. For of all the names in the world given to men, this is the only one by which we can be saved.'

This is the word of the Lord. *Acts 4:8-12*

Responsorial Psalm

℞ **The stone which the builders rejected has become the corner stone.**

or

℞ **Alleluia!**

1 Give thanks to the Lord for he is good,
for his love has no end.
It is better to take refuge in the Lord
than to trust in men:
it is better to take refuge in the Lord
than to trust in princes. ℞

2 I will thank you for you have given answer
and you are my saviour.
The stone which the builders rejected
has become the corner stone.
This is the work of the Lord,
a marvel in our eyes. ℞

3 Blessed in the name of the Lord
is he who comes.
We bless you from the house of the Lord;
I will thank you for you have given answer
and you are my saviour.
Give thanks to the Lord for he is good;
for his love has no end. ℞

Ps 117:1. 8-9. 21-23. 26. 28-29. ℞ v.22

SECOND READING

We read from the first letter of St John, chapter three.
*

Think of the love that the Father has lavished on us,
by letting us be called God's children;
and that is what we are.
Because the world refused to acknowledge him,
therefore it does not acknowledge us.
My dear people, we are already the children of God
but what we are to be in the future has not yet been revealed;
all we know is, that when it is revealed
we shall be like him
because we shall see him as he really is.

This is the word of the Lord.   *1 John 3:1-2*

Gospel Acclamation

Alleluia, alleluia!
I am the good shepherd, says the Lord;
I know my own sheep and my own know me.
Alleluia!   *Jn 10:14*

GOSPEL

We read from the holy Gospel according to John, chapter ten.
*

Jesus said:

'I am the good shepherd:
the good shepherd is one who lays down his life for his
    sheep.
The hired man, since he is not the shepherd
and the sheep do not belong to him,
abandons the sheep and runs away
as soon as he sees a wolf coming,
and then the wolf attacks and scatters the sheep;
this is because he is only a hired man
and has no concern for the sheep.
I am the good shepherd;
I know my own
and my own know me,
just as the Father knows me
and I know the Father;
and I lay down my life for my sheep.
And there are other sheep I have
that are not of this fold,

and these I have to lead as well.
They too will listen to my voice,
and there will be only one flock
and one shepherd.
The Father loves me,
because I lay down my life
in order to take it up again.
No one takes it from me;
I lay it down of my own free will,
and as it is in my power to lay it down,
so it is in my power to take it up again;
and this is the command I have been given by my Father.'

This is the Gospel of the Lord.   *John 10:11-18*

Fifth Sunday of Easter   B

Introduction to the Service

Most of us have brothers and sisters. We belong to our family. The same blood of our ancestors unites us, we talk the same language at home and keep the same customs.

I wonder, however, when I look at you. You come from different families and peoples. And yet you all have become brothers and sisters in the Church.

Christ tells us today why we belong together. He is the vine, he says, and we are the branches. His life, his blood and his spirit flow in us all, uniting us as members of one family.

Penitential Rite

Let us examine our conscience:

● Do I accept my fellow Christians as brothers and sisters? (*Silence*)

● Do I stand up for them when they are rejected or when they are in need? (*Silence*)

● Did I break my friendship and unity with Christ? (*Silence*)

Let us ask pardon for what we have done and for what we have failed to do. **I confess**...

FIRST READING

The vine, who is Christ, has some unusual branches. He has people as branches; often people whom we would not expect to belong to him.

We now read in the Acts of the Apostles how one such unusual person was introduced into the Christian community.

We read from chapter nine.

*

When Saul got to Jerusalem he tried to join the disciples, but they were all afraid of him: they could not believe he was really a disciple. Barnabas, however, took charge of him, introduced him to the apostles, and explained how the Lord had appeared to Saul and spoken to him on his journey, and how he had preached boldly at Damascus in the name of Jesus. Saul now started to go round with them in Jerusalem, preaching fearlessly in the name of the Lord. But after he had spoken to the Hellenists, and argued with them, they became determined to kill him. When the brothers knew, they took him to Caesarea, and sent him off from there to Tarsus.

The churches throughout Judaea, Galilee and Samaria were now left in peace, building themselves up, living in the fear of the Lord, and filled with the consolation of the Holy Spirit.

This is the word of the Lord.   *Acts 9:26-31*

Responsorial Psalm
℟   **You, Lord, are my praise in the great assembly.**

or

℟   **Alleluia!**

1   My vows I will pay before those who fear him.
The poor shall eat and shall have their fill.
They shall praise the Lord, those who seek him.
May their hearts live for ever and ever!   ℟

2   All the earth shall remember and return to the Lord,
all families of the nations worship before him.
They shall worship him, all the mighty of the earth;
before him shall bow all who go down to the dust.   ℟

3   And my soul shall live for him, my children serve him.
They shall tell of the Lord to generations yet to come,
declare his faithfulness to peoples yet unborn:
'These things the Lord has done.'   ℟

Ps 21:26-28. 30-32. ℟ v.26

SECOND READING

We read from the first letter of St John, chapter three.
*
My children,
our love is not to be just words or mere talk,
but something real and active;
only by this can we be certain
that we are the children of the truth
and be able to quieten our conscience in his presence,
whatever accusations it may raise against us,
because God is greater than our conscience and he knows
    everything.
My dear people,
if we cannot be condemned by our own conscience,
we need not be afraid in God's presence,
and whatever we ask him,
we shall receive,
because we keep his commandments
and live the kind of life that he wants.
His commandments are these:
that we believe in the name of his Son Jesus Christ
and that we love one another
as he told us to.
Whoever keeps his commandments
lives in God and God lives in him.
We know that he lives in us
by the Spirit that he has given us.

    This is the word of the Lord.   *1 John 3:18-24*

Gospel Acclamation
    Alleluia, alleluia!
    Make your home in me, as I make mine in you.
    Whoever remains in me bears fruit in plenty.
    Alleluia!   *Jn 15:4.5*

GOSPEL

We read from the holy Gospel according to John, chapter fifteen.
*
Jesus said to his disciples:

    'I am the true vine,
    and my Father is the vinedresser.
    Every branch in me that bears no fruit

he cuts away,
and every branch that does bear fruit he prunes
to make it bear even more.
You are pruned already,
by means of the word that I have spoken to you.
Make your home in me, as I make mine in you.
As a branch cannot bear fruit all by itself,
but must remain part of the vine,
neither can you unless you remain in me.
I am the vine,
you are the branches.
Whoever remains in me, with me in him,
bears fruit in plenty;
for cut off from me you can do nothing.
Anyone who does not remain in me
is like a branch that has been thrown away
– he withers;
these branches are collected and thrown on the fire,
and they are burnt.
If you remain in me
and my words remain in you,
you may ask what you will
and you shall get it.
It is to the glory of my Father that you should bear much
    fruit,
and then you will be my disciples.'

This is the Gospel of the Lord.   *John 15:1-8*

Sixth Sunday of Easter   B

Introduction to the Service

We want to love and to be loved by others.

Young people fall in love with each other. A husband and wife make a covenant of love and promise each other to remain in this love. Love makes life beautiful.

The Good News which Christ gives us today in our celebration is the same: he loves us intensely and invites us to remain in his love. He has no favourites, he loves the young and the old, black and white, the healthy and the sick. He loves all races and nations.

Christ is risen and is with us. He is willing to share his love with us.

Penitential Rite

Let us ask ourselves:

● Did we accept Christ as a loving friend?   (*Silence*)

● Did we remain in his love by praying?   (*Silence*)

● Did we turn our back on him by hating our neighbours?
(*Silence*)

Let us ask God's forgiveness and renew our friendship with
Christ.   **I confess**...

FIRST READING

The early Christians had a problem. They found it difficult to
understand that people of all races and nations would be accepted
by God. They thought that the Jews were the only people God had
chosen.

In our reading we hear Peter talking about this. After he had
baptised Cornelius, who was not a Jew, he explained why he had
done it.

Our reading is taken from the Acts of the Apostles, chapter ten.

As Peter reached the house Cornelius went out to meet him,
knelt at his feet and prostrated himself. But Peter helped him up.
'Stand up,' he said 'I am only a man after all!'

Then Peter addressed them: 'The truth I have now come to
realise' he said 'is that God does not have favourites, but that
anybody of any nationality who fears God and does what is right
is acceptable to him.'

While Peter was still speaking the Holy Spirit came down on all
the listeners. Jewish believers who had accompanied Peter were
all astonished that the gift of the Holy Spirit should be poured out
on the pagans too, since they could hear them speaking strange
languages and proclaiming the greatness of God. Peter himself
then said, 'Could anyone refuse the water of baptism to these
people, now they have received the Holy Spirit just as much as
we have?' He then gave orders for them to be baptised in the
name of Jesus Christ. Afterwards they begged him to stay on for
some days.

This is the word of the Lord.   *Acts 10:25-26. 34-35. 44-48*

Responsorial Psalm
℟ **The Lord has shown his salvation to the nations.**

or

℟ **Alleluia!**

1 Sing a new song to the Lord
for he has worked wonders.
His right hand and his holy arm
have brought salvation. ℟

2 The Lord has made known his salvation;
has shown his justice to the nations.
He has remembered his truth and love
for the house of Israel. ℟

3 All the ends of the earth have seen
the salvation of our God.
Shout to the Lord all the earth,
ring out your joy. ℟ *Ps 97:1-4. ℟ cf. v.2*

*When the Ascension of the Lord is celebrated on the Seventh
Sunday of Easter, the Second Reading and Gospel assigned to the
Seventh Sunday (see below, pp.337ff.) may be read on the Sixth
Sunday.*

SECOND READING

We read from the first letter of St John, chapter four.
*
My dear people,
let us love one another
since love comes from God
and everyone who loves is begotten by God and knows God.
Anyone who fails to love can never have known God,
because God is love.
God's love for us was revealed
when God sent into the world his only Son
so that we could have life through him;
this is the love I mean:
not our love for God,
but God's love for us when he sent his Son
to be the sacrifice that takes our sins away.

This is the word of the Lord. *1 John 4:7-10*

Gospel Acclamation
Alleluia, alleluia!
Jesus said: 'If anyone loves me he will keep my word,
and my Father will love him, and we shall come to him.
Alleluia!   *Jn 14:23*

GOSPEL
We read from the holy Gospel according to John, chapter fifteen.
*
Jesus said to his disciples:

'As the Father has loved me,
so I have loved you.
Remain in my love.
If you keep my commandments
you will remain in my love,
just as I have kept my Father's commandments
and remain in his love.
I have told you this
so that my own joy may be in you
and your joy be complete.
This is my commandment:
love one another,
as I have loved you.
A man can have no greater love
than to lay down his life for his friends.
You are my friends,
if you do what I command you.
I shall not call you servants any more,
because a servant does not know
his master's business;
I call you friends,
because I have made known to you
everything I have learnt from my Father.
You did not choose me,
no, I chose you;
and I commissioned you
to go out and to bear fruit,
fruit that will last;
and then the Father will give you
anything you ask him in my name.
What I command you
is to love one another.'

This is the Gospel of the Lord.   *John 15:9-17*

The Ascension of the Lord B

Introduction to the Service

There are great celebrations when the leader of a nation is installed. A king is led to his throne, a President has to swear an oath and other leaders are solemnly led into their new office. Sometimes the whole nation takes part by listening to the radio or watching the celebration on TV.

Today we celebrate the installation of Christ as the great Lord of all nations; Christ has ascended into heaven and takes his seat at the right hand of God. All honour and power are given to him.

On this day of Ascension we rejoice with all people in heaven and all nations on earth. We acclaim Jesus as our Lord.

Penetential Rite

We ask ourselves:

- Do we accept Jesus as our Lord by allowing him to rule our lives? (*Silence*)

- Do we trust in him in time of trouble? (*Silence*)

- Do we expect Christ to judge all our words and actions when he comes back in glory? (*Silence*)

Let us ask for mercy. **I confess**…

FIRST READING

When we say good-bye to friends we remain standing until they have gone out of sight.

We should NOT do the same when we celebrate the ascension of Jesus in heaven today. He is with us in a new way until he comes back in glory.

We read from the Acts of the Apostles, chapter one.

*

In my earlier work, Theophilus, I dealt with everything Jesus had done and taught from the beginning until the day he gave his instructions to the apostles he had chosen through the Holy Spirit, and was taken up to heaven. He had shown himself alive to them after his Passion by many demonstrations: for forty days he had continued to appear to them and tell them about the kingdom of God. When he had been at table with them, he had told them not to leave Jerusalem, but to wait there for what the

Father had promised. 'It is' he had said 'what you have heard me speak about: John baptised with water but you, not many days from now, will be baptised with the Holy Spirit.'

Now having met together, they asked him, 'Lord, has the time come? Are you going to restore the kingdom to Israel?' He replied, 'It is not for you to know times or dates that the Father has decided by his own authority, but you will receive power when the Holy Spirit comes on you, and then you will be my witnesses not only in Jerusalem but throughout Judaea and Samaria, and indeed to the ends of the earth.'

As he said this he was lifted up while they looked on, and a cloud took him from their sight. They were still staring into the sky when suddenly two men in white were standing near them and they said, 'Why are you men from Galilee standing here looking into the sky? Jesus who has been taken up from you into heaven, this same Jesus will come back in the same way as you have seen him go there.'

This is the word of the Lord.   *Acts 1:1-11*

Responsorial Psalm
℟   **God goes up with shouts of joy;**
    the Lord goes up with trumpet blast.

or

℟   **Alleluia!**

1   All peoples, clap your hands,
    cry to God with shouts of joy!
    For the Lord, the Most High, we must fear,
    great king over all the earth.   ℟

2   God goes up with shouts of joy;
    the Lord goes up with trumpet blast.
    Sing praise for God, sing praise,
    sing praise to our king, sing praise.   ℟

3   God is king of all the earth.
    Sing praise with all your skill.
    God is king over the nations;
    God reigns on his holy throne.   ℟   *Ps 46:2-3. 6-9. ℟ v.6*

SECOND READING

We read from the letter of St Paul to the Ephesians, chapter one.
*

May the God of our Lord Jesus Christ, the Father of glory, give you a spirit of wisdom and perception of what is revealed, to bring you to full knowledge of him. May he enlighten the eyes of your mind so that you can see what hope his call holds for you, what rich glories he has promised the saints will inherit and how infinitely great is the power that he has exercised for us believers. This you can tell from the strength of his power at work in Christ, when he used it to raise him from the dead and to make him sit at his right hand, in heaven, far above every Sovereignty, Authority, Power, or Domination, or any other name that can be named, not only in this age, but also in the age to come. He has put all things under his feet, and made him as the ruler of everything, the head of the Church; which is his body, the fullness of him who fills the whole creation.

This is the word of the Lord. *Ephesians 1:17-23*

Gospel Acclamation
Alleluia, alleluia!
Go, make disciples of all the nations;
I am with you always; yes, to the end of time.
Alleluia! *Mt 28:19-20*

GOSPEL

We read from the holy Gospel according to Mark, chapter sixteen.
*

Jesus showed himself to the Eleven, and said to them, 'Go out to the whole world; proclaim the Good News to all creation. He who believes and is baptised will be saved; he who does not believe will be condemned. These are the signs that will be associated with believers: in my name they will cast out devils; they will have the gift of tongues; they will pick up snakes in their hands, and be unharmed should they drink deadly poison; they will lay their hands on the sick, who will recover.'

And so the Lord Jesus, after he had spoken to them, was taken up into heaven: there at the right hand of God he took his place, while they, going out, preached everywhere, the Lord working with them and confirming the word by the signs that accompanied it.

This is the Gospel of the Lord. *Mark 16:15-20*

Seventh Sunday of Easter B

Introduction to the Service

Perhaps you have attended a meeting where office-bearers were chosen. This is always exciting. Each of us is asking ourselves the question: 'Will I be chosen?'. Of course, we also know that those chosen have to fulfil their task well and serve the whole group.

In our celebration today we hear the message that we are chosen by God and sent into the world. We have been chosen for a great task. The risen Christ has appointed us to be his messengers.

Penitential Rite

We ask ourselves:

- We live together with many people. Do we remember that God has sent us to serve them? (*Silence*)

- Many of us hold authority over other people at home and in our work. Do we remember that we are sent to show them the way of Christ? (*Silence*)

- Do we protect our friends from evil ways or do we lead them into sin? (*Silence*)

Let us ask for forgiveness for having failed to fulfil our task as Christians. **I confess**...

FIRST READING

In our reading we hear how the whole community was involved in electing Matthias to take the place of Judas. They did not nominate just anybody. They looked for somebody who was able to fulfil the task for which he was chosen.

We read from the Acts of the Apostles, chapter one.

*

One day Peter stood up to speak to the brothers – there were about a hundred and twenty persons in the congregation: 'Brothers, the passage of scripture had to be fulfilled in which the Holy Spirit, speaking through David, foretells the fate of Judas, who offered himself as a guide to the men who arrested Jesus – after having been one of our number and actually sharing this ministry of ours.

'In the Book of Psalms it says:

Let someone else take his office.

'We must therefore choose someone who has been with us the whole time that the Lord Jesus was travelling around with us, someone who was with us right from the time when John was baptising until the day when he was taken up from us – and he can act with us as a witness to his resurrection.'

Having nominated two candidates, Joseph known as Barsabbas, whose surname was Justus, and Matthias, they prayed, 'Lord, you can read everyone's heart; show us therefore which of these two you have chosen to take over this ministry and apostolate, which Judas abandoned to go to his proper place.' They then drew lots for them, and as the lot fell to Matthias, he was listed as one of the twelve apostles.

This is the word of the Lord.   *Acts 1:15-17. 20-26*

Responsorial Psalm
℟   **The Lord has set his sway in heaven.**

or

℟   **Alleluia!**

1   My soul, give thanks to the Lord;
     all my being, bless his holy name.
     My soul, give thanks to the Lord
     and never forget all his blessings.   ℟

2   For as the heavens are high above the earth
     so strong is his love for those who fear him.
     As far as the east is from the west
     so far does he remove our sins.   ℟

3   The Lord has set his sway in heaven
     and his kingdom is ruling over all.
     Give thanks to the Lord, all his angels,
     mighty in power, fulfilling his word.   ℟
                              Ps 102:1-2. 11-12. 19-20. ℟ v.19

SECOND READING
We read from the first letter of St John, chapter four.
*
My dear people,
since God has loved us so much,
we too should love one another.

No one has ever seen God;
but as long as we love one another
God will live in us
and his love will be complete in us.
We can know that we are living in him
and he is living in us
because he lets us share his Spirit.
We ourselves saw and we testify
that the Father sent his Son
as saviour of the world.
If anyone acknowledges that Jesus is the Son of God,
God lives in him, and he in God.
We ourselves have known and put our faith in
God's love towards ourselves.
God is love
and anyone who lives in love lives in God,
and God lives in him.

This is the word of the Lord. *1 John 4:11-16*

Gospel Acclamation
Alleluia, alleluia!
I will not leave your orphans, says the Lord;
I will come back to you, and your hearts will be full of joy.
Alleluia! *cf. Jn 14:18*

GOSPEL

We read from the holy Gospel according to John, chapter seventeen.
*
Jesus raised his eyes to heaven and said:

'Holy Father,
keep those you have given me true to your name,
so that they may be one like us.
While I was with them,
I kept those you had given me true to your name.
I have watched over them and not one is lost
except the one who chose to be lost,
and this was to fulfil the scriptures.
But now I am coming to you
and while still in the world I say these things
to share my joy with them to the full.

I passed your word on to them,
and the world hated them,
because they belong to the world
no more than I belong to the world.
I am not asking you to remove them from the world,
but to protect them from the evil one.
They do not belong to the world
any more than I belong to the world.
Consecrate them in the truth;
your word is truth.
As you sent me into the world,
I have sent them into the world,
and for their sake I consecrate myself
so that they too may be consecrated in truth.'

This is the Gospel of the Lord.   *John 17:11-19*

Pentecost Sunday   *B*

Mass during the Day

Introduction to the Service

Today we celebrate the great feast of Pentecost. It is the feast of
God's Spirit. The power of evil spirits has come to an end.

We know how the evil spirit of envy can poison our heart. We
know the evil spirits of anger and greed. The spirit of hatred
destroys happiness and peace. We are afraid of these spirits of evil
and death.

Today, however, we praise the great deeds of God. He breathes
over us with the spirit of power. His breath is like storm and fire.
Today, the evil spirits become afraid, their power is broken.

We have come together to open ourselves to God. We allow him
to breathe on us as he breathed upon the first Christians in
Jerusalem.

Penetential Rite

Let us prepare ourselves for the coming of the Spirit.

● Is there within us a spirit of joy and gratitude?   (*Silence*)

● Is there within us a spirit of love and unity?   (*Silence*)

● Is there within us a spirit of going out to other people, joyfully
  telling them about Christ?   (*Silence*)

Let us open ourselves to God by asking his forgiveness.
I confess…

FIRST READING

Our reading is challenging us.

Do we as Christians just come to church and sing and pray together? Or do we open the door and go out to other people who do not yet follow the way of Christ? When did we last talk about Christ to our children or our neighbours?

We read from the Acts of the Apostles, chapter two.
*
When Pentecost day came round, the apostles had all met in one room, when suddenly they heard what sounded like a powerful wind from heaven, the noise of which filled the entire house in which they were sitting; and something appeared to them that seemed like tongues of fire; these separated and came to rest on the head of each of them. They were all filled with the Holy Spirit, and began to speak foreign languages as the Spirit gave them the gift of speech.

Now there were devout men living in Jerusalem from every nation under heaven, and at this sound they all assembled, each one bewildered to hear these men speaking his own language. They were amazed and astonished. 'Surely' they said 'all these men speaking are Galileans? How does it happen that each of us hears them in his own native language? Parthians, Medes and Elamites; people from Mesopotamia, Judaea and Cappadocia, Pontus and Asia, Phrygia and Pamphylia, Egypt and the parts of Libya round Cyrene; as well as visitors from Rome – Jews and proselytes alike – Cretans and Arabs; we hear them preaching in our own language about the marvels of God.'

This is the word of the Lord. *Acts 2:1-11*

Responsorial Psalm
> ℟ **Send forth your Spirit, O Lord,
> and renew the face of the earth.**

or

> ℟ **Alleluia.**

1 Bless the Lord, my soul!
 Lord God, how great you are,
 How many are your works, O Lord!
 The earth is full of your riches. ℟

2   You take back your spirit, they die,
      returning to the dust from which they came.
      You send forth your spirit, they are created;
      and you renew the face of the earth. ℟

3   May the glory of the Lord last for ever!
      May the Lord rejoice in his works!
      May my thoughts be pleasing to him.
      I find my joy in the Lord. ℟

Ps 103:1. 24. 29-31. 34. ℟ cf v.30

The Second Reading and the Gospel may be taken from Year A, see above, pp.162ff. Alternatively, the Second Reading and the Gospel given below may be used.

SECOND READING

We read from the letter of St Paul to the Galatians, chapter five.
*
If you are guided by the Spirit you will be in no danger of yielding to self-indulgence, since self-indulgence is the opposite of the Spirit, the Spirit is totally against such a thing, and it is precisely because the two are so opposed that you do not always carry out your good intentions. If you are led by the Spirit, no law can touch you. When self-indulgence is at work the results are obvious: fornication, gross indecency and sexual irresponsibility; idolatry and sorcery; feuds and wrangling, jealousy, bad temper and quarrels; disagreements, factions, envy; drunkenness, orgies and similar things. I warn you now, as I warned you before: those who behave like this will not inherit the kingdom of God. What the Spirit brings is very different: love, joy, peace, patience, kindness, goodness, trustfulness, gentleness and self-control. There can be no law against things like that, of course. You cannot belong to Christ Jesus unless you crucify all self-indulgent passions and desire.

    Since the Spirit is our life, let us be directed by the Spirit.

    This is the word of the Lord.   *Galatians 5:16-25*

SEQUENCE

The sequence may be said or sung.

    Holy Spirit, Lord of light,
      From the clear celestial height
    Thy pure beaming radiance give.

Come, thou Father of the poor,
   Come with treasures which endure;
Come, thou light of all that live!

Thou, of all consolers best,
   Thou, the soul's delightful guest,
Dost refreshing peace bestow;

Thou in toil art comfort sweet;
   Pleasant coolness in the heat;
Solace in the midst of woe.

Light immortal, light divine,
   Visit thou these hearts of thine,
And our inmost being fill:

If thou take thy grace away,
   Nothing pure in man will stay;
All his good is turned to ill.

Heal our wounds, our strength renew;
   On our dryness pour thy dew;
Wash the stains of guilt away:

Bend the stubborn heart and will;
   Melt the frozen, warm the chill;
Guide the steps that go astray.

Thou, on us who evermore
   Thee confess and thee adore,
With thy sevenfold gifts descend:

Give us comfort when we die;
   Give us life with thee on high;
Give us joys that never end.

Gospel Acclamation

Alleluia, alleluia!
Come, Holy Spirit, fill the hearts of your faithful
and kindle in them the fire of your love.
Alleluia!

GOSPEL

We read from the holy Gospel according to John, chapters fifteen and sixteen.

Jesus said to his disciples:

'When the Advocate comes,
whom I shall send to you from the Father,
the Spirit of truth who issues from the Father,
he will be my witness.
And you too will be witnesses,
because you have been with me from the outset.

I still have many things to say to you
but they would be too much for you now.
But when the Spirit of truth comes
he will lead you to the complete truth,
since he will not be speaking as from himself
but will say only what he has learnt;
and he will tell you of the things to come.
He will glorify me,
since all he tells you
will be taken from what is mine.
Everything the Father has is mine;
that is why I said:
All he tells you
will be taken from what is mine.'

This is the Gospel of the Lord.   *John 15:26-27; 16:12-15*

SOLEMNITIES OF THE LORD IN ORDINARY TIME

The Most Holy Trinity   B

Introduction to the Service

Today we celebrate the feast of the Blessed Trinity. We rejoice that God is a loving community, Father, Son and Holy Spirit.

We all need a loving community and a home where we are accepted, where we find understanding, help and love. Just remember a time when you felt alone, abandoned by people, rejected by your friends and forgotten by your relatives!

The feast of the Blessed Trinity has a great message of joy and hope for us: God himself is a community and he has accepted us into his household. He marked us as his children when we were baptised in the name of the Father, the Son and the Holy Spirit.

God himself is our promised land, our home and shelter.

Penitential Rite

Let us ask ourselves:

● Do we keep the customs of God's household?   (*Silence*)

● Do we love one another as he commanded us?   (*Silence*)

● Do we care for our relatives and friends?   (*Silence*)

● Do we accept others as our brothers and sisters as God has accepted us?   (*Silence*)

Let us pray for each other that God may forgive us all. **I confess**…

FIRST READING

How lucky we are that the triune God has revealed himself to us as he is. Has God ever before revealed himself so deeply?

In our reading we hear Moses, too, reminding his people how lucky they are.

We read from the book of Deuteronomy, chapter four.
★
Moses said to the people: 'Put this question to the ages that are past, that went before you, from the time God created man on

earth: Was there ever a word so majestic, from one end of heaven to the other? Was anything ever heard? Did ever a people hear the voice of the living God speaking from the heart of the fire, as you heard it, and remain alive? Has any god ventured to take to himself one nation from the midst of another by ordeals, signs, wonders, war with mighty hand and outstretched arm, by fearsome terrors – all this that the Lord your God did for you before your eyes in Egypt?

'Understand this today, therefore, and take it to heart: The Lord is God indeed, in heaven above as on earth beneath, he and no other. Keep his laws and commandments as I give them to you today so that you and your children may prosper and live long in the land that the Lord your God gives you for ever.'

This is the word of the Lord.   *Deuteronomy 4:32-34. 39-40*

Responsorial Psalm
℞   **Happy the people the Lord has chosen as his own.**

1   The word of the Lord is faithful
and all his works to be trusted.
The Lord loves justice and right
and fills the earth with his love.   ℞

2   By his word the heavens were made,
by the breath of his mouth all the stars.
He spoke; and they came to be.
He commanded; they sprang into being.   ℞

3   The Lord looks on those who revere him,
on those who hope in his love,
to rescue their souls from death,
to keep them alive in famine.   ℞

4   Our soul is waiting for the Lord.
The Lord is our help and our shield.
May your love be upon us, O Lord,
as we place all our hope in you.   ℞
Ps 32:4-6. 9. 18-20. 22. ℞ v.12

SECOND READING

We read from the letter of St Paul to the Romans, chapter eight.
*
Everyone moved by the Spirit is a son of God. The spirit you received is not the spirit of slaves bringing fear into your lives

again; it is the spirit of sons, and it makes us cry out, 'Abba, Father!' The Spirit himself and our spirit bear united witness that we are children of God. And if we are children we are heirs as well: heirs of God and coheirs with Christ, sharing his sufferings so as to share his glory.

This is the word of the Lord. *Romans 8:14-17*

Gospel Acclamation

Alleluia, alleluia!
Glory be to the Father, and to the Son, and to the Holy
    Spirit,
the God who is, who was, and who is to come.
Alleluia! *cf Apoc 1:8*

GOSPEL

We read from the holy Gospel according to Matthew, chapter twenty-eight.
*
The eleven disciples set out for Galilee, to the mountain where Jesus had arranged to meet them. When they saw him they fell down before him, though some hesitated. Jesus came up and spoke to them. He said, 'All authority in heaven and on earth has been given to me. Go, therefore, make disciples of all the nations; baptise them in the name of the Father and of the Son and of the Holy Spirit, and teach them to observe all the commands I gave you. And know that I am with you always; yes, to the end of time.'

This is the Gospel of the Lord. *Matthew 28:16-20*

Thursday after Trinity Sunday *Solemnity*

The Body and Blood of Christ   B

Introduction to the Service

Today we celebrate the feast of *Corpus Christi*. *Corpus Christi* is the Latin for 'Body of Christ'. We could put this another way, saying: 'Today we celebrate in a special way the 'Blessed Sacrament of the Altar'.

When Mass is celebrated, we use a chalice. The chalice is the 'cup of the covenant' in which Jesus offers us the 'blood of the covenant'.

A 'covenant' is a solemn agreement or a solemn promise. For instance, a bride and bridegroom make such a covenant or solemn promise. They promise to remain faithful to each other. As a sign of faithfulness they wear a ring.

The sign of Christ's faithfulness to us, is the blood of the covenant. Christ says, as it were: I shall remain faithful to you even if you should kill me. My blood is the sign and seal of my faithfulness.

We have gathered together to renew our covenant with God. We are invited to give ourselves to Christ as he has given himself to us in his body and blood.

Penitential Rite

We ask ourselves:

● Do we receive the body of Christ with reverence and love? (*Silence*)

● Are we willing to give ourselves to Christ as he has given himself to us? (*Silence*)

Let us ask for forgiveness for receiving the body of Christ with too little reverence and love. **I confess**...

FIRST READING

In our reading we hear of the covenant or agreement between God and his people Israel. This happened at Mount Sinai. We also hear of the way in which this covenant was confirmed and sealed.

We read from the book of Exodus, chapter twenty-four.
*
Moses went and told the people all the commands of the Lord and all the ordinances. In answer, all the people said with one voice, 'We will observe all the commands that the Lord has decreed.' Moses put all the commands of the Lord into writing, and early next morning he built an altar at the foot of the mountain, with twelve standing-stones for the twelve tribes of Israel. Then he directed certain young Israelites to offer holocausts and to immolate bullocks to the Lord as communion sacrifices. Half of the blood Moses took up and put into basins, the other half he cast on the altar. And taking the Book of the Covenant he read it to the listening people, and they said, 'We will observe all that the Lord has decreed; we will obey.' Then Moses took the blood and cast it towards the people. 'This' he said 'is the blood of the Covenant that the Lord has made with you, containing all these rules.'

This is the word of the Lord.   *Exodus 24:3-8*

Responsorial Psalm
> ℟ **The cup of salvation I will raise;**
> **I will call on the Lord's name.**

or

> ℟ **Alleluia!**

1 How can I repay the Lord
for his goodness to me?
The cup of salvation I will raise;
I will call on the Lord's name. ℟

2 O precious in the eyes of the Lord
is the death of his faithful.
Your servant, Lord, your servant am I;
you have loosened my bonds. ℟

3 A thanksgiving sacrifice I make:
I will call on the Lord's name.
My vows to the Lord I will fulfil
before all his people. ℟   *Ps 115:12-13. 15-18 ℟ v.13*

SECOND READING

We read from the letter to the Hebrews, chapter nine.
*
Now Christ has come, as the high priest of all the blessings which were to come. He has passed through the greater, the more perfect tent, which is better than one made by men's hands because it is not of this created order; and he has entered the sanctuary once and for all, taking with him not the blood of goats and bull calves, but his own blood, having won an eternal redemption for us. The blood of goats and bulls and the ashes of a heifer are sprinkled on those who have incurred defilement and they restore the holiness of their outward lives; how much more effectively the blood of Christ, who offered himself as the perfect sacrifice to God through the eternal Spirit, can purify our inner self from dead actions so that we do our service to the living God.

He brings a new covenant, as the mediator, only so that the people who were called to an eternal inheritance may actually receive what was promised: his death took place to cancel the sins that infringed the earlier covenant.

This is the word of the Lord.   *Hebrews 9:11-15*

The sequence, Sing forth, O Zion, *may be said or sung in its longer or shorter form. See above, pp. 170.*

Gospel Acclamation

Alleluia, alleluia!
I am the living bread which has come down from heaven,
says the Lord.
Anyone who eats this bread will live for ever.
Alleluia!   Jn 6:51-52

GOSPEL

We read from the holy Gospel according to Mark, chapter fourteen.
✶
On the first day of Unleavened Bread, when the Passover lamb
was sacrificed, his disciples said to Jesus, 'Where do you want us
to go and make the preparations for you to eat the passover?' So
he sent two of his disciples, saying to them, 'Go into the city and
you will meet a man carrying a pitcher of water. Follow him, and
say to the owner of the house which he enters, "The Master says:
Where is my dining room in which I can eat the passover with my
disciples?" He will show you a large upper room furnished with
couches, all prepared. Make the preparations for us there.' The
disciples set out and went to the city and found everything as he
had told them, and prepared the Passover.

And as they were eating he took some bread, and when he
had said the blessing he broke it and gave it to them. 'Take it,' he
said 'this is my body.' Then he took a cup, and when he had
returned thanks he gave it to them, and all drank from it, and he
said to them, 'This is my blood, the blood of the covenant, which
is to be poured out for many. I tell you solemnly, I shall not drink
any more wine until the day I drink the new wine in the kingdom
of God.'

After psalms had been sung they left for the Mount of Olives.

This is the Gospel of the Lord.   Mark 14:12-16. 22-26

Friday after the Second Sunday after Pentecost   *Solemnity*

The Sacred Heart of Jesus   B

Introduction to the Service

Today we celebrate the feast of the Sacred Heart of Jesus. This
feast reveals the tender and warm love God has for us. He loves us
with a human heart of flesh and blood, he loves us as a mother
loves her children, he loves us as a bridegroom loves his bride.

There are many ways of depicting the Sacred Heart. One of the best, however, is a crucifix, where we see the pierced heart of Jesus. It is a heart overflowing with love.

Penitential Rite
We ask ourselves:

● How do we deal with people?
    Do we sometimes give them a warm smile?
    Or do we approach them with a bitter face?   (*Silence*)

● How do we imagine God?
    Do we think of God as being far away and unapproachable?
    Or do we accept the warm and tender love of God?   (*Silence*)

Let us ask for forgiveness for not loving God with all our heart as he loves us.   **I confess**…

FIRST READING
There is a conflict in God's mind: should he destroy the unfaithful people of Israel as he destroyed the people of Sodom and Gomorrah and the cities of Admah and Zeboiim?
    There is a conflict between anger and love in God's heart. In our reading, the prophet Hosea tells us what eventually happened.

We read from the book of Hosea, chapter eleven.
*
Listen to the word of the Lord:

When Israel was a child I loved him,
and I called my son out of Egypt.
I myself taught Ephraim to walk,
I took them in my arms;
yet they have not understood that I was the one looking after
    them.
I led them with reins of kindness,
with leading-strings of love.
I was like someone who lifts an infant close against his
    cheek;
stooping down to him I gave him his food.
How could I treat you like Admah,
or deal with you like Zeboiim?
My heart recoils from it,
my whole being trembles at the thought.
I will not give rein to my fierce anger,

I will not destroy Ephraim again,
for I am God, not man:
I am the Holy One in your midst
and have no wish to destroy.

This is the word of the Lord.   *Hosea 11:1.3-4. 8-9*

Responsorial Psalm
℟   **With joy you will draw water**
    from the wells of the Saviour.

1   Truly God is my salvation,
    I trust, I shall not fear.
    For the Lord is my strength, my song,
    he became my saviour.
    With joy you will draw water
    from the wells of salvation.   ℟

2   Give thanks to the Lord, give praise to his name!
    Make his mighty deeds known to the peoples!
    Declare the greatness of his name.   ℟

3   Sing a psalm to the Lord
    for he has done glorious deeds;
    make them known to all the earth!
    People of Zion, sing and shout for joy
    for great in your midst is the Holy One of Israel.   ℟

                                                Is 12:2-6. ℟ v.3

SECOND READING
We read from the letter of St Paul to the Ephesians, chapter three.
*
I, Paul, who am less than the least of all the saints, have been
entrusted with this special grace, not only of proclaiming to the
pagans the infinite treasure of Christ but also of explaining how
the mystery is to be dispensed. Through all the ages, this has
been kept hidden in God, the creator of everything. Why? So that
the Sovereignties and Powers should learn only now, through
the Church, how comprehensive God's wisdom really is, exactly
according to the plan which he had had from all eternity in Christ
Jesus our Lord. This is why we are bold enough to approach God
in complete confidence, through our faith in him.

This, then, is what I pray, kneeling before the Father, from
whom every family, whether spiritual or natural, takes its name:
Out of his infinite glory, may he give you the power through

his Spirit for your hidden self to grow strong, so that Christ may live in your hearts through faith, and then, planted in love and built on love, you will with all the saints have strength to grasp the breadth and the length, the height and the depth; until, knowing the love of Christ, which is beyond all knowledge, you are filled with the utter fullness of God.

This is the word of the Lord.   *Ephesians 3:8-12. 14-19*

Gospel Acclamation
Alleluia, alleluia!
Shoulder my yoke and learn from me,
for I am gentle and humble in heart.
Alleluia!   *Mt 11:29*

Alternative Gospel Acclamation
Alleluia, alleluia!
This is the love I mean:
God's love for us when he sent his Son
to be the sacrifice that takes our sins away.
Alleluia!   *1 Jn 4:10*

GOSPEL

We read from the holy Gospel according to John, chapter nineteen.
*
It was Preparation Day, and to prevent the bodies remaining on the cross during the sabbath since that sabbath was a day of special solemnity – the Jews asked Pilate to have the legs broken and the bodies taken away. Consequently the soldiers came and broke the legs of the first man who had been crucified with him and then of the other. When they came to Jesus, they found he was already dead, and so instead of breaking his legs one of the soldiers pierced his side with a lance; and immediately there came out blood and water. This is the evidence of one who saw it – trustworthy evidence, and he knows he speaks the truth – and he gives it so that you may believe as well. Because all this happened to fulfil the words of scripture:

Not one bone of his will be broken;

and again, in another place scripture says:

They will look on the one whom they have pierced.

This is the Gospel of the Lord.   *John 19:31-37*

SUNDAYS IN ORDINARY TIME

First Sunday in Ordinary Time

The Baptism of the Lord

See above, pp. 47.

Second Sunday in Ordinary Time   B

Introduction to the Service

There are many ways in which we may be called. People may call us by telephone or send a letter. They may call us by silent signs or send somebody to call us to them.

How is God calling us?

In our celebration today we shall hear of different ways in which God calls people. He calls them to come to him and to live with him.

Penitential Rite

Let us ask ourselves:

● Were we open to God's call?
   Are we ready for God and is our prayer: 'Speak Lord, your servant is listening?'   (*Silence*)

● We ask many favours from God.
   Do we also ask what God wants us to do?   (*Silence*)

● Do we help others to find the right way; calling them back to Christ?   (*Silence*)

We ask for forgiveness for closing our ears and hearts; for not listening to God's call.   **I confess**…

FIRST READING

The young boy Samuel had a strange experience in the Temple. A similar thing may have happened to us. In the silence of the night, or in the silence of prayer, we may have experienced God's presence. Suddenly we may have understood what God wanted us to do.

We read from the first book of Samuel, chapter three.
*
Samuel was lying in the sanctuary of the Lord where the ark of God was, when the Lord called, 'Samuel! Samuel!' He answered, 'Here I am.' Then he ran to Eli and said, 'Here I am, since you called me.' Eli said, 'I did not call. Go back and lie down.' So he went and lay down. Once again the Lord called, 'Samuel! Samuel!' Samuel got up and went to Eli and said, 'Here I am, since you called me.' He replied, 'I did not call you, my son; go back and lie down.' Samuel had as yet no knowledge of the Lord and the word of the Lord had not yet been revealed to him. Once again the Lord called, the third time. He got up and went to Eli and said, 'Here I am, since you called me.' Eli then understood that it was the Lord who was calling the boy, and he said to Samuel, 'Go and lie down, and if someone calls say, "Speak, Lord, your servant is listening." ' So Samuel went and lay down in his place.

The Lord then came and stood by, calling as he had done before, 'Samuel! Samuel!' Samuel answered, 'Speak, Lord, your servant is listening.'

Samuel grew up and the Lord was with him and let no word of his fall to the ground.

This is the word of the Lord. *1 Samuel 3:3-10. 19*

Responsorial Psalm
℟ **Here I am, Lord!**
I come to do your will.

1 I waited, I waited for the Lord
   and he stooped down to me;
   he heard my cry.
   He put a new song into my mouth,
   praise of our God. ℟

2 You do not ask for sacrifice and offerings,
   but an open ear.
   You do not ask for holocaust and victim.
   Instead, here am I. ℟

3 In the scroll of the book it stands written
   that I should do your will.
   My God, I delight in your law
   in the depth of my heart. ℟

4   Your justice I have proclaimed
    in the great assembly.
    My lips I have not sealed;
    you know it, O Lord. ℞   *Ps 39:2. 4. 7-10. ℞ vv. 8. 9*

SECOND READING

We read from the first letter of St Paul to the Corinthians, chapter six.
*
The body is not meant for fornication; it is for the Lord, and the
Lord for the body. God who raised the Lord from the dead, will
by his power raise us up too.

    You know, surely, that your bodies are members making up
the body of Christ; anyone who is joined to the Lord is one spirit
with him.

    Keep away from fornication. All the other sins are committed
outside the body; but to fornicate is to sin against your own body.
Your body, you know, is the temple of the Holy Spirit, who is in
you since you received him from God. You are not your own
property; you have been bought and paid for. That is why you
should use your body for the glory of God.

    This is the word of the Lord.   *1 Corinthians 6:13-15.17-20*

Gospel Acclamation
    Alleluia, alleluia!
    Speak, Lord, your servant is listening:
    you have the message of eternal life.
    Alleluia!   *1 Sam 3:9; Jn 6:68*

or

    Alleluia, alleluia!
    We have found the Messiah – which means the Christ –
    grace and truth have come through him.
    Alleluia!   *Jn 1:41.17*

GOSPEL

We read from the holy Gospel according to John, chapter one.
*
As John stood with two of his disciples, Jesus passed, and John
stared hard at him and said, 'Look, there is the lamb of God.'
Hearing this, the two disciples followed Jesus. Jesus turned
round, saw them following and said, 'What do you want?' They
answered, 'Rabbi,' – which means Teacher – 'where do you live?'
'Come and see' he replied; so they went and saw where he lived,

and stayed with him the rest of that day. It was about the tenth hour.

One of these two who became followers of Jesus after hearing what John had said was Andrew, the brother of Simon Peter. Early next morning, Andrew met his brother and said to him, 'We have found the Messiah' – which means the Christ – and he took Simon to Jesus. Jesus looked hard at him and said, 'You are Simon son of John; you are to be called Cephas' – meaning Rock.

This is the Gospel of the Lord.   *John 1:35-42*

Third Sunday in Ordinary Time   B

Introduction to the Service

We all have our own little kingdoms. If we can have our own way, we feel great, like little kings. In our kingdom we are in control; we feel secure and independent.

In our own little kingdom we solve problems by retaliation, fighting and wars. In our little kingdoms we make money the way we want to – it doesn't matter if we push others aside and oppress them. In our little kingdoms we are concerned only for ourselves and not for other people.

In our celebration today, Christ calls us out of our little kingdoms. He says: 'Repent, the Kingdom of God is at hand'.

There were people at the Sea of Galilee who heard him saying this and who understood him. They left their little kingdoms and accepted Christ as their leader. They left their nets and followed him.

Penitential Rite

Let us ask ourselves:

● Is there something in my life which is like a 'little kingdom' where I refuse to allow even God to enter?   (*Silence*)

● What still prevents me from following Christ whole-heartedly?   (*Silence*)

Let us repent and come back to the Lord by asking for forgiveness.   **I confess**…

FIRST READING

When Jesus told people to 'repent', he added a joyful promise: 'because the kingdom of God is close at hand.'

This is a much more beautiful invitation to repentance than the one which we will hear now in our reading: Jonah tells the people of the city of Nineveh: 'Your city will be destroyed'.

We read from the book of Jonah, chapter three.

*
The word of the Lord was addressed to Jonah: 'Up!' he said 'Go to Nineveh, the great city, and preach to them as I told you to.' Jonah set out and went to Nineveh in obedience to the word of the Lord. Now Nineveh was a city great beyond compare: it took three days to cross it. Jonah went on into the city, making a day's journey. He preached in these words, 'Only forty days more and Nineveh is going to be destroyed.' And the people of Nineveh believed in God; they proclaimed a fast and put on sackcloth, from the greatest to the least.

God saw their efforts to renounce their evil behaviour. And God relented: he did not inflict on them the disaster which he had threatened.

This is the word of the Lord.   *Jonah 3:1-5. 10*

Responsorial Psalm
℟   **Lord, make me know your ways.**

1   Lord, make me know your ways.
     Lord, teach me your paths.
     Make me walk in your truth, and teach me:
     for you are God my saviour.   ℟

2   Remember your mercy, Lord,
     and the love you have shown from of old.
     In your love remember me,
     because of your goodness, O Lord.   ℟

3   The Lord is good and upright.
     He shows the path to those who stray,
     he guides the humble in the right path;
     he teaches his way to the poor.   ℟   *Ps 24:4-9. ℟ v.4*

SECOND READING

We read from the first letter of St Paul to the Corinthians, chapter seven.
*

Brothers: our time is growing short. Those who have wives should live as though they had none, and those who mourn should live as though they had nothing to mourn for; those who are enjoying life should live as though there were nothing to laugh about; those whose life is buying things should live as though they had nothing of their own; and those who have to deal with the world should not become engrossed in it. I say this because the world as we know it is passing away.

This is the word of the Lord.   *1 Corinthians 7:29-31.*

Gospel Acclamation
   Alleluia, alleluia!
   The kingdom of God is close at hand;
   believe the Good News.
   Alleluia!   *Mk 1:15*

GOSPEL

We read from the holy Gospel according to Mark, chapter one.
*

After John had been arrested, Jesus went into Galilee. There he proclaimed the Good News from God. 'The time has come' he said 'and the kingdom of God is close at hand. Repent, and believe the Good News.'

As he was walking along by the Sea of Galilee he saw Simon and his brother Andrew casting a net in the lake – for they were fishermen. And Jesus said to them, 'Follow me and I will make you into fishers of men.' And at once they left their nets and followed him.

Going on a little further, he saw James son of Zebedee and his brother John; they too were in their boat, mending their nets. He called them at once and, leaving their father Zebedee in the boat with the men he employed, they went after him.

This is the Gospel of the Lord.   *Mark 1:14-20*

Fourth Sunday in Ordinary Time   B

Introduction to the Service

It is not always easy to trust in people and to believe what they promise in their speeches. They may be brilliant and powerful speakers, but often we need to ask ourselves: might these brilliant speakers not be mistaken? Who gave them the authority to tell us what is true and what is false? Too often people have disappointed us. They may have broken their promises or even have deceived us with their beautiful words. Is there really anybody in whose word we can trust?

This is the Good News which we proclaim today in our celebration: there is one in whom we can trust, whose words are true, who speaks with authority. It is Christ the Lord. He is not a false prophet. His words are filled with the power of God. He does not need police and soldiers to enforce his word. His word created the world. His word is casting out unclean spirits. He talks with authority.

We are encouraged today to open ourselves to God and to experience the power of his word.

Penitential Rite

Let us ask ourselves:

● Do we allow God to touch our hearts when we read the Bible or when we listen to God's word in church?   (*Silence*)

● Do we appreciate God's word of forgiveness in the Sacrament of Reconciliation?   (*Silence*)

Let us ask for forgiveness for not taking God's word seriously.   **I confess**…

FIRST READING

In our reading Moses talks about the true prophet whom God was going to bring up among the people. Moses spoke about Christ, who was to come into the world at some point in the future.

At the end of our reading we shall also hear a warning against false prophets. They pretend to talk in the name of God. They talk as if they themselves were little gods.

We read from the book of Deuteronomy, chapter eighteen.
*
Moses said to the people: 'Your God will raise up for you a

prophet like myself, from among yourselves, from your own brothers; to him you must listen. This is what you yourselves asked of the Lord your God at Horeb on the day of the Assembly. "Do not let me hear again" you said "the voice of the Lord my God, nor look any longer on this great fire, or I shall die"; and the Lord said to me, "All they have spoken is well said. I will raise up a prophet like yourself for them from their own brothers; I will put my words into his mouth and he shall tell them all I command him. The man who does not listen to my words that he speaks in my name, shall be held answerable to me for it. But the prophet who presumes to say in my name a thing I have not commanded him to say, or who speaks in the name of other gods, that prophet shall die." '

This is the word of the Lord.   *Deuteronomy 18:15-20*

Responsorial Psalm
℞   **O that today you would listen to his voice!**
     Harden not your hearts.

1   Come, ring out our joy to the Lord;
     hail the rock who saves us.
     Let us come before him, giving thanks,
     with songs let us hail the Lord.   ℞

2   Come in; let us kneel and bend low;
     let us kneel before the God who made us
     for he is our God and we
     the people who belong to his pasture,
     the flock that is led by his hand.   ℞

3   O that today you would listen to his voice!
     'Harden not your hearts as at Meribah,
     as on that day at Massah in the desert
     when your fathers put me to the test;
     when they tried me, though they saw my work.'   ℞
                                        Ps 94:1-2. 6-9. ℞ v.9

SECOND READING
We read from the first letter of St Paul to the Corinthians, chapter seven.
*
I would like to see you free from all worry. An unmarried man can devote himself to the Lord's affairs, all he need worry about is pleasing the Lord; but a married man has to bother about the

world's affairs and devote himself to pleasing his wife: he is torn two ways. In the same way an unmarried woman, like a young girl, can devote herself to the Lord's affairs; all she need worry about is being holy in body and spirit. The married woman, on the other hand, has to worry about the world's affairs and devote herself to pleasing her husband. I say this only to help you, not to put a halter round your necks, but simply to make sure that everything is as it should be, and that you give your undivided attention to the Lord.

This is the word of the Lord.   *1 Corinthians 7:32-35*

Gospel Acclamation
Alleluia, alleluia!
Blessed are you, Father,
Lord of heaven and earth,
for revealing the mysteries of the kingdom
to mere children.
Alleluia!   *cf. Mt 11:25*

or

Alleluia, alleluia!
The people that lived in darkness
has seen a great light;
on those who dwell in the land and shadow of death
a light has dawned.
Alleluia!   *Mt 4.16*

GOSPEL
We read from the holy Gospel according to Mark, chapter one.
*
Jesus and his followers went as far as Capernaum, and as soon as the sabbath came Jesus went to the synagogue and began to teach. And his teaching made a deep impression on them because, unlike the scribes, he taught them with authority.

In their synagogue just then there was a man possessed by an unclean spirit, and it shouted, 'What do you want with us, Jesus of Nazareth? Have you come to destroy us? I know who you are: the Holy One of God.' But Jesus said sharply, 'Be quiet! Come out of him!' And the unclean spirit threw the man into convulsions and with a loud cry went out of him. The people were so astonished that they started asking each other what it all meant. 'Here is a teaching that is new' they said 'and with authority behind it: he gives orders even to unclean spirits and they obey him.' And his reputation rapidly spread everywhere, through all the surrounding Galilean countryside.

This is the Gospel of the Lord. *Mark 1:21-28*

Fifth Sunday in Ordinary Time   B

Introduction to the Service

Life can be miserable. For many it involves suffering and disappointment. Many silently ask themselves: 'What is the purpose of life, what can make me really happy? Life is boring. The only things I can look forward to are my wages, food and drink.'

In our celebration today we see the example of Christ. His life was not boring. He was anxious to go to people who needed him. He helped them without looking for profit or fame. From time to time he withdrew from the noisy crowd and had a long talk with God – often early in the morning, long before the sun came up behind the mountains. This gave him direction, strength and joy. Prayer gave him courage again to go back to people and love them. In this way, Christ made a success of his life.

Penitential Rite

Let us ask ourselves:

● Are we always busy with our own affairs or do we have time for other people who need us?   (*Silence*)

● Do we get so absorbed in our work that we have no time for prayer?   (*Silence*)

● Do we give time to our Christian community when we are asked to attend meetings or do something in church?   (*Silence*)

Let us ask God's forgiveness for all that we have failed to do. **I confess**...

FIRST READING

In our reading we hear Job complaining about the many things which went wrong in his life. He reminds us of ourselves and how we feel about life sometimes.

This reading is a mirror in which we see people who have not yet met Christ.

We read from the book of Jòb, chapter seven.
*
Job began to speak:

> Is not man's life on earth nothing more than pressed service,
> his time no better than hired drudgery?
> Like the slave, sighing for the shade,
> or the workman with no thought but his wages,
> months of delusion I have assigned to me,
> nothing for my own but nights of grief.
> Lying in bed I wonder, 'When will it be day?'
> Risen I think, 'How slowly evening comes!'
> Restlessly I fret till twilight falls.
> Swifter than a weaver's shuttle my days have passed,
> and vanished, leaving no hope behind.
> Remember that my life is but a breath,
> and that my eyes will never again see joy.

This is the word of the Lord.   *Job 7:1-4. 6-7*

Responsorial Psalm
℟ **Praise the Lord who heals the broken-hearted.**

or

℟ **Alleluia!**

1 Praise the Lord for he is good;
  sing to our God for he is loving:
  to him our praise is due. ℟

2 The Lord builds up Jerusalem
  and brings back Israel's exiles,
  he heals the broken-hearted,
  he binds up all their wounds.
  He fixes the number of the stars;
  he calls each one by its name. ℟

3 Our Lord is great and almighty;
  his wisdom can never be measured.
  The Lord raises the lowly;
  he humbles the wicked to the dust. ℟   *Ps 146:1-6. ℟ v.3*

SECOND READING

We read from the first letter of St Paul to the Corinthians, chapter nine.
*
I do not boast of preaching the gospel, since it is a duty which has been laid on me; I should be punished if I did not preach it! If I had chosen this work myself, I might have been paid for it, but as I have not, it is a responsibility which has been put into my hands. Do you know what my reward is? It is this: in my preaching, to be able to offer the Good News free, and not insist on the rights which the gospel gives me.

So though I am not a slave of any man I have made myself the slave of everyone so as to win as many as I could. For the weak I made myself weak. I made myself all things to all men in order to save some at any cost; and I still do this, for the sake of the gospel, to have a share in its blessing.

This is the word of the Lord.   *1 Corinthians 9:16-19. 22-23*

Gospel Acclamation
  Alleluia, alleluia!
  I am the light of the world, says the Lord,
  anyone who follows me
  will have the light of life.
  Alleluia!   *Jn 8:12*

or

  Alleluia, alleluia!
  He took our sicknesses away,
  and carried our diseases for us.
  Alleluia!   *Mt 8:17*

GOSPEL

We read from the holy Gospel according to Mark, chapter one.
*
On leaving the synagogue, Jesus went with James and John straight to the house of Simon and Andrew. Now Simon's mother-in-law had gone to bed with fever, and they told him about her straightaway. He went to her, took her by the hand and helped her up. And the fever left her and she began to wait on them.

That evening, after sunset, they brought to him all who were sick and those who were possessed by devils. The whole town came crowding round the door, and he cured many who were suffering from diseases of one kind or another; he also cast out many devils, but he would not allow them to speak, because they knew who he was.

In the morning, long before dawn, he got up and left the house, and went off to a lonely place and prayed there. Simon and his companions set out in search of him, and when they found him they said, 'Everybody is looking for you.' He answered, 'Let us go elsewhere, to the neighbouring country towns, so that I can preach there too, because that is why I came.' And he went all through Galilee, preaching in their synagogues and casting out devils.

This is the Gospel of the Lord.   *Mark 1:29-39*

Sixth Sunday in Ordinary Time B

Introduction to the Service

We may all have experienced a time when we felt not wanted; rejected by other people. We may have felt very hurt. Just remember when your friends did not come to a meal you had prepared for them. Or think of a day when you greeted your neighbours but they turned their backs on you.

How deeply hurt must children feel who are abandoned by their parents. Old people suffer in the same way when they are forgotten and neglected by their own children.

In every society we find 'outcasts', people who are ignored or even despised by the rest. How must people feel who are forced by poverty to live in shacks. How must people feel when they are rejected because they have a different colour skin or belong to a different nation?

Outcasts today are like lepers in olden times. People were afraid to come near them.

In our celebration today we hear Good News. Jesus has joined the outcasts, he stays with them.

Penitential Rite

Let us ask ourselves:

- Are we quick to cast people aside if they do not agree with us?   (*Silence*)

- Are there unjust laws or customs which make people outcasts in our society?   (*Silence*)

Let us ask God to forgive us and to accept us inspite of all our failings. **I confess**...

FIRST READING

In former times lepers could not be healed. People were afraid of contracting this disease which covers the body with ugly sores. For this reason lepers were forced to live outside the settlement. They became 'outcasts'.

We read from the book of Leviticus, chapter thirteen.
★
The Lord said to Moses and Aaron, 'If a swelling or scab or shiny spot appears on a man's skin, a case of leprosy of the skin is to be suspected. The man must be taken to Aaron, the priest, or to one of the priests who are his sons.

'The man is leprous: he is unclean. The priest must declare him unclean; he is suffering from leprosy of the head. A man infected with leprosy must wear his clothing torn and his hair disordered; he must shield his upper lip and cry, "Unclean, unclean." As long as the disease lasts he must be unclean; and therefore he must live apart; he must live outside the camp.'

This is the word of the Lord.   *Leviticus 13:1-2.44-46*

Responsorial Psalm
   ℟   **You are my refuge, O Lord;**
        you fill me with the joy of salvation.

1   Happy the man whose offence is forgiven,
     whose sin is remitted.
     O happy the man to whom the Lord
     imputes no guilt,
     in whose spirit is no guile.   ℟

2   But now I have acknowledged my sins;
     my guilt I did not hide.
     I said: 'I will confess
     my offence to the Lord.'
     And you, Lord, have forgiven
     the guilt of my sin.   ℟

3   Rejoice, rejoice in the Lord,
     exult, you just!
     O come, ring out your joy,
     all you upright of heart.   ℟   *Ps 31:1-2. 5. 11. ℟ v.7*

SECOND READING

We read from the first letter of St Paul to the Corinthians, chapters ten and eleven.

*
Whatever you eat, whatever you drink, whatever you do at all, do it for the glory of God. Never do anything offensive to anyone – to Jews or Greeks or to the Church of God; just as I try to be helpful to everyone at all times, not anxious for my own advantage but for the advantage of everybody else, so that they may be saved.

Take me for your model, as I take Christ.

This is the word of the Lord. *1 Corinthians 10:31-11:1*

Gospel Acclamation

Alleluia, alleluia!
May the Father of our Lord Jesus Christ
enlighten the eyes of our mind,
so that we can see what hope his call holds for us.
Alleluia! *cf. Eph 1:17. 18*

or

Alleluia, alleluia!
A great prophet has appeared among us;
God has visited his people.
Alleluia! *Lk 7:16*

GOSPEL

We read from the holy Gospel according to Mark, chapter one.

*
A leper came to Jesus and pleaded on his knees: 'If you want to' he said 'you can cure me.' Feeling sorry for him, Jesus stretched out his hand and touched him. 'Of course I want to!' he said. 'Be cured!' And the leprosy left him at once and he was cured. Jesus immediately sent him away and sternly ordered him, 'Mind you say nothing to anyone, but go and show yourself to the priest, and make the offering for your healing prescribed by Moses as evidence of your recovery.' The man went away, but then started talking about it freely and telling the story everywhere, so that Jesus could no longer go openly into any town, but had to stay outside in places where nobody lived. Even so, people from all around would come to him.

This is the Gospel of the Lord. *Mark 1:40-45*

Seventh Sunday in Ordinary Time   B

Introduction to the Service

We often say: 'How beautiful our world could be. Why must there be so much strife between people?'

We know that much of the great misery and suffering in the world is caused by people themselves. Human weakness and loss of self-control destroy the health of our body, the happiness in our families and peace among nations. There is something wrong within us. The Bible calls it 'sin'.

Sin is the root of all misery. Sin disturbs our friendship with people and our friendship with God.

In our celebration today we meet our Saviour. We see him pulling out the root of all evil, sin. He forgives the sins of the paralysed man on the stretcher and makes him walk again.

Penitential Rite

Let us go to the Lord and ask him to heal us:

● Lord we have come to you in faith. You know our human weakness.   (*Silence*)
   Lord, have mercy...

● Lord we have caused other people to suffer through our wrong words and wrong deeds.   (*Silence*)
   Christ, have mercy...

● Lord, there is so much trouble in the world among races and nations because we think only of ourselves.   (*Silence*)
   Lord, have mercy...

FIRST READING

In our reading we hear the prophet talking to the people of Israel who were in deep trouble. Many of them had been led away in chains and made slaves in Babylon.

The prophet gives them hope. But he also tells them the cause of their national disaster.

We read from the book of Isaiah, chapter forty-three.
★
Thus says the Lord:
   No need to recall the past,
   no need to think about what was done before.
   See, I am doing a new deed,
   even now it comes to light; can you not see it?

Yes, I am making a road in the wilderness,
paths in the wilds.
The people I have formed for myself
will sing my praises.
Jacob, you have not invoked me,
you have not troubled yourself, Israel, on my behalf.
Instead you have burdened me with your sins,
troubled me with your iniquities.
I it is, I it is, who must blot out everything
and not remember your sins.

This is the word of the Lord. *Isaiah 43:18-19. 21-22. 24-25*

Responsorial Psalm
℞ **Heal my soul for I have sinned against you.**

1 Happy the man who considers the poor and the weak.
   The Lord will save him in the day of evil,
   will guard him, give him life, make him happy in the land
   and will not give him up to the will of his foes. ℞

2 The Lord will help him on his bed of pain,
   he will bring him back from sickness to health.
   As for me, I said: 'Lord, have mercy on me,
   heal my soul for I have sinned against you.' ℞

3 If you uphold me I shall be unharmed
   and set in your presence for evermore.
   Blessed be the Lord, the God of Israel
   from age to age. Amen. Amen. ℞   *Ps 40:2-5. 13-14. ℞ v.5*

SECOND READING

We read from the second letter of St Paul to the Corinthians, chapter one.
*
I swear by God's truth, there is no Yes and No about what we say to you. The Son of God, the Christ Jesus that we proclaimed among you – I mean Silvanus and Timothy and I – was never Yes and No: with him it was always Yes, and however many the promises God made, the Yes to them all is in him. That is why it is 'through him' that we answer Amen to the praise of God. Remember it is God himself who assures us all, and you, of our standing in Christ, and has anointed us, marking us with his seal and giving us the pledge, the Spirit, that we carry in our hearts.

This is the word of the Lord.   *2 Corinthians 1:18-22*

Gospel Acclamation
Alleluia, alleluia!
The Word was made flesh and lived among us;
to all who did accept him
he gave power to become children of God.
Alleluia!

Jn 1:14. 12

or

Alleluia, alleluia!
The Lord has sent me to bring the good news to the poor,
to proclaim liberty to captives.
Alleluia!

cf Lk 4:18

GOSPEL

We read from the holy Gospel according to Mark, chapter two.
*

When Jesus returned to Capernaum, word went round that he was back; and so many people collected that there was no room left, even in front of the door. He was preaching the word to them when some people came bringing him a paralytic carried by four men, but as the crowds made it impossible to get the man to him, they stripped the roof over the place where Jesus was; and when they had made an opening, they lowered the stretcher on which the paralytic lay. Seeing their faith, Jesus said to the paralytic, 'My child, your sins are forgiven.' Now some scribes were sitting there, and they thought to themselves, 'How can this man talk like that? He is blaspheming. Who can forgive sins but God?' Jesus, inwardly aware that this was what they were thinking, said to them, 'Why do you have these thoughts in your hearts? Which of these is easier: to say to the paralytic, "Your sins are forgiven" or to say, "Get up, pick up your stretcher and walk?" But to prove to you that the Son of Man has authority on earth to forgive sins,' – he said to the paralytic – 'I order you: get up, pick up your stretcher, and go off home.' And the man got up, picked up his stretcher at once and walked out in front of everyone, so that they were all astounded and praised God saying, 'We have never seen anything like this.'

This is the Gospel of the Lord.

Mark 2:1-12

Eighth Sunday in Ordinary Time   B

Introduction to the Service

How do we imagine God?

Some people think of God as a grand old man, others imagine God as a strict master who lays down rules and regulations. For others again God may look like a policeman who is ready to catch them.

How wrong all these pictures are! In our celebration today there is real Good News for all who have a wrong and distorted picture of God. This is the message we hear today: God is the great lover, full of tenderness and love.

Christ compares himself to a bridegroom who is feasting with his bride. Christ proclaims the new law, the law of love. He tells the people that his message is new, that it is not like the teaching of the Pharisees who only talked about laws and regulations.

Penitential Rite

Let us ask ourselves:

● Have we ever experienced in our lives that God is love? (*Silence*)

● Do we wrongly think that human love has nothing to do with God? (*Silence*)

● Do we help others with a cold heart and a stern face, without showing warmth and tenderness? (*Silence*)

We ask for forgiveness for not reflecting God's tender love in our lives.   **I confess**...

FIRST READING

Our reading is written by a prophet who married a prostitute. By remaining faithful to her, Hosea wanted to show God's faithfulness and tender love for his people. The reading is like a love-letter which God has written to every Christian.

We read from the book of Hosea, chapter two.
*
Thus says the Lord:
I am going to lure her
and lead her out into the wilderness
and speak to her heart.

There she will respond to me as she did when she was
   young,
as she did when she came out of the land of Egypt.
I will betroth you to myself for ever,
betroth you with integrity and justice,
with tenderness and love;
I will betroth you to myself with faithfulness,
and you will come to know the Lord.

   This is the word of the Lord.   *Hosea 2:16-17. 21-22*

Responsorial Psalm
   ℟   **The Lord is compassion and love.**

1   My soul, give thanks to the Lord,
    all my being, bless his holy name.
    My soul, give thanks to the Lord
    and never forget all his blessings.   ℟

2   It is he who forgives all your guilt,
    who heals every one of your ills,
    who redeems your life from the grave,
    who crowns you with love and compassion.   ℟

3   The Lord is compassion and love,
    slow to anger and rich in mercy.
    He does not treat us according to our sins
    nor repay us according to our faults.   ℟

4   So far as the east is from the west
    so far does he remove our sins.
    As a father has compassion on his sons,
    the Lord has pity on those who fear him.   ℟
                              Ps 102:1-4. 8. 10. 12-13. ℟v.8

SECOND READING

We read from the second letter of St Paul to the Corinthians, chapter
three.
*
Unlike other people, we need no letters of recommendation
either to you or from you, because you are yourselves our letter,
written in our hearts, that anybody can see and read, and it is
plain that you are a letter from Christ, drawn up by us, and
written not with ink but with the Spirit of the living God, not on
stone tablets but on the tablets of your living hearts.

Before God, we are confident of this through Christ: not that we are qualified in ourselves to claim anything as our own work: all our qualifications come from God. He is the one who has given us the qualifications to be the administrators of this new covenant, which is not a covenant of written letters but of the Spirit: the written letters bring death, but the Spirit gives life.

This is the word of the Lord.   *2 Corinthians 3:1-6*

Gospel Acclamation
Alleluia, alleluia!
The sheep that belong to me listen to my voice,
says the Lord,
I know them and they follow me.
Alleluia!   *Jn 10:27*

or

Alleluia, alleluia!
By his own choice the Father made us his children
by the message of the truth,
so that we should be a sort of first-fruits
of all that he created.
Alleluia!   *James 1:18*

GOSPEL
We read from the holy Gospel according to Mark, chapter two.
*
One day when John's disciples and the Pharisees were fasting, some people came and said to Jesus, 'Why is it that John's disciples and the disciples of the Pharisees fast, but your disciples do not?' Jesus replied, 'Surely the bridegroom's attendants would never think of fasting while the bridegroom is still with them? As long as they have the bridegroom with them, they could not think of fasting. But the time will come for the bridegroom to be taken away from them, and then, on that day, they will fast. No one sews a piece of unshrunken cloth on an old cloak; if he does, the patch pulls away from it, the new from the old, and the tear gets worse. And nobody puts new wine into old wineskins; if he does, the wine will burst the skins, and the wine is lost and the skins too. No! New wine, fresh skins!'

This is the Gospel of the Lord.   *Mark 2:18-22*

Ninth Sunday in Ordinary Time   B

Introduction to the Service

Why do we have laws and regulations in our country? What is the purpose of these laws?

Laws are meant to help people and to protect them. For instance, traffic laws make it possible for cars to drive safely on the road. Without such laws there would be chaos on the roads.

The same is true with God's laws, the commandments. Without them there would be chaos in the world.

Today, Jesus tells us that these commandments are made to help people. He also shows us that people are more important than the laws. If a law oppresses people it must be changed. Of course, the authorities everywhere do not like this. In some countries people who criticise their laws are put into prison or even killed.

We should not be surprised at this. The same thing happened even to Jesus. He dared to tell the Pharisees that God's laws are made to help people and not to oppress them.

Penitential Rite

Let us ask ourselves:

- Did we ever thank God for his guiding words and his commandments? (*Silence*)

- Do we have the courage to speak out against unjust laws? (*Silence*)

Let us ask for forgiveness for not following God's way. **I confess**…

FIRST READING

It is wonderful to see how God shows concern for people and even for animals. We see this care in the third commandment: 'Keep the Sabbath holy.'

God does not want people to work seven days a week. He wants them to have time to be happy and to have a good rest.

We read from the book of Deuteronomy, chapter five.
*
The Lord says this: 'Observe the sabbath day and keep it holy, as the Lord your God has commanded you. For six days you shall labour and do all your work, but the seventh day is a sabbath for the

Lord your God. You shall do no work that day, neither you nor your son nor your daughter nor your servants, men or women, nor your ox nor your donkey nor any of your animals, nor the stranger who lives with you. Thus your servant, man or woman, shall rest as you do. Remember that you were a servant in the land of Egypt, and that the Lord your God brought you out from there with mighty hand and outstretched arm; because of this, the Lord your God has commanded you to keep the sabbath day.'

This is the word of the Lord.   *Deuteronomy 5:12-15*

Responsorial Psalm
  ℟   **Ring out your joy to God our strength.**

1   Raise a song and sound the timbrel,
      the sweet-sounding harp and the lute,
      blow the trumpet at the new moon,
      when the moon is full, on our feast.   ℟

2   For this is Israel's law,
      a command of the God of Jacob.
      He imposed it as a rule on Joseph,
      when he went out against the land of Egypt.   ℟

3   A voice I did not know said to me:
      'I freed your shoulder from the burden;
      your hands were freed from the load.
      You called in distress and I saved you.   ℟

4   'Let there be no foreign god among you,
      no worship of an alien god.
      I am the Lord your God,
      who brought you from the land of Egypt.'   ℟
                                            Ps 80:3-8. 10-11. ℟ v.2

SECOND READING
We read from the second letter of St Paul to the Corinthians, chapter four.
*
It is the same God that said, 'Let there be light shining out of darkness,' who has shone in our minds to radiate the light of the knowledge of God's glory, the glory on the face of Christ.

We are only the earthenware jars that hold this treasure, to make it clear that such an overwhelming power comes from God and not from us. We are in difficulties on all sides, but never cornered; we see no answer to our problems, but never despair; we have been persecuted, but never deserted; knocked down, but never killed; always, wherever we may be, we carry with us in our body the death of Jesus, so that the life of Jesus, too, may always be seen in our body. Indeed, while we are still alive, we are consigned to our death every day, for the sake of Jesus, so that in our mortal flesh the life of Jesus, too, may be openly shown.

This is the word of the Lord.   *2 Corinthians 4:6-11*

Gospel Acclamation

Alleluia, alleluia!
Your words are spirit, Lord,
and they are life:
you have the message of eternal life.
Alleluia!
                                                    cf. Jn 6:63. 68

or

Alleluia, alleluia!
Your word is truth, O Lord,
consecrate us in the truth.
Alleluia!
                                                    cf. Jn 17:17

GOSPEL

We read from the holy Gospel according to Mark chapters two and three.
*
*One sabbath day Jesus happened to be taking a walk through the cornfields, and his disciples began to pick ears of corn as they went along. And the Pharisees said to him, 'Look, why are they doing something on the sabbath day that is forbidden?' And he replied, 'Did you ever read what David did in his time of need when he and his followers were hungry – how he went into the house of God when Abiathar was high priest, and ate the loaves of offering which only the priests are allowed to eat, and how he also gave some to the men with him?'

And he said to them, 'The sabbath was made for man, not man for the sabbath; so the Son of Man is master even of the sabbath.'*

He went again into a synagogue, and there was a man there who had a withered hand. And they were watching him to see if he would cure him on the sabbath day, hoping for something to use against him. He said to the man with the withered hand, 'Stand up out in the middle!' Then he said to them, 'Is it against the law on the sabbath day to do good, or to do evil; to save life, or to kill?' But they said nothing. Then, grieved to find them so obstinate, he looked angrily round at them, and said to the man, 'Stretch out your hand.' He stretched it out and his hand was better. The Pharisees went out and at once began to plot with the Herodians against him, discussing how to destroy him.

| *This is the Gospel of the Lord.*   *Mark 2:23-3:6*

*Shorter Form, verses 23-28, read between *.

Tenth Sunday in Ordinary Time   B

Introduction to the Service

There are many fights and wars among both people and nations. What are they fighting for?

Some say it is because there is enmity between the rich and the poor, between those of different race, between the strong and the weak.

Why can people not live together as brothers and sisters? The situation seems to be hopeless.

In our celebration today we shall hear of the real reason behind all the troubles in the world. It is our rebellion against God's plan. It is the evil spirit in us whom we allow to rule our hearts. It is Satan, whom Christ calls the prince of this world. Satan is the old snake that Christ has come to destroy.

There is no reason for dispair. Christ has overpowered the evil spirits. He shows us how we can live together as brothers and sisters.

Penitential Rite

Let us examine our conscience:

● Do we allow evil spirits to rule us? (*Silence*)

● Do we accept our fellow Christians as brothers and sisters? (*Silence*)

Let us ask our brothers and sisters to pray for us. **I confess**...

FIRST READING

People of many nations have asked the question: 'Where does evil come from?' They have tried to answer this question by using different stories which talk about the beginning of evil in the world.

Our reading is one such story which was current among the Israelites.

This reading is also called the 'First Gospel' for in it our salvation is proclaimed for the very first time in the Bible.

We read from the book of Genesis, chapter three.
*
The Lord God called to the man after he had eaten of the tree. 'Where are you?' he asked. 'I heard the sound of you in the garden;' he replied 'I was afraid because I was naked, so I hid.' 'Who told you that you were naked?' he asked. 'Have you been eating of the tree I forbade you to eat?' The man replied, 'It was the woman you put with me; she gave me the fruit, and I ate it.' Then the Lord God asked the woman, 'What is this you have done?' The woman replied, 'The serpent tempted me and I ate.'

Then the Lord God said to the serpent, 'Because you have done this,

'Be accursed beyond all cattle,
all wild beasts.
You shall crawl on your belly and eat dust
every day of your life.
I will make you enemies of each other:
you and the woman,
your offspring and her offspring.
It will crush your head
and you will strike its heel.'

This is the word of the Lord. *Genesis 3:9-15*

Responsorial Psalm
℟ **With the Lord there is mercy
and fullness of redemption.**

1 Out of the depths I cry to you, O Lord,
Lord, hear my voice!
O let your ears be attentive
to the voice of my pleading. ℟

2 If you, O Lord, should mark our guilt,
Lord, who would survive?

But with you is found forgiveness:
for this we revere you. ℟

3 My soul is waiting for the Lord,
   I count on his word.
   My soul is longing for the Lord
   more than watchman for daybreak. ℟

4 Because with the Lord there is mercy
   and fullness of redemption,
   Israel indeed he will redeem
   from all its iniquity. ℟   *Ps 129. ℟ v.7*

SECOND READING

We read from the second letter of St Paul to the Corinthians, chapters four and five.

*
As we have the same spirit of faith that is mentioned in scripture
– I believed, and therefore I spoke – we too believe and therefore
we too speak, knowing that he who raised the Lord Jesus to life
will raise us with Jesus in our turn, and put us by his side and you
with us. You see, all this is for your benefit, so that the more
grace is multiplied among people, the more thanksgiving there
will be, to the glory of God.

That is why there is no weakening on our part, and instead,
though this outer man of ours may be falling into decay, the inner
man is renewed day by day. Yes, the troubles which are soon
over, though they weigh little, train us for the carrying of a
weight of eternal glory which is out of all proportion to them.
And so we have no eyes for things that are visible, but only for
things that are invisible; for visible things last only for a time, and
the invisible things are eternal.

For we know that when the tent that we live in on earth is
folded up, there is a house built by God for us, an everlasting
home not made by human hands, in the heavens.

This is the word of the Lord.   *2 Corinthians 4:13–5:1*

Gospel Acclamation
   Alleluia, alleluia!
   If anyone loves me he will keep my word,
   and my Father will love him,
   and we shall come to him.
   Alleluia!
                                              Jn 14:23

or

Alleluia, alleluia!
Now the prince of this world is to be overthrown,
says the Lord.
And when I am lifted up from the earth,
I shall draw all men to myself.
Alleluia!

Jn 12:31.32

GOSPEL

We read from the holy Gospel according to Mark, chapter three.
*

Jesus went home with his disciples, and such a crowd collected that they could not even have a meal. When his relatives heard of this, they set out to take charge of him, convinced he was out of his mind.

The scribes who had come down from Jerusalem were saying,'Beelzebul is in him,' and, 'It is through the prince of devils that he casts devils out.' So he called them to him and spoke to them in parables, 'How can Satan cast out Satan? If a kingdom is divided against itself, that kingdom cannot last. And if a household is divided against itself, that household can never stand. Now if Satan has rebelled against himself and is divided, he cannot stand either – it is the end of him. But no one can make his way into a strong man's house and burgle his property unless he has tied up the strong man first. Only then can he burgle his house.

'I tell you solemnly, all men's sins will be forgiven, and all their blasphemies; but let anyone blaspheme against the Holy Spirit and he will never have forgiveness: he is guilty of an eternal sin.' This was because they were saying, 'An unclean spirit is in him.'

His mother and brothers now arrived and, standing outside, sent in a message asking for him. A crowd was sitting round him at the time the message was passed to him, 'Your mother and brothers and sisters are outside asking for you.' He replied, 'Who are my mother and my brothers?' And looking round at those sitting in a circle about him, he said, 'Here are my mother and my brothers. Anyone who does the will of God, that person is my brother and sister and mother.'

This is the Gospel of the Lord.

Mark 3:20-35

Eleventh Sunday in Ordinary Time   B

Introduction to the Service

A small seed is a wonder of nature. It is scarcely visible in your hand and yet it has the potential to grow into a mighty tree, complete with roots, trunk, branches and leaves. What an amazing thought: the power of life hidden within a little seed.

The tiny seed of God's Kingdom is Christ himself. We hear today how powerful this seed is. It will grow and grow, penetrating the whole world. It will grow into a mighty tree under which all nations will find a home. Christ's message today gives us hope that the world will not end in disaster. The seed of the Kingdom is too strong and cannot be destroyed.

Penitential Rite

We ask ourselves:

● Did I appreciate God's wisdom which is hidden in nature? (*Silence*)

● Did I allow the seed of God's Kingdom to grow in me?   (*Silence*)

● Did I nourish God's seed in me by prayer and by listening carefully to his message?   (*Silence*)

Let us ask for forgiveness for neglecting God's seed in us. **I confess**…

FIRST READING

In our reading the prophet Ezekiel is talking about the coming of Christ. He compares Christ with the very small top of a tree which God took in order to plant it and make it into a big and fruitful tree.

We read from the book of Ezekiel, chapter seventeen.
*
The Lord says this:

'From the top of the cedar,
from the highest branch I will take a shoot
and plant it myself on a very high mountain.
I will plant it on the high mountain of Israel.
It will sprout branches and bear fruit,
and become a noble cedar.
Every kind of bird will live beneath it,

every winged creature rest in the shade of its branches.
And every tree of the field will learn that I, the Lord, am the
  one
who stunts tall trees and makes the low ones grow,
who withers green trees and makes the withered green.
I, the Lord, have spoken, and I will do it.'

This is the word of the Lord.   *Ezekiel 17:22-24*

Responsorial Psalm
R̸ **It is good to give you thanks, O Lord.**

1 It is good to give thanks to the Lord
   to make music to your name, O Most High,
   to proclaim your love in the morning
   and your truth in the watches of the night. R̸

2 The just will flourish like the palm-tree
   and grow like a Lebanon cedar. R̸

3 Planted in the house of the Lord
   they will flourish in the courts of our God,
   still bearing fruit when they are old,
   still full of sap, still green,
   to proclaim that the Lord is just.
   In him, my rock, there is no wrong. R̸

Ps 91:2-3. 13-16. R̸ cf. v.2

SECOND READING
We read from the second letter of St Paul to the Corinthians, chapter
five.
*
We are always full of confidence when we remember that to live
in the body means to be exiled from the Lord, going as we do by
faith and not by sight – we are full of confidence, I say, and
actually want to be exiled from the body and make our home with
the Lord. Whether we are living in the body or exiled from it, we
are intent on pleasing him. For all the truth about us will be
brought out in the law court of Christ, and each of us will get
what he deserves for the things he did in the body, good or bad.

This is the word of the Lord.   *2 Corinthians 5:6-10*

Gospel Acclamation
Alleluia, alleluia!
I call you friends, says the Lord,

because I have made known to you
everything I have learnt from my Father.
Alleluia!   *Jn 15:15*

or

Alleluia, alleluia!
The seed is the word of God, Christ the sower;
whoever finds the seed will remain for ever.
Alleluia!

GOSPEL

We read from the holy Gospel according to Mark, chapter four.
*
Jesus said to the crowds: 'This is what the kingdom of God is like.
A man throws seed on the land. Night and day, while he sleeps,
when he is awake, the seed is sprouting and growing; how, he
does not know. Of its own accord the land produces first the
shoot, then the ear, then the full grain in the ear. And when the
crop is ready, he loses no time: he starts to reap because the
harvest has come.'

He also said, 'What can we say the kingdom of God is like?
What parable can we find for it? It is like a mustard seed which at
the time of its sowing in the soil is the smallest of all the seeds on
earth; yet once it is sown it grows into the biggest shrub of them
all and puts out big branches so that the birds of the air can
shelter in its shade.'

Using many parables like these, he spoke the word to them,
so far as they were capable of understanding it. He would not
speak to them except in parables, but he explained everything to
his disciples when they were alone.

This is the Gospel of the Lord.   *Mark 4:26-34*

Twelfth Sunday in Ordinary Time   B

Introduction to the Service

We are afraid of storms. Lightning might strike our house or wind
blow the roof off. We are frightened.

There are different types of storms. Our hearts may be torn by
fear and anxiety. Wars, famine, sickness, oppression and persecution may sweep over a country like a fierce storm.

The early Christians experienced the same fear. Many of them were persecuted and killed. But then they remembered that Jesus is powerful. They remembered that it was Jesus commanding the storm, lightning and waves. This gave them courage in their difficulties.

In our celebration today, Jesus asks us the question: 'You people of this parish in ... Why are you frightened? How is it that you have no faith?'

Penitential Rite
Let us ask ourselves:

- What do I fear most in my life?   (*Silence*)

- Do I put all my trust in the Lord?   (*Silence*)

- Do I only trust in my own clever plans, my money and power?   (*Silence*)

Let us ask God's forgiveness for having little faith.   **I confess**...

FIRST READING
Job was nearly crushed by suffering and pain. When he cried out to God he received the answer: 'Do you not know that I can check the floodwaters of the sea, command the mist in the sky and the waves of the ocean?'

We read from the book of Job, chapter three.

From the heart of tempest the Lord gave Job his answer. He said:

Who pent up the sea behind closed doors
when it leapt tumultuous out of the womb,
when I wrapped it in a robe of mist
and made black clouds its swaddling bands;
when I marked the bounds it was not to cross
and made it fast with a bolted gate?
Come thus far, I said, and no farther:
here your proud waves shall break.

This is the word of the Lord.   *Job 3:1. 8-11*

Responsorial Psalm
℞ **O give thanks to the Lord,**
for his love endures for ever.

or

℞ **Alleluia!**

1 Some sailed to the sea in ships
to trade on the mighty waters.
These men have seen the Lord's deeds,
the wonders he does in the deep. ℞

2 For he spoke; he summoned the gale.
tossing the waves of the sea
up to heaven and back into the deep;
their soul melted away in their distress. ℞

3 Then they cried to the Lord in their need
and he rescued them from their distress
He stilled the storm to a whisper:
all the waves of the sea were hushed. ℞

4 They rejoiced because of the calm
and he led them to the haven they desired.
Let them thank the Lord for his love,
the wonders he does for men. ℞   *Ps 106:23-26. 28-31. ℞ v.1*

SECOND READING

We read from the second letter of St Paul to the Corinthians, chapter five.
*
The love of Christ overwhelms us when we reflect that if one man has died for all, then all men should be dead; and the reason he died for all was so that living men should live no longer for themselves, but for him who died and was raised to life for them.

From now onwards, therefore, we do not judge anyone by the standards of the flesh. Even if we did once know Christ in the flesh, that is not how we know him now. And for anyone who is in Christ, there is a new creation; the old creation has gone, and now the new one is here.

This is the word of the Lord.   *2 Corinthians 5:14-17*

Gospel Acclamation
Alleluia, alleluia!
May the Father of our Lord Jesus Christ
enlighten the eyes of our mind,

so that we can see what hope his call holds for us.
Alleluia!

cf. Eph 1:17. 18

or

Alleluia, alleluia!
A great prophet has appeared among us;
God has visited his people.
Alleluia!

Lk 7:16

GOSPEL

We read from the holy Gospel according to Mark, chapter four.

★

With the coming of evening, Jesus said to his disciples, 'Let us cross over to the other side.' And leaving the crowd behind they took him, just as he was, in the boat; and there were other boats with him. Then it began to blow a gale and the waves were breaking into the boat so that it was almost swamped. But he was in the stern, his head on the cushion, asleep. They woke him and said to him, 'Master, do you not care? We are going down!' And he woke up and rebuked the wind and said to the sea, 'Quiet now! Be calm!' And the wind dropped, and all was calm again. Then he said to them, 'Why are you so frightened? How is it that you have no faith?' They were filled with awe and said to one another, 'Who can this be? Even the wind and the sea obey him.'

This is the Gospel of the Lord.

Mark 4:35-41

Thirteenth Sunday in Ordinary Time B

Introduction to the Service

What is our greatest enemy? It is death.

What is our most powerful enemy? It is death.

We may have the money to buy the most expensive medicines and call the best doctors but we shall still lose the battle against death.

There are even people who say: 'Accept death as natural. There is no life after death. Death is the end of all. Never mind.'

But we know from deep in our hearts how wrong such people are. We know that we are not created for death. We are created for life. This is the message of our celebration today.

Penitential Rite

We ask ourselves:

● Do I ever think of the day when I will die? (*Silence*)

● Do I pray for those people who have died before me?   (*Silence*)

● What should I remove from my life so that God can accept me and raise me up to life after death?   (*Silence*)

Let us ask for forgiveness and surrender ourselves into God's merciful hands.   **I confess**...

FIRST READING

Many people have asked the question: 'Where does death come from, who makes us die, why must we die at all?'
Our reading discusses the same question.

We read from the book of Wisdom, chapters one and two.
*
Death was not God's doing,
he takes no pleasure in the extinction of the living.
To be – for this he created all;
the world's created things have health in them,
in them no fatal poison can be found,
and Hades holds no power on earth;
for virtue is undying.
Yet God did make man imperishable,
he made him in the image of his own nature;
it was the devil's envy that brought death into the world,
as those who are his partners will discover.

This is the word of the Lord.   *Wisdom 1:13-15; 2:23-24*

Responsorial Psalm
   ℟   **I will praise you, Lord, you have rescued me.**

1   I will praise you, Lord, you have rescued me
    and have not let my enemies rejoice over me.
    O Lord, you have raised my soul from the dead,
    restored me to life from those who sink into the grave.   ℟

2   Sing psalms to the Lord, you who love him,
    give thanks to his holy name.
    His anger lasts but a moment; his favour through life.
    At night there are tears, but joy comes with dawn.   ℟

3   The Lord listened and had pity.
    The Lord came to my help.
    For me you have changed my mourning into dancing,
    O Lord my God, I will thank you for ever.   ℟
                              Ps 29:2. 4-6. 11-13. ℟ v.2

SECOND READING

We read from the second letter of St Paul to the Corinthians, chapter eight.
*
You always have the most of everything – of faith, of eloquence, of understanding, of keenness for any cause, and the biggest share of our affection – so we expect you to put the most into this work of mercy too. Remember how generous the Lord Jesus was: he was rich, but he became poor for your sake, to make you rich out of his poverty. This does not mean that to give relief to others you ought to make things difficult for yourselves: it is a question of balancing what happens to be your surplus now against their present need, and one day they may have something to spare that will supply your own need. That is how we strike a balance: as scripture says: The man who gathered much had none too much, the man who gathered little did not go short.

This is the word of the Lord.   *2 Corinthians 8:7. 9. 13-15*

Gospel Acclamation
Alleluia, alleluia!
Your words are spirit, Lord,
and they are life:
you have message of eternal life.
Alleluia!   *cf. Jn 6:63. 68*
or

Alleluia, alleluia!
Our Saviour Christ Jesus abolished death,
and he has proclaimed life through the Good News.
Alleluia!   *cf. 2 Tim 1:10*

GOSPEL

We read from the holy Gospel according to Mark, chapter five.
*
When Jesus had crossed in the boat to the other side, a large crowd gathered round him and he stayed by the lakeside. Then one of the synagogue officials came up, Jairus by name, and seeing him, fell at his feet and pleaded with him earnestly, saying, 'My little daughter is desperately sick. Do come and lay your hands on her to make her better and save her life.' Jesus went with him and a large crowd followed him; they were pressing all round him.

Now there was a woman who had suffered from a haemorrhage for twelve years; after long and painful treatment under various doctors, she had spent all she had without being any the better for it, in fact, she was getting worse. She had heard about Jesus, and she came up behind him through the crowd and touched his cloak. 'If I can touch even his clothes,' she had told herself 'I shall be well again.' And the source of the bleeding dried up instantly, and she felt in herself that she was cured of her complaint. Immediately aware that power had gone out from him Jesus turned round in the crowd and said, 'Who touched my clothes?' His disciples said to him, 'You see how the crowd is pressing round you and yet you say, "Who touched me?" ' But he continued to look all round to see who had done it. Then the woman came forward, frightened and trembling because she knew what had happened to her, and she fell at his feet and told him the whole truth. 'My daughter,' he said 'your faith has restored you to health; go in peace and be free from your complaint.'

*While he was still speaking some people arrived from the house of the synagogue offical to say, 'Your daughter is dead: why put the Master to any further trouble?' But Jesus had overheard this remark of theirs and he said to the official, 'Do not be afraid; only have faith.' And he allowed no one to go with him except Peter and James and John the brother of James. So they came to the official's house and Jesus noticed all the commotion, with people weeping and wailing unrestrainedly. He went in and said to them, 'Why all this commotion and crying? The child is not dead, but asleep.' But they laughed at him. So he turned them all out and, taking with him the child's father and mother and his own companions, he went into the place where the child lay. And taking the child by the hand he said to her, 'Talitha, kum!' which means, 'Little girl, I tell you to get up.' The little girl got up at once and began to walk about, for she was twelve years old. At this they were overcome with astonishment, and he ordered them strictly not to let anyone know about it, and told them to give her something to eat.

This is the Gospel of the Lord.*   *Mark 5:21-43*

*Shorter Form, verses 21-24. 35-43. Read between *.

Fourteenth Sunday in Ordinary Time **B**

Introduction to the Service

There is no community in which everything is right. Many things can go wrong. Some people may feel they are being pushed aside, others may feel ill-treated and oppressed. People in power may look after their own interests and no one else's. The young may no longer know what is right and what is wrong. People rebel against God.

In such situations there must be somebody who stands up and tries to put things right.

The Jews called such a person a prophet. But will people listen to him? Especially if he tries to put things right in his home town, where he is thought of as just an ordinary person? We shall hear in our reading today how this is what happened to Jesus: he was rejected as a prophet in his home town.

Should he have kept quiet? Should he not have proclaimed the truth in his home town? If things are wrong can we keep silent?

Penitential Rite

We ask ourselves:

- Was I afraid to stand up for those who were ill-treated? (*Silence*)

- Did I show people God's way when I saw them doing wrong? (*Silence*)

- Was I too proud to accept the advice of somebody whom God may have sent to show me the right way? (*Silence*)

Let us ask God to come to our aid and to forgive us. **I confess…**

FIRST READING

In our reading we hear of the prophet Ezekiel.

He did not say: 'I am afraid, I will not go, I will not speak, it is not my business.'

We read from the book of Ezekiel, chapter two.

*
The spirit came into me and made me stand up, and I heard the Lord speaking to me. He said, 'Son of man, I am sending you to the Israelites, to the rebels who have turned against me. Till now they and their ancestors have been in revolt against me. The sons

are defiant and obstinate; I am sending you to them, to say, "The Lord says this." Whether they listen or not, this set of rebels shall know there is a prophet among them.'

This is the word of the Lord. *Ezekiel 2:2-5*

Responsorial Psalm

℟ **Our eyes are on the Lord**
   till he show us his mercy.

1 To you have I lifted up my eyes,
   you who dwell in the heavens:
   my eyes, like the eyes of slaves
   on the hand of their lords. ℟

2 Like the eyes of a servant
   on the hand of her mistress,
   so our eyes are on the Lord our God
   till he show us his mercy. ℟

3 Have mercy on us, Lord, have mercy.
   We are filled with contempt.
   Indeed all too full is our soul
   with the scorn of the rich,
   with the proud man's disdain. ℟ *Ps 122. ℟ v.2*

SECOND READING

We read from the second letter of St Paul to the Corinthians, chapter twelve.
*
In view of the extraordinary nature of these revelations, to stop me from getting too proud I was given a thorn in the flesh, an angel of Satan to beat me and stop me from getting too proud! About this thing, I have pleaded with the Lord three times for it to leave me, but he has said, 'My grace is enough for you: my power is at its best in weakness.' So I shall be very happy to make my weaknesses my special boast so that the power of Christ may stay over me, and that is why I am quite content with my weaknesses, and with insults, hardships, persecutions, and the agonies I go through for Christ's sake. For it is when I am weak that I am strong.

This is the word of the Lord. *2 Corinthians 12:7-10*

Gospel Acclamation
>Alleluia, alleluia!
>The Word was made flesh and lived among us;
>to all who did accept him
>he gave power to become children of God.
>Alleluia!

Jn 1:14. 12

or

>Alleluia, alleluia!
>The Lord has sent me to bring the good news to the poor,
>to proclaim liberty to captives.
>Alleluia!

cf. Lk 4:18

GOSPEL

We read from the holy Gospel according to Mark, chapter six.
★
Jesus went to his home town and his disciples accompanied him. With the coming of the sabbath he began teaching in the synagogue and most of them were astonished when they heard him. They said, 'Where did the man get all this? What is this wisdom that has been granted him, and these miracles that are worked through him? This is the carpenter, surely, the son of Mary, the brother of James and Joset and Jude and Simon? His sisters, too, are they not here with us?' And they would not accept him. And Jesus said to them, 'A prophet is only despised in his own country among his own relations and in his own house'; and he could work no miracle there, though he cured a few sick people by laying his hands on them. He was amazed at their lack of faith.

This is the Gospel of the Lord.

Mark 6:1-6

Fifteenth Sunday in Ordinary Time   B

Introduction to the Service
>If the congregation in our church held a meeting today and decided to ask one or two of us to go to a neighbouring town or village to preach the gospel there, would you be prepared to go?
>   Wouldn't most of us say: I am an ordinary worker, an ordinary farmer, an ordinary housewife. I can't do this. How would I preach? I come to church to listen to God's Word but I cannot go to other people and preach to them.

And yet this is exactly what happens in the reading we hear today: an ordinary sheep farmer was sent, ordinary fishermen were sent.

We can all be sent and have in fact already been sent. God is with us. We do not need to be afraid. We should be grateful for being sent to go out and to invite people to choose God's path.

Penitential Rite

We ask ourselves:

- Did I show others the right way or did I say: 'That is not my business?' (*Silence*)

- Can I work together with other people in church, like the Apostles who were sent out two by two? (*Silence*)

Let us ask for forgiveness for not bringing other people back to God. **I confess**...

FIRST READING

The prophet Amos was not afraid of telling the king the truth. For that reason Amos was hated by the king.

Amos, however, explained who had sent him.

We read from the book of Amos, chapter seven

*

Amaziah, the priest of Bethel, said to Amos, 'Go away, seer; get back to the land of Judah; earn your bread there, do your prophesying there. We want no more prophesying in Bethel; this is the royal sanctuary, the national temple.' 'I was no prophet, neither did I belong to any of the brotherhoods of prophets,' Amos replied to Amaziah. 'I was a shepherd, and looked after sycamores: but it was the Lord who took me from herding the flock, and the Lord who said, "Go, prophesy to my people Israel." '

This is the word of the Lord.   *Amos 7:12-15*

Responsorial Psalm

℞ **Let us see, O Lord, your mercy
and give us your saving help.**

1 I will hear what the Lord God has to say,
a voice that speaks of peace,
peace for his people.

His help is near for those who fear him
and his glory will dwell in our land. ℟

2 Mercy and faithfulness have met;
justice and peace have embraced.
Faithfulness shall spring from the earth
and justice look down from heaven. ℟

3 The Lord will make us prosper
and our earth shall yield its fruit.
Justice shall march before him
and peace shall follow his steps. ℟   *Ps 84:9-14. ℟ v.8*

SECOND READING

We read from the letter of St Paul to the Ephesians, chapter one.
*
*Blessed be God the Father of our Lord Jesus Christ,
who has blessed us with all the spiritual blessings of heaven in
    Christ.
Before the world was made, he chose us, chose us in Christ,
to be holy and spotless, and to live through love in his presence,
determining that we should become his adopted sons, through
    Jesus Christ
for his own kind purposes,
to make us praise the glory of his grace,
his free gift to us in the Beloved
in whom, through his blood, we gain our freedom, the
    forgiveness of our sins.
Such is the richness of the grace
which he has showered on us
in all wisdom and insight.
He has let us know the mystery of his purpose,
the hidden plan he so kindly made in Christ from the beginning
to act upon when the times had run their course to the end:
that he would bring everything together under Christ, as head,
everything in the heavens and everything on earth.*

And it is in him that we were claimed as God's own,
chosen from the beginning,
under the predetermined plan of the one who guides all things
as he decides by his own will;
chosen to be,
for his greater glory,
the people who would put their hopes in Christ before he came.

Now you too, in him,
have heard the message of the truth and the good news of your
    salvation,
and have believed it:
and you too have been stamped with the seal of the Holy Spirit
    of the Promise,
the pledge of our inheritance
which brings freedom for those whom God has taken for his
    own,
to make his glory praised.

This is the word of the Lord.   *Ephesians 1:3-14*

*Shorter Form, verses 3-10. Read between *.*

Gospel Acclamation
Alleluia, alleluia!
Your words are spirit, Lord,
and they are life:
you have the message of eternal life.
Alleuia!   *cf. Jn 6:63. 68*

or

Alleluia, alleluia!
May the Father of our Lord Jesus Christ
enlighten the eyes of our mind,
so that we can see what hope his call holds for us.
Alleluia!   *cf. Eph 1:17.18*

GOSPEL
We read from the holy Gospel according to Mark, chapter six.
*
Jesus summoned the Twelve and began to send them out in pairs
giving them authority over the unclean spirits. And he instructed
them to take nothing for the journey except a staff – no bread, no
haversack, no coppers for their purses. They were to wear
sandals but, he added, 'Do not take a spare tunic.' And he said to
them, 'If you enter a house anywhere, stay there until you leave
the district. And if any place does not welcome you and people
refuse to listen to you, as you walk away shake off the dust from
under your feet as a sign to them.' So they set off to preach
repentance; and they cast out many devils, and anointed many
sick people with oil and cured them.

This is the Gospel of the Lord.   *Mark 6:7-13*

Sixteenth Sunday in Ordinary Time   B

Introduction to the Service

We need leaders in the Church and in public office. We want them to be good leaders. However, what is a good leader? What qualities should they have? What do we expect from them?

We expect good leaders to care for people, to have time for them and to worry about them. Good leaders forget themselves and have only the wellbeing of their people in mind. They do not make themselves big and rich at the expense of other people. Good leaders live for their people. Such leaders are a blessing in the Church and in public office.

In our celebration today we see Jesus giving us an example of good leadership. He did not even have time to eat. He was always ready to serve his people.

We shall also hear today of a prophet who had the courage to stand up against the bad leaders of his time.

Penitential Rite

We ask ourselves:

● If I have people working under me – do I care for them? (*Silence*)

● If I work as a clerk in public service – do I serve the poor people in the same way as I serve the rich? (*Silence*)

● If I am a leader in the Church – do I allow others to grow and to develop as leaders? (*Silence*)

Let us ask for forgiveness for not caring for people. **I confess...**

FIRST READING

When we listen to our reading some people may think that the prophet Jeremiah is talking politics. Jeremiah, however, is fully prepared to suffer for criticising the leaders of his nation.

We read from the book of Jeremiah, chapter twenty-three.

*
'Doom for the shepherds who allow the flock of my pasture to be destroyed and scattered – it is the Lord who speaks! This, therefore, is what the Lord, the God of Israel, says about the shepherds in charge of my people: You have let my flock be scattered and go wandering and have not taken care of them.

Right, I will take care of you for your misdeeds – it is the Lord who speaks! But the remnant of my flock I myself will gather from all the countries where I have dispersed them, and will bring them back to their pastures: they shall be fruitful and increase in numbers. I will raise up shepherds to look after them and pasture them; no fear, no terror for them any more; not one shall be lost – it is the Lord who speaks!

'See, the days are coming – it is the Lord who speaks –
when I will raise a virtuous Branch for David,
who will reign as true king and be wise,
practising honesty and integrity in the land.
In his days Judah will be saved
and Israel dwell in confidence.
And this is the name he will be called:
The Lord-our-integrity.'

This is the word of the Lord. *Jeremiah 23:1-6*

Responsorial Psalm

℟ **The Lord is my shepherd;
there is nothing I shall want.**

1 The Lord is my shepherd;
there is nothing I shall want.
Fresh and green are the pastures
where he gives me repose.
Near restful waters he leads me,
to revive my drooping spirit. ℟

2 He guides me along the right path;
he is true to his name.
If I should walk in the valley of darkness
no evil would I fear.
You are there with your crook and your staff;
with these you give me comfort. ℟

3 You have prepared a banquet for me
in the sight of my foes.
My head you have anointed with oil;
my cup is overflowing. ℟

4 Surely goodness and kindness shall follow me
all the days of my life.
In the Lord's own house shall I dwell
for ever and ever. ℟

Ps 22. ℟ v.2

SECOND READING

We read from the letter of St Paul to the Ephesians, chapter two.
*

In Christ Jesus, you that used to be so far apart from us have been brought very close, by the blood of Christ. For he is the peace between us, and has made the two into one and broken down the barrier which used to keep them apart, actually destroying in his own person the hostility caused by the rules and decrees of the Law. This was to create one single New Man in himself out of the two of them and by restoring peace through the cross, to unite them both in a single Body and reconcile them with God. In his own person he killed the hostility. Later he came to bring the good news of peace, peace to you who were far away and peace to those who were near at hand. Through him, both of us have in the one Spirit our way to come to the Father.

This is the word of the Lord. *Ephesians 2:13-18*

Gospel Acclamation
Alleluia, alleluia!
The sheep that belong to me listen to my voice,
says the Lord,
I know them and they follow me.
Alleluia! *Jn 10:27*

GOSPEL

We read from the holy Gospel according to Mark, chapter six.
*

The apostles rejoined Jesus and told him all they had done and taught. Then he said to them, 'You must come away to some lonely place all by yourselves and rest for a while'; for there were so many coming and going that the apostles had no time even to eat. So they went off in a boat to a lonely place where they could be by themselves. But people saw them going, and many could guess where; and from every town they all hurried to the place on foot and reached it before them. So as he stepped ashore he saw a large crowd; and he took pity on them because they were like sheep without a shepherd, and he set himself to teach them at some length.

This is the Gospel of the Lord. *Mark 6:30-34*

Seventeenth Sunday in Ordinary Time   B

Introduction to the Service

It is disgraceful that there are many people in the world who have no food to eat. Many even die of hunger. There are plenty of guns – but not enough loaves of bread. There are plenty of bullets – but not enough pounds of butter.

In our celebration today the Word of God and the example of Jesus challenge us. When Jesus saw the five thousand hungry people he was moved to help them. He multiplied the fishes and the loaves.

Even today, bread can be multiplied. If people love one another and work together in peace, everybody will have more than enough to eat.

Let us reflect again on how sad it is that there are people in the world who have to die of hunger.

Penitential Rite

We ask ourselves:

● What do I do to feed the hungry or to help people in their daily needs?   (*Silence*)

● Do I buy useless and unecessary things for myself while others around me have nothing to eat or to wear?   (*Silence*)

● Do I profit by pushing others aside?   (*Silence*)

Let us ask God to make right what we have done wrong. **I confess**...

FIRST READING

In our reading we hear of a prophet who was given bread as a present. He did not keep it for himself but shared it with others. For this reason still greater things happened to him.

We read from the second book of Kings, chapter four.
*
A man came from Baal-shalishah, bringing Elisha, the man of God, bread from the first-fruits, twenty barley loaves and fresh grain in the ear. 'Give it to the people to eat,' Elisha said. But his servant replied, 'How can I serve this to a hundred men?' 'Give it to the people to eat' he insisted 'for the Lord says this, "They will eat and have some left over." ' He served them; they ate and had some over, as the Lord had said.

This is the word of the Lord.   *2 Kings 4:42-44*

Responsorial Psalm
℟ **You open wide your hand, O Lord,
and grant our desires.**

1 All your creatures shall thank you, O Lord,
and your friends shall repeat their blessing.
They shall speak of the glory of your reign
and declare your might, O God. ℟

2 The eyes of all creatures look to you
and you give them their food in due time.
You open wide your hand,
grant the desires of all who live. ℟

3 The Lord is just in all his ways
and loving in all his deeds.
He is close to all who call him,
who call on him from their hearts. ℟

Ps 144:10-11. 15-18. ℟ v. 16

SECOND READING

We read from the letter of St Paul to the Ephesians, chapter four.
*
I, the prisoner in the Lord, implore you to lead a life worthy of
your vocation. Bear with one another charitably, in complete
selflessness, gentleness and patience. Do all you can to preserve
the unity of the Spirit by the peace that binds you together. There
is one Body, one Spirit, just as you were all called into one and
the same hope when you were called. There is one Lord, one
faith, one baptism, and one God who is Father of all, through all
and within all.

This is the word of the Lord.   *Ephesians 4:1-6*

Gospel Acclamation
Alleluia, alleluia!
Your words are spirit, Lord,
and they are life:
you have the message of eternal life.
Alleluia!   *cf. Jn 6:63. 68*

or

Alleluia, alleluia!
A great prophet has appeared among us;
God has visited his people.
Alleluia!   *Lk 7:16*

GOSPEL

We read from the holy Gospel according to John, chapter six.

*

Jesus went off to the other side of the Sea of Galilee – or of Tiberias – and a large crowd followed him, impressed by the signs he gave by curing the sick. Jesus climbed the hillside, and sat down there with his disciples. It was shortly before the Jewish feast of Passover.

Looking up, Jesus saw the crowds approaching and said to Philip, 'Where can we buy some bread for these people to eat?' He only said this to test Philip; he himself knew exactly what he was going to do. Philip answered, 'Two hundred denarii would only buy enough to give them a small piece each.' One of his disciples, Andrew, Simon Peter's brother, said, 'There is a small boy here with five barley loaves and two fish; but what is that between so many?' Jesus said to them, 'Make the people sit down.' There was plenty of grass there, and as many as five thousand men sat down. Then Jesus took the loaves, gave thanks, and gave them out to all who were sitting ready; he then did the same with the fish, giving out as much as was wanted. When they had eaten enough he said to the disciples, 'Pick up the pieces left over, so that nothing gets wasted.' So they picked them up, and filled twelve hampers with scraps left over from the meal of five barley loaves. The people, seeing this sign that he had given, said, 'This really is the prophet who is to come into the world.' Jesus, who could see they were about to come and take him by force and make him king, escaped back to the hills by himself.

This is the Gospel of the Lord.   *John 6:1-15*

Eighteenth Sunday in Ordinary Time   B

Introduction to the Service

There are people who say: 'Why should I go to church and wait for heaven. I am hungry now. I am oppressed now. The Church should join us in our struggle against injustice and help us to fill our bellies!'

In our celebration today we shall hear of such people who only demanded food from God. Sure enough, he gave them food. He created many things for his people, and he saw that it was good. God wants everybody to have enough food. However, God offers still more. A happy life does not only mean food and drink.

In our celebration today Jesus advises us: 'Do not work for food that cannot last.'

Penitential Rite

Let us examine our conscience:

● What are my ideals in life? Do I only want to satisfy the needs of my body? (*Silence*)

● What efforts did I make last week to keep in contact with God. Did I think of God? Pray? Read the Bible? (*Silence*)

● Did I help people without being paid for it? (*Silence*)

Let us ask God to be merciful to us. **I confess**...

FIRST READING

The people of Israel stood up against Moses in the desert. It was almost like a riot. The flesh-pots of Egypt were more attractive to the people than the freedom of the desert.

We read from the book of Exodus, chapter sixteen.
*
The whole community of the sons of Israel began to complain against Moses and Aaron in the wilderness and said to them, 'Why did we not die at the Lord's hand in the land of Egypt, when we were able to sit down to pans of meat and could eat bread to our heart's content! As it is, you have brought us to this wilderness to starve this whole company to death!'

Then the Lord said to Moses, 'Now I will rain down bread for you from the heavens. Each day the people are to go out and gather the day's portion; I propose to test them in this way to see whether they will follow my law or not.'

'I have heard the complaints of the sons of Israel. Say this to them, "Between the two evenings you shall eat meat, and in the morning you shall have bread to your heart's content. Then you will learn that I, the Lord, am your God." ' And so it came about: quails flew up in the evening, and they covered the camp; in the morning there was a coating of dew all round the camp. When the coating of dew lifted, there on the surface of the desert was a thing delicate, powdery, as fine as hoarfrost on the ground. When they saw this, the sons of Israel said to one another, 'What is that?' not knowing what it was. 'That' said Moses to them 'is the bread the Lord gives you to eat.'

This is the word of the Lord.   *Exodus 16:2-4*

Responsorial Psalm
℟ **The Lord gave them bread from heaven.**

1 The things we have heard and understood,
   the things our fathers have told us,
   we will tell to the next generation:
   the glories of the Lord and his might. ℟

2 He commanded the clouds above
   and opened the gates of heaven.
   He rained down manna for their food,
   and gave them bread from heaven. ℟

3 Mere men ate the bread of angels.
   He sent them abundance of food.
   He brought them to his holy land,
   to the mountain which his right hand had won. ℟

                              Ps 77:3-4. 23-25. 54. ℟ v.24

SECOND READING

We read from the letter of St Paul to the Ephesians, chapter four.
*

I want to urge you in the name of the Lord, not to go on living the
aimless kind of life that pagans live. Now that is hardly the way
you have learnt from Christ, unless you failed to hear him
properly when you were taught what the truth is in Jesus. You
must give up your old way of life; you must put aside your old
self, which gets corrupted by following illusory desires. Your
mind must be renewed by a spiritual revolution so that you can
put on the new self that has been created in God's way, in the
goodness and holiness of the truth.

    This is the word of the Lord.   *Ephesians 4:17. 20-24*

Gospel Acclamation
   Alleluia, alleluia!
   I am the Way, the Truth and the Life, says the Lord;
   no one can come to the Father except through me.
   Alleluia!   *Jn 14:5*

or

   Alleluia, alleluia!
   Man does not live on bread alone,
   but on every word that comes from the mouth of God.
   Alleluia!   *Mt 4:4*

GOSPEL

We read from the holy Gospel according to John, chapter six.

*

When the people saw that neither Jesus nor his disciples were there, they got into boats and crossed to Capernaum to look for Jesus. When they found him on the other side, they said to him, 'Rabbi, when did you come here?' Jesus answered:

'I tell you most solemnly,
you are not looking for me
because you have seen the signs
but because you had all the bread you wanted to eat.
Do not work for food that cannot last,
but work for food that endures to eternal life,
the kind of food the Son of Man is offering you,
for on him the Father, God himself, has set his seal.'

Then they said to him, 'What must we do if we are to do the works that God wants?' Jesus gave them this answer, 'This is working for God: you must believe in the one he has sent.' So they said, 'What sign will you give to show us that we should believe in you? What work will you do? Our fathers had manna to eat in the desert; as scripture says: He gave them bread from heaven to eat.'

Jesus answered:

'I tell you most solemnly,
it was not Moses who gave you bread from heaven,
it is my Father who gives you the bread from heaven,
the true bread;
for the bread of God
is that which comes down from heaven
and gives life to the world.'

'Sir,' they said 'give us that bread always.' Jesus answered:

'I am the bread of life.
He who comes to me will never be hungry;
he who believes in me will never thirst.'

This is the Gospel of the Lord.   *John 6:24-35*

Nineteenth Sunday in Ordinary Time   B

Introduction to the Service

Our life is rather like a long, long journey over mountains and hills. Sometimes the road is easy, sometimes difficult. On every journey we need food, bread and drink. Without food and water we would die on the way, so if we are going on a long journey we prepare our provisions very carefully.

In our celebration today, Christ offers us his provision for our journey through life. He tells us: 'I am the living bread'.

Christ gives us hope when we have lost hope. Christ strengthens us when we have become weak. Christ shows us the aim of our journey at times when we walk in darkness and despair. Therefore he says: 'I am the living bread.'

Penitential Rite

Let us ask ourselves:

● Do I invite God to join me on my journey through life? (*Silence*)

● Do I accept God's food, God's Word and God's advice on my way?   (*Silence*)

● Do I remember during the day that I have received the living bread of Christ in Holy Communion?   (*Silence*)

Let us ask for forgiveness for forgetting God on our way through life.   **I confess**...

FIRST READING

In our reading we meet the prophet Elijah on his journey through the desert. He was fed up with life. He was tired of being a prophet. He refused to do God's work any longer. He ran away from his work because the king wanted to kill him.

We read from the first book of Kings, chapter nineteen.
*
Elijah went into the wilderness, a day's journey, and sitting under a furze bush wished he were dead. 'Lord,' he said 'I have had enough. Take my life; I am no better than my ancestors.' Then he lay down and went to sleep. But an angel touched him and said, 'Get up and eat.' He looked round, and there at his head was a scone baked on hot stones, and a jar of water. He ate and drank and then lay down again. But the angel of the Lord

came back a second time and touched him and said, 'Get up and eat, or the journey will be too long for you.' So he got up and ate and drank, and strengthened by that food he walked for forty days and forty nights until he reached Horeb, the mountain of God.

This is the word of the Lord.   *1 Kings 19:4-8*

Responsorial Psalm

℟ **Taste and see that the Lord is good.**

1   I will bless the Lord at all times,
      his praise always on my lips;
      in the Lord my soul shall make its boast.
      The humble shall hear and be glad.   ℟

2   Glorify the Lord with me.
      Together let us praise his name.
      I sought the Lord and he answered me;
      from all my terrors he set me free.   ℟

3   Look towards him and be radiant;
      let your faces not be abashed.
      This poor man called; the Lord heard him
      and rescued him from all his distress.   ℟

4   The angel of the Lord is encamped
      around those who revere him, to rescue them.
      Taste and see that the Lord is good.
      He is happy who seeks refuge in him.   ℟   *Ps 33:2-9. ℟ v.9*

SECOND READING

We read from the letter of St Paul to the Ephesians, chapters four and five.
*
Do not grieve the Holy Spirit of God who has marked you with his seal for you to be set free when the day comes. Never have grudges against others, or lose your temper, or raise your voice to anybody, or call each other names, or allow any sort of spitefulness. Be friends with one another, and kind, forgiving each other as readily as God forgave you in Christ.

Try, then, to imitate God, as children of his that he loves, and follow Christ by loving as he loved you, giving himself up in our place as a fragrant offering and a sacrifice to God.

This is the word of the Lord.   *Ephesians 4:30–5:2*

Gospel Acclamation
Alleluia, alleluia!
If anyone loves me he will keep my word,
and my Father will love him,
and we shall come to him.
Alleluia!   *Jn 14-23*

or

Alleluia, alleluia!
I am the living bread which has come down from heaven,
says the Lord.
Anyone who eats this bread will live for ever.
Alleluia!   *Jn 6:51*

GOSPEL

We read from the holy Gospel according to John, chapter six.
✝
The Jews were complaining to each other about Jesus, because he
had said, 'I am the bread that came down from heaven.' 'Surely
this is Jesus son of Joseph' they said. 'We know his father and
mother. How can he now say, "I have come down from
heaven"?' Jesus said in reply, 'Stop complaining to each other.

'No one can come to me
unless he is drawn by the Father who sent me,
and I will raise him up at the last day.
It is written in the prophets:
They will all be taught by God,
and to hear the teaching of the Father,
and learn from it,
is to come to me.
Not that anybody has seen the Father,
except the one who comes from God:
he has seen the Father.
I tell you most solemnly,
everybody who believes has eternal life.
I am the bread of life.
Your fathers ate the manna in the desert
and they are dead;
but this is the bread that comes down from heaven,
so that a man may eat it and not die.
I am the living bread which has come down from heaven.
Anyone who eats this bread will live for ever;

and the bread that I shall give
is my flesh, for the life of the world.'

This is the Gospel of the Lord. *John 6:41-51*

Twentieth Sunday in Ordinary Time   B

Introduction to the Service

We all want to be wise people. We do not want to be called 'fools'.

For instance, we would be fools if we bought plastic bread instead of real bread. Wise people know how to distinguish between useless things and things of real value. We need lots of wisdom when we listen to the clever advertisements on the radio or on TV. They tempt us to buy things which very often are useless and which we do not really need.

We are here today to listen to God's wisdom. The Lord will tell us: 'I am the living bread. Anyone who eats this bread will live for ever.' He invites us, saying: 'Take and eat'.

Penitential Rite

We ask ourselves:

- Do I act like a fool by chasing after things which cannot bring real happiness?   (*Silence*)

- Do I believe too quickly the promises which are made by clever advertisements?   (*Silence*)

- Do I reject the treasures which God is offering me?   (*Silence*)

Let us ask for forgiveness for rejecting God's wisdom. **I confess**…

FIRST READING

The wisdom of God is like a loving mother. She goes around the city calling back her children who chase after silly things. She calls the ignorant and those who make fools of themselves. She invites them to come and eat the real food.

We read from the book of Proverbs, chapter nine.
*
Wisdom has built herself a house,
she has erected her seven pillars,
she has slaughtered her beasts, prepared her wine,

she has laid her table.
She has despatched her maidservants
and proclaimed from the city's heights:
'Who is ignorant? Let him step this way.'
To the fool she says,
'Come and eat my bread,
drink the wine I have prepared!
Leave your folly and you will live,
walk in the ways of perception.'

This is the word of the Lord.   *Proverbs 9:1-6*

Responsorial Psalm
℟   **Taste and see that the Lord is good.**

1   I will bless the Lord at all times,
    his praise always on my lips;
    in the Lord my soul shall make its boast.
    The humble shall hear and be glad.   ℟

2   Revere the Lord, you his saints.
    They lack nothing, those who revere him.
    Strong lions suffer want and go hungry
    but those who seek the Lord lack no blessing.   ℟

3   Come, children, and hear me
    that I may teach you the fear of the Lord.
    Who is he who longs for life
    and many days, to enjoy his prosperity?   ℟

4   Then keep your tongue from evil
    and your lips from speaking deceit.
    Turn aside from evil and do good;
    seek and strive after peace.   ℟   *Ps 33:2-3. 10-15. ℟ v.9*

SECOND READING
We read from the letter of St Paul to the Ephesians, chapter five.
*
Be very careful about the sort of lives you lead, like intelligent and
not like senseless people. This may be a wicked age, but your
lives should redeem it. And do not be thoughtless but recognise
what is the will of the Lord. Do not drug yourselves with wine,
this is simply dissipation; be filled with the Spirit. Sing the words
and tunes of the psalms and hymns when you are together, and
go on singing and chanting to the Lord in your hearts, so that

always and everywhere you are giving thanks to God who is our Father in the name of our Lord Jesus Christ.

This is the word of the Lord.

Ephesians 5:15-20

Gospel Acclamation

Alleluia, alleluia!
The Word was made flesh and lived among us;
to all who did accept him
he gave power to become children of God.
Alleluia!

Jn 1:14. 12

or

Alleluia, alleluia!
He who eats my flesh and drinks my blood
lives in me, and I live in him,
says the Lord.
Alleluia!

Jn 6:56

GOSPEL

We read from the holy Gospel according to John, chapter six.
✦
Jesus said to the crowd:

'I am the living bread which has come down from heaven.
Anyone who eats this bread will live for ever;
and the bread that I shall give
is my flesh, for the life of the world.'

Then the Jews started arguing with one another: 'How can this man give us his flesh to eat?' they said. Jesus replied:

'I tell you most solemnly,
if you do not eat the flesh of the Son of Man
and drink his blood,
you will not have life in you.
Anyone who does eat my flesh and drink my blood
has eternal life,
and I shall raise him up on the last day.
For my flesh is real food
and my blood is real drink.
He who eats my flesh and drinks my blood
lives in me
and I live in him.
As I, who am sent by the living Father,
myself draw life from the Father,

so whoever eats me will draw life from me.
This is the bread come down from heaven;
not like the bread our ancestors ate:
they are dead,
but anyone who eats this bread will live for ever.'

This is the Gospel of the Lord.   *John 6:51-58*

Twenty-First Sunday in Ordinary Time   B

Introduction to the Service

There are people who say: 'The teaching of Christ and his Church is too hard. We cannot keep all the demands of the Gospel. After all, times have changed. We have different ideas today about life, money, sex, marriage and many other things. We cannot follow the Christian way of life.'

The same thing happened even in Christ's lifetime. People found his teaching too hard and too demanding. Many left him. Jesus, however, did not soften his demands in order to please everybody.

Christ will ask us today in our celebration the same question which he put to the people of his time: 'Do you want to go away too?'

Penitential Rite

Let us examine our conscience:

- Which demands of Christ do we simply ignore, saying: 'These are too hard for me?'   (*Silence*)

- Do we follow public opinion without asking ourselves if it is right or wrong?   (*Silence*)

Let us ask God's forgiveness for following Christ half-heartedly and with little conviction.   **I confess**...

FIRST READING

When the people of Israel arrived in Canaan, the Promised Land, they had to live among people who venerated many little gods and idols. They had to make a choice as to whom they wanted to follow and in whom they wished to put their trust.

Joshua, the successor of Moses, challenged them on this question as we shall hear in our reading.

We read from the book of Joshua, chapter twenty-four.
*
Joshua gathered all the tribes of Israel together at Shechem; then he called the elders, leaders, judges and scribes of Israel, and they presented themselves before God. Then Joshua said to all the people: 'If you will not serve the Lord, choose today whom you wish to serve, whether the gods that your ancestors served beyond the River, or the gods of the Amorites in whose land you are now living. As for me and my House, we will serve the Lord.'

The people answered, 'We have no intention of deserting the Lord our God who brought us and our ancestors out of the land of Egypt, the house of slavery, who worked those great wonders before our eyes and preserved us all along the way we travelled and among all the peoples through whom we journeyed. We too will serve the Lord, for he is our God.'

This is the word of the Lord.   *Joshua 24:1-2. 15-18*

Responsorial Psalm
℟   **Taste and see that the Lord is good.**

1 I will bless the Lord at all times,
     his praise always on my lips;
     in the Lord my soul shall make its boast.
     The humble shall hear and be glad.   ℟

2 The Lord turns his face against the wicked
     to destroy their remembrance from the earth.
     The Lord turns his eyes to the just
     and his ears to their appeal.   ℟

3 They call and the Lord hears
     and rescues them in all their distress.
     The Lord is close to the broken-hearted;
     those whose spirit is crushed he will save.   ℟

4 Many are the trials of the just man
     but from them all the Lord will rescue him.
     He will keep guard over all his bones,
     not one of his bones shall be broken.   ℟

5 Evil brings death to the wicked;
     those who hate the good are doomed.
     The Lord ransoms the souls of his servants.
     Those who hide in him shall not be condemned.   ℟

                                   Ps 33:2-3. 16-23. ℟ v.9

SECOND READING

We read from the letter of St Paul to the Ephesians, chapter five.

*

Give way to one another in obedience to Christ. Wives should regard their husbands as they regard the Lord, since as Christ is head of the Church and saves the whole body, so is a husband the head of his wife; and as the Church submits to Christ, so should wives to their husbands, in everything. Husbands should love their wives just as Christ loved the Church and sacrificed himself for her to make her holy. He made her clean by washing her in water with a form of words, so that when he took her to himself she would be glorious, with no speck or wrinkle or anything like that, but holy and faultless. In the same way, husbands must love their wives as they love their own bodies; for a man to love his wife is for him to love himself. A man never hates his own body, but he feeds it and looks after it; and that is the way Christ treats the Church, because it is his body – and we are its living parts. For this reason, a man must leave his father and mother and be joined to his wife, and the two will become one body. This mystery has many implications; but I am saying it applies to Christ and the Church.

This is the word of the Lord.   *Ephesians 5:21-32*

Gospel Acclamation
　　Alleluia, alleluia!
　　Your words are spirit, Lord,
　　and they are life:
　　you have the message of eternal life.
　　Alleluia!   *cf. Jn 6:63. 68*

GOSPEL

We read from the holy Gospel according to John, chapter six.

*

After hearing his doctrine many of the followers of Jesus said, 'This is intolerable language. How could anyone accept it?' Jesus was aware that his followers were complaining about it and said, 'Does this upset you? What if you should see the Son of Man ascend to where he was before?

　　'It is the spirit that gives life,
　　the flesh has nothing to offer.
　　The words I have spoken to you are spirit
　　and they are life.

'But there are some of you who do not believe.' For Jesus knew from the outset those who did not believe, and who it was that would betray him. He went on, 'This is why I told you that no one could come to me unless the Father allows him.' After this, many of his disciples left him and stopped going with him.

Then Jesus said to the Twelve, 'What about you, do you want to go away too?' Simon Peter answered, 'Lord, who shall we go to? You have the message of eternal life, and we believe; we know that you are the Holy One of God.'

This is the Gospel of the Lord.   *John 6:60-69*

Twenty-Second Sunday in Ordinary Time   B

Introduction to the Service
All societies and nations have their own customs and traditions. It sometimes happens, however, that people maintain customary practices without understanding them. Some will keep the most unimportant customs very faithfully. The really important traditions, however, are often ignored if people do not like them or find them too difficult to maintain.

This problem can occur within our church community. We too have traditions and customs and in the same way it can happen that we keep up the unimportant traditions whilst ignoring those which really matter. For example, too much emphasis can be given to holy pictures and holy water or to shrines and relics. The danger is that we forget about the important traditions: love, unity, forgiveness, prayer. How well do we, in our church community, keep up these important traditions?

There is also a danger that we give pride of place to the traditions of our society and not to those of God. We are reminded of this today when Christ says: 'You put aside the commandment of God to cling to human traditions.'

Penitential Rite
We ask ourselves:

● In our meetings, are we more concerned with our constitution than with keeping God's law of unity and love?   *(Silence)*

● Do we only pray with our lips, without raising our hearts to God?   *(Silence)*

Let us ask for forgiveness for doing holy things whilst our hearts are far away from God. **I confess**...

FIRST READING

In our reading we shall hear how precious God's commandments are. They give us real life. They are customs which make us wise and prudent.

We read from the book of Deuteronomy, chapter four.

*
Moses said to the people: 'Now, Israel, take notice of the laws and customs that I teach you today, and observe them, that you may have life and may enter and take possession of the land that the Lord the God of your fathers is giving you. You must add nothing to what I command you, and take nothing from it, but keep the commandments of the Lord your God just as I lay them down for you. Keep them, observe them, and they will demonstrate to the peoples your wisdom and understanding. When they come to know of all these laws they will exclaim, "No other people is as wise and prudent as this great nation." And indeed, what great nation is there that has its gods so near as the Lord our God is to us whenever we call to him? And what great nation is there that has laws and customs to match this whole Law that I put before you today?'

This is the word of the Lord.   *Deuteronomy 4:1-2. 6-8*

Responsorial Psalm
℟   **The just will live in the presence of the Lord.**

1   Lord, who shall dwell on your holy mountain?
    He who walks without fault;
    he who acts with justice
    and speaks the truth from his heart.   ℟

2   He who does no wrong to his brother,
    who casts no slur on his neighbour,
    who holds the godless in disdain,
    but honours those who fear the Lord.   ℟

3   He who keeps his pledge, come what may;
    who takes no interest on a loan
    and accepts no bribes against the innocent.
    Such a man will stand firm for ever.   ℟   *Ps 14:2-5. ℟ v.1*

SECOND READING

We read from the letter of St James, chapter one.
★

It is all that is good, everything that is perfect, which is given us from above; it comes down from the Father of all light; with him there is no such thing as alteration, no shadow of a change. By his own choice he made us his children by the message of the truth so that we should be a sort of first-fruits of all that he had created.

Accept and submit to the word which has been planted in you and can save your souls. But you must do what the word tells you, and not just listen to it and deceive yourselves.

Pure unspoilt religion, in the eyes of God our Father is this: coming to the help of orphans and widows when they need it, and keeping oneself uncontaminated by the world.

This is the word of the Lord. *James 1:17-18. 21-22. 27*

Gospel Acclamation
Alleluia, alleluia!
Your words are spirit, Lord,
and they are life:
you have the message of eternal life.
Alleluia! *cf. Jn 6:63. 68*

or

Alleluia, alleluia!
By his own choice the Father made us his children
by the message of the truth,
so that we should be a sort of first-fruits
of all that he created.
Alleluia! *James 1:18*

GOSPEL

We read from the holy Gospel according to Mark, chapter seven.
★

The Pharisees and some of the scribes who had come from Jerusalem gathered round Jesus, and they noticed that some of his disciples were eating with unclean hands, that is, without washing them. For the Pharisees, and the Jews in general, follow the tradition of the elders and never eat without washing their arms as far as the elbow; and on returning from the market place they never eat without first sprinkling themselves. There are also many other observances which have been handed down to them concerning the washing of cups and pots and bronze dishes. So these Pharisees and scribes asked him, 'Why do your disciples not respect the tradition of the elders but eat their food with unclean hands?' He answered, 'It was of you hypocrites that Isaiah so rightly prophesied in this passage of scripture:

This people honours me only with lip-service,
while their hearts are far from me.
The worship they offer me is worthless,
the doctrines they teach are only human regulations.

You put aside the commandment of God to cling to human traditions.'

He called the people to him again and said, 'Listen to me, all of you, and understand. Nothing that goes into a man from outside can make him unclean; it is the things that come out of a man that make him unclean. For it is from within, from men's hearts, that evil intentions emerge: fornication, theft, murder, adultery, avarice, malice, deceit, indecency, envy, slander, pride, folly. All these evil things come from within and make a man unclean.'

This is the Gospel of the Lord.   *Mark 7:1-8. 14-15. 21-23*

Twenty-Third Sunday in Ordinary Time   B

Introduction to the Service

There are people who reject religion and the Church. They say that religion talks only about heaven and forgets the troubles which we have on earth. Religion, they say, is like a sleeping pill.

In our celebration today we hear the opposite. We see Christ doing all things well: healing the sick, loosening the tongue of a man who could not speak properly. Isaiah had foreseen all this in a vision. He saw the eyes of the blind opened, the ears of the deaf unsealed and the lame made healthy again.

It is this example of Christ which has inspired countless Christians of all times to open schools for the deaf and dumb, schools for the blind and schools for the handicapped. It was religion, the love of God, which urged them to do all things well.

When we listen to the message of God today we should allow ourselves to be urged and inspired by the same example of Christ.

Penitential Rite

Let us ask ourselves:

- Do we ever thank God for giving us eyes to see and a tongue to speak?   (*Silence*)

- How do we use our tongue? Do we use it to hurt and destroy others?   (*Silence*)

Let us ask God's forgiveness for being blind to the needs of our neighbours; for being dumb when we should speak a word of appreciation.   **I confess**...

FIRST READING

Our reading does not say: 'People, suffer on earth and wait for heaven!' It proclaims the message that our God is coming to us, opening the eyes of the blind, the ears of the deaf and making the lame walk.

We read from the book of Isaiah, chapter thirty-five.

*

Say to all faint hearts,
'Courage! Do not be afraid.

'Look, your God is coming,
vengeance is coming,
the retribution of God;
he is coming to save you.'

Then the eyes of the blind shall be opened,
the ears of the deaf unsealed,
then the lame shall leap like a deer
and the tongues of the dumb sing for joy;

for water gushes in the desert,
streams in the wasteland,
the scorched earth becomes a lake,
the parched land springs of water.

This is the word of the Lord.

Isaiah 35:4-7

Responsorial Psalm
℟   **My soul, give praise to the Lord.**

or

℟   **Alleluia!**

1   It is the Lord who keeps faith for ever,
     who is just to those who are oppressed.
     It is he who gives bread to the hungry,
     the Lord, who sets prisoners free. ℟

2   It is the Lord who gives sight to the blind,
     who raises up those who are bowed down,
     the Lord who loves the just,
     the Lord, who protects the stranger. ℟

3   The Lord upholds the widow and orphan,
     but thwarts the path of the wicked.
     The Lord will reign for ever,
     Zion's God, from age to age. ℟   *Ps 145:7-10. ℟ v.1*

SECOND READING

We read from the letter of St James, chapter two.
*
My brothers, do not try to combine faith in Jesus Christ, our
glorified Lord, with the making of distinctions between classes of
people. Now suppose a man comes into your synagogue, beauti-
fully dressed and with a gold ring on, and at the same time a poor
man comes in, in shabby clothes, and you take notice of the
well-dressed man, and say, 'Come this way to the best seats;'
then you tell the poor man, 'Stand over there' or 'You can sit on
the floor by my foot-rest.' Can't you see that you have used two
different standards in your mind, and turned yourselves into
judges, and corrupt judges at that?

     Listen, my dear brothers: it was those who are poor according
to the world that God chose, to be rich in faith and to be the heirs
to the kingdom which he promised to those who love him.

     This is the word of the Lord.   *James 2:1-5*

Gospel Acclamation
     Alleluia, alleluia!
     Speak, Lord, your servant is listening:
     you have the message of eternal life.
     Alleluia!   *1 Sam 3:9; Jn 6:68*

or

Alleluia, alleluia!
Jesus proclaimed the Good News of the kingdom,
and cured all kinds of sickness among the people.
Alleluia!

cf. Mt 4:23

GOSPEL

We read from the holy Gospel according to Mark, chapter seven.
*

Returning from the district of Tyre, Jesus went by way of Sidon
towards the Sea of Galilee, right through the Decapolis region.
And they brought him a deaf man who had an impediment in his
speech; and they asked him to lay his hand on him. He took him
aside in private, away from the crowd, put his fingers into the
man's ears and touched his tongue with spittle. Then looking up
to heaven he sighed; and he said to him, 'Ephphatha,' that is, 'Be
opened.' And his ears were opened, and the ligament of his
tongue was loosened and he spoke clearly. And Jesus ordered
them to tell no one about it, but the more he insisted, the more
widely they published it. Their admiration was unbounded. 'He
has done all things well,' they said 'he makes the deaf hear and
the dumb speak.'

This is the Gospel of the Lord.

Mark 7:31-37

Twenty-Fourth Sunday in Ordinary Time   B

Introduction to the Service

We have our own way of solving problems. When somebody
insults us we feel justified in retaliating by insulting them. We
quickly say that the other person started all the trouble.

When somebody uses a gun against us, we want to do the same
against them. When one country feels threatened by another, both
prepare their deadly weapons: guns, bullets and bombs.

We want to overcome evil by evil. This is the world's way of
solving problems. Christ tells us today that it is the way of Satan.

The Lord shows us a different way through his word and
example. He breaks the unending chain of evil and retaliation by
accepting the cross. He wants to overcome evil with good. He
overcomes darkness with light. This is his way. It is God's way of
doing things.

Penitential Rite

We ask ourselves:

- How do we react when people hurt us by word or deed? (*Silence*)

- Do we have the strength to take the first step towards reconciliation, even if we feel completely innocent? (*Silence*)

Let us ask for forgiveness for rejecting God's way of solving problems. **I confess**…

FIRST READING

As we listen to our reading it may be helpful if we imagine Christ on his way to the cross. We might also imagine people who are suffering in silence. Or we can imagine all the brave people who have been put into prison because they stood up against injustice.

We read from the book of Isaiah, chapter fifty.
*
The Lord has opened my ear.

For my part, I made no resistance,
neither did I turn away.
I offered my back to those who struck me,
my cheeks to those who tore at my beard;
I did not cover my face
against insult and spittle.

The Lord comes to my help,
so that I am untouched by the insults.
So, too, I set my face like flint;
I know I shall not be shamed.

My vindicator is here at hand. Does anyone start proceedings
against me?
Then let us go to court together.
Who thinks he has a case against me?
Let him approach me.
The Lord is coming to my help,
who dare condemn me?

This is the word of the Lord. *Isaiah 50:5-9*

Responsorial Psalm

℟   **I will walk in the presence of the Lord,**
       in the land of the living.

or

℟   **Alleluia!**

1   I love the Lord for he has heard
     the cry of my appeal;
     for he turned his ear to me
     in the day when I called him.   ℟

2   They surrounded me, the snares of death,
     with the anguish of the tomb;
     they caught me, sorrow and distress.
     I called on the Lord's name.
     O Lord my God, deliver me!   ℟

3   How gracious is the Lord, and just;
     our God has compassion.
     The Lord protects the simple hearts;
     I was helpless so he saved me.   ℟

4   He has kept my soul from death,
     my eyes from tears
     and my feet from stumbling.
     I will walk in the presence of the Lord
     in the land of the living.   ℟   *Ps 114:1-6. 8-9. ℟ v.9*

SECOND READING

We read from the letter of St James, chapter two.
*
Take the case, my brothers, of someone who has never done a
single good act but claims that he has faith. Will that faith save
him? If one of the brothers or one of the sisters is in need of
clothes and has not enough food to live on, and one of you says
to them, 'I wish you well; keep yourself warm and eat plenty,'
without giving them these bare necessities of life, then what good
is that? Faith is like that: if good works do not go with it, it is quite
dead.

This is the way to talk to people of that kind: 'You say you
have faith and I have good deeds; I will prove to you that I have
faith by showing you my good deeds – now you prove to me that
you have faith without any good deeds to show.'

This is the word of the Lord.   *James 2:14-18*

Gospel Acclamation

Alleluia, alleluia!
I am the Way, the Truth and the Life, says the Lord;
no one can come to the Father except through me.
Alleluia!

Jn 14:5

or

Alleluia, alleluia!
The only thing I can boast about is the cross of our Lord,
through whom the world is crucified to me, and I to the
world.
Alleluia!

Gal 6:14

GOSPEL

We read from the holy Gospel according to Mark, chapter eight.
✶
Jesus and his disciples left for the villages round Caesarea
Philippi. On the way he put this question to his disciples, 'Who
do people say I am?' And they told him. 'John the Baptist,' they
said 'others Elijah; others again, one of the prophets.' 'But you,'
he asked 'who do you say I am?' Peter spoke up and said to him,
'You are the Christ.' And he gave them strict orders not to tell
anyone about him.

And he began to teach them that the Son of Man was destined
to suffer grievously, to be rejected by the elders and the chief
priests and the scribes, and to be put to death, and after three
days to rise again; and he said all this quite openly. Then, taking
him aside, Peter started to remonstrate with him. But, turning
and seeing his disciples, he rebuked Peter and said to him, 'Get
behind me, Satan! Because the way you think is not God's way
but man's.'

He called the people and his disciples to him and said, 'If
anyone wants to be a follower of mine, let him renounce himself
and take up his cross and follow me. For anyone who wants to
save his life will lose it; but anyone who loses his life for my sake,
and for the sake of the gospel, will save it.'

This is the Gospel of the Lord.

Mark 8:27-35

Twenty-Fifth Sunday in Ordinary Time   B

Introduction to the Service

Let me begin with a question.

How do you react when somebody criticises you and tells you you are wrong? Perhaps you are grateful to be told. It may also be, however, that you get very angry. You do not want to be criticised and react sharply against your critic.

The same thing happens in public life. Some people in authority may appreciate the help of the opposition. Other leaders, however, are annoyed with their critics and put them into prison.

This is exactly what happened to many prophets and above all to Christ himself. He criticised the ways of the religious leaders. As a result they hated him and made a plan to kill him. Christ, however, kept on showing them the right way. This was his mission. He wanted to serve the people and to help them, even if because of this they sought to harm him. 'He who wants to be first', he says, 'he must make himself last of all and servant of all.'

Penitential Rite

Let us examine our conscience:

- How do we react when we are criticised?
  Do we have the courage to take criticism?   (*Silence*)

- Do we avoid or hate people who have criticised us?
  Do we push them aside or even illtreat them?   (*Silence*)

Let us ask God's forgiveness for being too proud or touchy to take criticism.   **I confess**…

FIRST READING

If somebody lives a truly good life, he must know that his life-style will be seen as a threat and as an accusation by others. Should he or she then be afraid and give up?

We read from the book of Wisdom, chapter two.
*
The godless say to themselves,

'Let us lie in wait for the virtuous man, since he annoys us
and opposes our way of life,
reproaches us for our breaches of the law
and accuses us of playing false to our upbringing.

Let us see if what he says is true,
let us observe what kind of end he himself will have.
If the virtuous man is God's son, God will take his part
and rescue him from the clutches of his enemies.
Let us test him with cruelty and with torture,
and thus explore this gentleness of his
and put his endurance to the proof.
Let us condemn him to a shameful death
since he will be looked after – we have his word for it.'

This is the word of the Lord. *Wisdom 2:12. 17-20*

Responsorial Psalm
℟ **The Lord upholds my life.**

1 O God, save me by your name;
by your power, uphold my cause.
O God, hear my prayer;
listen to the words of my mouth. ℟

2 For proud men have risen against me,
ruthless men seek my life.
They have no regard for God. ℟

3 But I have God for my help.
The Lord upholds my life.
I will sacrifice to you with willing heart
and praise your name for it is good. ℟ *Ps 53:3-6. 8. ℟ v.6*

SECOND READING
We read from the letter of St James, chapters three and four.
*
Wherever you find jealousy and ambition, you find disharmony,
and wicked things of every kind being done; whereas the
wisdom that comes down from above is essentially something
pure; it also makes for peace, and is kindly and considerate; it is
full of compassion and shows itself by doing good; nor is there
any trace of partiality or hypocrisy in it. Peacemakers, when they
work for peace, sow the seeds which will bear fruit in holiness.
    Where do these wars and battles between yourselves first
start? Isn't it precisely in the desires fighting inside your own
selves? You want something and you haven't got it; so you are
prepared to kill. You have an ambition that you cannot satisfy; so
you fight to get your way by force. Why you don't have what you

want is because you don't pray for it; when you do pray and don't get it, it is because you have not prayed properly, you have prayed for something to indulge your own desires.

This is the word of the Lord.

James 3:16 - 4:3

Gospel Acclamation
Alleluia, alleluia!
I am the light of the world, says the Lord,
anyone who follows me
will have the light of life.
Alleluia!

Jn 8:12

or

Alleluia, alleluia!
Through the Good News God called us
to share the glory of our Lord Jesus Christ.
Alleluia!

cf. 2 Thess 2:14

GOSPEL

We read from the holy Gospel according to Mark, chapter nine.
✶
After leaving the mountain Jesus and his disciples made their way through Galilee; and he did not want anyone to know, because he was instructing his disciples; he was telling them, 'The Son of Man will be delivered into the hands of men; they will put him to death; and three days after he has been put to death he will rise again.' But they did not understand what he said and were afraid to ask him.

They came to Capernaum, and when he was in the house he asked them, 'What were you arguing about on the road?' They said nothing because they had been arguing which of them was the greatest. So he sat down, called the Twelve to him and said, 'If anyone wants to be first, he must make himself last of all and servant of all.' He then took a little child, set him in front of them, put his arms round him, and said to them, 'Anyone who welcomes one of these little children in my name, welcomes me; and anyone who welcomes me welcomes not me but the one who sent me.'

This is the Gospel of the Lord.

Mark 9:30-37

Twenty-Sixth Sunday in Ordinary Time   B

Introduction to the Service

Jealousy is like poison. It destroys happiness in our hearts and causes strife amongst people and nations. A jealous look kills and destroys like frost in the winter.

We need not be surprised to find jealousy even among Church communities and Church leaders. Jealousy is an ugly enemy that the Israelites in the desert and even the Apostles themselves had to fight.

What shall we do with a jealous eye which causes us to sin? Christ gives us a radical answer: 'If your eye should cause you to sin, tear it out.' God does not want us to be stingy or jealous. He wants us to be generous like him. He is not a stingy God with a jealous eye. He is a God with a big wide heart, filled with boundless generosity.

Penitential Rite

Let us examine our conscience:

- Did I hurt others with words and deeds because I was jealous? (*Silence*)

- Did I allow others to share in my responsibility for work in the Church or did I want to do everything alone, without training others? (*Silence*)

We ask the Lord to take away our jealous eyes and our wicked hearts and to forgive us our sins.   **I confess**...

FIRST READING

Moses was prepared to share his spirit of leadership with other men. He felt that it was too much for him to lead the people of Israel on his own. Some of his best friends did not like that. They complained and grumbled.

We read from the book of Numbers, chapter eleven.
*
The Lord came down in the Cloud. He spoke with Moses, but took some of the spirit that was on him and put it on the seventy elders. When the spirit came on them they prophesied, but not again.

Two men had stayed back in the camp; one was called Eldad and the other Medad. The spirit came down on them; though they had not gone to the Tent, their names were enrolled among the rest. These began to prophesy in the camp. The young man ran to tell this to Moses, 'Look,' he said 'Eldad and Medad are prophesying in the camp.' Then said Joshua the son of Nun, who had served Moses from his youth, 'My Lord Moses, stop them!' Moses answered him, 'Are you jealous on my account? If only the whole people of the Lord were prophets, and the Lord gave his Spirit to them all!'

This is the word of the Lord. *Numbers 11:25-29*

Responsorial Psalm
℟ **The precepts of the Lord gladden the heart.**

1 The law of the Lord is perfect,
   it revives the soul.
   The rule of the Lord is to be trusted,
   it gives wisdom to the simple. ℟

2 The fear of the Lord is holy,
   abiding for ever.
   The decrees of the Lord are truth
   and all of them just. ℟

3 So in them your servant finds instruction;
   great reward is in their keeping.
   But who can detect all his errors?
   From hidden faults acquit me. ℟

4 From presumption restrain your servant
   and let it not rule me.
   Then shall I be blameless,
   clean from grave sin. ℟ *Ps 18:8. 10. 12-14. ℟ v.9*

SECOND READING
We read from the letter of St James, chapter five.
*
An answer for the rich. Start crying, weep for the miseries that are coming to you. Your wealth is all rotting, your clothes are all eaten up by moths. All your gold and your silver are corroding away, and the same corrosion will be your own sentence, and eat into your body. It was a burning fire that you stored up as your treasure for the last days. Labourers mowed your fields, and you cheated them – listen to the wages that you kept back, calling out;

realise that the cries of the reapers have reached the ears of the Lord of hosts. On earth you have had a life of comfort and luxury; in the time of slaughter you went on eating to your heart's content. It was you who condemned the innocent and killed them; they offered you no resistance.

This is the word of the Lord.   *James 5:1-6*

Gospel Acclamation
Alleluia, alleluia!
Your word is truth, O Lord,
consecrate us in the truth.
Alleluia!   *cf. Jn 17:17*

GOSPEL
We read from the holy Gospel according to Mark, chapter nine.
*
John said to Jesus, 'Master, we saw a man who is not one of us casting out devils in your name; and because he was not one of us we tried to stop him.' But Jesus said, 'You must not stop him: no one who works a miracle in my name is likely to speak evil of me. Anyone who is not against us is for us.

'If anyone gives you a cup of water to drink just because you belong to Christ, then I tell you solemnly, he will most certainly not lose his reward.

'But anyone who is an obstacle to bring down one of these little ones who have faith, would be better thrown into the sea with a great millstone round his neck. And if your hand should cause you to sin, cut it off; it is better for you to enter into life crippled, than to have two hands and go to hell, into the fire that cannot be put out. And if your foot should cause you to sin, cut it off; it is better for you to enter into life lame, than to have two feet and be thrown into hell. And if your eye should cause you to sin, tear it out; it is better for you to enter into the kingdom of God with one eye, than to have two eyes and be thrown into hell where their worm does not die nor their fire go out.'

This is the Gospel of the Lord.   *Mark 9:38-43. 45. 47-48.*

Twenty-Seventh Sunday in Ordinary Time   B

Introduction to the Service

In our celebration today God wants to advise us about marriage.

In the past there were clear and firm customs about marriage. Nobody doubted them. There were traditions which were kept.

Today many things seem to have changed. People have different ideas about marriage. There is great disappointment and confusion about marriage. Young people may even ask: 'What's the use of getting married. So many marriages end in divorce.' Many girls complain, saying 'Traditional marriage oppresses the woman.'

In this confusion it is worth listening to God's plan for men and women.

Penitential Rite

To prepare ourselves for this message, let us ask ourselves:

● Do we regard marriage just as a thing of the world, or as a call from God?   (*Silence*)

● What does our congregation do to prepare young people for marriage?   (*Silence*)

Let us ask for forgiveness for all our failures and wrong ideas about love between men and women.   **I confess**…

FIRST READING

The people of Israel knew that the creation of man and woman is a great mystery. Therefore they talked only in a hidden way about it, as we shall hear in our reading.

This reading wants to make one point very clear: God has created man and woman for each other. They belong together.

We read from the book of Genesis, chapter two.
*
The Lord God said, 'It is not good that the man should be alone. I will make him a helpmate.' So from the soil the Lord God fashioned all the wild beasts and all the birds of heaven. These he brought to the man to see what he would call them; each one was to bear the name the man would give it. The man gave names to all the cattle, all the birds of heaven and all the wild beasts. But no

helpmate suitable for man was found for him. So the Lord God made the man fall into a deep sleep. And while he slept, he took one of his ribs and enclosed it in flesh. The Lord God built the rib he had taken from the man into a woman, and brought her to the man. The man exclaimed:

'This at last is bone from my bones
and flesh from my flesh!
This is to be called woman,
for this was taken from man.'

This is why a man leaves his father and mother and joins himself to his wife, and they become one body.

This is the word of the Lord. *Genesis 2:18-24*

Responsorial Psalm
℟ **May the Lord bless us**
all the days of our life.

1 O blessed are those who fear the Lord
and walk in his ways!
by the labour of your hands you shall eat.
You will be happy and prosper. ℟

2 Your wife will be like a fruitful vine
in the heart of your house;
your children like shoots of the olive,
around your table. ℟

3 Indeed thus shall be blessed
the man who fears the Lord.
May the Lord bless you from Zion
in a happy Jerusalem
all the days of your life!
May you see your children's children.
On Israel, peace! ℟ *Ps 127.℟ v.5*

SECOND READING

We read from the letter to the Hebrews, chapter two.
*
We see in Jesus one who was for a short while made lower than the angels and is now crowned with glory and splendour because he submitted to death; by God's grace he had to experience death for all mankind.

As it was his purpose to bring a great many of his sons into glory, it was appropriate that God, for whom everything exists and through whom everything exists, should make perfect, through suffering, the leader who would take them to their salvation. For the one who sanctifies, and the ones who are sanctified, are of the same stock; that is why he openly calls them brothers.

This is the word of the Lord. *Hebrews 2:9-11*

Gospel Acclamation
Alleluia, alleluia!
Your word is truth, O Lord,
consecrate us in the truth.
Alleluia! *cf. Jn 17:17*

or

Alleluia, alleluia!
As long as we love one another
God will live in us
and his love will be complete in us.
Alleluia! *1 Jn 4:12*

GOSPEL

We read from the holy Gospel according to Mark, chapter ten.
*
Some Pharisees approached Jesus and asked, 'Is it against the law for a man to divorce his wife?' They were testing him. He answered them, 'What did Moses command you?' 'Moses allowed us' they said 'to draw up a writ of dismissal and so to divorce.' Then Jesus said to them, 'It was because you were so unteachable that he wrote this commandment for you. But from the beginning of creation God made them male and female. This is why a man must leave father and mother, and the two become one body. They are no longer two, therefore, but one body. So then, what God has united, man must not divide.' Back in the house the disciples questioned him again about this, and he said to them, 'The man who divorces his wife and marries another is guilty of adultery against her. And if a woman divorces her husband and marries another she is guilty of adultery too.'

People were bringing little children to him, for him to touch them. The disciples turned them away, but when Jesus saw this he was indignant and said to them, 'Let the little children come to me; do not stop them; for it is to such as these that the kingdom of God belongs. I tell you solemnly, anyone who does not welcome the kingdom of God like a little child will never enter it.' Then he put his arms round them, laid his hands on them and gave them his blessing.

This is the Gospel of the Lord.   Mark 10:2-16

*Shorter Form, verses 2-12. Read between *.

Twenty-Eighth Sunday in Ordinary Time   B

Introduction to the Service

There are many people who cannot understand why priests, or other Christian men and women they know, do not get married.

Why do they not get married? Do they despise marriage or do they look for an easier life?

The answer is not easy. We need God's wisdom to understand it because it is a matter of love.

Even now, there are boys and girls, men and women who experience the love of Christ in a special way. They meet him in the same way as the man whom we hear about in today's Gospel reading. Jesus looked steadily at this man and loved him and he said: 'Go and sell everything – then come and follow me.'

Penitential Rite

Let us prepare ourselves for this message by asking for forgiveness:

● Lord Jesus, how often did you look at us and love us yet we did not recognise you?   (*Silence*)
    Lord, have mercy...

● Lord Jesus, how often did you invite us to do what is good yet we rejected your invitation.   (*Silence*)
    Christ, have mercy...

● Lord Jesus, often we had no time for you because we were too busy with our own plans.   (*Silence*)
    Lord, have mercy...

FIRST READING

Our reading talks about a person who prays for wisdom. The wisdom of God was more precious to him than money, health or beauty.

We read from the book of Wisdom, chapter seven.
*
I prayed, and understanding was given me;
I entreated, and the spirit of Wisdom came to me.
I esteemed her more than sceptres and thrones;
compared with her, I held riches as nothing.
I reckoned no priceless stone to be her peer,
for compared with her, all gold is a pinch of sand,
and beside her silver ranks as mud.
I loved her more than health or beauty,
preferred her to the light,
since her radiance never sleeps.
In her company all good things came to me,
at her hands riches not to be numbered.

This is the word of the Lord. *Wisdom 7:7-11*

Responsorial Psalm
℞   **Fill us with your love that we may rejoice.**

1   Make us know the shortness of our life
    that we may gain wisdom of heart.
    Lord, relent! Is your anger for ever?
    Show pity to your servants.   ℞

2   In the morning, fill us with your love;
    we shall exult and rejoice all our days.
    Give us joy to balance our affliction
    for the years when we knew misfortune.   ℞

3   Show forth your work to your servants;
    let your glory shine on their children.
    Let the favour of the Lord be upon us:
    give success to the work of our hands.   ℞

Ps 89:12-17. ℞ *v.14*

SECOND READING

We read from the letter to the Hebrews, chapter four.
*
The word of God is something alive and active: it cuts like any double-edged sword but more finely: it can slip through the place

where the soul is divided from the spirit, or joints from the marrow; it can judge the secret emotions and thoughts. No created thing can hide from him; everything is uncovered and open to the eyes of the one to whom we must give account of ourselves.

This is the word of the Lord. *Hebrews 4:12-13*

Gospel Acclamation
Alleluia, alleluia!
Blessed are you, Father,
Lord of heaven and earth,
for revealing the mysteries of the kingdom
to mere children.
Alleluia! *cf. Mt 11:25*

or

Alleluia, alleluia!
How happy are the poor in spirit;
theirs is the kingdom of heaven.
Alleluia! *Mt 5:3*

GOSPEL

We read from the holy Gospel according to Mark, chapter ten.
*
*Jesus was setting out on a journey when a man ran up, knelt before him and put this question to him, 'Good master, what must I do to inherit eternal life?' Jesus said to him, 'Why do you call me good? No one is good but God alone. You know the commandments: You must not kill; You must not commit adultery; You must not steal; You must not bring false witness; You must not defraud; Honour your father and mother.' And he said to him, 'Master, I have kept all these from my earliest days.' Jesus looked steadily at him and loved him, and he said, 'There is one thing you lack. Go and sell everything you own and give the money to the poor, and you will have treasure in heaven; then come, follow me.' But his face fell at these words and he went away sad, for he was a man of great wealth.

Jesus looked round and said to his disciples, 'How hard it is for those who have riches to enter the kingdom of God!' The disciples were astounded by these words, but Jesus insisted, 'My children,' he said to them, 'how hard it is to enter the kingdom of God! It is easier for a camel to pass through the eye of a needle than for a rich man to enter the kingdom of God.' They were more astonished than ever. 'In that case' they said to one another 'who can be saved?' Jesus gazed at them. 'For men' he said 'it is impossible, but not for God: because everything is possible for God.'*

Peter took this up. 'What about us?' he asked him. 'We have left everything and followed you.' Jesus said, 'I tell you solemnly, there is no one who has left house, brothers, sisters, father, children or land for my sake and for the sake of the gospel who will not be repaid a hundred times over, houses, brothers, sisters, mothers, children and land – not without persecutions – now in this present time and, in the world to come, eternal life.'

This is the Gospel of the Lord.   Mark 10:17-30

*Shorter Form, verses 17-27. Read between *.*

Twenty-Ninth Sunday in Ordinary Time   B

Introduction to the Service

Who is the greatest among us? The person who is richest? Those with the best academic qualifications? Those in high position in government office? They are great, but they may not be the greatest.

What about a good mother at home? She cares for her family, works for her husband and children, prepares food and cares for all in the house who are sick or in trouble. She makes herself a servant of all. Her children may talk of her later, saying: 'There was nobody greater than our mother. She was super.'

In our celebration today Jesus talks about this kind of greatness which comes from unselfish love. Such a love will suffer for others and even die for them.

Penitential Rite

Let us ask ourselves:

● Do we despise the poor and simple while we admire the rich and powerful?   (*Silence*)

● How do we treat people who are working under us? Do we just use them like tools? Do we worry about them when they are in trouble?   (*Silence*)

Let us ask God's forgiveness for making ourselves great in words and actions whilst belittling others.   **I confess**…

FIRST READING

Our reading talks about Christ. He became our servant by taking the beatings which we deserved. This made him the greatest.

We read from the book of Isaiah, chapter fifty-three.
★
The Lord has been pleased to crush his servant with suffering.
If he offers his life in atonement,
he shall see his heirs, he shall have a long life
and through him what the Lord wishes will be done.
His soul's anguish over
he shall see the light and be content.
By his sufferings shall my servant justify many,
taking their faults on himself.

This is the word of the Lord.   *Isaiah 53:10-11*

Responsorial Psalm
℟   **May your love be upon us, O Lord,
as we place all our hope in you.**

1   The word of the Lord is faithful
and all his works to be trusted.
The Lord loves justice and right
and fills the earth with his love.   ℟

2   The Lord looks on those who revere him,
on those who hope in his love,
to rescue their souls from death,
to keep them alive in famine.   ℟

3   Our soul is waiting for the Lord.
The Lord is our help and our shield.
May your love be upon us, O Lord,
as we place all our hope in you.   ℟
Ps 32:4-5. 18-20. 22. ℟ v.22

SECOND READING

We read from the letter to the Hebrews, chapter four.
★
Since in Jesus, the Son of God, we have the supreme high priest
who has gone through to the highest heaven, we must never let
go of the faith that we have professed. For it is not as if we had a
high priest who was incapable of feeling our weaknesses with us;
but we have one who has been tempted in every way that we are,
though he is without sin. Let us be confident, then, in approach-

ing the throne of grace, that we shall have mercy from him and find grace when we are in need of help.

> This is the word of the Lord. *Hebrews 4:14-16*

Gospel Acclamation
> Alleluia, alleluia!
> I am the Way, the Truth and the Life, says the Lord;
> no one can come to the Father except through me.
> Alleluia! *Jn 14:6*

or

> Alleluia, alleluia!
> The Son of Man came to serve,
> and to give his life as a ransom for many.
> Alleluia! *Mk 10:45*

GOSPEL

We read from the holy Gospel according to Mark, chapter ten.

*
James and John, the sons of Zebedee, approached Jesus. 'Master,' they said to him 'we want you to do us a favour.' He said to them, 'What is it you want me to do for you?' They said to him, 'Allow us to sit one at your right hand and the other at your left in your glory.' 'You do not know what you are asking' Jesus said to them. 'Can you drink the cup that I must drink, or be baptised with the baptism with which I must be baptised?' They replied, 'We can.' Jesus said to them, 'The cup that I must drink you shall drink, and with the baptism with which I must be baptised you shall be baptised, but as for seats at my right hand or my left, these are not mine to grant; they belong to those to whom they have been allotted.'

When the other ten heard this they began to feel indignant with James and John, so *Jesus called them to him and said to them, 'You know that among the pagans their so-called rulers lord it over them, and their great men make their authority felt. This is not to happen among you. No; anyone who wants to become great among you must be your servant, and anyone who wants to be first among you must be slave to all. For the Son of Man himself did not come to be served but to serve, and to give his life as a ransom for many.'*

> This is the Gospel of the Lord.* *Mark 10:35-45*

***Shorter Form, verses 42-45. Read between *.**

Thirtieth Sunday in Ordinary Time B

Introduction to the Service

There are many blind people in the world. More than we think. We ourselves may be one of them.

For instance, remember an occasion when we insisted emphatically that we were right. Next day, however, we find out that we were wrong. That has happened to each one of us.

Here is another example of our blindness: we are very quick to judge and to condemn people. We do so without knowing all the details or having listened to the other side. We are blind and do not see their good intentions.

In our celebration today let us ask the Lord to open our eyes as he opened the eyes of the blind man sitting at the side of the road.

Penitential Rite

Together with this blind man we cry out to Christ for mercy:

● Lord we your people stand here before you. Open our eyes that we may see all the good things you have done for us. (*Silence*)
   Lord, have mercy...

● Lord, open our eyes that we may see what is right and what is wrong. (*Silence*)
   Christ, have mercy...

● Lord, open our eyes that we may see all the good which is in other people. (*Silence*)
   Lord, have mercy...

FIRST READING

Our reading is addressed to the people of Israel who were living in exile, far away from home. It is a solemn promise that God will gather them together again and lead them home, even the blind and the lame.

We read from the book of Jeremiah, chapter thirty-one.
*
The Lord says this:

Shout with joy for Jacob!
Hail the chief of nations!
Proclaim! Praise! Shout!
'The Lord has saved his people,

the remnant of Israel!'
See, I will bring them back
from the land of the North
and gather them from the far ends of earth;
all of them: the blind and the lame,
women with child, women in labour:
a great company returning here.
They had left in tears,
I will comfort them as I lead them back;
I will guide them to streams of water,
by a smooth path where they will not stumble.
For I am a father to Israel,
and Ephraim is my first-born son.

This is the word of the Lord.   *Jeremiah 31:7-9*

Responsorial Psalm

℟   **What marvels the Lord worked for us!**
Indeed we were glad.

1   When the Lord delivered Zion from bondage,
it seemed like a dream.
Then was our mouth filled with laughter,
on our lips there were songs.   ℟

2   The heathens themselves said: 'What marvels
the Lord worked for them!'
What marvels the Lord worked for us!
Indeed we were glad.   ℟

3   Deliver us, O Lord, from our bondage
as streams in dry land.
Those who are sowing in tears
will sing when they reap.   ℟

4   They go out, they go out, full of tears,
carrying seed for the sowing:
they come back, they come back, full of song,
carrying their sheaves.   ℟

Ps 125. ℟ v. 3

SECOND READING

We read from the letter to the Hebrews, chapter five.
*
Every high priest has been taken out of mankind and is
appointed to act for men in their relations with God, to offer gifts

and sacrifices for sins; and so he can sympathise with those who are ignorant or uncertain because he too lives in the limitations of weakness. That is why he has to make sin offerings for himself as well as for the people. No one takes this honour on himself, but each one is called by God, as Aaron was. Nor did Christ give himself the glory of becoming high priest, but he had it from the one who said to him: You are my son, today I have become your father, and in another text: You are a priest of the order of Melchizedek, and for ever.

This is the word of the Lord.   *Hebrews 5:1-6*

Gospel Acclamation
　Alleluia, alleluia!
　I am the light of the world, says the Lord,
　anyone who follows me
　will have the light of life.
　Alleluia!   *Jn 8:12*

or

　Alleluia, alleluia!
　Our Saviour Christ Jesus abolished death,
　and he has proclaimed life through the Good News.
　Alleluia!   *cf. 2 Tim 1:10*

GOSPEL
We read from the holy Gospel according to Mark, chapter ten.
*
As Jesus left Jericho with his disciples and a large crowd, Bartimaeus (that is, the son of Timaeus), a blind beggar, was sitting at the side of the road. When he heard that it was Jesus of Nazareth, he began to shout and to say, 'Son of David, Jesus, have pity on me.' And many of them scolded him and told him to keep quiet, but he only shouted all the louder, 'Son of David, have pity on me.' Jesus stopped and said, 'Call him here.' So they called the blind man. 'Courage,' they said 'get up; he is calling you.' So throwing off his cloak, he jumped up and went to Jesus. Then Jesus spoke, 'What do you want me to do for you?' 'Rabbuni,' the blind man said to him 'Master, let me see again.' Jesus said to him, 'Go; your faith has saved you.' And immediately his sight returned and he followed him along the road.

This is the Gospel of the Lord.   *Mark 10:46-52*

Thirty-First Sunday in Ordinary Time   B

Introduction to the Service

The whole world talks about love. Love songs are composed, love-stories are written. Young people fall in love and tell each other: 'I love you'.

Human love is something wonderful. It fills people's hearts, penetrates their minds and inspires their actions. Yes, indeed, many people talk about love – but few talk about God.

And yet, God is the source of all love. Human love is only a spark of the fire of love which burns in God. God is love. Love is the way God lives.

In our celebration today, the Lord invites us to take part in God's great love. His love is the way to the Promised Land.

Penitential Rite

Let us ask ourselves:

● Did we ever thank God for the gift of human love?   (*Silence*)

● Did we look for love in the wrong way?   (*Silence*)

● Did we love ourselves but not our neighbours?   (*Silence*)

Let us ask God's forgiveness for having so little love. **I confess**…

FIRST READING

It sounds strange to us that God commands love. Can love be commanded?

When we listen to our reading we should remember that God's commandments are like sign-posts. They command us by showing us the right direction to take in order to find life.

We read from the book of Deuteronomy, chapter six.
*
Moses said to the people: 'If you fear the Lord your God all the days of your life and if you keep all his laws and commandments which I lay on you, you will have a long life, you and your son and your grandson. Listen then, Israel, keep and observe what will make you prosper and give you great increase, as the Lord God of your fathers has promised you, giving you a land where milk and honey flow.

'Listen, Israel: The Lord our God is the one Lord. You shall love the Lord your God with all your heart, with all your soul, with all your strength. Let these words I urge on you today be written on your heart.'

This is the word of the Lord.   *Deuteronomy 6:2-6*

Responsial Psalm
℞   **I love you, Lord, my strength.**

1   I love you, Lord, my strength,
      my rock, my fortress, my saviour.
      My God is the rock where I take refuge;
      my shield, my mighty help, my stronghold.
      The Lord is worthy of all praise:
      when I call I am saved from my foes.   ℞

2   Long life to the Lord, my rock!
      Praised be the God who saves me.
      He has given great victories to his king
      and shown his love for his anointed.   ℞

                            Ps 17:2-4. 47. 51. ℞ v.2

SECOND READING
We read from the letter to the Hebrews, chapter seven.
*
There used to be a great number of priests under the former
covenant, because death put an end to each one of them; but this
one, Christ, because he remains for ever, can never lose his
priesthood. It follows then, that his power to save is utterly
certain, since he is living for ever to intercede for all who come to
God through him.

   To suit us, the ideal high priest would have to be holy,
innocent and uncontaminated, beyond the influence of sinners,
and raised up above the heavens; one who would not need to
offer sacrifices every day, as the other high priests do for their
own sins and then for those of the people, because he has done
this once and for all by offering himself. The Law appoints high
priests who are men subject to weakness; but the promise on
oath, which came after the Law, appointed the Son who is made
perfect for ever.

   This is the word of the Lord.   *Hebrews 7:23-28*

Gospel Acclamation
      Alleluia, alleluia!
      Your words are spirit, Lord,
      and they are life:

you have the message of eternal life.
Alleluia!   *cf. Jn 6:63.68*

or

Alleluia, alleluia!
If anyone loves me he will keep my word,
and my Father will love him,
and we shall come to him.
Alleluia!   *Jn 14:23*

GOSPEL

We read from the holy Gospel according to Mark, chapter twelve.
*

One of the scribes came up to Jesus and put a question to him,
'Which is the first of all the commandments?' Jesus replied, 'This
is the first: Listen, Israel, the Lord our God is the one Lord, and
you must love the Lord your God with all your heart, with all
your soul, with all your mind and with all your strength. The
second is this: You must love your neighbour as yourself. There is
no commandment greater than these.' The scribe said to him,
'Well spoken, Master; what you have said is true: that he is one
and there is no other. To love with all your heart, with all your
understanding and strength and to love your neighbour as
yourself, this is far more important than any holocaust or
sacrifice.' Jesus, seeing how wisely he had spoken said, 'You are
not far from the kingdom of God.' And after that no one dared to
question him any more.

This is the Gospel of the Lord.   *Mark 12:28-34*

Thirty-Second Sunday in Ordinary Time   B

Introduction to the Service

There are many ways in which we can help others. We can give
them money or food. We can also give them our time.

For example, some give up their time to teach the catechism,
others visit the sick or serve on the parish council. Others again
give their talents to the community and serve as readers. All those
who give their time in serving others give something from
themselves: they share their love, their faith and their talents.

If we want to follow Christ, we have to give ourselves to others.

Today, we celebrate and remember how Christ gives himself
completely. He gives himself away in the most radical way. He
gives away all he possesses: his life, his love, his body and blood.

Penitential Rite

Let us ask ourselves:

● How do I help people who need me?
    Do I give my time to them?
    Do I give my time to the Church community by serving on a
church council or by teaching the catechism?   (*Silence*)

● Am I prepared to give myself completely to the service of God if
he calls me?   (*Silence*)

Let us ask pardon from the Lord for not giving ourselves to
others as he has shown us.   **I confess**...

FIRST READING

How can people give away the last of their food, knowing they will
need it themselves? It seems a foolish thing to do. However, we
may have experienced this already ourselves and discovered that
when we gave away the last we had, we were provided for again
in abundance.

We read from the first book of Kings, chapter seventeen.

Elijah the Prophet went off to Sidon. And when he reached the
city gate, there was a widow gathering sticks; addressing her he
said, 'Please bring a little water in a vessel for me to drink.' She
was setting off to bring it when he called after her. 'Please' he said
'bring me a scrap of bread in your hand.' 'As the Lord your God
lives,' she replied 'I have no baked bread, but only a handful of
meal in a jar and a little oil in a jug; I am just gathering a stick or
two to go and prepare this for myself and my son to eat, and then
we shall die.' But Elijah said to her, 'Do not be afraid, go and do
as you have said; but first make a little scone of it for me and bring
it to me, and then make some for yourself and for your son. For
thus the Lord speaks, the God of Israel:

"Jar of meal shall not be spent,
jug of oil shall not be emptied,
before the day when the Lord sends
rain on the face of the earth." '

The woman went and did as Elijah told her and they ate the
food, she, himself and her son. The jar of meal was not spent nor
the jug of oil emptied, just as the Lord had foretold through
Elijah.

This is the word of the Lord.   *1 Kings 17:10-16*

Responsorial Psalm

℞ My soul, give praise to the Lord.

or

℞ Alleluia!

1 It is the Lord who keeps faith for ever,
who is just to those who are oppressed.
It is he who gives bread to the hungry,
the Lord, who sets prisoners free. ℞

2 It is the Lord who gives sight to the blind,
who raises up those who are bowed down.
It is the Lord who loves the just,
the Lord, who protects the stranger. ℞

3 The Lord upholds the widow and orphan
but thwarts the path of the wicked.
The Lord will reign for ever,
Zion's God, from age to age. ℞   *Ps 145:7-10.* ℞ *v.2*

SECOND READING

We read from the letter to the Hebrews, chapter nine.

✶

It is not as though Christ had entered a man-made sanctuary
which was only modelled on the real one; but it was heaven itself,
so that he could appear in the actual presence of God on our
behalf. And he does not have to offer himself again and again,
like the high priest going into the sanctuary year after year with
the blood that is not his own, or else he would have had to suffer
over and over again since the world began. Instead of that, he has
made his appearance once and for all, now at the end of the last
age, to do away with sin by sacrificing himself. Since men only
die once, and after that comes judgement, so Christ, too, offers
himself only once to take the faults of many on himself, and
when he appears a second time, it will not be to deal with sin but
to reward with salvation those who are waiting for him.

This is the word of the Lord.   *Hebrews 9: 24-28*

Gospel Acclamation

Alleluia, alleluia!
Even if you have to die, says the Lord,
keep faithful, and I will give you
the crown of life.
Alleluia!   *Apoc 2:10*

or

Alleluia, alleluia!
How happy are the poor in spirit;
theirs is the kingdom of heaven.
Alleluia!

Mt 5:3

GOSPEL

We read from the holy Gospel according to Mark, chapter twelve.
*
In his teaching Jesus said, 'Beware of the scribes who like to walk about in long robes, to be greeted obsequiously in the market squares, to take the front seats in the synagogues and the places of honour at banquets; these are the men who swallow the property of widows, while making a show of lengthy prayers. The more severe will be the sentence they receive.'

*He sat down opposite the treasury and watched the people putting money into the treasury, and many of the rich put in a great deal. A poor widow came and put in two small coins, the equivalent of a penny. Then he called his disciples and said to them, 'I tell you solemnly, this poor widow has put more in than all who have contributed to the treasury; for they have all put in money they had over, but she from the little she had has put in everything she possessed, all she had to live on.'

This is the Gospel of the Lord.*

Mark 12:38-44

*Shorter Form, verses 41-44. Read between *.

Thirty-Third Sunday in Ordinary Time B

Introduction to the Service

If you have a really good friend, you will be very anxious to ensure that your friendship lasts forever. If you truly love your wife or your husband, you are most anxious that the bond of love between you should last forever. You look into the future and say: never mind what the future brings us, as long as the bond between us lasts for ever.

Such thoughts come into our mind on these last Sundays of the Church year, when we look into the future and read about the end of the world. We read of frightening events: 'The sun will be darkened, the moon will lose its brightness ... then they will see the Son of Man coming in the clouds'.

This is the time to which we, as Christians, look forward with anxiety, saying: if only our friendship with Christ will last … never mind what else happens; if only our union with Christ will last for ever.

Penitential Rite

To prepare ourselves for this service, let us ask ourselves:

● Are we ready to welcome Christ when he comes back in glory on the clouds of heaven?   (*Silence*)

● Of which things in our lives shall we be ashamed when Christ comes back in glory?   (*Silence*)

Let us ask the Lord to take from us all the things of which we are ashamed.   **I confess**…

FIRST READING

Our reading tells us of a good way to prepare ourselves for the Day of Judgement. If we instruct others in virtue, we shall shine as brightly as stars for all eternity.

We read from the book of Daniel, chapter twelve.

*
'At that time Michael will stand up, the great prince who mounts guard over your people. There is going to be a time of great distress, unparalleled since nations first came into existence. When that time comes, your own people will be spared, all those whose names are found written in the Book. Of those who lie sleeping in the dust of the earth many will awake, some to everlasting life, some to shame and everlasting disgrace. The learned will shine as brightly as the vault of heaven, and those who have instructed many in virtue, as bright as stars for all eternity.'

This is the word of the Lord.   *Daniel 12:1-13*

Responsorial Psalm

℟   **Preserve me, God, I take refuge in you.**

1   O Lord, it is you who are my portion and cup;
    it is you yourself who are my prize.
    I keep the Lord ever in my sight:
    since he is at my right hand, I shall stand firm.   ℟

2   And so my heart rejoices, my soul is glad;
    even my body shall rest in safety.
    For you will not leave my soul among the dead,
    nor let your beloved know decay.   ℟

3   You will show me the path of life,
    the fullness of joy in your presence,,
    at your right hand happiness for ever.   ℟

Ps 15:5. 8-11. ℟ v.1

SECOND READING

We read from the letter to the Hebrews, chapter ten.
*
All the priests stand at their duties every day, offering over and
over again the same sacrifices which are quite incapable of taking
sins away. Christ, on the other hand, has offered one single
sacrifice for sins, and then taken his place for ever, at the right
hand of God, where he is now waiting until his enemies are made
into a footstool for him. By virtue of that one single offering, he
has achieved the eternal perfection of all whom he is sanctifying.
When all sins have been forgiven, there can be no more sin
offerings.

This is the word of the Lord.   *Hebrews 10:11-14. 18*

Gospel Acclamation
    Alleluia, alleluia!
    Stay awake and stand ready,
    because you do not know the hour
    when the Son of Man is coming.
    Alleluia!   *Mt 24:42. 44*

or

    Alleluia, alleluia!
    Stay awake, praying at all times
    for the strength to stand with confidence
    before the Son of Man.
    Alleluia!   *Lk 21:36*

GOSPEL

We read from the holy Gospel according to Mark, chapter thirteen.
*
Jesus said to his disciples: 'In those days, after the time of
distress, the sun will be darkened, the moon will lose its

brightness, the stars will come falling from heaven and the powers in the heavens will be shaken. And then they will see the Son of Man coming in the clouds with great power and glory; then too he will send the angels to gather his chosen from the four winds, from the ends of the world to the ends of heaven.

'Take the fig tree as a parable: as soon as its twigs grow supple and its leaves come out, you know that summer is near. So with you, when you see these things happening: know that he is near, at the very gates. I tell you solemnly, before this generation has passed away all these things will have taken place. Heaven and earth will pass away, but my words will not pass away.

'But as for that day or hour, nobody knows it, neither the angels of heaven, nor the Son; no one but the Father.'

This is the Gospel of the Lord.   *Mark 13:24-32*

Thirty-Fourth Sunday in Ordinary Time   *Solemnity*

Our Lord Jesus Christ, Universal King   B

Introduction to the Service

Today we celebrate the great feast of Christ the King. It is also the last Sunday of the Church year.

In our celebration today, we look ahead to the Last Day when Christ will come back in glory. He will not come with powerful armies. He will not need them. He will not come with deadly weapons, guns and bombs. He will not need them. The King of kings will come like the sun rising after a long night. He will destroy all darkness with the glory of his light.

This is the truth which we proclaim today.

'Yes I am a King,' says the Lord, 'All who are on the side of truth listen to my voice.'

Penitential Rite

Let us come before the judgement seat of Christ the King and ask for his forgiveness and mercy:

● Lord Jesus, King of kings! Forgive us and accept us into your kingdom.
       Lord, have mercy....

● Lord Jesus, Lord of lords! So often we have ignored you in our lives.
       Christ, have mercy...

● Lord Jesus, King of heaven and earth! Your kingdom come. Forgive us our trespasses as we forgive those who trespass against us.

    Lord have mercy...

FIRST READING

Our reading records one of the famous visions of the prophet Daniel.

    To understand the reading better it may be helpful to know what Daniel saw in an earlier vision: he saw the powerful kingdoms of this world rising from the sea like ugly beasts and monsters, breathing out fire. They were eating human flesh, crushing people to death and trampling nations underfoot. After that he saw the vision which is written down for us in our reading.

We read from the book of Daniel, chapter seven.
*
I gazed into the visions of the night.
And I saw, coming on the clouds of heaven,
one like a son of man.
He came to the one of great age
and was led into his presence.
On him was conferred sovereignty,
glory and kingship,
and men of all peoples, nations and languages became his
    servants.
His sovereignty is an eternal sovereignty
which shall never pass away,
nor will his empire be destroyed.

    This is the word of the the Lord.   *Daniel 7:13-14*

Responsorial Psalm
  ℟ **The Lord is king, with majesty enrobed.**

1 The Lord is king, with majesty enrobed;
    the Lord has robed himself with might,
    he has girded himself with power.   ℟

2 The world you made firm, not to be moved;
    your throne has stood firm from of old.
    From all eternity, O Lord, you are.   ℟

3 Truly your decrees are to be trusted.
    Holiness is fitting to your house,
    O Lord, until the end of time.   ℟   *Ps 92:1-2. 5. ℟ v.1*

SECOND READING

We read from the book of the Apocalypse, chapter one.
*
Jesus Christ is the faithful witness, the First-born from the dead, the Ruler of the kings of the earth. He loves us and has washed away our sins with his blood, and made us a line of kings, priests to serve his God and Father; to him, then, be glory and power for ever and ever. Amen. It is he who is coming on the clouds; everyone will see him, even those who pierced him, and all the races of the earth will mourn over him. This is the truth. Amen. 'I am the Alpha and the Omega' says the Lord God, who is, who was, and who is to come, the Almighty.

This is the word of the Lord. *Apocalypse 1:5-8*

Gospel Acclamation

Alleluia, alleluia!
Blessings on him who comes in the name of the Lord!
Blessings on the coming kingdom of our father David!
Alleluia! *Mk 11:9. 10*

GOSPEL

We read from the holy Gospel according to John, chapter eighteen.
*
'Are you the king of the Jews?' Pilate asked. Jesus replied, 'Do you ask this of your own accord, or have others spoken to you about me?' Pilate answered, 'Am I a Jew? It is your own people and the chief priests who have handed you over to me: what have you done?' Jesus replied, 'Mine is not a kingdom of this world; if my kingdom were of this world, my men would have fought to prevent my being surrendered to the Jews. But my kingdom is not of this kind.' 'So you are a king then?' said Pilate. 'It is you who say it' answered Jesus. 'Yes, I am a king. I was born for this, I came into the world for this: to bear witness to the truth; and all who are on the side of truth listen to my voice.'

This is the Gospel of the Lord. *John 18:33-37*

About the Response After the First Reading

The purpose of the RESPONSE after the First Reading is to help us meditate in our hearts on the Word of God which we have heard.

The purpose is to let the very words which we have heard re-echo within us.

The purpose is to allow ourselves to be touched by the message which we have heard.

The purpose is to have time to sense how we could reply to God in word and deed.

The purpose is to give us time to let a response arise in our hearts.

● **Therefore the RESPONSE should contain the message of the reading**

It should not just be any hymn.
It should not always be the same chant, hymn or psalm.

● **Therefore the RESPONSE should come from the community**

It should not be read or sung by the reader.
It should be sung by the community, by a choir or by a 'cantor'.

● **Therefore the RESPONSE should lead to some kind of meditation**

The simplest form of meditation is the repetition of the message.
Singing is usually better than speaking.
Meditative singing is better than other kinds of singing.

The Alleluia or Gospel Acclamation

The Acclamation before the Gospel has a different purpose to the Response: in the Acclamation we greet the Risen Lord who will speak to us in the Gospel.

In order to make it very clear that the Acclamation and the Gospel belong together, some congregations have introduced a simple gesture:

On his way to the lectern the deacon or priest halts in the centre, before the altar, turns to the congregation and lifts up the lectionary or Bible.

The choir waits until this moment and then sings the Alleluia and its verse.

In some places, the deacon or priest holds up the lectionary or Bible again, after he has proclaimed the Gospel, while the choir and the people repeat the Alleluia.

Ways of preparing for a meaningful expression of the GOSPEL ACCLAMATION

● Choose an existing hymn which expresses the message of the reading.

● Choose a psalm which expresses this message; singing or reciting the antiphon in between the psalm verses.

● Compose an antiphon which expresses the message of the Reading.

● The readers meet with the choir to plan an INTRODUCTION and a RESPONSE which express the same message.

(There are parishes where the choir-master asks the priest every week, what the main message of the following Sunday's Gospel will be. The choir-master composes a tune for it and practises with the choir during the week. On Sundays this tune is sung as an 'antiphon' between the psalm verses.)

THE SEASON OF ADVENT

First Sunday of Advent   C

Introduction to the Service

'There will be honesty in the land; there will be integrity in the land.'

What a daring promise this sounds to us, because the reality is quite different. When we listen to people talking in the streets, we hear them saying, 'There is no honesty, you are cheated everywhere, you cannot trust anybody, people do not keep their promises, they do not tell you the truth...'

'He will practise honesty and integrity in the land.' This is the powerful message of today, the first Sunday of Advent. 'You will see the Son of Man coming in a cloud with power and great glory.' Creation will be renewed, is the message of Advent. Honesty and integrity will come to the land.

Penitential Rite

Advent is a time when we must examine our sense of hope. Let us offer ourselves into the Lord's presence:

- Lord, in our work for honesty and integrity you want us never to give up or to lose hope.   (*Silence*)
  Lord, have mercy...

- Christ, while we are busy improving our land, you want us to put all our trust in you. Forgive us for trusting in our own strength.   (*Silence*)
  Christ, have mercy...

- Lord, you want us to wait in joyful hope for your coming. Forgive us for losing this joy and hope.   (*Silence*)
  Lord, have mercy...

FIRST READING

In Advent we hear of the wonderful visions of the prophets. In these visions, the prophets see what is going to happen in the future. But what is the value of these wonderful visions as we read them now in Advent?

These visions are a powerful reminder about our life today: many things which are happening now are not right. They must be changed.

We read from the book of Jeremiah, chapter thirty-three.
*
See, the days are coming – it is the Lord who speaks – when I am
going to fulfil the promise I made to the House of Israel and the
House of Judah:

> 'In those days and at that time,
> I will make a virtuous Branch grow for David,
> who shall practise honesty and integrity in the land.
> In those days Judah shall be saved
> and Israel shall dwell in confidence.
> And this is the name the city will be called:
> The Lord-our-integrity.'

This is the word of the Lord.   *Jeremiah 33:14-16*

Responsorial Psalm
℞   **To you, O Lord, I lift up my soul.**

1   Lord, make me know your ways.
    Lord, teach me your paths.
    Make me walk in your truth, and teach me:
    for you are God my saviour.   ℞

2   The Lord is good and upright.
    He shows the path to those who stray,
    he guides the humble in the right path;
    he teaches his way to the poor.   ℞

3   His ways are faithfulness and love
    for those who keep his covenant and will.
    The Lord's friendship is for those who revere him;
    to them he reveals his covenant.   ℞

                    Ps 24:4-5. 8-9. 10. 14. ℞ v.1

SECOND READING

We read from the first letter of St Paul to the Thessalonians, chapters
three and four.
*
May the Lord be generous in increasing your love and make you
love one another and the whole human race as much as we love
you. And may he so confirm your hearts in holiness that you may
be blameless in the sight of our God and Father when our Lord
Jesus Christ comes with all his saints.

    Finally, brothers, we urge you and appeal to you in the Lord
Jesus to make more and more progress in the kind of life that you

are meant to live: the life that God wants, as you learnt from us, and as you are already living it. You have not forgotten the instructions we gave you on the authority of the Lord Jesus.

This is the word of the Lord.   *1 Thessalonians 3:12–4:2*

Gospel Acclamation
    Alleluia, alleluia!
    Let us see, O Lord, your mercy
    and give us your saving help.
    Alleluia!   *Ps 84:8*

GOSPEL

We read from the holy Gospel according to Luke, chapter twenty-one.
*
Jesus said to his disciples: 'There will be signs in the sun and moon and stars; on earth nations in agony, bewildered by the clamour of the ocean and its waves; men dying of fear as they await what menaces the world, for the powers of heaven will be shaken. And then they will see the Son of Man coming in a cloud with power and great glory. When these things begin to take place, stand erect, hold your heads high, because your liberation is near at hand.'

'Watch yourselves, or your hearts will be coarsened with debauchery and drunkenness and the cares of life, and that day will be sprung on you suddenly, like a trap. For it will come down on every living man on the face of the earth. Stay awake, praying at all times for the strength to survive all that is going to happen, and to stand with confidence before the Son of Man.'

This is the Gospel of the Lord.   *Luke 21:25-28. 34-36*

Second Sunday of Advent   C

Introduction to the Service
    'There is no way' people say. 'Prepare the way' is God's reply. 'There is no way of improving life in this area' people say. 'Then prepare a way, make a way' is God's reply. 'There is no way of making people friendlier', we say. 'There is no way of making marriages happier, of finding work for the many unemployed, of securing just laws for our country ...'
    If there is no way, then make a way, is the message of this second Sunday of Advent: 'Prepare a way for the Lord.'

Penitential Rite

Let us begin our service by asking for forgiveness for our passivity:

- Did we often fail to prepare a way for God, by leaving wrong things unchanged? (*Silence*)

- Did we offend God by saying too easily that nothing could be done to overcome evil? (*Silence*)

We confess that we have sinned. **I confess**...

FIRST READING

How can you give new hope to people who are in despair? How can you rouse them to new hope and action?

We hear now about the people of Jerusalem; how they were told to wake up from despair.

We read from the prophet Baruch, chapter five.
*
Jerusalem, take off your dress of sorrow and distress,
put on the beauty of the glory of God for ever,
wrap the cloak of the integrity of God around you,
put the diadem of the glory of the Eternal on your head:
since God means to show your splendour to every nation under
    heaven,
since the name God gives you for ever will be,
'Peace through integrity, and honour through devotedness'.
Arise, Jerusalem, stand on the heights
and turn your eyes to the east:
see your sons reassembled from west and east
at the command of the Holy One, jubilant that God has
    remembered them.
Though they left you on foot,
with enemies for an escort,
now God brings them back to you
like royal princes carried back in glory.
For God has decreed the flattening
of each high mountain, of the everlasting hills,
the filling of the valleys to make the ground level
so that Israel can walk in safety under the glory of God.
And the forests and every fragrant tree will provide shade
for Israel at the command of God;
for God will guide Israel in joy by the light of his glory

with his mercy and integrity for escort.

This is the word of the Lord.   *Baruch 5:1-9*

Responsorial Psalm
  ℟ **What marvels the Lord worked for us!**
      Indeed we were glad.

1 When the Lord delivered Zion from bondage,
    it seemed like a dream.
    Then was our mouth filled with laughter,
    on our lips there were songs. ℟

2 The heathens themselves said: 'What marvels
    the Lord worked for them!'
    What marvels the Lord worked for us!
    Indeed we were glad. ℟

3 Deliver us, O Lord, from our bondage
    as streams in dry land.
    Those who are sowing in tears
    will sing when they reap. ℟

4 They go out, they go out, full of tears
    carrying seed for the sowing:
    they come back, they come back, full of song,
    carrying their sheaves. ℟   *Ps 125. ℟ v.3*

SECOND READING
We read from the letter of St Paul to the Philippians, chapter one.
*
Every time I pray for all of you, I pray with joy, remembering
how you have helped to spread the Good News from the day you
first heard it right up to the present. I am quite certain that the
One who began this good work in you will see that it is finished
when the Day of Christ Jesus comes. God knows how much I
miss you all, loving you as Christ Jesus loves you. My prayer is
that your love for each other may increase more and more and
never stop improving your knowledge and deepening your
perception so that you can always recognise what is best. This
will help you to become pure and blameless, and prepare you for
the Day of Christ, when you will reach the perfect goodness
which Jesus Christ produces in us for the glory and praise of God.

This is the word of the Lord.   *Philippians 1:3-6. 8-11*

Gospel Acclamation
Alleluia, alleluia!
Prepare a way for the Lord,
make his paths straight,
and all mankind shall see the salvation of God.
Alleluia!

Lk 3:4. 6

GOSPEL

We read from the holy Gospel according to Luke, chapter three.
*

In the fifteenth year of Tiberius Caesar's reign, when Pontius
Pilate was governor of Judaea, Herod tetrarch of Galilee, his
brother Philip tetrarch of the lands of Ituraea and Trachonitis,
Lysanias tetrarch of Abilene, during the pontificate of Annas and
Caiaphas, the word of God came to John son of Zechariah, in the
wilderness. He went through the whole Jordan district proclaiming a baptism of repentance for the forgiveness of sins, as it is
written in the book of the sayings of the prophet Isaiah:

A voice cries in the wilderness;
Prepare a way for the Lord,
make his paths straight.
Every valley will be filled in,
every mountain and hill be laid low,
winding ways will be straightened
and rough roads made smooth.
And all mankind shall see the salvation of God.

This is the Gospel of the Lord.

Luke 3:1-6

Third Sunday of Advent   C

Introduction to the Service
Every day we see people waiting. Some we see waiting for the
arrival of a bus; we find others waiting for the opening of a
meeting; we find others waiting for the arrival of a person.

You can notice a great difference between people waiting; some
wait with bored faces, some even in sadness, while others wait
with joy on their faces.

In which way do we wait, during this time of waiting which is
called 'Advent'? Should we belong to those who wait in sadness
or to those who wait with a sense of joy?

The hymns and readings of this third Sunday of Advent give a
resounding reply: 'Shout for joy' while you wait! 'Be happy,
always happy in the Lord'.

Penitential Rite

Let us examine ourselves to see whether we have this sense of joyful waiting:

● Lord, you give us the firm promise that our longing for justice and happiness will be fulfilled. Forgive us our loss of hope. (*Silence*)

    Lord, have mercy...

● Christ, we know that the time will come when we will be fully united with you and with all whom we love. Forgive us for forgetting this joyful hope. (*Silence*)

    Christ, have mercy...

● Lord, we firmly believe that the whole of creation will be renewed. We want to take part in renewing it, with a sense of joy. (*Silence*)

    Lord, have mercy...

FIRST READING

It is not easy to arouse a sense of joy in a nation which is threatened by enemies who want to destroy it. Yet the prophet Zephaniah is sure that the nation of Israel will be forgiven by God and will survive. He even calls Israel 'the daughter of Zion' to indicate that God loves her like a bride. Great joy lies ahead of her.

We read from prophet Zephaniah, chapter three.
*
Shout for joy, daughter of Zion,
Israel, shout aloud!
Rejoice, exult with all your heart,
daughter of Jerusalem!
The Lord has repealed your sentence;
he has driven your enemies away.
The Lord, the king of Israel, is in your midst;
you have no more evil to fear.
When that day comes, word will come to Jerusalem:
Zion, have no fear,
do not let your hands fall limp.
The Lord your God is in your midst,
a victorious warrior.
He will exult with joy over you,
he will renew you by his love;
he will dance with shouts of joy for you
as on a day of festival.

    This is the word of the Lord.   *Zephaniah 3:14-18*

Responsorial Psalm
℟ **Sing and shout for joy**
for great in your midst is the Holy One of Israel.

1 Truly, God is my salvation,
I trust, I shall not fear.
For the Lord is my strength, my song,
he became my saviour.
With joy you will draw water
from the wells of salvation. ℟

2 Give thanks to the Lord, give praise to his name!
Make his mighty deeds known to the peoples!
Declare the greatness of his name. ℟

3 Sing a psalm to the Lord
for he has done glorious deeds,
make them known to all the earth!
People of Zion, sing and shout for joy
for great in your midst is the Holy One of Israel. ℟

Is 12:2-6. ℟ v.6

SECOND READING

We read from the letter of St Paul to the Philippians, chapter four.
*
I want you to be happy, always happy in the Lord; I repeat, what I want is your happiness. Let your tolerance be evident to everyone: the Lord is very near. There is no need to worry; but if there is anything you need, pray for it, asking God for it with prayer and thanksgiving, and that peace of God, which is so much greater than we can understand, will guard your hearts and your thoughts, in Christ Jesus.

This is the word of the Lord. *Philippians 4:4-7*

Gospel Acclamation
Alleluia, alleluia!
The spirit of the Lord has been given to me.
He has sent me to bring good news to the poor.
Alleluia! *Is 61:1 (Lk 4:18)*

GOSPEL

We read from the holy Gospel according to Luke, chapter three.
*
When all the people asked John, 'What must we do?' he answered, 'If anyone has two tunics he must share with the man

who has none, and the one with something to eat must do the same.' There were tax collectors too who came for baptism, and these said to him, 'Master what must we do?' He said to them, 'Exact no more than your rate.' Some soldiers asked him in their turn, 'What about us? What must we do?' He said to them, 'No intimidation! No extortion! Be content with your pay!'

A feeling of expectancy had grown among the people, who were beginning to think that John might be the Christ, so John declared before them all, 'I baptise you with water, but someone is coming, someone who is more powerful than I am, and I am not fit to undo the strap of his sandals; he will baptise you with the Holy Spirit and fire. His winnowing-fan is in his hand to clear his threshing-floor and to gather the wheat into his barn; but the chaff he will burn in a fire that will never go out.' As well as this, there were many other things he said to exhort the people and to announce the Good News to them.

This is the Gospel of the Lord.   *Luke 3:10-18*

Fourth Sunday of Advent   C

Introduction to the Service
Today is the fourth Sunday of Advent, the last Sunday before Christmas. The time of waiting is nearing its end. But we still wish to understand more deeply in what way we, as Christians, should wait; in what spirit we should live our Advent.

We find an answer by looking at Mary. How did she await the birth of her child, the Saviour? She waited by giving help to her relative, Elizabeth. She did not wait passively. And she did not wait in a selfish way, only concerned about herself. Instead she hurried to the hill country and for three months helped in Elizabeth's household. What a model of active waiting.

Penitential Rite
Let us look at our own lives:

● Do we also await the Saviour by giving help to our neighbour?   (*Silence*)

● Do we await the Saviour by remaining where we are or do we, like Mary, move out to meet him and his people?   (*Silence*)

Let us admit our wrong ways by saying together: **I confess**…

FIRST READING

Mary was not rich or famous but was one of the least among the people. In the same way it will be from one of the least tribes, the tribe of Ephrata, and in one of the least towns, the tiny Bethlehem, that the great Prince of Peace will be born. God exalts the lowly, those who await him in sincerity.

We read from the book of Micah, chapter five.
*
The Lord says this:

You, Bethlehem Ephrathah,
the least of the clans of Judah,
out of you will be born for me
the one who is to rule over Israel;
his origin goes back to the distant past,
to the days of old.
The Lord is therefore going to abandon them
till the time when she who is to give birth gives birth.
Then the remnant of his brothers will come back
to the sons of Israel.
He will stand and feed his flock
with the power of the Lord,
with the majesty of the name of his God.
They will live secure, for from then on he will extend his
     power
to the ends of the land.
He himself will be peace.

This is the word of the Lord. *Micah 5:1-4*

Responsorial Psalm

℟ **God of hosts, bring us back;**
let your face shine on us and we shall be saved.

1 O shepherd of Israel, hear us,
shine forth from your cherubim throne.
O Lord, rouse up your might,
O Lord, come to our help. ℟

2 God of hosts, turn again, we implore,
look down from heaven and see.
Visit this vine and protect it,
the vine your right hand has planted. ℟

3 May your hand be on the man you have chosen,
the man you have given your strength.

And we shall never forsake you again:
give us life that we may call upon your name. ℟

Ps 79:2-3. 15-16. 18-19. ℟ v.4

SECOND READING

We read from the letter to the Hebrews, chapter ten.
*
This is what Christ said, on coming into the world:

> You who wanted no sacrifice or oblation,
> prepared a body for me.
> You took no pleasure in holocausts or sacrifices for sin;
> then I said,
> just as I was commanded in the scroll of the book,
> 'God, here I am! I am coming to obey your will.'

Notice that he says first: You did not want what the Law lays down as the things to be offered, that is: the sacrifices, the oblations, the holocausts and the sacrifices for sin, and you took no pleasure in them; and then he says: Here I am! I am coming to obey your will. He is abolishing the first sort to replace it with the second. And this will was for us to be made holy by the offering of his body made once and for all by Jesus Christ.

This is the word of the Lord.   *Hebrews 10:5-10*

Gospel Acclamation
Alleluia, alleluia!
I am the handmaid of the Lord:
let what you have said be done to me.
Alleluia!   *Lk 1:38*

GOSPEL

We read from the holy Gospel according to Luke, chapter one.
*
Mary set out and went as quickly as she could to a town in the hill country of Judah. She went into Zechariah's house and greeted Elizabeth. Now as soon as Elizabeth heard Mary's greeting, the child leapt in her womb and Elizabeth was filled with the Holy Spirit. She gave a loud cry and said, 'Of all women you are the most blessed, and blessed is the fruit of your womb. Why should I be honoured with a visit from the mother of my Lord? For the moment your greeting reached my ears, the child in my womb leapt for joy. Yes, blessed is she who believed that the promise made her by the Lord would be fulfilled.'

This is the Gospel of the Lord.   *Luke 1:39-44*

THE SEASON OF CHRISTMAS

Christmas Day

See above, pp. 25.

Sunday in the Octave of Christmas Feast

The Holy Family of Jesus, Mary and Joseph C

Where there is no Sunday occurring between 25 December and 1 January, this feast is celebrated on 30 December, with one reading only before the Gospel.

Introduction to the Service

We all belong to a family. We grew up in a family and know the people who are related to us. We also know the difficulties which families have to face. There are misunderstandings and troubles between parents and children, between father and mother, between one family and another.

Jesus also belonged to a family. Joseph the carpenter, Mary and Jesus are called the Holy Family of Nazareth. Today we remember this Holy Family in our celebration.

We know that there were difficulties even in the Holy Family. Jesus, for instance, remained behind in the Temple without the permission of his parents. But we can also be sure that Mary, Joseph and Jesus could sort out possible misunderstandings and difficulties. With Jesus in their midst, the family of Nazareth was able to do things well and to solve their problems in a spirit of love.

Penitential Rite

Let us examine our conscience:

- What are we doing at home in order to keep Jesus in our midst? Do we pray together at home? Do we read and share God's Word together? *(Silence)*

- Do we appreciate the Sacrament of Marriage as a sign of Christ's presence in our families? *(Silence)*

Let us ask for forgiveness for so often excluding Christ from our families. **I confess**...

The First Reading, Psalm, Second Reading and Gospel Acclamation given for Year A, pp.34ff., may be used, with the Gospel below. Or the alternative readings given below may be used.

FIRST READING

Why do parents bring their children to church to be baptised? Is it a mere formality, just an empty ceremony? In our reading, we hear of a woman who is an example to all parents who present their children for baptism.

We read from the first book of Samuel, chapter one.
*
Hannah conceived and gave birth to a son, and called him Samuel 'since' she said 'I asked the Lord for him.'

When a year had gone by, the husband Elkanah went up again with all his family to offer the annual sacrifice to the Lord and to fulfil his vow. Hannah, however, did not go up, having said to her husband, 'Not before the child is weaned. Then I will bring him and present him before the Lord and he shall stay there for ever.'

When she had weaned him, she took him up with her together with a three-year old bull, an ephah of flour and a skin of wine, and she brought him to the temple of the Lord at Shiloh; and the child was with them. They slaughtered the bull and the child's mother came to Eli. She said, 'If you please, my lord. As you live, my lord, I am the woman who stood here beside you, praying to the Lord. This is the child I prayed for, and the Lord granted me what I asked him. Now I make him over to the Lord for the whole of his life. He is made over to the Lord.'

There she left him, for the Lord.

This is the word of the Lord.   *1 Samuel 1:20-22. 24-28*

Responsorial Psalm
   ℟   **They are happy who dwell in your house, O Lord.**

1   How lovely is your dwelling place,
    Lord, God of hosts.
    My soul is longing and yearning,
    is yearning for the courts of the Lord.
    My heart and my soul ring out their joy
    to God, the living God.   ℟

2   They are happy, who dwell in your house,
for ever singing your praise.
They are happy, whose strength is in you;
they walk with ever growing strength.   ℞

3   O Lord, God of hosts, hear my prayer,
give ear, O God of Jacob.
Turn your eyes, O God, our shield,
look on the face of your anointed.   ℞

Ps 83:2-3. 5-6. 9-10 ℞ v.5

SECOND READING

We read from the first letter of St John, chapter three.
*

Think of the love that the Father has lavished on us,
by letting us be called God's children;
and that is what we are.
Because the world refused to acknowledge him,
therefore it does not acknowledge us.
My dear people, we are already the children of God
but what we are to be in the future has not yet been revealed,
all we know is, that when it is revealed
we shall be like him
because we shall see him as he really is.

My dear people,
if we cannot be condemned by our own conscience,
we need not be afraid in God's presence,
and whatever we ask him,
we shall receive,
because we keep his commandments
and live the kind of life that he wants.
His commandments are these:
that we believe in the name of his Son Jesus Christ
and that we love one another
as he told us to.
Whoever keeps his commandments
lives in God and God lives in him.
We know that he lives in us
by the Spirit that he has given us.

This is the word of the Lord.   *1 John 3:1-2. 21-24*

Gospel Acclamation
Alleluia, alleluia!
Open our heart, O Lord,
to accept the words of your Son.
Alleluia!

cf. Acts 16:14

GOSPEL

We read from the holy Gospel according to Luke, chapter two.
*
Every year the parents of Jesus used to go to Jerusalem for the feast of the Passover. When he was twelve years old, they went up for the feast as usual. When they were on their way home after the feast, the boy Jesus stayed behind in Jerusalem without his parents knowing it. They assumed he was with the caravan, and it was only after a day's journey that they went to look for him among their relations and acquaintances. When they failed to find him they went back to Jerusalem looking for him everywhere.

Three days later, they found him in the Temple, sitting among the doctors, listening to them, and asking them questions; and all those who heard him were astounded at his intelligence and his replies. They were overcome when they saw him, and his mother said to him, 'My child, why have you done this to us? See how worried your father and I have been, looking for you.' 'Why were you looking for me?' he replied. 'Did you not know that I must be busy with my Father's affairs?' But they did not understand what he meant.

He then went down with them and came to Nazareth and lived under their authority. His mother stored up all these things in her heart. And Jesus increased in wisdom, in stature, and in favour with God and men.

This is the Gospel of the Lord.

Luke 2:41-52

1 January: Octave of Christmas

Solemnity of Mary, Mother of God

See above, pp. 37.

Second Sunday after Christmas

See above, pp. 40.

6 January (or Sunday between 2 January and 8 January)

The Epiphany of the Lord

See above, pp. 44.

Sunday after 6 January   First Sunday in Ordinary Time   Feast

The Baptism of the Lord   C

This feast is omitted when the Epiphany is celebrated on this Sunday.

Introduction to the Service

Today we celebrate the feast of our Lord's baptism in the river Jordan. We could also think of it as the feast of our Lord's baptism *and* confirmation.

Many of us remember the day when we were confirmed. Others in our community are preparing themselves for receiving this great sacrament of confirmation.

Baptism and confirmation belong together. This we can clearly see on the occasion when Jesus was baptised in the river Jordan. After John had baptised him, the Holy Spirit came down on Jesus and strengthened him.

Today, Jesus publicly began his mission. He was sent by the Father to overcome evil with good, to proclaim the will of God, to face jealousy, persecution and death. It was for this task that Jesus was strengthened at his baptism by the Holy Spirit.

This feast of our Lord's baptism, therefore, reminds us of our own baptism and confirmation.

Penitential Rite

Let us ask ourselves:

● In baptism God has accepted us as his beloved sons and daughters. Do we behave as God's children? (*Silence*)

● We are called to stand up against evil and hatred as Christ did. Do we accept this task for which we were strengthened in the sacrament of confirmation? (*Silence*)

We ask for forgiveness for forgetting the task which God gave us in the sacrament of baptism and confirmation.   **I confess**...

The First Reading, Psalm, Second Reading and Gospel Acclamation given for Year A, pp.47ff., may be used, with the Gospel below. Or the alternative readings given below may be used.

FIRST READING

When Jesus was baptised in the river Jordan, he was baptised and confirmed to fulfil a great task. What was this task? What was he sent to do?

We read from the prophet Isaiah, chapter forty.

*
'Console my people, console them'
says your God.
'Speak to the heart of Jerusalem
and call to her
that her time of service is ended,
that her sin is atoned for,
that she has received from the hand of the Lord
double punishment for all her crimes.'

A voice cries, 'Prepare in the wilderness
a way for the Lord.
Make a straight highway for our God
across the desert.
Let every valley be filled in,
every mountain and hill be laid low,
let every cliff become a plain,
and the ridges a valley;
then the glory of the Lord shall be revealed
and all mankind shall see it;
for the mouth of the Lord has spoken.'

Go up on a high mountain,
joyful messenger to Zion.
Shout with a loud voice,
joyful messenger to Jerusalem.
Shout without fear,
say to the towns of Judah,
'Here is your God.'
Here is the Lord coming with power,
his arm subduing all things to him.
The prize of his victory is with him,
his trophies all go before him.
He is like a shepherd feeding his flock,
gathering lambs in his arms,
holding them against his breast
and leading to their rest the mother ewes.

This is the word of the Lord.   *Isiah 40:1-5. 9-11*

Responsorial Psalm
℞ **Bless the Lord, my soul!**
Lord God, how great you are.

1 Lord God, how great you are,
   clothed in majesty and glory,
   wrapped in light as in a robe!
   You stretch out the heavens like a tent. ℞

2 Above the rains you build your dwelling.
   You make the clouds your chariot,
   you walk on the wings of the wind,
   you make the winds your messengers
   and flashing fire your servants. ℞

3 How many are your works, O Lord!
   In wisdom you have made them all.
   The earth is full of your riches.
   There is the sea, vast and wide,
   with its moving swarms past counting,
   living things great and small. ℞

4 All of these look to you
   to give them their food in due season.
   You give it, they gather it up:
   you open your hand, they have their fill. ℞

5 You take back your spirit, they die,
   returning to the dust from which they came.
   You send forth your spirit, they are created;
   and you renew the face of the earth. ℞

Ps 103:1-2. 3-4. 24-25. 27-30. ℞ v.1

SECOND READING

We read from the letter of St Paul to Titus, chapters two and three.
*
God's grace has been revealed, and it has made salvation possible for the whole human race and taught us that what we have to do is to give up everything that does not lead to God, and all our worldly ambitions; we must be self-restrained and live good and religious lives here in this present world, while we are waiting in hope for the blessing which will come with the Appearing of the glory of our great God and saviour Christ Jesus. He sacrificed himself for us in order to set us free from all wickedness and to purify a people so that it could be his very

own and would have no ambition except to do good.

When the kindness and love of God our saviour for mankind were revealed, it was not because he was concerned with any righteous actions we might have done ourselves; it was for no reason except his own compassion that he saved us, by means of the cleansing water of rebirth and by renewing us with the Holy Spirit which he has so generously poured over us through Jesus Christ our saviour. He did this so that we should be justified by his grace, to become heirs looking forward to inheriting eternal life.

This is the word of the Lord. *Titus 2:11-14. 3:4-7*

Gospel Acclamation
Alleluia, alleluia!
Someone is coming, said John, someone greater than I.
He will baptize you with the Holy Spirit and with fire.
Alleluia! *cf. Lk 3:16*

GOSPEL

We read from the holy Gospel according to Luke, chapter three.
*
A feeling of expectancy had grown among the people, who were beginning to think that John might be the Christ, so John declared before them all, 'I baptise you with water, but someone is coming, someone who is more powerful than I am and I am not fit to undo the strap of his sandals; he will baptise you with the Holy Spirit and fire.'

Now when all the people had been baptised and while Jesus after his own baptism was at prayer, heaven opened and the Holy Spirit descended on him in bodily shape, like a dove. And a voice came from heaven, 'You are my Son, the Beloved; my favour rests on you'.

This is the Gospel of the Lord. *Luke 3:15-16. 21-22*

THE SEASON OF LENT

Ash Wednesday

See above, pp. 51.

First Sunday of Lent   C

Introduction to the Service

The Passover was always a great feast for the Jews, because then they remembered that they were freed from slavery. We, too, celebrate our liberation at Easter. We begin today, on this first Sunday of Lent, to prepare ourselves for Easter, the feast of our liberation.

On this first Sunday of Lent we read about the one person who was completely free and who never became a slave. Satan wanted to make Jesus a slave by tempting him. But Jesus was stronger than Satan and remained free.

Penitential Rite

Let us now look at our own lives and ask for the Lord's mercy:

● Lord Jesus, we were tempted like you but we confess that we often allowed ourselves to be overpowered by Satan and to be enslaved by him.   (*Silence*)

Lord, have mercy...

● Lord Jesus, you replied to Satan: 'Man does not live by bread alone'. Forgive us for the times when we only cared for our bodily needs and failed to live by the words that come from your mouth.   (*Silence*)

Christ, have mercy...

● Satan offered you riches, and power over people. You rejected this temptation, but we often give in to it.   (*Silence*)

Lord, have mercy...

FIRST READING

The Jews were liberated from the slavery of Egypt, and they wanted to make sure that they would never forget this liberation. Therefore each Jew had to stand in front of his brethren at harvest time each year and offer up to God some of his harvest in a basket, whilst at the same time declaring in a loud voice how his forefathers were liberated.

In our reading from the book of Deuteronomy, chapter twenty-six, we will hear the very words with which each one had to proclaim his liberation.

★

Moses said to the people: 'The priest shall take the pannier from your hand and lay it before the altar of the Lord your God. Then, in the sight of the Lord your God, you must make this pronouncement:

"My father was a wandering Aramaean. He went down into Egypt to find refuge there, few in numbers; but there he became a nation, great, mighty, and strong. The Egyptians ill-treated us, they gave us no peace and inflicted harsh slavery on us. But we called on the Lord, the God of our fathers. The Lord heard our voice and saw our misery, our toil and our oppression; and the Lord brought us out of Egypt with mighty hand and outstretched arm, with great terror, and with signs and wonders. He brought us here and gave us this land, a land where milk and honey flow. Here then I bring the first-fruits of the produce of the soil that you, Lord, have given me." You must then lay them before the Lord your God, and bow down in the sight of the Lord your God.'

This is the word of the Lord.   *Deuteronomy 26:4-10*

Responsorial Psalm
℞ **Be with me, O Lord, in my distress.**

1 He who dwells in the shelter of the Most High
   and abides in the shade of the Almighty
   says to the Lord: 'My refuge,
   my stronghold, my God in whom I trust!'   ℞

2 Upon you no evil shall fall,
   no plague approach where you dwell.
   For you has he commanded his angels,
   to keep you in all your ways.   ℞

3 They shall bear you upon their hands
   lest you strike your foot against a stone.
   On the lion and the viper you will tread
   and trample the young lion and the dragon.   ℞

4 His love he set on me, so I will rescue him;
   protect him for he knows my name.

When he calls I shall answer: 'I am with you.'
I will save him in distress and give him glory. ℟
Ps 90:1-2. 10-15. ℟ v.15

SECOND READING

We read from the letter of St Paul to the Romans, chapter ten.
*
Scripture says: The word, that is the faith we proclaim, is very
near to you, it is on your lips and in your heart. If your lips
confess that Jesus is Lord and if you believe in your heart that
God raised him from the dead, then you will be saved. By
believing from the heart you are made righteous; by confessing
with your lips you are saved. When scripture says: those who
believe in him will have no cause for shame, it makes no
distinction between Jew and Greek: all belong to the same Lord
who is rich enough, however many ask for his help, for everyone
who calls on the name of the Lord will be saved.

This is the word of the Lord.   *Romans 10:8-13*

Gospel Acclamation

Praise to you, O Christ, king of eternal glory!
Man does not live on bread alone
but on every word that comes from the mouth of God.
Praise to you, O Christ, king of eternal glory!   *Mt 4:4*

GOSPEL

We read from the holy Gospel according to Luke, chapter four.
*
Filled with the Holy Spirit, Jesus left the Jordan and was led by
the Spirit through the wilderness, being tempted there by the
devil for forty days. During that time he ate nothing and at the
end he was hungry. Then the devil said to him, 'If you are the
Son of God, tell this stone to turn into a loaf.' But Jesus replied,
'Scripture says: Man does not live on bread alone.'

Then leading him to a height, the devil showed him in a
moment of time all the kingdoms of the world and said to him, 'I
will give you all this power and the glory of these kingdoms, for it
has been committed to me and I give it to anyone I choose.
Worship me, then, and it shall all be yours.' But Jesus answered
him. 'Scripture says:

You must worship the Lord your God,
and serve him alone.'

Then he led him to Jerusalem and made him stand on the parapet of the Temple. 'If you are the Son of God', he said to him 'throw yourself down from here, for scripture says:

He will put his angels in charge of you
to guard you,

and again:

They will hold you up on their hands
in case you hurt your foot against a stone.'

But Jesus answered him, 'It has been said:

You must not put the Lord your God to the test.'

Having exhausted all these ways of tempting him, the devil left him, to return at the appointed time.

This is the Gospel of the Lord.   *Luke 4:1-13*

Second Sunday of Lent   C

Introduction to the Service
How would you feel if you knew that soon you would have to suffer very severely and that your life would be in danger? If you knew that this suffering could not be avoided, what would you do? Would you not look for somebody to be with you? Would you not look for any sign of hope?

When Christ approached the time of his suffering, he received such a sign. On the mountain, while he was praying, God's glory became visible in him, Christ was transfigured and the Father's voice was heard above him. Truly, a powerful sign of hope before the beginning of his suffering.

Penitential Rite
Are not we, too, in need of such a divine sign in our times of suffering? Because we do not always bear our suffering in the right way. Let us reflect:

● When we have to bear suffering, do we remember that God is always close to us?   (*Silence*)

● In times of suffering, do we often remember that God's glory is hidden in us?   (*Silence*)

Together we admit that we have sinned.   **I confess**...

FIRST READING

Like Christ, Abraham went up a mountain, ready to give up all he had, ready to suffer.

As we listen to this reading about Abraham's sacrifice on the mountain, let us be aware that we, too, are sometimes called to go up the mountain of suffering. We will be called to go up, trusting that God will not forsake us.

We read from the book of Genesis, chapter fifteen.

*
Taking Abram outside the Lord said, 'Look up to heaven and count the stars if you can. Such will be your descendants' he told him. Abram put his faith in the Lord, who counted this as making him justified.

'I am the Lord' he said to him 'who brought you out of Ur of the Chaldaeans to make you heir to this land.' 'My Lord, the Lord' Abram replied 'how am I to know that I shall inherit it?' He said to him, 'Get me a three-year-old heifer, a three-year-old goat, a three-year-old ram, a turtledove and a young pigeon.' He brought him all these, cut them in half and put half on one side and half facing it on the other; but the birds he did not cut in half. Birds of prey came down on the carcasses but Abram drove them off.

Now as the sun was setting Abram fell into a deep sleep, and terror seized him. When the sun had set and darkness had fallen, there appeared a smoking furnace and a firebrand that went between the halves. That day the Lord made a Covenant with Abram in these terms:

'To your descendants I give this land,
from the wadi of Egypt to the Great River.'

This is the word of the Lord.   *Genesis 15:5-12. 17-18.*

Responsorial Psalm
    ℟   **The Lord is my light and my help.**

1   The Lord is my light and my help;
      whom shall I fear?
      The Lord is the stronghold of my life;
      before whom shall I shrink?   ℟

2   O Lord, hear my voice when I call;
      have mercy and answer.
      Of you my heart has spoken:
      'Seek his face.'   ℟

3   It is your face, O Lord, that I seek;
    hide not your face.
    Dismiss not your servant in anger;
    you have been my help.   ℟

4   I am sure I shall see the Lord's goodness
    in the land of the living.
    Hope in him, hold firm and take heart.
    Hope in the Lord!   ℟   *Ps 26:1. 7-9. 13-14. ℟ v.1*

SECOND READING

We read from the letter of St Paul to the Philippians, chapters three and
four.
*
My brothers, be united in following my rule of life. Take as your
models everybody who is already doing this and study them as
you used to study us. I have told you often, and I repeat it today
with tears, there are many who are behaving as the enemies of
the cross of Christ. They are destined to be lost. They make foods
into their god and they are proudest of something they ought to
think shameful; the things they think important are earthly
things. *For us, our homeland is in heaven, and from heaven
comes the saviour we are waiting for, the Lord Jesus Christ, and
he will transfigure these wretched bodies of ours into copies of
his glorious body. He will do that by the same power with which
he can subdue the whole universe.

So then, my brothers and dear friends, do not give way but
remain faithful in the Lord. I miss you very much, dear friends;
you are my joy and my crown.

This is the word of the Lord.*   *Philippians 3:17–4:1*

*Shorter Form, 3:20–4:1. Read between *.

Gospel Acclamation
    Glory and praise to you, O Christ!
    From the bright cloud, the Father's voice was heard:
    'This is my Son, the Beloved. Listen to him!'
    Glory and praise to you, O Christ!   *Mt 17:5*

GOSPEL

We read from the holy Gospel according to Luke, chapter nine.
*
Jesus took with him Peter and John and James and went up the

mountain to pray. As he prayed, the aspect of his face was changed and his clothing became brilliant as lightning. Suddenly there were two men there talking to him; they were Moses and Elijah appearing in glory, and they were speaking of his passing which he was to accomplish in Jerusalem. Peter and his companions were heavy with sleep, but they kept awake and saw his glory and the two men standing with him. As these were leaving him, Peter said to Jesus, 'Master, it is wonderful for us to be here; so let us make three tents, one for you, one for Moses and one for Elijah.' – He did not know what he was saying. As he spoke, a cloud came and covered them with shadow; and when they went into the cloud the disciples were afraid. And a voice came from the cloud saying, 'This is my Son, the Chosen One. Listen to him'. And after the voice had spoken, Jesus was found alone. The disciples kept silence and, at that time, told no one what they had seen.

This is the Gospel of the Lord.   *Luke 9:28-36*

Third Sunday of Lent   C

Introduction to the Service

'Unless you repent, you will all perish.' These hard words come from the mouth of Jesus. We read them today because we are approaching Easter and it is already the third Sunday of Lent.

We will try to repent. We will try to approach Easter in the way in which Moses approached God in the burning bush. Moses showed us what it meant to repent. He fell to the ground. He respected God. He asked him what to do. He surrendered to him.

Penitential Rite

Let us approach God in the same way now, at the beginning of this service.

● Lord, as Moses fell to the ground before you, we too, humble ourselves before you. We ask for forgiveness because we exalted ourselves and forgot how small we are before you. (*Silence*)
    Lord, have mercy...

● As Moses took off his shoes before the holy place, we too take off our pride before you and ask pardon.   (*Silence*)
    Christ, have mercy...

● As Moses remembered your holiness and his unworthiness, we, too, remember how holy you are and how unworthily we stand before you.   (*Silence*)

    Lord, have mercy...

FIRST READING

Easter is like the burning bush which Moses approached. As we listen now to this reading about the burning bush, let us see ourselves in the figure of Moses. We, too, are called to approach the Holy God.

We read from the book of Exodus, chapter three.

Moses was looking after the flock of Jethro, his father-in-law, priest of Midian. He led his flock to the far side of the wilderness and came to Horeb, the mountain of God. There the angel of the Lord appeared to him in the shape of a flame of fire, coming from the middle of a bush. Moses looked; there was the bush blazing but it was not being burnt up. 'I must go and look at this strange sight,' Moses said 'and see why the bush is not burnt.' Now the Lord saw him go forward to look, and God called to him from the middle of the bush. 'Moses, Moses!' he said. 'Here I am' he answered. 'Come no nearer' he said. 'Take off your shoes, for the place on which you stand is holy ground. I am the God of your father,' he said 'the God of Abraham, the God of Isaac and the God of Jacob.' At this Moses covered his face, afraid to look at God.

    And the Lord said, 'I have seen the miserable state of my people in Egypt. I have heard their appeal to be free of their slave-drivers. Yes, I am well aware of their sufferings. I mean to deliver them out of the hands of the Egyptians and bring them up out of that land to a land rich and broad, a land where milk and honey flow.'

    Then Moses said to God, 'I am to go, then, to the sons of Israel and say to them, "The God of your fathers has sent me to you." But if they ask me what his name is, what am I to tell them?' And God said to Moses, 'I Am who I Am. This' he added 'is what you must say to the sons of Israel: "The Lord, the God of your fathers, the God of Abraham, the God of Isaac, and the God of Jacob, has sent me to you." This is my name for all time; by this name I shall be invoked for all generations to come.'

This is the word of the Lord.   *Exodus 3:1-8. 13-15*

Responsorial Psalm
℟   **The Lord is compassion and love.**

1   My soul, give thanks to the Lord,
    all my being, bless his holy name.
    My soul give thanks to the Lord
    and never forget all his blessings.   ℟

2   It is he who forgives all your guilt,
    who heals every one of your ills,
    who redeems your life from the grave,
    who crowns you with love and compassion.   ℟

3   The Lord does deeds of justice,
    gives judgement for all who are oppressed.
    He made known his ways to Moses
    and his deeds to Israel's sons.   ℟

4   The Lord is compassion and love,
    slow to anger and rich in mercy.
    For as the heavens are high above the earth
    so strong is his love for those who fear him.   ℟

Ps 102:1-4. 6-8. 11. ℟ v.8

SECOND READING

We read from the first letter of St Paul to the Corinthians, chapter ten.
*

I want to remind you, brothers, how our fathers were all guided
by a cloud above them and how they all passed through the sea.
They were all baptised into Moses in this cloud and in this sea; all
ate the same spiritual food and all drank the same spiritual drink,
since they all drank from the spiritual rock that followed them as
they went, and that rock was Christ. In spite of this, most of them
failed to please God and their corpses littered the desert.

These things all happened as warnings for us, not to have the
wicked lusts for forbidden things that they had. You must never
complain: some of them did, and they were killed by the
Destroyer.

All this happened to them as a warning and it was written
down to be a lesson for us who are living at the end of the age.
The man who thinks he is safe must be careful that he does not
fall.

This is the word of the Lord.   *1 Corinthians 10:1-6. 10-12.*

Gospel Acclamation
Glory to you, O Christ, you are the Word of God!
Repent, says the Lord,
for the kingdom of heaven is close at hand.
Glory to you, O Christ, you are the Word of God!   Mt 4:17

GOSPEL
We read from the holy Gospel according to Luke, chapter thirteen.
*
Some people arrived and told Jesus about the Galileans whose blood Pilate had mingled with that of their sacrifices. At this he said to them, 'Do you suppose these Galileans who suffered like that were greater sinners than any other Galileans? They were not, I tell you. No; but unless you repent you will all perish as they did. Or those eighteen on whom the tower at Siloam fell and killed them? Do you suppose that they were more guilty than all the other people living in Jerusalem? They were not, I tell you. No; but unless you repent you will all perish as they did.'

He told this parable: 'A man had a fig tree planted in his vineyard and he came looking for fruit on it but found none. He said to the man who looked after the vineyard, "Look here, for three years now I have been coming to look for fruit on this fig tree and finding none. Cut it down: why should it be taking up the ground?" "Sir," the man replied "leave it one more year and give me time to dig round it and manure it: it may bear fruit next year; if not, then you can cut it down." '

This is the Gospel of the Lord.   *Luke 13:1-9*

Fourth Sunday of Lent   C
Introduction to the Service
Christ told us that there will be a feast in heaven if one sinner returns home to the Father. Easter is such a feast of the reunion between God and those who were far from him. We are preparing for this feast.

It is the fourth Sunday of Lent, and there are only three weeks left before Easter. Every day we are called upon to prepare ourselves by self-denial, by good works, and by reflecting.

Penitential Rite
Let us think about the way in which we should return to the Father:

- The prodigal son returned home because he remembered how good his home was and how merciful his Father was. How much do we think about our heavenly Father and his invitation to return to him? (*Silence*)

- The prodigal son was invited to the feast of reconciliation because he returned and had the courage to confess his sin. Are we ready to confess our sins, or are we trying to deny them? (*Silence*)

Let us confess that we have sinned: **I confess**...

FIRST READING

Two things happened to the prodigal son: his shame was taken away and a feast was held to celebrate his return. God had done the same two things long ago with the people of Israel when they returned from Egypt: God took away the shame of their slavery and he celebrated the feast of Passover in their midst.

We read from the book of Joshua, chapter five.

The Lord said to Joshua, 'Today I have taken the shame of Egypt away from you.'

The Israelites pitched their camp at Gilgal and kept the Passover there on the fourteenth day of the month, at evening in the plain of Jericho. On the morrow of the Passover they tasted the produce of that country, unleavened bread and roasted ears of corn, that same day. From that time, from their first eating of the produce of that country, the manna stopped falling. And having manna no longer, the Israelites fed from that year onwards on what the land of Canaan yielded.

This is the word of the Lord.   *Joshua 5:9-12*

Responsorial Psalm
  ℟ **Taste and see that the Lord is good.**

1 I will bless the Lord at all times,
   his praise always on my lips;
   in the Lord my soul shall make its boast.
   The humble shall hear and be glad. ℟

2 Glorify the Lord with me.
   Together let us praise his name.
   I sought the Lord and he answered me;

from all my terrors he set me free.   ℟

3   Look towards him and be radiant;
    let your faces not be abashed.
    This poor man called; the Lord heard him
    and rescued him from all his distress.   ℟   *Ps 33:2-7. ℟ v.9*

SECOND READING

We read from the second letter of St Paul to the Corinthians, chapter
five.
*
For anyone who is in Christ, there is a new creation; the old
creation has gone, and now the new one is here. It is all God's
work. It was God who reconciled us to himself through Christ
and gave us the work of handing on his reconciliation. In other
words, God in Christ was reconciling the world to himself, not
holding men's faults against them, and he has entrusted to us the
news that they are reconciled. So we are ambassadors for Christ;
it is as though God were appearing through us, and the appeal
that we make in Christ's name is: be reconciled to God. For our
sake God made the sinless one into sin, so that in him we might
become the goodness of God.

This is the word of the Lord.   *2 Corinthians 5:17-21*

Gospel Acclamation
    Praise and honour to you, Lord Jesus!
    I will leave this place and go to my father and say:
    'Father, I have sinned against heaven and against you.'
    Praise and honour to you, Lord Jesus!   *Lk 15:18*

GOSPEL

We read from the holy Gospel according to Luke, chapter fifteen.
*
The tax collectors and the sinners were all seeking the company
of Jesus to hear what he had to say, and the Pharisees and the
scribes complained. 'This man' they said 'welcomes sinners and
eats with them.' So he spoke this parable to them:
    'A man had two sons. The younger said to his father, "Father,
let me have the share of the estate that would come to me." So
the father divided the property between them. A few days later,
the younger son got together everything he had and left for a
distant country where he squandered his money on a life of
debauchery.

'When he had spent it all, that country experienced a severe famine, and now he began to feel the pinch, so he hired himself out to one of the local inhabitants who put him on his farm to feed the pigs. And he would willingly have filled his belly with the husks the pigs were eating but no one offered him anything. Then he came to his senses and said, "How many of my father's paid servants have more food than they want, and here am I dying of hunger! I will leave this place and go to my father and say: Father, I have sinned against heaven and against you; I no longer deserve to be called your son; treat me as one of your paid servants." So he left the place and went back to his father.

'While he was still a long way off, his father saw him and was moved with pity. He ran to the boy, clasped him in his arms and kissed him tenderly. Then his son said, "Father, I have sinned against heaven and against you. I no longer deserve to be called your son." But the father said to his servants, "Quick! Bring out the best robe and put it on him; put a ring on his finger and sandals on his feet. Bring the calf we have been fattening, and kill it; we are going to have a feast, a celebration, because this son of mine was dead and has come back to life; he was lost and is found." And they began to celebrate.

'Now the elder son was out in the fields, and on his way back, as he drew near the house, he could hear music and dancing. Calling one of the servants he asked what it was all about. "Your brother has come" replied the servant "and your father has killed the calf we had fattened because he has got him back safe and sound." He was angry then and refused to go in, and his father came out to plead with him; but he answered his father, "Look, all these years I have slaved for you and never once disobeyed your orders, yet you never offered me so much as a kid for me to celebrate with my friends. But for this son of yours, when he comes back after swallowing up your property – he and his women – you kill the calf we had been fattening."

'The father said, "My son, you are with me always and all I have is yours. But it is only right we should celebrate and rejoice, because your brother here was dead and has come to life; he was lost and is found." '

This is the Gospel of the Lord.   *Luke 15:1-3. 11-32*

Fifth Sunday of Lent   C

Introduction to the Service

As we are gathered here, how do we appear to God? We have put on our best clothes, because it is Sunday. It is a joy to look at us as we are gathered together in church. But God does not look at our outward appearance. He looks at our hearts. How do we appear to him?

The Gospel reading for this fifth Sunday of Lent gives us a wonderful reply: God sees in us nothing of our evil past. He sees only the love which is present in us now.

Easter is a feast of forgiveness. It is the feast of our completely new life. We are like the woman who was caught committing a serious sin for which she was condemned to death. But she was totally forgiven. She could begin a completely new life. In the same way God, as he looks at us now, sees only the new spirit which is in us. Are we grateful for this?

Penitential Rite

- Lord, you do not recall our past deeds. You have completely forgiven us. We praise you for your mercy.   (*Silence*)
  Lord, have mercy...

- Christ, you have given us a new spirit and a new heart. We praise you for your mercy.   (*Silence*)
  Christ, have mercy...

- Lord, in the same way as you have forgiven us, help us to show your mercy to our neighbours.   (*Silence*)
  Lord, have mercy...

FIRST READING

In our reading we do not hear the words 'forgiveness' or 'mercy'. And yet the reading does speak about forgiveness and mercy. When it says 'there is no need to recall the past', it is saying that our evil past is completely wiped out.

We read from prophet Isaiah, chapter forty-three.
*
Thus says the Lord,
who made a way through the sea,
a path in the great waters;
who put chariots and horse in the field

and a powerful army,
which lay there never to rise again,
snuffed out, put out like a wick:

> No need to recall the past,
> no need to think about what was done before.
> See, I am doing a new deed,
> even now it comes to light; can you not see it?
> Yes, I am making a road in the wilderness,
> paths in the wilds.

> The wild beasts will honour me,
> jackals and ostriches,
> because I am putting water in the wilderness
> (rivers in the wild)
> to give my chosen people drink.
> The people I have formed for myself
> will sing my praises.

This is the word of the Lord.   *Isaiah 43:16-21*

Responsorial Psalm
℟   **What marvels the Lord worked for us!**
    Indeed we were glad.

1   When the Lord delivered Zion from bondage,
    it seemed like a dream.
    Then was our mouth filled with laughter,
    on our lips there were songs. ℟

2   The heathens themselves said: 'What marvels
    the Lord worked for them!'
    What marvels the Lord worked for us!
    Indeed we were glad. ℟

3   Deliver us, O Lord, from our bondage
    as streams in dry land.
    Those who are sowing in tears
    will sing when they reap. ℟

4   They go out, they go out, full of tears,
    carrying seed for the sowing:
    they come back, they come back, full of song,
    carrying their sheaves. ℟   *Ps 125. ℟ v.3*

SECOND READING

We read from the letter of St Paul to the Philippians, chapter three.

*
I believe nothing can happen that will outweigh the supreme advantage of knowing Christ Jesus my Lord. For him I have accepted the loss of everything, and I look on everything as so much rubbish if only I can have Christ and be given a place in him. I am no longer trying for perfection by my own efforts, the perfection that comes from the Law, but I want only the perfection that comes through faith in Christ, and is from God and based on faith. All I want is to know Christ and the power of his resurrection and to share his sufferings by reproducing the pattern of his death. That is the way I can hope to take my place in the resurrection of the dead. Not that I have become perfect yet: I have not yet won, but I am still running, trying to capture the prize for which Christ Jesus captured me. I can assure you my brothers, I am far from thinking that I have already won. All I can say is that I forget the past and I strain ahead for what is still to come; I am racing for the finish, for the prize to which God calls us upwards to receive in Christ Jesus.

This is the word of the Lord. *Philippians 3:8-14*

Gospel Acclamation

Praise to you, O Christ, king of eternal glory!
Seek good and not evil so that you may live,
and that the Lord God of hosts may really be with you.
Praise to you, O Christ, king of eternal glory! *cf. Amos 5:14*

or

Praise to you, O Christ, king of eternal glory!
Now, now – it is the Lord who speaks –
come back to me with all your heart,
for I am all tenderness and compassion.
Praise to you, O Christ, king of eternal glory! *Joel 2:12-13*

GOSPEL

We read from the holy Gospel according to John, chapter eight.

*
Jesus went to the Mount of Olives. At daybreak he appeared in the Temple again; and as all the people came to him, he sat down and began to teach them.

The scribes and Pharisees brought a woman along who had been caught committing adultery; and making her stand there in full view of everybody, they said to Jesus, 'Master, this woman was caught in the very act of committing adultery, and Moses has ordered us in the Law to condemn women like this to death by stoning. What have you to say?' They asked him this as a test, looking for something to use against him. But Jesus bent down and started writing on the ground with his finger. As they persisted with their question, he looked up and said, 'If there is one of you who has not sinned, let him be the first to throw a stone at her.' Then he bent down and wrote on the ground again. When they heard this they went away one by one, beginning with the eldest, until Jesus was left alone with the woman, who remained standing there. He looked up and said, 'Woman, where are they? Has no one condemned you?' 'No one, sir,' she replied. 'Neither do I condemn you,' said Jesus 'go away, and don't sin any more.'

This is the Gospel of the Lord. *John 8:1-11*

HOLY WEEK

Passion Sunday (Palm Sunday)
See above, pp. 74.

THE EASTER TRIDUUM

Holy Thursday
(Mass of the Lord's Supper)

See above, pp. 103.

Good Friday
(Celebration of the Lord's Passion)

See above, pp. 107.

The Easter Vigil
See above, pp. 116.

Easter Day
See above, pp. 135.

THE SEASON OF EASTER

Second Sunday of Easter   C

Introduction to the Service

There are pictures which you see and forget but there are other pictures which you cannot forget. There are some pictures you cannot get out of your mind.

Today, on this second Sunday of Easter, we are given such a picture: Jesus, risen from the dead, standing among the disciples.

This picture is so powerful because it is happening right now as we are gathered here, 'Jesus came and stood among them'. Where does he stand? Not only over there, inside the tabernacle but also right here among us. Here, where the young man from your neighbourhood stands, here where your husband or wife stands, here where the worker from the same factory stands, here where you see the pupil from the same school next to you. What a powerful and true picture: 'Jesus came and stood among them.'

Penitential Rite

Do we always recognise Jesus among us?

● When we meet Christians in our neighbourhood, in the same flat, in the house next to us, do we remember that Christ lives among us? (*Silence*)

● When people differ from us, when our interests clash, when others offend us, do we remember that Christ still stands among us? (*Silence*)

Let us confess our failures.   **I confess**…

FIRST READING

When Christians meet, you cannot see with your eyes that Christ is there among them. You can only see it from signs happening in that group.

We will now read about the meetings of the early Christian community and while we listen, we reflect: by which signs could one conclude that the risen Christ stood among them?

We read from chapter five of the Acts of the Apostles.
*
The faithful all used to meet by common consent in the Portico of Solomon. No one else ever dared to join them, but the people

were loud in their praise and the numbers of men and women who came to believe in the Lord increased steadily. So many signs and wonders were worked among the people at the hands of the apostles that the sick were even taken out into the streets and laid on beds and sleeping-mats in the hope that at least the shadow of Peter might fall across some of them as he went past. People even came crowding in from the towns round about Jerusalem, bringing with them their sick and those tormented by unclean spirits, and all of them were cured.

This is the word of the Lord.   *Acts 5:12-16*

Responsorial Psalm
℟   **Give thanks to the Lord for he is good,**
       for his love has no end.

or

℟   **Alleluia, alleluia, alleluia!**

1   Let the sons of Israel say:
     'His love has no end.'
     Let the sons of Aaron say:
     'His love has no end.'
     Let those who fear the Lord say:
     'His love has no end.'   ℟

2   The stone which the builders rejected
     has become the corner stone.
     This is the work of the Lord,
     a marvel in our eyes.
     This day was made by the Lord;
     we rejoice and are glad.   ℟

3   O Lord, grant us salvation;
     O Lord grant success.
     Blessed in the name of the Lord
     is he who comes.
     We bless you from the house of the Lord;
     the Lord God is our light.   ℟   *Ps 117:2-4. 22-27. ℟ v.1*

SECOND READING
We read from the book of the Apocalypse, chapter one.
*
My name is John, and through our union in Jesus I am your brother and share your sufferings, your kingdom, and all you

endure. I was on the island of Patmos for having preached God's word and witnessed for Jesus; it was the Lord's day and the Spirit possessed me, and I heard a voice behind me, shouting like a trumpet, 'Write down all that you see in a book.' I turned round to see who had spoken to me, and when I turned I saw seven golden lamp-stands and, surrounded by them, a figure like a Son of man, dressed in a long robe tied at the waist with a golden girdle.

When I saw him, I fell in a dead faint at his feet, but he touched me with his right hand and said, 'Do not be afraid; it is I, the First and the Last; I am the Living One. I was dead and now I am to live for ever and ever, and I hold the keys of death and of the underworld. Now write down all that you see of present happenings and things that are still to come.'

This is the word of the Lord.　　　　　*Apocalypse 1:9-13. 17-19*

Gospel Acclamation
Alleluia, alleluia!
Jesus said: 'You believe because you can see me.
Happy are those who have not seen and yet believe.'
Alleluia!　　　　　*Jn 20:29*

GOSPEL

We read from the holy Gospel according to John, chapter twenty.
*
In the evening of that same day, the first day of the week, the doors were closed in the room where the disciples were, for fear of the Jews. Jesus came and stood among them. He said to them, 'Peace be with you,' and showed them his hands and his side. The disciples were filled with joy when they saw the Lord, and he said to them again, 'Peace be with you.

'As the Father sent me,
so am I sending you.'

After saying this he breathed on them and said:

'Receive the Holy Spirit.
For those whose sins you forgive,
they are forgiven;
for those whose sins you retain,
they are retained.'

Thomas, called the Twin, who was one of the Twelve, was not

with them when Jesus came. When the disciples said, 'We have seen the Lord', he answered, 'Unless I see the holes that the nails made in his hands and can put my finger into the holes they made, and unless I can put my hand into his side, I refuse to believe.' Eight days later the disciples were in the house again and Thomas was with them. The doors were closed, but Jesus came in and stood among them. 'Peace be with you' he said. Then he spoke to Thomas, 'Put your finger here; look, here are my hands. Give me your hand; put it into my side. Doubt no longer but believe.' Thomas replied, 'My Lord and my God!' Jesus said to him:

'You believe because you can see me.
Happy are those who have not seen and yet believe.'

There were many other signs that Jesus worked and the disciples saw, but they are not recorded in this book. These are recorded so that you may believe that Jesus is the Christ, the Son of God, and that believing this you may have life through his name.

This is the Gospel of the Lord.   *John 20:19-31*

Third Sunday of Easter   C

Introduction to the Service

So many people struggle to get their daily bread, and all too often they fail. The fishermen go out in their boats every day to catch fish, sometimes failing, sometimes succeeding. The farmers plant food for their families, unsure that they will reap a harvest. The unemployed look for work every day. Will they succeed?

In John's Gospel we will read today how Christ, risen from the dead at Easter, meets the unsuccessful fishermen. He tells them to try again.

Is Christ not present in our cities, in our suburbs, in our villages, where people struggle, like the fishermen of Galilee, to find their daily bread?

Penitential Rite

Christ is present, but it may be that sometimes we have not recognised him. Let us call on his mercy.

● There were times when we did not succeed in our daily work.

You were there, but we did not see you.   (*Silence*)
Lord, have mercy...

- There were times when we gave up hope and said that we would not try again.   (*Silence*)
Christ, have mercy...

- There were times when we were so busy with our hunt for success that we said we had no time to meet you, Lord. (*Silence*)
Lord, have mercy.

FIRST READING

It is when trouble comes, when you are in need, that you find out whether or not somebody is a real friend. In our reading, we see the apostles in trouble. They have to decide whether or not to continue their friendship with the risen Christ.

We read from the Acts of the Apostles, chapter five.

*

The high priest demanded an explanation of the apostles. 'We gave you a formal warning,' he said 'not to preach in this name, and what have you done? You have filled Jerusalem with your teaching, and seem determined to fix the guilt of this man's death on us.' In reply Peter and the apostles said, 'Obedience to God comes before obedience to men; it was the God of our ancestors who raised up Jesus, but it was you who had him executed by hanging on a tree. By his own right hand God has now raised him up to be leader and saviour, to give repentance and forgiveness of sins through him to Israel. We are witnesses to all this, we and the Holy Spirit whom God has given to those who obey him.' They warned the apostles not to speak in the name of Jesus and released them. And so they left the presence of the Sanhedrin glad to have had the honour of suffering humiliation for the sake of the name.

This is the word of the Lord.   *Acts 5:27-32. 40-41*

Responsorial Psalm
℟   **I will praise you, Lord,**
      you have rescued me.

or

℟   **Alleluia!**

1   I will praise you, Lord, you have rescued me
    and have not let my enemies rejoice over me.
    O Lord, you have raised my soul from the dead,
    restored me to life from those who sink into the grave.   ℟

2   Sing psalms to the Lord, you who love him,
    give thanks to his holy name.
    His anger lasts but a moment; his favour through life.
    At night there are tears, but joy comes with dawn.   ℟

3   The Lord listened and had pity.
    The Lord came to my help.
    For me you have changed my mourning into dancing;
    O Lord my God, I will thank you for ever.   ℟

Ps 29:2. 4-6. 11-13. ℟ v.2

SECOND READING

We read from the book of the Apocalypse, chapter five.
*
In my vision, I, John, heard the sound of an immense number of
angels gathered round the throne and the animals and the elders;
there were ten thousand times ten thousand of them and
thousands upon thousands, shouting, 'The Lamb that was sacrificed is worthy to be given power, riches, wisdom, strength,
honour, glory and blessing.' Then I heard all the living things in
creation – everything that lives in the air, and on the ground, and
under the ground, and in the sea, crying, 'To the One who is
sitting on the throne and to the Lamb, be all praise, honour, glory
and power, for ever and ever.' And the four animals said,
'Amen'; and the elders prostrated themselves to worship.

This is the word of the Lord.   *Apocalypse 5:11-14*

Gospel Acclamation
   Alleluia, alleluia!
   Lord Jesus, explain the scriptures to us.
   Make our hearts burn within us as you talk to us.
   Alleluia!
or
   Alleluia, alleluia!
   Christ has risen: he who created all things,
   and has granted his mercy to men.
   Alleluia!
                                      cf. Lk 24:32

GOSPEL

We read from the holy Gospel according to John, chapter twenty-one.

*
*Jesus showed himself again to the disciples. It was by the Sea of Tiberias, and it happened like this: Simon Peter, Thomas called the Twin, Nathanael from Cana in Galilee, the sons of Zebedee and two more of his disciples were together. Simon Peter said, 'I'm going fishing.' They replied, 'We'll come with you.' They went out and got into the boat but caught nothing that night.

It was light by now and there stood Jesus on the shore, though the disciples did not realise that it was Jesus. Jesus called out, 'Have you caught anything, friends?' And when they answered, 'No', he said, 'Throw the net out to starboard and you'll find something.' So they dropped the net, and there were so many fish that they could not haul it in. The disciple Jesus loved said to Peter, 'It is the Lord.' At these words 'It is the Lord', Simon Peter, who had practically nothing on, wrapped his cloak round him and jumped into the water. The other disciples came on in the boat, towing the net and the fish; they were only about a hundred yards from land.

As soon as they came ashore they saw that there was some bread there, and a charcoal fire with fish cooking on it. Jesus said, 'Bring some of the fish you have just caught.' Simon Peter went aboard and dragged the net to the shore, full of big fish, one hundred and fifty-three of them; and in spite of there being so many the net was not broken. Jesus said to them, 'Come and have breakfast.' None of the disciples was bold enough to ask, 'Who are you?'; they knew quite well it was the Lord. Jesus then stepped forward, took the bread and gave it to them, and the same with the fish. This was the third time that Jesus showed himself to the disciples after rising from the dead.*

After the meal Jesus said to Simon Peter, 'Simon son of John, do you love me more than these others do?' He answered, 'Yes Lord, you know I love you.' Jesus said to him, 'Feed my lambs.' A second time he said to him, 'Simon son of John, do you love me?' He replied 'Yes, Lord, you know I love you.' Jesus said to him, 'Look after my sheep.' Then he said to him a third time, 'Simon son of John, do you love me?' Peter was upset that he asked him the third time, 'Do you love me?' and said, 'Lord, you know everything; you know I love you.' Jesus said to him, 'Feed my sheep.

'I tell you most solemnly,

when you were young
you put on your own belt
and walked where you liked;
but when you grow old
you will stretch out your hands,
and somebody else will put a belt round you
and take you where you would rather not go.'

In these words he indicated the kind of death by which Peter would give glory to God. After this he said, 'Follow me.'

| *This is the Gospel of the Lord.* *John 21:1-19*

*Shorter Form, verses 1-14. Read between *.

Fourth Sunday of Easter   C

Introduction to the Service

Have you ever experienced the joy of somebody really listening to you? You had something important to tell and the other person looked at you, and you felt that he or she was eager to hear every word you said. The other person wanted to understand what you said and why you said it; wanted to be with you and to be one with you. Was it a joyful experience to be listened to in such a genuine way? Did you not feel that such listening created a bond between you?

When Jesus said: 'The sheep that belong to me listen to my voice' he surely wanted to create such a deep bond between us and him. It is the fourth Sunday of Easter and we try to learn in this Easter season how to create such a deep bond with him who rose from the dead and who now lives among us. Listening to Christ means to live closely with him.

Penitential Rite

Do we truly listen to Jesus?

● He speaks to us not only in words but also through the needs of other people. Do we hear his voice in the needs of others? (*Silence*)

● He speaks to us through the events happening in our town and in our country, in the discussions about work, about laws, and about what is right or wrong. Do we try to hear his voice among the many other voices?   (*Silence*)

We admit that we have not always listened to Christ. **I confess**...

FIRST READING

Not everybody listens to God's message with an open ear. Even devout believers such as the Jews, were sometimes unable to detect God's call. The word of Christ can therefore cause division, as we will now hear in our reading.

We read from Acts of the Apostles, chapter thirteen.

*
Paul and Barnabas carried on from Perga till they reached Antioch in Pisidia. Here they went to synagogue on the sabbath and took their seats.

When the meeting broke up, many Jews and devout converts joined Paul and Barnabas, and in their talks with them Paul and Barnabas urged them to remain faithful to the grace God had given them.

The next sabbath almost the whole town assembled to hear the word of God. When they saw the crowds, the Jews, prompted by jealousy, used blasphemies and contradicted everything Paul said. Then Paul and Barnabas spoke out boldly, 'We had to proclaim the word of God to you first, but since you have rejected it, since you do not think yourselves worthy of eternal life, we must turn to the pagans. For this is what the Lord commanded us to do when he said:

I have made you a light for the nations,
so that my salvation may reach the ends of the earth.'

It made the pagans very happy to hear this and they thanked the Lord for his message; all who were destined for eternal life became believers. Thus the word of the Lord spread through the whole countryside.

But the Jews worked upon some of the devout women of the upper classes and the leading men of the city and persuaded them to turn against Paul and Barnabas and expel them from their territory. So they shook the dust from their feet in defiance and went off to Iconium; but the disciples were filled with joy and the Holy Spirit.

This is the word of the Lord.   *Acts 13:14. 43-52*

Responsorial Psalm

℟   **We are his people, the sheep of his flock.**

or

℟   **Alleluia!**

1   Cry out with joy to the Lord, all the earth.
     Serve the Lord with gladness.
     Come before him, singing for joy.   ℟

2   Know that he, the Lord, is God.
     He made us, we belong to him,
     we are his people, the sheep of his flock.   ℟

3   Indeed, how good is the Lord,
     eternal his merciful love.
     He is faithful from age to age.   ℟   *Ps 99:1-3. 5. ℟v.3*

SECOND READING

We read from the book of the Apocalypse, chapter seven.
*

I, John, saw a huge number, impossible to count, of people from
every nation, race, tribe and language; they were standing in
front of the throne and in front of the Lamb, dressed in white
robes and holding palms in their hands. One of the elders said to
me, 'These are the people who have been through the great
persecution, and because they have washed their robes white
again in the blood of the Lamb, they now stand in front of God's
throne and serve him day and night in his sanctuary; and the One
who sits on the throne will spread his tent over them. They will
never hunger or thirst again; neither the sun nor scorching wind
will ever plague them, because the Lamb who is at the throne will
be their shepherd and will lead them to springs of living water;
and God will wipe away all tears from their eyes.'

This is the word of the Lord.   *Apocalypse 7:9. 14-17*

Gospel Acclamation

   Alleluia, alleluia!
   I am the good shepherd, says the Lord;
   I know my own sheep and my own know me.
   Alleluia!   *Jn 10:14*

GOSPEL

We read from the holy Gospel according to John, chapter ten.

★

Jesus said:

> 'The sheep that belong to me listen to my voice;
> I know them and they follow me.
> I give them eternal life;
> they will never be lost
> and no one will ever steal them from me.
> The Father who gave them to me is greater than anyone,
> and no one can steal from the Father.
> The Father and I are one.'

This is the Gospel of the Lord. *John 10:27-30*

Fifth Sunday of Easter C

Introduction to the Service

We all long for a beautiful home and a pleasant neighbourhood, where people help one another, respect one another and have time for one another. We long for a group of people where we need not be afraid of others, but can trust everyone. We long for a country where different nations treat one another as equals and respect one another.'

It is not only you and I who want such good relationships between people. God wants it. In the Gospel today, Christ says: 'I give you a new commandment: love one another. Just as I have loved you, you also must love one another.'

Penitential Rite

Christ is risen and lives among us. He wants his word to come true, first of all among us, his disciples. Let us call on his mercy:

● During this week when we met people of a different race or nation, did we show them respect? *(Silence)*

Lord, have mercy...

● During this week people may have longed for a sign of love from us. Did we ignore them? *(Silence)*

Christ, have mercy...

● During this week did we try to create a more friendly atmosphere in our families and at our places of work? *(Silence)*

Lord, have mercy...

FIRST READING

When you are treated badly by others, you can easily become disappointed. You start to retaliate, and your spirit of love becomes weaker and weaker because of these hardships.

In our reading we hear how somebody tries to prepare one of the early Christian communities for such hardships.

We read from the Acts of the Apostles, chapter fourteen.

*

Paul and Barnabas went back through Lystra and Iconium to Antioch. They put fresh heart into the disciples, encouraging them to persevere in the faith. 'We all have to experience many hardships' they said 'before we enter the kingdom of God.' In each of these churches they appointed elders, and with prayer and fasting they commended them to the Lord in whom they had come to believe.

They passed through Pisidia and reached Pamphylia. Then after proclaiming the word at Perga they went down to Attalia and from there sailed for Antioch, where they had originally been commended to the grace of God for the work they had now completed.

On their arrival they assembled the church and gave an account of all that God had done with them, and how he had opened the door of faith to the pagans.

This is the word of the Lord.   *Acts 14:21-27*

Responsorial Psalm
℟   **I will bless your name for ever, O God my King.**
or
℟   **Alleluia!**

1   The Lord is kind and full of compassion,
    slow to anger, abounding in love.
    How good is the Lord to all,
    compassionate to all his creatures.   ℟

2   All your creatures shall thank you, O Lord,
    and your friends shall repeat their blessing.
    They shall speak of the glory of your reign
    and declare your might, O God,
    to make known to men your mighty deeds
    and the glorious splendour of your reign.   ℟

3   Yours is an everlasting kingdom;
    your rule lasts from age to age.   ℟   *Ps 144:8-13. ℟ cf. v.1*

SECOND READING

We read from the book of the Apocalypse, chapter twenty-one.
*
I, John, saw a new heaven and a new earth; the first heaven and the first earth had disappeared now, and there was no longer any sea. I saw the holy city, and the new Jerusalem, coming down from God out of heaven, as beautiful as a bride all dressed for her husband. Then I heard a loud voice call from the throne, 'You see this city? Here God lives among men. He will make his home among them; they shall be his people, and he will be their God; his name is God-with-them. He will wipe away all tears from their eyes; there will be no more death, and no more mourning or sadness. The world of the past has gone.'

Then the One sitting on the throne spoke: 'Now I am making the whole of creation new'.

This is the word of the Lord.   *Apocalypse 21:1-5*

Gospel Acclamation
Alleluia, alleluia!
Jesus said: 'I give you a new commandment:
love one another, just as I have loved you.'
Alleluia!   *Jn 13:34*

GOSPEL

We read from the holy Gospel according to John, chapter thirteen.
*
When Judas had gone Jesus said:

'Now has the Son of Man been glorified,
and in him God has been glorified.
If God has been glorified in him,
God will in turn glorify him in himself,
and will glorify him very soon.
My little children,
I shall not be with you much longer.
I give you a new commandment:
love one another;
just as I have loved you,
you also must love one another.
By this love you have for one another,
everyone will know that you are my disciples.'

This is the Gospel of the Lord.   *John 13:31-35*

Sixth Sunday of Easter C

Introduction to the Service

One of the most beautiful names by which Christians can be called is 'peacemakers'. It is a wonderful name, but we are afraid of it, because we live surrounded by so many different conflicts. There is a lack of peace between nations, between workers and employers, between rich and poor. There is also a lack of peace in our homes, between husband and wife, and between parents and children. The name 'peacemakers' seems too demanding.

But the lighted Easter candle reminds us that Christ stands in our midst and says: 'My peace I give you.'

Penitential Rite

Let us reflect on how we promoted Christ's peace:

● Did we first of all make sure that we ourselves live in peace with God?   (*Silence*)

● When conflicts arose between people, did we remember that we are sent to bring peace?   (*Silence*)

Let us confess our failures.   **I confess**…

FIRST READING

Even in the Church peace can be threatened. A difference in teaching can cause disagreement in the Church, as we will hear in our reading.

What did the apostles and the communities do in order to restore peace in the Church?

We read from the Acts of the Apostles, chapter fifteen.
*

Some men came down from Judaea and taught the brothers, 'Unless you have yourselves circumcised in the tradition of Moses you cannot be saved.' This led to disagreement, and after Paul and Barnabas had had a long argument with these men it was arranged that Paul and Barnabas and others of the church should go up to Jerusalem and discuss the problem with the apostles and elders.

Then the apostles and elders decided to choose delegates to send to Antioch with Paul and Barnabas; the whole church concurred with this. They chose Judas known as Barsabbas and Silas, both leading men in the brotherhood, and gave them this letter to take with them:

'The apostles and elders, your brothers, send greetings to the brothers of pagan birth in Antioch, Syria and Cilicia. We hear that some of our members have disturbed you with their demands and have unsettled your minds. They acted without any authority from us, and so we have decided unanimously to elect delegates and to send them to you with Barnabas and Paul, men we highly respect who have dedicated their lives to the name of our Lord Jesus Christ. Accordingly we are sending you Judas and Silas, who will confirm by word of mouth what we have written in this letter. It has been decided by the Holy Spirit and by ourselves not to saddle you with any burden beyond these essentials: you are to abstain from food sacrificed to idols, from blood, from the meat of strangled animals and from fornication. Avoid these, and you will do what is right. Farewell.'

This is the word of the Lord.   *Acts 15:1-2. 22-29*

Responsorial Psalm

℟   **Let the peoples praise you, O God;**
     let all the peoples praise you.

or

℟   **Alleluia!**

1   O God, be gracious and bless us
     and let your face shed its light upon us.
     So will your ways be known upon earth.
     and all nations learn your saving help.   ℟

2   Let the nations be glad and exult
     for you rule the world with justice.
     With fairness you rule the peoples,
     you guide the nations on earth.   ℟

3   Let the peoples praise you, O God;
     let all the peoples praise you.
     May God still give us his blessing
     till the ends of the earth revere him.   ℟

                                  Ps 66:2-3. 5-6. 8. ℟ v.4

When the Ascension of the Lord is celebrated on the Seventh Sunday of Easter, the Second Reading and Gospel assigned to the Seventh Sunday (see below pp.513ff.) may be read on the Sixth Sunday.

SECOND READING

We read from the book of the Apocalypse, chapter twenty-one.

*

In the spirit, the angel took me to the top of an enormous high mountain and showed me Jerusalem, the holy city, coming down from God out of heaven. It had all the radiant glory of God and glittered like some precious jewel of crystal-clear diamond. The walls of it were of a great height, and had twelve gates; at each of the twelve gates there was an angel, and over the gates were written the names of the twelve tribes of Israel; on the east there were three gates, on the north three gates, on the south three gates, and on the west three gates. The city walls stood on twelve foundation stones, each one of which bore the name of one of the twelve apostles of the Lamb.

I saw that there was no temple in the city since the Lord God Almighty and the Lamb were themselves the temple, and the city did not need the sun or the moon for light, since it was lit by the radiant glory of God and the Lamb was a lighted torch for it.

This is the word of the Lord.   *Apocalypse 21:10-14. 22-23*

Gospel Acclamation

Alleluia, alleluia!
Jesus said: 'If anyone loves me he will keep my word,
and my Father will love him, and we shall come to him.
Alleluia!   *Jn 14:23*

GOSPEL

We read from the holy Gospel according to John, chapter fourteen.

*

Jesus said to his disciples:

'If anyone loves me he will keep my word,
and my Father will love him,
and we shall come to him
and make our home with him.
Those who do not love me do not keep my words.
And my word is not my own:
it is the word of the one who sent me.
I have said these things to you
while still with you;
but the Advocate, the Holy Spirit,
whom the Father will send in my name,
will teach you everything

and remind you of all I have said to you.
Peace I bequeath to you,
my own peace I give you,
a peace the world cannot give, this is my gift to you.
Do not let your hearts be troubled or afraid.
You heard me say:
I am going away, and shall return.
If you loved me you would have been glad to know that I am
     going to the Father,
for the Father is greater than I.
I have told you this now before it happens,
so that when it does happen you may believe.'

This is the Gospel of the Lord.   *John 14:23-29*

The Ascension of the Lord   C

Introduction to the Service

There are great celebrations when the leader of a nation is installed. A king is led to his throne, a President has to swear an oath and other leaders are solemnly led into their new office. Sometimes the whole nation takes part by listening to the radio or watching the celebration on TV.

Today we celebrate the installation of Christ as the great Lord of all nations; Christ has ascended into heaven and takes his seat at the right hand of God. All honour and power are given to him.

On this day of Ascension we rejoice with all people in heaven and all nations on earth. We acclaim Jesus as our Lord.

Penetential Rite

We ask ourselves:

- Do we accept Jesus as our Lord by allowing him to rule our lives?   (*Silence*)

- Do we trust in him in time of trouble?   (*Silence*)

- Do we expect Christ to judge all our words and actions when he comes back in glory?   (*Silence*)

Let us ask for mercy.   **I confess**...

FIRST READING

When we say good-bye to a friend we remain standing until they have gone out of sight.

We should NOT do the same when we celebrate the ascension of Jesus in heaven today. He is with us in a new way until he comes back in glory.

We read from the Acts of the Apostles, chapter one.

★
In my earlier work, Theophilus, I dealt with everything Jesus had done and taught from the beginning until the day he gave his instructions to the apostles he had chosen through the Holy Spirit, and was taken up to heaven. He had shown himself alive to them after his Passion by many demonstrations: for forty days he had continued to appear to them and tell them about the kingdom of God. When he had been at table with them, he had told them not to leave Jerusalem, but to wait there for what the Father had promised. 'It is,' he had said, 'what you have heard me speak about: John baptised with water but you, not many days from now, will be baptised with the Holy Spirit.'

Now having met together, they asked him, 'Lord, has the time come? Are you going to restore the kingdom to Israel?' He replied, 'It is not for you to know times or dates that the Father has decided by his own authority, but you will receive power when the Holy Spirit comes on you, and then you will be my witnesses not only in Jerusalem but throughout Judaea and Samaria, and indeed to the ends of the earth.'

As he said this he was lifted up while they looked on, and a cloud took him from their sight. They were still staring into the sky when suddenly two men in white were standing near them and they said, 'Why are you men from Galilee standing here looking into the sky? Jesus who has been taken up from you into heaven, this same Jesus will come back in the same way as you have seen him go there.'

This is the word of the Lord.

Acts 1:1-11

Responsorial Psalm
℟ **God goes up with shouts of joy;**
the Lord goes up with trumpet blast.

or

℟ **Alleluia!**

1 All peoples, clap your hands,
cry to God with shouts of joy!
For the Lord, the Most High, we must fear,
great king over all the earth. ℟

2 God goes up with shouts of joy;
the Lord goes up with trumpet blast.
Sing praise for God, sing praise,
sing praise to our king, sing praise. ℟

3 God is king of all the earth.
Sing praise with all your skill.
God is king over the nations;
God reigns on his holy throne. ℟ *Ps 46:2-3. 6-7. 8-9. ℟ v.6*

SECOND READING

We read from the letter of St Paul to the Ephesians, chapter one.
*

May the God of our Lord Jesus Christ, the Father of glory, give
you a spirit of wisdom and perception of what is revealed, to
bring you to full knowledge of him. May he enlighten the eyes of
your mind so that you can see what hope his call holds for you,
what rich glories he has promised the saints will inherit and how
infinitely great is the power that he has exercised for us believers.
This you can tell from the strength of his power at work in Christ,
when he used it to raise him from the dead and to make him sit at
his right hand, in heaven, far above every Sovereignty, Authority, Power, or Domination, or any other name that can be
named, not only in this age, but also in the age to come. He has
put all things under his feet, and made him, as the ruler of
everything, the head of the Church; which is his body, the
fullness of him who fills the whole creation.

This is the word of the Lord. *Ephesians 1:17-23*

Gospel Acclamation
Alleluia, alleluia!
Go, make disciples of all the nations;

I am with you always; yes, to the end of time.
Alleluia!

Mt 28:19. 20

GOSPEL

We read from the holy Gospel according to Luke, chapter twenty-four.
∗
Jesus said to his disciples: 'You see how it is written that the Christ would suffer and on the third day rise from the dead, and that, in his name, repentance for the forgiveness of sins would be preached to all the nations, beginning from Jerusalem. You are witnesses to this.

'And now I am sending down to you what the Father has promised. Stay in the city then, until you are clothed with the power from on high.' Then he took them out as far as the outskirts of Bethany, and lifting up his hands he blessed them. Now as he blessed them, he withdrew from them and was carried up to heaven. They worshipped him and then went back to Jerusalem full of joy; and they were continually in the Temple praising God.

This is the Gospel of the Lord.

Luke 24:46-53

Seventh Sunday of Easter   C

Introduction to the Service

When a father leaves his family for a long time, he will choose carefully what last message of encouragement to give his family. Very often it will be a message about unity. 'Stay together' will be the final word. Be one, because you are all my children. Be one, because you are brothers and sisters. Be one.

Christ did the same. In his final exhortation to his disciples he urged them to remain one. We remember this call to unity, especially now, in this time between Ascension and Pentecost.

We call this week, 'unity week'. Today we reflect on how sad it is that Christians are not one Church, but are divided into many different denominations. Brothers and sisters are disunited and do not eat at one table.

Penitential Rite

We all share the guilt for this division in some way. Therefore we all ask for forgiveness:

● Lord, you said we should be one as you are with the Father and

the Spirit, but we are divided.   (*Silence*)
Lord, have mercy...

● Christ, you died for all Christians, and yet they are in disagreement with one another.   (*Silence*)
Christ, have mercy...

● Lord, you live in all Christians through the Spirit. We know you cannot accept the division of the churches.   (*Silence*)
Lord, have mercy...

FIRST READING

Stephen was threatened with death. His fellow Jews threatened to kill him if he continued to preach about Jesus. What should he do? Should he abandon Jesus to be one with the Jewish nation? Should he abandon the truth for the sake of harmony? It was a bitter choice for Stephen.

We read about the decisive moment of his choice, in the seventh chapter of the Acts of the Apostles.
*
Stephen, filled with the Holy Spirit, gazed into heaven and saw the glory of God, and Jesus standing at God's right hand. 'I can see heaven thrown open' he said 'and the Son of Man standing at the right hand of God.' At this all the members of the council shouted out and stopped their ears with their hands; then they all rushed at him, sent him out of the city and stoned him. The witnesses put down their clothes at the feet of a young man called Saul. As they were stoning him, Stephen said in invocation, 'Lord Jesus, receive my spirit.' Then he knelt down and said aloud, 'Lord, do not hold this sin against them'; and with these words he fell asleep.

This is the word of the Lord.   *Acts 7:55-60*

Responsorial Psalm
    ℟   **The Lord is king, most high above all the earth.**

or

    ℟   **Alleluia!**

1   The Lord is king, let earth rejoice,
    the many coastlands be glad.
    His throne is justice and right.   ℟

2   The skies proclaim his justice;

all peoples see his glory.
All you spirits, worship him.   ℟

3   For you indeed are the Lord
most high above all the earth
exalted far above all spirits.   ℟   *Ps 96:1-2. 6-7. 9. ℟ vv.1. 9*

SECOND READING

We read from the book of the Apocalypse, chapter twenty-two.
*

I, John, heard a voice speaking to me: 'Very soon now, I shall be with you again, bringing the reward to be given to every man according to what he deserves. I am the Alpha and the Omega, the First and the Last, the Beginning and the End. Happy are those who will have washed their robes clean, so that they will have the right to feed on the tree of life and can come through the gates into the city.'

I, Jesus, have sent my angel to make these revelations to you for the sake of the churches. I am of David's line, the root of David and the bright star of the morning.

The Spirit and the Bride say, 'Come.' Let everyone who listens answer, 'Come.' Then let all who are thirsty come; all who want it may have the water of life, and have it free.

The one who guarantees these revelations repeats his promise: I shall indeed be with you soon. Amen; come, Lord Jesus.

This is the word of the Lord.   *Apocalypse 22:12-14. 16-17. 20*

Gospel Acclamation
Alleluia, alleluia!
I will not leave you orphans, says the Lord;
I will come back to you, and your hearts will be full of joy.
Alleluia!   *cf. Jn 14:18*

GOSPEL

We read from the holy Gospel according to John, chapter seventeen.
*
Jesus raised his eyes to heaven and said:

'Holy Father,
I pray not only for these,
but for those also
who through their words will believe in me.
May they all be one.

Father, may they be one in us,
as you are in me and I am in you,
so that the world may believe it was you who sent me.
I have given them the glory you gave to me,
that they may be one as we are one.
With me in them and you in me,
may they be so completely one
that the world will realise that it was you who sent me
and that I have loved them as much as you love me.
Father,
I want those you have given me
to be with me where I am,
so that they may always see the glory
you have given me
because you loved me
before the foundation of the world.
Father, Righteous One,
the world has not known you,
but I have known you,
and these have known
that you have sent me.
I have made your name known to them
and will continue to make it known,
so that the love with which you loved me may be in them,
and so that I may be in them.'

This is the Gospel of the Lord.   *John 17:20-26*

Pentecost Sunday   C

Mass during the Day

Introduction to the Service

Today we celebrate the great feast of Pentecost. It is the feast of
God's Spirit. The power of evil spirits has come to an end.

We know how the evil spirit of envy can poison our heart. We
know the evil spirits of anger and greed. The spirit of hatred
destroys happiness and peace. We are afraid of these spirits of evil
and death.

Today, however, we praise the great deeds of God. He breathes
over us with the spirit of power. His breath is like storm and fire.
Today, the evil spirits become afraid, their power is broken.

We have come together to open ourselves to God. We allow him to breathe on us as he breathed upon the first Christians in Jerusalem.

Penetential Rite
Let us prepare ourselves for the coming of the Spirit.

● Is there within us a spirit of joy and gratitude? (*Silence*)

● Is there within us a spirit of love and unity? (*Silence*)

● Is there within us a spirit of going out to other people, joyfully telling them about Christ? (*Silence*)

Let us open ourselves to God by asking his forgiveness. **I confess**…

FIRST READING
Our reading is challenging us.
Do we as Christians just come to church and sing and pray together? Or do we open the door and go out to other people who do not yet follow the way of Christ? When did we last talk about Christ to our children or our neighbours?

We read from the Acts of the Apostles, chapter two.
*
When Pentecost day came round, the apostles had all met in one room, when suddenly they heard what sounded like a powerful wind from heaven, the noise of which filled the entire house in which they were sitting; and something appeared to them that seemed like tongues of fire; these separated and came to rest on the head of each of them. They were all filled with the Holy Spirit, and began to speak foreign languages as the Spirit gave them the gift of speech.

Now there were devout men living in Jerusalem from every nation under heaven, and at this sound they all assembled, each one bewildered to hear these men speaking his own language. They were amazed and astonished. 'Surely' they said 'all these men speaking are Galileans? How does it happen that each of us hears them in his own native language? Parthians, Medes and Elamites; people from Mesopotamia, Judaea and Cappadocia, Pontus and Asia, Phrygia and Pamphylia, Egypt and the parts of Libya round Cyrene; as well as visitors from Rome – Jews and proselytes alike – Cretans and Arabs; we hear them preaching in our own language about the marvels of God.'

This is the word of the Lord.   *Acts 2:1-11*

Responsorial Psalm
℟ Send forth your Spirit, O Lord,
    and renew the face of the earth.

or

℟ Alleluia.

1 Bless the Lord, my soul!
   Lord God, how great you are,
   How many are your works, O Lord!
   The earth is full of your riches. ℟

2 You take back your spirit, they die,
   returning to the dust from which they came.
   You send forth your spirit, they are created;
   and you renew the face of the earth. ℟

3 May the glory of the Lord last for ever!
   May the Lord rejoice in his works!
   May my thoughts be pleasing to him.
   I find my joy in the Lord. ℟

                    Ps 103:1. 24. 29-31. 34. ℟ cf v.30

The Second Reading and Gospel may be taken from Year A, see above pp.162ff. Alternatively, the Second Reading and Gospel given below may be used.

SECOND READING

We read from the letter of St Paul to the Romans, chapter eight.
*
People who are interested only in unspiritual things can never be pleasing to God. Your interests, however, are not in the unspiritual, but in the spiritual, since the Spirit of God has made his home in you. In fact, unless you possessed the Spirit of Christ you would not belong to him. Though your body may be dead it is because of sin, but if Christ is in you then your spirit is life itself because you have been justified; and if the Spirit of him who raised Jesus from the dead is living in you, then he who raised Jesus from the dead will give life to your own mortal bodies through his Spirit living in you.

So then, my brothers, there is no necessity for us to obey our unspiritual selves or to live unspiritual lives. If you do live in that way, you are doomed to die; but if by the Spirit you put an end to the misdeeds of the body you will live.

Everyone moved by the Spirit is a son of God. The spirit you received is not the spirit of slaves bringing fear into your lives again; it is the spirit of sons, and it makes us cry out, 'Abba, Father!' The Spirit himself and our spirit bear united witness that we are children of God. And if we are children we are heirs as well: heirs of God and coheirs with Christ, sharing his sufferings so as to share his glory.

This is the word of the Lord. *Romans 8:8-17*

SEQUENCE

The sequence may be said or sung.

Holy Spirit, Lord of light,
    From the clear celestial height
Thy pure beaming radiance give.

Come, thou Father of the poor,
    Come with treasures which endure;
Come, thou light of all that live!

Thou, of all consolers best,
    Thou, the soul's delightful guest,
Dost refreshing peace bestow;

Thou in toil art comfort sweet;
    Pleasant coolness in the heat;
Solace in the midst of woe.

Light immortal, light divine,
    Visit thou these hearts of thine,
And our inmost being fill:

If thou take thy grace away,
    Nothing pure in man will stay;
All his good is turned to ill.

Heal our wounds, our strength renew;
    On our dryness pour thy dew;
Wash the stains of guilt away:

Bend the stubborn heart and will;
    Melt the frozen, warm the chill;
Guide the steps that go astray.
Thou, on us who evermore
    Thee confess and thee adore,
With thy sevenfold gifts descend:

Give us comfort when we die;
  Give us life with thee on high;
Give us joys that never end.

Gospel Acclamation

Alleluia, alleluia!
Come, Holy Spirit, fill the hearts of your faithful
and kindle in them the fire of your love.
Alleluia!

GOSPEL

We read from the holy Gospel according to John, chapter fourteen.
*
Jesus said to his disciples

'If you love me you will keep my commandments.
I shall ask the Father
and he will give you another Advocate
to be with you for ever.

'If anyone loves me he will keep my word,
and my Father will love him,
and we shall come to him
and make our home with him.
Those who do not love me do not keep my words.
And my word is not my own;
it is the word of the one who sent me.
I have said these things to you
while still with you;
but the Advocate, the Holy Spirit,
whom the Father will send in my name,
will teach you everything
and remind you of all I have said to you.'

This is the Gospel of the Lord.   *John 14:15-16. 23-26*

SOLEMNITIES OF THE LORD IN ORDINARY TIME

The Most Holy Trinity   C

Introduction to the Service

Today we celebrate the feast of the Most Holy Trinity: God the Father, Son and Holy Spirit. We celebrate this feast today, because now the time of Easter is over and we want to acknowledge that Easter was not the work of the Son alone; it was the loving action of all three: the Father, the Son and the Holy Spirit.

You or I may ask: what has the Trinity to do with me and my life? The reply we should be given is: the Trinity is not just connected with my life, it is my life. Because the Father is not any father, but my Father; the Son is not just any son, but Son with me, of the same Father; and the Spirit is not just any spirit, but the Spirit living in me.

Penitential Rite

Let us admit to God that we were not always aware how closely we live with him:

● Father, you are our own Father, but we sometimes forget that you are so close to us.   (*Silence*)

● Son of God, you are our brother. We did not always remember this wonderful truth.   (*Silence*)

● Spirit of God, you breathe in us, but we sometimes forget your presence in us.   (*Silence*)

Let us admit our failures.   **I confess**...

FIRST READING

In the books of the Old Testament there are no readings which speak about God as the Trinity. God had not revealed himself so fully at that time. But there are books of the Old Testament which speak about the Wisdom of God. Is this Wisdom of God the Holy Spirit?

We read from the book of Proverbs, chapter eight.

*

The Wisdom of God cries aloud:

    The Lord created me when his purpose first unfolded,
    before the oldest of his works.
    From everlasting I was firmly set,
    from the beginning, before earth came into being.
    The deep was not, when I was born,
    there were no springs to gush with water.
    Before the mountains were settled,
    before the hills, I came to birth;
    before he made the earth, the countryside,
    or the first grains of the world's dust.
    When he fixed the heavens firm, I was there,
    when he drew a ring on the surface of the deep,
    when he thickened the clouds above,
    when he fixed fast the springs of the deep.
    when he assigned the sea its boundaries
    – and the waters will not invade the shore –
    when he laid down the foundations of the earth,
    I was by his side, a master craftsman,
    delighting him day after day,
    ever at play in his presence,
    at play everywhere in his world,
    delighting to be with the sons of men.

    This is the word of the Lord.   *Proverbs 8:22-31*

Responsorial Psalm
    ℟ **How great is your name, O Lord our God,**
        through all the earth!

1   When I see the heavens, the work of your hands,
    the moon and the stars which you arranged,
    what is man that you should keep him in mind,
    mortal man that you care for him? ℟

2   Yet you have made him little less than a god;
    with glory and honour you crowned him,
    gave him power over the works of your hand,
    put all things under his feet. ℟

3   All of them, sheep and cattle,
    yes, even the savage beasts,

birds of the air, and fish
that make their way through the waters.   ℟   *Ps 8:4-9. ℟ v.2*

SECOND READING

We read from the letter of St Paul to the Romans, chapter five.
*
Through our Lord Jesus Christ, by faith we are judged righteous
and at peace with God, since it is by faith and through Jesus that
we have entered this state of grace in which we can boast about
looking forward to God's glory. But that is not all we can boast
about; we can boast about our sufferings. These sufferings bring
patience, as we know, and patience brings perseverance, and
perseverance brings hope, and this hope is not deceptive,
because the love of God has been poured into our hearts by the
Holy Spirit which has been given us.

This is the word of the Lord.   *Romans 5:1-5*

Gospel Acclamation
Alleluia, alleluia!
Glory be to the Father, and to the Son, and to the Holy
    Spirit,
the God who is, who was, and who is to come.
Alleluia!   *cf. Apoc 1:8*

GOSPEL

We read from the holy Gospel according to John, chapter sixteen.
*
Jesus said to his disciples:

'I still have many things to say to you
but they would be too much for you now.
But when the Spirit of truth comes
he will lead you to the complete truth,
since he will not be speaking as from himself
but will say only what he has learnt;
and he will tell you of the things to come.
He will glorify me
since all he tells you
will be taken from what is mine.
Everything the Father has is mine;
that is why I said:
All he tells you
will be taken from what is mine.'

This the Gospel of the Lord.   *John 16:12-15*

Thursday after Trinity Sunday   *Solemnity*

The Body and Blood of Christ   C

Introduction to the Service

Before we eat a meal in our homes, we say a prayer, thanking God for the food prepared for us. Although we are so used to having food every day, we still pray before eating, because we want to remember that this food is a gift from God.

Today we are doing something similar here in church. Our celebration is called *Corpus Christi* in Latin, which means the 'Body of Christ'. We give special thanks today to God for giving us this holy food of the body and blood of Christ at every holy communion.

Penitential Rite

Are we sometimes lacking in gratitude for this wonderful sacrament? Let us ask God's forgiveness.

- For the times when we forgot how great this gift was to us, of the body and blood of Christ.   (*Silence*)
  Lord, have mercy...

- For the times when we participated in Holy Mass without respect.   (*Silence*)
  Christ, have mercy...

- For the times when we did not try to understand what this sacrament meant for us.   (*Silence*)
  Lord, have mercy...

FIRST READING

Comparisons and examples can help us to grasp the meaning of the sacrament of the body and blood of Christ. We now read one famous and very old example. It is the offering made by Melchizedek. He was a pagan king, who lived three thousand years ago. Yet his offering was very similar to the one we make at the altar.

We read from the book of Genesis, chapter fourteen.

*
Melchizedek king of Salem brought bread and wine; he was a priest of God Most High. He pronounced this blessing:

'Blessed be Abraham by God Most High, creator of heaven
   and earth,

and blessed be God Most High for handing over your
    enemies to you.'

And Abraham gave him a tithe of everything.

> This is the word of the Lord.   *Genesis 14:18-20*

Responsorial Psalm
> ℟ **You are a priest for ever,**
>   **a priest like Melchizedek of old.**

1 The Lord's revelation to my Master:
    'Sit on my right:
    I will put your foes beneath your feet.'   ℟

2 The Lord will send from Zion
    your sceptre of power:
    rule in the midst of all your foes.   ℟

3 A prince from the day of your birth
    on the holy mountains;
    from the womb before the daybreak I begot you.   ℟

4 The Lord has sworn an oath he will not change.
    'You are a priest for ever,
    a priest like Melchizedek of old.'   ℟   *Ps 109:1-4. ℟ v.4*

SECOND READING

We read from the first letter of St Paul to the Corinthians, chapter
eleven.
*

This is what I received from the Lord, and in turn passed on to
you: that on the same night that he was betrayed, the Lord Jesus
took some bread, and thanked God for it and broke it, and he
said, 'This is my body, which is for you; do this as a memorial of
me.' In the same way he took the cup after supper, and said,
'This cup is the new covenant in my blood. Whenever you drink
it, do this as a memorial of me.' Until the Lord comes, therefore,
every time you eat this bread and drink this cup, you are
proclaiming his death.

> This is the word of the Lord.   *1 Corinthians 11:23-26*

The sequence, Sing forth, O Zion, *may be said or sung in its longer
or shorter form. See above, p. 170.*

Gospel Acclamation
Alleluia, alleluia!
I am the living bread which has come down from heaven,
says the Lord.
Anyone who eats this bread will live for ever.
Alleluia!

Jn 6:51-52

GOSPEL
We read from the holy Gospel according to Luke, chapter nine.

*
Jesus made the crowds welcome and talked to them about the
kingdom of God; and he cured those who were in need of
healing.

It was late afternoon when the Twelve came to him and said,
'Send the people away, and they can go to the villages and farms
round about to find lodging and food; for we are in a lonely place
here.' He replied, 'Give them something to eat yourselves.' But
they said, 'We have no more than five loaves and two fish, unless
we are to go ourselves and buy food for all these people.' For
there were about five thousand men. But he said to his disciples,
'Get them to sit down in parties of about fifty.' They did so and
made them all sit down. Then he took the five loaves and the two
fish, raised his eyes to heaven, and said the blessing over them;
then he broke them and handed them to his disciples to distribute
among the crowd. They all ate as much as they wanted, and
when the scraps remaining were collected they filled twelve
baskets.

This is the Gospel of the Lord.

Luke 9:11-17

Friday after the Second Sunday after Pentecost   *Solemnity*

The Sacred Heart of Jesus   C

Introduction to the Service
Shepherds are not all the same. Some are cruel to their sheep and
want to show that they can treat them as they please. Others are
very different; they have a kind heart for their flock.

When people looked for examples to illustrate what kind of
leader Christ was, they pointed to this example of the shepherd
who has a heart for his flock. He has a heart for each single
member of his flock.

It is this heart of Christ which we remember today in a special feast day. We celebrate the feast of the Sacred Heart of Christ.

We look at this difference between leaders who have no heart, and leaders who have a heart for others. We recognise the difference between a leader who pushes others down, and a leader who, out of the goodness of his heart, lifts others up. We see this difference, because it exists also in each one of us.

Penitential Rite
Let us reflect:

● Do we have a heart for others, even when they are weak and we have power over them?　(*Silence*)

● Do we show respect to everybody, even to the poor and the weak?　(*Silence*)

Let us confess that we have sinned.　**I confess**…

FIRST READING
There were times when the nation of the Israelites was so defeated and scattered that all other nations despised them and laughed at them. But God had a heart for them. He uplifted them although they had offended him.

In the book of Ezekiel, chapter thirty-four, we read what God promised to do for the Israelites.

*
The Lord God says this: I am going to look after my flock myself and keep all of it in view. As a shepherd keeps all his flock in view when he stands up in the middle of his scattered sheep, so shall I keep my sheep in view. I shall rescue them from wherever they have been scattered during the mist and darkness. I shall bring them out of the countries where they are; I shall gather them together from foreign countries and bring them back to their own land. I shall pasture them on the mountains of Israel, in the ravines and in every inhabited place in the land. I shall feed them in good pasturage; the high mountains of Israel will be their grazing ground. There they will rest in good grazing ground; they will browse in rich pastures on the mountains of Israel. I myself will pasture my sheep, I myself will show them where to rest – it is the Lord who speaks. I shall look for the lost one, bring back the stray, bandage the wounded and make the weak strong. I shall watch over the fat and healthy. I shall be a true shepherd to them.

This is the word of the Lord.　　　　　　　　*Ezekiel 34:11-16*

Responsorial Psalm

℟ **The Lord is my shepherd;**
there is nothing I shall want.

1 The Lord is my shepherd;
   there is nothing I shall want.
   Fresh and green are the pastures
   where he gives me repose.
   Near restful waters he leads me,
   to revive my drooping spirit. ℟

2 He guides me along the right path;
   he is true to his name.
   If I should walk in the valley of darkness
   no evil would I fear.
   You are there with your crook and your staff;
   with these you give me comfort. ℟

3 You have prepared a banquet for me
   in the sight of my foes.
   My head you have anointed with oil;
   my cup is overflowing. ℟

4 Surely goodness and kindness shall follow me
   all the days of my life.
   In the Lord's own house shall I dwell
   for ever and ever. ℟   *Ps 22. ℟ v.1*

i

SECOND READING

We read from the letter of St Paul to the Romans, chapter five.

*
The love of God has been poured into our hearts by the Holy
Spirit which has been given us. We were still helpless when at his
appointed moment Christ died for sinful men. It is not easy to die
even for a good man – though of course for someone really
worthy, a man might be prepared to die – but what proves that
God loves us is that Christ died for us while we were still sinners.
Having died to make us righteous, is it likely that he would now
fail to save us from God's anger? When we were reconciled to
God by the death of his Son, we were still enemies; now that we
have been reconciled, surely we may count on being saved by the
life of his Son? Not merely because we have been reconciled but
because we are filled with joyful trust in God, through our Lord

Jesus Christ, through whom we have already gained our reconciliation.

This is the word of the Lord. *Romans 5:5-11*

Gospel Acclamation
Alleluia, alleluia!
Shoulder my yoke and learn from me,
for I am gentle and humble in heart.
Alleluia! *Mt 11:29*

Alternative Gospel Acclamation
Alleluia, alleluia!
I am the good shepherd, says the Lord;
I know my own sheep and my own know me.
Alleluia! *Jn 10:14*

GOSPEL

We read from the holy Gospel according to Luke, chapter fifteen.
★
Jesus spoke this parable to the scribes and Pharisees:
'What man among you with a hundred sheep, losing one, would not leave the ninety-nine in the wilderness and go after the missing one till he found it? And when he found it, would he not joyfully take it on his shoulders and then, when he got home, call together his friends and neighbours? "Rejoice with me," he would say "I have found my sheep that was lost." In the same way, I tell you, there will be more rejoicing in heaven over one repentant sinner than over ninety-nine virtuous men who have no need of repentance.'

This is the Gospel of the Lord. *Luke 15:3-7*

How can People's Daily Experience Flow into our Sunday Worship?

Suggestions

1 Ask a House Group to read the Sunday Readings in advance, and to be ready to share their thoughts with the congregation on Sunday. Their findings will reflect the daily experience of people.

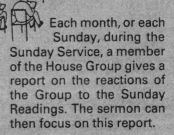

Each month, or each Sunday, during the Sunday Service, a member of the House Group gives a report on the reactions of the Group to the Sunday Readings. The sermon can then focus on this report.

Other possibilities

2 The priest prepares the homily with the special groups active in different aspects of life in the area.

3 The priest prepares the homily in conjunction with one of the Basic Christian Communities or Small Groups.

4 Background reports. After the readings, one or more members of the congregation come forward and give a concrete report on a life-situation related to the readings. This report has been prepared in advance with the aim of enriching the understanding of the congregation. The sermon can then be based on this report together with the readings.

5 A special introduction to the readings is compiled by the group of readers. These introductions try to reflect the people's lives and experience, and the questions they are asking.

6 The whole Sunday liturgy is compiled by the group of readers who try and relate the liturgy to the lives and experiences of the people of a particular area.

Lay Ministry is Not Merely a Liturgical Task

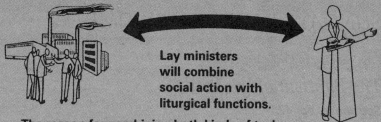

Lay ministers will combine social action with liturgical functions.

The reason for combining both kinds of tasks are

● The announcing of the Kingdom must be clearly linked with the building of the Kingdom.

● The building of a more just society should not be separated from the celebration of God's action for justice. Otherwise it will appear as a mere human undertaking.

● Similarly, our celebration of God's renewal of the world should not be separated from actively working to renew it. Otherwise the message of God who transforms the world will appear as a purely spiritual teaching, unrelated to the lives of people today.

Practical Suggestions

● Each lay minister should be involved in groups which work for development, justice, improvement of living conditions, or acts of mercy.

● Each lay minister should belong to a Basic Christian Community, which relates the Gospel to life, and takes action.

● The training of lay ministers to include the study of the Church's responsibility for a more human and just society.

● The group of lay ministers should ensure they are informed about the conditions of life, and the issues which touch the lives of people.

● The group of lay ministers should search for ways of making the Gospel relevant to people of today.

SUNDAYS IN ORDINARY TIME

First Sunday in Ordinary Time

The Baptism of the Lord

See above, pp. 47.

Second Sunday in Ordinary Time   C

Introduction to the Service

What are we, as we stand here before God at the beginning of this service? We, the Church, what are we? With what words or phrases could one explain what we are before God?

One could say we are God's people, or his followers, or his servants, or his children. But there is one much more beautiful word by which we can be called: we are God's bride. Today's readings remind us that God is like a bridegroom to us, and we, all of us together, are his bride, invited to the wedding feast.

Penitential Rite

Let us reflect:

● Do we look at God only in fear, or do we learn to look at him in love?   (*Silence*)

● Do we speak to God only when we need him, or do we want to be close to God at all times, like somebody who loves him?   (*Silence*)

Let us confess that we have failed and sinned.   **I confess**…

FIRST READING

When somebody speaks to us with words of love, how do we feel? When God himself addresses us as if we were his own bride, are we not filled with joy?

Let us listen to the prophet Isaiah, chapter sixty-two.
*
About Zion I will not be silent.
about Jerusalem I will not grow weary,
until her integrity shines out like the dawn
and her salvation flames like a torch.

The nations then will see your integrity,
all the kings your glory,
and you will be called by a new name,
one which the mouth of the Lord will confer.
You are to be a crown of splendour in the hand of the Lord,
a princely diadem in the hand of your God;
no longer are you to be named 'Forsaken',
nor your land 'Abandoned',
but you shall be called 'My Delight'
and your land 'The Wedded';
for the Lord takes delight in you
and your land will have its wedding.
Like a young man marrying a virgin,
so will the one who built you wed you,
and as the bridegroom rejoices in his bride,
so will your God rejoice in you.

       This is the word of the Lord.

                                    Isaiah 62:1-5

Responsorial Psalm
   ℟ **Proclaim the wonders of the Lord**
      among all the peoples.

1   O sing a new song to the Lord,
    sing to the Lord all the earth.
    O sing to the Lord, bless his name. ℟

2   Proclaim his help day by day,
    tell among the nations his glory
    and his wonders among all the peoples. ℟

3   Give the Lord, you families of peoples,
    give the Lord glory and power,
    give the Lord the glory of his name. ℟

4   Worship the Lord in his temple.
    O earth, tremble before him.
    Proclaim to the nations: 'God is king.'
    He will judge the peoples in fairness. ℟

                                Ps 95:1-3. 7-10. ℟ v.3

SECOND READING

We read from the first letter of St Paul to the Corinthians, chapter twelve.
*
There is a variety of gifts but always the same Spirit; there are all

sorts of service to be done, but always to the same Lord; working in all sorts of different ways in different people, it is the same God who is working in all of them. The particular way in which the Spirit is given to each person is for a good purpose. One may have the gift of preaching with wisdom given him by the Spirit; another may have the gift of preaching instruction given him by the same Spirit; and another the gift of faith given by the same Spirit; another again the gift of healing, through this one Spirit; one, the power of miracles; another, prophecy; another the gift of recognising spirits; another the gift of tongues and another the ability to interpret them. All these are the work of one and the same Spirit, who distributes different gifts to different people just as he chooses.

This is the word of the Lord.   *1 Corinthians 12:4-11*

Gospel Acclamation
Alleluia, alleluia!
Your words are spirit, Lord,
and they are life:
you have the message of eternal life.
Alleluia!   *cf. Jn 6:63. 68*

or

Alleluia, alleluia!
Through the Good News God called us
to share the glory of our Lord Jesus Christ.
Alleluia!   *cf. 2 Thess 2:14*

GOSPEL
We read from the holy Gospel according to John, chapter two.
*
There was a wedding at Cana in Galilee. The mother of Jesus was there, and Jesus and his disciples had also been invited. When they ran out of wine, since the wine provided for the wedding was all finished, the mother of Jesus said to him, 'They have no wine.' Jesus said, 'Woman why turn to me? My hour has not come yet.' His mother said to the servants, 'Do whatever he tells you.' There were six stone water jars standing there, meant for the ablutions that are customary among the Jews; each could hold twenty or thirty gallons. Jesus said to the servants, 'Fill the jars with water,' and they filled them to the brim. 'Draw some out now' he told them 'and take it to the steward.' They did this; the

steward tasted the water, and it had turned into wine. Having no idea where it came from – only the servants who had drawn the water knew – the steward called the bridegroom and said, 'People generally serve the best wine first, and keep the cheaper sort till the guests have had plenty to drink; but you have kept the best wine till now.'

This was the first of the signs given by Jesus: it was given at Cana in Galilee. He let his glory be seen, and his disciples believed in him.

This is the Gospel of the Lord.   *John 2:1-11*

Third Sunday in Ordinary Time   C

Introduction to the Service

When people have a truly great leader, they gather round the leader as the plan of action is explained to them.

We, Christians, have such a great leader. We gather round Christ this morning as Christ unfolds his plan of action with the words 'I am sent to bring the good news to the poor. I am sent to proclaim liberty to captives, and to the blind new sight.'

Christ says these words to us, because we are sent with him: I am sent and you are sent. We are sent to bring the good news to the poor.

Penitential Rite

Let us look at the Lord. He has sent us. Did we go where he sent us?

● Lord, you sent us to bring good news to the poor. Often, we failed to go to them.   (*Silence*)

Lord, have mercy...

● Christ, you sent us to liberate captives. Did we care about them?   (*Silence*)

Christ, have mercy...

● Lord, you sent us to the downtrodden. Were we willing to go to them?   (*Silence*)

Lord, have mercy...

FIRST READING

It is a most important occasion when a new set of laws is given to a nation. The laws provide a new plan for the way in which the people should live. On such an occasion, how do people show their interest in this new plan? How do they show their approval or disapproval?

We read of such an occasion in the book of Nehemiah, chapter eight.

*

Ezra the priest brought the Law before the assembly, consisting of men, women, and children old enough to understand. This was the first day of the seventh month. On the square before the Water Gate, in the presence of the men and women, and children old enough to understand, he read from the book from early morning till noon; all the people listened attentively to the Book of the Law.

Ezra the scribe stood on a wooden dais erected for the purpose. In full view of all the people – since he stood higher than all the people – Ezra opened the book; and when he opened it all the people stood up. Then Ezra blessed the Lord, the great God, and all the people raised their hands and answered, 'Amen! Amen!'; then they bowed down and, face to the ground, prostrated themselves before the Lord. And Ezra read from the Law of God, translating and giving the sense, so that the people understood what was read.

Then Nehemiah – His Excellency – and Ezra, priest and scribe (and the Levites who were instructing the people) said to all the people, 'This day is sacred to the Lord your God. Do not be mournful, do not weep.' For the people were all in tears as they listened to the words of the Law.

He then said, 'Go, eat the fat, drink the sweet wine, and send a portion to the man who has nothing prepared ready. For this day is sacred to our Lord. Do not be sad: the joy of the Lord is your stronghold.'

This is the word of the Lord.   *Nehemiah 8:2-6. 8-10*

Responsorial Psalm
  ℞ **Your words are spirit, Lord,**
      and they are life.

1   The law of the Lord is perfect,
    it revives the soul.
    The rule of the Lord is to be trusted,
    it gives wisdom to the simple.   ℞

2 The precepts of the Lord are right,
   they gladden the heart.
   The command of the Lord is clear,
   it gives light to the eyes. ℟

3 The fear of the Lord is holy,
   abiding for ever.
   The decrees of the Lord are truth
   and all of them just. ℟

4 May the spoken words of my mouth,
   the thoughts of my heart,
   win favour in your sight, O Lord,
   my rescuer, my rock! ℟   *Ps 18:8-10. 15. ℟ Jn 6:63*

SECOND READING

We read from the first letter of St Paul to the Corinthians, chapter twelve.

*Just as a human body, though it is made up of many parts is a single unit because all these parts, though many, make one body, so it is with Christ. In the one Spirit we were all baptised, Jews as well as Greeks, slaves as well as citizens, and one Spirit was given to us all to drink.

Nor is the body to be identified with any one of its many parts.* If the foot were to say, 'I am not a hand and so I do not belong to the body', would that mean that it stopped being part of the body? If the ear were to say, 'I am not an eye, and so I do not belong to the body,' would that mean that it is not a part of the body? If your whole body was just one eye, how would you hear anything? If it was just one ear, how would you smell anything?

Instead of that, God put all the separate parts into the body on purpose. If all the parts were the same, how could it be a body? As it is, the parts are many but the body is one. The eye cannot say to the hand, 'I do not need you,' nor can the head say to the feet, 'I do not need you.'

What is more, it is precisely the parts of the body that seem to be the weakest which are the indispensable ones; and it is the least honourable parts of the body that we clothe with the greatest care. So our more improper parts get decorated in a way that our more proper parts do not need. God has arranged the body so that more dignity is given to the parts which are without it, and so that there may not be disagreements inside the body, but that each part may be equally concerned for all the others. If one part is hurt, all parts are hurt with it. If one part is given special honour, all parts enjoy it.

Now you together are Christ's body; but each of you is a different part of it. In the Church, God has given the first place to apostles, the second to prophets, the third to teachers; after them, miracles, and after them the gift of healing; helpers, good leaders, those with many languages. Are all of them apostles, or all of them prophets, or all of them teachers? Do they all have the gift of miracles, or all have the gift of healing? Do all speak strange languages, and all interpret them?

This is the word of the Lord.   *1 Corinthians 12:12-30*

*Shorter Form, verses 12-14. 17. Read between *.*

Gospel Acclamation
Alleluia, alleluia!
The Lord has sent me to bring the good news to the poor,
to proclaim liberty to captives.
Alleluia!   *Lk 4:18*

GOSPEL
We read from the holy Gospel according to Luke, chapters one and four.
*
Seeing that many others have undertaken to draw up accounts of the events that have taken place among us, exactly as these were handed down to us by those who from the outset were eyewitnesses and ministers of the word, I in my turn, after carefully going over the whole story from the beginning, have decided to write an ordered account for you, Theophilus, so that your Excellency may learn how well founded the teaching is that you have received.

Jesus, with the power of the Spirit in him, returned to Galilee; and his reputation spread throughout the countryside. He taught in their synagogues and everyone praised him.

He came to Nazara, where he had been brought up, and went into the synagogue on the sabbath day as he usually did. He stood up to read, and they handed him the scroll of the prophet Isaiah. Unrolling the scroll he found the place where it is written:

The spirit of the Lord has been given to me, for he has

anointed me.
He has sent me to bring the good news to the poor,
to proclaim liberty to captives
and to the blind new sight,
to set the downtrodden free,
to proclaim the Lord's year of favour.

He then rolled up the scroll, gave it back to the assistant and sat down. And all eyes in the synagogue were fixed on him. Then he began to speak to them, 'This text is being fulfilled today even as you listen.'

This is the Gospel of the Lord. *Luke 1:1-4; 4:14-21*

Fourth Sunday in Ordinary Time   C

Introduction to the Service

It must be a frightening experience if you are sent to people with an important message for them, but they will not allow you to speak. Or they reject what you say. Would we be strong enough to bear such a rejection?

When Jesus came to preach in Nazareth, his home town, he was rejected. And yet he continued his work.

We, too, as we are assembled here, are sent to announce the Good News. How do we react when difficulties arise?

Penitential Rite

● When others show no interest in the faith or laugh about it, do we remain strong in our faith, or are we weakened by their disbelief? (*Silence*)

● When our faith demands difficult things from us, how do we react? (*Silence*)

Let us confess our weakness and our sins. **I confess**...

FIRST READING

When you send somebody to fulfil an important task for you, how can you strengthen them if they become weak? You can speak to them. You can remind them that they are not acting on their own behalf by saying: 'It is I who send you. I appoint you.'

When the prophet Jeremiah was in danger of getting weak, God strengthened him, just as even now he is strengthening us.

We read from the prophet Jeremiah, chapter one.
*
In the days of Josiah, the word of the Lord was addressed to me,
saying,

> 'Before I formed you in the womb I knew you;
> before you came to birth I consecrated you;
> I have appointed you as prophet to the nations.
> So now brace yourself for action.
> Stand up and tell them
> all I command you.
> Do not be dismayed at their presence,
> or in their presence I will make you dismayed.
> I, for my part, today will make you
> into a fortified city,
> a pillar of iron,
> and a wall of bronze
> to confront all this land:
> the kings of Judah, its princes,
> its priests and the country people.
> They will fight against you
> but shall not overcome you,
> for I am with you to deliver you –
> it is the Lord who speaks.'

This is the word of the Lord.   *Jeremiah 1:4-5. 17-19*

Responsorial Psalm
　　℟　**My lips will tell of your help.**

1　In you, O Lord, I take refuge;
　　let me never be put to shame.
　　In your justice rescue me, free me:
　　pay heed to me and save me.　℟

2　Be a rock where I can take refuge,
　　a mighty stronghold to save me;
　　for you are my rock, my stronghold.
　　Free me from the hand of the wicked.　℟

3　It is you, O Lord, who are my hope,
　　my trust, O Lord, since my youth.
　　On you I have leaned from my birth,
　　from my mother's womb you have been my help.　℟

4   My lips will tell of your justice
    and day by day of your help.
    O God, you have taught me from my youth
    and I proclaim your wonders still.   ℞ *Ps 70:1-6. 15. 17.* ℞ *v.15*

SECOND READING

We read from the first letter of St Paul to the Corinthians, chapters twelve and thirteen.
*
Be ambitious for the higher gifts. And I am going to show you a way that is better than any of them.

If I have all the eloquence of men or of angels, but speak without love, I am simply a gong booming or a cymbal clashing. If I have the gift of prophecy, understanding all the mysteries there are, and knowing everything, and if I have faith in all its fulness, to move mountains, but without love, then I am nothing at all. If I give away all that I possess, piece by piece, and if I even let them take my body to burn it, but am without love, it will do me no good whatever.

*Love is always patient and kind: it is never jealous; love is never boastful or conceited; it is never rude or selfish; it does not take offence, and is not resentful. Love takes no pleasure in other people's sins but delights in the truth; it is always ready to excuse, to trust, to hope, and to endure whatever comes.

Love does not come to an end. But if there are gifts of prophecy, the time will come when they must fail; or the gift of languages, it will not continue for ever; and knowledge – for this, too, the time will come when it must fail. For our knowledge is imperfect and our prophesying is imperfect; but once perfection comes, all imperfect things will disappear. When I was a child, I used to talk like a child, and think like a child, and argue like a child, but now I am a man, all childish ways are put behind me. Now we are seeing a dim reflection in a mirror; but then we shall be seeing face to face. The knowledge that I have now is imperfect; but then I shall know as fully as I am known.

In short, there are three things that last: faith, hope and love; and the greatest of these is love.

This is the word of the Lord.*   *1 Corinthians 12:31-13:13*

Shorter Form, verses 4-13, read between.

Gospel Acclamation
Alleluia, alleluia!
I am the Way, the Truth and the Life, says the Lord;
no one can come to the Father except through me.
Alleluia!

Jn 14:5

or

Alleluia, alleluia!
The Lord has sent me to bring the good news to the poor,
to proclaim liberty to captives.
Alleluia!

Lk 4:18

GOSPEL

We read from the holy Gospel according to Luke, chapter four.
*
Jesus began to speak in the synagogue, 'This text is being fulfilled today even as you listen.' And he won the approval of all, and they were astonished by the gracious words that came from his lips.

They said, 'This is Joseph's son, surely?' But he replied, 'No doubt you will quote me the saying, "Physician, heal yourself" and tell me, "We have heard all that happened in Capernaum, do the same here in your own countryside." ' And he went on, 'I tell you solemnly, no prophet is ever accepted in his own country.

'There were many widows in Israel, I can assure you, in Elijah's day, when heaven remained shut for three years and six months and a great famine raged throughout the land, but Elijah was not sent to any one of these: he was sent to a widow at Zarephath, a Sidonian town. And in the prophet Elisha's time there were many lepers in Israel, but none of these was cured, except the Syrian, Naaman.'

When they heard this everyone in the synagogue was enraged. They sprang to their feet and hustled him out of the town; and they took him up to the brow of the hill their town was built on, intending to throw him down the cliff, but he slipped through the crowd and walked away.

This is the Gospel of the Lord.

Luke 4:21-30

Fifth Sunday in Ordinary Time C

Introduction to the Service

When we entered the church building today, we bent our knees. Why did we do so? Because we know that this is a holy place. It is a place of God's presence. By bending the knee we are lowering ourselves. We acknowledge that God is higher, we are lower.

Isn't it surprising that the greatest friends of God, like Isaiah and Peter, began in the same way. First they fell to their knees, then they were sent by God.

We, too, began this service by bending our knees and at the end we too are sent: go forth, you are sent.

Penitential Rite

We are now at the beginning of this service. We have already bent our knees. Let us also bend our heads and ask for the Lord's mercy.

● Lord, you alone are holy, living in unapproachable light. (*Silence*)
> Lord, have mercy...

● Christ, you have made us holy, but we have not lived holy lives. (*Silence*)
> Christ, have mercy...

● Lord, we ask for forgiveness for our unholy thoughts, words, and deeds. (*Silence*)
> Lord, have mercy.

FIRST READING

We have all wondered, at one time or another, how it would be if suddenly we could see God, just for a moment.

We now read how Isaiah was allowed this experience in a vision. Let us pay attention to the two things happening to Isaiah in this vision: first he becomes conscious of his unworthiness, and secondly he is sent.

We read from Isaiah, chapter six.
*
In the year of King Uzziah's death I saw the Lord seated on a high throne; his train filled the sanctuary; above him stood seraphs, each one with six wings.

And they cried out one to another in this way,

'Holy, holy, holy is the Lord of hosts.
His glory fills the whole earth.'

The foundations of the threshold shook with the voice of the one who cried out, and the Temple was filled with smoke. I said:

'What a wretched state I am in! I am lost,
for I am a man of unclean lips
and I live among a people of unclean lips,
and my eyes have looked at the King, the Lord of hosts.'

Then one of the seraphs flew to me, holding in his hand a live coal which he had taken from the altar with a pair of tongs. With this he touched my mouth and said:

'See now, this has touched your lips,
your sin is taken away,
your iniquity is purged.'

Then I heard the voice of the Lord saying:

'Whom shall I send? Who will be our messenger?'

I answered, 'Here I am, send me.'

This is the word of the Lord.   *Isaiah 6:1-8*

Responsorial Psalm
℟ **Before the angels I will bless you, O Lord.**

1 I thank you, Lord, with all my heart,
   you have heard the words of my mouth.
   Before the angels I will bless you.
   I will adore before your holy temple. ℟

2 I thank you for your faithfulness and love
   which excel all we ever knew of you.
   On the day I called, you answered;
   you increased the strength of my soul. ℟

3 All earth's kings shall thank you
   when they hear the words of your mouth.
   They shall sing of the Lord's ways:
   'How great is the glory of the Lord!' ℟

4 You stretch out your hand and save me,
   your hand will do all things for me.
   Your love, O Lord, is eternal,
   discard not the work of your hand. ℟   *Ps 137:1-5. 7-8. ℟ v.1*

SECOND READING

We read from the first letter of St Paul to the Corinthians, chapter fifteen.

*
Brothers, I want to remind you of the gospel I preached to you, the gospel that you received and in which you are firmly established; because the gospel will save you only if you keep believing exactly what I preached to you – believing anything else will not lead to anything.

Well then, *in the first place, I taught you what I had been taught myself, namely that Christ died for our sins, in accordance with the scriptures; that he was buried; and that he was raised to life on the third day, in accordance with the scriptures; that he appeared first to Cephas and secondly to the Twelve. Next he appeared to more than five hundred of the brothers at the same time, most of whom are still alive, though some have died; then he appeared to James, and then to all the apostles; and last of all he appeared to me too; it was as though I was born when no one expected it.*

I am the least of the apostles; in fact, since I persecuted the Church of God, I hardly deserve the name apostle; but by God's grace that is what I am, and the grace that he gave me has not been fruitless. On the contrary, I, or rather the grace of God that is with me, have worked harder than any of the others; *but what matters is that I preach what they preach, and this is what you all believed.

This is the word of the Lord.*　　　　　　　*1 Corinthians 15:1-11*

*Shorter Form, verses 3-8. 11, read between *.*

Gospel Acclamation
　　Alleluia, alleluia!
　　I call you friends, says the Lord,
　　because I have made known to you
　　everything I have learnt from my Father.
　　Alleluia!　　　　　　　　　　　　　　　　*Jn 15:15*
or

　　Alleluia, alleluia!
　　Follow me, says the Lord,
　　and I will make you fishers of men.
　　Alleluia!
　　　　　　　　　　　　　　　　　　　　　　Mt 4:19

GOSPEL

We read from the holy Gospel according to Luke, chapter five.

*
Jesus was standing one day by the lake of Gennesaret, with the crowd pressing round him listening to the word of God, when he caught sight of two boats close to the bank. The fishermen had gone out of them and were washing their nets. He got into one of the boats – it was Simon's – and asked him to put out a little from the shore. Then he sat down and taught the crowds from the boat.

When he had finished speaking he said to Simon, 'Put out into deep water and pay out your nets for a catch.' 'Master,' Simon replied 'we worked hard all night long and caught nothing, but if you say so, I will pay out the nets.' And when they had done this they netted such a huge number of fish that their nets began to tear, so they signalled to their companions in the other boats to come and help them; when these came, they filled the two boats to sinking point.

When Simon Peter saw this he fell at the knees of Jesus saying, 'Leave me, Lord; I am a sinful man.' For he and all his companions were completely overcome by the catch they had made; so also were James and John, sons of Zebedee, who were Simon's partners. But Jesus said to Simon, 'Do not be afraid; from now on it is men you will catch.' Then, bringing their boats back to land, they left everything and followed him.

This is the Gospel of the Lord.   *Luke 5:1-11*

Sixth Sunday in Ordinary Time   C

Introduction to the Service

At the opening of this service, everyone was greeted. We tried to greet each other in a friendly way and in a prayerful way. But our greeting and our welcome can never be as beautiful as the welcome and blessing which Jesus himself pronounced. He pronounced it over the crowds as they came from all directions to the hill at the lakeside. He looked at his disciples and said: 'Blessed are you! How happy are you!' Eight times he said this blessing over them, as we will hear in today's Gospel reading.

Penitential Rite

We want to be worthy of such blessings. Therefore, at the beginning of this service we reflect:

- Are we among those who are blessed because we are hungry for the kingdom of God? *(Silence)*

- Are we in any way those poor to whom Christ gave his blessing? *(Silence)*

Let us confess our unworthiness before God. **I confess…**

FIRST READING

The opposite of a blessing is a curse. The very word frightens us, and we hardly dare speak of it. We are deeply afraid of a curse, and we wish only to receive a blessing. But who is the kind of person who deserves a blessing? And who is the kind of person who deserves a curse? The prophet Jeremiah gives us an answer.

We read from Jeremiah chapter seventeen.
*
The Lord says this:

'A curse on the man who puts his trust in man,
who relies on things of flesh,
whose heart turns from the Lord.
He is like dry scrub in the wastelands:
if good comes, he has no eyes for it,
he settles in the parched places of the wilderness,
a salt land, uninhabited.

'A blessing on the man who puts his trust in the Lord,
with the Lord for his hope.
He is like a tree by the waterside
that thrusts its roots to the stream:
when the heat comes it feels no alarm,
its foliage stays green;
it has no worries in a year of drought,
and never ceases to bear fruit.'

This is the word of the Lord.   *Jeremiah 17:5-8*

Responsorial Psalm
℟ **Happy the man who has placed
his trust in the Lord.**

1   Happy indeed is the man
who follows not the counsel of the wicked;
nor lingers in the way of sinners
nor sits in the company of scorners,

but whose delight is the law of the Lord
and who ponders his law day and night.   ℟

2   He is like a tree that is planted
beside the flowing waters,
that yields its fruit in due season
and whose leaves shall never fade;
and all that he does shall prosper.   ℟

3   Not so are the wicked, not so!
For they like winnowed chaff
shall be driven away by the wind.
For the Lord guards the way of the just
but the way of the wicked leads to doom.   ℟

Ps 1:1-4. 6. ℟ Ps 39:5

SECOND READING

We read from the first letter of St Paul to the Corinthians, chapter
fifteen.
*
If Christ raised from the dead is what has been preached, how
can some of you be saying that there is no resurrection of the
dead? For if the dead are not raised, Christ has not been raised,
and if Christ has not been raised, you are still in your sins. And
what is more serious, all who have died in Christ have perished.
If our hope in Christ has been for this life only, we are the most
unfortunate of all people.

But Christ has in fact been raised from the dead, the first-fruits
of all who have fallen asleep.

This is the word of the Lord.   *1 Corinthians 15:12. 16-20*

Gospel Acclamation
Alleluia, alleluia!
Blessed are you, Father,
Lord of heaven and earth,
for revealing the mysteries of the kingdom
to mere children.
Alleluia!   *cf. Mt 11:25*

or

Alleluia, alleluia!
Rejoice and be glad:
your reward will be great in heaven.
Alleluia!   *Lk 6:23*

GOSPEL

We read from the holy Gospel according to Luke, chapter six.
★

Jesus came down with the Twelve and stopped at a piece of level ground where there was a large gathering of his disciples with a great crowd of people from all parts of Judaea and from Jerusalem and from the coastal region of Tyre and Sidon who had come to hear him and to be cured of their diseases.

Then fixing his eyes on his disciples he said:

'How happy are you who are poor; yours is the kingdom of God.
Happy you who are hungry now: you shall be satisfied.
Happy you who weep now: you shall laugh.

'Happy are you when people hate you, drive you out, abuse you, denounce your name as criminal, on account of the Son of Man. Rejoice when that day comes and dance for joy, for then your reward will be great in heaven. This was the way their ancestors treated the prophets.

'But alas for you who are rich: you are having your consolation now.
Alas for you who have your fill now: you shall go hungry.
Alas for you who laugh now: you shall mourn and weep.

'Alas for you when the world speaks well of you! This was the way their ancestors treated the false prophets.'

This is the Gospel of the Lord.   *Luke 6:17.20-26*

Seventh Sunday in Ordinary Time   C

Introduction to the Service

For friends it is easy to come together as we have come together now for this service. Friends like to meet. It is not so easy, however, to meet people whom we dislike. The biggest challenge is to meet those who consider us an enemy. But Jesus goes even further when he says that we should not only meet them, but that we should love them. 'Love your enemy' is the message to us today, on this Sunday.

Penitential Rite

Before we approach the altar, let us examine our conscience and call on the Lord's mercy:

● Lord, we remember times when we kept grudges in our hearts against others. (*Silence*)
 Lord, have mercy…

● Christ, we remember times when we allowed thoughts of revenge to grow in us. (*Silence*)
 Christ, have mercy…

● Lord, there were times when we should have loved our enemies, but we failed to do so. (*Silence*)
 Lord, have mercy…

FIRST READING

Young David knew that King Saul was his enemy, because Saul considered David to be a rival for the throne. For a long time David had to flee for his life, pursued by Saul, his enemy. But one night there came a chance for revenge. Saul lay asleep, defenceless, at the feet of David. What would David do with his enemy?

We read from the first book of Samuel, chapter twenty-six.
*
Saul set off and went down to the wilderness of Ziph, accompanied by three thousand men chosen from Israel to search for David in the wilderness of Ziph.

So in the dark David and Abishai made their way towards the force, where they found Saul asleep inside the camp, his spear stuck in the ground beside his head, with Abner and the troops lying round him.

Then Abishai said to David, 'Today God has put your enemy in your power; so now let me pin him to the ground with his own spear. Just one stroke! I will not need to strike him twice.' David answered Abishai, 'Do not kill him, for who can lift his hand against the Lord's anointed and be without guilt?' David took the spear and the pitcher of water from beside Saul's head, and they made off. No one saw, no one knew, no one woke up; they were all asleep, for a deep sleep from the Lord had fallen on them.

David crossed to the other side and halted on the top of the mountain a long way off; there was a wide space between them. David then called out, 'Here is the king's spear. Let one of the soldiers come across and take it. The Lord repays everyone for his uprightness and loyalty. Today the Lord put you in my power, but I would not raise my hand against the Lord's anointed.'

This is the word of the Lord.   *1 Samuel 26:2. 7-9. 12-13. 22-33*

Responsorial Psalm
℟   **The Lord is compassion and love.**

1   My soul, give thanks to the Lord,
    all my being, bless his holy name.
    My soul, give thanks to the Lord
    and never forget all his blessings.   ℟

2   It is he who forgives all your guilt,
    who heals every one of your ills,
    who redeems your life from the grave,
    who crowns you with love and compassion.   ℟

3   The Lord is compassion and love,
    slow to anger and rich in mercy.
    He does not treat us according to our sins
    nor repay us according to our faults.   ℟

4   As far as the east is from the west
    so far does he remove our sins.
    As a father has compassion on his sons,
    the Lord has pity on those who fear him.   ℟

Ps 102:1-4. 8. 10. 12-13. ℟ v.8

SECOND READING

We read from the first letter of St Paul to the Corinthians, chapter fifteen.
*
The first man, Adam, as scripture says, became a living soul; but the last Adam has become a life-giving spirit. That is, first the one with the soul, not the spirit, and after that, the one with the spirit. The first man, being from the earth, is earthly by nature; the second man is from heaven. As this earthly man was, so are we on earth; and as the heavenly man is, so are we in heaven. And we, who have been modelled on the earthly man, will be modelled on the heavenly man.

This is the word of the Lord.   *1 Corinthians 15:45-49*

Gospel Acclamation
   Alleluia, alleluia!
   Open our heart, O Lord,
   to accept the words of your Son.
   Alleluia!   *cf. Acts 16:14*

or

Alleluia, alleluia!
I give you a new commandment:
love one another,
just as I have loved you,
says the Lord.
Alleluia!

Jn 13:34

GOSPEL

We read from the holy Gospel according to Luke, chapter six.
*
Jesus said to his disciples: 'I say this to you who are listening: Love your enemies, do good to those who hate you, bless those who curse you, pray for those who treat you badly. To the man who slaps you on one cheek, present the other cheek too; to the man who takes your cloak from you, do not refuse your tunic. Give to everyone who asks you, and do not ask for your property back from the man who robs you. Treat others as you would like them to treat you. If you love those who love you, what thanks can you expect? Even sinners love those who love them. And if you do good to those who do good to you, what thanks can you expect? For even sinners do that much. And if you lend to those from whom you hope to receive, what thanks can you expect? Even sinners lend to sinners to get back the same amount. Instead, love your enemies and do good, and lend without any hope of return. You will have a great reward, and you will be sons of the Most High, for he himself is kind to the ungrateful and the wicked.

'Be compassionate as your Father is compassionate. Do not judge, and you will not be judged yourselves; do not condemn, and you will not be condemned yourselves; grant pardon, and you will be pardoned. Give, and there will be gifts for you: a full measure, pressed down, shaken together, and running over, will be poured into your lap; because the amount you measure out is the amount you will be given back.'

This is the Gospel of the Lord.

Luke 6:27-38

Eighth Sunday in Ordinary Time C

Introduction to the Service

To what can we compare our assembly as we come together today for our Sunday celebration?

Today's readings compare us to a field from which good fruit is expected. God has planted this field. We are glad to be God's field, and we have come together to give thanks to God for having made us his people, his field.

Penitential Rite

What does this field produce? Where is the good fruit produced by this field during this past week?

● During this week did we show genuine love towards somebody who was in need? (*Silence*)

● During this week did we bring the fruit of peace to others? (*Silence*)

Let us confess our failures and sins. **I confess**...

FIRST READING

How do you distinguish good fruit from bad fruit? Sometimes this is easy but sometimes you need to test it in some way.

For the quality of people's lives, too, there are tests, and our reading explains such tests to us.

We read from the book of Ecclesiasticus, chapter twenty-seven.
*
In a shaken sieve the rubbish is left behind,
so too the defects of a man appear in his talk.
The kiln tests the work of the potter,
the test of a man is in his conversation.
The orchard where the tree grows is judged on the quality of its
    fruit,
similarly a man's words betray what he feels.
Do not praise a man before he has spoken,
since this is the test of men.

This is the word of the Lord. *Ecclesiasticus 27:4-7*

Responsorial Psalm
℟́ **It is good to give you thanks, O Lord.**

1   It is good to give thanks to the Lord
    to make music to your name, O Most High,
    to proclaim your love in the morning
    and your truth in the watches of the night.   ℟

2   The just will flourish like the palm-tree
    and grow like a Lebanon cedar.   ℟

3   Planted in the house of the Lord
    they will flourish in the courts of our God,
    still bearing fruit when they are old,
    still full of sap, still green,
    to proclaim that the Lord is just.
    In him, my rock, there is no wrong.   ℟
                                    Ps 91:2-3. 13-16. ℟ cf. v.2

SECOND READING

We read from the first letter of St Paul to the Corinthians, chapter fifteen.

When this perishable nature has put on imperishability, and when this mortal nature has put on immortality, then the words of scripture will come true: Death is swallowed up in victory. Death, where is your victory? Death, where is your sting? Now the sting of death is sin, and sin gets its power from the Law. So let us thank God for giving us the victory through our Lord Jesus Christ.

Never give in then, my dear brothers, never admit defeat; keep on working at the Lord's work always, knowing that, in the Lord, you cannot be labouring in vain.

This is the word of the Lord.   *1 Corinthians 15:54-58*

Gospel Acclamation
Alleluia, alleluia!
Open our hearts, O Lord,
to accept the words of your Son.
Alleluia!
                                    cf. Acts 16:14

or

Alleluia, alleluia!
You will shine in the world like bright stars

because you are offering it the word of life.
Alleluia!

Phil 2:15-16

GOSPEL

We read from the holy Gospel according to Luke, chapter six.

*
Jesus told a parable to his disciples. 'Can one blind man guide another? Surely both will fall into a pit? The disciple is not superior to his teacher; the fully trained disciple will always be like his teacher. Why do you observe the splinter in your brother's eye and never notice the plank in your own? How can you say to your brother, "Brother, let me take out the splinter that is in your eye," when you cannot see the plank in your own? Hypocrite! Take the plank out of your own eye first, and then you will see clearly enough to take out the splinter that is in your brother's eye.

'There is no sound tree that produces rotten fruit, nor again a rotten tree that produces sound fruit. For every tree can be told by its own fruit; people do not pick figs from thorns, nor gather grapes from brambles. A good man draws what is good from the store of goodness in his heart; a bad man draws what is bad from the store of badness. For a man's words flow out of what fills his heart.'

This is the Gospel of the Lord.

Luke 6:39-45

Ninth Sunday in Ordinary Time   C

Introduction to the Service

We greeted each other and welcomed each other at the beginning of this service. We greet each other because we are one family of Christians.

But today a question is put to us – a kind of test of a real Christian community: do we welcome strangers into our family? How welcome is a foreigner among us?

Today we will read about two events in the Bible, where foreigners wanted to be accepted among the believers.

Penitential Rite

Let us examine our attitude towards others: during this week did we extend God's friendliness even to those who are not close to us?   *(Silence)*

● Lord, you accepted us as your children even when we were still strangers to you. Forgive us for the times when we did not do the same and were not kind to strangers.

Lord, have mercy…

● Christ, you died for all nations without distinction. Forgive us for not treating people as equals.

Christ, have mercy…

● Lord, you have compassion on all, especially those in need. Forgive us our lack of compassion to strangers who were in need.

Lord, have mercy…

FIRST READING

King Solomon was a Jew, and Jews did not easily welcome people of other nations into their homes. So all the more do we admire the words of Solomon, as he promises a welcome to foreigners who come to the newly built temple.

We read from the first book of Kings, chapter eight.
*
Solomon stood before the altar of the Lord and, stretching out his hands towards heaven, said:

'If a foreigner, not belonging to your people Israel, comes from a distant country for the sake of your name – for men will hear of your name, of your mighty hand and outstretched arm – if he comes and prays in this Temple, hear from heaven where your home is, and grant all the foreigner asks, so that all the peoples of the earth may come to know your name and, like your people Israel, revere you, and know that your name is given to the Temple I have built.'

This is the word of the Lord.   *1 Kings 8:41-43*

Responsorial Psalm
℞ **Go out to the whole world
    and proclaim the Good News.**

or

℞ **Alleluia!**

1 O praise the Lord, all you nations,
   acclaim him all you peoples! ℞

2 Strong is his love for us;
   he is faithful for ever. ℞   *Ps 116:1-2. ℞ Mk. 16:15*

SECOND READING

We read from the letter of St Paul to the Galatians, chapter one.
*

From Paul to the churches of Galatia, and from all the brothers who are here with me, an apostle who does not owe his authority to men or his appointment to any human being but who has been appointed by Jesus Christ and by God the Father who raised Jesus from the dead.

I am astonished at the promptness with which you have turned away from the one who called you and have decided to follow a different version of the Good News. Not that there can be more than one Good News; it is merely that some troublemakers among you want to change the Good News of Christ; and let me warn you that if anyone preaches a version of the Good News different from the one we have already preached to you, whether it be ourselves or an angel from heaven, he is to be condemned. I am only repeating what we told you before: if anyone preaches a version of the Good News different from the one you have already heard, he is to be condemned. So now whom am I trying to please – man, or God? Would you say it is men's approval I am looking for? If I still wanted that, I should not be what I am – a servant of Christ.

This is the word of the Lord.   *Galatians 1:1-2. 6-10*

Gospel Acclamation

Alleluia, alleluia!
The Word was made flesh and lived among us;
to all who did accept him
he gave power to become children of God.
Alleluia!   *Jn 1:14. 12*

or

Alleluia, alleluia!
God loved the world so much
that he gave his only Son
so that everyone who believes in him
may have eternal life.
Alleluia!   *Jn 3:16*

GOSPEL

We read from the holy Gospel according to Luke, chapter seven.

*

When Jesus had come to the end of all he wanted the people to hear, he went into Capernaum. A centurion there had a servant, a favourite of his, who was sick and near death. Having heard about Jesus he sent some Jewish elders to him to ask him to come and heal his servant. When they came to Jesus they pleaded earnestly with him. 'He deserves this of you,' they said 'because he is friendly towards our people; in fact, he is the one who built the synagogue.' So Jesus went with them, and was not very far from the house when the centurion sent word to him by some friends: 'Sir,' he said 'do not put yourself to trouble; because I am not worthy to have you under my roof; and for this same reason I did not presume to come to you myself; but give the word and let my servant be cured. For I am under authority myself, and have soldiers under me; and I say to one man: Go, and he goes; to another: Come here, and he comes; to my servant: Do this, and he does it.' When Jesus heard these words he was astonished at him and, turning round, said to the crowd following him, 'I tell you, not even in Israel have I found faith like this.' And when the messengers got back to the house they found the servant in perfect health.

This is the Gospel of the Lord.   *Luke 7:1-10*

Tenth Sunday in Ordinary Time C

Introduction to the Service

You can only follow a leader you know. The better you know the leader, the better you will be able to follow him or her. This is why we, when we meet for our Sunday celebration, want to get to know Christ more and more.

Christ is not just a leader like any other. Today we look at an action of his which shows clearly how far Christ is beyond all other kinds of leaders. When Jesus came to a town and saw a funeral procession approaching, he was so moved by the grief of the bereaved mother that he raised her son to life.

What does this mean for us, his followers, gathered for our Sunday celebration? What does it mean for you and me, busy with our daily tasks the whole week? What does it mean for each one of us whether young or old, working or at home, parent or child.

Penitential Rite

As we prepare ourselves for the Eucharist, we immediately become aware of our lack of belief in Christ, and our lack of trust in him. Let us reflect:

● We say we believe in Christ who raises even the dead to life. Yet are we not often without hope? Are we not often overcome by a sense of despair? (*Silence*)

● We say we believe in the power of Christ, who is stronger than death. But are we not often overwhelmed by fear? Are we not often lacking in trust in him? (*Silence*)

Let us confess that we have sinned. **I confess**…

FIRST READING

How did the widow of Zarephath react when her son died? We may disagree with her reaction but who can say they would not have reacted as she did? She blamed the prophet Elijah for the death of her son. Did she forget God's presence in this dark hour?

We read from first book of Kings, chapter seventeen.
★
The son of the mistress of the house fell sick; his illness was so severe that in the end he had no breath left in him. And the woman said to Elijah, 'What quarrel have you with me, man of God? Have you come here to bring my sins home to me and to kill my son?' 'Give me your son,' he said, and taking him from her lap, carried him to the upper room where he was staying and laid him on his own bed. He cried out to the Lord, 'Lord my God, do you mean to bring grief to the widow who is looking after me by killing her son?' He stretched himself on the child three times and cried out to the Lord, 'Lord my God, may the soul of this child, I beg you, come into him again!' The Lord heard the prayer of Elijah and the soul of the child returned to him again and he revived. Elijah took the child, brought him down from the upper room into the house, and gave him to his mother. 'Look,' Elijah said 'your son is alive.' And the woman replied, 'Now I know you are a man of God and the word of the Lord in your mouth is truth itself.'

This is the word of the Lord. *1 Kings 17:17-24*

Responsorial Psalm
℟ **I will praise you, Lord,**
you have rescued me.

1 I will praise you, Lord, you have rescued me
and have not let my enemies rejoice over me.
O Lord, you have raised my soul from the dead,
restored me to life from those who sink into the grave. ℟

2 Sing psalms to the Lord, you who love him,
give thanks to his holy name.
His anger lasts a moment; his favour through life.
At night there are tears, but joy comes with dawn. ℟

3 The Lord listened and had pity.
The Lord came to my help.
For me you have changed my mourning into dancing;
O Lord my God, I will thank you for ever. ℟

Ps 29:2. 4-6. 11-13. ℟ v.2

SECOND READING

We read from the letter of St Paul to the Galatians, chapter one.
*
The Good News I preached is not a human message that I was
given by men, it is something I learnt only through a revelation of
Jesus Christ. You must have heard of my career as a practising
Jew, how merciless I was in persecuting the Church of God, how
much damage I did to it, how I stood out among other Jews of my
generation, and how enthusiastic I was for the traditions of my
ancestors.

Then God, who had specially chosen me while I was still in
my mother's womb, called me through his grace and chose to
reveal his Son in me, so that I might preach the Good News about
him to the pagans. I did not stop to discuss this with any human
being, nor did I go up to Jerusalem to see those who were already
apostles before me, but I went off to Arabia at once and later went
straight back from there to Damascus. Even when after three
years I went up to Jerusalem to visit Cephas and stayed with him
for fifteen days, I did not see any of the other apostles; I only saw
James, the brother of the Lord.

This is the word of the Lord. *Galatians 1:11-19*

Gospel Acclamation
Alleluia, alleluia!
May the Father of our Lord Jesus Christ
enlighten the eyes of our mind,
so that we can see what hope his call holds for us.
Alleluia!

cf. Eph 1:17. 18

or

Alleluia, alleluia!
A great prophet has appeared among us;
God has visited his people.
Alleluia!

Lk 7:16

GOSPEL

We read from the holy Gospel according to Luke, chapter seven.
✳

Jesus went to a town called Nain, accompanied by his disciples and a great number of people. When he was near the gate of the town it happened that a dead man was being carried out for burial, the only son of his mother, and she was a widow. And a considerable number of the townspeople were with her. When the Lord saw her he felt sorry for her. 'Do not cry' he said. Then he went up and put his hand on the bier and the bearers stood still, and he said, 'Young man, I tell you to get up.' And the dead man sat up and began to walk, and Jesus gave him to his mother. Everyone was filled with awe and praised God saying, 'A great prophet has appeared among us; God has visited his people.' And this opinion of him spread throughout Judaea and all over the countryside.

This is the Gospel of the Lord.

Luke 7:11-17

Eleventh Sunday in Ordinary Time   C

Introduction to the Service
We come to the Sunday service well-dressed. For all important occasions we want to appear respectable before other people.

This desire to make a good impression on others is surely a good desire. It only becomes harmful when we want to appear better than we are. Then we become like the Pharisee who sat at the table with Jesus, but who was unwilling to admit that he needed help.

This is not how we want to stand before God, now, during this service. Instead we will rather humble ourselves like the repentant woman who knelt down at the feet of Jesus. Jesus saw how, with her whole heart, she was resolved to return to God.

Penitential Rite

God sees us now, at this moment, as we stand before him, ready to begin our Holy Mass. How does he see us?

- Lord, we are afraid to look into your eyes, because nothing is hidden from you.   (*Silence*)
  Lord, have mercy...

- Christ, you remind us of our failures, not in order to condemn us, but in order to heal us.   (*Silence*)
  Christ, have mercy...

- Lord, you do not want us to lose hope because of our sins. Instead you give us the courage to make a new start.   (*Silence*)
  Lord, have mercy...

FIRST READING

A king was a highly respected person, so much so that some kings thought they could do what they liked. King David, too, fell into this error and thought that he could not be blamed for his crimes. As we will read now, he needed a long and severe warning from the prophet Nathan, before he admitted his sin.

We read from the second book of Samuel, chapter twelve.
*
Nathan said to David, 'The Lord the God of Israel says this, "I anointed you king over Israel; I delivered you from the hands of Saul; I gave your master's house to you, his wives into your arms; I gave you the House of Israel and of Judah; and if this were not enough, I would add as much again for you. Why have you shown contempt for the Lord, doing what displeases him? You have struck down Uriah the Hittite with the sword, taken his wife for your own, and killed him with the sword of the Ammonites. So now the sword will never be far from your House, since you have shown contempt for me and taken the wife of Uriah the Hittite to be your wife." '

David said to Nathan, 'I have sinned against the Lord.' Then Nathan said to David, 'The Lord, for his part, forgives your sin; you are not to die.'

This is the word of the Lord.   *2 Samuel 12:7-10. 13*

Responsorial Psalm
℟ **Forgive, Lord, the guilt of my sin.**

1 Happy the man whose offence is forgiven
whose sin is remitted.
O happy the man to whom the Lord
imputes no guilt,
in whose spirit is no guile. ℟

2 But now I have acknowledged my sins:
my guilt I did not hide.
I said: 'I will confess
my offence to the Lord.'
And you, Lord, have forgiven
the guilt of my sin. ℟

3 You are my hiding place, O Lord;
you save me from distress.
You surround me with cries of deliverance. ℟

4 Rejoice, rejoice in the Lord,
exult, you just!
O come, ring out your joy,
all you upright of heart. ℟   *Ps 31:1-2. 5. 7. 11. ℟ cf. v.5*

SECOND READING

We read from the letter of St Paul to the Galatians, chapter two.
*
We acknowledge that what makes a man righteous is not obedience to the Law, but faith in Jesus Christ. We had to become believers in Christ Jesus no less than you had, and now we hold that faith in Christ rather than fidelity to the Law is what justifies us, and that no one can be justified by keeping the Law. In other words, through the Law I am dead to the Law, so that now I can live for God. I have been crucified with Christ, and I live now not with my own life but with the life of Christ who lives in me. The life I now live in this body I live in faith: faith in the Son of God who loved me and who sacrificed himself for my sake. I cannot bring myself to give up God's gift: if the Law can justify us, there is no point in the death of Christ.

This is the word of the Lord.   *Galatians 2:16. 19-21*

Gospel Acclamation
    Alleluia, alleluia!
    I am the Way, the Truth and the Life, says the Lord;
    no one can come to the Father except through me.
    Alleluia!   *Jn 14:6*

or

    Alleluia, alleluia!
    God so loved us when he sent his Son
    to be the sacrifice that takes our sins away.
    Alleluia!   *1 Jn 4:10*

GOSPEL

We read from the holy Gospel according to Luke, chapters seven and eight.
*
*One of the Pharisees invited Jesus to a meal. When he arrived at the Pharisee's house and took his place at table, a woman came in, who had a bad name in the town. She had heard he was dining with the Pharisee and had brought with her an alabaster jar of ointment. She waited behind him at his feet, weeping, and her tears fell on his feet, and she wiped them away with her hair; then she covered his feet with kisses and anointed them with the ointment.

When the Pharisee who had invited him saw this, he said to himself, 'If this man were a prophet, he would know who this woman is that is touching him and what a bad name she has.' Then Jesus took him up and said, 'Simon, I have something to say to you.' 'Speak Master' was the reply. 'There was once a creditor who had two men in his debt; one owed him five hundred denarii, the other fifty. They were unable to pay, so he pardoned them both. Which of them will love him more?' 'The one who was pardoned more, I suppose' answered Simon. Jesus said, 'You are right.'

Then he turned to the woman. 'Simon', he said 'you see this woman? I came into your house, and you poured no water over my feet, but she has poured out her tears over my feet and wiped them away with her hair. You gave me no kiss, but she has been covering my feet with kisses ever since I came in. You did not anoint my head with oil, but she has anointed my feet with ointment. For this reason I tell you that her sins, her many sins, must have been forgiven her, or she would not have shown such great love. It is the man who is forgiven little who shows little love.' Then he said to her, 'Your sins are forgiven.' Those who were with him at table began to say to themselves, 'Who is this man, that he even forgives sins?' But he said to the woman 'Your faith has saved you; go in peace.'*

Now after this he made his way through towns and villages, preaching, and proclaiming the Good News of the kingdom of God. With him went the Twelve, as well as certain women who had been cured of evil spirits and ailments: Mary surnamed the Magdalene, from whom seven demons had gone out, Joanna the wife of Herod's steward Chuza, Susanna, and several others who provided for them out of their own resources.

This is the Gospel of the Lord.   *Luke 7:36–8:3*

*Shorter Form, verses 36-50, read between *.

Twelfth Sunday in Ordinary Time   C

Introduction to the Service

It is a joy to be a Christian, and this morning we have come together to give thanks for being called to Christ.

Yet what are we to do when our faith does not bring us joy, but brings us suffering instead? How shall we react when our belief in Christ brings us disadvantages, or rejection or even persecution? Christ has said: 'Who follows me must be ready to carry the cross.' We want to think about this word today.

Penitential Rite

At the beginning of this service we will ask for forgiveness for not having borne our difficulties in the right way:

● Lord, when difficulties came over us, we forgot that you are with us always.   (*Silence*)
    Lord, have mercy…

● Christ, when we had to suffer because of your name, we even looked for ways of denying you.   (*Silence*)
    Christ, have mercy…

● Lord, when we suffered disadvantages because of our faith, we lost joy in our faith.   (*Silence*)
    Lord, have mercy….

FIRST READING

The suffering of a just person can lead others to conversion. This is why we will hear in our reading: 'They will look on the one whom they have pierced.' The prophet had to suffer, but his suffering helped others, because they looked with horror on the one whom they had pierced. As a result of the prophet's suffering, they were converted. Even today the suffering of a Christian can lead others to conversion.

We read in the twelfth and thirteenth chapters of the prophet Zechariah.
*
It is the Lord who speaks: 'Over the House of David and the citizens of Jerusalem I will pour out a spirit of kindness and prayer. They will look on the one whom they have pierced; they will mourn for him as for an only son, and weep for him as people weep for a first-born child. When that day comes, there will be great mourning in Judah, like the mourning of Hadadrimmon in the plain of Megiddo. When that day comes, a fountain will be opened for the House of David and the citizens of Jerusalem, for sin and impurity.'

This is the word of the Lord.   *Zechariah 12:10-11; 13:1*

Responsorial Psalm
    ℟ **For you my soul is thirsting,**
        O God, my God.

1 O God, you are my God, for you I long;
    for you my soul is thirsting.
    My body pines for you
    like a dry, weary land without water. ℟

2 So I gaze on you in the sanctuary
    to see your strength and your glory.
    For your love is better than life,
    my lips will speak your praise. ℟

3 So I will bless you all my life,
    in your name I will lift up my hands.
    My soul shall be filled as with a banquet,
    my mouth shall praise you with joy. ℟

4 For you have been my help;
    in the shadow of your wings I rejoice.
    My soul clings to you;
    your right hand holds me fast. ℟   *Ps 62:2-6. 8-9. ℟ v.2*

SECOND READING

We read from the letter of St Paul to the Galatians, chapter three.
*

You are, all of you, sons of God through faith in Christ Jesus. All baptised in Christ, you have all clothed yourselves in Christ, and there are no more distinctions between Jew and Greek, slave and free, male and female, but all of you are one in Christ Jesus. Merely by belonging to Christ you are the posterity of Abraham, the heirs he was promised.

This is the word of the Lord.   *Galatians 3:26-29*

Gospel Acclamation
Alleluia, alleluia!
I am the light of the world, says the Lord,
anyone who follows me
will have the light of life.
Alleluia!
                                                         Jn 8:12

or

Alleluia, alleluia!
The sheep that belong to me listen to my voice,
says the Lord,
I know them and they follow me.
Alleluia!
                                                         Jn 10:27

GOSPEL

We read from the holy Gospel according to Luke, chapter nine.
*

One day when Jesus was praying alone in the presence of his disciples he put this question to them, 'Who do the crowds say I am?' And they answered, 'John the Baptist; others Elijah; and others say one of the ancient prophets come back to life.' 'But you,' he said 'who do you say I am?' It was Peter who spoke up. 'The Christ of God' he said. But he gave them strict orders not to tell anyone anything about this.

'The Son of Man' he said 'is destined to suffer grievously, to be rejected by the elders and chief priests and scribes and to be put to death, and to be raised up on the third day.'

Then to all he said, 'If anyone wants to be a follower of mine, let him renounce himself and take up his cross every day and follow me. For anyone who wants to save his life will lose it; but anyone who loses his life for my sake, that man will save it.'

This is the Gospel of the Lord.   *Luke 9:18-24*

Thirteenth Sunday in Ordinary Time   C

Introduction to the Service

We came to this service because we are followers of Christ. Christ goes ahead of us and we follow in the path he chose. We came together this morning to thank Christ for putting us on the right path, and to renew our determination to follow him.

Penitential Rite

● The question we must first ask ourselves is: how did we follow him in the past week? Were we on his path or on another one?   (*Silence*)

Let us confess that we have sinned.   **I confess…**

FIRST READING

If somebody has grown up ploughing the fields, he will love his fields and his ploughs. It will be very difficult to persuade him to give up his work and do something else. But we will read about such a person in our reading today.

We read about Elisha who was called to leave his plough and to follow the prophet. His heart was with his fields, with his plough and with his oxen. Will he be able to leave them to follow the new call?

We read from the first book of Kings, chapter nineteen.
*
The Lord said the Elijah: 'Go, you are to anoint Elisha son of Shaphat, of Abel Meholah, as prophet to succeed you.'

Leaving there, Elijah came on Elisha son of Shaphat as he was ploughing behind twelve yoke of oxen, he himself being with the twelfth. Elijah passed near to him and threw his cloak over him. Elisha left his oxen and ran after Elijah. 'Let me kiss my father and mother, then I will follow you' he said. Elijah answered, 'Go, go back; for have I done anything to you?' Elisha turned away, took the pair of oxen and slaughtered them. He used the plough for cooking the oxen, then gave to his men, who ate. He then rose, and followed Elijah and became his servant.

This is the word of the Lord.   *1 Kings 19:16. 19-21*

Responsorial Psalm

℞   **O Lord, it is you who are my portion.**

1   Preserve me, God, I take refuge in you.
    I say to the Lord: 'You are my God.'
    O Lord, it is you who are my portion and cup;
    it is you yourself who are my prize. ℟

2   I will bless the Lord who gives me counsel,
    who even at night directs my heart.
    I keep the Lord ever in my sight:
    since he is at my right hand, I shall stand firm. ℟

3   And so my heart rejoices, my soul is glad;
    even my body shall rest in safety.
    For you will not leave my soul among the dead,
    nor let your beloved know decay. ℟

4   You will show me the path of life,
    the fullness of joy in your presence,
    at your right hand happiness for ever. ℟

Ps 15:1-2. 5. 7-11. ℟ cf. v.5

SECOND READING

We read from the letter of St Paul to the Galatians, chapter five.
*

When Christ freed us, he meant us to remain free. Stand firm, therefore, and do not submit again to the yoke of slavery.

My brothers, you were called, as you know, to liberty; but be careful, or this liberty will provide an opening for self-indulgence. Serve one another, rather, in works of love, since the whole of the Law is summarised in a single command: Love your neighbour as yourself. If you go snapping at each other and tearing each other to pieces, you had better watch or you will destroy the whole community.

Let me put it like this: if you are guided by the Spirit you will be in no danger of yielding to self-indulgence, since self-indulgence is the opposite of the Spirit, the Spirit is totally against such a thing, and it is precisely because the two are so opposed that you do not always carry out your good intentions. If you are led by the Spirit, no law can touch you.

This is the word of the Lord. *Galatians 5:1. 13-18*

Gospel Acclamation
    Alleluia, alleluia!
    Speak, Lord, your servant is listening:

you have the message of eternal life.
Alleluia!   *1 Sam 3:9; Jn 6:68*

GOSPEL

We read from the holy Gospel according to Luke, chapter nine.
*
As the time drew near for him to be taken up to heaven, Jesus resolutely took the road for Jerusalem and sent messengers ahead of him. These set out, and they went into a Samaritan village to make preparations for him, but the people would not receive him because he was making for Jerusalem. Seeing this, the disciples James and John said, 'Lord, do you want us to call down fire from heaven to burn them up?' But he turned and rebuked them, and they went off to another village.

As they travelled along they met a man on the road who said to him, 'I will follow you wherever you go.' Jesus answered, 'Foxes have holes and the birds of the air have nests, but the Son of Man has nowhere to lay his head.'

Another to whom he said, 'Follow me,' replied, 'Let me go and bury my father first.' But he answered, 'Leave the dead to bury their dead; your duty is to go and spread the news of the kingdom of God.'

Another said, 'I will follow you, sir, but first let me go and say good-bye to my people at home.' Jesus said to him, 'Once the hand is laid on the plough, no one who looks back is fit for the kingdom of God.'

This is the Gospel of the Lord.   *Luke 9:51-62*

Fourteenth Sunday in Ordinary Time   C

Introduction to the Service

Our congregation this morning consists of very different kinds of people: young and old, women and men, workers and students... But there is something we all have in common: we are all Christians and we are all sent to bring the peace of God to others.

Today we read how the Lord sent out not only the twelve disciples but a further seventy-two. He sent them out to every village and every house, to bring people his peace.

Penitential Rite

We ask ourselves: have we always fulfilled his command? Have we really brought peace to others?   (*Silence*)

- Lord, you have sent us to bring your peace to others, but often we have brought discord instead.   (*Silence*)
  Lord, have mercy...

- We have received peace from you, but often we forgot that we should have handed on this peace to others.   (*Silence*)
  Christ, have mercy...

- Lord, sometimes we did intend to bring peace to others but we did not succeed.   (*Silence*)
  Lord, have mercy...

FIRST READING

When we expect a visitor who is not known to us, we ask ourselves: will he bring peace to our house, or sorrow?

Our reading speaks of somebody who expects a visitor. He is told 'rejoice' because your visitor brings peace: 'Behold, I send peace, flowing like a river' to you.

We, Christians, are sent to bring such a river of peace to others.

We read from the prophet Isaiah, chapter sixty-six.
*
Rejoice, Jerusalem,
be glad for her, all you who love her!
Rejoice, rejoice for her,
all you who mourned her!

That you may be suckled, filled,
from her consoling breast,
that you may savour with delight
her glorious breasts.

For thus says the Lord:
Now towards her I send flowing
peace, like a river,
and like a stream in spate
the glory of the nations.

At her breast will her nurslings be carried
and fondled in her lap.
Like a son comforted by his mother
will I comfort you.
And by Jerusalem you will be comforted.

At the sight your heart will rejoice,
and your bones flourish like the grass.

To his servants the Lord will reveal his hand.

This is the word of the Lord.   *Isaiah 66:10-14*

Responsorial Psalm

℟   **Cry out with joy to God all the earth.**

1   Cry out with joy to God all the earth,
    O sing to the glory of his name.
    O render him glorious praise.
    Say to God: 'How tremendous your deeds!   ℟

2   'Before you all the earth shall bow;
    shall sing to you, sing to your name!'
    Come and see the works of God,
    tremendous his deeds among men.   ℟

3   He turned the sea into dry land,
    they passed through the river dry-shod.
    Let our joy then be in him;
    he rules for ever by his might.   ℟

4   Come and hear, all who fear God.
    I will tell what he did for my soul.
    Blessed be God who did not reject my prayer
    nor withhold his love from me.   ℟   *Ps 65:1-7. 16. 20. ℟ v.1*

SECOND READING

We read from the letter of St Paul to the Galatians, chapter six.
*
The only thing I can boast about is the cross of our Lord Jesus
Christ, through whom the world is crucified to me, and I to the
world. It does not matter if a person is circumcised or not; what
matters is for him to become an altogether new creature. Peace
and mercy to all who follow this rule, who form the Israel of God.

I want no more trouble from anybody after this; the marks on
my body are those of Jesus. The grace of our Lord Jesus Christ be
with your spirit, my brothers. Amen.

This is the word of the Lord.   *Galatians 6:14-18*

Gospel Acclamation

Alleluia, alleluia!
I call you friends, says the Lord,
because I have made known to you

everything I have learnt from my Father.
Alleluia!

Jn 15:15

or

Alleluia, alleluia!
May the peace of Christ
reign in your hearts,
because it is for this that you were called together
as parts of one body.
Alleluia!

Col 3:15. 16

GOSPEL

We read from the holy Gospel according to Luke, chapter ten.
*
The Lord appointed seventy-two others and sent them out ahead of him, in pairs, to all the towns and places he himself was to visit. He said to them, 'The harvest is rich but the labourers are few, so ask the Lord of the harvest to send labourers to his harvest. Start off now, but remember, I am sending you out like lambs among wolves. Carry no purse, no haversack, no sandals. Salute no one on the road. Whatever house you go into, let your first words be, "Peace to this house!" And if a man of peace lives there, your peace will go and rest on him; if not, it will come back to you. Stay in the same house, taking what food and drink they have to offer, for the labourer deserves his wages; do not move from house to house. Whenever you go into a town where they make you welcome, eat what is set before you. Cure those in it who are sick, and say, "The kingdom of God is very near to you." But whenever you enter a town and they do not make you welcome, go out into its streets and say, "We wipe off the very dust of your town that clings to our feet, and leave it with you. Yet be sure of this: the kingdom of God is very near." I tell you, that on that day it will not go as hard with Sodom as with that town.'

The seventy-two came back rejoicing. 'Lord,' they said 'even the devils submit to us when we use your name.' He said to them, 'I watched Satan fall like lightning from heaven. Yes, I have given you power to tread underfoot serpents and scorpions and the whole strength of the enemy; nothing shall ever hurt you. Yet do not rejoice that the spirits submit to you; rejoice rather that your names are written in heaven.'

This is the Gospel of the Lord.

Luke 10:1-2. 17-20

*Shorter Form, verses 1-9, read between *.

Fifteenth Sunday in Ordinary Time   C

Introduction to the Service

Not one of us lives entirely alone. We live in a community with others, and we meet people wherever we go. Some of those whom we meet are in need, and we ask ourselves whether we should go out of our way to help them or whether we should pass them by. We ask ourselves: 'Is that person who is in trouble really my neighbour?' We know, of course, the answer which Jesus gave in the parable of the traveller from the foreign country of Samaria, who showed mercy although he was a stranger.

Penitential Rite

● We have gathered here this morning because we are Christians. We have been touched by Christ's word and we want to listen to Christ again today. We begin by asking ourselves: did we show mercy to those in need?   (*Silence*)

Let us confess that we have sinned.   **I confess**...

FIRST READING

When we hear the parable of the merciful Samaritan, we ask ourselves whether our Lord is not perhaps asking too much of us. Is his word not perhaps beyond what we are able to do?

A passage from the book of Deuteronomy gives us an answer.

We read from chapter thirty.
*
Moses said to the people: 'Obey the voice of the Lord your God, keeping those commandments and laws of his that are written in the Book of this Law, and you shall return to the Lord your God with all your heart and soul.

'For this Law that I enjoin on you today is not beyond your strength or beyond your reach. It is not in heaven, so that you need to wonder, "Who will go up to heaven for us and bring it down to us, so that we may hear it and keep it?" Nor is it beyond the seas, so that you need to wonder, "Who will cross the seas for us and bring it back to us, so that we may hear it and keep it?" No, the Word is very near to you, it is in your mouth and in your heart for your observance.'

This is the word of the Lord.   *Deuteronomy 30:10-14*

Responsorial Psalm
℟   **Seek the Lord, you who are poor,**
and your hearts will revive.

1   This is my prayer to you,
my prayer for your favour.
In your great love, answer me, O God,
with your help that never fails:
Lord, answer, for your love is kind;
in your compassion, turn towards me.   ℟

2   As for me in my poverty and pain
let your help, O God, lift me up.
I will praise God's name with a song;
I will glorify him with thanksgiving.   ℟

3   The poor when they see it will be glad
and God-seeking hearts will revive;
for the Lord listens to the needy
and does not spurn his servants in their chains.   ℟

4   For God will bring help to Zion
and rebuild the cities of Judah.
The sons of his servants shall inherit it;
those who love his name shall dwell there.   ℟

Ps 68:14. 17. 30-31. 33-34. 36-37. ℟ cf. v.33

Alternative Responsorial Psalm
℟   **The precepts of the Lord**
gladden the heart.

1   The law of the Lord is perfect,
it revives the soul.
The rule of the Lord is to be trusted,
it gives wisdom to the simple.   ℟

2   The precepts of the Lord are right,
they gladden the heart.
The command of the Lord is clear,
it gives light to the eyes.   ℟

3   The fear of the Lord is holy,
abiding for ever.
The decrees of the Lord are truth
and all of them just.   ℟

4   They are more to be desired than gold,
     than the purest of gold
     and sweeter are they than honey,
     than honey from the comb. ℟   *Ps 18:8-11. ℟ v.9*

SECOND READING

We read from the letter of St Paul to the Colossians, chapter one.
*
Christ Jesus is the image of the unseen God
and the first-born of all creation,
for in him were created
all things in heaven and on earth:
everything visible and everything invisible,
Thrones, Dominations, Sovereignties, Powers –
all things were created through him and for him.
Before anything was created, he existed,
and he holds all things in unity.
Now the Church is his body,
he is its head.
As he is the Beginning,
he was first to be born from the dead,
so that he should be first in every way;
because God wanted all perfection
to be found in him
and all things to be reconciled through him and for him,
everything in heaven and everything on earth,
when he made peace
by his death on the cross.

    This is the word of the Lord.   *Colossians 1:15-20*

Gospel Acclamation
    Alleluia, alleluia!
    The sheep that belong to me listen to my voice,
    says the Lord,
    I know them and they follow me.
    Alleluia!   *Jn 10:27*

or

    Alleluia, alleluia!
    Your words are spirit, Lord,
    and they are life:

you have the message of eternal life.
Alleluia!

cf. Jn 6:63. 68

GOSPEL

We read from the holy Gospel according to Luke, chapter ten.
*

There was a lawyer who, to disconcert Jesus, stood up and said to him, 'Master, what must I do to inherit eternal life?' He said to him, 'What is written in the law? What do you read there?' He replied, 'You must love the Lord your God with all your heart, with all your soul, with all your strength, and with all your mind, and your neighbour as yourself.' 'You have answered right,' said Jesus, 'do this and life is yours.'

But the man was anxious to justify himself and said to Jesus, 'And who is my neighbour?' Jesus replied, 'A man was once on his way down from Jerusalem to Jericho and fell into the hands of brigands; they took all he had, beat him and then made off, leaving him half dead. Now a priest happened to be travelling down the same road, but when he saw the man, he passed by on the other side. In the same way a Levite who came to the place saw him, and passed by on the other side. But a Samaritan traveller who came upon him was moved with compassion when he saw him. He went up and bandaged his wounds, pouring oil and wine on them. He then lifted him on to his own mount, carried him to the inn and looked after him. Next day, he took out two denarii and handed them to the innkeeper. "Look after him," he said "and on my way back I will make good any extra expense you have." Which of these three, do you think, proved himself a neighbour to the man who fell into the brigands' hands?' 'The one, who took pity on him' he replied. Jesus said to him, 'Go, and do the same yourself.'

This is the Gospel of the Lord.

Luke 10:25-37

Sixteenth Sunday in Ordinary Time   C

Introduction to the Service

How does one welcome a friend? We all know what to do. There are many ways of showing somebody that we welcome them as a friend. But what do we do if it is not just anybody at all who comes to us, but God himself? How does one welcome God?

We who are gathered here this morning, have actually gathered for this very purpose: to welcome God.

Penitential Rite

Immediately our thoughts will go back to our past week. Even during this week there were times when we should have met God: in our prayer and in our contacts with other people. Did we meet God in the right way?

● Lord, you visit us in our contacts with other people. Forgive us for the times when we did not recognise you when you came to us through a person who needed our help.   (*Silence*)
    Lord, have mercy...

● You always speak to us. Yet we sometimes fail to listen to you, especially when you want us to recognise the injustice we do.   (*Silence*)
    Christ, have mercy...

● Lord, you wish to speak to us in prayer. Forgive us for neglecting prayer.   (*Silence*)
    Lord, have mercy...

FIRST READING

When we open the Bible and look for stories where people met God, or occasions when they welcomed him, we find several such stories.
    We now read one of the oldest of these stories.

We read from the book of Genesis, chapter eighteen.
*
The Lord appeared to Abraham at the Oak of Mamre while he was sitting by the entrance of the tent during the hottest part of the day. He looked up, and there he saw three men standing near him. As soon as he saw them he ran from the entrance of the tent to meet them, and bowed to the ground. 'My Lord,' he said 'I beg you, if I find favour with you, kindly do not pass your servant by. A little water shall be brought; you shall wash your feet and lie down under the tree. Let me fetch a little bread and you shall refresh yourselves before going further. That is why you have come in your servant's direction.' They replied, 'Do as you say.'

Abraham hastened to the tent to find Sarah. 'Hurry,' he said 'knead three bushels of flour and make loaves.' Then running to the cattle Abraham took a fine and tender calf and gave it to the servant, who hurried to prepare it. Then taking cream, milk and the calf he had prepared, he laid all before them, and they ate while he remained standing near them under the tree.

'Where is your wife Sarah?' they asked him. 'She is in the tent' he replied. Then his guest said, 'I shall visit you again next year without fail and your wife will then have a son.'

This is the word of the Lord.   *Genesis 18:1-10*

Responsorial Psalm
  ℟   **The just will live in the presence of the Lord.**

1   Lord, who shall dwell on your holy mountain?
    He who walks without fault;
    he who acts with justice
    and speaks the truth from his heart;
    he who does not slander with his tongue.   ℟

2   He who does no wrong to his brother,
    who casts no slur on his neighbour,
    who holds the godless in disdain,
    but honours those who fear the Lord.   ℟

3   He who keeps his pledge, come what may;
    who takes no interest on a loan
    and accepts no bribes against the innocent.
    Such a man will stand firm for ever.   ℟   *Ps 14:2-5. ℟ v.1*

SECOND READING

We read from the letter of St Paul to the Colossians, chapter one.
*
It makes me happy to suffer for you, as I am suffering now, and in my body to do what I can to make up all that has still to be undergone by Christ for the sake of his body, the Church. I became the servant of the Church when God made me responsible for delivering God's message to you, the message which was a mystery hidden for generations and centuries and has now been revealed to his saints. It was God's purpose to reveal it to them and to show all the rich glory of this mystery to pagans. The mystery is Christ among you, your hope of glory: this is the Christ we proclaim, this is the wisdom in which we thoroughly train everyone and instruct everyone, to make them all perfect in Christ.

This is the word of the Lord.   *Colossians 1:24-28*

Gospel Acclamation
    Alleluia, alleluia!
    Open our heart, O Lord,

to accept the words of your Son.
Alleluia!   *cf. Acts 16:14*

or

Alleluia, alleluia!
Blessed are those who,
with a noble and generous heart,
take the word of God to themselves
and yield a harvest through their perseverance.
Alleluia!   *cf. Lk 8:15*

GOSPEL

We read from the holy Gospel according to Luke, chapter ten.

*
Jesus came to a village, and a woman named Martha welcomed
him into her house. She had a sister called Mary, who sat down at
the Lord's feet and listened to him speaking. Now Martha who
was distracted with all the serving said, 'Lord, do you not care
that my sister is leaving me to do the serving all by myself? Please
tell her to help me.' But the Lord answered: 'Martha, Martha,' he
said 'you worry and fret about so many things, and yet few are
needed, indeed only one. It is Mary who has chosen the better
part; it is not to be taken from her.'

This is the Gospel of the Lord.   *Luke 10:38-42*

Seventeenth Sunday in Ordinary Time   C

Introduction to the Service

We have come together on this Sunday, because we are God's
people. He knows us. We know him. He speaks to us and we speak
to him. And yet, we are like the apostles. We ask again and again:
Lord, teach us how to pray, teach us how to speak to you. We want
to learn more about the ways in which we can pray.

Penitential Rite

During the whole service we will be speaking to God, in our
singing and in our prayers. As we begin to do so, we look back on
the past week:

● Did we often speak with God?   (*Silence*)

● Were we honest when we talked with him?   (*Silence*)

Let us confess our failures.   **I confess**…

FIRST READING

We are still learning how to speak to God. For instance, is it right to bargain with God? With a good friend we do this, but is it right to do it with God?

Let us now read about the way in which Abraham spoke to God.

We read from the book of Genesis, chapter eighteen.

The Lord said, 'How great an outcry there is against Sodom and Gomorrah! How grievous is their sin! I propose to go down and see whether or not they have done all that is alleged in the outcry against them that has come up to me. I am determined to know.'

The men left there and went to Sodom while Abraham remained standing before the Lord. Approaching him he said, 'Are you really going to destroy the just man with the sinner? Perhaps there are fifty just men in the town. Will you really overwhelm them, will you not spare the place for the fifty just men in it? Do not think of doing such a thing: to kill the just man with the sinner, treating just and sinner alike! Do not think of it! Will the judge of the whole earth not administer justice?' The Lord replied, 'If at Sodom I find fifty just men in the town, I will spare the whole place because of them.'

Abraham replied, 'I am bold indeed to speak like this to my Lord, I who am dust and ashes. But perhaps the fifty just men lack five: will you destroy the whole city for five?' 'No,' he replied, 'I will not destroy it if I find forty-five just men there.' Again Abraham said to him, 'Perhaps there will only be forty there.' 'I will not do it' he replied 'for the sake of the forty.'

Abraham said, 'I trust my Lord will not be angry, but give me leave to speak: perhaps there will only be thirty there.' 'I will not do it' he replied 'if I find thirty there.' He said, 'I am bold indeed to speak like this, but perhaps there will only be twenty there.' 'I will not destroy it' he replied 'for the sake of the twenty.' He said, 'I trust my Lord will not be angry if I speak once more: perhaps there will only be ten.' 'I will not destroy it' he replied 'for the sake of the ten.'

This is the word of the Lord.   *Genesis 18:20-32*

Responsorial Psalm
℞   **On the day I called,**
    you answered me, O Lord.

1   I thank you, Lord, with all my heart,
    you have heard the words of my mouth.
    Before the angels I will bless you.
    I will adore before your holy temple.   ℞

2   I thank you for your faithfulness and love
    which excel all we ever knew of you.
    On the day I called, you answered;
    you increased the strength of my soul.   ℞

3   The Lord is high yet he looks on the lowly
    and the haughty he knows from afar.
    Though I walk in the midst of affliction
    you give me life and frustrate my foes.   ℞

4   You stretch out your hand and save me,
    your hand will do all things for me.
    Your love, O Lord, is eternal,
    discard not the work of your hands.   ℞

Ps 137:1-3. 6-8. ℞ v.3

SECOND READING

We read from the letter of St Paul to the Colossians, chapter two.
*
You have been buried with Christ, when you were baptised; and
by baptism, too, you have been raised up with him through your
belief in the power of God who raised him from the dead. You
were dead, because you were sinners and had not been circumcised: he has brought you to life with him, he has forgiven us all
our sins.

He has overridden the Law, and cancelled every record of the
debt that we had to pay; he has done away with it by nailing it to
the cross.

This is the word of the Lord.   *Colossians 2:12-14*

Gospel Acclamation
    Alleluia, alleluia!
    The Word was made flesh and lived among us;
    to all who did accept him
    he gave power to become children of God.
    Alleluia!   *Jn 1:14. 12*

or

Alleluia, alleluia!
The spirit you received is the spirit of sons,
and it makes us cry out, 'Abba, Father!'
Alleluia!   *Rom 8:15*

GOSPEL

We read from the holy Gospel according to Luke, chapter eleven.
*
Once Jesus was in a certain place praying, and when he had
finished, one of his disciples said, 'Lord, teach us to pray, just as
John taught his disciples.' He said to them, 'Say this when you
pray:

"Father, may your name be held holy,
your kingdom come;
give us each day our daily bread,
and forgive us our sins,
for we ourselves forgive each one who is in debt to us.
And do not put us to the test." '

He also said to them, 'Suppose one of you has a friend and
goes to him in the middle of the night to say, "My friend, lend me
three loaves because a friend of mine on his travels has just
arrived at my house and I have nothing to offer him"; and the
man answers from inside the house, "Do not bother me. The
door is bolted now, and my children and I are in bed; I cannot get
up to give it to you," I tell you, if the man does not get up and
give it him for friendship's sake, persistence will be enough to
make him get up and give his friend all he wants.

'So I say to you: Ask, and it will be given to you; search, and
you will find; knock, and the door will be opened to you. For the
one who asks always receives; the one who searches always
finds; the one who knocks will always have the door opened to
him. What father among you would hand his son a stone when
he asked for bread? Or hand him a snake instead of a fish? Or
hand him a scorpion if he asked for an egg? If you then, who are
evil, know how to give your children what is good, how much
more will the heavenly Father give the Holy Spirit to those who
ask him!'

This is the Gospel of the Lord.   *Luke 11:1-13*

Eighteenth Sunday in Ordinary Time C

Introduction to the Service

We have come together to praise God. Today we particularly want to praise God for the many things he allows us to use as our possessions: the fields and their fruit, the animals, the things our hands can make, the clothing we wear, our houses, our provisions, everything we have.

Penitential Rite

On this Sunday, however, we are also reminded of our mistakes concerning possessions. We are particularly reminded of our wrong desire to own more than we need.   (*Silence*)

● Lord, every day we use the things which you created for us, and yet we often forget that they are not completely our own, but are only lent to us.   (*Silence*)
  Lord, have mercy...

● Christ, forgive us for the many times when we wanted to own more than we needed.   (*Silence*)
  Christ, have mercy...

● Lord, sometimes our hearts were tied more to the things we possessed than to you.   (*Silence*)
  Lord, have mercy...

FIRST READING

The Bible uses a strong word to describe the attitude of somebody who thinks of nothing else but his possessions. The Bible calls this attitude 'vanity'.

The text which we will read now, was written more than two thousand years ago, and yet even at that time the believers realised how wrong it was to long only for possessions.

We read from the book of Ecclesiastes, chapters one and two.
*
Vanity of vanities, the Preacher says. Vanity of vanities. All is vanity!

For so it is that a man who has laboured wisely, skilfully and successfully must leave what is his own to someone who has not toiled for it at all. This, too, is vanity and great injustice; for what does he gain for all the toil and strain that he has undergone under the sun? What of all his laborious days, his cares of office, his restless nights? This, too, is vanity.

This is the word of the Lord. *Ecclesiastes 1:2; 2: 21-23*

Responsorial Psalm

℟ **O Lord, you have been our refuge
from one generation to the next.**

1 You turn men back into dust
and say: 'Go back, sons of men.'
To your eyes a thousand years
are like yesterday, come and gone,
no more than a watch in the night. ℟

2 You sweep men away like a dream,
like grass which springs up in the morning.
In the morning it springs up and flowers:
by evening it withers and fades. ℟

3 Make us know the shortness of our life
that we may gain wisdom of heart.
Lord, relent! Is your anger for ever?
Show pity to your servants. ℟

4 In the morning, fill us with your love;
we shall exult and rejoice all our days.
Let the favour of the Lord be upon us:
give success to the work of our hands. ℟

Ps 89:3-6. 12-14. 17. ℟ v. 1

Alternative Responsorial Psalm

℟ **O that today you would listen to his voice!
Harden not your hearts.**

1 Come, ring out our joy to the Lord;
hail the rock who saves us.
Let us come before him, giving thanks,
with songs let us hail the Lord. ℟

2 Come in; let us bow and bend low;
let us kneel before the God who made us
for he is our God and we
the people who belong to his pasture,
the flock that is led by his hand. ℟

3   O that today you would listen to his voice!
    'Harden not your hearts at Meribah,
    as on that day at Massah in the desert
    when your fathers put me to the test;
    when they tried me, though they saw my work.'   ℟

Ps 94:1-2. 6-9. ℟ vv. 7-8

SECOND READING

We read from the letter of St Paul to the Colossians, chapter three.
*
Since you have been brought back to true life with Christ, you
must look for the things that are in heaven, where Christ is,
sitting at God's right hand. Let your thoughts be on heavenly
things, not on the things that are on the earth, because you have
died, and now the life you have is hidden with Christ in God. But
when Christ is revealed – and he is your life – you too will be
revealed in all your glory with him.

That is why you must kill everything in you that belongs only
to earthly life: fornication, impurity, guilty passion, evil desires
and especially greed, which is the same thing as worshipping a
false god; and never tell each other lies. You have stripped off
your old behaviour with your old self, and you have put on a new
self which will progress towards true knowledge the more it is
renewed in the image of its creator; and in that image there is no
room for distinction between Greek and Jew, between the
circumcised or the uncircum cised, or between barbarian and
Scythian, slave and free man. There is only Christ: he is everything and he is in everything.

This is the word of the Lord.   *Colossians 3:1-5. 9-11*

Gospel Acclamation
    Alleluia, alleluia!
    Your word is truth, O Lord,
    consecrate us in the truth.
    Alleluia!   *cf. Jn 17:17*

or

    Alleluia, alleluia!
    How happy are the poor in spirit;
    theirs is the kingdom of heaven.
    Alleluia!   *Mt 5:3*

GOSPEL

We read from the holy Gospel according to Luke, chapter twelve.
✶
A man in the crowd said to Jesus, 'Master, tell my brother to give me a share of our inheritance.' 'My friend,' he replied 'who appointed me your judge, or the arbitrator of your claims?' Then he said to them, 'Watch, and be on your guard against avarice of any kind, for a man's life is not made secure by what he owns, even when he has more than he needs.'

Then he told them a parable: 'There was once a rich man who, having had a good harvest from his land, thought to himself, "What am I to do? I have not enough room to store my crops." Then he said, "This is what I will do: I will pull down my barns and build bigger ones, and store all my grain and my goods in them, and I will say to my soul: My soul, you have plenty of good things laid by for many years to come; take things easy, eat, drink, have a good time." But God said to him, "Fool! This very night the demand will be made for your soul; and this hoard of yours, whose will it be then?" So it is when a man stores up treasure for himself in place of making himself rich in the sight of God.'

This is the Gospel of the Lord. *Luke 12:13-21*

Nineteenth Sunday in Ordinary Time C

Introduction to the Service
Jesus called his group of disciples 'a little flock'. Let us look at our congregation, as we have gathered today for our Sunday service. Are we a large flock or a small one?
What really matters is not the number of the flock but the attitude we have. Jesus says: 'Do not be afraid, little flock, for it has pleased the Father to give you the kingdom.'

Penitential Rite
The words 'do not be afraid' make us think about the quality of our faith. Let us reflect:

● In times of danger, do we perhaps lack trust in God? (*Silence*)

● In times of danger, do we firmly believe that God will always do the best for us? (*Silence*)

Let us confess our lack of faith by saying: **I confess**…

FIRST READING

We are not the first to be called the little flock of God. The Israelites were also such a little flock, especially when they were oppressed in Egypt; when they had to hold their prayer meetings at night and in secret.

We read about them in the book of Wisdom, chapter eighteen.
*
That night had been foretold to our ancestors, so that,
once they saw what kind of oaths they had put their trust in
they would joyfully take courage.
This was the expectation of your people,
the saving of the virtuous and the ruin of their enemies;
for by the same act with which you took vengeance on our foes
you made us glorious by calling us to you.
The devout children of worthy men offered sacrifice in secret
and this divine pact they struck with one accord:
that the saints would share the same blessings and dangers
    alike;
and forthwith they had begun to chant the hymns of the fathers.

This is the word of the Lord.   *Wisdom 18:6-9*

Responsorial Psalm
℟   **Happy are the people the Lord has chosen as his own.**

1 Ring out your joy to the Lord, O you just;
    for praise is fitting for loyal hearts.
    They are happy, whose God is the Lord,
    the people he has chosen as his own.   ℟

2 The Lord looks on those who revere him,
    on those who hope in his love,
    to rescue their souls from death,
    to keep them alive in famine.   ℟

3 Our soul is waiting for the Lord.
    The Lord is our help and our shield.
    May your love be upon us, O Lord,
    as we place all our hope in you.   ℟
                    Ps 32:1. 12. 18-20. 22. ℟ v.12

SECOND READING

We read from the letter to the Hebrews, chapter eleven.
*
*Only faith can guarantee the blessings that we hope for, or prove the existence of the realities that at present remain unseen.

It was for faith that our ancestors were commended.

It was by faith that Abraham obeyed the call to set out for a country that was the inheritance given to him and his descendants, and that he set out without knowing where he was going. By faith he arrived, as a foreigner, in the Promised Land, and lived there as if in a strange country, with Isaac and Jacob, who were heirs with him of the same promise. They lived there in tents while he looked forward to a city founded, designed and built by God.

It was equally by faith that Sarah, in spite of being past the age, was made able to conceive, because she believed that he who had made the promise would be faithful to it. Because of this, there came from one man, and one who was already as good as dead himself, more descendants than could be counted, as many as the stars of heaven or the grains of sand on the seashore.*

All these died in faith, before receiving any of the things that had been promised, but they saw them in the far distance and welcomed them, recognising that they were only strangers and nomads on earth. People who use such terms about themselves make it quite plain that they are in search of their real homeland. They can hardly have meant the country they came from, since they had the opportunity to go back to it; but in fact they were longing for a better homeland, their heavenly homeland. That is why God is not ashamed to be called their God, since he has founded the city for them.

It was by faith that Abraham, when put to the test, offered up Isaac. He offered to sacrifice his only son even though the promises had been made to him and he had been told: It is through Isaac that your name will be carried on. He was confident that God had the power even to raise the dead; and so, figuratively speaking, he was given back Isaac from the dead.

This is the word of the Lord.   *Hebrews 11:1-2. 8-19*

*Shorter Form, verses 1-2, 8-12. Read between *.

Gospel Acclamation
  Alleluia, alleluia!
  Blessed are you, Father,
  Lord of heaven and earth,
  for revealing the mysteries of the kingdom
  to mere children.
  Alleluia!   *cf. Mt 11:25*

or

Alleluia, alleluia!
Stay awake and stand ready,
because you do not know the hour
when the Son of Man is coming.
Alleluia!   *Mt 24:42. 44*

GOSPEL

We read from the holy Gospel according to Luke, chapter twelve.

Jesus said to his disciples: 'There is no need to be afraid, little flock, for it has pleased your Father to give you the kingdom.

'Sell your possessions and give alms. Get yourselves purses that do not wear out, treasure that will not fail you, in heaven where no thief can reach it and no moth destroy it. For where your treasure is, there will your heart be also.

'See that you are dressed for action and have your lamps lit. Be like men waiting for their master to return from the wedding feast, ready to open the door as soon as he comes and knocks. Happy those servants whom the master finds awake when he comes. I tell you solemnly, he will put on an apron, sit them down at table and wait on them. It may be in the second watch he comes, or in the third, but happy those servants if he finds them ready. You may be quite sure of this, that if the householder had known at what hour the burglar would come, he would not have let anyone break through the wall of his house. You too must stand ready, because the Son of Man is coming at an hour you do not expect.

Peter said, 'Lord, do you mean this parable for us, or for everyone?' The Lord replied, 'What sort of steward, then, is faithful and wise enough for the master to place him over his household to give them their allowance of food at the proper time? Happy that servant if his master's arrival finds him at this employment. I tell you truly, he will place him over everything he owns. But as for the servant who says to himself, "My master is taking his time coming", and sets about beating the menservants and the maids, and eating and drinking and getting drunk, his master will come on a day he does not expect and at an hour he does not know. The master will cut him off and send him to the same fate as the unfaithful.

'The servant who knows what his master wants, but has not even started to carry out those wishes, will receive very many strokes of the lash. The one who did not know, but deserves to be beaten for what he has done, will receive fewer strokes. When a man has had a great deal given him, a great deal will be demanded of him; when a man has had a great deal given him on trust, even more will be expected of him.'

This is the Gospel of the Lord.   *Luke 12:32-48*

*Shorter Form, verses 35-40. Read between *.

Twentieth Sunday in Ordinary Time   C

Introduction to the Service

We left our homes this morning to come to church. For many of us this was easy, but for others it was not. It may even have caused quarrels. Your friends may have wanted you to stay with them while you wanted to go to church. Although God's call is for peace, it can cause friction and division.

Jesus foretold this, when he said: 'I have come to bring fire on earth.' Although Jesus' intention is peace, we have to expect that his message will cause opposition. Are we prepared for such opposition? (*Silence*)

Penitential Rite

● Lord, there were times when we should have said openly what our faith demands, but we were afraid of causing offence.
Lord, have mercy...

● There were times when we were more afraid of losing other friends than of losing you.
Christ, have mercy...

● Lord, there were times when we were confused and did not know what to do. We still lack a clear understanding of your plans.
Lord, have mercy...

FIRST READING

The prophet Jeremiah knew very well that it would cause uproar and opposition if he foretold the truth. He knew it, and yet he openly proclaimed the truth. In our reading we will hear how he had to suffer for this.

We read in the thirty-eighth chapter of the book of Jeremiah.

*

The king's leading men spoke to the king. 'Let Jeremiah be put to death: he is unquestionably disheartening the remaining soldiers in the city, and all the people too, by talking like this. The fellow does not have the welfare of this people at heart so much as its ruin.' 'He is in your hands as you know,' King Zedekiah answered 'for the king is powerless against you.' So they took Jeremiah and threw him into the well of Prince Malchiah in the Court of the Guard, letting him down with ropes. There was no water in the well, only mud, and into the mud Jeremiah sank.

Ebed-melech came out from the palace and spoke to the king. 'My lord king,' he said 'these men have done a wicked thing by treating the prophet Jeremiah like this: they have thrown him into the well where he will die.' At this the king gave Ebed-melech the Cushite the following order: 'Take three men with you from here and pull the prophet Jeremiah out of the well before he dies.'

This is the word of the Lord.   ·   *Jeremiah 38: 4-6. 8-10*

Responsorial Psalm
℞   **Lord, come to my aid!**

1   I waited, I waited for the Lord
    and he stooped down to me;
    he heard my cry.   ℞

2   He drew me from the deadly pit,
    from the miry clay.
    He set my feet upon a rock
    and made my footsteps firm.   ℞

3   He put a new song into my mouth,
    praise of our God.
    Many shall see and fear
    and shall trust in the Lord.   ℞

4   As for me, wretched and poor,
    the Lord thinks of me.
    You are my rescuer, my help,   ·
    O God, do not delay.   ℞   *Ps 39:2-4. 18. ℞ v.14*

SECOND READING

We read from the letter to the Hebrews, chapter twelve.
*

With so many witnesses in a great cloud on every side of us, we too, then, should throw off everything that hinders us, especially the sin that clings so easily, and keep running steadily in the race we have started. Let us not lose sight of Jesus, who leads us in our faith and brings it to perfection: for the sake of the joy which was still in the future, he endured the cross, disregarding the shamefulness of it, and from now on has taken his place at the right of God's throne. Think of the way he stood such opposition from sinners and then you will not give up for want of courage. In the fight against sin, you have not yet had to keep fighting to the point of death.

This is the word of the Lord. *Hebrews 12: 1-4*

Gospel Acclamation
Alleluia, alleluia!
Open our heart, O Lord,
to accept the words of your Son.
Alleluia! *cf. Acts 16:14*

or

Alleluia, alleluia!
The sheep that belong to me listen to my voice,
says the Lord,
I know them and they follow me.
Alleluia! *Jn 10:27*

GOSPEL

We read from the holy Gospel according to Luke, chapter twelve.
*

Jesus said to his disciples: 'I have come to bring fire to the earth, and how I wish it were blazing already! There is a baptism I must still receive, and how great is my distress till it is over!

'Do you suppose that I am here to bring peace on earth? No, I tell you, but rather division. For from now on a household of five will be divided: three against two and two against three; the father divided against the son, son against father, mother against daughter, daughter against mother, mother-in-law against daughter-in-law, daughter-in-law against mother-in-law.'

This is the Gospel of the Lord. *Luke 12:49-53*

Twenty-First Sunday in Ordinary Time   C

Introduction to the Service

As we gather for this service we are full of joy. We come together to praise God and to give him thanks.

Yet sometimes we have to read those passages of scripture which are not joyful, but which act as warnings to us. Today Christ warns us to choose the narrow path of truth, for otherwise he will say to us: 'I do not know you – away from me.'

Penitential Rite

● Is there anything in our lives which could cause the Lord to say these hard words to us: 'I do not know you – away from me'?   (*Silence*)

Let us ask for forgiveness for our sins: **I confess**...

FIRST READING

The Jews despised the pagan nations, saying that those nations did not know God. But God warns the Jews in our reading. God says that those pagan nations are in fact closer to him than the Jews, that he knows them and gathers them to him. The last of these nations will in fact be the first.

We read from Isaiah, chapter sixty-six.

*
The Lord says this: I am coming to gather the nations of every language. They shall come to witness my glory. I will give them a sign and send some of their survivors to the nations: to Tarshish, Put, Lud, Moshech, Rosh, Tubal, and Javan, to the distant islands that have never heard of me or seen my glory. They will proclaim my glory to the nations. As an offering to the Lord they will bring all your brothers, in horses, in chariots, in litters, on mules, on dromedaries, from all the nations to my holy mountain in Jerusalem, says the Lord, like Israelites bringing oblations in clean vessels to the Temple of the Lord. And of some of them I will make priests and Levites, says the Lord.

This is the word of the Lord.   *Isaiah 66:18-21*

Responsorial Psalm

℟   **Go out to the whole world;
proclaim the Good News.**

or

℟ **Alleluia!**

1 O praise the Lord, all you nations,
   acclaim him all you peoples! ℟

2 Strong is his love for us;
   he is faithful for ever. ℟   *Ps 116. ℟ Mk 16:15*

SECOND READING

We read from the letter to the Hebrews, chapter twelve.
*
Have you forgotten that encouraging text in which you are
addressed as sons? My son, when the Lord corrects you, do not
treat it lightly; but do not get discouraged when he reprimands
you. For the Lord trains the ones that he loves and he punishes
all those that he acknowledges as his sons. Suffering is part of
your training; God is treating you as his sons. Has there ever
been any son whose father did not train him? Of course, any
punishment is most painful at the time, and far from pleasant;
but later, in those on whom it has been used, it bears fruit in
peace and goodness. So hold up your limp arms and steady your
trembling knees and smooth out the path you tread; then the
injured limb will not be wrenched, it will grow strong again.

This is the word of the Lord.   *Hebrews 12: 5-7. 11-13*

Gospel Acclamation
   Alleluia, alleluia!
   If anyone loves me he will keep my word,
   and my Father will love him,
   and we shall come to him.
   Alleluia!   *Jn 14:23*

or

   Alleluia, alleluia!
   I am the Way, the Truth and the Life, says the Lord;
   no one can come to the Father except through me.
   Alleluia!   *Jn 14:6*

GOSPEL

We read from the holy Gospel according to Luke, chapter thirteen.
*
Through towns and villages Jesus went teaching, making his way
to Jerusalem. Someone said to him, 'Sir, will there be only a few

saved?' He said to them, 'Try your best to enter by the narrow door, because I tell you, many will try to enter and will not succeed.

'Once the master of the house has got up and locked the door, you may find yourself knocking on the door, saying, "Lord, open to us" but he will answer, "I do not know where you come from." Then you will find yourself saying, "We once ate and drank in your company; you taught in our streets" but he will reply, "I do not know where you come from. Away from me, all you wicked men!"

'Then there will be weeping and grinding of teeth, when you see Abraham and Isaac and Jacob and all the prophets in the kingdom of God, and yourselves turned outside. And men from east and west, from north and south, will come to take their places at the feast in the kingdom of God.

'Yes, there are those now last who will be first, and those now first who will be last.'

This is the Gospel of the Lord. *Luke 13:22-30*

Twenty-Second Sunday in Ordinary Time C

Introduction to the Service

When we come to church on Sunday, we dress well. We put on our best clothes. This is a good custom, but it is not important in the eyes of God. God does not look at our clothes. In fact God is not pleased if we try to appear higher or greater than others. On the contrary, he loves the humble.

Penitential Rite

In today's readings we will hear passages of the Bible which show how God prefers those who are humble. Are we truly humble? (*Silence*)

● Lord, we ask your forgiveness for the times when we despised others and thought too highly of ourselves.

Lord, have mercy...

● We often forgot how holy and great you are, our God, and how small we are before you.

Christ, have mercy...

• Lord, we are often overpowered by our desire to appear greater than we are.

    Lord, have mercy...

FIRST READING

Why should we be humble? Why should we not exalt ourselves even if we are important among people?

    Ben Sirach, a teacher of the Old Testament, tries to give us an answer.

We read from the third chapter of his book, Ecclesiasticus.
*

My son, be gentle in carrying out your business,
and you will be better loved than a lavish giver.
The greater you are, the more you should behave humbly,
and then you will find favour with the Lord;
for great though the power of the Lord is,
he accepts the homage of the humble.
There is no cure for the proud man's malady,
since an evil growth has taken root in him.
The heart of a sensible man will reflect on parables,
an attentive ear is the sage's dream.

    This is the word of the Lord.   *Ecclesiasticus 3:17-20. 28-29*

Responsorial Psalm
   ℟ **In your goodness, O God, you prepared a home for the poor.**

1   The just shall rejoice at the presence of God,
     they shall exult and dance for joy.
     O sing to the Lord, make music to his name;
     rejoice in the Lord, exult at his presence. ℟

2   Father of the orphan, defender of the widow,
     such is God in his holy place.
     God gives the lonely a home to live in;
     he leads the prisoners forth into freedom. ℟

3   You poured down, O God, a generous rain:
     when your people were starved you gave them new life.
     It was there that your people found a home,
     prepared in your goodness, O God, for the poor. ℟
                      Ps 67:4-7. 10-11. ℟ cf. v.11

SECOND READING

We read from the letter to the Hebrews, chapter twelve.
*
What you have come to is nothing known to the senses: not a blazing fire, or a gloom turning to total darkness, or a storm; or trumpeting thunder or the great voice speaking which made everyone that heard it beg that no more should be said to them. But what you have come to is Mount Zion and the city of the living God, the heavenly Jerusalem where the millions of angels have gathered for the festival, with the whole Church in which everyone is a 'first-born son' and a citizen of heaven. You have come to God himself, the supreme Judge, and been placed with spirits of the saints who have been made perfect; and to Jesus, the mediator who brings a new covenant.

This is the word of the Lord.   *Hebrews 12: 18-19. 22-24*

Gospel Acclamation
    Alleluia, alleluia!
    If anyone loves me he will keep my word,
    and my Father will love him,
    and we shall come to him.
    Alleluia!   *Jn 14:23*

or

    Alleluia, alleluia!
    Shoulder my yoke and learn from me,
    for I am gentle and humble in heart.
    Alleluia!   *Mt 11:29*

GOSPEL

We read from the holy Gospel according to Luke, chapter fourteen.
*
On a sabbath day Jesus had gone for a meal to the house of one of the leading Pharisees; and they watched him closely. He then told the guests a parable, because he had noticed how they picked the places of honour. He said this, 'When someone invites you to a wedding feast, do not take your seat in the place of honour. A more distinguished person than you may have been invited, and the person who invited you both may come and say, "Give up your place to this man." And then, to your embarrassment, you would have to go and take the lowest place. No; when you are a guest, make your way to the lowest place and sit there, so that, when your host comes, he may say, "My friend, move

up higher.'' In that way, everyone with you at the table will see you honoured. For everyone who exalts himself will be humbled, and the man who humbles himself will be exalted.'

Then he said to his host, 'When you give a lunch or a dinner, do not ask your friends, brothers, relations or rich neighbours, for fear they repay your courtesy by inviting you in return. No; when you have a party, invite the poor, the crippled, the lame, the blind; that they cannot pay you back means that you are fortunate, because repayment will be made to you when the virtuous rise again.'

This is the Gospel of the Lord. *Luke 14:1. 7-14*

Twenty-Third Sunday in Ordinary Time   C

Introduction to the Service

We who have gathered here today in this room, are called by the same name. We are called 'Christians'. The word means that we are followers of Christ. He is the Christ. We are the Christians.

Today we reflect on another similarity we have with Christ. It is a very important similarity: Christ carried his cross and we have to carry our cross. We read today the words of Christ: 'Anyone who does not carry his cross and come after me, cannot be my disciple.'

Penitential Rite

● Are we really carrying our cross and are we following Christ? (*Silence*)

● Or were there times when we were unwilling to carry any burden for the sake of our faith? (*Silence*)

We confess that we have failed and we ask for forgiveness: **I confess**...

FIRST READING

Why should we have to carry a cross in our lives? Why is there any suffering at all on this earth?

Such questions are beyond our understanding. We will therefore read about somebody who also found it difficult to understand God's ways.

We read from the book of Wisdom, chapter nine.
*
What man can know the intentions of God?
Who can divine the will of the Lord?
The reasonings of mortals are unsure
and our intentions unstable;
for a perishable body presses down the soul,
and this tent of clay weighs down the teeming mind.
It is hard enough for us to work out what is on earth,
laborious to know what lies within our reach;
who, then, can discover what is in the heavens?
As for your intention, who could have learnt it, had you not
    granted Wisdom
and sent your holy spirit from above?
Thus have the paths of those on earth been straightened
and men been taught what pleases you,
and saved, by Wisdom.

    This is the word of the Lord.   *Wisdom 9:13-18*

Responsorial Psalm
  ℟   **O Lord, you have been our refuge**
      from one generation to the next.

1   You turn men back into dust
    and say: 'Go back, sons of men.'
    To your eyes a thousand years
    are like yesterday, come and gone,
    no more than a watch in the night. ℟

2   You sweep men away like a dream,
    like grass which springs up in the morning.
    In the morning it springs up and flowers:
    by evening it withers and fades.   ℟

3   Make us know the shortness of our life
    that we may gain wisdom of heart.
    Lord, relent! Is your anger for ever?
    Show pity to your servants.   ℟

4   In the morning, fill us with your love;
    we shall exult and rejoice all our days.
    Let the favour of the Lord be upon us:
    give success to the work of our hands. ℟

                    Ps 89:3-6. 12-14. 17. ℟ v.1

SECOND READING

We read from the letter of St Paul to Philemon, chapter nine.
✶
This is Paul writing, an old man now and, what is more, still a prisoner of Christ Jesus. I am appealing to you for a child of mine, whose father I became while wearing these chains: I mean Onesimus. I am sending him back to you, and with him – I could say – a part of my own self. I should have liked to keep him with me; he could have been a substitute for you, to help me while I am in the chains that the Good News has brought me. However, I did not want to do anything without your consent; it would have been forcing your act of kindness, which should be spontaneous. I know you have been deprived of Onesimus for a time, but it was only so that you could have him back for ever, not as a slave any more, but something much better than a slave, a dear brother; especially dear to me, but how much more to you, as a blood-brother as well as a brother in the Lord. So if all that we have in common means anything to you, welcome him as you would me.

This is the word of the Lord.   *Philemon 9-10. 12-17*

Gospel Acclamation
    Alleluia, alleluia!
    I call you friends, says the Lord,
    because I have made known to you
    everything I have learnt from my Father.
    Alleluia!   *Jn 15:15*
or

    Alleluia, alleluia!
    Let your face shine on your servant,
    and teach me your decrees.
    Alleluia!   *Ps 118:135*

GOSPEL

We read from the holy Gospel according to Luke, chapter fourteen.
✶
Great crowds accompanied Jesus on his way and he turned and spoke to them. 'If any man comes to me without hating his father, mother, wife, children, brothers, sisters, yes and his own life too, he cannot be my disciple. Anyone who does not carry his cross and come after me cannot be my disciple.

    'And indeed, which of you here, intending to build a tower,

would not first sit down and work out the cost to see if he had enough to complete it? Otherwise, if he laid the foundation and then found himself unable to finish the work, the onlookers would all start making fun of him and saying, "Here is a man who started to build and was unable to finish." Or again, what king marching to war against another king would not first sit down and consider whether with ten thousand men he could stand up to the other who advanced against him with twenty thousand? If not, then while the other king was still a long way off, he would send envoys to sue for peace. So in the same way, none of you can be my disciple unless he gives up all his possessions.'

This is the Gospel of the Lord.   *Luke 14:25-33*

Twenty-Fourth Sunday in Ordinary Time   C

Introduction to the Service

We welcome all who have come here for holy communion, for this sacred meal. But let me begin with a question: is this a meal for good people or a meal for sinners?

We expect Jesus to sit down at table only with good people. But in today's Gospel we hear people accusing Jesus: 'This man welcomes sinners and eats with them.'

So, what is our communion today? Is it a meal for good people or a meal for sinners? We can perhaps reply: 'It is a meal for sinners who are trying to turn away from sin.'

Penitential Rite

Let us call on our merciful Lord.

● Lord, if you do not refuse to eat with sinners, we too must not refuse to accept others.

Lord, have mercy...

● You are one with the Father, the Father who welcomed the prodigal son. We, too, want to welcome those who have gone astray.

Christ, have mercy...

● Lord, you are always merciful even if we fail repeatedly. We will try to imitate your mercy.

    Lord, have mercy...

FIRST READING

The people of the Old Testament were afraid of God's anger when they did something wrong.

    In our reading we hear of such an occasion when the people of Israel became afraid of God. However, they also knew that in the end God would not give way to wrath and anger but would show mercy.

We read from the book of Exodus, chapter thirty-two.
*
The Lord spoke to Moses, 'Go down now, because your people whom you brought out of Egypt have apostasised. They have been quick to leave the way I marked out for them; they have made themselves a calf of molten metal and have worshipped it and offered it sacrifice. "Here is your God, Israel," they have cried "who brought you up from the land of Egypt!" I can see how headstrong these people are! Leave me, now, my wrath shall blaze out against them and devour them; of you, however, I will make a great nation.'

    But Moses pleaded with the Lord his God. 'Lord,' he said, 'why should your wrath blaze out against this people of yours whom you brought out of the land of Egypt with arm outstretched and mighty hand? Remember Abraham, Isaac and Jacob, your servants to whom by your own self you swore and made this promise: I will make your offspring as many as the stars of heaven, and all this land which I promised I will give to your descendants, and it shall be their heritage for ever.' So the Lord relented and did not bring on his people the disaster he had threatened.

    This is the word of the Lord.   *Exodus 32:7-11. 13-14*

Responsorial Psalm
    ℞   **I will leave this place and go to my father.**

1   Have mercy on me, God, in your kindness.
    In your compassion blot out my offence.
    O wash me more and more from my guilt
    and cleanse me from my sin.   ℞

2 A pure heart create for me, O God,
   put a steadfast spirit within me.
   Do not cast me away from your presence,
   nor deprive me of your holy spirit. ℟

3 O Lord, open my lips
   and my mouth shall declare your praise.
   My sacrifice is a contrite spirit;
   a humbled, contrite heart you will not spurn. ℟
                                    Ps 50:3-4. 12-13. 17. 19. ℟ Lk 15:18

SECOND READING

We read from the first letter of St Paul to Timothy, chapter one.
*
I thank Christ Jesus our Lord, who has given me strength, and
who judged me faithful enough to call me into his service even
though I used to be a blasphemer and did all I could to injure and
discredit the faith. Mercy, however, was shown me, because
until I became a believer I had been acting in ignorance; and the
grace of our Lord filled me with faith and with the love that is in
Christ Jesus. Here is a saying that you can rely on and nobody
should doubt: that Christ Jesus came into the world to save
sinners. I myself am the greatest of them; and if mercy has been
shown to me, it is because Jesus Christ meant to make me the
greatest evidence of his inexhaustible patience for all the other
people who would later have to trust in him to come to eternal
life. To the eternal King, the undying, invisible and only God, be
honour and glory for ever and ever. Amen.

This is the word of the Lord.   *1 Timothy 1:12-17*

Gospel Acclamation
   Alleluia, alleluia!
   May the Father of our Lord Jesus Christ
   enlighten the eyes of our mind,
   so that we can see what hope his call holds for us.
   Alleluia!   *cf. Eph 1:17. 18*

or

   Alleluia, alleluia!
   God in Christ was reconciling the world to himself,
   and he has entrusted to us the news that they are reconciled.
   Alleluia!   *2 Cor 5:19*

GOSPEL

We read from the holy Gospel according to Luke, chapter fifteen.

*The tax collectors and the sinners were all seeking the company of Jesus to hear what he had to say, and the Pharisees and the scribes complained. 'This man' they said 'welcomes sinners and eats with them.' So he spoke this parable to them:

'What man among you with a hundred sheep, losing one, would not leave the ninety-nine in the wilderness and go after the missing one till he found it? And when he found it, would he not joyfully take it on his shoulders and then, when he got home, call together his friends, and neighbours? "Rejoice with me," he would say "I have found my sheep that was lost." In the same way, I tell you, there will be more rejoicing in heaven over one repentant sinner than over ninety-nine virtuous men who have no need of repentance.

'Or again, what woman with ten drachmas would not, if she lost one, light a lamp and sweep out the house and search thoroughly till she found it? And then, when she had found it, call together her friends and neighbours? "Rejoice with me," she would say "I have found the drachma I lost." In the same way, I tell you, there is rejoicing among the angels of God over one repentant sinner.'*

He also said, 'A man had two sons. The younger said to his father, "Father, let me have the share of the estate that would come to me." So the father divided the property between them. A few days later, the younger son got together everything he had and left for a distant country where he squandered his money on a life of debauchery.

'When he had spent it all, that country experienced a severe famine, and now he began to feel the pinch, so he hired himself out to one of the local inhabitants who put him on his farm to feed the pigs. And he would willingly have filled his belly with the husks the pigs were eating but no one offered him anything. Then he came to his senses and said, "How many of my father's paid servants have more food than they want, and here am I dying of hunger! I will leave this place and go to my father and say: Father, I have sinned against heaven and against you; I no longer deserve to be called your son; treat me as one of your paid servants.' So he left the place and went back to his father.

'While he was still a long way off, his father saw him and was moved with pity. He ran to the boy, clasped him in his arms and kissed him tenderly. Then his son said, "Father, I have sinned against heaven and against you. I no longer deserve to be called your son." But the father said to his servants, "Quick! Bring out the best robe and put it on him; put a ring on his finger and sandals on his feet. Bring the calf we have been fattening, and kill it; we are going to have a feast, a celebration, because this son of mine was dead and has come back to life; he was lost and is found." And they began to celebrate.

'Now the elder son was out in the fields, and on his way back, as he drew near the house, he could hear music and dancing. Calling one of the servants he asked what it was all about. "Your brother has come" replied the servant "and your father has killed the calf we had fattened because he has got him back safe and sound." He was angry then and refused to go in, and his father came out to plead with him; but he answered his father, "Look, all these years I have slaved for you and never once disobeyed your orders, yet you never offered me so much as a kid for me to celebrate with my friends. But, for this son of yours, when he comes back after swallowing up your property – he and his women – you kill the calf we had been fattening."

'The father said, "My son, you are with me always and all I have is yours. But it was only right we should celebrate and rejoice, because your brother here was dead and has come to life; he was lost and is found."'

This is the Gospel of the Lord.   *Luke 15:1-32*

*Shorter Form, verses 1-10. Read between *.

Twenty-Fifth Sunday in Ordinary Time   C

Introduction to the Service

In the world today one can only live if one has money. As we stand here to begin our Sunday service, we look at ourselves and see that almost all we have is bought with money: the clothes we wear are bought with money, the building is built with money as are the books we use, the candles, the vestments. We even have a collection of money during our service.

This makes it all the more important for us to listen to Christ's warning to be careful how we deal with money. We cannot be the slave of both God and money.

Penitential Rite

● We reflect: how have we dealt with money? Has money become our master? Has it become our most valued possession? Have we used it only for ourselves, or to help others as well? (*Silence*)

We confess that we have sinned: **I confess**…

FIRST READING

What are those people like, who can be called 'slaves of money'? The prophet Amos describes them for us in our reading today.

We read from chapter eight of Amos' prophetic book.
*

Listen to this, you who trample on the needy
and try to suppress the poor people of the country,
you who say, 'When will New Moon be over
so that we can sell our corn,
and sabbath, so that we can market our wheat?
Then by lowering the bushel, raising the shekel,
by swindling and tampering with the scales,
we can buy up the poor for money,
and the needy for a pair of sandals,
and get a price even for the sweepings of the wheat.'
The Lord swears it by the pride of Jacob,
'Never will I forget a single thing you have done.'

This is the word of the Lord.   *Amos 8:4-7*

Responsorial Psalm
℞   **Praise the Lord, who raises the poor.**

or

℞   **Alleluia!**

1 Praise, O servants of the Lord,
   praise the name of the Lord!
   May the name of the Lord be blessed
   both now and for evermore!   ℞

2 High above all nations is the Lord,
   above the heavens his glory.
   Who is like the Lord, our God,
   who has risen on high to his throne

yet stoops from the heights to look down,
to look down upon heaven and earth?   ℞

3   From the dust he lifts up the lowly,
    from the dungheap he raises the poor
    to set him in the company of princes,
    yes, with the princes of his people.   ℞

Ps 112:1-2. 4-8. ℞ cf. vv.1. 7

SECOND READING

We read from the first letter of St Paul to Timothy, chapter two.
*

My advice is that, first of all, there should be prayers offered for
everyone – petitions, intercessions and thanksgiving – and
especially for kings and others in authority, so that we may be
able to live religious and reverent lives in peace and quiet. To do
this is right, and will please God our saviour: he wants everyone
to be saved and reach full knowledge of the truth. For there is
only one God, and there is only one mediator between God and
mankind, himself a man, Christ Jesus, who sacrificed himself as a
ransom for them all. He is the evidence of this, sent at the
appointed time, and I have been named a herald and apostle of it
and – I am telling the truth and no lie – a teacher of the faith and
the truth to the pagans.

In every place, then, I want the men to lift their hands up
reverently in prayer, with no anger or argument.

This is the word of the Lord.   *1 Timothy 2:1-8*

Gospel Acclamation
    Alleluia, alleluia!
    Open our heart, O Lord,
    to accept the words of your Son,
    Alleluia!   *cf. Acts 16:14*

or

    Alleluia, alleluia!
    Jesus Christ was rich,
    but he became poor for your sake,
    to make you rich out of his poverty.
    Alleluia!   *2 Cor 8:9*

GOSPEL

We read from the holy Gospel according to Luke, chapter sixteen.

Jesus said to his disciples, 'There was a rich man and he had a steward who was denounced to him for being wasteful with his property. He called for the man and said, "What is this I hear about you? Draw me up an account of your stewardship because you are not to be my steward any longer." Then the steward said to himself, "Now that my master is taking the stewardship from me, what am I to do? Dig? I am not strong enough. Go begging? I should be too ashamed. Ah, I know what I will do to make sure that when I am dismissed from office there will be some to welcome me into their homes."

'Then he called his master's debtors one by one. To the first he said, "How much do you owe my master?" "One hundred measures of oil" was the reply. The steward said, "Here, take your bond; sit down straight away and write fifty." To another he said, "And you, sir, how much do you owe?" "One hundred measures of wheat" was the reply. The steward said, "Here, take your bond and write eighty."

'The master praised the dishonest steward for his astuteness. For the children of this world are more astute in dealing with their own kind than are the children of light.

'And so I tell you this: use money, tainted as it is, to win you friends, and thus make sure that when it fails you, they will welcome you into the tents of eternity. *The man who can be trusted in little things can be trusted in great; the man who is dishonest in little things will be dishonest in great. If then you cannot be trusted with money, that tainted thing, who will trust you with genuine riches? And if you cannot be trusted with what is not yours, who will give you what is your very own?

'No servant can be the slave of two masters: he will either hate the first and love the second, or treat the first with respect and the second with scorn. You cannot be the slave both of God and of money.'

This is the Gospel of the Lord.* Luke 16: 1-13

*Shorter Form, verses 10-13. Read between *.

Twenty-Sixth Sunday in Ordinary Time   C

Introduction to the Service

It is very enjoyable to come together for a meal. Today we come with joy to this holy communion, because it is God's meal with us.

But although it is true that every meal should be something enjoyable, something beautiful, it is also true that even a meal can become something ugly. It can become ugly, if, for instance, there is no sharing, no love. We read today the shocking story of one such ugly meal – the meal of the rich man who ignored the poor Lazarus standing at his gate.

As we are about to approach the table of the Lord, to receive the food which comes from God, we promise God that we will not close our eyes to those in need. We also ask for forgiveness for our failure to share in the past.

Penitential Rite

● Lord, you have shared with us so generously. Forgive us our failure to share with others.   (*Silence*)
   Lord, have mercy...

● You bowed down low to lift us up from our need, but we sometimes refuse to bow down to uplift others.   (*Silence*)
   Christ, have mercy...

● Lord, you cannot look on idly when you see people in need, but we sometimes remain passive.   (*Silence*)
   Lord, have mercy...

FIRST READING

At the time of the prophet Amos there was a tremendous gap between the few rich people and the many very poor.

We read now how Amos warned the rich in the name of God.

Our reading is from Amos chapter six.
*
The almighty Lord says this:

Woe to those ensconced so snugly in Zion
and to those who feel so safe on the mountain of Samaria.
Lying on ivory beds
and sprawling on their divans,
they dine on lambs from the flock,
and stall-fattened veal;

they bawl to the sound of the harp,
they invent new instruments of music like David,
they drink wine by the bowlful,
and use the finest oil for anointing themselves,
but about the ruin of Joseph they do not care at all.
That is why they will be the first to be exiled;
the sprawlers' revelry is over.

   This is the word of the Lord.

                                 Amos 6:1. 4-7

Responsorial Psalm
   ℟   **My soul, give praise to the Lord.**

or

   ℟   **Alleluia!**

1   It is the Lord who keeps faith for ever,
    who is just to those who are oppressed.
    It is he who gives bread to the hungry,
    the Lord, who sets prisoners free. ℟

2   It is the Lord who gives sight to the blind,
    who raises up those who are bowed down.
    It is the Lord who loves the just,
    the Lord, who protects the stranger. ℟

3   He upholds the widow and orphan
    but thwarts the path of the wicked.
    The Lord will reign for ever,
    Zion's God, from age to age. ℟   *Ps 145:6-10. ℟ v.2*

SECOND READING

We read from the first letter of St Paul to Timothy, chapter six.
*

As a man dedicated to God, you must aim to be saintly and
religious, filled with faith and love, patient and gentle. Fight the
good fight of the faith and win for yourself the eternal life to
which you were called when you made your profession and
spoke up for the truth in front of many witnesses. Now, before
God the source of all life and before Jesus Christ, who spoke up
as a witness for the truth in front of Pontius Pilate, I put to you
the duty of doing all that you have been told, with no faults or
failures, until the Appearing of our Lord Jesus Christ,

   who at the due time will be revealed

by God, the blessed and only Ruler of all,
the King of kings and the Lord of lords,
who alone is immortal,
whose home is in inaccessible light,
whom no man has seen and no man is able to see:
to him be honour and everlasting power. Amen.

This is the word of the Lord.   *1 Timothy 6:11-16*

Gospel Acclamation
Alleluia, alleluia!
The sheep that belong to me listen to my voice,
says the Lord,
I know them and they follow me.
Alleluia!   *Jn 10:27*

or

Alleluia, alleluia!
Jesus Christ was rich,
but he became poor for your sake,
to make you rich out of his poverty.
Alleluia!   *2 Cor 8:9*

GOSPEL

We read from the holy Gospel according to Luke, chapter sixteen.
*
Jesus said to the Pharisees: 'There was a rich man who used to
dress in purple and fine linen and feast magnificently every day.
And at his gate there lay a poor man called Lazarus, covered with
sores, who longed to fill himself with the scraps that fell from the
rich man's table. Dogs even came and licked his sores. Now the
poor man died and was carried away by the angels to the bosom
of Abraham. The rich man also died and was buried.

'In his torment in Hades he looked up and saw Abraham a
long way off with Lazarus in his bosom. So he cried out, "Father
Abraham, pity me and send Lazarus to dip the tip of his finger in
water and cool my tongue, for I am in agony in these flames."
"My son," Abraham replied "remember that during your life
good things came your way, just as bad things came the way of
Lazarus. Now he is being comforted here while you are in agony.
But that is not all: between us and you a great gulf has been fixed,
to stop anyone, if he wanted to, crossing from our side to yours,
and to stop any crossing from your side to ours."

'The rich man replied, "Father, I beg you then to send Lazarus to my father's house, since I have five brothers, to give them warning so that they do not come to this place of torment too." "They have Moses and the prophets," said Abraham "let them listen to them." "Ah no, father Abraham," said the rich man "but if someone comes to them from the dead, they will repent." Then Abraham said to him, "If they will not listen either to Moses or to the prophets, they will not be convinced even if someone should rise from the dead." '

This is the Gospel of the Lord.   *Luke 16:19-31*

Twenty-Seventh Sunday in Ordinary Time   C

Introduction to the Service

What brought us together this morning is our faith. Each one of us has joined this community because of our faith in Jesus Christ.

But although we already have faith, there are still many questions in our minds regarding our faith. How should faith be visible in our daily lives? What does faith mean when we are in difficulties? How can we grow in faith?

During our service today we will reflect specifically on these questions about faith.

Penitential Rite

We begin by listening to the voice of our conscience:

● Did we fail to remain faithful during the past week?   (*Silence*)

● Did we turn a deaf ear to the demands of our faith?   (*Silence*)

● Did we truly trust in God?   (*Silence*)

We confess our failures and sins.   **I confess**…

FIRST READING

What does it mean for an oppressed person to have faith? To find an answer we will read a conversation between such an oppressed person and God.

The oppressed person complains to God: 'How long must I cry to you and you do not listen?' Does a person who has faith speak in this way? God replies to him and shows him what faith means.

We read from the prophet Habakkuk, chapters one and two.
*
How long, Lord, am I to cry for help
while you will not listen;
to cry 'Oppression!' in your ear
and you will not save?
Why do you set injustice before me,
why do you look on where there is tyranny?
Outrage and violence, this is all I see,
all is contention, and discord flourishes.
Then the Lord answered and said,

> 'Write the vision down,
> inscribe it on tablets
> to be easily read,
> since this vision is for its own time only:
> eager for its own fulfilment, it does not deceive;
> if it comes slowly, wait,
> for come it will, without fail.
> See how he flags, he whose soul is not at rights,
> but the upright man will live by his faithfulness.'

This is the word of the Lord.   *Habakkuk 1:2-3; 2:2-4*

Responsorial Psalm
℟   **O that today you would listen to his voice!
Harden not your hearts.**

1   Come, ring out our joy to the Lord;
hail the rock who saves us.
Let us come before him, giving thanks,
with songs let us hail the Lord.   ℟

2   Come in; let us bow and bend low;
let us kneel before the God who made us
for he is our God and we
the people who belong to his pasture,
the flock that is led by his hand.   ℟

3   O that today you would listen to his voice!
'Harden not your hearts as at Meribah,
as on that day at Massah in the desert
when your fathers put me to the test;
when they tried me, though they saw my work.'   ℟
                              Ps 94:1-2. 6-9. ℟ *v.8*

SECOND READING

We read from the second letter of St Paul to Timothy, chapter one.
*

I am reminding you to fan into a flame the gift that God gave you when I laid my hands on you. God's gift was not a spirit of timidity, but the Spirit of power, and love, and self-control. So you are never to be ashamed of witnessing to the Lord, or ashamed of me for being his prisoner; but with me, bear the hardships for the sake of the Good News, relying on the power of God.

Keep as your pattern the sound teaching you have heard from me, in the faith and love that are in Christ Jesus. You have been trusted to look after something precious; guard it with the help of the Holy Spirit who lives in us.

This is the word of the Lord. *2 Timothy 1:6-8. 13-14*

Gospel Acclamation
Alleluia, alleluia!
Speak, Lord, your servant is listening:
you have the message of eternal life.
Alleluia! *1 Sam 3:9; Jn 6:68*

or

Alleluia, alleluia!
The word of the Lord remains for ever:
What is this word?
It is the Good News that has been brought to you.
Alleluia! *1 Peter 1:25*

GOSPEL

We read from the holy Gospel according to Luke, chapter seventeen.
*

The apostles said to the Lord, 'Increase our faith.' The Lord replied, 'Were your faith the size of a mustard seed you could say to this mulberry tree, "Be uprooted and planted in the sea," and it would obey you.

'Which of you, with a servant ploughing or minding sheep, would say to him when he returned from the fields, "Come and have your meal immediately?" Would he not be more likely to say, "Get my supper laid; make yourself tidy and wait on me while I eat and drink. You can eat and drink yourself afterwards?" Must he be grateful to the servant for doing what he was told? So with you: when you have done all you have been told to do, say, "We are merely servants: we have done no more than our duty." '

This is the Gospel of the Lord. *Luke 17:5-10*

Twenty-Eighth Sunday in Ordinary Time   C

Introduction to the Service

When people give you a lot of help, what do you do? You don't just say a quick thank you, but instead you visit them and thank them properly, or perhaps you send them a little present. You try and show them as clearly as possible how grateful you are for their help.

It is for this reason that we have come together today. We want to thank God and to show him that we appreciate what he has done for us.

In our readings today, we will hear of people who went out of their way to show their gratitude. These readings will encourage us still more to offer up our thanks to God.

A good way of showing our gratitude to God is to ask his forgiveness for all those times when we were ungrateful to him.

Penitential Rite

Let us reflect in silence for a few moments on whether we have been ungrateful to people and to God during the past week. (*Silence*)

● Lord, we receive so many gifts from you every day that we become used to them and no longer thank you for them. Lord, have mercy...

● The gifts which we most easily overlook are actually the greatest ones: the spiritual gifts you give us.   (*Silence*) Christ, have mercy...

● Lord, we know that we should not only thank you in words, but also in our deeds. But often we have failed to do so.   (*Silence*) Lord, have mercy...

FIRST READING

In the story which we will now read, the grateful person is a pagan, an army commander in Syria. If pagans can be so grateful, how much more should we, Christians, be thankful.

We read from the second book of Kings, chapter five.
*
Naaman the leper went down and immersed himself seven times in the Jordan, as Elisha had told him to do. And his flesh became clean once more like the flesh of a little child.

Returning to Elisha with his whole escort, he went in and stood before him. 'Now I know' he said 'that there is no God in all the earth except in Israel. Now, please, accept a present from your servant.' But Elisha replied, 'As the Lord lives, whom I serve, I will accept nothing.' Naaman pressed him to accept, but he refused. Then Naaman said, 'Since your answer is "No," allow your servant to be given as much earth as two mules may carry, because your servant will no longer offer holocaust or sacrifice to any god except the Lord.'

This is the word of the Lord.   *2 Kings 5:14-17*

Responsorial Psalm
    ℟   **The Lord has shown his salvation to the nations.**

1   Sing a new song to the Lord
      for he has worked wonders.
      His right hand and his holy arm
      have brought salvation.   ℟

2   The Lord has made known his salvation;
      has shown his justice to the nations.
      He has remembered his truth and love
      for the house of Israel.   ℟

3   All the ends of the earth have seen
      the salvation of our God.
      Shout to the Lord all the earth,
      ring out your joy.   ℟   *Ps 97:1-4. ℟ cf. v.2*

SECOND READING

We read from the second letter of St Paul to Timothy, chapter two.
*
Remember the Good News that I carry, 'Jesus Christ risen from the dead, sprung from the race of David'; it is on account of this that I have my own hardships to bear, even to being chained like a criminal – but they cannot chain up God's news. So I bear it all for the sake of those who are chosen, so that in the end they may have the salvation that is in Christ Jesus and the eternal glory that comes with it.

Here is a saying that you can rely on:

If we have died with him, then we shall live with him.
If we hold firm, then we shall reign with him.
If we disown him, then he will disown us.
We may be unfaithful, but he is always faithful,
for he cannot disown his own self.

This is the word of the Lord.   *2 Timothy 2:8-13*

Gospel Acclamation
Alleluia, alleluia!
Your words are spirit, Lord,
and they are life:
you have the message of eternal life.
Alleluia!   *cf. Jn 6:63. 68*

or

Alleluia, alleluia!
For all things give thanks,
because this is what God expects you to do in Christ Jesus.
Alleluia!   *1 Thess 5:18*

GOSPEL

We read from the holy Gospel according to Luke, chapter seventeen.
*
On the way to Jerusalem Jesus travelled along the border
between Samaria and Galilee. As he entered one of the villages,
ten lepers came to meet him. They stood some way off and called
to him, 'Jesus! Master! Take pity on us.' When he saw them he
said 'Go and show yourselves to the priests.' Now as they were
going away they were cleansed. Finding himself cured, one of
them turned back praising God at the top of his voice and threw
himself at the feet of Jesus and thanked him. The man was a
Samaritan. This made Jesus say, 'Were not all ten made clean?
The other nine, where are they? It seems that no one has come
back to give praise to God, except this foreigner.' And he said to
the man, 'Stand up and go on your way. Your faith has saved
you.'

This is the Gospel of the Lord.   *Luke 17: 11-19*

Twenty-Ninth Sunday in Ordinary Time   C

Introduction to the Service

God's people are prayerful people. Our congregation today is a gathering of people who pray. The importance of prayer is revealed in our Gospel reading today, where we will hear the message: 'God will see justice done to his chosen ones who cry to him day and night, even when he delays to help them.' Are we among the chosen ones of God, who call on him day and night?

Penitential Rite

Let us reflect:

- During this week, were there long periods when we did not think of God?   (*Silence*)

- Were there times when we only prayed that justice would be done to us, but failed to pray that we, too, would do justice to others?   (*Silence*)

Let us confess that we have sinned.   **I confess**...

FIRST READING

When we look in the Bible for instances of God's people praying continuously, day and night, we find the example of Moses and Aaron.

We read of their prayer in the book of Exodus, chapter seventeen.
*
The Amalekites came and attacked Israel at Rephidim. Moses said to Joshua, 'Pick out men for yourself, and tomorrow morning march out to engage Amalek. I, meanwhile, will stand on the hilltop, the staff of God in my hand.' Joshua did as Moses told him and marched out to engage Amalek, while Moses and Aaron and Hur went up to the top of the hill. As long as Moses kept his arms raised, Israel had the advantage; when he let his arms fall, the advantage went to Amalek. But Moses' arms grew heavy, so they took a stone and put it under him and on this he sat, Aaron and Hur supporting his arms, one on one side, one on the other; and his arms remained firm till sunset. With the edge of the sword Joshua cut down Amalek and his people.

This is the word of the Lord.   *Exodus 17:8-13*

Responsorial Psalm
℞   **Our help is in the name of the Lord
who made heaven and earth.**

1   I lift up my eyes to the mountains:
from where shall come my help?
My help shall come from the Lord
who made heaven and earth.   ℞

2   May he never allow you to stumble!
Let him sleep not, your guard.
No, he sleeps not nor slumbers,
Israel's guard.   ℞

3   The Lord is your guard and your shade;
at your right side he stands.
By day the sun shall not smite you
nor the moon in the night.   ℞

4   The Lord will guard you from evil,
he will guard your soul.
The Lord will guard your going and coming
both now and for ever.   ℞   *Ps 120. ℞ cf. v.2*

SECOND READING

We read from the second letter of St Paul to Timothy, chapters three
and four.
*
You must keep to what you have been taught and know to be
true; remember who your teachers were, and how, ever since you
were a child, you have known the holy scriptures – from these
you can learn the wisdom that leads to salvation through faith in
Christ Jesus. All scripture is inspired by God and can profitably
be used for teaching, for refuting error, for guiding people's lives
and teaching them to be holy. This is how the man who is
dedicated to God becomes fully equipped and ready for any good
work.

Before God and before Christ Jesus who is to be judge of the
living and the dead, I put this duty to you, in the name of his
Appearing and of his kingdom: proclaim the message and,
welcome or unwelcome, insist on it. Refute falsehood, correct
error, call to obedience – but do all with patience and with the
intention of teaching.

This is the word of the Lord.   *2 Timothy 3:14—4:2*

Gospel Acclamation
Alleluia, alleluia!
May the Father of our Lord Jesus Christ
enlighten the eyes of our mind,
so that we can see what hope his call holds for us.
Alleluia! *cf. Eph 1:17. 18*

or

Alleluia, alleluia!
The word of God is something alive and active;
it can judge secret emotions and thoughts.
Alleluia! *Heb 4:12*

GOSPEL

We read from the holy Gospel according to Luke, chapter eighteen.
*

Jesus told his disciples a parable about the need to pray continually and never lose heart. 'There was a judge in a certain town' he said 'who had neither fear of God nor respect for man. In the same town there was a widow who kept on coming to him and saying, "I want justice from you against my enemy!" For a long time he refused, but at last he said to himself, "Maybe I have neither fear of God nor respect for man, but since she keeps pestering me I must give this widow her just rights, or she will persist in coming and worry me to death."'

And the Lord said, 'You notice what the unjust judge has to say? Now will not God see justice done to his chosen who cry to him day and night even when he delays to help them? I promise you, he will see justice done to them, and done speedily. But when the Son of Man comes, will he find any faith on earth?'

This is the Gospel of the Lord. *Luke 18:1-8*

Thirtieth Sunday in Ordinary Time   C

Introduction to the Service
When we look at our congregation, we sometimes feel proud of it, sometimes sad about it. We feel proud of it when the church is full, when people are well dressed, when the singing is lively, when the whole service is beautiful.

God looks at us in a very different way. He is not deceived by outward appearances. He looks for different things. He looks at the inner spirit of our community, at the real, innermost aim we have when coming to him.

Penitential Rite

Let us reflect for a few moments on how God may, at this moment, see you and me. *(Silence)*

● Lord, nothing is hidden before you.
   Lord, have mercy...

● You can see clearly whether we only talk of love, or whether we truly have love.
   Christ, have mercy...

● Lord, we pray with the tax-collector in the temple: 'God be merciful to me, a sinner.'
   Lord, have mercy...

FIRST READING

If we select somebody to be a judge, we look for a person who is good. It should be someone who is not deceived by people's outward appearance, who does not judge the poor harshly and let the rich get away lightly. A good judge will rarely be deceived.

However, there is a judge who can never be deceived, who will always judge in the right way. It is the Lord our God.

This is the message of our reading from the book of Ecclesiasticus, chapter thirty-five.

*
The Lord is a judge
who is no respecter of personages.
He shows no respect of personages to the detriment of a poor man,
he listens to the plea of the injured party.
He does not ignore the orphan's supplication,
nor the widow's as she pours out her story.

The man who with his whole heart serves God will be accepted,
his petitions will carry to the clouds.
The humble man's prayer pierces the clouds,
until it arrives he is inconsolable,
nor will he desist until the Most High takes notice of him,
acquits the virtuous and delivers judgement.
And the Lord will not be slow,
nor will he be dilatory on their behalf.

This is the word of the Lord.   *Ecclesiasticus 35:12-14. 16-19*

Responsorial Psalm
  ℟ **This poor man called; the Lord heard him.**

1 I will bless the Lord at all times,
  his praise always on my lips;
  in the Lord my soul shall make its boast.
  The humble shall hear and be glad.   ℟

2 The Lord turns his face against the wicked
  to destroy their remembrance from the earth.
  The just call and the Lord hears
  and rescues them in all their distress.   ℟

3 The Lord is close to the broken-hearted;
  those whose spirit is crushed he will save.
  The Lord ransoms the souls of his servants.
  Those who hide in him shall not be condemned.   ℟

Ps 32:2-3. 17-19. 23. ℟ v.7

SECOND READING

We read from the second letter of St Paul to Timothy, chapter four.
*
My life is already being poured away as a libation, and the time
has come for me to be gone. I have fought the good fight to the
end; I have run the race to the finish; I have kept the faith; all
there is to come now is the crown of righteousness reserved for
me, which the Lord, the righteous judge, will give to me on that
Day; and not only to me but to all those who have longed for his
Appearing.

The first time I had to present my defence, there was not a
single witness to support me. Every one of them deserted me –
may they not be held accountable for it. But the Lord stood by me
and gave me power, so that through me the whole message
might be proclaimed for all the pagans to hear; and so I was
rescued from the lion's mouth. The Lord will rescue me from all
evil attempts on me, and bring me safely to his heavenly
kingdom. To him be glory for ever and ever. Amen.

This is the word of the Lord.   *2 Timothy 4:6-8. 16-18*

Gospel Acclamation
  Alleluia, alleluia!
  Blessed are you, Father,
  Lord of heaven and earth,

for revealing the mysteries of the kingdom
to mere children.
Alleluia!   *cf. Mt 11:25*

or

Alleluia, alleluia!
God in Christ was reconciling the world to himself,
and he has entrusted to us the news that they are reconciled.
Alleluia!   *2 Cor 5:19*

GOSPEL
We read from the holy Gospel according to Luke, chapter eighteen.
*
Jesus spoke the following parable to some people who prided
themselves on being virtuous and despised everyone else. 'Two
men went up to the Temple to pray, one a Pharisee, the other a
tax collector. The Pharisee stood there and said this prayer to
himself, "I thank you, God, that I am not grasping, unjust,
adulterous like the rest of mankind, and particularly that I am not
like this tax collector here. I fast twice a week; I pay tithes on all I
get." The tax collector stood some distance away, not daring even
to raise his eyes to heaven; but he beat his breast and said, "God,
be merciful to me, a sinner." This man, I tell you, went home
again at rights with God; the other did not. For everyone who
exalts himself will be humbled, but the man who humbles
himself will be exalted.'

This is the Gospel of the Lord.   *Luke 18:9-14*

Thirty-First Sunday in Ordinary Time C

Introduction to the Service
This morning, as we are gathered here, we are like the family of
Zacchaeus. Jesus passes the door of our community, and says:
'Today I want to be your guest. I want to stay with you, to sit down
with you at table, and to eat with you. I know, of course, that you
have quite a few faults, and I know what people say about you.
Yet, I want to help you and to be with you.'

Like Zacchaeus, we are pleased to hear that Jesus wants to stay
with us. We tell Jesus: 'Come to us, we welcome you with joy.' But
then we add, quickly, as Zacchaeus did: 'Lord, whatever we did
wrong, we shall put right again.'

Penitential Rite

●Let us be silent for a few moments so that each one of us can think: what can I put right in my life? (*Silence*)

Let us tell the Lord that we have sinned and that we want to convert. **I confess**...

FIRST READING

If there is someone in a group who continually offends the others, what will they do? They will expel that person, abandon him.

Why doesn't God do the same thing? Our reading today explains the many reasons why God does not throw anybody out, not even the worse type of Zacchaeus. Why not?

We read from the eleventh and twelfth chapters of the book of Wisdom.
*

In your sight, Lord, the whole world is like a grain of dust that
    tips the scales,
like a drop of morning dew falling on the ground.
Yet you are merciful to all, because you can do all things
and overlook men's sins so that they can repent.
Yes, you love all that exists, you hold nothing of what you have
    made in abhorrence,
for had you hated anything, you would not have formed it.
And how, had you not willed it, could a thing persist,
how be conserved if not called forth by you?
You spare all things because all things are yours, Lord, lover of
    life,
you whose imperishable spirit is in all.
Little by little, therefore, you correct those who offend,
you admonish and remind them of how they have sinned,
so that they may abstain from evil and trust in you, Lord.

This is the word of the Lord.   *Wisdom 11:22-12:2*

Responsorial Psalm
    ℟   **I will bless your name for ever,**
         O God my King.

1   I will give you glory, O God my King,
     I will bless your name for ever.
     I will bless you day after day
     and praise your name for ever.   ℟

2   The Lord is kind and full of compassion,
    slow to anger, abounding in love.
    How good is the Lord to all,
    compassionate to all his creatures.   ℟

3   All your creatures shall thank you, O Lord,
    and your friends shall repeat their blessing.
    They shall speak of the glory of your reign
    and declare your might, O God.   ℟

4   The Lord is faithful in all his words
    and loving in all his deeds.
    The Lord supports all who fall
    and raises all who are bowed down.   ℟

Ps 144:1-2. 8-11. 13-14. ℟ cf. v.1

SECOND READING

We read from the second letter of St Paul to the Thessalonians, chapters one and two.
*
We pray continually that our God will make you worthy of his call, and by his power fulfil all your desires for goodness and complete all that you have been doing through faith; because in this way the name of our Lord Jesus Christ will be glorified in you and you in him; by the grace of our God and the Lord Jesus Christ.

To turn now, brothers, to the coming of our Lord Jesus Christ and how we shall all be gathered round him: please do not get excited too soon or alarmed by any prediction or rumour or any letter claiming to come from us, implying that the Day of the Lord has already arrived.

This is the word of the Lord.   *2 Thessalonians 1:11-2:2*

Gospel Acclamation
    Alleluia, alleluia!
    Blessings on the King who comes,
    in the name of the Lord!
    Peace in heaven
    and glory in the highest heavens!
    Alleluia!   *Lk 19:38; 2:14*

or

    Alleluia, alleluia!
    God loved the world so much

that he gave his only Son,
so that everyone who believes in him
may have eternal life.
Alleluia!

Jn 3:16

GOSPEL

We read from the holy Gospel according to Luke, chapter nineteen.
★
Jesus entered Jericho and was going through the town when a man whose name was Zacchaeus made his appearance; he was one of the senior tax collectors and a wealthy man. He was anxious to see what kind of man Jesus was, but he was too short and could not see him for the crowd; so he ran ahead and climbed a sycamore tree to catch a glimpse of Jesus who was to pass that way. When Jesus reached the spot he looked up and spoke to him: 'Zacchaeus, come down. Hurry, because I must stay at your house today.' And he hurried down and welcomed him joyfully. They all complained when they saw what was happening. 'He has gone to stay at a sinner's house' they said. But Zacchaeus stood his ground and said to the Lord, 'Look, sir, I am going to give half my property to the poor, and if I have cheated anybody I will pay him back four times the amount.' And Jesus said to him, 'Today salvation has come to this house, because this man too is a son of Abraham; for the Son of Man has come to seek out and save what was lost.'

This is the Gospel of the Lord.

Luke 19:1-10

Thirty-Second Sunday in Ordinary Time C

Introduction to the Service

We always begin our service with a word of welcome to those who are present. But who, exactly, is present at this moment? We know that we are here, and we know that God the Father, the Son and the Holy Spirit are present.

But there are many others present, whom we easily forget: they are those who have died, who now live with God. Today's readings remind us that they are risen and live with God. They are, where God is. If God is in our midst then they too are standing in our midst.

You are here with us, you Saints of God. You are here with us, you our forefathers, who were found worthy to rise and live with God. We know that you are here with us, you, our deceased parents and relatives who live with God. You are risen. You live in God. You are present with us today. Your presence reminds us that we, too, are called to rise and live with God and with you.

Penitential Rite
Let us call on the Lord who is the first who rose from the dead:

- Lord, you alone make us worthy to join you in rising from death. (*Silence*)
  Lord, have mercy...

- It is you alone who can make us worthy to become united with our deceased forefathers and relatives. (*Silence*)
  Christ, have mercy...

- Lord, if we sin, we are separated from you. If we return to you we will rise and live with you. (*Silence*)
  Lord, have mercy...

FIRST READING
Hope in resurrection can be a powerful force in our lives. We now read how this hope of resurrection has enabled young people to face even torture and death.

We read from the second book of Maccabees, chapter seven.
*
There were seven brothers who were arrested with their mother. The king tried to force them to taste pig's flesh, which the Law forbids, by torturing them with whips and scourges. One of them, acting as spokesman for the others, said, 'What are you trying to find out from us? We are prepared to die rather than break the Law of our ancestors.'

With his last breath the second brother exclaimed, 'Inhuman fiend, you may discharge us from this present life, but the King of the world will raise us up, since it is for his laws that we die, to live again for ever.'

After him, they amused themselves with the third, who on being asked for his tongue promptly thrust it out and boldly held out his hands, with these honourable words, 'It was heaven that gave me these limbs; for the sake of his laws I disdain them; from him I hope to receive them again.' The king and his attendants were astounded at the young man's courage and his utter indifference to suffering.

When this one was dead they subjected the fourth to the same savage torture. When he neared his end he cried, 'Ours is the better choice, to meet death at men's hands, yet relying on God's promise that we shall be raised up by him; whereas for you there can be no resurrection, no new life.'

This is the word of the Lord.   *2 Maccabees 7:1-2. 9-14*

Responsorial Psalm
℞   **I shall be filled, when I awake,**
    with the sight of your glory, O Lord.

1   Lord, hear a cause that is just,
    pay heed to my cry.
    Turn your ear to my prayer:
    no deceit is on my lips.   ℞

2   I kept my feet firmly in your paths;
    there was no faltering in my steps.
    I am here and I call, you will hear me, O God.
    Turn your ear to me; hear my words.   ℞

3   Guard me as the apple of your eye.
    Hide me in the shadow of your wings.
    As for me, in my justice I shall see your face
    and be filled, when I awake, with the sight of your glory.   ℞
                                    Ps 16:1. 5-6. 8. 15. ℞ v.15

SECOND READING

We read from the second letter of St Paul to the Thessalonians, chapters two and three.
*
May our Lord Jesus Christ himself, and God our Father who has given us his love and, through his grace, such inexhaustible comfort and such sure hope, comfort you and strengthen you in everything good that you do or say.

Finally, brothers, pray for us; pray that the Lord's message may spread quickly, and be received with honour as it was among you; and pray that we may be preserved from the interference of bigoted and evil people, for faith is not given to everyone. But the Lord is faithful, and he will give you strength and guard you from the evil one, and we, in the Lord, have every confidence that you are doing and will go on doing all that we tell you. May the Lord turn your hearts towards the love of God and the fortitude of Christ.

This is the word of the Lord.   *Thessalonians 2:16-3:5*

Gospel Acclamation
Alleluia, alleluia!
Stay awake, praying at all times
for the strength to stand with confidence before the Son of
    Man.
Alleluia!   *Lk 21:36*

or

Alleluia, alleluia!
Jesus Christ is the First-born from the dead;
to him be glory and power for ever and ever.
Alleluia!   *Apoc 1:5. 6*

GOSPEL

We read from the holy Gospel according to Luke, chapter twenty.
*
*Some Sadducees – those who say that there is no resurrection –
approached Jesus and they put this question to him,* 'Master, we
have it from Moses in writing, that if a man's married brother dies
childless, the man must marry the widow to raise up children for
his brother. Well, then, there were seven brothers. The first,
having married a wife, died childless. The second and then the
third married the widow. And the same with all seven, they died
leaving no children. Finally the woman herself died. Now, at the
resurrection, to which of them will she be wife since she had been
married to all seven?'

*Jesus replied, 'The children of this world take wives and
husbands, but those who are judged worthy of a place in the
other world and in the resurrection from the dead do not marry
because they can no longer die, for they are the same as the
angels, and being children of the resurrection they are sons of
God. And Moses himself implies that the dead rise again, in the
passage about the bush where he calls the Lord the God of
Abraham, the God of Isaac and the God of Jacob. Now he is God,
not of the dead, but of the living; for to him all men are in fact
alive.'

This is the Gospel of the Lord.*   *Luke 20:27-38*

Shorter Form, verses 27, 34-38. Read between *.

Thirty-Third Sunday in Ordinary Time   C

Introduction to the Service

We are nearing the end of the Church year; next Sunday will be the last Sunday of the year, the feast of Christ the King. The Sunday after next will be the first Sunday of Advent.

In these last weeks of the Church's year, we reflect on the 'last days' of the world. As Christians we look forward to these final days and we prepare ourselves. Will we be worthy of the Lord's coming?

Penitential Rite

● Let us observe a short silence and ask for forgiveness for our sins.   (*Silence*)

We confess that we have sinned.   **I confess**...

FIRST READING

When the Bible uses the expression 'the day is coming, it usually means the final day of the world. Will that final day be a day of joy for us, or a day of sorrow?

We read from the third chapter of the prophet Malachi.

*

The day is coming now, burning like a furnace; and all the arrogant and the evil-doers will be like stubble. The day that is coming is going to burn them up, says the Lord of hosts, leaving them neither root nor stalk. But for you who fear my name, the sun of righteousness will shine out with healing in its rays.

This is the word of the Lord.   *Malachi 3:19-20*

Responsorial Psalm

℟   **The Lord comes to rule the peoples with fairness.**

1   Sing psalms to the Lord with the harp
    with the sound of music.
    With trumpets and the sound of the horn
    acclaim the King, the Lord.   ℟

2   Let the sea and all within it, thunder;
    the world, and all its peoples.
    Let the rivers clap their hands

and the hills ring out their joy
at the presence of the Lord.   ℟

3   For the Lord comes,
he comes to rule the earth.
He will rule the world with justice
and the peoples with fairness.   ℟   *Ps 97:5-9. ℟ cf. v.9*

SECOND READING

We read from the second letter of St Paul to the Thessalonians, chapter three.
*
You know how you are supposed to imitate us: now we were not idle when we were with you, nor did we ever have our meals at anyone's table without paying for them; no, we worked night and day, slaving and straining, so as not to be a burden on any of you. This was not because we had no right to be, but in order to make ourselves an example for you to follow.

We gave you a rule when we were with you: not to let anyone have any food if he refused to do any work. Now we hear that there are some of you who are living in idleness, doing no work themselves but interfering with everyone else's. In the Lord Jesus Christ, we order and call on people of this kind to go on quietly working and earning the food that they eat.

This is the word of the Lord.   *2 Thessalonians 3:7-12*

Gospel Acclamation
Alleluia, alleluia!
Stay awake, praying at all times
for the strength to stand with confidence
before the Son of Man.
Alleluia!   *Lk 21:36*

or

Alleluia, alleluia!
Stand erect, hold your heads high,
because your liberation is near at hand.
Alleluia!   *Lk 21:28*

GOSPEL

We read from the holy Gospel according to Luke, chapter twenty-one.
*
When some were talking about the Temple, remarking how it was adorned with fine stonework and votive offerings, Jesus

said, 'All these things you are staring at now – the time will come when not a single stone will be left on another: everything will be destroyed.' And they put to him this question: 'Master,' they said 'when will this happen, then, and what sign will there be that this is about to take place?'

'Take care not to be deceived,' he said 'because many will come using my name and saying, "I am he" and, "The time is near at hand." Refuse to join them. And when you hear of wars and revolutions, do not be frightened, for this is something that must happen but the end is not so soon.' Then he said to them, 'Nation will fight against nation, and kingdom against kingdom. There will be great earthquakes and plagues and famines here and there; there will be fearful sights and great signs from heaven.

'But before all this happens, men will seize you and persecute you; they will hand you over to the synagogues and to imprisonment, and bring you before kings and governors because of my name – and that will be your opportunity to bear witness. Keep this carefully in mind: you are not to prepare your defence, because I myself shall give you an eloquence and a wisdom that none of your opponents will be able to resist or contradict. You will be betrayed even by parents and brothers, relations and friends; and some of you will be put to death. You will be hated by all men on account of my name, but not a hair of your head will be lost. Your endurance will win you your lives.'

This is the Gospel of the Lord.   *Luke 21:5-19*

Thirty-Fourth Sunday in Ordinary Time   *Solemnity*

Our Lord Jesus Christ, Universal King   C

Introduction to the Service

A family or tribe may be able to trace its history back to one person, from whom all its members have their origin. In the beginning there was only that one person, then his offspring multiplied and became a huge family or tribe. All members of that family or tribe now venerate him as their founding member.

In a similar way Christ is our King, because we all come from him. We celebrate today the feast of Christ the King. It is the last Sunday of the Church year. We look back on this year and say: Christ is the origin of all that we experienced during this year, and indeed the origin of all that exists. Christ is the first-born of all creation. We give thanks to him today and promise our faithfulness to him as our king.

Penitential Rite
Let us reflect on how we have accepted Christ as our king.

● When we made use of all the gifts of this world, of all its beauty and its wonders, did we remember that Christ is the source and the king of all creation?   (*Silence*)

● When we found that our king did not force us to do what is good, but left us free to decide for ourselves how to act, what did we do? Did we follow Christ or did we ignore him and do our own will?   (*Silence*)

Let us confess that we have sinned.   **I confess**…

FIRST READING
We now read how David was anointed king. Once David was anointed, all had to accept him as king and follow him.
   Christ was not anointed by any human being. He was anointed king before all time and therefore all creation must accept and follow him.

We read from the second book of Samuel, chapter five.
*
All the tribes of Israel came to David at Hebron. 'Look' they said 'we are your own flesh and blood. In days past when Saul was our king, it was you who led Israel in all their exploits; and the Lord said to you, "You are the man who shall be shepherd of my people Israel, you shall be the leader of Israel." ' So all the elders of Israel came to the king at Hebron, and King David made a pact with them at Hebron in the presence of the Lord, and they anointed David king of Israel.

This is the word of the Lord.   *2 Samuel 5:1-3*

Responsorial Psalm
   ℟   **I rejoiced when I heard them say:**
        'Let us go to God's house.'

1   I rejoiced when I heard them say:
     'Let us go to God's house.'
     And now our feet are standing
     within your gates, O Jerusalem.   ℟

2 Jerusalem is built as a city
   strongly compact.
   It is there that the tribes go up,
   the tribes of the Lord. ℟

3 For Israel's law it is,
   there to praise the Lord's name.
   There were set the thrones of judgement
   of the house of David. ℟   *Ps 121:1-5. ℟ cf. v.2*

SECOND READING

We read from the letter of St Paul to the Colossians, chapter one.
*
We give thanks to the Father who has made it possible for you to
join the saints and with them to inherit the light.

Because that is what he has done: he has taken us out of the
power of darkness and created a place for us in the kingdom of
the Son that he loves, and in him, we gain our freedom, the
forgiveness of our sins.

He is the image of the unseen God
and the first-born of all creation,
for in him were created
all things in heaven and on earth:
everything visible and everything invisible,
Thrones, Dominations, Sovereignties, Powers –
all things were created through him and for him.
Before anything was created, he existed,
and he holds all things in unity.
Now the Church is his body,
he is its head.
As he is the Beginning,
he was first to be born from the dead,
so that he should be first in every way;
because God wanted all perfection
to be found in him
and all things to be reconciled through him and for him,
everything in heaven and everything on earth,
when he made peace
by his death on the cross.

This is the word of the Lord.   *Colossians 1: 12-20*

Gospel Acclamation
Alleluia, alleluia!
Blessings on him who comes in the name of the Lord!
Blessings on the coming kingdom of our father David!
Alleluia!   *Mk 11:9. 10*

GOSPEL
We read from the holy Gospel according to Luke, chapter twenty-three.
*
The people stayed there before the cross watching Jesus. As for
the leaders, they jeered at him. 'He saved others,' they said 'let
him save himself if he is the Christ of God, the Chosen One.' The
soldiers mocked him too, and when they approached to offer him
vinegar they said, 'If you are the king of the Jews, save yourself.'
Above him there was an inscription: 'This is the King of the Jews.'

One of the criminals hanging there abused him. 'Are you not
the Christ?' he said. 'Save yourself and us as well.' But the other
spoke up and rebuked him. 'Have you no fear of God at all?' he
said, 'You got the same sentence as he did, but in our case we
deserved it: we are paying for what we did. But this man has
done nothing wrong. Jesus,' he said 'remember me when you
come into your kingdom.' 'Indeed, I promise you,' he replied
'today you will be with me in paradise.'

This is the Gospel of the Lord.   *Luke 23:35-43*

FEASTS OF THE LORD AND SOLEMNITIES

2 February   *Feast*

Presentation of the Lord

Introduction to the service

We have assembled here today to celebrate the Lord's presentation in the Temple. We see Mary and Joseph entering the Temple, carrying Jesus in their arms and offering him to God the Father.

We do not need just to stand and watch from afar, for we are invited to take part in what is happening.

With Simeon and Anna we open our arms and hearts to receive the Lord as the light of our lives. With Simeon we praise the Lord as the light of all peoples on earth.

It is for this reason that we bless and light our candles today.

(Here follows the blessing of candles.)

FIRST READING

You may have been going to church for many years. Yet you may never have felt the truth of what you believe: that God really is close to you. Despite all your prayer, all your worship, God may have seemed to be far away.

Perhaps that was true, too, for Simeon and Anna, who spent their whole lives praying and waiting in the Temple. But then things changed as they may also change with us. Our reading puts it this way: 'And the Lord you are seeking will suddenly enter his temple.'

Let us listen to the words of the prophet Malachi, chapter three.

★
The Lord God says this: Look, I am going to send my messenger to prepare a way before me. And the Lord you are seeking will suddenly enter his Temple; and the angel of the covenant whom you are longing for, yes, he is coming, says the Lord of hosts. Who will be able to resist the day of his coming? Who will remain standing when he appears? For he is like the refiner's fire and the fullers' alkali. He will take his seat as refiner and purifier; he will purify the sons of Levi and refine them like gold and silver, and then they will make the offering to the Lord as it should be made. The offering of Judah and Jerusalem will then be welcomed by the Lord as in former days, as in the years of old.

This is the word of the Lord.   *Malachi 3:1-4*

637

Responsorial Psalm
 ℟ **Who is the king of glory?**
 It is the Lord.

1 O gates, lift up your heads;
 grow higher, ancient doors.
 Let him enter, the king of glory! ℟

2 Who is the king of glory?
 The Lord, the mighty, the valiant,
 the Lord, the valiant in war. ℟

3 O gates, lift high your heads;
 grow higher, ancient doors.
 Let him enter, the king of glory! ℟

4 Who is he, the king of glory?
 He, the Lord of armies,
 he is the king of glory. ℟   *Ps 23:7-10. ℟ v.8*

SECOND READING

When Mary and Joseph presented Jesus in the Temple they
fulfilled an old custom of Abraham's children. By keeping these
customs we see that Jesus wanted to be completely like his
brothers and sisters. God, who seemed to be so far away, has
become one of us.

We read from the letter to the Hebrews, chapter two.
*
Since all the children share the same blood and flesh, Jesus too
shared equally in it, so that by his death he could take away all
the power of the devil, who had power over death, and set free
all those who had been held in slavery all their lives by the fear of
death. For it was not the angels that he took to himself; he took to
himself descent from Abraham. It was essential that he should in
this way become completely like his brothers so that he could be a
compassionate and trustworthy high priest of God's religion, able
to atone for human sins. That is, because he has himself been
through temptation he is able to help others who are tempted.

This is the word of the Lord.   *Hebrews 2:14-18*

Gospel Acclamation
 Alleluia, alleluia!
 The light to enlighten the Gentiles
 and give glory to Israel, your people.
 Alleluia!   *Lk 2:32*

GOSPEL
We read from the holy Gospel according to Luke, chapter two.

*When the day came for them to be purified as laid down by the Law of Moses, the parents of Jesus took him up to Jerusalem to present him to the Lord – observing what stands written in the Law of the Lord: Every first-born male must be consecrated to the Lord – and also to offer in sacrifice, in accordance with what is said in the Law of the Lord, a pair of turtledoves or two young pigeons. Now in Jerusalem there was a man named Simeon. He was an upright and devout man; he looked forward to Israel's comforting and the Holy Spirit rested on him. It had been revealed to him by the Holy Spirit that he would not see death until he had set eyes on the Christ of the Lord. Prompted by the Spirit he came to the Temple; and when the parents brought in the child Jesus to do for him what the law required, he took him into his arms and blessed God; and he said:

'Now, Master, you can let your servant go in peace,
just as you promised;
because my eyes have seen the salvation
which you have prepared for all the nations to see,
a light to enlighten the pagans
and the glory of your people Israel.'*

As the child's father and mother stood there wondering at the things that were being said about him, Simeon blessed them and said to Mary his mother, 'You see this child: he is destined for the fall and for the rising of many in Israel, destined to be a sign that is rejected – and a sword will pierce your own soul too – so that the secret thoughts of many may be laid bare.'

There was a prophetess also, Anna the daughter of Phanuel, of the tribe of Asher. She was well on in years. Her days of girlhood over, she had been married for seven years before becoming a widow. She was now eighty-four years old and never left the Temple, serving God night and day with fasting and prayer. She came by just at that moment and began to praise God; and she spoke of the child to all who looked forward to the deliverance of Jerusalem.

When they had done everything the Law of the Lord required, they went back to Galilee, to their own town of Nazareth. Meanwhile the child grew to maturity, and he was filled with wisdom; and God's favour was with him.

This is the Gospel of the Lord.   *Luke 2:22-40*
*Shorter Form, Luke 2:22-32. Read between *.*

St Joseph Husband of the Blessed Virgin Mary

Introduction to the Service

Today we celebrate a very humble and simple man. His neighbours could not see anything extraordinary in his life. He was a carpenter. When he married, he left his home for some time but he returned to the village after a while, with his wife and a boy. This man was Joseph whose feast we celebrate today.

We celebrate Joseph as the loving husband of Mary and as the brave protector of his family. We know more about him than his neighbours did. We know him as a man who fully surrendered to God's will. We know him as a husband who must have had a very deep and unselfish love for his wife.

In the life of Joseph we see that obedience to God does not destroy human love but makes it develop and brings it to perfection.

Penitential Rite

Remembering the unselfish love of Joseph, we ask ourselves:

● Are we ready to obey God – even if we cannot fully understand his will?   (*Silence*)

● Are we ready to accept and to protect other people even if they do not belong to our family or nation?   (*Silence*)

●Do we allow God to purify and to perfect our human love?   (*Silence*)

We ask for forgiveness for all the occasions when we did not allow God to guide us.   **I confess** ...

FIRST READING

The prophet Nathan gave King David an important promise. He said: 'Your House will never die out and your power as king will be secure for ever.'

At the time when David received this promise he must have thought that it would come about through an unbroken line of kings. However, it came true in another way. It came true through the humble carpenter, Joseph.

We read from the second book of Samuel, chapter two.
*
The word of the Lord came to Nathan:
'Go and tell my servant David, "Thus the Lord speaks: When

your days are ended and you are laid to rest with your ancestors, I will preserve the offspring of your body after you and make his sovereignty secure. (It is he who shall build a house for my name, and I will make his royal throne secure for ever.) I will be a father to him and he a son to me. Your House and your sovereignty will always stand secure before me and your throne be established for ever." '

This is the word of the Lord.   *2 Samuel 7:4-5. 12-14. 16*

Responsorial Psalm
   ℟ **His dynasty shall last for ever.**

1   I will sing for ever of your love, O Lord;
    through all ages my mouth will proclaim your truth.
    Of this I am sure, that your love lasts for ever,
    that your truth is firmly established as the heavens. ℟

2   'I have made a covenant with my chosen one;
    I have sworn to David my servant:
    I will establish your dynasty for ever
    and set up your throne through all ages.' ℟

3   He will say to me: 'You are my father,
    my God, the rock who saves me.'
    I will keep my love for him always;
    for him my covenant shall endure. ℟ *Ps 88:2-5. 27. 29.* ℟ *v.37*

SECOND READING

We read from the letter of St Paul to the Romans, chapter four.
*
The promise of inheriting the world was not made to Abraham and his descendants on account of any law but on account of the righteousness which consists in faith. That is why what fulfils the promise depends on faith, so that it may be a free gift and be available to all of Abraham's descendants, not only those who belong to the Law but also those who belong to the faith of Abraham who is the Father of all of us. As scripture says: I have made you the ancestor of many nations – Abraham is our father in the eyes of God, in whom he put his faith, and who brings the dead to life and calls into being what does not exist.

Though it seemed Abraham's hope could not be fullfilled, he hoped and he believed, and through doing so he did become the father of many nations exactly as he had been promised: Your descendants will be as many as the stars. This is the faith that was 'considered as justifying him'.

This is the word of the Lord.   *Romans 4:13. 16-18. 22*

Gospel Acclamation
Glory and praise to you, O Christ.
They are happy who dwell in your house, O Lord,
for ever singing your praise.
Glory and praise to you, O Christ.   *Ps 83:5*

GOSPEL

We read from the holy Gospel according to Matthew, chapter one.
*
Jacob was the father of Joseph the husband of Mary; of her was born Jesus who is called Christ.

This is how Jesus Christ came to be born. His mother Mary was betrothed to Joseph; but before they came to live together she was found to be with child through the Holy Spirit. Her husband Joseph, being a man of honour and wanting to spare her publicity, decided to divorce her informally. He had made up his mind to do this when the angel of the Lord appeared to him in a dream and said, 'Joseph son of David, do not be afraid to take Mary home as your wife, because she has conceived what is in her by the Holy Spirit. She will give birth to a son and you must name him Jesus, because he is the one who is to save his people from their sins.' When Joseph woke up he did what the angel of the Lord had told him to do.

This is the Gospel of the Lord.   *Matthew 1:16. 18-21. 24*

Alternative Gospel, Matthew 1:16. 18-21. 24.

25 March   *Solemnity*

The Annunciation of the Lord

Introduction to the Service
Today we have come together to remember an event which happened very silently, unnoticed by other people. And yet it was an event which was as powerful as the creation of the world at the beginning of time.

We celebrate today the feast of the Annunciation. It is the day when the angel announced his message to Mary, the beautiful woman of Nazareth. It is the day Mary said her great *yes* to God's plan, when she said to the angel 'I am the handmaid of the Lord, let what you have said be done to me.'

In great silence and unnoticed by the world around, the Word became flesh in the womb of the Virgin Mary and dwelt among us.

Penitential Rite

Mary said *yes* to God and to his great plan. It is, however, our misery and sin that we often say *no* to God. Therefore let us ask for forgiveness:

● Lord God, loving Father, how often do you want to advise and guide us through the people whom you have sent to us. But we say no and reject your guidance.

Lord, have mercy...

● Lord Jesus, how often do you want to announce your good news to us by giving us your word in the Bible. We, however, do not take the time to listen to your message. We say no to you.

Christ, have mercy...

● Holy Spirit, who lives within us. How often do you want to inspire us in the depth of our hearts. We, however, say no to you and do not want to listen to your invitation.

Lord, have mercy...

FIRST READING

In our first reading we hear how God gave his people a great promise: a wonderful child will be born for them.

Today, on the feast of the Annunciation, this promise was fulfilled.

We read from the book of Isaiah, chapter seven.

*
The Lord spoke to Ahaz and said, 'Ask the Lord your God for a sign for yourself coming either from the depths of Sheol or from the heights above.' 'No,' Ahaz answered, 'I will not put the Lord to the test.'

Then Isaiah said:

Listen now, House of David:
are you not satisfied with trying the patience of men
without trying the patience of my God, too?
The Lord himself, therefore,
will give you a sign.
It is this: the maiden is with child
and will soon give birth to a son
whom she will call Emmanuel,
a name which means, 'God-is-with-us'.

This is the word of the Lord.   *Isaiah 7:10-14. 8:10*

Responsorial Psalm
℟ **Here I am, Lord!**
  I come to do your will.

1 You do not ask for sacrifice and offerings,
  but an open ear.
  You do not ask for holocaust and victim.
  Instead, here am I. ℟

2 In the scroll of the book it stands written
  that I should do your will.
  My God, I delight in your law
  in the depth of my heart. ℟

3 Your justice I have proclaimed
  in the great assembly.
  My lips I have not sealed;
  you know it, O Lord. ℟

4 I have not hidden your justice in my heart
  but declared your faithful help.
  I have not hidden your love and your truth
  from the great assembly. ℟   *Ps 39:7-11. ℟ vv.8. 9.*

SECOND READING

We read from the letter to the Hebrews, chapter ten.
*
Bulls' blood and goats' blood are useless for taking away sins,
and this is what Christ said, on coming into the world:

  You who wanted no sacrifice or oblation,
  prepared a body for me.
  You took no pleasure in holocausts or sacrifices for sin;
  then I said,
  just as I was commanded in the scroll of the book,
  'God, here I am! I am coming to obey your will.'

Notice that he says first: You did not want what the Law lays
down as the things to be offered, that is: the sacrifices, the
oblations, the holocausts and the sacrifices for sin, and you took
no pleasure in them; and then he says: Here I am! I am coming to
obey your will. He is abolishing the first sort to replace it with the
second. And this will was for us to be made holy by the offering
of his body made once and for all by Jesus Christ.

  This is the word of the Lord.   *Hebrews 10:4-10*

Gospel Acclamation
Praise to you, O Christ, king of eternal glory!
The Word was made flesh,
he lived among us,
and we saw his glory.
Praise to you, O Christ, king of eternal glory!   *Jn 1:14. 12*

GOSPEL

We read from the holy Gospel according to Luke, chapter one.

★
The angel Gabriel was sent by God to a town in Galilee called
Nazareth, to a virgin betrothed to a man named Joseph, of the
House of David; and the virgin's name was Mary. He went in and
said to her, 'Rejoice, so highly favoured! The Lord is with you.'
She was deeply disturbed by these words and asked herself what
this greeting could mean, but the angel said to her, 'Mary, do not
be afraid; you have won God's favour. Listen! You are to conceive
and bear a son, and you must name him Jesus. He will be great
and will be called Son of the Most High. The Lord God will give
him the throne of his ancestor David; he will rule over the House
of Jacob for ever and his reign will have no end.' Mary said to the
angel, 'But how can this come about, since I am a virgin?' 'The
Holy Spirit will come upon you,' the angel answered, 'and the
power of the Most High will cover you with its shadow. And so
the child will be holy and will be called Son of God. Know this
too: your kinswoman Elizabeth has, in her old age, herself
conceived a son, and she whom people called barren is now in
her sixth month, for nothing is impossible to God.' 'I am the
handmaid of the Lord,' said Mary, 'let what you have said be
done to me.' And the angel left her.

This is the Gospel of the Lord.   *Luke 1:26-38*

24 June   *Solemnity*

The Birth of John the Baptist

Introduction to the Service
When a child is born we anxiously ask the following question:
'What will this child turn out to be?' Of course, we are unable to
answer the question. We can only hope and see.

Today we celebrate the birth of John the Baptist. The same
question was asked by his family when he was born: 'What

will this child turn out to be?'

God alone knows the answer. This is the message of our celebration today: God knows the name of a child long before he or she is born. God calls every boy and girl by name – calling them to a certain task in life. God has a wonderful plan for each one of them, nobody is just thrown into life like a piece of wood thrown into floodwaters.

Jesus says that John is the greatest man ever borne by a woman. John is great because he has fulfilled in his life the plan which God had mapped out for him long before he was born.

Penitential Rite

Let us examine our conscience in the light of this message:

- Do we just look for jobs in life without asking God what his plans for us are? (*Silence*)

- When we plan the futures of our children – do we ask God what his plans for them are? (*Silence*)

- When a child is born into our family – do we commend this child into the loving hands of God? (*Silence*)

Let us ask for forgiveness for not allowing God to guide our lives. **I confess**…

FIRST READING

What was the task which John the Baptist had to fulfil in life? What plan did God have for him?

Our reading talks about this plan which God had for John the Baptist and for the whole people of Israel.

We read from the prophet Isaiah, chapter forty-nine.
*
Islands, listen to me,
pay attention, remotest peoples.
The Lord called me before I was born,
from my mother's womb he pronounced my name.

He made my mouth a sharp sword,
and hid me in the shadow of his hand.
He made me into a sharpened arrow,
and concealed me in his quiver.

He said to me, 'You are my servant (Israel)
in whom I shall be glorified';

while I was thinking 'I have toiled in vain,
I have exhausted myself for nothing';
and all the while my cause was with the Lord,
my reward with my God.
I was honoured in the eyes of the Lord,
my God was my strength.

And now the Lord has spoken,
he who formed me in the womb to be his servant,
to bring Jacob back to him,
to gather Israel to him:
'It is not enough for you to be my servant,
to restore the tribes of Jacob and bring back the survivors of
    Israel;
I will make you the light of the nations
so that my salvation may reach to the ends of the earth.'

    This is the word of the Lord.   *Isaiah 49:1-6*

Responsorial Psalm
    ℟   **I thank you for the wonder of my being.**

1   O Lord, you search me and you know me,
      you know my resting and my rising,
      you discern my purpose from afar.
      You mark when I walk or lie down,
      all my ways lie open to you.   ℟

2   For it was you who created my being,
      knit me together in my mother's womb.
      I thank you for the wonder of my being,
      for the wonders of all your creation.   ℟

3   Already you knew my soul,
      my body held no secret from you
      when I was being fashioned in secret
      and moulded in the depths of the earth.   ℟
                  Ps 138:1-3. 13-15. ℟ v.14

SECOND READING
We read from the Acts of the Apostles.
*
Paul said: 'God made David the king of our ancestors, of whom
he approved in these words, "I have selected David son of Jesse,
a man after my own heart, who will carry out my whole

purpose." To keep his promise, God has raised up for Israel one of David's descendants, Jesus, as Saviour, whose coming was heralded by John when he proclaimed a baptism of repentance for the whole people of Israel. Before John ended his career he said, "I am not the one you imagine me to be; that one is coming after me and I am not fit to undo his sandal."

'My brothers, sons of Abraham's race, and all you who fear God, this message of salvation is meant for you.'

This is the word of the Lord. *Acts 13:22-26*

Gospel Acclamation
Alleluia, alleluia!
As for you, little child, you shall be called
a prophet of God, the Most High.
You shall go ahead of the Lord
to prepare his ways before him.
Alleluia! *cf. Lk 1:76*

GOSPEL

We read from the holy Gospel according to Luke.
✢
The time came for Elizabeth to have her child, and she gave birth to a son; and when her neighbours and relations heard that the Lord had shown her so great a kindness, they shared her joy.

Now on the eighth day they came to circumcise the child; they were going to call him Zechariah after his father, but his mother spoke up. 'No,' she said 'he is to be called John.' They said to her, 'But no one in your family has that name', and made signs to his father to find out what he wanted him called. The father asked for a writing tablet and wrote, 'His name is John.' And they were all astonished. At that instant his power of speech returned and he spoke and praised God. All their neighbours were filled with awe and the whole affair was talked about throughout the hill country of Judaea. All those who heard of it treasured it in their hearts. 'What will this child turn out to be?' they wondered. And indeed the hand of the Lord was with him. The child grew up and his spirit matured. And he lived out in the wilderness until the day he appeared openly to Israel.

This is the Gospel of the Lord. *Luke 1:57-66. 80*

29 *June*   *Solemnity*

Saints Peter and Paul, Apostles

Introduction to the Service

Today we celebrate the feast of the Apostles Peter and Paul. It is a joyful feast for our Christian family because these two apostles are the great ancestors or forefathers of our Christian community.

There are still strong bonds which unite us with Peter and Paul. Whenever we proclaim the Apostles' Creed, we proclaim the faith which was handed down to us by the apostles and for which they died as martyrs.

Peter and Paul still explain to us their faith in Christ. The Gospel of St Mark, for instance, is regarded as the written report of the sermons which St Peter preached in Rome. Nearly every Sunday we listen to the inspiring and encouraging letters of St Paul.

There is also a very concrete, visible and living bond which unites us with St Peter. This living bond is the Bishop of Rome, the Pope. All who are in unity with the Bishop of Rome are united with Peter, whom the Lord called the 'rock' on which he wanted to build his Church.

Penitential Rite

Let us prepare ourselves for celebrating this feast of Peter and Paul.

- Lord, Peter and Paul died rather than abandon their faith in you. We confess that we are people of little faith.   (*Silence*)
  Lord have mercy…

- Christ, Peter and Paul never got tired of proclaiming the good news of your love. Forgive us for not helping others to find you.   (*Silence*)
  Christ have mercy…

- Lord, help us to strengthen our bond with the successor of Peter, our Pope.   (*Silence*)
  Lord have mercy…

FIRST READING

Peter and Paul are called the two princes of the apostles.

Our readings tell us that leadership in the Church does not mean splendour and glory or the ability to boss others. On the contrary, it means following the Lord in a special way, even in suffering.

We read from the Acts of the Apostles, chapter twelve.
*
King Herod started persecuting certain members of the Church.
He beheaded James the brother of John, and when he saw that
this pleased the Jews he decided to arrest Peter as well. This was
during the days of Unleavened Bread, and he put Peter in prison,
assigning four squads of four soldiers each to guard him in turns.
Herod meant to try Peter in public after the end of Passover
week. All the time Peter was under guard the Church prayed to
God for him unremittingly.

On the night before Herod was to try him, Peter was sleeping
between two soldiers, fastened with double chains, while guards
kept watch at the main entrance to the prison. Then suddenly the
angel of the Lord stood there, and the cell was filled with light.
He tapped Peter on the side and woke him. 'Get up!' he said
'Hurry!' – and the chains fell from his hands. The angel then said,
'Put on your belt and sandals.' After he had done this, the angel
next said, 'Wrap your cloak round you and follow me.' Peter
followed him, but had no idea that what the angel did was all
happening in reality; he thought he was seeing a vision. They
passed through two guard posts one after the other, and reached
the iron gate leading to the city. This opened of its own accord;
they went through it and had walked the whole length of one
street when suddenly the angel left him. It was only then that
Peter came to himself. 'Now I know it is all true,' he said. 'The
Lord really did send his angel and has saved me from Herod and
from all that the Jewish people were so certain would happen to
me.'

This is the word of the Lord.   *Acts 12:1-11*

Responsorial Psalm
   ℟ **From all my terrors the Lord set me free.**

or

   ℟ **The angel of the Lord rescues those who revere him.**

1 I will bless the Lord at all times,
    his praise always on my lips;
    in the Lord my soul shall make its boast.
    The humble shall hear and be glad. ℟

2 Glorify the Lord with me.
    Together let us praise his name.
    I sought the Lord and he answered me;
    from all my terrors he set me free. ℟

3   Look towards him and be radiant;
     let your faces not be abashed.
     This poor man called; the Lord heard him
     and rescued him from all his distress. ℟

4   The angel of the Lord is encamped
     around those who revere him, to rescue them.
     Taste and see that the Lord is good.
     He is happy who seeks refuge in him. ℟

                                          Ps 33:2-9. ℟ v.5. Alt. ℟ v.8

SECOND READING

We read from the second letter of St Paul to Timothy, chapter four.
*

My life is already being poured away as a libation, and the time
has come for me to be gone. I have fought the good fight to the
end; I have run the race to the finish; I have kept the faith; all
there is to come now is the crown of righteousness reserved for
me, which the Lord, the righteous judge, will give to me on that
Day; and not only to me but to all those who have longed for his
Appearing.

    The Lord stood by me and gave me power, so that through me
the whole message might be proclaimed for all the pagans to
hear; and so I was rescued from the lion's mouth. The Lord will
rescue me from all evil attempts on me, and bring me safely to his
heavenly kingdom. To him be glory for ever and ever. Amen

    This is the word of the Lord.   *2 Timothy 4:6-8. 17-18*

Gospel Acclamation
    Alleluia, alleluia!
    You are Peter and on this rock I will build my Church.
    And the gates of the underworld can never hold out against
      it.
    Alleluia!

GOSPEL

We read from the holy Gospel according to Matthew, chapter sixteen.
*

When Jesus came to the region of Caesarea Philippi he put this
question to his disciples, 'Who do people say the Son of Man is?'
And they said, 'Some say he is John the Baptist, some Elijah, and
others Jeremiah or one of the prophets.' 'But you,' he said 'who
do you say I am?' Then Simon Peter spoke up, 'You are the

Christ,' he said 'the Son of the living God.' Jesus replied, 'Simon son of Jonah, you are a happy man! Because it was not flesh and blood that revealed this to you but my Father in heaven. So I now say to you: You are Peter and on this rock I will build my Church. And the gates of the underworld can never hold out against it. I will give you the keys of the kingdom of heaven: whatever you bind on earth shall be considered bound in heaven; whatever you loose on earth shall be considered loosed in heaven.'

This is the Gospel of the Lord.   *Matthew 16:13-19*

6 August   *Feast*

The Transfiguration of the Lord

Introduction to the Service

There are people who love mountain-climbing. They do not mind difficulties and hardships on the way. Heat and sweat do not matter to them. On top of the mountain a new world appears before them. The horizon widens, new villages and valleys appear below them.

Today we are invited to accompany the Lord on his way to Mount Tabor because we are celebrating the feast of the Lord's transfiguration.

On top of Mount Tabor the Lord widens our narrow human horizons. We shall see things which we have never seen before. For a short moment we shall see the glory of the Lord which is still hidden from us. It is the glory of a new world into which God wants to lead us – if we listen to Jesus and follow him.

Penitential Rite

Let us prepare ourselves to celebrate this feast of the Lord's transfiguration on Mount Tabor.

● Are we ready to follow the Lord even if it seems to be difficult?   (*Silence*)

● Do greed and envy darken our eyes so that we cannot see the glory of the Lord?   (*Silence*)

● Did we ever experience the glory of the Lord in silent and humble prayer?   (*Silence*)

Let us ask the Lord to make us worthy of following him to Mount Tabor.   **I confess**…

FIRST READING

What the three apostles saw on Mount Tabor was also seen by the prophet Daniel when he gazed 'into the visions of the night'.

In this vision, the prophet sees the final victory of God over all the powers of evil on earth. The Son of Man receives all glory and kingship. It is this same glory which the apostles saw on Mount Tabor.

We read from the seventh chapter of the book of Daniel.
★
As I watched:
Thrones were set in place
and one of great age took his seat.
His robe was white as snow,
the hair of his head as pure as wool.
His throne was a blaze of flames,
its wheels were a burning fire.
A stream of fire poured out,
issuing from his presence.
A thousand thousand waited on him,
ten thousand times ten thousand stood before him.
A court was held and the books were opened.
I gazed into the visions of the night.
And I saw, coming on the clouds of heaven,
one like a son of man.
He came to the one of great age
and was led into his presence
On him was conferred sovereignty,
glory and kingship,
and men of all peoples, nations and languages became his
   servants.
His sovereignty is an eternal sovereignty
which shall never pass away,
nor will his empire ever be destroyed.

This is the word of the Lord.   *Daniel 7:9-10. 13-14*

Responsorial Psalm
 ℞   **The Lord is king,**
       most high above all the earth.

1   The Lord is king, let earth rejoice,
     let all the coastlands be glad.
     Cloud and darkness are his raiment;
     his throne, justice and right.   ℞

2   The mountains melt like wax
    before the Lord of all the earth.
    The skies proclaim his justice;
    all peoples see his glory. ℟

3   For you indeed are the Lord
    most high above all the earth
    exalted far above all spirits. ℟   *Ps 96:1-2. 5-6. 9. ℟ vv.1.9*

SECOND READING

We read from the second letter of St Peter, chapter one.

*

It was not any cleverly invented myths that we were repeating when we brought you the knowledge of the power and the coming of our Lord Jesus Christ; we had seen his majesty for ourselves. He was honoured and glorified by God the Father, when the Sublime Glory itself spoke to him and said, 'This is my Son, the Beloved; he enjoys my favour.' We heard this ourselves, spoken from heaven, when we were with him on the holy mountain.

So we have confirmation of what was said in prophecies; and you will be right to depend on prophecy and take it as a lamp for lighting a way through the dark until the dawn comes and the morning star rises in your minds.

This is the word of the Lord.   *2 Peter 1:16-19*

Gospel Acclamation
    Alleluia, alleluia!
    This is my Son, the Beloved,
    he enjoys my favour;
    listen to him.
    Alleluia!   *Mt 17:5*

GOSPEL

Year A

We read from the holy Gospel according to Matthew, chapter seventeen.

*

Jesus took with him Peter and James and his brother John and led them up a high mountain where they could be alone. There in their presence he was transfigured: his face shone like the sun and his clothes became as white as the light. Suddenly Moses and Elijah appeared to them; they were talking with him. Then Peter spoke to Jesus. 'Lord,' he said 'it is wonderful for us to be here; if you wish, I will make three tents here, one for you, one for Moses and one for Elijah.' He was still speaking when suddenly a bright cloud covered them with shadow, and from the cloud there came a voice which said, 'This is my Son; the Beloved; he enjoys my favour. Listen to him.' When they heard this, the disciples fell on their faces, overcome with fear. But Jesus came up and touched them. 'Stand up,' he said 'do not be afraid.' And when they raised their eyes they saw no one but only Jesus.

As they came down from the mountain Jesus gave them this order, 'Tell no one about the vision until the Son of Man has risen from the dead.'

This is the Gospel of the Lord. *Matthew 17:1-9*

Year B

We read from the holy Gospel according to Mark, chapter nine.
*

Jesus took with him Peter and James and John and led them up a high mountain where they could be alone by themselves. There in their presence he was transfigured: his clothes became dazzlingly white, whiter than any earthly bleacher could make them. Elijah appeared to them with Moses; and they were talking with Jesus. Then Peter spoke to Jesus: 'Rabbi,' he said 'it is wonderful for us to be here; so let us make three tents, one for you, one for Moses and one for Elijah.' He did not know what to say; they were so frightened. And a cloud came, covering them in shadow; and there came a voice from the cloud, 'This is my Son, the Beloved. Listen to him.' Then suddenly, when they looked round, they saw no one with them any more but only Jesus.

As they came down from the mountain he warned them to tell no one what they had seen, until after the Son of Man had risen from the dead. They observed the warning faithfully, though among themselves they discussed what 'rising from the dead' could mean.

This is the Gospel of the Lord. *Mark 9:2-10*

Year C

We read from the holy Gospel according to Luke, chapter nine.

*

Jesus took with him Peter and John and James and went up the mountain to pray. As he prayed, the aspect of his face was changed and his clothing became brilliant as lightning. Suddenly there were two men there talking to him; they were Moses and Elijah appearing in glory, and they were speaking of his passing which he was to accomplish in Jerusalem. Peter and his companions were heavy with sleep, but they kept awake and saw his glory and the two men standing with him. As these were leaving him, Peter said to Jesus, 'Master, it is wonderful for us to be here; so let us make three tents, one for you, one for Moses and one for Elijah.' – He did not know what he was saying. As he spoke, a cloud came and covered them with shadow; and when they went into the cloud the disciples were afraid. And a voice came from the cloud, saying, 'This is my Son, the Chosen One. Listen to him.' And after the voice had spoken, Jesus was found alone. The disciples kept silence and, at that time, told no one what they had seen.

This is the Gospel of the Lord. *Luke 9:28-36*

15 August *Solemnity*

The Assumption of the Blessed Virgin Mary

Introduction to the Service

Today we celebrate the great feast of the Assumption of Mary. We remember with joy that the mother of our Lord was taken up into heaven in body and soul.

We take great care of our bodies. We want to look good. We try to improve the beauty of our bodies by washing ourselves, by buying good and attractive clothes and by decorating ourselves – for example with rings and necklaces. This is good. God loves our body. Christ has not come just to redeem our soul. He died and is risen to redeem soul *and* body.

The Assumption of Mary into heaven shows us, strikingly, what God has planned for all of us. He will make our bodies perfect and beautiful. God wants us all to live with him in body and soul.

It is for this reason that we sing today, with Mary, her song of praise, the 'Magnificat': 'My soul proclaims the greatness of the Lord, for the Almighty has done great things for me.'

Penitential Rite

We ask ourselves:

- Do we accept our bodies as gifts from God and as temples of the Holy Spirit?   (*Silence*)

- Do we accept Mary as our example of a perfect and most beautiful woman and mother?   (*Silence*)

Let us ask for forgiveness for all that we have done wrong by using our body in the wrong way.   **I confess**...

FIRST READING

Our reading records a vision of the apostle John. He sees the great battle which is going on between Satan and the woman who has given birth to the saviour of the world.

We read from the book of the Apocalypse, chapters eleven and twelve.

*
The sanctuary of God in heaven opened, and the ark of the covenant could be seen inside it.

Now a great sign appeared in heaven: a woman, adorned with the sun, standing on the moon, and with the twelve stars on her head for a crown. She was pregnant, and in labour, crying aloud in the pangs of childbirth. Then a second sign appeared in the sky, a huge red dragon which had seven heads and ten horns, and each of the seven heads crowned with a coronet. Its tail dragged a third of the stars from the sky and dropped them to the earth, and the dragon stopped in front of the woman as she was having the child, so that he could eat it as soon as it was born from its mother. The woman brought a male child into the world, the son who was to rule all the nations with an iron sceptre, and the child was taken straight up to God and to his throne, while the woman escaped into the desert, where God had made a place of safety ready. Then I heard a voice shout from heaven, 'Victory and power and empire for ever have been won by our God, and all authority for his Christ.'

This is the word of the Lord.   *Apocalypse 11:19; 12:1-6. 10*

Responsorial Psalm
℟ **On your right stands the queen,
in garments of gold.**

1 The daughters of kings are among your loved ones.
On your right stands the queen in gold of Ophir.
Listen, O daughter, give ear to my words:
forget your own people and your father's house. ℟

2 So will the king desire your beauty:
He is your lord, pay homage to him.
They are escorted amid gladness and joy;
they pass within the palace of the king. ℟

Ps 44:10-12. 16. ℟ *v.10*

SECOND READING

We read from the first letter of St Paul to the Corinthians, chapter fifteen.
*
Christ has been raised from the dead, the first-fruits of all who have fallen asleep. Death came through one man and in the same way the resurrection of the dead has come through one man. Just as all men die in Adam, so all men will be brought to life in Christ; but all of them in their proper order: Christ as the first-fruits and then, after the coming of Christ, those who belong to him. After that will come the end, when he hands over the kingdom to God the Father, having done away with every sovereignty, authority and power. For he must be king until he has put all his enemies under his feet and the last of the enemies to be destroyed is death, for everything is to be put under his feet.

This is the word of the Lord. *1 Corinthians 15:20-26*

Gospel Acclamation
Alleluia, alleluia!
Mary has been taken up into heaven;
all the choirs of angels are rejoicing.
Alleluia!

GOSPEL

We read from the holy Gospel according to Luke, chapter one.
*
Mary set out and went as quickly as she could to a town in the hill

country of Judah. She went into Zechariah's house and greeted Elizabeth. Now as soon as Elizabeth heard Mary's greeting, the child leapt in her womb and Elizabeth was filled with the Holy Spirit. She gave a loud cry and said, 'Of all women you are the most blessed, and blessed is the fruit of your womb. Why should I be honoured with a visit from the mother of my Lord? From the moment your greeting reached my ears, the child in my womb leapt for joy. Yes, blessed is she who believed that the promise made her by the Lord would be fulfilled.'
And Mary said:

'My soul proclaims the greatness of the Lord
and my spirit exults in God my saviour;
because he has looked upon his lowly handmaid.
Yes, from this day forward all generations will call me blessed,
for the Almighty has done great things for me.
Holy is his name,
and his mercy reaches from age to age for those who fear him.
He has shown the power of his arm,
he has routed the proud of heart.
He has pulled down princes from their thrones and exalted the lowly.
The hungry he has filled with good things, the rich sent empty away.
He has come to the help of Israel his servant, mindful of his mercy
– according to the promise he made to our ancestors –
of his mercy to Abraham and to his descendants for ever.'

Mary stayed with Elizabeth about three months and then went back home.

>This is the Gospel of the Lord. *Luke 1:39-56*

14 September *Feast*

The Triumph of the Cross

Introduction to the Service

Today we have gathered together to celebrate the Holy Cross in a special way. We celebrate the feast of the 'Triumph of the Cross'.

For us, Christians, the cross is not a sign of death and disaster. It is the sign of victory and of triumph over death and evil.

We may all have experienced times of trouble, when our last

hope was the Lord on the cross.

A young priest, for instance, experienced the victory of the cross when he was called to a dying woman who had lost contact with the Church many, many years before. She could not speak any more and her relatives thought she was already dead. The priest placed a crucifix in her hands. To the surprise of all, the woman firmly grasped the crucifix with both hands and pressed it against her lips. The Lord on the cross became her hope and security in the hour of her death.

Penitential Rite
By receiving forgiveness for our sins we take part in the triumph of the cross here and now. Therefore, let us pray:

● Lord on the cross, you were forsaken and rejected. Forgive us and accept us into your kingdom.
   Lord have mercy...

● Lord on the cross, you were pierced with a sword, give us the love of your heart.
   Christ, have mercy...

● Lord on the cross, help us to change our lives and let us rise with you to new life.
   Lord have mercy...

FIRST READING
Our first reading sounds very strange. It talks about a bronze-serpent which Moses lifted up on a high pole. All who looked at it with a sorrowful heart were saved from the deadly snakes.

This bronze-serpent on the pole reminds us of Christ on the cross, of whom psalm twenty-two says: 'Here am I, now more worm than man, despised and scorned by everyone'. It is the Psalm which the Lord may have prayed while hanging on the cross.

Our reading is taken from the book of Numbers, chapter twenty-one.
*
On the way through the wilderness, the Israelites lost patience. They spoke against God and against Moses, 'Why did you bring us out of Egypt to die in this wilderness? For there is neither bread nor water here; we are sick of this unsatisfying food.'

At this God sent fiery serpents among the people; their bite brought death to many in Israel. The people came and said to Moses, 'We have sinned by speaking against the Lord and against you. Intercede for us with the Lord to save us from these serpents.' Moses interceded for the people, and the Lord answered him, 'Make a fiery serpent and put it on a standard. If anyone is bitten and looks at it, he shall live.' So Moses fashioned a bronze serpent which he put on a standard, and if anyone was bitten by a serpent, he looked at the bronze serpent and lived.

This is the word of the Lord.   *Numbers 21:4-9*

Responsorial Psalm
℟ **Never forget the deeds of the Lord.**

1   Give heed, my people, to my teaching;
     turn your ear to the words of my mouth.
     I will open my mouth in a parable
     and reveal hidden lessons of the past.   ℟

2   When he slew them then they would seek him,
     return and seek him in earnest.
     They would remember that God was their rock,
     God the Most High their redeemer.   ℟

3   But the words they spoke were mere flattery;
     they lied to him with their lips.
     For their hearts were not truly with him;
     they were not faithful to his covenant.   ℟

4   Yet he who is full of compassion
     forgave their sin and spared them.
     So often he held back his anger
     when he might have stirred up his rage.   ℟
                         Ps 77:1-2. 34-38. ℟ *v.7*

SECOND READING
We read from the letter of St Paul to the Philippians, chapter two.
*
The state of Jesus Christ was divine,
yet he did not cling
to his equality with God
but emptied himself
to assume the condition of a slave,
and became as men are;
and being as all men are,
he was humbler yet,
even to accepting death,
death on a cross.

But God raised him high
and gave him the name
which is above all other names
so that all beings
in the heavens, on earth and in the underworld,
should bend the knee at the name of Jesus
and that every tongue should acclaim
Jesus Christ as Lord,
to the glory of God the Father.

This is the word of the Lord. *Philippians 2:6-11*

Gospel Acclamation
Alleluia, alleluia!
We adore you, O Christ,
and we bless you;
because by your cross
you have redeemed the world.
Alleluia!

GOSPEL

We read from the holy Gospel according to John, chapter three.

Jesus said to Nicodemus:

'No one has gone up to heaven
except the one who came down from heaven,
the Son of Man who is in heaven;
and the Son of Man must be lifted up
as Moses lifted up the serpent in the desert,
so that everyone who believes may have eternal life in him.
Yes, God loved the world so much
that he gave his only Son,
so that everyone who believes in him may not be lost
but may have eternal life.
For God sent his Son into the world
not to condemn the world,
but so that through him the world might be saved.'

This is the Gospel of the Lord. *John 3:13-17*

All Saints

Introduction to the Service

Today we celebrate the Feast of All Saints. It is a great feast for our whole Christian community. We remember with joy the countless multitudes of men and women, boys and girls, who have gone before us to God.

Among these saints there may be those from our community whose names have long been forgotten; those who died poor and lonely; those tiny babies of whom nobody speaks much.

But today, we speak of them. God has done great things for them.

In our celebration today the Lord also tells us what kind of person a saint is and what people must do to become saints. There are the humble ones, the poor, the gentle, those who suffer, those who make peace, those with a pure heart, those who suffered because they stood up against evil and injustice.

Penitential Rite

Let us ask ourselves:

- If we were to die today – could God accept us as we are now? (*Silence*)

- Could God praise us and say: come, you were merciful to others, I shall be merciful to you? (*Silence*)

- Could God say to us: come into my joy because you were a peace-maker? (*Silence*)

Let us present ourselves to God and ask him to make right what we have done wrong. **I confess…**

FIRST READING

Our reading is an account of a vision of the apostle John. John sees God sending his angels into the world to seal the friends of God and put a mark on their foreheads.

When we hear this reading we can also think of ourselves. We, too, have received God's mark in baptism. We belong to him and have washed ourselves in the blood of the Lamb, who is Christ.

We read from the book of the Apocalypse, chapter seven.
*
I, John, saw another angel rising where the sun rises, carrying the

seal of the living God; he called in a powerful voice to the four angels whose duty was to devastate land and sea, 'Wait before you do any damage on land or at sea or to the trees, until we have put the seal on the foreheads of the servants of our God.' Then I heard how many were sealed: a hundred and forty-four thousand, out of all the tribes of Israel.

After that I saw a huge number, impossible to count, of people from every nation, race, tribe and language; they were standing in front of the throne and in front of the Lamb, dressed in white robes and holding palms in their hands. They shouted aloud, 'Victory to our God, who sits on the throne, and to the Lamb!' And all the angels who were standing in a circle round the throne, surrounding the elders and the four animals, prostrated themselves before the throne, and touched the ground with their foreheads, worshipping God with these words: 'Amen. Praise and glory and wisdom and thanksgiving and honour and power and strength to our God for ever and ever. Amen.'

One of the elders then spoke, and asked me, 'Do you know who these people are, dressed in white robes, and where they have come from?' I answered him, 'You can tell me, my Lord.' Then he said, 'These are the people who have been through the great persecution, and they have washed their robes white again in the blood of the Lamb.'

This is the word of the Lord. *Apocalypse 7:2-4. 9-14*

Responsorial Psalm
℞̂ **Such are the men who seek your face, O Lord.**

1 The Lord's is the earth and its fullness,
   the world and all its peoples.
   It is he who set it on the seas;
   on the waters he made it firm. ℞̂

2 Who shall climb the mountain of the Lord?
   Who shall stand in his holy place?
   The man with clean hands and pure heart,
   who desires not worthless things. ℞̂

3 He shall receive blessings from the Lord
   and reward from the God who saves him.
   Such are the men who seek him,
   seek the face of the God of Jacob. ℞̂   *Ps 23:1-6. ℞̂ cf. v.6*

SECOND READING

We read from the first letter of St John, chapter three.
*

Think of the love that the Father has lavished on us,
by letting us be called God's children;
and that is what we are.
Because the world refused to acknowledge him,
therefore it does not acknowledge us.
My dear people, we are already the children of God
but what we are to be in the future has not yet been revealed;
all we know is, that when it is revealed
we shall be like him
because we shall see him as he really is.
Surely everyone who entertains this hope
must purify himself, must try to be as pure as Christ.

This is the word of the Lord.   *1 John 3:1-3*

Gospel Acclamation
Alleluia, alleluia!
Come to me, all you who labour and are overburdened,
and I will give you rest, says the Lord.
Alleluia!   *Mt 11:28*

GOSPEL

We read from the holy Gospel according to Matthew, chapter five.
*

Seeing the crowds, Jesus went up the hill. There he sat down and
was joined by his disciples. Then he began to speak. This is what
he taught them:

'How happy are the poor in spirit;
theirs is the kingdom of heaven.
Happy the gentle:
they shall have the earth for their heritage.
Happy those who mourn:
they shall be comforted.
Happy those who hunger and thirst for what is right:
they shall be satisfied.
Happy the merciful:
they shall have mercy shown them.
Happy the pure in heart:
they shall see God.
Happy the peacemakers:

they shall be called sons of God
Happy those who are persecuted in the cause of right:
theirs is the kingdom of heaven.

'Happy are you when people abuse you and persecute you and speak all kinds of calumny against you on my account. Rejoice and be glad, for your reward will be great in heaven.'

This is the Gospel of the Lord.   *Matthew 5:1-12*

2 November

The Commemoration of all the Faithful Departed

Introduction to the Service

Death is a cruel enemy. Death inflicts on us deep wounds which never seem to heal. Our hearts rebel against the fact that people whom we loved and with whom we lived should just vanish and go away without returning.

There were bonds of love and friendship which united us with our dead brothers and sisters. Are all these bonds broken and destroyed by death? Is there no way left in which we can communicate with them?

Indeed, there is, on this day of All Souls we do much more than just remembering the dead. With them we are united around the Altar, together with them we stand under the cross of the Lord when we celebrate the Eucharist. It is the cross of Christ which bridges the dark valley of death and unites the living and the dead.

Penitential Rite

United with our dead relatives and friends we cry out to the Lord on the cross and ask for mercy and forgiveness.

● Lord, you have prepared for us a place in your father's house. Forgive us our sins and make us worthy of entering into the glory of your father.   (*Silence*)
   Lord have mercy…

● Jesus, you accepted the good thief who died beside you. We humbly ask, accept us too, and do not forget our dead brothers and sisters.   (*Silence*)
   Christ, have mercy…

● Lord forgive us as we forgive those who sinned against us, be they alive or dead.   (*Silence*)

Lord, have mercy…

FIRST READING

There is a bridge leading across the dark valley of death. But what is on the other side?

In our reading, the prophet Isaiah shares with us a vision of the other side. He sees a mountain which is higher than all other mountains.

On this mountain we shall meet our deceased friends. This is our Christian hope and our prayer today.

We read from the book of Isaiah, chapter twenty-five.
*

On this mountain,
the Lord of hosts will prepare for all peoples
a banquet of rich food.
On this mountain he will remove
the mourning veil covering all peoples,
and the shroud enwrapping all nations,
he will destroy Death for ever.
The Lord will wipe away
the tears from every cheek;
he will take away his people's shame
everywhere on earth,
for the Lord has said so.
That day, it will be said: See, this is our God
in whom we hoped for salvation;
the Lord is the one in whom we hoped.
We exult and we rejoice
that he has saved us.

This is the word of the Lord.   *Isaiah 25:6-9*

Responsorial Psalm
℟   **The Lord is my light and my help.**

or

℟   **I am sure I shall see the Lord's goodness
in the land of the living.**

1   The Lord is my light and my help;
whom shall I fear?
The Lord is the stronghold of my life;
before whom shall I shrink?   ℟

2   There is one thing I ask of the Lord,
    for this I long,
    to live in the house of the Lord,
    all the days of my life,
    to savour the sweetness of the Lord,
    to behold his temple.   ℟

3   O Lord, hear my voice when I call;
    have mercy and answer.
    It is your face, O Lord, that I seek;
    hide not your face.   ℟

4   I am sure I shall see the Lord's goodness
    in the land of the living.
    Hope in him, hold firm and take heart.
    Hope in the Lord!   ℟

                              Ps 26:1. 4. 7-9. 13-14.. ℟ v.1. Alt. ℟ v.13

SECOND READING

We read from the letter of St Paul to the Romans.
*
Hope is not deceptive, because the love of God has been poured
into our hearts by the Holy Spirit which has been given us. We
were still helpless when at his appointed moment Christ died for
sinful men. It is not easy to die even for a good man – though of
course for someone really worthy, a man might be prepared to
die – but what proves that God loves us is that Christ died for us
while we were still sinners. Having died to make us righteous, is
it likely that he would now fail to save us from God's anger?
When we were reconciled to God by the death of his Son, we
were still enemies; now that we have been reconciled, surely we
may count on being saved by the life of his Son? Not merely
because we have been reconciled but because we are filled with
joyful trust in God, through our Lord Jesus Christ, through
whom we have already gained our reconciliation.

     This is the word of the Lord.   *Romans 5:5-11*

Gospel Acclamation
    Alleluia, alleluia!
    It is my Father's will, says the Lord,
    that I should lose nothing of all that he has given to me,
    and that I should raise it up on the last day.
    Alleluia!   *Jn 6:39*

GOSPEL

Year A: Matthew 11:25-30, see Fourteenth Sunday of Year A, p.214 above.

Year B

We read from the holy Gospel according to Mark, chapters fifteen and sixteen.

*
When the sixth hour came there was darkness over the whole land until the ninth hour. And at the ninth hour Jesus cried out in a loud voice, 'Eloi, Eloi, lama sabachthani?' which means, 'My God, my God, why have you deserted me?' When some of those who stood by heard this, they said, 'Listen, he is calling on Elijah.' Someone ran and soaked a sponge in vinegar and, putting it on a reed, gave it him to drink saying, 'Wait and see if Elijah will come to take him down.' But Jesus gave a loud cry and breathed his last. And the veil of the Temple was torn in two from top to bottom. The centurion, who was standing in front of him, had seen how he had died and he said, 'In truth this man was a son of God.'

When the sabbath was over, Mary of Magdala, Mary the mother of James, and Salome, bought spices with which to go and anoint him. And very early in the morning on the first day of the week they went to the tomb, just as the sun was rising.

They had been saying to one another, 'Who will roll away the stone for us from the entrance to the tomb?' But when they looked they could see that the stone – which was very big – had already been rolled back. On entering the tomb they saw a young man in a white robe seated on the right-hand side, and they were struck with amazement. But he said to them, 'There is no need for alarm. You are looking for Jesus of Nazareth, who was crucified: he has risen, he is not here. See, here is the place where they laid him.'

This is the Gospel of the Lord.   *Mark 15:33-39; 16:1-6*

**Shorter Form, verses 33-39. Read between *.*

Year C: Luke 7:11-17, see Tenth Sunday of Year C, p.560 above.

8 December   *Solemnity*

The Immaculate Conception of the Blessed Virgin Mary

Introduction to the Service

If we expect an important visitor to arrive, we clean our home and decorate the room where he or she is going to stay. We prepare for such a visitor in the best way we can.

Today, on the feast of the Immaculate Conception of Mary, we ask the question: how did God prepare a place for his Son? Wasn't Mary the place where Jesus found his very first home on earth? How did God prepare and decorate the place where his beloved son was going to say?

This is our catholic faith: God had made Mary most beautiful already, in her mother's womb. She was conceived and born to her parents without original sin, without ever being touched by the evil one. In other words: from the moment Mary began to grow under the heart of her mother Anne, God decorated her with immaculate beauty. This is our joy today when we celebrate the feast of the Immaculate Conception of Mary. It was for Christ's sake that God protected Mary from original sin. It is for Christ's sake that we, too, are freed from the grip of the evil one.

Penitential Rite

Let us ask ourselves:

● Do we ever give joyful thanks that we, too, were freed from original sin in baptism?   (*Silence*)

● Do we ever give thanks to God because he has given us great interior beauty and splendour, through the Holy Spirit dwelling in us?   (*Silence*)

● Do we destroy God's gift within us by evil plans and evil words and actions?   (*Silence*)

Let us ask God to renew in us his beauty and splendour. **I confess**…

FIRST READING

We will now read a sad story, a story of failure and of punishment. But we will listen to this story with joy, because that failure never occurred in Mary's life. The evil one never overpowered her.

We read from the book of Genesis, chapter three.
*
After Adam had eaten of the tree, the Lord God called to him. 'Where are you?' he asked. 'I heard the sound of you in the

garden,' he replied. 'I was afraid because I was naked, so I hid.' 'Who told you that you were naked?' he asked. 'Have you been eating of the tree I forbade you to eat?' The man replied, 'It was the woman you put with me; she gave me the fruit, and I ate it.' Then the Lord God asked the woman, 'What is this you have done?' The woman replied, 'The serpent tempted me and I ate.'

Then the Lord God said to the serpent, 'Because you have done this,

'Be accursed beyond all cattle,
all wild beasts.
You shall crawl on your belly and eat dust
every day of your life.
I will make you enemies of each other:
you and the woman,
your offspring and her offspring.
It will crush your head
and you will strike its heel.'

The man named his wife 'Eve' because she was the mother of all those who live.

This is the word of the Lord.   *Genesis 3:9-15. 20*

Responsorial Psalm
℟ **Sing a new song to the Lord**
   for he has worked wonders.

1 Sing a new song to the Lord
   for he has worked wonders.
   His right hand and his holy arm
   have brought salvation.   ℟

2 The Lord has made known his salvation;
   has shown his justice to the nations.
   He has remembered his truth and love
   for the house of Israel.   ℟

3 All the ends of the earth have seen
   the salvation of our God.
   Shout to the Lord all the earth,
   ring out your joy.   ℟   *Ps 97:1-4. ℟ v.1*

SECOND READING
We read from the letter of St Paul to the Ephesians, chapter one.
*
Blessed be God the Father of our Lord Jesus Christ,
who has blessed us with all the spiritual blessings of heaven in
   Christ.

Before the world was made, he chose us, chose us in Christ,
to be holy and spotless, and to live through love in his presence,
determining that we should become his adopted sons, through
　　Jesus Christ
for his own kind purposes,
to make us praise the glory of his grace,
his free gift to us in the Beloved.
And it is in him that we were claimed as God's own,
chosen from the beginning,
under the predetermined plan of the one who guides all things
as he decides by his own will;
chosen to be,
for his greater glory,
the people who would put their hopes in Christ before he came.

　　This is the word of the Lord.　　　　　　*Ephesians 1:3-6. 11-12*

Gospel Acclamation
　　Alleluia, alleluia!
　　Hail, Mary, full of grace; the Lord is with thee!
　　Blessed art thou among women.
　　Alleluia!　　　　　　　　　　　　　　　　　*cf. Lk 1:28*

GOSPEL

We read from the holy Gospel according to Luke, chapter one.

*
The angel Gabriel was sent by God to a town in Galilee called
Nazareth, to a virgin betrothed to a man named Joseph, of the
House of David; and the virgin's name was Mary. He went in and
said to her, 'Rejoice, so highly favoured! The Lord is with you.'
She was deeply disturbed by these words and asked herself what
this greeting could mean, but the angel said to her, 'Mary, do not
be afraid; you have won God's favour. Listen! You are to conceive
and bear a son, and you must name him Jesus. He will be great
and will be called Son of the Most High. The Lord God will give
him the throne of his ancestor David; he will rule over the House
of Jacob for ever and his reign will have no end.' Mary said to the
angel, 'But how can this come about, since I am a virgin?' 'The
Holy Spirit will come upon you,' the angel answered, 'and the
power of the Most High will cover you with its shadow. And so
the child will be holy and will be called Son of God. Know this
too: your kinswoman Elizabeth has, in her old age, herself
conceived a son, and she whom people called barren is now in
her sixth month, for nothing is impossible to God.' 'I am the
handmaid of the Lord,' said Mary, 'let what you have said be
done to me.' And the angel left her.

　　This is the Gospel of the Lord.　　　　　　*Luke 1:26-38*